PAGE
38

ON THE ROAD

YOUR COMPLETE DESTINATION GUIDE
In-depth reviews, detailed listings
and insider tips

Norte Grande
p142

**Easter Island
(Rapa Nui)**
p401

Norte Chico
p193

Santiago
p40

Middle Chile
p87

Sur Chico
p223

Chiloé
p284

Northern Patagonia
p305

Southern Patagonia
p339

Tierra del Fuego

Language

THIS EDITION WRITTEN AND RESEARCHED BY

Carolyn McCarthy,
Jean-Bernard Carillet, Bridget Gleeson,
Anja Mutić, Kevin Raub

welcome to Chile

Meet A Land of Extremes

Preposterously thin and unreasonably long, Chile stretches from the belly of South America to its foot, reaching from the driest desert on earth to vast southern glacial fields. It's nature on a symphonic scale. Diverse landscapes unfurl over a 4300km stretch: parched dunes, fertile valleys, volcanoes, ancient forests, clear rivers, massive glaciers and fjords. For the traveler, there's wonder in every detail. Trace the sculpted contours of a glacier, watch a condor skate from crumbling cliffs or scramble up the Andes to scan a full 360 degrees without a human mark. And it's boggling to think how so much has stayed intact for so long. The very human quest for development could imperil these treasures sooner than we think. For now, Chile guards parts of our planet that remain the most pristine, and they shouldn't be missed.

La Buena Onda

In Chile, close borders foster intimacy. No matter where you go, it feels a little like a backyard. Bookended by the Andes and the Pacific, the country averages just 175km wide. No wonder you start greeting the same faces. Kick back in one place and it starts to feel like home. Perhaps it's because you have landed at the end of the continent, but one thing that stands out

Chile is nature on a colossal scale, but travel here is surprisingly easy. Your trip can be as hardcore or as pampered as you like, but you'll always feel welcome.

(left) Vicuña, Parque Nacional Lauca (p159)
(below) Centro Cultural Palacio La Moneda (p48), Santiago

is hospitality. *Buena onda* (good vibes) means putting forth a welcoming attitude. While in many destinations on the globe the traveler might feel like a commodity, here you are still a guest. In the city, diners linger over table conversations and bottles of wine. Patagonians share round upon round of *maté* tea. These rituals – of relating and relaxing – are so integral to the fabric of local life, that they are hardly even noticed. But they do say one thing: stay and let your guard down.

Slow Adventure

In Chile, adventure is what happens on the way to having an adventure. Pedal the chunky gravel of the Carretera Austral and end up sharing ferries with SUVs and oxcarts, taking a wrong turn and finding heaven in an anonymous orchard. Plans may be made, but try being just as open to experience. Set out to find sweeping desert solitude, climb craggy Andean summits or wander the sacred forests of poet Pablo Neruda. Surf, paddle or sail your way up or down the seemingly endless coast. Explore the mysteries of Easter Island, stargaze, soak in natural hot springs or watch glaciers calve. Then if you can stay still long enough, Chile might regale you with a moment of clarity.

⟩Chile & Easter Island

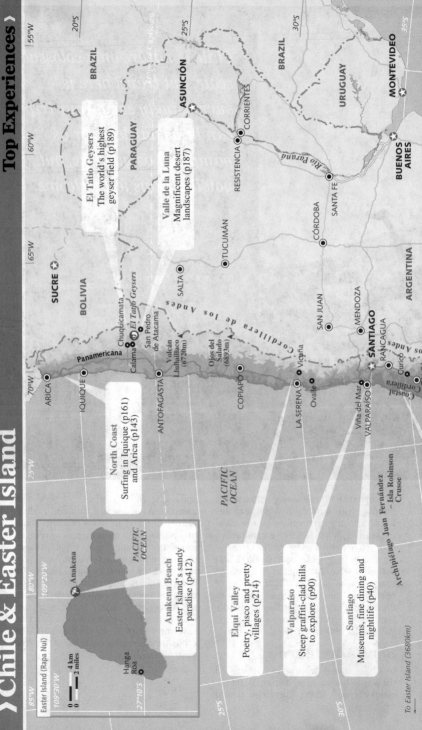

El Tatio Geysers
The world's highest geyser field (p189)

Valle de la Luna
Magnificent desert landscapes (p187)

North Coast
Surfing in Iquique (p161) and Arica (p143)

Elqui Valley
Poetry, pisco and pretty villages (p214)

Valparaíso
Steep graffiti-clad hills to explore (p90)

Santiago
Museums, fine dining and nightlife (p40)

Anakena Beach
Easter Island's sandy paradise (p412)

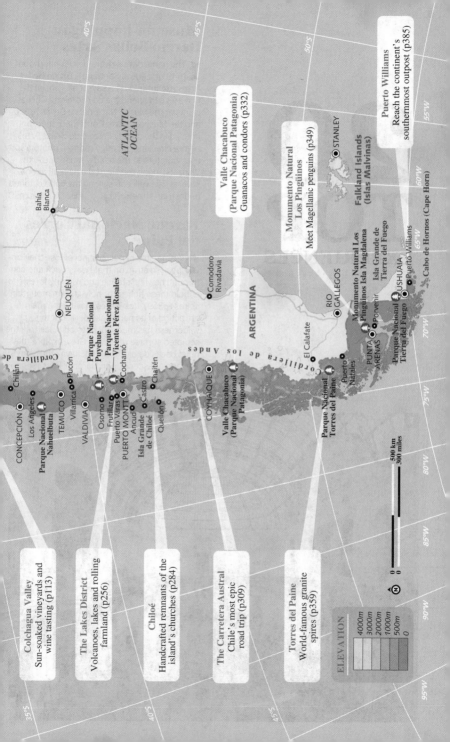

Colchagua Valley
Sun-soaked vineyards and wine tasting (p113)

The Lakes District
Volcanoes, lakes and rolling farmland (p256)

Chiloé
Handcrafted remnants of the island's churches (p284)

The Carretera Austral
Chile's most epic road trip (p309)

Torres del Paine
World-famous granite spires (p359)

Valle Chacabuco
(Parque Nacional Patagonia)
Guanacos and condors (p332)

Monumento Natural Los Pingüinos
Meet Magellanic penguins (p349)

Puerto Williams
Reach the continent's southernmost outpost (p385)

ATLANTIC OCEAN

Bahía Blanca

NEUQUÉN

Comodoro Rivadavia

ARGENTINA

Cordillera de los Andes

RÍO GALLEGOS

STANLEY

Falkland Islands (Islas Malvinas)

El Calafate

Puerto Natales

PUNTA ARENAS

Porvenir

Isla Grande de Tierra del Fuego

USHUAIA

Puerto Williams

Monumento Natural Los Pingüinos Isla Magdalena

Parque Nacional Tierra del Fuego

Cabo de Hornos (Cape Horn)

CONCEPCIÓN

Chillán

Los Angeles

Parque Nacional Nahuelbuta

TEMUCO

Villarrica

Pucón

VALDIVIA

Osorno

Frutillar

Puerto Varas

PUERTO MONTT

Cochamó

Parque Nacional Puyehue

Parque Nacional Vicente Pérez Rosales

Ancud

Castro

Isla Grande de Chiloé

Quellón

Chaitén

COYHAIQUE

Valle Chacabuco (Parque Nacional Patagonia)

Parque Nacional Torres del Paine

Cordillera de

500 km
300 miles

N

ELEVATION

4000m
3000m
2000m
1000m
500m
0

20 TOP EXPERIENCES

Museum-hopping in Barrio Bellas Artes

1 The name of this riverside neighborhood (p49) in central Santiago – Barrio Bellas Artes (Beautiful Art) – says it all. Fans of the fine arts can spend the day admiring Chilean works at the Museo Nacional de Bellas Artes and the Museo de Arte Contemporáneo, both housed in the stately Palacio de Bellas Artes, before checking out edgy modern photography and sculpture at the nearby Museo de Artes Visuales. Along the way, take a break at one of several sidewalk cafes along the cobblestoned pedestrian streets. Palacio de Bellas Artes (p50)

Parque Nacional Torres del Paine

2 Some rites of passage never lose their appeal, so strap on that heavy pack and hike through howling steppe and winding forests to behold these holiest-of-holy granite mountain spires (p359). Las Torres may be the main attraction of its namesake park, but this vast wilderness has much more to offer. Ice trek the sculpted surface of Glacier Grey, explore the quiet backside of the circuit, kayak the calm Río Serrano or ascend John Gardner Pass for gaping views of the southern ice field.

JOHN ELK III / LONELY PLANET IMAGES ©

Moai

3 The strikingly enigmatic *moai* (statues) are the most pervasive image of Easter Island (Rapa Nui; p411). Dotted all around the island, these massive carved figures stand on stone platforms, like colossal puppets on a supernatural stage. They emanate mystical vibes and it is thought that they represent clan ancestors. The biggest question is: how were these giant statues moved from where they were carved to their platforms? It's a never-ending debate among specialists.

Climbing Volcán Villarrica

4 Few things are as menacing as a growling volcano, especially an eye-to-eye encounter from the crater's edge. That's exactly the sort of spectacular confrontation you volunteer for on the rewarding climb to the summit of Volcán Villarrica (p235). Nothing quite prepares you for the snow-capped edge of a 2847m sulfur-spewing menace, and it's just that thrill – along with the snow-toboggan glaciating slide back down the mountain – that insures heart rates remain on overdrive. But don't worry – it hasn't erupted since 1984!

North Coast Surfing

5 Hit the potent tubes in northern Chile's duo of surf capitals, Iquique (p164) and Arica (p147). Surf dudes come in droves year-round for the consistent swell and a string of perfect gnarly reef breaks that break close to the desert shore. We're talking huge, hollow and nearly all left waves of board-breaking variety, especially in July and August when the hardcore surfers storm the coast. But do bring booties and wetsuits – the shallow reefs are full of urchins and the water is cold, courtesy of the Humboldt Current. Arica

The Churches of Chiloé

6 No matter how many European cathedrals, Buddhist monasteries or Islamic mosques you've seen, the 14 17th- and 18th-century wooden churches that make up Chiloé's (p287) Unesco World Heritage site will be unlike any previously encountered. Each an architectural marvel marrying European and indigenous design, boasting unorthodox colors and construction, these cathedrals were built by Jesuit missionaries working to convert pagans to the papacy. Their survival mirrors the Chilote people's own uncanny resilience. Iglesia de Nuestra Señora del Patrocinio, Tenaún (p293)

Wine Tasting in Colchagua Valley

7 Anyone who's tasted Chilean wine is already familiar with the charms of the Colchagua Valley (p113), whether or not they're aware of it. The bright sunshine and rich soil of Chile's best-established wine region, located several hours south of Santiago, is responsible for some of the richest Cabernet Sauvignon in South America. Taste this famous vino straight from the barrels at wineries like the posh Lapostolle, the old-fashioned Viu Manent, or the up-and-coming Emiliana, an organic vineyard employing innovative biodynamic growing techniques.

8

9

Swoon over Valle de la Luna

8 See the desert don its surrealist cloak as you stand atop a giant sand dune, with the sun slipping below the horizon and multicolored hues bathing the sands, all with a backdrop of distant volcanoes and the rippling Cordillera de la Sal. In Valle de la Luna (p187), the moment the color show kicks in – intense purples, golds, pinks and yellows stretch as far as your eye can see – you'll forget the crowds around you, all squeezing in to catch sundown in the valley.

Elqui Valley

9 Spend a few languid days in the lush Elqui Valley (p214) and you'll start to wax lyrical, or even channel the late Nobel Prize–winning poet Gabriela Mistral who grew up in these parts. Infused by poetry, pisco, pretty villages and star-sprinkled night skies, this is a wholesome land of spiritual retreats, ecofriendly inns, hilltop observatories and artisanal distilleries of the potent little grape. Sample food cooked solely by sun rays, get your aura cleaned, feast on herb-infused Andean fusion fare and ride the valley's mystic wave.

BETHUNE CARMICHAEL / LONELY PLANET IMAGES ©

JOHN ELK III / LONELY PLANET IMAGES ©

La Araucanía's National Park Trifecta

10 Sur Chico boasts seven national parks, none more otherworldly than Reserva Nacional Malalcahuello-Nalcas (p233) and Parque Nacional Conguillío (p231), whose charred desertscapes were born from volcanic eruptions, Lonquimay and Llaima among them. Along with Parque Nacional Tolhuaca (p230), flush with araucarias and intensely hued lagoons, this stunning trifecta – easily accessed via a base along the road to Lonquimay – is a microcosm of all that's beautiful about Sur Chico. Parque Nacional Conguillío

La Chascona

11 Pablo Neruda's Santiago house (p51), built at the foot of Cerro San Cristobal, paid tribute to two of his great loves: his wife Matilde (the name 'La Chascona' refers to her unruly hair) and the sea. No matter that this house, unlike his others in Chile, is nowhere near the ocean – the living room feels like a lighthouse, while the dining room resembles a ship's cabin. The great Chilean poet's quirky collections of colored glass, seashells and nautical equipment are also on display.

PRISMA BILDAGENTUR AG / ALAMY ©

Road-tripping the Carretera Austral

12 Find out what adventures wait on this 1240km romp through Andean backcountry dotted with parks and pioneer homesteads. Every wanderer's dream, this dusty washboard road to nowhere (p309) was created in the 1980s under the Pinochet regime, in an attempt to link the country's most isolated residents to the rest of the country. Now the connection is tenuous. If you have the time, offshoot roads to glaciers, seaside villages and mountain hamlets are worthy detours.

Santiago Dining and Nightlife

13 Though the Chilean capital may not be known as a party-all-night city like Buenos Aires or Rio de Janeiro, the scene is picking up momentum. A night out on the town, Santiago-style: world-class chefs modernize Chilean seafood classics at organic eateries in Providencia (p68), beautiful people crowd the rooftop of the W Hotel (p71) for pisco cocktails and stunning views of the Andes, and the party rolls on through dawn at the rustic bars and alternative music venues of Bellavista (p70). Liguria (p68), Providencia

Puerto Williams, the Southernmost Spot

14 At the Americas' southernmost outpost (p384), colts roam Main St, yachties trade round-the-world tales and wilderness looms larger than life. Part of the appeal is getting there, which means crossing the Beagle Channel by ferry or small boat. As villages go, Puerto Williams is the kind of place where people know your name within days of your arrival. For adventure, you can trek right out of town onto the Dientes de Navarino circuit, a five-day walk through wild high country fringed by razor-faced peaks.

El Tatio Geysers

15 Dress warmly and catch daybreak on a frigid walk through the gurgling geysers, gnarly craters and gassy fumaroles of the Tatio (p189), the world's highest geyser field ringed by pointy volcanoes and mighty mountains at 4300m above sea level. Hear this giant steam bath hiss, groan, spit and grumble as it shoots up white-vapor jets of steam, while the sun rises over the surrounding cordillera and bathes it in a sudden and surreal splash of reds, violets, greens, chartreuses and blues.

Valle Chacabuco (Parque Nacional Patagonia)

16 Dubbed the Serengetti of the Southern Cone (p332), this new park is the best place to spot amazing Patagonian wildlife – like guanacos, condors and flamingos. Once a down-and-out cattle and sheep ranch, its meticulous restoration is making it a model park worthy of worldwide recognition. Put aside a few days to take the trails to turquoise lagoons, undulating steppe and ridgetops, or just see the wildlife along the main road which climbs to the border of Argentina near Ruta 40.

15

JOHN ELK III / LONELY PLANET IMAGES ©

16

CAROLYN McCARTHY / LONELY PLANET IMAGES ©

Anakena Beach

17 Got a fantasy of an idyllic white-sand beach? You've just pictured Anakena beach (p412). Easter Island's biggest and most popular beach is a wide curve of white sand and sparkling turquoise sea backed by a lovely coconut grove on the north coast. It has food kiosks, picnic shelters and a few facilities. What makes Anakena beach so special, though, are the two major archaeological sites that form the picture-perfect backdrop. A stunning beach with grandiose *moai* – it's hard to think of a more compelling sight.

Monumento Natural Los Pingüinos

18 Every year, 60,000 Magellanic penguin couples convene just off the coast of Punta Arenas on Isla Magdelena (p349). Watching them waddle around, guard their nests, feed their fluffy and oversized offspring and turn a curious eye towards visitors makes for a great outing. There's also a historic lighthouse-turned-visitor center worth exploring. Ferries go regularly from the mainland. The penguins reside on the island between the months of October and March.

The Lakes District

19 Don't judge a district by its name. The Lakes District (p256), known as Los Lagos in Spanish, only tells a part of the story. While turquoise glacial lakes dominate the landscape, they're hardly the only attraction. Towering, perfectly conal, snowcapped volcanoes, charming lakeside hamlets, spectacular national parks, a long list of outdoor adventures and a unique, German-influenced Latin culture make for a cinematic region far beyond the *agua* (water). Lago Todos Los Santos and Volcán Puntiagudo (p270)

The Hills of Valparaíso

20 It's the busy port that put Valparaíso (p90) on the map, but it's the city's steep *cerros* (hills) that have inspired generations of poets, artists, and philosophers. A maze of winding paths, colorfully painted cottages, antique elevators and glowing streetlamps climb up the hills, offering ever more dramatic views of the sea below – and eerily quiet moments in which you might find your own poetic inspiration. Go ahead, try to use a map. You'll probably get lost halfway uphill, and that's part of the charm.

need to know

Currency
» Chilean peso (CH$)

Language
» Spanish

When to Go

Iquique
GO Year-round

San Pedro de Atacama
GO Mar–Dec

Easter Island
GO Oct–Jun

Santiago
GO Year-round

Puerto Montt
GO Nov–Mar

Desert, dry climate
Dry climate
Warm to hot summers, mild winters
Mild year round
Cold climate

Punta Arenas
GO Nov–Apr

High Season
(Nov–Feb)

» Patagonia is best (and most expensive) December to February

» Beaches throng with crowds from late December through January

» Best time for ski resorts is June to August

Shoulder (Sep–Nov & Mar–May)

» Temperature-wise, these are the best times to visit Santiago

» The Lakes District is pleasant September to November; April's fall foliage in the south

» Wine country has its grape harvests and wine festivals (March)

Low Season
(Jun–Aug)

» A good time to visit the North (along with the shoulder seasons)

» Services are few on Carretera Austral, and mountain passes can be blocked by snow

» Transportation and accommodation are busy in July during winter vacation

Your Daily Budget

Budget
CH$20,000–30,000

» Inexpensive *hospedaje* room/dorm bed CH$10,000

» Budget-restaurant dinner main CH$5000

» Set lunches are good value; supermarkets have takeout

» Some free sights and parks

Midrange
CH$60,000–75,000

» Double room in midrange hotel or B&B CH$45,000

» Midrange-restaurant dinner main CH$8000

» Car rentals start at CH$20,000 per day

Top End Over
CH$100,000

» Double room in top-end hotel CH$65,000

» Fine-restaurant dinner main CH$12,000

» Hire an outfitter for outdoor adventures

Money
» ATMs widely available. Credit cards accepted at higher-end hotels, some restaurants and shops. Travelers checks *not* widely accepted.

Visas
» Generally not required for stays of up to 90 days. Citizens of the US, Australia and Canada must pay a 'reciprocity fee' when arriving by air.

Cell Phones
» Local SIM cards (and top-up credits) are cheap and widely available, and can be used on unlocked GSM 850/1900 compatible phones.

Transportation
» Internal flights and buses are convenient and frequent. Drive on the right; steering wheel is on the left side of the car.

Websites
» **Chile Information Project** (www.chip.cl) Umbrella for English-language *Santiago Times*; discusses everything from human rights to souvenirs.

» **Go Chile** (www.gochile.cl) General tourist information.

» **Interpatagonia** (www.interpatagonia.com) All things touristy in Patagonia.

» **Lonely Planet** (www.lonelyplanet.com) Has travel news and tips.

» **Sernatur** (www.chile.travel/en.html) The national tourism organization, in French, Spanish or English.

Exchange Rates

Australia	A$1	CH$505
Canada	C$1	CH$488
Euro zone	€1	CH$640
Japan	¥100	CH$606
New Zealand	NZ$1	CH$399
UK	UK£1	CH$800
US	US$1	CH$517

For current exchange rates see www.xe.com

Important Numbers

Chile Country Code	☑56
International Access Code	three-digit carrier + ☑0
Directory Assistance	☑103
National Tourist Information (in Santiago)	☑562-731-8310
Police	☑133

Arriving in Chile
» **Aeropuerto Internacional Arturo Merino Benítez**
Minibus shuttle – frequent connections to downtown Santiago in 40 minutes; CH$6000
Local Bus – for penny-pinchers only, one hour to downtown; CH$1600
Transantiago buses – fare around CH$600, paid with Bip! card
Metro – located on lower level of bus terminals. Fare around CH$600.
Taxi – CH$16,000

Don't Leave Home Without...
» Warm waterproof gear – indispensable year-round in Patagonia
» Bomber sunblock, lip block and sun hat for high altitudes and the southerly ozone hole
» A cozy sleeping bag in winter, even if you're not camping
» Camping gear – it's available but expensive, so best bring it from home
» Essentials such as a Swiss Army knife
» Toilet paper, since public bathrooms may lack it
» Zoom lens or binoculars to capture Chile's more bashful wildlife
» Medical items
» Adaptor for chargers

if you like...

Urban Exploration

South American life spills into the streets as pop-up graffiti murals, sprawling food markets, narrow winding staircases and leafy museum neighborhoods in the vibrant Chilean cities of Santiago and Valparariso. Want to dip in yourself? Check out:

La Vega Central Browse this market for the visual feast of ripe figs, avocados and chirimoya arranged in towers and hawked by bellowing vendors. Just cross the bridge to the Mercado Central for authentic fish-market lunches (p50)

Museum Strolling Soak up culture in Santiago's great museums. The breathtaking artifacts at the Museo Chileno de Arte Precolombino contrast with the funky energy of the Museo de Arte Contemporáneo and fashion-forward Museo de la Moda (p44)

Graffiti Art Bright, funny and sometimes sad, compelling graffiti murals flank the alleys and steep staircases of Valparaíso, making any stroll an exploration (p93)

Night Cycling After the sun sets, Santiago traffic eases, the air cools and the city lights up – the perfect time to tour the city on two wheels (p59)

Hiking

Sure, Torres del Paine may be the continent's number one hiking destination, but guess what? Chile has 4000km of mountains bumping down its spine. From desert to temperate rainforest, trails are everywhere, so expand your itinerary to include a lesser-known route. You won't regret it.

Putre Make this miniature altiplano village base camp for high altitude desert treks, you will see far fewer souls than in San Pedro de Atacama (p156)

Siete Tazas Near wine country, a clear river drops through seven pools carved of black basalt, and Sendero Los Chiquillanes takes you there (p123)

Cochamó Valley Also a mecca for climbers, this pristine valley of waterfalls and granite panoramas boasts well-marked trails, though the mud is infamous (p272)

Cerro Castillo In the heart of Patagonia, trekking around this cathedral peak provides a top-notch four day adventure (p327)

Animal Encounters

While the great Andean condor soars all along the spine of the Andes, other wildlife inhabits concentrated areas. The cold Humboldt Current means abundant marine life, from sea lions to migrating blue whales. On land, Chile is home to a variety of camelids, diverse bird species and the endangered national symbol – the huemul.

Lago Chungará Teeming with birdlife, including the flamboyant Chilean flamingo, this surreal mirror lake sits high in the altiplano near the Bolivian border (p159)

Reserva Nacional Las Vicuñas Over 20,000 of the park's namesake camelids roam this high desert reserve surrounded by sky-hugging volcanoes (p160)

Chiloe Both Magellanic and Humboldt penguins nest near the northern end of the island, while pudú and abundant avian life inhabit the south-central Parque Tantauco (p303)

Valle Chacabuco From guanaco, fox and Andean condor to the more elusive puma and huemul, this former ranch is now a treasure of Patagonian wildlife (p332)

CHRIS BEALL / LONELY PLANET IMAGES ©

» Llama, Lago Chungará, Parque Nacional Lauca (p159)

Food & Nightlife

Foodies don't fear, though Chile is a gourmet late-bloomer, it does boast some of the freshest and finest ingredients (like the Central Valley's California-style produce and abundant seafood in the south). Nightlife ranges from rustic to sophisticate, predictably hitting its apogee in the capital.

Norte Chico With firewood scarce, women in the desert village of Villaseca power up solar ovens to rave reviews (p216)

Santiago From the glittering cityscape at W Hotel's rooftop bar to the barrio-pleaser Bar Constitución, something for everyone (p70)

Lakes District While German in influence, there's more than sauerkraut and sausages. *Asados* (barbecues) feature tender locally raised beef, berry pies and organic summer salads. (p256)

Patagonia A Chilean staple, *cocinas custombristas* are rudimentary restaurants banked on the talent of grandma, who's slaving in the back over steaming, fragrant concoctions of seafood stew (p313)

Memorable Landscapes

Potent scenery is not hard to find in Chile, where the climate ranges from parched desert to glacial peaks.

Atacama Desert The red rock canyons, cactus scrub and copper mountains are a sharp contrast to the piercing blue of the sky, here in the world's driest desert (p170)

Archipelago of Chiloé From western cliffs on the charging Pacific to quiet eastern inlets pocked with stilt houses and fishing boats, these green isles feed the imagination (p284)

Lakes District A rustic and sometimes rainy destination, with rolling countryside marked by dozens of deep-blue lakes and snowcapped volcanoes that stand sentinel (p256)

Patagonian Andes This amazing range is strung along the whole of South America, but reaches its dramatic crescendo in the deepest south (p359)

Tierra del Fuego Both rugged and mystical, this is a last frontier destination of remote isles and wind-sculpted landscapes (p378)

Remote Getaways

With over 90% of its population concentrated in the middle, Chile has escapes in every direction. To the north, you can explore the dry, wild expanse of the Atacama. To the south, the remote heart of Patagonia and its maze of fjords gives way to barren Tierra del Fuego. Or escape to the remotest Pacific isle – Easter Island (Rapa Nui).

Belén Precordillera Off the beaten path, visit ancient pictographs, old colonial churches and lovely landscapes (p155)

North Coast of Easter Island This eerie stretch north of Ahu Tenai passes towering *moai* (large anthropomorphic statues), climbs hills of overgrown grass and gazes out on the vast Pacific (p411)

Raul Marín Balmaceda With overgrown ferns and streets of sand, this lost village sits on a fjord flanked by otters, dolphins and sea lions (p318)

Caleta Tortel Built entirely on boardwalks, this ocean hamlet over teal waters was once the home of canoe-traveling Alacalufes (p335)

If you like... wilderness, don't miss the turquoise rivers, pristine lakes and glaciated peaks of the Carretera Austral.

Wine Country

The sky a delirious blue, a bicycle rolls by neat rows of grapes growing robust on the vine. With tall poplars and snowclad peaks shimmering in the distance, the languorous landscape says California or northern Italy. Guess again. Chile's wine country spans from the grand estates of family dynasties to upstart garage wines. Uncork it and savour.

Ruta del Vino Link up with local experts touring the powerhouse wine region responsible for the country's best reds (p113)

Lapastolle Winery A posh and lovely setting to acquaint yourself with Chile's richest terroir (p114)

Cabablanca Valley A hub of excellent cool-climate winemaking and a quick getaway from Santiago (p107)

Museo de Cochagua Take a break from sipping reds and check out the fascinating 'El Gran Rescate' exhibit with key memorabilia from the amazing rescue of the 33 miners in 2011 (p114)

Living History

Chile has its share of museum treasures, particularly found in Santiago or in the archeological collections of the north. But sometimes you just want to explore. Out of doors, history lives in the old naval ship *Esmeralda* (docked in Iquique), in the well-worn Patagonian trails first forged by pioneers and in Chilote villages still using their ancestral inventions. And there's more.

Humberstone This whole nitrate boomtown gone ghost city whets the traveler's imagination (p170)

Ascensor Concepcion Relive Valparaíso's glory days climbing above the city on its oldest cable-car elevator (p90)

Orongo Ceremonial Village Serene and surreal, this ancient village places you in the geographical heart of Easter Island's strange bird cult culture (p411)

Lago Llanquihue Once German colonies, the historic villages around Lago Llanquihue confound anyone's Latin sensibilities with unique architecture and German sweets (p262)

Pure Adrenaline

With high-quality outfitters, wild geography and pristine settings, Chile is a natural playground for adventure sports.

For a more extensive list of activities and destinations, check out the Chile Outdoors chapter (p28).

Skiing & Snowboarding Chile's top ski resorts include Valle Nevado (p85), Portillo (p112) and hot-springs mecca Nevados de Chillán (p126)

Glacier Treks The best known ice hike scrambles up Torres del Paine's Glacier Grey (p363), but on the Carretera Austral, you can now hike to Glaciar San Rafael (p327) and access remote glaciers from Puerto Guadal (p331); both with a boat/hike combo.

Surfing Ride some of South America's best waves at Pichilemu (p121) or Iquique (p164); or discover the quiet surf-shack style of Buchupureo (p128)

Rafting & Kayaking Hit the white water hard in Santiago's Cajón de Maipo (p83), around Puerto Varas (p264) and on the world-class Futaleufú (p314)

month by month

Top Events

1 **New Year's Eve in Valparaíso**, December

2 **Fiestas Patrias**, September

3 **Carnaval Ginga**, February

4 **Campeonato Nacional de Rodeo**, March

5 **Tapati Rapa Nui**, February

January

In summer peak season, Chileans start flocking to beaches. In January and February annual celebrations break out in every Chilean town and city with live music, special feasts and fireworks. It's also high season in Patagonia.

Santiago a Mil
Latin America's biggest theater festival (www.stgoamil.cl), brings acts to the street, plus international works, emerging theater and acrobats, in Santiago.

Semanas Musicales
All month, prestigious international acts ranging from classical to hip-hop come south to perform in Frutillar's stunning Teatro de Frutillar (www.semanasmusicales.cl) with sublime lake and volcano views.

Brotes de Chile
One of Chile's biggest folk festivals takes place in the second week of January and includes traditional dances, food and crafts in Angol.

February

It's Chileans' favorite month to vacation. With unrelenting heat from the north to Santiago, people flock south, particularly to Pucón and the Lakes District. Beaches fill and Santiago nightlife transplants to Viña del Mar and Valparaíso.

Fiesta de la Candelaria
A religious festival in early February, most fervently celebrated in Copiapó, where thousands of pilgrims and dancers converge.

Festival Internacional de la Canción
This fancy star-studded concert series held in Viña del Mar showcases top names in Latin American pop.

Festival Costumbrista
Perhaps the Carretera Austral's best rural fete, with dancing, music and an authentic Patagonian rodeo in Villa Cerro Castillo.

Carnaval
Putre puts out highland merriment and flour bombs, ending with the burning of the *momo* – a figure symbolizing the frivolity of Carnaval.

Tapati Rapa Nui
The premier festival on Easter Island is an incredibly colorful event that keeps the party going for two weeks, with a series of dance, music and cultural contests.

Festival Costumbrista
Castro struts Chiloé's distinctive folk music and dance, plying revelers with heaps of traditional foods in mid-February.

Carnaval Ginga
Held in Arica, in mid-February, this festival features the musical skills of regional *comparsas* (traditional dancing groups).

March

A great month to travel Chile. As fall ushers in, summer crowds disperse. Though all of Chile cools a bit, usually southern Patagonia is still dry and less windy, with great hiking weather. The Central Valley's grape harvest begins.

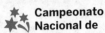 **Campeonato Nacional de Rodeo**

In Rancagua in late March, the National Rodeo Championship features feasting, *cueca* (a playful, handkerchief-waving dance that imitates the courtship of a rooster and hen) and, most importantly, Chilean cowboys showing off their fancy horse skills.

 Fiesta de la Vendimia

Santa Cruz celebrates the grape harvest with stands from local wineries in the plaza, a crowned harvest queen, songs and folk dancing.

April

Bright reds and yellows highlight the forests of Northern Patagonia, though rain will come any day now. The south is clearing out but you might get lucky with decent hiking weather. Santiago and the Central Valley enjoy still-pleasant temperatures.

⭐ **Lollapalooza Chile**

Chile rocks this international edition (www.lollapaloozacl.com), with 60 bands playing Santiago's Parque O'Higgins; kids get their hair punked at the adjoining Kidsapalooza.

June

Winter begins. With days at their shortest, nightlife and cultural events pick up. The world-class ski resorts around Santiago start gearing up and it's still a good time to visit the desert.

 Fiesta de San Pedro y San Pablo

In San Pedro de Atacama, folk-dancing groups, a rodeo and solemn processions mark this animated religious festival held on June 29.

July

Chilean winter vacation means family travel hits full-swing. Ski resorts run full-swing and those who brave Patagonia will find lovely winter landscapes without the infamous wind of summer.

 Festival de la Virgen del Carmen

Some 40,000 pilgrims pay homage to Chile's virgin with lots of street dancing, curly-horned devil masks with flashing eyes and spangly cloaks. Held in La Tirana in mid-July.

⭐ **Carnaval de Invierno**

Punta Arenas gets through the longest nights with fireworks, music and parades in late July.

September

Spring comes to Santiago, with mild, sunny days. Though low season throughout Chile, it's not a bad time to travel. Everything closes and people get boisterous the week of the national holiday.

 Fiestas Patrias

Chilean Independence is feted at Fiestas Patrias (week of September 18), with a week of big barbecues, *terremotos* (potent wine punch) and merrymaking all over Chile.

October

A fine time to travel with spring flowers in Northern and Central Chile.

🍺 **Oktoberfest**

Join the swillers and oompah bands in Puerto Varas and Valdivia for live music in lederhosen and beer festivals.

November

Chile's south is in full bloom though the weather is still crisp. It's a good time to visit the beach resorts and Patagonia, since the crowds and high prices are still a month or so away.

December

Summer begins and services return to the Carretera Austral. It's still quiet but also ideal for outdoor activities in the Lake District and Patagonia.

 New Year's Eve

December 31 means the year's biggest bash in Valparaíso, where revelers fill open balconies and streets to dance, drink and watch fireworks on the bay.

itineraries

Whether you've got six days or 60, these itineraries provide a starting point for the trip of a lifetime. Want more inspiration? Head online to lonelyplanet. com/thorntree to chat with other travelers.

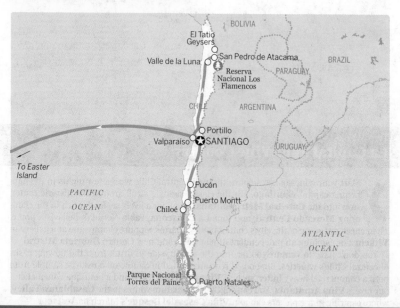

Four Weeks
Best of Chile

Skate through Chile's amazing diversity in one month. From **Santiago**, feed your creative yen wandering around boho capital **Valparaíso**. If it's winter, explore nearby powder stashes at top Andean resorts like **Portillo**.

Then turn up the dial with desert heat. Fly or bus to the highland village of **San Pedro de Atacama**. Absorb altiplano ambiance visiting the moonlike **Valle de la Luna**, the steaming and strange **El Tatio geysers** and the stark **Reserva Nacional Los Flamencos**. Wind up days of hiking, horseback riding or volcano climbing with mellow evening bonfires and star-stocked skies.

Delve into temperate rainforest in **Pucón**, where rafting, hiking and hot springs fill up your Lakes District dance card. From **Puerto Montt**, detour to folklore capital **Chiloé**; or cruise on a four-day ferry ride through glacier-laced fjords to **Puerto Natales**. By now you are probably in top shape for **Parque Nacional Torres del Paine**. Take up to a week on the trails of this world-famous hiking destination. Then barrel back to Santiago and hop a plane to **Easter Island (Rapa Nui)** to puzzle over its archaeological treasures for five days.

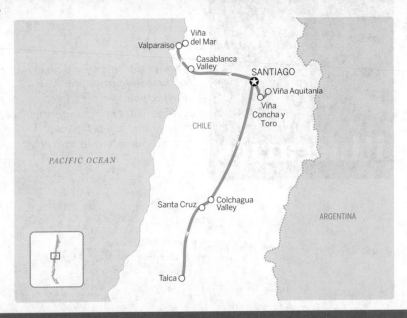

Two Weeks
La Capital and Wine Country

> Start your wine-soaked sojourn through Central Chile with a few nights in the happening capital, **Santiago**. Hit the classic sights – stroll around the historic center, stop into the **Catedral Metropolitana**, break for a lively seafood lunch in the clamoring **Mercado Central**, and tour **La Chascona**, Pablo Neruda's Bellavista home. Then check out some of the city's contemporary charms, sipping champagne at a gallery in **Vitacura** or catching an independent film at the brand-new **Centro Gabriela Mistral**.

You don't have to venture too far into the countryside to drink from the flowing casks of central Chile's wineries. Big-bodied reds are crafted in Santiago's outskirts; sample from both a commercial heavy hitter, such as **Viña Concha y Toro** and a boutique winemaker – our fave is **Viña Aquitania**. You can sip Chile's signature whites in the **Casablanca Valley**, where aspiring grape pickers can join **Viña Casas del Bosque's** March harvest tour.

Explore the de facto Chilean wine capital on a **Colchagua Valley** wine tour in **Santa Cruz**. Highlights include a carriage ride through **Viu Manent's** vineyards, the organic, biodynamic wines at **Emiliana** and the haute hand-picked approach of **Casa Lapostolle**. Half the fun is getting there – the Santa Cruz steam engine **Tren del Vino** offers doorstop delivery (with shuttles) as well as on-board wine tasting.

Recover from the overindulgence by heading to the seaside and climbing up one of **Valparaíso's** famously steep hills – but make sure you also catch a ride on one of the city's antique elevators, like **Cerro Concepción**, Valparaíso's oldest – at least once. Wander the charming alleyways, taking in stunning ocean views around nearly every corner, then step into Neruda's **La Sebastiana** getaway before feasting on freshly caught seafood.

Exhausted from the urban hiking? Unwind at the nearby resort city of **Viña del Mar** – Santiaguinos' favorite for a quick beach getaway, with little pressure to sightsee. Simply pull up a chair at **Enjoy del Mar**, strategically located where the sea meets the Río Marga, and toast your travels with yet another pisco sour.

Other acclaimed tours take in **Talca**, where lovers of a fine vintage get a varied experience; at Viña Gillmore you can even get wine therapy at the spa!

» (above) Parque Nacional Queulat
(p320)
» (left) Wine cellar, Viña Concha y Toro
(p82), Pirque

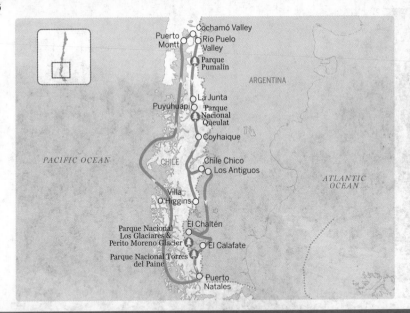

Four Weeks
Pioneer Patagonia

If you wish to travel only back roads, if you desire getting dirty, almost lost and awe-inspired, look no further than this four-week plan. Following the **Carretera Austral**, this route criss-crosses its little-known offshoots and gives you plenty of time on the hoof. Summer, with more-frequent transportation connections and warm weather, is the best time to go.

Leave **Puerto Montt** or Puerto Varas for the **Cochamó** or **Río Puelo** valleys, where you can hike or horseback ride, camping or staying at remote lodgings. From Puerto Montt, ferry to **Parque Pumalín** and camp in an ancient forest with boardwalk trails to booming waterfalls. Ramble the Carretera Austral to **La Junta**, where a farmstay and lazy river run will put you in the Huck Finn mode. Check out the hot-springs options near **Puyuhuapi** or if you're not ready to come clean, camp under the hanging glacier at **Parque Nacional Queulat**.

Coyhaique is the next major hub. After making connections to **Chile Chico** on the enormous Lago General Carrera, hop the border to **Los Antiguos** and travel Argentina's classic Ruta 40 to **El Chaltén** for hiking around the gnarled tooth of Cerro Fitz Roy. Take two days to visit **El Calafate**, spending one under the spell of the magnificent glacier **Perito Moreno** in the **Parque Nacional Los Glaciares**. While you're there, feast on giant steaks and bottles of peppery Malbec. From El Calafate it's an easy bus connection to **Parque Nacional Torres del Paine** via **Puerto Natales**. Hike the 'W' route or go for the full week-long circuit. By now you're in prime hiking shape – enjoy passing others on the trail. Return to Natales for post-trek pampering, namely handcrafted beer, hot tubs and thin-crust pizza. If you have time, head back to Puerto Montt via the **Navimag ferry**. Otherwise, fly from Punta Arenas.

An alternative route would be to skip Chile Chico and follow the Carretera Austral to its southern terminus – **Villa O'Higgins**. Relax, go fishing and hike. From here, a rugged boat-hike combination can get you across the border to El Chaltén, where you can rejoin the itinerary a week behind schedule.

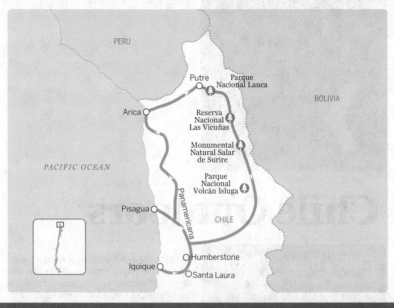

Desert Solitaire

How about a few weeks sleeping under star-crazy skies, following condor shadows along desert mountaintops? You'll need a 4WD and plenty of food, water and extra gas. Start with a surfboard in **Iquique** to sample the swells of Playa Cavancha and Playa Huaiquique, and then jump off a cliff on a tandem paragliding jaunt. With the adrenaline rush in place, slow things down with a contemplative wander around nitrate ghost towns **Humberstone** and **Santa Laura**, where you can poke around the creepy abandoned buildings of these once flourishing spots and explore their crumbling grandeur.

Head further north from here, stopping in the isolated coastal town of **Pisagua**, once a bustling nitrate-era port, then a penal colony and today a nearly abandoned and strangely lyrical place where algae gatherers work alongside the ruins of busted mansions; don't miss the windswept old cemetery sloping forlorn on a nearby hill. Cheer up in sunny **Arica**, where plenty of surf awaits below the dramatic headland of El Morro lording it over the city and remarkably preserved Chinchorro mummies lie in situ at the small museum just below the hill. From the coast, head inland via Hwy 11, passing geoglyphs, colonial chapels and misty mountain hamlets, to the pretty Andean village of **Putre**. Take a day or two here to catch your breath, literally, as Putre sits at a dizzying altitude of 3530m. Once you've adjusted to the height, head to nearby **Parque Nacional Lauca**, where you can take in the perfect cone of Volcán Parinacota, wander through the tiny Aymara village with the same name and walk around the lovely Lago Chungará, all paired with awesome wildlife sightings in this Unesco Biosphere Reserve.

Further south, the remote **Reserva Nacional Las Vicuñas** shelters thousands of these flighty creatures and few interlopers to spook them, so go easy. Heading south on tough terrain through dazzling landscapes, through the isolated salt flat of **Monumento Natural Salar de Surire** with its three flamingo species (best seen between December and April), your reward for an adventurous ride is reaching the ultra-removed **Parque Nacional Volcán Isluga**, before looping back to Iquique.

Chile Outdoors

Chile's Biggest Thrills

Hiking Valle Frances In Torres del Paine, this valley rimmed by steep summits inspires awe.

Climbing a Volcano Chile's Ojos del Salado is the highest volcano in the world, but dozens more are well-equipped for exploration.

Exploring the Atacama Scale massive dunes, admire petroglyphs and question the shimmering visions of oases.

Surfing Pichilemu Punta de Lobos is considered a perfect left break.

A Powder day at Portillo Steep and deep terrain is the delight of boarders and skiers.

Diving off Easter Island The water around stunning sea stack Motu Kao Kao boasts 60m visibility.

Cycling the Carretera Austral Every summer, more cyclists take up the challenge of this epic journey of journeys.

In Chile, the outdoors means dazzling geography. The empty expanse of the Atacama Desert stretches to temperate rainforest and the glacier-studded south. The Pacific is one constant. Surf the many breaks and kayak southern fjords dotted with wild isles or head inland to white-water raft, or soak in sublime hot springs. The other constant is the Andes. Here adventurers get vertical climbing volcanoes, biking scenic routes, skiing world-class resorts and hiking the hills and valleys. The possibilities are only limited by the time at hand. If you plan carefully for seasonal changes, equipment needs and access to expertise, this world is your oyster.

Hiking & Trekking

Some of the most inspirational and iconic hiking trails in the world are here. All this exquisite beauty is worth the heavy packs and sore legs. What follows barely touches the extent of the possibilities but should tantalize you enough to pack those heavy boots.

The sublime Torres del Paine is one of the continent's most beloved hiking destinations, graced by glaciers, gemstone lakes and the world-famous granite spires. The park has decent transportation links, *refugios* (rustic shelters) and campsites that allow for day hikes and multiday circuit treks. However, its popularity has led to summer overcrowding. For awe-inspiring isolation, Tierra del Fuego's Dientes de Navarino hiking circuit is equally stunning but harder to get to.

RESPONSIBLE TREKKING

To help preserve Chile's pristine wilderness, consider the following tips.

» Take the utmost care not to cook or smoke near dried grass or other combustible materials, especially in the windy Patagonian steppe.

» Don't depend on open fires for cooking. Cook on a lightweight camp stove and dispose of butane cartridges responsibly.

» Carry out all rubbish. Don't overlook easily forgotten items such as silver paper, orange peel, cigarette butts and plastic wrappers.

» Contamination of water sources by human waste can lead to the transmission of all sorts of nasties. Where there is a toilet, please use it. Where there is none, bury your feces. Dig a small hole 15cm deep and at least 100m from any watercourse. Cover the waste with soil and a rock. Pack out toilet paper.

» For washing, use biodegradable soap and a water container at least 50m away from any watercourses. Disperse the waste water widely to allow the soil to filter it fully.

» Do not feed the wildlife as this can lead to animals becoming dependent on handouts, to unbalanced populations and to diseases.

» Some trails pass through private property. It's polite to ask residents before crossing their property and leave all livestock gates as you found them.

Within the northern corner of Patagonia, Parque Pumalín has some great day hikes, and now it's possible to go up the recently active Volcan Chaitén with local guides.

The Lakes District abounds with trails and tantalizing terrain. Highlights include Parque Nacional Conguillío along the Valdivian coast. Volcanic activity in Cordón Caulle may limit access to Parque Nacional Puyehue.

The citybound can escape above Santiago's smog line with jaunts to nearby Monumento Natural El Morado or Parque Nacional La Campana. Altos de Lircay, in Chile's middle, has a great backcountry circuit. In the north, desert oasis San Pedro de Atacama has a number of intriguing hikes, as does Parque Nacional Lauca. Fly to the Pacific for great hiking in Parque Nacional Juan Fernández and on Easter Island.

Opportunities are not limited to the national parks: check out the Sendero de Chile and opportunities for rural community tourism in the south. Private reserves, such as Chiloé's Parque Tantauco and El Mirador de Chepú, as well as future Parque Nacional Patagonia near Cochrane, and others are preserving top-notch destinations.

Some regional Conaf offices (p453) have reasonable trail maps, and the JLM maps also have trail indicators on the more specific tourist-oriented maps (see p457).

Trekkers can go further afield with Lonely Planet's *Trekking in the Patagonian Andes*, where you will find detailed descriptions and maps of extensive walks in Chile, plus others across the border in Argentina.

Mountaineering & Climbing

Chile is prime mountaineering and ice-climbing territory. There are hundreds of peaks to choose from, including 50 active volcanoes. They range from the picture-perfect cone of dormant Parinacota in the northern altiplano, which has a twin just across the Bolivian border, to the challenging trek up Ojos del Salado.

A charm bracelet of lower volcanic cones also rises through La Araucanía and the Lakes District and Torres del Paine. The most popular climbs here are Volcán Osorno, which has summit ice caves, and Volcán Villarrica, which still smolders ominously. Meanwhile ice-climbers can look into the Loma Larga and Plomo massifs, just a few hours' drive from Santiago.

Climbers intending to scale border peaks like the Pallachatas or Ojos del Salado must have permission from Chile's **Dirección de Fronteras y Límites** (Difrol; ☎02-671-4110; www.difrol.cl, in Spanish; Bandera 52, 4th fl, Santiago). It's possible to request permission prior to arriving in Chile; a request form can be accessed on the agency's website.

For more information, contact the **Federación de Andinismo** (☎02-222-9140; www.feach.cl, in Spanish; Almirante Simpson 77, Providencia, Santiago).

For detailed stats, route descriptions and inspirational photos of mountaineering, volcaneering and ice-climbing throughout Chile, visit www.escalando.cl.

Skiing & Snowboarding

Powder junkies rejoice. World-class resorts in the Chilean Andes offer myriad possibilities for skiing, snowboarding, and even heliskiing. Don't expect too many bargains though; many resorts have prices to match their quality.

Most resorts are within an hour's drive of Santiago, including a wide variety of runs at family-oriented La Parva, all-levels El Colorado and Valle Nevado, with a lot of terrain and renowned heliskiing. Legendary Portillo, the site of several downhill speed records and summer training base for many of the northern hemisphere's top skiers, is northeast of Santiago near the Argentine border crossing to Mendoza. Termas de Chillán, just east of Chillán, is a more laid-back spot with several beginners' slopes, while Parque Nacional Villarrica, near the resort town of Pucón, has the added thrill of skiing on a smoking volcano. Volcanoes Osorno and Antillanca, east of Osorno, have open terrain with incredible views and a family atmosphere. The last four places mentioned have the added bonus of being close to hot springs, a godsend after a hard day of descents.

The perfect cone of Volcán Osorno offers great family skiing. Coyhaique has its own small resort, while Punta Arenas can lay claim to having one of the few places where one can ski with an ocean view. 'First descents' of Chilean Patagonia's numerous mountains is a growing (but limited) trend. Ski novices can also find suitable terrain and cheaper prices at Volcán Lonquimay, while well-kept secret Chapa Verde near Rancagua is another low-key, cheap alternative with a variety of slopes.

Ski season runs from June to October. Santiago has some rental shops; otherwise resorts rent full packages.

A good website to gather general information on Chile and Argentina's big ski resorts is www.andesweb.com, with photo essays, reviews and trail maps.

Cycling & Mountain Biking

Whether you are looking to slowly pedal your way around tranquil lakeside trails or bomb down still-smoking volcanoes, there's plenty of opportunity to get around on two wheels. A favorite mountain-biking destination in the north is San Pedro de Atacama. Bikers can enjoy any number of fabulous trips in the Lakes District, accessing pristine areas that have limited public transportation. The new bike lane around Lago Llanquihue is

BUT WAIT, THERE'S MORE...

» **Canyoning** Navigate Southern Chile's stream canyons by jumping into clear pools and rappelling alongside gushing waterfalls. Hotspots are near Puerto Varas and Pucón.

» **Canopy** Popular in the Lakes District and La Araucanía, where zip-lines take you through the treetops with a by-product of a full adrenaline rush. Go with well-recommended tour operators. Minimal gear is a secure harness with two straps that attach to the cable (one is a safety strap), a hard hat and gloves.

» **Paragliding & Landsailing** With its steep coastal escarpment, rising air currents and soft, extensive dunes, Iquique ranks among the continent's top spots for paragliding, and a good spot for desert land-sailing and kite-buggying.

» **Fly-fishing** The Lakes District is a prime destination for anglers who want to reel in monster trout (brown and rainbow) and Atlantic salmon (a non-native species). The season generally runs from November to May.

» **Sand-boarding** Be prepared to get sand in places you never imagined possible. Try it in San Pedro de Atacama or Iquique.

» **Diving** Exciting dive sites can be found on the Juan Fernández archipelago and around Easter Island. On the Chilean mainland, check out the coast of Norte Chico.

» **Swimming** Chile's almost endless coastline has sandy beaches, but the Humboldt Current makes waters cold, except in the far north around Arica.

» (above) Horseback riding, Parque
   Nacional Torres del Paine (p363)
» (left) Skiing, Termas de Chillán (p126)

very popular (though it still doesn't make the whole circumference), as is the Ojos de Caburgua loop near Pucón. The long, challenging, but extremely rewarding Carretera Austral has become an iconic route for international cyclists, and is well worth the effort.

More and more bikers are taking on the ultimate challenge: to cycle Chile's entire length. Most large towns have bike-repair shops and sell basic parts, but packing a comprehensive repair kit is essential. See p467 for more details of cycling through Chile, renting bikes and transporting them.

Horseback Riding

Saddling up and following in the path of Chile's *huasos* (cowboys) is a fun and easy way to experience the wilderness. Chilean horses are compact and sturdy, with amazing skill fording rivers and climbing Andean steeps. Now more than ever, multiday horseback-riding trips explore cool circuits, sometimes crossing the Andes to Argentina, on terrain that would be inaccessible otherwise. Except in the far north, opportunities can be found just about everywhere.

With strong initiatives for community-based rural tourism in the south, guided horseback riding and trekking with packhorses is a great way to discover remote areas. Rural guides charge affordable rates, provide family lodging in their own homes and offer invaluable cultural insight. Check out offerings in Río Cochamó, Palena and Coyhaique.

Adventure outfitters offer multilingual guides and a more elaborate range of services. Most places offer first-time riders preliminary lessons before taking to the trails. Favorites for single- or multiday horse treks are: Pucón, Puelo Valley, Valle Elqui, Hurtado, San Pedro de Atacama and around Torres del Paine. The island of Chiloé is also popular.

Rafting & Kayaking

The wealth of scenic rivers, lakes, fjords and inlets in southern Chile make it a water-lover's dream destination. And white-water junkies agree that Chile's rivers, raging through narrow canyons from the Andes, are world class. While hydroelectric projects are mercilessly taming many excellent rivers,

Northern Patagonia's Futaleufú River still offers world-class runs with plenty of Class IV and V water to get the blood racing. Other popular runs include those outside Pucón and the beautiful Petrohué, Puerto Varas in the Lakes District. Also worth investigating are Río Simpson and Río Baker in the Aisén region. Even near Santiago, the Cajón del Maipo offers a gentle but enjoyable run.

Agencies in Santiago, Pucón, Puerto Varas and elsewhere offer trips for different levels. Since there is no certifying body for guides, check to see if the company has specialized river safety and first-aid training and verify that equipment is high quality.

Meanwhile the southern fjords and bays of southern Chile are a sea-kayaker's paradise. Popular spots include the fjords in Parque Pumalín and around the sheltered bays of Chiloé, though more intrepid kayakers have been known to paddle their way around Cape Horn. Lake kayaking is also terrific throughout the Lakes District.

Surfing & Kitesurfing

With breaks lining the long Pacific Coast, Chile nurtures some serious surf culture. Developed surf scenes, however, are best found along the coast of middle and northern Chile. With big breaks and long left-handers, surf capital Pichilemu hosts the national surfing championship. Pilgrims crowd the perfect left break at Pichilemu's Punta de Lobos, but beginners can also have a go nearby at La Puntilla. Iquique has a shallow reef break; bring booties to spare yourself from the sea urchins. Coastal Ruta 1 is lined with surfing beaches and, unfortunately, mountains of trash from careless campers. Only at Arica is the water comfortably warm, so wetsuits are imperative. The biggest breaks are seen in July. Rough surf and rip currents also make some areas inadvisable, and it's best not to surf alone anywhere. You can buy or hire boards and track down lessons in all these surfing hotspots.

Chile also has opportunities for kitesurfing, although equipment and lessons are harder to come by: try Pichilemu and Puclaro (near Vicuña). Spanish-speakers can find more information on www.kitesurf.cl.

Travel with Children

Best Regions for Kids

Santiago Brimming with children's museums, parks and winter resorts with easy terrain, fun events and kids' classes.

Sur Chico For horseback riding, lake dips, ziplines and volcano thrills. Lake towns Pucón or Puerto Varas provide the best bases to explore the region.

Norte Chico Seaside resorts provide beach fun and some surf. Kids love playing in the tide pools of La Piscina in Bahía Inglesa. The gentle, sunny climate here helps keep your plans on target.

In Chile, travelers find that bringing children offers up some distinct advantages. Throughout the whole country, little ones are welcome and treasured. Empathy for parents is usually keen; strangers don't hesitate to help out and hotels and services tend to accommodate. Chile is a great place for kids to explore and interact with lots of water sports, adventures and family-oriented resorts and lodgings.

Chile for Kids

Chile is as kid-friendly as a destination gets, though it's best to take all the same travel precautions you would at home. Free or reduced admission rates are often given at events and performances. For Santiago tips, see p61.

Adventure

Routine travel, like crossing fjords on a ferry or riding the subway, can amount to adventure for kids. Many of the activites aimed at adults can be scaled down for children. Activities like guided horse rides (usually for kids aged eight and up) and canyoning usually have age limits but are invariably fine for teenagers.

In rural areas, agrotourism can be a great option, which can involve farm chores or just hiking with pack horses taking all the load. Some rivers may be suitable for children to float or raft, make sure outfitters have life vests and wet suits in appropriate sizes.

Practicalities

In Chile, people are helpful on public transportation; often someone will give up a seat for parent and child. Expecting mothers enjoy a boon of special parking spaces and grocery store lines.

Though the upper-middle class usually employ a *nana* (live in or daily childcare), finding last-minute help is not easy. Babysitting services or children's activity clubs tend to be limited to upmarket hotels and ski resorts. If you're comfortable with an informal approach, trusted acquaintances can recommend sitters.

Formula, baby food and disposable diapers are easy to find. In general, public toilets are poorly maintained; always carry toilet paper, which is almost nonexistent. While a woman may take a young boy into the ladies' room, it would be socially unacceptable for a man to take a girl into the men's room.

Dining

While restaurants don't offer special kids' meals, most offer a variety of dishes suitable for children, none are spicy. It is perfectly acceptable to order a meal to split between two children or an adult and a child; most portions are abundant. High chairs are rarely available. The only challenge to dining families is the Latin hours. Restaurants open for dinner no earlier than 7pm, sometimes 8pm, and service can be quite slow.

Safety

There are no special food and health concerns, but bottled water is a good idea for delicate stomachs. Street dogs are common but usually mild-mannered and after food scraps.

Children's Highlights

Adventure

» Rafting the Petrohué River

» Horseback riding in the Andean foothills

» Ski resort Valle Nevado's terrain park and family barbecues

Entertainment

» Rodeos in *medialuna* (half moon) stadiums in summer

» The kids' booth at Lollapalooza

» Santiago's free tours and Parque Bicentenario

Dining

» *Asados* (barbecues) with oversized grills and backyard ambiance

» Burgers eaten on the shiny stools of a *fuente de soda* (soda fountain)

» Fresh berry *küchen* (sweet, German-style cakes) served in the Lakes District tea houses

Rainy-Day Refuges

» Interactive museum Museo Interactivo Mirador in Santiago

» Kids' workshops at Teatro del Lago in Frutillar

» Making masterpieces in the kids' studio of Museo Artequín in Santiago

Planning

Keep the kids in mind as you plan your itinerary or include them in the trip planning from the get-go. If renting a car, communicate ahead if you will need a child's seat, as they are not always available. Lonely Planet's *Travel with Children,* by Cathy Lanigan, provides good information, advice and anecdotes.

If you don't want to be tied town to a schedule while traveling, plenty of activities can be booked just a few days in advance.

When to Go

☐ Summer (December to February) for good weather and outdoor fun

☐ The desert north can be visited year-round

☐ Off-season travel throughout Chile isn't bad

☐ Try to avoid the south during the rainiest months (May to July)

☐ Winter (June to August) is fun as kids try out skis and see fumaroles puff from white landscapes.

Accommodation

☐ Hotels often give discounts for families and some can provide cribs.

☐ Cabins are widely available in summer, and often have self-catering options

☐ Campgrounds in the south may have *quinchos* (barbecue huts) for some shelter from the rain.

What to Pack

☐ Bathing suit, sunhat and warm clothing

☐ Bug spray

☐ Good walking shoes that are already broken in

☐ Baby backpacks (as strollers aren't always that convenient)

regions at a glance

Skinny Chile unfurls toward Cape Horn, cartwheeling from the stargazing center of the world's driest desert to patchwork vineyards and farms, the deep green of temperate rainforest and the cool blue of glacial fields. Throughout, there's the constant blue of the roiling Pacific and the ragged bulwark of the Andes. With the country's population cinched in the middle, Santiago keeps humming unto the wee hours. Yet Valparaíso is a close challenger for urban cool, with its narrow, graffiti-cloaked passages. Roam in any direction for vibrant country life, in villages where time seems to tick a little slower and wilderness that begs exploration.

Santiago

History ✓✓
Arts ✓✓✓
Nightlife ✓✓

History
From the early independence from Spain to Salvador Allende's deposition in 1973 and the years of military government, Chile's history is displayed at the museums of Santiago.

Arts
Santiago has the best of old and new. Pre-Colombian objects and Chilean masterpieces abound at traditional museums, while up-and-coming artists, photographers and filmmakers show at contemporary centers and galleries.

Nightlife
Chile's lively capital pulls all-nighters. Find *carrete* (nightlife) in the down-to-earth bars of Bellavista and Barrio Brasil, the posh cocktail lounges of Vitacura and rocking live-music venues about town.

p40

Middle Chile

Wine ✓✓✓
Beaches ✓✓
Outdoors ✓✓

Wine
Red or white? These welcoming wineries literally overflow with both. The Maule Valley specializes in Cabernet Sauvignon, while Casablanca Valley produces Chardonnay and Sauvignon Blanc.

Beaches
The coast is famous for fantastic surf breaks and laid-back villages. Grab a board in Pichilemu or Buchupureo. Head to lower-key Maitencillo to learn how to catch a wave.

Outdoors
Dare to brave South America's longest ski slope (14km) run. In summer, travelers bolt for Chile's star outdoor attractions – Torres del Paine and the Atacama – leaving Central Chile's national parks crowd-free.

p87

Norte Grande

Landscapes ✓✓✓
Activities ✓✓✓
History ✓✓

Landscapes
Take in the diversity and drama of Norte Grande's landscapes – from the heights of the altiplano to the desert sunsets and the star-studded night skies.

Activities
Norte Grande offers up a healthy dose of adrenaline, from hitting Arica's waves and paragliding off Iquique's cliff to sand boarding near San Pedro de Atacama and horseback riding through the world's driest desert.

History
Wander around the nitrate-era ghost towns of Humberstone and Santa Laura, tour the storied *Esmeralda* ship in Iquique's harbor and take in creepy Chinchorro mummies in situ at an Arica museum.

p142

Norte Chico

Beaches ✓✓
Activities ✓✓✓
Architecture ✓

Beaches
A string of pretty beaches lines the coast of Norte Chico, including activity hubs like buzzy La Serena as well as virtually virgin strips of sand and hip beach hideaways like the tiny Bahía Inglesa.

Activities
You can climb the world's highest active volcano, Ojos del Salado, sail the coast around Bahía Inglesa, hop on a boat to see Humboldt penguins, and windsurf off the coast of La Serena.

Architecture
From the colonial charms of leafy La Serena to Caldera's neoclassical mansions from the early mining era, Norte Chico showcases a hodgepodge of eye-candy for architecture buffs.

p193

Sur Chico

Parks ✓✓✓
Outdoors ✓✓✓
Lakes ✓✓✓

Parks
Sur Chico parks offer a wealth of landscapes. Climb Volcán Villarrica and peer into its gas-spewing crater. Other parks showcase alpine lakes, araucaria forests and ski slopes.

Outdoors
While trekkers relish the laundry list of trails, rafting, kayaking, canopy zip lines, mountain biking and volcano climbing are other great options here. Pucón is Chile's high-adrenaline epicenter, while Puerto Varas is a close cousin.

Lakes
Deep-blue and jade-green lakes pepper the region, but there are also hot springs, none more enticing than Termas Geométricas. Rivers are rich with trout and waterfalls.

p223

Chiloé

Churches ✓✓✓
Culture ✓✓
Nature ✓✓

Churches
These Unesco Word Heritage site churches will have you worshipping architecture. Each village centerpiece was built at the call of Jesuit missionaries in the 17th and 18th centuries.

Culture
Chiloé's distinctive flavor, notable in mythology and folklore, lives in the architecture of churches and *palafitos* (stilt houses). Cuisine dates to pre-Hispanic cultures, with seafood and potatoes, famously in *curanto* (meat, potato and seafood stew).

Nature
Parque Nacional Chiloé and Parque Tantauco protect rainforest with native wildlife. To meet Magellanic and Humboldt penguins, visit Monumento Natural Islotes de Puñihuil.

p284

Northern Patagonia

Culture ✓✓
Outdoors ✓✓✓
Nature ✓✓

Culture

Long the most isolated part of Chile, Patagonia's northern region is a cowboy stronghold. Visit rural settlers off the grid who live in harmony with a wicked and whimsical mother nature.

Outdoors

Land the big one fly-fishing, raft wild rivers or mosey into the backcountry on a fleece-mounted saddle. Scenery and real adventure abound on the Carretera Austral, Chile's unpaved southern road.

Nature

Patagonia can get pretty wild. The best wildlife watching is in the Valle Chacabuco (Parque Nacional Patagonia), home to guanaco and flamingos. Near Raul Marín Balmaceda, observe dolphins and sea lions at play from your kayak.

p305

Southern Patagonia

Seafaring ✓✓
Trekking ✓✓✓
Parks ✓✓✓

Seafaring

Sailors of yore mythologized these channels rife with craggy isles, whales and dolphins. Today ferry trips go to Puerto Montt and Puerto Williams. Kayakers can paddle still sounds and glacier-strewn bays.

Trekking

Between Torres del Paine and Argentina's Fitz Roy range, the trekking doesn't get any better. Snug *refugios* (rustic shelters) make the day's work a little easier. Or go off the beaten path in Pali Aike or to Cabo Froward.

Parks

Glaciers, rock spires and rolling steppe. Southern Patagonia is a feast for the eye, and Torres del Paine and Argentina's Parque Nacional Los Glaciares rate among the finest parks on the continent.

p339

Tierra del Fuego

Wilderness ✓✓✓
History ✓✓
Landscapes ✓✓✓

Wilderness

Whether you are backpacking the rugged Dientes de Navarino circuit, observing penguins or boating among glaciers and sea lions, this special spot on the planet connects you to your wild side.

History

The past is ever-present in this far-flung isle. Coastal shell middens remain from native inhabitants. Trace its history in Puerto Williams' Museo Martín Guisinde and Ushuaia's former jail Museo del Presido.

Landscapes

From steep snow-bound peaks and tawny plains to labyrinthine channels scattered with rugged isles, the scenery of the land of fire is breathtaking. Take it in on a trek, coastal stroll or long boat ride.

p378

Easter Island

History ✓✓✓
Landscapes ✓✓
Outdoors ✓✓

History

Easter Island (Rapa Nui) is an open-air museum, with archaeological remains dating from pre-European times. Think *moai* (large anthropomorphic statues), large *ahu* (ceremonial platforms) and burial cairns.

Landscapes

Ready your wide-angle lens for some shutter-blowing landscapes. For the most dramatic, stand on the edge of Rano Kau, a lake-filled crater, or walk across the beautiful Península Poike.

Outdoors

Outdoorsy types will be in seventh heaven. Hike up Mt Terevaka for extraordinary views. Learn to surf, then snorkel or dive in crystal-clear waters. Clip clop around Península Poike and bike your way around the island.

p401

> Every listing is recommended by our authors, and their favourite places are listed first

> Look out for these icons:

 Our author's top recommendation

 A green or sustainable option

 No payment required

See the Index for a full list of destinations covered in this book.

On the Road

Santiago

Includes »

Best Places to Eat

» Liguria (p68)

» Peluquería Francesa (p67)

» Azul Profundo (p67)

» Astrid y Gastón (p68)

» Tiramisú (p69)

» Aquí Está Coco (p68)

Best Places to Stay

» W Hotel Santiago (p65)

» Aubrey Hotel (p63)

» Vilafranca Petit Hotel (p64)

» Bellavista Home (p63)

Why Go?

Surprise: the Chilean capital is suddenly cool. Santiago has always had its measured charms – fine dining, perfectly landscaped gardens, a famous seafood market, the stunning backdrop of the Andes – but in the past few years it has undergone a cultural metamorphosis. In celebration of Chile's bicentennial, the city poured millions of pesos into the construction of sleek new cultural centers, thoughtful museums and gorgeous green parks. The upscale neighborhoods of Vitacura and El Golf bloomed with stylish new art galleries, the new W Hotel started drawing A-list celebrities to its rooftop bar, and the faded but beautiful Barrio Brasil was infused with vibrant public art and funky youth hostels. True, Santiago may never be as glamorous as Rio or as dynamic as Buenos Aires, but now it's more than a stopoff on the way to Chilean Patagonia or the Atacama. Understated but up-and-coming, Santiago just became a destination in its own right.

When to Go
Santiago

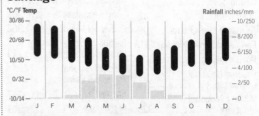

| **Mar–Aug** The wine harvest kicks off in March, while May brings ski season to Tres Valles. | **Sep–Nov** Comfortable temperatures make the shoulder season ideal for sightseeing. | **Dec–Feb** Summer in Santiago sees street festivals and getaways to the Cajón del Maipo. |

Santiago Cuisine

With cuisines from all of Chile represented at the table and a generation of innovative new chefs experimenting with classic dishes, the capital city is a gourmet's playground. Whether you're eating lunch at a plastic table inside the bustling seafood market or dining at a high-end eatery in Providencia, it is customary to begin the meal with a pisco sour and *machas a la parmesana* (razor clams baked in parmesan cheese and white wine) or an *empanada de pino* (stuffed with ground beef, onions and hard-boiled eggs) before moving onto a main course of *paila marina* (seafood stew), *pastel de choclo* (a baked casserole made of corn, meat and cheese) or fresh grilled fish, preferably paired with a fine wine from the Colchagua Valley. For dessert, try cake or ice cream topped with *manjar,* the Chilean version of *dulce de leche* (but don't expect espresso! Chileans are crazy for Nescafé instant coffee.)

PARQUE POR LA PAZ

During Chile's last dictatorship some 4500 political prisoners were tortured and 266 were executed at Villa Grimaldi by the now-disbanded DINA (National Intelligence Directorate). The compound was razed to conceal evidence in the last days of Pinochet's dictatorship, but since the return of democracy it has been turned into a powerful memorial park known as **Parque por la Paz** (📞292-5229; www.villagrimaldi.cl, in Spanish; Av Arrieta 8401; ⏰10am-6pm). Each element of the park symbolizes one aspect of the atrocities that occurred there and visits here are fascinating but harrowing – be sensitive about taking pictures as other visitors may be former detainees or family members. Check the website ahead of time to arrange a guided tour. Take the yellow bus D09 (you need a Bip! card) from right outside the Av Vespucio exit of Plaza Egaña metro station; it drops you opposite.

Santiago's Best Museums

» Museo de la Moda (p55)
» Museo de la Memoria y Derechos Humanos (p53)
» Museo Nacional de Bellas Artes (p50)
» Museo de Arte Contemporáneo (p50)
» Museo Chileno de Arte Precolombino (p45)
» Museo de Artes Visuales (p51)

Main Points of Entry

» Aeropuerto Internacional Arturo Merino Benítez: International airport.
» Terminal de Buses Santiago: The main bus station.
» Estación Central: Train station with connections to south-central Chile.

Fast Facts

» Population: 5,883,000
» Area: 2030 sq m
» Elevation: 543m
» Telephone code: 📞02

Top Tip

» Most first-time visitors to Chile will have to pay a 'reciprocity fee' (US$140 for American citizens) when going through passport control at the Santiago airport. Credit cards and cash are accepted; the stamp is valid for the life of the passport. Once in the arrivals hall, avoid the taxi stand and go straight to the desks for flat-rate taxis or shared shuttles.

Resources

» www.lonelyplanet.com/chile/Santiago
» www.chile.travel
» www.santiagotimes.cl
» www.eatwineguides.com
» www.chile-travel.com/santiago

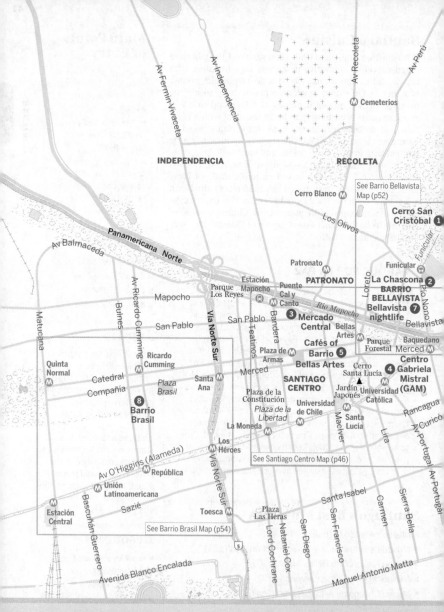

Santiago Highlights

1 Gaze out over Santiago from the breathtaking summit of **Cerro San Cristóbal** (p51)

2 Walk in Pablo Neruda's footsteps at **La Chascona** (p51), the one-time home of Chile's legendary poet

3 Sample *paila marina* (seafood stew) and watch locals bargain for fresh fish at the clamoring **Mercado Central** (p45)

4 Catch a Chilean art film at the sleek new **Centro Gabriela Mistral** (GAM; p50)

5 People-watch over coffee and cake in the quaint cafes of **Barrio Bellas Artes** or **Barrio Lastarria** (p69)

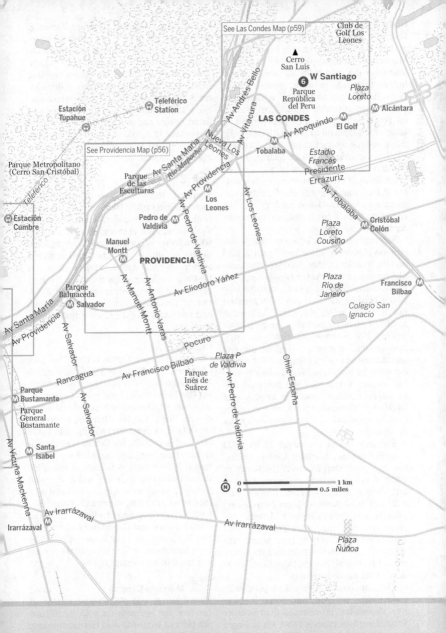

6 Drink in sunset views of the Andes – and a pisco sour or two – from the rooftop bar at the **W Santiago** (p71)

7 Trace the roots of Chilean culture through the preconquest art of the **Museo Chileno de Arte Precolombino** (p45)

8 Dine, drink, and dance till dawn in *carrete* (party) central **Bellavista** (p70)

9 Tear up the slopes at Chile's top ski resort, **Valle Nevado** (p85)

History

Nomadic hunter-gatherers wandered here as early as 10,000 BC, but only in 800 BC did Mapuche-related peoples settle here. Not long after the Inka made the area a major hub on their road network, Spanish soldier Pedro de Valdivia arrived and founded the city of Santiago de la Nueva Extremadura on February 12, 1541, then marched off to attack the Mapuche to the south. Mapuche living nearby weren't happy and attacked: Valdivia's girlfriend, Inés de Suárez, turned out to be as bloodthirsty as he was, and led the defense of the city, personally decapitating at least one Mapuche chief. Despite ongoing attacks, floods and earthquakes, the conquistadores didn't budge, and eventually Santiago began to grow.

Santiago was the backdrop for Chile's declaration of independence from Spain in 1810 and the final battle that overthrew the colonial powers in 1818. As the population grew, public-works projects transformed the city, which became the hub of Chile's growing rail network before displacing Valparaíso as Chile's financial capital in the early 20th century. Not everyone prospered, however. Impoverished farmers flocked to the city and the upper classes migrated to the eastern suburbs. Rapid post-WWII industrialization created urban jobs, but never enough to satisfy demand, resulting in scores of squatter settlements known as *callampas* ('mushrooms,' so-called because they sprang up virtually overnight).

Santiago was at the center of the 1973 coup that deposed Salvador Allende. During the dark years that followed, thousands of political prisoners were executed, and torture centers and clandestine prisons were scattered throughout Santiago. Despite this, military commander-in-chief General Augusto Pinochet was Chile's president until 1990. Chile's democratic government was restored in 1990 when Patricio Aylwin was elected president; Pinochet continued on as head of the nation's military.

The gap between rich and poor widened during the '90s, and social inequality – though less pronounced than in other Latin American cities – looks set to linger for some time at least. Still, relative economic prosperity has sparked something of a renaissance in Santiago, particularly in the period leading up to Chile's bicentennial celebration in 2010. Recent years have seen a plethora of brand-new parks and museums popping up around town, a cleaned-up riverfront, construction of super-modern apartment buildings and large-scale projects like the Costanera Center (which, when finished, will be the tallest building in South America) and the ongoing development of posh business and residential zones like Vitacura and Dehesa. In fact, thanks to smart design and strict building codes, the earthquake that struck central Chile in February 2010 left surprisingly minimal damage in the capital city.

◉ Sights

Thanks to the recent wave of construction surrounding Chile's bicentennial, Santiago is alive with ultra-modern cultural centers, sleek museums and vast green parks dotted with colorful sculptures and locals basking in the sunshine. The city's food markets, leafy residential streets, outdoor cafes and bustling shopping strips are often the best places to witness the particular mix of distinctly Latin American hustle-and-bustle and more Old World reticence that defines Santiago.

CENTRO

The wedge-shaped Centro is the oldest part of Santiago, and the busiest. It is hemmed in by three fiendishly hard-to-cross borders: the Río Mapocho and Autopista Central expressway, which have only occasional bridges over them, and the Alameda, where the central railing puts your vaulting skills to the test. Architecturally, the Centro is exuberant rather than elegant: haphazardly maintained 19th-century buildings sit alongside the odd glittering high-rise, and its crowded *paseos* (pedestrian precincts) are lined with inexpensive clothing stores and several fast-food joints. Government offices, the presidential palace and the banking district are also here, making it the center of civic life; most tourists come here to make the rounds to a handful of standout sights.

TOP CHOICE Mercado Central   MARKET

(Central Market; Map p46; ◎7am-5pm Mon-Sat, 7am-3pm Sun; Ⓜ Puente Cal y Canto) Gleaming piles of fresh fish and crustaceans atop mounds of sparkling ice thrill foodies, fishers and photographers alike at the Mercado Central, which is bordered by 21 de Mayo, San Pablo, Paseo Puente and Valdés Vergara. Fishmongers compete noisily for customers in one half of the market, while touts for its

SANTIAGO IN...

Two Days

Start your day in the heart of town, at the bustling **Plaza de Armas**. Visit the **Museo Chileno de Arte Precolombino**, or have a coffee and check out contemporary art and fair-trade crafts at the **Centro Cultural Palacio La Moneda**. Have a seafood lunch at the **Mercado Central**, then hotfoot it up **Cerro Santa Lucía** to see the city from above. Take a break for afternoon tea and people-watching at a **Barrio Bellas Artes cafe**. Head to Bellavista for a classic Chilean dinner at **Galindo**, then get down at **Bar Constitución**. Get inspiration for your second day at Pablo Neruda's house, **La Chascona**, then take in more great views atop **Cerro San Cristóbal**. After a ceviche lunch at **Azul Profundo**, check out the **Centro Cultural Gabriela Mistral**. Later, have a pisco sour at the W Hotel's **Red2One** cocktail bar before dining with stylish Santiaguinos at **Tiramisú**.

Four Days

On your third day visit the **Cajón del Maipo** or a **winery**. In winter, head for the snow at **Tres Valles**. Spend your fourth day admiring street art in **Barrio Brasil**, stopping for lunch at antique **Peluquería Francesa**. Toast your stay in Santiago with drinks at Providencia's **Bar:Liguria**.

many seafood restaurants make an equal racket in the other. (For a slightly more authentic dining experience, skip the central restaurants and check out the peripheral seafood eateries that are packed with locals at lunchtime.)

Plaza de Armas   PLAZA
(Map p46; Ⓜ Plaza de Armas) Since the city's founding in 1541, the Plaza de Armas has been its symbolic heart. In colonial times a gallows was the square's grisly centerpiece; today it's a fountain celebrating *libertador* (liberator) Simón Bolívar, shaded by more than a hundred Chilean palm trees. Parallel pedestrian precincts Paseo Ahumada and Paseo Estado disgorge scores of strolling Santiaguinos onto the square on weekends and sunny weekday afternoons: clowns, helium-balloon sellers and snack stands keep them entertained.

Catedral Metropolitana   CHURCH
(Map p46; Plaza de Armas; ⊗ 9am-7pm Mon-Sat, 9am-noon Sun; Ⓜ Plaza de Armas) Overlooking the Plaza de Armas is the neoclassical Catedral Metropolitana, built between 1748 and 1800. Bishops celebrating mass on the lavish main altar may feel uneasy: beneath them is the crypt where their predecessors are buried.

Museo Chileno de Arte
Precolombino   MUSEUM
(Chilean Museum of Pre-Columbian Art; Map p46; ☎ 928-1500; www.precolombino.cl; Bandera 361;

adult/child CH$3000/free; ⊗ 10am-6pm Tue-Sat, 10am-2pm Sun; Ⓜ Plaza de Armas) Exquisite pottery from most major pre-Columbian cultures is the backbone of Santiago's best museum, the Museo Chileno de Arte Precolombino. As well as dozens of intricately molded anthropomorphic vessels, star exhibits include hefty Mayan stone stele and a fascinating Andean textile display. More unusual are the wooden vomit spatulas used by Amazonian shamans before taking psychoactive powders. At the time of writing, the museum was closed while it was undergoing a major expansion; it is set to reopen in 2013. Check the museum's website for updates.

Cerro Santa Lucía   HILL
(Map p46; entrances cnr Alameda & Santa Lucía, & cnr Santa Lucía & Subercaseaux; ⊗ 9am-7pm Mar-Sep, 9am-8pm Oct-Feb; Ⓜ Santa Lucía or Bellas Artes) Rising out of the eastern side of the Centro is Cerro Santa Lucía. It was a rocky hill until 19th-century city mayor Benjamín Vicuña Mackenna had it transformed into a beautifully landscaped park where the grassy verges are still a favorite with canoodling local couples. A web of trails and steep stone stairs leads you up through terraces to the Torre Mirador at the top. Charles Darwin proclaimed the view from here 'certainly most striking' in 1833 – it's still well worth the climb.

Santiago Centro

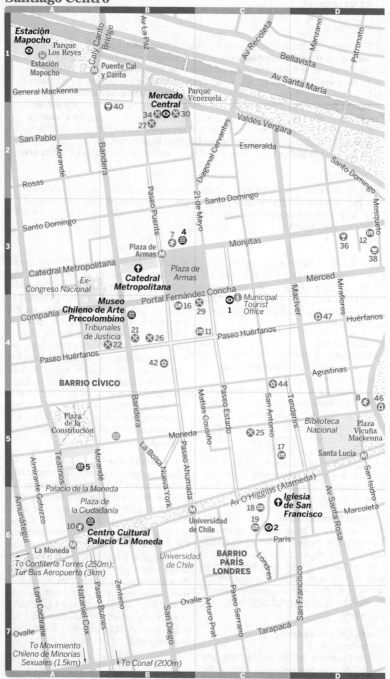

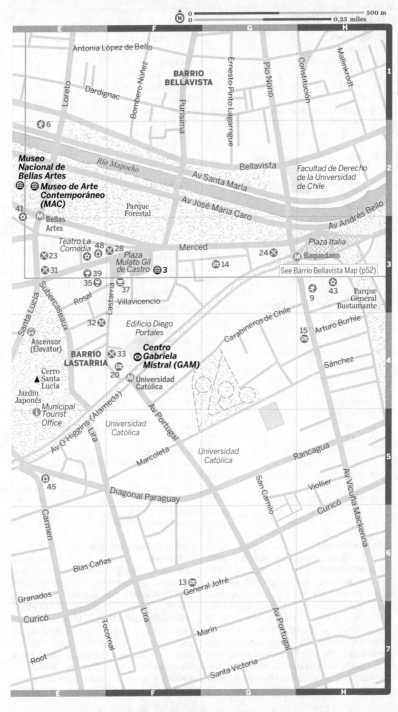

SANTIAGO

0
0

500 m
0.25 miles

Antonia López de Bello

BARRIO
BELLAVISTA

Loreto

Dardignac

Bombero Núñez

Purísima

Ernesto Pinto Lagarrigue

Pío Nono

Constitución

Mallinkrodt

6

Museo
Nacional de
Bellas Artes

Río Mapocho

Bellavista

Av Santa María

Facultad de Derecho
de la Universidad
de Chile

Museo de Arte
Contemporáneo
(MAC)

Av José María Caro

Av Andrés Bello

41

Parque
Forestal

M Bellas
Artes

Teatro La
Comedia

48 28

Merced

24

Plaza Italia

M Baquedano

23

Plaza
Mulato Gil
de Castro

3

14

See Barrio Bellavista Map (p52)

31

39

35

37

9

43

Parque
General
Bustamante

Rosal

Lastarria

Villavicencio

Carabineros de Chile

15

Arturo Burhle

Santa Lucía

Subercaseaux

32

Edificio Diego
Portales

Sánchez

Ascensor
(Elevator)

BARRIO
LASTARRIA

33

Centro
Gabriela
Mistral (GAM)

Cerro
Santa
Lucía

20

M Universidad
Católica

Jardín
Japonés

Municipal
Tourist
Office

Av O'Higgins (Alameda)

Lira

Universidad
Católica

Av Portugal

Universidad
Católica

Rancagua

45

Marcoleta

San Camilo

Viollier

Av Vicuña Mackenna

Diagonal Paraguay

Curicó

Carmen

Blas Cañas

Granados

13

General Jofré

Curicó

Tocornal

Lira

Marín

Av Portugal

Root

Santa Victoria

E F G H

Santiago Centro

Estación Mapocho CULTURAL BUILDING
(Mapocho Station; Map p46; ☎787-0000; www.
estacionmapocho.cl, in Spanish; Plaza de la Cultura s/n; ⓂPuente Cal y Canto) Rail services
north once left from Estación Mapocho.
Earthquake damage and the decay of the
rail system led to its closure, but it's been
reincarnated as a cultural center which
hosts art exhibitions, major concerts and
trade expos. The soaring cast-iron structure
of the main hall was built in France then assembled in Santiago behind its golden beaux
arts–style stone facade.

**Centro Cultural Palacio
La Moneda** ARTS CENTER
(Map p46; ☎355-6500; www.ccplm.cl; Plaza de la
Ciudadanía 26; exhibitions adult/child & student
CH$1000/CH$500, free 9am-noon Mon-Fri, cinema tickets adult/child & student CH$2000/1000;
⏰9am-7:30pm; ⓂLa Moneda) Underground art
takes on a new meaning in one of Santiago's
newer cultural spaces: the Centro Cultural
Palacio La Moneda is beneath **Plaza de la
Ciudadanía**. A glass-slab roof floods the
vaultlike space with natural light, and ramps
wind down through the central atrium past

the Cineteca Nacional, a state-run art-house movie theater, to two large temporary exhibition spaces. The uppermost level contains a fair-trade crafts shop, a few cafes and a gallery celebrating Chilean folk singer, artist and activist Violeta Parra.

Barrio París-Londres   NEIGHBORHOOD
Immediately south of the Iglesia de San Francisco is the Barrio París-Londres, a pocket-sized neighborhood that developed on the grounds of the Franciscan convent of **Iglesia San Francisco**. It's made up of two intersecting cobbled streets called – yes, you guessed it – París and Londres. They're lined by graceful European-style townhouses built in the 1920s, some of which now contain old-fashioned hotels. Look for the memorial at **Londres 38** (www.londres38.cl, in Spanish; ☺10am-1pm & 3-6pm Tue-Fri), a building that served as a torture center during Pinochet's government.

Iglesia de San Francisco   CHURCH
(Map p46; Alameda 834; ☺11am-6pm Mon-Sat, 10am-1pm Sun; ⓂUniversidad de Chile) The first stone of the austere Iglesia de San Francisco was laid in 1586, making it Santiago's oldest surviving colonial building. Its sturdy walls have weathered some powerful earthquakes, although the current clock tower, finished in 1857, is the fourth. On the main altar look for the carving of the Virgen del Socorro (Our Lady of Perpetual Help), which Santiago's founder Pedro de Valdivia brought to Chile on his 1540 conquistador mission to protect him from attacks.

FREE **Palacio de la Moneda**   PALACE
(Map p46; ☏690-4000; Morandé 130; ☺10am-6pm Mon-Fri; ⓂLa Moneda) Chile's presidential offices are in the Palacio de la Moneda. The ornate neoclassical building was designed by Italian architect Joaquín Toesca in the late 18th century, and was originally the official mint – its name means 'the coin.' The north facade was badly damaged by air-force missile attacks during the 1973 military coup when President Salvador Allende – who refused to leave – was overthrown here. A monument honoring Allende now stands opposite in **Plaza de la Constitución**.

Museo Histórico Nacional   MUSEUM
(National History Museum; Map p46; ☏411-7010; www.dibam.cl/historico_nacional, in Spanish; Plaza de Armas 951; adult/child CH$600/300; ☺10am-5:30pm Tue-Sun; ⓂPlaza de Armas) Colonial furniture, weapons, paintings, historical objects and models chart Chile's colonial and republican history at the Museo Histórico Nacional. After a perfunctory nod to pre-Columbian culture, the ground floor covers the conquest and colony. Upstairs goes from independence through Chile's industrial revolution right up to the 1973 military coup but no further – Allende's broken glasses are the chilling final exhibit.

Casa Colorada   HISTORIC BUILDING
(Red House; Map p46; Merced 860) Few colonial houses are still standing in Santiago, but the simple, oxblood-colored Casa Colorada is a happy exception, although only the front half of the original 18th-century building has survived.

BARRIO LASTARRIA & BARRIO BELLAS ARTES
Home to three of the city's best museums, these postcard-pretty neighborhoods near Cerro Santa Lucía are also Santiago's twin hubs of hip. East of the Cerro, Barrio Lastarria takes its name from its cobbled main drag JV Lastarria, lined with arty bars and restaurants. The intersecting street, Merced, adds a few funky shops and some cafes to the mix. The real center of Santiago cafe culture, however, is over at Barrio Bellas Artes, as the few blocks north of Cerro Santa Lucía are now known. JM de la Barra is the main axis.

THE LAY OF THE LAND

Greater Santiago is wedged between two mountain ranges, the Andes and the coastal cordillera. Although it's made up of some 32 comunas (districts), most sights and activities are concentrated in a few of the central neighborhoods.

East–west thoroughfare Av O'Higgins (better known as the Alameda) is the city's main axis; east of Plaza Italia it becomes Av Providencia and then Av Apoquindo. Metro Línea 1 runs under it for much of its length. Flowing roughly parallel to the north is the highly polluted Río Mapocho, which effectively acts as the border between downtown and the northern suburbs.

Two hills punctuate the otherwise flat cityscape: Cerro San Cristóbal, a major recreational park, and the smaller Cerro Santa Lucía.

BARRIO RECOLETA

Bustling Korean eateries and Middle Eastern takeaway counters, a happening market-place overflowing with ripe fruit, a colorful jumble of street vendors, an achingly hip cocktail lounge – this burgeoning barrio just west of Bellavista is a slight detour off the beaten path. Here are a few spots you shouldn't miss.

Patronato (Map p52; MPatronato) This barrio within a barrio, roughly bordered by Recoleta, Loreto, Bellavista and Dominica streets, is the heart of Santiago's immigrant populations, particularly Koreans, Chinese and Arabs. The colorful, slightly run-down blocks are lined with antique buildings and illuminated by neon signs; a soundtrack of cumbia always seems to keep the beat in the background. Come to poke around the bare-bones ethnic supermarkets, feast on street food, or wander through the clothing market to watch the locals haggling over *quinceañera* (15th birthday) dresses and Chinese slippers.

La Vega Central (☺6am-6pm Mon-Sat, 6am-3pm Sun; MPatronato) Raspberries, quinces, figs, peaches, persimmons, custard apples… if it grows in Chile, you'll find it at La Vega Central, which is bordered by Dávila Baeza, Nueva Rengifo, López de Bello and Salas. Go early to see the hollering vendors in full swing.

Vietnam Discovery (Map p52; ✆737-2037; www.vietnamdiscovery.cl; Loreto 324; mains CH$4800-7600; ☺lunch only Sat; MPatronato; ✍) Hip Santiaguinos were already lined up around the block when a French-Thai couple opened this intimate new eatery. It's a young, stylish twist on the barrio's traditional ethnic restaurant, serving inspired Thai and Vietnamese dishes. Book ahead, using the online form, or you'll never see the inside.

Restobar KY (Map p52; www.restobarky.cl; Av Perú 631; ☺closed Mon; MCerro Blanco) Also taking inspiration from the barrio's southeast Asian flavor is this stunning new cocktail bar. The photographer owner has done wonders with a rambling old house – the interior is otherworldly, glowing with Chinese lanterns and the soft light of antique chandeliers, and filled with a fascinating mix of vintage chairs, exotic plants, carved wooden furnishings and vibrant artwork. Choose a Thai-inspired libation from the cocktail menu, then sit back to watch the beautiful people cavorting under the gaze of a Buddha statue.

Museo Nacional de Bellas Artes MUSEUM (National Museum of Fine Art; Map p46; ✆499-1600; www.mnba.cl, in Spanish; Parque Forestal s/n; adult/child CH$600/300; ☺10am-6:50pm Tue-Sun; MBellas Artes) In the park's center is the stately neoclassical **Palacio de Bellas Artes**, built as part of Chile's centenary celebrations in 1910. Two of Santiago's art museums, the Museo Nacional de Bellas Artes and the Museo de Arte Contemporáneo, share the premises. The National Museum of Fine Art features an excellent permanent collection of Chilean art; look out for works by Luis Vargas Rosas, erstwhile director of the museum and a member of the Abstraction Creation group, along with fellow Chilean Roberto Matta, whose work is also well represented.

Museo de Arte Contemporáneo MUSEUM (MAC, Contemporary Art Museum; Map p46; ✆977-1741; www.mac.uchile.cl, in Spanish; Mosqueto s/n; admission by donation; ☺11am-7pm Tue-Sat, 11am-6pm Sun; MBellas Artes) Temporary exhibitions showcasing contemporary photography, design, sculpture, installations and web art are often held at the Museo de Arte Contemporáneo, also located inside the Palacio de Bellas Artes. Its pristine galleries are the result of extensive restoration work to reverse fire and earthquake damage. Twentieth century Chilean painting forms the bulk of the permanent collection.

FREE **Centro Gabriela Mistral** ARTS CENTER (GAM; Map p46; ✆566-5500; www.gam.cl, in Spanish; Av O'Higgins 227; ☺plazas 8am-midnight, exhibition spaces 10am-8pm Tue-Sat, from 11am Sun; MUniversidad Católica) This striking cultural center – named for Chilean poet Gabriela Mistral, the first Latin American woman to win the Nobel Prize in Literature – is an exciting new addition to Santiago's art scene. In addition to two large exhibition spaces and airy outdoor plazas, super-contemporary GAM comprises a delightful bookstore, a cool cafe and eatery, a wine shop and a small outdoor antiques fair. Free tours of the center leave every hour; inquire at the information desk.

Museo de Artes Visuales MUSEUM
(MAVI, Visual Arts Museum; Map p46; ☎638-3502; www.mavi.cl; Lastarria 307, Plaza Mulato Gil de Castro, Centro; adult/child CH$1000/500, free Sun; ☺10:30am-6:30pm Tue-Sun, closed Feb; ⓜBellas Artes) Exposed concrete, stripped wood and glass are the materials local architect Cristián Undurraga chose for the stunningly simple Museo de Artes Visuales. The contents of the four open-plan galleries are as winsome as the building: top-notch modern engravings, sculptures, paintings and photography form the regularly changing temporary exhibitions. Admission includes the **Museo Arqueológico de Santiago** (MAS; Santiago Archeological Museum), tucked away on the top floor. The low-lighted room with dark stone walls and floors makes an atmospheric backdrop for a small but quality collection of Diaguita, San Pedro and Molle ceramics, Mapuche jewelry and Easter Island carvings.

Parque Forestal PARK
(Map p46) On weekend afternoons, the temperature rises in Parque Forestal, a narrow green space wedged between Río Mapocho and Merced. The rest of the week it's filled with joggers and power walkers.

BARRIO BELLAVISTA
Tourists associate Bellavista with Pablo Neruda's house and the Virgin Mary statue looming over the city from the soaring hilltop park on Cerro San Cristóbal. For locals, Bellavista equals *carrete* (nightlife). Partying to the wee hours makes Bellavista's colorful streets and cobbled squares deliciously sleepy by day. Toss your map aside: the leafy residential streets east of Constitución are perfect for aimless wandering, while the graffitied blocks west of it are a photographer's paradise.

La Chascona HISTORIC BUILDING
(Map p52; ☎777-8741; www.fundacionneruda.org; Fernando Márquez de La Plata 0192; admission by tour only, adult/child in Spanish CH$2500/1500, in English CH$3500, students & seniors CH$1500; ☺10am-7pm Tue-Sun Jan & Feb, 10am-6pm Tue-Sun Mar-Dec; ⓜBaquedano) When poet Pablo Neruda needed a secret hideaway to spend time with his mistress Matilde Urrutia, he built La Chascona (loosely translated as 'messy hair'), the name inspired by her unruly curls. Neruda, of course, was a great lover of the sea, so the dining room is modeled on a ship's cabin and the living room on a lighthouse. Guided tours take you through the history of the building and the collection of colored glass, shells, furniture and artworks by famous friends that fills it – sadly much more was lost when the house was ransacked during the dictatorship. The Fundación Neruda, which maintains Neruda's houses, has its headquarters here and runs a lovely cafe and gift shop. Book at least one day ahead using the online form or by calling directly.

Cerro San Cristóbal MOUNTAIN
(Map p52; ☎730-1331; www.parquemet.cl, in Spanish) Bellavista entrance (Pío Nono 450, Barrio Bellavista; ⓜBaquedano); Providencia entrance (Av Pedro de Valdivia & El Cerro, Providencia; ⓜPedro de Valdivia) The best sweeping views over Santiago are from the peaks and viewpoints of the **Parque Metropolitano**, better known as Cerro San Cristóbal. At 722 hectares, the park is Santiago's largest green space, but it's still decidedly urban: a funicular carries you between different landscaped sections, and roads through it are aimed at cars rather than hikers. The park lies north of Bellavista and Providencia and has entrances in both neighborhoods.

A snowy white 14m-high statue of the **Virgen de la Inmaculada Concepción** (Map p52) towers atop the *cumbre* (summit) at the Bellavista end of the park. The benches at its feet are the outdoor church where Pope John Paul II said mass in 1984.

For years, the preferred mode of transportation to the summit were gondola-style cable cars; at the time of writing, the *teleférico* was out of service and the only public transportation to and from the top was the **funicular train** (Map p52; adult/child round-trip CH$1800/1100; ☺10am-8pm Tue-Sun, 1-8pm Mon) that climbs 284m from Plaza Caupolicán at the north end of Pío Nono. It stops halfway up at the small **Zoológico Nacional** (National Zoo; Map p52; ☎730-1334; Parque Metropolitano; adult/child CH$3000/1500; ☺10am-6pm Tue-Sun; ⓜBaquedano). Though the zoo isn't too impressive, it may be one of the only places in Chile where you're assured a glimpse of the pint-sized pudú deer, Chile's national mascot. Note that the funicular stops at the zoo on the way up, but not on the way down.

Other attractions on the hillside include the **Jardín Botánico Mapulemu**, a botanical garden; the child-oriented **Plaza de Juegos**

Barrio Bellavista

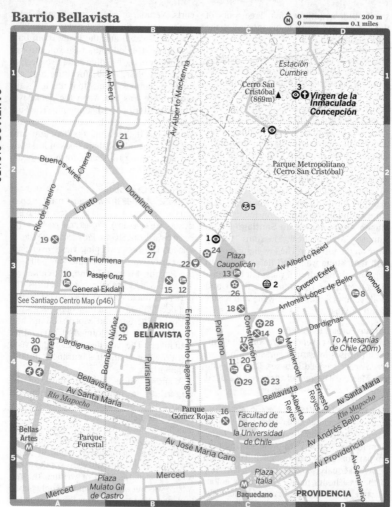

Infantiles Gabriela Mistral featuring attractive wooden playground equipment and an interactive water fountain; and two huge public swimming pools, the **Piscina Tupahue** and **Piscina Antilén** (see p58). The small but perfectly landscaped **Jardín Japonés** (Japanese Garden; Map p46) is 400m east.

There are snack stands near the cable-car stations, but Cerro San Cristóbal is also a prime picnicking spot – pick up your provisions down in Bellavista before ascending. Near the top of the funicular is the **Terraza Bellavista** (Map p52) where there are extraordinary views across the city.

Patio Bellavista CULTURAL BUILDING
(Map p52; ☏249-8700; www.patiobellavista.cl; Constitución 30-70; ⏱11am-2am Sun-Wed, 10am-4am Thu-Sat; Ⓜ Baquedano) Upmarket eateries and posh souvenir shops ranged around a huge courtyard make up Patio Bellavista, a clear attempt by developers to spruce up the barrio. True, it's very 'for export,' but they've kept things classy enough to make it worth a wander. Check the online schedule for full listings and the schedule of live music and theatre performances.

BARRIO BRASIL & BARRIO YUNGAY

Toss aside the map, but don't forget your camera – wandering through these slightly sleepy barrios west of the center is like stepping back in time. Characterized by vibrant street art, crumbling old-fashioned houses, down-to-earth outdoor markets and a range of hole-in-the-wall ethnic eateries, these *barrios históricos* (historic neighborhoods) offer a charming counterpoint to the high-rise glitz of Santiago's business sector. True, the area is short on tourist sights and has a dodgy reputation after dark – but a stroll through the neighborhood offers a glimpse of faded grandeur you're unlikely to find elsewhere in the Chilean capital.

A spindly monkey-puzzle tree shades **Plaza Brasil**, the green heart of the 'hood. A wave of urban renovation is slowly sweeping the surrounding streets, where more and more bars and hip hostels are popping up. Incongruous among the car-parts shops between here and the Alameda is pint-sized **Barrio Concha y Toro**, featuring a gorgeous little square fed by cobblestone streets and overlooked by art deco and beaux arts mansions.

FREE Museo de la Memoria y los Derechos Humanos   MUSEUM
(Museum of Memory & Human Rights; Map p54; ☑597-9600; www.museodelamemoria.cl, in Spanish; Matucana 501; ☉10am-8pm Tue-Sun; ⓜRicardo Cumming) Opened in 2010, this brand-new museum isn't for the faint of heart: the exhibits expose the terrifying human rights violations and large-scale 'disappearances' that took place under Chile's military government between the years of 1973 and 1990. There's no way around it – learning about the 40,000 victims subjected to torture and execution is positively chilling – but a visit to this carefully curated museum helps to contextualize Chile's tumultuous recent history.

Parque Quinta Normal   PARK
(Map p54; ⓜQuinta Normal) Strolls, picnics, pedal-boating, soccer kickabouts and soapbox rants are all popular activities at the 40-hectare Parque Quinta Normal, just west of Barrio Brasil. Several museums are also located here, though they're not up to the standard of the offerings elsewhere in the city. For information on the child-oriented Museo Artequín, see p61.

Museo de Arte Contemporáneo Espacio Quinta Normal   MUSEUM
(Museum of Contemporary Art, Quinta Normal Branch; Map p54; ☑681-7813; www.mac.uchile.cl, in Spanish; Matucana 464; admission by donation; ☉11am-7pm Tue-Sat, 11am-6pm Sun; ⓜRicardo Cumming) This branch of the downtown Museo de Arte Contemporáneo specializes in

Barrio Brasil

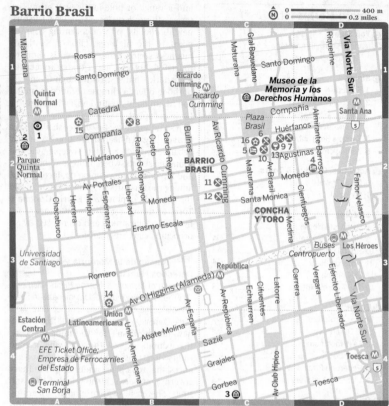

offbeat and experimental exhibitions. It's housed in the **Palacio Versailles**, declared a national monument in 2004.

FREE **Centro Cultural**
Matucana 100   ARTS CENTER
(Map p54; ☎682-4502; www.m100.cl, in Spanish; Matucana 100; ticket prices to performances vary; ⊙11am-1pm & 2-9pm; ⓜQuinta Normal & Estación Central) One of Santiago's hippest alternative arts venues, the huge red-brick Centro Cultural Matucana 100 gets its gritty industrial look from its previous incarnation as government warehouses. Renovated as part of Chile's bicentennial project, it now contains a hangarlike gallery and a theater for art-house film cycles, concerts and fringe productions.

PROVIDENCIA

Head east from the Centro, and Santiago's neighborhoods slowly get swisher. First up: Providencia, a traditionally upper-middle-

class area that's short on sights but very long indeed on drinking and dining possibilities. The '70s and '80s tower blocks along the area's main artery, Av Providencia, aren't aesthetically interesting, but the more residential side streets contain some lovely early-20th-century buildings.

FREE **Parque de las Esculturas**
Exhibition Hall   ART, PARK
(Sculpture Park; Map p56; ☎340-7303; Av Santa María 2205; ⊙10am-7:30pm; ⓜPedro de Valdivia) On the north side of the Río Mapocho lies a rare triumph in city landscaping: the Parque de las Esculturas, a green stretch along the river decorated with 20 unique sculptures by noted Chilean artists.

Casa Museo Eduardo Frei
Montalva   HISTORIC BUILDING
(off Map p56; ☎881-8674; www.casamuseoedu ardofrei.cl; Hindenburg 683; adult/child & sen-

Barrio Brasil

ior CH$1300/700, free last Sun of every month; ⊙10am-6pm Tue-Sun, closed Feb; MPedro de Valdivia) This historic former home of Chilean president Eduardo Frei Montalva (elected in 1964) houses a collection of his original furniture, textiles, paintings, glassware and cutlery alongside family photographs and mementos from his official travels.

LAS CONDES, BARRIO EL GOLF & VITACURA

Glittering skyscrapers, security-heavy apartment blocks and spanking-new malls: Las Condes is determined to be the international face of Chile's phenomenal economic growth. In addition to posh eateries and American chain restaurants, these ritzy neighborhoods also contain Santiago's most exclusive shopping street, Av Alonso de Córdova – not to mention a steady stream of business travelers who take up temporary residence in the area's gleaming high-rise hotels. The tongue-in-cheek nickname 'Sanhattan' is sometimes used to describe the financial district around the Costanera Center, about to be the tallest building in South America.

TOP CHOICE **Museo de la Moda** MUSEUM
(Museum of Fashion; off Map p59; ☑218-5500; www.museodelamoda.cl; Av Vitacura 4562, Vitacura; adult/student & senior/child CH$3500/2000/free, CH$1800 for all visitors on Wed & Sun; ⊙10am-6pm Tue-Fri, 11am-7pm Sat & Sun; MEscuela Militar) This slick, privately operated fashion museum comprises a vast and exquisite permanent collection of Western clothing – 20th-century designers are particularly well-represented. Star attractions include John Lennon's jacket from 1966, the 'cone bra' Jean Paul Gaultier designed for Madonna, and an evening gown donned by Lady Diana in 1981 (but note that only a fraction of items from the 10,000-piece collection are on display at any given time.) Lighthearted temporary exhibits have ranged from a Michael Jackson tribute to a 'Back to the 80s' show to a *fútbol*-themed exhibit featuring athletic wear from the World Cup held in Chile in 1962. The airy on-site cafe is a fashionable spot for coffee or lunch.

WORTH A TRIP

CEMENTERIO GENERAL

More than just a graveyard, Santiago's **Cementerio General** (☑737-9469; www.cementeriogeneral.cl; Av Profesor Alberto Zañartu 951; ⊙8:30am-6pm; MCementerios) is a veritable city of tombs, many adorned with works by famous local sculptors. The names above the crypts read like a who's who of Chilean history: its most tumultuous moments are attested to by Salvador Allende's tomb and the **Memorial del Detenido Desaparecido y del Ejecutado Político**, a memorial to the 'disappeared' of Pinochet's dictatorship. To reach the memorial from the main entrance, walk down Av Lima, turning right into Horvitz for another 200m; it's over the bridge to the right.

Providencia

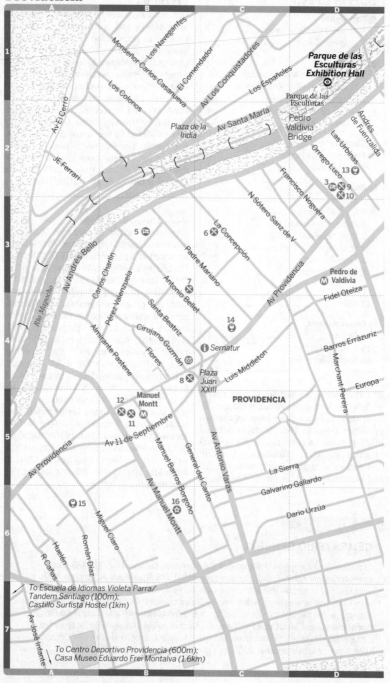

Parque de las
Esculturas
Exhibition Hall

To Escuela de Idiomas Violeta Parra/
Tandem Santiago (100m);
Castillo Surfista Hostel (1km)

To Centro Deportivo Providencia (600m);
Casa Museo Eduardo Frei Montalva (1.6km)

Providencia

◉ Top Sights
Parque de las Esculturas
Exhibition Hall....................D1

◔ Activities, Courses & Tours
1 Santiago Adventures...........................E3

◰ Sleeping
2 Andes Suites E3
3 Hotel Orly..D2
4 Intiwasi Hotel...................................F3
5 Vilafranca Petit Hotel B3

◔ Eating
6 Aquí Está Coco.................................C3
7 Astrid y Gastón B3
8 Doner House.....................................B4
9 El Huerto...D2
10 Liguria...D2
11 Liguria...B5
12 Voraz Pizza......................................B5

◔ Drinking
Bar:Liguria .... (see 10)
13 California Cantina...............................D2
14 Phone Box Pub................................... C4
15 Santo Remedio.................................A6

◔ Entertainment
16 Mito Urbano......................................B6

◔ Shopping
Contrapunto ....(see 17)
Galería del Patio.........................(see 14)
17 Galería Drugstore E2

From Escuela Militar metro, grab a taxi, or take bus 305 from the west side of Américo Vespucio (you need a Bip! card) and get off at the intersection with Av Vitacura.

Parque Bicentenario   PARK
(Bicentennial Park; off Map p59; Andrés Bello 2461; ⓜTobalaba) This gorgeous urban oasis was created, as the name suggests, in celebration of the Chilean bicentennial. In addition to more than 4000 trees, a peaceful location alongside the Río Mapocho, and access to city bike paths, the park features inviting chaise lounges and sun umbrellas to lounge under, plus state-of-the-art playground equipment for kids. It's a quick taxi ride from the Tobalaba metro station, or hop on bus 405 and get off at Alonso de Córdova. Keep walking in the direction of the bus until you turn onto Av Bicentenario, a few blocks from the park.

Costanera Center
ARCHITECTURE

(Map p59; Andrés Bello 2461; MTobalaba) Financial woes have halted construction several times on this ambitious project: the four skyscrapers that make up the future Costanera Center include **Gran Torre Santiago**, set to be the tallest building in South America (300m) when it's completed. Though building was still underway at the time of writing, the towers will include luxury apartments, a pair of high-end hotels, a large shopping mall and a food court with panoramic views.

BARRIO ESTACIÓN CENTRAL

Museo de la Solidaridad
Salvador Allende
MUSEUM

(Map p54; ☑689-8761; www.museodelasolidaridad.cl; Av República 475; adult/student & senior CH$1000/free, free Sun; ☉10am-6pm Tue-Sun; MRepública) Picasso, Miró, Tàpies and Matta are some of the artistic heavyweights who gave works to the Museo de la Solidaridad Salvador Allende. Begun as a populist art initiative during Allende's presidency – and named in his honor – the incredible collection was taken abroad during the dictatorship, where it became a symbol of Chilean resistance. The 2000 works finally found a home in 2006, when the Fundación Allende bought and remodeled this grand old townhouse. The permanent collection sometimes goes on tour and is replaced by temporary exhibitions, and there's a darkened room with an eerie display of Allende's personal effects. Guided tours (email ahead) visit the basement, where you can see tangled telephone wires and torture instruments left over from when the house was used by the dictatorship's notorious DINA as a listening station.

Palacio Cousiño
PALACE

(☑698-5063; www.palaciocousino.co.cl; Dieciocho 438; admission on guided tour only; ☉9:30am-1:30pm & 2:30-5pm Tue-Fri, 9:30am-1:30pm Sat & Sun, last tours leave an hour before closing; MToesca) 'Flaunt it' seems to have been the main idea behind the shockingly lavish Palacio Cousiño. It was built between 1870 and 1878 by the prominent Cousiño-Goyenechea family after they'd amassed a huge fortune from wine-making and coal and silver mining, and it's a fascinating glimpse of how Chile's 19th-century elite lived. Carrara marble columns, a half-tonne Bohemian crystal chandelier, Chinese cherrywood furniture, solid gold cutlery, and the first electrical fittings in Chile are just some of the ways they found to fritter away their fortune.

 ## Activities

Swimming

There are fabulous views from the two huge, open-air pools atop Cerro San Cristóbal, **Piscina Tupahue** (☑732-0998; adult/child CH$6000/3500; ☉10am-7:30pm Tue-Sun Nov-Mar) and **Piscina Antilén** (☑732-0998; adult/child CH$7500/4000; ☉10am-7:30pm Tue-Sun Nov-Mar). Both are more for splashing about than serious training.

Centro Deportivo Providencia
SWIMMING

(off Map p56; ☑341-4790; www.cdprovidencia.cl; Santa Isabel 0830; day pass CH$5000-7000; ☉6:30am-10pm Mon-Fri, 9am-6pm Sat & Sun) You can do your lengths year-round at this 25m indoor pool.

Walking, Running & Cycling

Locals run, walk and cycle along the Río Mapocho (especially through the Parque Forestal), in Parque Quinta Normal and along the steep roads of Cerro San Cristóbal. In town on the first Tuesday of the month? Join the crowds of cyclists who cruise through the city on two wheels, part of the **Movimiento Furiosos Ciclistas** (Furious Bikers Movement; www.furiosos.cl). Check in with La Bicicleta Verde for more information.

La Bicicleta Verde
CYCLING

(Map p52; ☑570-9338; www.labicicletaverde.cl; cnr Loreto & Santa María, Bellavista; half-day CH$4000-9000, per day CH$9000-15,000; MBellas Artes) You can rent bikes and helmets here or choose from highly recommended guided tours like Bike at Night (CH$30,000).

Courses

Although Santiago isn't the cheapest place to kick-start your Spanish, these language schools have excellent reputations.

Escuela de Idiomas Violeta
Parra/Tandem Santiago
LANGUAGE COURSE

(Map p56; ☑236-4241; www.tandemsantiago.cl; Triana 863, Providencia; enrollment fee US$50, single one-on-one lesson from US$20, intensive weeklong course with accommodations from US$365; MSalvador) Combines an outstanding academic record with a friendly vibe and cultural activities. Accommodations (optional) are in shared or private apartments. Check the website for special courses like 'Spanish for Lawyers' or 'Medical Spanish.'

Natalislang
LANGUAGE COURSE

(Map p46; ☑222-8721; www.natalislang.com; Av Vicuña Mackenna 6, 7th fl, Oficina 4, Centro; tradi-

Las Condes

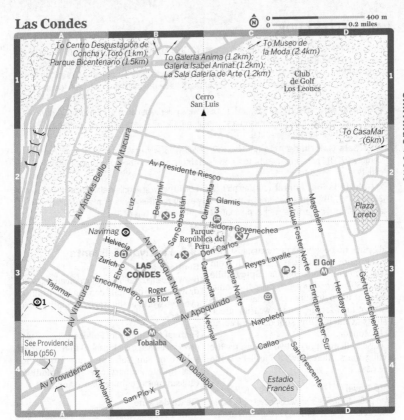

tional weeklong course from CH\$99,000, intensive 3-day traveler crash course from CH\$150,000) Great for quick, intense courses. The website has an extensive list of options.

Instituto Chileno-Británico LANGUAGE COURSE
(Map p46; ☎413-2350; www.britanico.cl, in Spanish; Huérfanos 554, Centro; ⓂSanta Lucía) Qualified English teachers may find work at this language school. There's also a library with some English-language newspapers and periodicals.

☞ Tours

A few new companies offer free walking tours in English that take in the city's central tourist sights. Guides work for tips only, so travelers are simply encouraged to offer them some gratuity for the service.

Free Tour Santiago (☎236-8789; www.freetoursantiago.cl) runs tours every day at 10am

---

Las Condes

⊙ Sights
1 Costanera Center A3

⊟ Sleeping
2 Ritz Carlton...C3
3 W Hotel Santiago C2

⊗ Eating
4 Café Melba...B3
5 Dominó...B2
6 Liguria..B4
7 Tiramisú C3

⊕ Drinking
Red2One ....(see 3)

⊙ Shopping
8 Andesgear...B3
Mundo del Vino ....(see 3)

ART GALLERY HOP

Ground zero for the exhibition of contemporary Chilean art – and a choice spot to observe a fashionable crowd of Santiaguinos in their natural habitat – is the gallery circuit around Alonso de Córdova. Drop by one of these art spaces for an opening to see the champagne-fueled scene at its most happening. Check the galleries' websites for upcoming events and times.

» **Galería Animal** (off Map p59; ☑371-9090; www.galeriaanimal.com; Alonso de Córdova 3105) Edgy contemporary works in a stunning multilevel space complete with a rooftop terrace facing the Andes.

» **La Sala Galería de Arte** (off Map p59; ☑246-7013; www.galerialasala.cl; Alonso de Córdova 2700) Featuring the photography, sculpture and painting of rising Chilean artists.

» **Galería Isabel Aninat** (off Map p59; ☑481-9870; www. galeriaisabelaninat.cl; Espoz 3100) Since 1983, this well-known gallery has exhibited the works of major Chilean and international artists, including Joan Miró and Antoni Gaudí.

and 3pm – no booking is necessary, just look for the guides wearing red shirts in front of the Catedral Metropolitana. **Spicy Chile** (☑342-3307; www.spicychile.cl) does the same, leaving at 10am and 2pm every day but Sunday. Just look for the guides wearing green T-shirts at the meeting spot outside Palacio de la Moneda.

For excellent tours on two wheels, try the cycling tours offered by La Bicicleta Verde (see p58).

Chip Travel   TOUR
(Map p46; ☑737-5649; www.chiptravel.cl; Av Santa María 227, Oficina 11; Ⓜ Bellas Artes) This excellent tour operator's refreshing slogan is 'No more buses. No more name tags.' They run independent tours including a human rights–themed circuit (from CH$35,000 per person) that combines Parque por la Paz, a memorial for victims of the last dictatorship (see boxed text, p41), with a stop at the Fundación Pinochet.

Santiago Adventures   TOUR
(Map p56; ☑244-2750; www.santiagoadventures. com; Guardia Vieja 255, Oficina 403, Providencia; Ⓜ Los Leones) Savvy English-speaking tour guides lead personalized tours covering the city's food and wine, as well as day trips to the coast.

Turistik   BUS TOUR
(☑220-1000; www.turistik.cl; day pass from CH$17,100; ⊙9:30am-6pm) Hop-on hop-off double-decker bus tours run to 13 stops between the Centro district and Parque Arauco mall. Check the online map for further information.

✵ Festivals & Events

Santiago a Mil   THEATER
(www.stgoamil.cl) This major theater festival draws experimental companies from all over the world to the stages of Santiago each January.

Festival Nacional del Folklore   MUSIC
(www.sanbernardo.cl, in Spanish) In the southern suburb of San Bernardo, this five-day festival in late January celebrates traditional Chilean music, culture, dance and food.

Fiesta del Vino   WINE
(www.fiestadelvinodepirque.cl, in Spanish) This wine festival in Pirque, one of many taking place around Santiago during harvest time, also features traditional cuisine and folkloric music.

Rodeo Season   RODEO
(www.rodeochileno.cl, in Spanish) In Chile, March is all about *huasos* (cowboys) and bucking broncos. The focus of the action is Rancagua, 145km south of Santiago, but events also take place in Santiago.

Lollapalooza Chile   MUSIC
(www.lollapaloozacl.com) The famous music festival now has a Chilean edition; national and international acts roll into Santiago at the end of March.

Santiago Festival Internacional de Cine   FILM
(SANFIC; www.sanfic.cl) Each August, Santiago's weeklong film festival showcases choice independent cinema throughout several movie theaters.

Festival de Jazz de Ñuñoa   MUSIC
(www.ccn.cl, in Spanish) Free concerts that showcase jazz and blues from some of Chile's top musicians take place at the Teatro Municipal de Ñuñoa over a weekend in August.

Feria Internacional de Artesanía   ART
Talented craftspeople show off their creations each November in Parque Bustamente, Providencia.

Feria Internacional del Libro   BOOKS
(www.camlibro.cl) Scores of publishing houses and authors from throughout the Spanish-speaking world move into the Estación Mapocho and set up in the last week of November.

🛏 Sleeping

For longer stays, consider renting a furnished apartment. **Contact Chile** (☎264-1719; www.contactchile.cl) and **Lastarria 43** (Map p46; ☎639-3132; www.apartmentsantiago.cl; Lastarria 43, Centro) are two reliable rental services, while **Ameristar** (Map p46; ☎581-3715; www.ameristar.cl) provides furnished mini-apartments that are in a perfectly located building in Barrio Lastarria.

CENTRO
Hostel Plaza de Armas   HOSTEL $
(Map p46; ☎671-4436; www.plazadearmashostel.com; Compañía 960, Apt 607, Plaza de Armas; dm CH$8800, d or apt incl breakfast CH$29,000; @🛜; MPlaza de Armas) You'll think you're in the wrong place when you show up to this busy apartment building on Santiago's main square. Take the elevator to the 6th floor to reach this cheery hostel – once a large apartment – with tiny dorms, a well-equipped communal kitchen, and great balconies with views over the Plaza de Armas. The self-contained doubles can be hit or miss; ask to see the room first.

SANTIAGO FOR CHILDREN

Santiaguinos are family-oriented and usually welcome travelers with children. Kids stay up late and often accompany their parents to parties or restaurants, where they order from the regular menu rather than a separate one for children. That said, most kiddy-oriented activities here are helpful distractions rather than standout sights. In a pinch, children also love creamy Chilean ice cream, which is available everywhere, and the clowns and acrobats that put on performances in the Plaza de Armas and Parque Forestal on weekends.

Fantasilandia (☎476-8600; www.fantasilandia.cl; Av Beaucheff 938; adult/child from CH$7900/4400, children under 90cm free; ⊙noon-9pm daily Jan–mid-Feb, noon-7pm daily mid-Feb–Mar, noon-7pm Sat & Sun Apr-Jun; MParque O'Higgins) Give your children their dose of adrenaline and cotton candy at this colorful amusement park. Check the Fantasilandia website for further information, updates, frequent promotions and discounts.

Parque Metropolitano Your one-stop shop for good clean fun is the Parque Metropolitano (p51), which combines a modest zoo, two great outdoor swimming pools and a well-maintained playground with interesting transport – a creaky cable car and a funicular. Toffee-apple vendors and fee-charging, photogenic llamas crowd the Bellavista entrance on weekends.

Museo Interactivo Mirador (MIM, Mirador Interactive Museum; ☎828-8000; www.mim.cl; Punta Arenas 6711, La Granja; adult/child CH$3900/2600, tickets half-price Wed; ⊙9:30am-6:30pm Tue-Sun; MMirador) The stimulus is more intellectual – but still fun – at the Museo Interactivo Mirador. Forget 'do not touch': you can handle, push, lie on and even get inside most of the exhibits.

Museo Artequín (Map p54; ☎681-8656; www.artequin.cl; Av Portales 3530; adult/child CH$800/500; ⊙9am-5pm Tue-Fri, 11am-6pm Sat & Sun, closed Feb; MQuinta Normal) Education and entertainment also come together at the Museo Artequín – a museum that showcases copies of famous artworks, hung at children's height in a striking cast-iron and glass structure that was once used as Chile's pavilion in the 1889 Paris Exhibition.

GAY & LESBIAN SANTIAGO

Although Santiago is still not on the Latin American gaydar in the same way as Buenos Aires or Rio, the scene's surprisingly good for a country that's still ultra-Catholic and fairly socially conservative.

Every June, thousands take part in the **Marcha del Orgullo Gay** (Gay Pride Parade), organized by the **Movimiento Chileno de Minorías Sexuales** (Movilh; Map p46; www.movilh.org, in Spanish; Coquimbo 1410, Centro). The website has links to social events. There's another annual parade in late November, the **Open Mind Fest** (www.movilh.cl/gayparade, in Spanish), which is one big electronic street party. **Sitiosgay** (www.sitiosgay.cl, in Spanish) has listings of Chilean gay and gay-friendly organizations, hotels, pubs and bars, clubs, salons and more. For listings in English, try **Queer City** (www.santiago.queercity.info).

The heart of the nightlife action is Bellavista, home to the bar-lined street Bombero Núñez as well as several other bars and clubs. In addition to the places mentioned below, **Blondie** (p72) also draws in a decent gay crowd.

Vox Populi (Map p52; ☎738-0562; Ernesto Pinto Lagarrigue 364, Bellavista; ☻from 9pm Tue-Sat; Ⓜ Baquedano) Tucked away on a side street in Bellavista, you will walk right past this place if you're not paying attention; the low-key entrance adds to the cool factor. An old house filled with mismatched furniture is the setting for this relaxed bar, popular with an arty crowd, both gay and straight. In summer, you can sip your cocktails on a plant-filled patio. The volume gets turned up on weekends.

Bokhara (Map p52; www.bokhara.cl, in Spanish; Pío Nono 430, Bellavista; ☻10pm-4am Mon-Sun; Ⓜ Baquedano) Although local connoisseurs may think it is slightly passé, Bokhara is still the automatic choice for mid-week clubbing. House and techno music are the main beats that are spun on its two floors; there are live shows every night at 11:30pm and 2:30am. If you buy a drink, the CH$2000 cover is waived.

Bunker (Map p52; www.bunker.cl, in Spanish; Bombero Núñez 159, Bellavista; cover CH$5000-7000; ☻from 11pm Fri & Sat; Ⓜ Baquedano) The hippest gay club night in town draws a mix of well-dressed local people (including minor celebrities), as well as visitors who love the high-octane music, glamorous dancers and theme nights ('Whitney Houston Forever,' in honor of the late pop singer, was drawing crowds at the time of writing).

Hotel Vegas
HOTEL **$$**

(Map p46; ☎632-2514; www.hotelvegas.net; Londres 49; s/d incl breakfast CH$37,000/46,200, apt for 2/3 people CH$32,900/37,800; Ⓟ❄@☎; Ⓜ Universidad de Chile) There's a vintage twist to the grand old rooms at the Hotel Vegas – think wood paneling, beige bathrooms and lime green accents. Apart from some travelers' complaints of noise at night, this antique building in the classy Barrio París-Londres has a lot going for it – spacious quarters, a decent breakfast, friendly staff and a high standard of cleanliness. The affiliated apartments (in another building down the road) are excellent value; note that there's a three-day minimum stay.

Hostal Río Amazonas
HOSTEL **$**

(Map p46; ☎635-1631; www.hostalrioamazonas.cl; Av Vicuña Mackenna 47; s/d/q incl breakfast CH$19,000/25,000/43,000; @☎; Ⓜ Baquedano) Families and couples make up most of the guests at this mock-Tudor mansion painted a warm orangey-yellow. Rooms are plain but bright and have lovely parquet floors; double-glazed windows keep the sounds of the avenue at bay.

Hotel Galerías
HOTEL **$$$**

(Map p46; ☎470-7400; www.hotelgalerias.cl; San Antonio 65; s/d incl breakfast CH$78,000/88,000; ❄@☎❄❄; Ⓜ Santa Lucía) This hotel is certainly proud to be Chilean: mock *moai* (Easter Island statues) guard the entrance, the restaurant specializes in regional cuisine, and the simple but well-appointed rooms are accented with traditional weavings and hardwood furniture. Thanks to the outdoor swimming pool and the fact that kids under 10 stay free with their parents, it's also a solid family pick.

Hotel Plaza San Francisco
LUXURY HOTEL **$$$**

(Map p46; ☎639-3832; www.plazasanfrancisco.cl; Alameda 816; d incl breakfast CH$91,500; ❄@☎❄; Ⓜ Universidad de Chile) An oak-paneled reception, hunting prints and sober maroon and mustard furnishings in the rooms: this hotel is angling for the English drawing-room look. The impeccably mannered staff are a match for any butler, the fitness center is convenient, the buffet breakfast and on-site restaurant are excellent, but overall the place feels overdue for some updates.

BARRIO LASTARRIA & BARRIO BELLAS ARTES

Hostal Forestal
HOSTEL $
(Map p46; ☑638-1347; www.hostalforestal.cl; Coronel Santiago Bueras 120; dm/s without bathroom CH$6000/18,000, d with/without bathroom CH$13,500/11,000 per person; @☎; MBaquedano) Recent renovations and colorful new wall-sized murals have added some visual appeal to this lively hostel. Dorms with bunkbeds are functional and bathrooms basic; the private single and doubles offer slightly more charm. Also on the menu are Chilean cooking classes, live music, bike rentals, weekly *asados* (barbecues) and poetry readings.

Andes Hostel
HOSTEL $
(Map p46; ☑633-1976; www.andeshostel.com; Monjitas 506; dm CH$8250, d with/without bathroom CH$31,500/24,100, apt for 1-4 people CH$36,300-65,300; @☎☒; MBellas Artes) Pistachio-colored walls, a zebra-print rug, mismatched retro sofas and a mosaic-tiled bar are some of the pop-art charms of this centrally located hostel. Unfortunately, dorms look better than they feel – without air-con, they're rather airless on hot nights. It's worth splashing out more for an Andes apartment on the next block, especially as you'll get swimming pool access and possibly a private balcony.

BELLAVISTA

TOP CHOICE Bellavista Home
B&B $$
(Map p52; ☑735-9259; www.bellavistahome.cl; Capellán Abarzúa 143; d with/without bathroom CH$35,000/45,000, tr without bathroom CH$45,000; @☎♿; MBaquedano) This four-room B&B, housed inside an antique building that once contained artists' workshops, is a tranquil and family-friendly respite from the *carrete* and crowds of Bellavista. Breezy rooms are outfitted with pristine white linens, colorful throw rugs and brightly painted wooden doors. All guests have kitchen access; an adorable breakfast and round-the-clock coffee and tea can be

enjoyed on the pretty garden patio. Prices include breakfast.

The Aubrey Hotel
LUXURY HOTEL $$$
(Map p52; ☑940-2800; www.theaubrey.com; Constitución 299-317; d incl breakfast US$240-350, ste US$450-550; @☎☒; MBaquedano) The Aubrey garnered international attention when it made Condé Nast's Hot List in 2010. Indeed, an award seems in order for the extensive restorations that transformed this Spanish-style patrician mansion and the adjacent art deco house, both dating from 1927, into an ultra-sleek boutique hotel. The luxury amenities are standard for the price range; true standout features include the lovely (and well-heated) outdoor swimming pool, tech-forward lighting throughout, romantic alfresco dining at the on-site Italian restaurant, and the stunning location at the foot of Cerro San Cristóbal.

Bellavista Hostel
HOSTEL $
(Map p52; ☑732-8737; www.bellavistahostel.com; Dardignac 0184; dm CH$8000, s/d without bathroom CH$15,000/25,000; @; MBaquedano) A Bellavista classic. Brightly painted walls crammed with colorful paintings and graffiti announce this hostel's relaxed, arty vibe. The city's best bars and clubs are on your doorstep and so, sometimes, are their clients – peaceful slumbers are not the main aim here, though rooms in the annex are quieter. Prices include breakfast.

Hotel del Patio
BOUTIQUE HOTEL $$
(Map p52; ☑732-7571; www.hoteldelpatio.cl; Pío Nono 61; s/d/tr incl breakfast from CH$53,200/55,600/62,900; @; MBaquedano) This design-conscious boutique, converted from a rambling 19th-century house, comprises 10 guest rooms situated around a courtyard. The original

native wood floors remain, but flat-screen TVs and contemporary hues like cerulean, emerald, pistachio and chocolate add a modern spin. The buffet breakfast is a treat, but be forewarned: the thin walls often let in significant nighttime noise.

Hostal Caracol
HOSTEL $

(Map p52; ☎732-4644; www.hostalcaracol.cl/hostel_santiago; General Ekdhal 151; dm CH$8000, d/q from CH$28,000/CH$44,000; @☎; MPatronato) This well-located hostel is nearly brand-new, and it shows. The beds and bathrooms feel like they've hardly been used. Sleeping quarters can be tight – the place is, after all, a restored house from the 1920s – but you won't care if you've scored one of the en suite doubles with a lovely private balcony. A grassy yard, spacious terrace and a sparkling-clean open kitchen round out the offerings. Prices include breakfast.

La Chimba
HOSTEL $

(Map p52; ☎735-8978; www.lachimba.com; Ernesto Pinto Lagarrigue 262; dm CH$7000-8000, d CH$20,000; @☎; MBaquedano) Extra-wide bunks with well-sprung mattresses and feather quilts practically guarantee sweet dreams at this small hostel (though the beats from nearby clubs always filter in on weekends). The red-painted living room is cozy and the kitchen small but well-equipped. If only they'd put the same effort into the broken door handles or leaking showers... Still, the friendly staff bend over backwards to help. Prices include breakfast.

BARRIO BRASIL & BARRIO YUNGAY

Happy House Hostel
HOSTEL $

(Map p54; ☎688-4849; www.happyhousehostel.cl; Moneda 1829, Barrio Brasil; dm without breakfast CH$8000, dm/s/d/tr incl breakfast CH$10,000/23,000/25,000/35,000; @☎✉; MLos Héroes) Happy news indeed: this popular hostel has moved on from its original Barrio Brasil location. And with the new digs come slightly cheaper prices and welcome features: open terraces, spacious doubles outfitted with cutting-edge decor, a swimming pool and luggage storage services. Did we mention the building itself is a gorgeous restored townhouse redone with eye-popping colors and funky chandeliers? If you're here during ski season, note that only common areas and private rooms are heated.

La Casa Roja
HOSTEL $

(Map p54; ☎696-4241; www.lacasaroja.cl; Agustinas 2113; dm CH$6800, d with/without bathroom

CH$23,100/18,800; @☎; MRicardo Cumming) With its swimming pool, airy patios, outdoor bar, garden and a huge, well-designed kitchen, it's easy to see why this Aussie-owned outfit is backpacker central – even if travelers perennially complain about the grumpy staff. Serious socializing isn't the only appeal: with its sweeping staircases and sky-high molded ceilings, the lovingly restored 19th-century mansion oozes character. Especially great value are the doubles, fitted with stylish retro furniture and bijoux bathrooms.

PROVIDENCIA

Vilafranca Petit Hotel
B&B $$

(Map p56; ☎235-1413; www.vilafranca.cl; Pérez Valenzuela 1650; s CH$41,000, d CH$49,000-53,000; @☎; MPedro de Valdivia) Why can't all B&Bs be this good? Squishy sofas in the living room and wooden steamer chairs in a plant-filled patio invite you to make yourself at home. The rooms feel deliciously Merchant Ivory: think sage-colored walls hung with dried flowers, time-worn parquet and artfully mismatched antique furniture. Prices include breakfast.

Castillo Surfista Hostel
HOSTEL $

(off Map p56; ☎893-3350; www.castillosurfista.com; Maria Luisa Santander 0329; dm CH$8000-9000, d without bathroom from CH$20,000-24,000; @☎; MBaquedano) If Santiago is a layover on your journey towards Chile's famous waves – or if you're just looking for a spotless, friendly place to sleep – this brand-new hostel is your place. Run by a California surfer, the renovated house features homey dorms and doubles, tidy communal areas and laid-back hosts who can help you access the surf scene (the owner even runs shuttle service to his favorite breaks). The slightly off-the-beaten-path location means you can actually get a good night's sleep here.

Intiwasi Hotel
BOUTIQUE HOTEL $$

(Map p56; ☎985-5285; www.intiwasihotel.com; Josue Smith Solar 380; d CH$34,000-37,400; ❋@☎; MLos Leones) This cozy, centrally located hotel is more like a boutique hostel for grown-ups. The proud owners are eager to help you plan your travels, and the look is native Chilean – Intiwasi means 'house of the sun' in Quechua – with indigenous textiles, dark wood and bright hues of red and orange throughout. Rooms have private bathrooms and LCD televisions.

Hotel Orly
LUXURY HOTEL $$$

(Map p56; ☎231-8947; www.orlyhotel.com; Av Pedro de Valdivia 027; s/d incl breakfast US$120/135, apt incl breakfast US$110; ❄@; MPedro de Valdivia) This stately hotel will catch your eye from the street. The look is classic, with dark wood furnishings, crisp white linens and heavy maroon drapes; guest rooms feature luxurious details like renovated bathrooms with big marble sinks and windows made of soundproof glass. There's coffee, tea and cake available all day in the breakfast room. Slightly more affordable are the Orly's 12 apartments down the block; service includes breakfast at the hotel.

Andes Suites
APARTMENT $$$

(Map p56; ☎761-7070; www.andes-suites.cl; Diego de Velázquez 2071; 1-/2-bedroom apt incl breakfast US$95/105; ❄❄; MPedro de Valdivia) An upscale hotel runs these furnished apartments, so you get the best of both worlds, including daily maid service and breakfast. Kitchens could be better equipped, but there's a gorgeous rooftop pool with views over the Andes. Weekly rates are significantly cheaper.

LAS CONDES, BARRIO EL GOLF & VITACURA

W Hotel Santiago
LUXURY HOTEL $$$

(Map p59; ☎770-0000; www.starwoodhotels.com; Isidora Goyenechea 3000, Las Condes; r from US$269; ❄@❄❄; MEl Golf) With three hipper-than-thou eateries and a pair of happening cocktail bars, plus a chic spa, salon, fitness center and rooftop infinity pool with panoramic views of the Andes, this W outpost quickly became one of the most prominent landmarks on Santiago's social scene when it opened in late 2009. Like its sister hotels around the world, the W has a sophisticated air and an artistic edge; this particular branch brings in local flavor with Chilean tapestries in the lobby and to-die-for pisco sours and ceviche on the menu. Sleek guest rooms and suites feature tech-friendly amenities and killer mountain views. And if that weren't enough, it's also a pet-friendly hotel employing environmentally sound practices from water conservation to recycling.

Ritz-Carlton
LUXURY HOTEL $$$

(Map p59; ☎470-8500; www.ritzcarlton.com/santiago; El Alcalde 15; r from US$398; ❄@❄❄; MEl Golf) A glittering symbol of Chile's soaring economy, the Ritz is the luxury choice in Santiago. Detail is what it does best: the king-sized beds have Egyptian cotton sheets and deliciously comfortable mattresses, and there's even a menu of bath treatments. The jewel in the crown is the top-floor health club and pool, with a vaulted glass roof that means you can swim beneath the stars. If you prefer liquid treats that come in a glass, the bar's novelty pisco sours are legendary.

BARRIO ESTACIÓN CENTRAL

Ecohostel
HOSTEL $

(Map p46; ☎222-6833; www.ecohostel.cl; General Jofré 349B; dm/d without bathroom CH$7000/20,000; @❄; MUniversidad Católica) Backpackers and families looking to chill love this hostel's friendly, personalized service, cozy couches and sunny patio (complete with hammock). Dorms in the converted old house can be dark, but bunks and lockers are both big and there are plenty of well-divided bathrooms. Trash gets separated here, hence the name.

Eating

More than ever before, Santiago is a foodie wonderland. In recent years, the arrival of creative restaurateurs from Peru, Argentina and Europe has added extra flair to the city's already excellent restaurant scene, and while traditional Chilean seafood still reigns supreme, modern Peruvian and Japanese are also having a moment, as is sophisticated cafe fare.

The best high-end restaurants are concentrated in Lastarria, Bellavista and Providencia – you can sample many of them for less by going for midweek set lunch menus. More classic Chilean food experiences include cheap and cheerful seafood lunches at the central fish market, empanadas from takeaway counters around the city and *completos* (hot dogs piled high with avocado) at downtown diners.

CENTRO

From local office workers lunching on the clock to tourists needing a bite between sights, downtown diners are mainly interested in getting their food fast. A good bet for a midday meal is one of the Centro's vintage *fuente de sodas* (soda fountains), atmospheric diner-style eateries where businessmen feast on sandwiches and Chilean comfort food. At night, you'll find better cuisine elsewhere in the city.

Some of the cheapest meals in town come from the string of food stands that line the Portal Fernández Concha, the arcade along the north side of Plaza de Armas. Supersized empanadas, *completos* and pizza slices are the staples here, day and night.

Mercado Central
MARKET $

(Central Market; Map p46; www.mercadocentral. cl; ☻food stands & restaurants 9am-5pm Mon-Fri, 7am-3:30pm Sat & Sun; ⓜPuente Cal y Canto) Santiago's wrought-iron fish market is a classic for seafood lunches (and hangover-curing fish stews like the tomato- and potato-based *caldillo de congrio*, Pablo Neruda's favorite). Skip the touristy restaurants in the middle and head for one of the tiny, low-key stalls around the market's periphery, such as the cheap and delicious **Tio Willy** (Local 120-75; mains CH$2500-4000). The market is bordered by 21 de Mayo, San Pablo, Paseo Puente and Valdés Vergara.

⌂TOP CHOICE Bar Nacional
DINER $

(Map p46; www.barnacional1.cl; Bandera 317; mains CH$3400-4500; ☻7am-11pm Mon-Sat; ⓜPlaza de Armas) From the chrome counter to the waitstaff of old-timers, this *fuente de soda* is as vintage as they come. It has been churning out Chilean specialties like *lomo a lo pobre* (steak and fries topped with fried egg) for years. To save a buck (or a few hundred pesos) ask for the sandwich menu. There's a second branch, **Bar Nacional 2** (☎696-5986; Paseo Huérfanos 1151).

Empanadas Zunino
BAKERY $

(Map p46; www.empanadaszunino.cl; Puente 801; empanadas CH$850-1600; ⓜPuente Cal y Canto) Founded in the 1930s, this classic bakery makes fantastic empanadas – Chilean food journalists recently awarded them second place in a contest for the best empanadas in Santiago.

El Naturista
VEGETARIAN $

(www.elnaturista.cl; mains CH$3000-4000; ☻9am-8pm Mon-Fri, 10am-3pm Sat) Huérfanos (Map p46; Huérfanos 1046; ⓜPlaza de Armas); Moneda (Map p46; Moneda 846; ⓜSanta Lucía) A downtown vegetarian classic for decades, El Naturista does simple but filling soups, sandwiches, salads, tarts and fresh-squeezed juices, plus light breakfasts and fruit-infused ice cream.

BARRIO LASTARRIA & BARRIO BELLAS ARTES

These stylish neighborhoods boast some of the city's culinary hot spots, not to mention a range of contemporary cafes, several ethnic eateries and a wealth of lovely sidewalk tables for dining alfresco.

Opera
FRENCH $$

(Map p46; ☎664-3048; Merced 395; mains CH$9200-12,000; ☻1-3:30pm & 8-11pm Mon-Fri, 8pm-midnight Sat; ⓜBellas Artes) From the first mouthful of foie gras to the last smear of crème brûlée, the food at Opera bears the mark of classic French cooking, but it's made with the best Chilean ingredients. Hefty mains include lamb shank in a Cabernet reduction or the perfectly pink veal ribchop in a buttery béarnaise. The upstairs sister bar, Catedral (p70), does simpler but equally excellent food. The stunning antique corner building is a national historic landmark.

Sur Patagónico
CHILEAN $$

(Map p46; Lastarria 92; mains CH$3800-7500; ☻1pm-1am Mon-Tue, 11am-4am Wed, noon-1pm Thu-Sun; ⓜUniversidad Católica) Service is notoriously slow here, but if you can score one of the pretty sidewalk tables on this well-traveled corner, you might not mind – the people-watching is fantastic, especially if you have a cold Chilean microbrew in hand. The steamed mussels are ideal for sharing; more substantial Patagonian-inspired options range from mushroom risotto to steak and lamb seared on the *parrilla* (grill). Indoors, you'll find a pleasantly rustic dining room resembling an antique general store.

Café Bistro de la Barra
CAFE $

(Map p46; JM de la Barra 455; sandwiches CH$3500-7000; ☻9am-9:30pm Mon-Fri, 10am-9:30pm Sat & Sun; ⓜBellas Artes; ☛) Worn old floor tiles, a velvet sofa, 1940s swing and light fittings made from cups and teapots make a quirky-but-pretty backdrop for some of the best brunches and *onces* (afternoon tea) in town. The rich sandwiches include salmon-filled croissants or Parma ham and arugula on flaky green olive bread, but make sure you save room for the perfectly firm, berry-drenched cheesecake.

Tambo
PERUVIAN $$

(Map p46; www.tambochile.cl; Lastarria 65; mains CH$4000-7500; ☻9am-11pm Mon-Sat, to 4:30pm Sun; ⓜUniversidad Católica) Occupying a prime spot along one of Lastarria's most scenic passages, this contemporary Peruvian eatery offers spicy twists on dishes and drinks that Chileans have since adopted – go ahead, taste-test the fantastic ceviche. Kick off your sampling from the other side of the border with a delicious *maracuyá* (passion fruit)-spiked pisco sour.

Emporio La Rosa
BAKERY $

(Map p46; Merced 291; ice cream CH$900-1800, salads & sandwiches CH$2500-3900; ☺8am-9pm Mon-Wed, 8am-10pm Thu & Fri, 9am-10pm Sat & Sun; ⓂBellas Artes; ➔) Choco-chili, strawberry and black pepper, and rose petal are some of the fabulous flavors of this extra-creamy handmade ice cream, which has been known to cause addiction. Flaky *pains-au-chocolat* and squishy focaccia sandwiches are two more reasons to plonk yourself at the chrome tables.

BELLAVISTA

Bellavista is a hot spot for eating and drinking around the clock. Restaurants fit into a few categories: family-run classics that have been popular with locals for years, posh new eateries that come and go along Constitución and Dardignac, and finally, on Pío Nono, the rough-and-ready staples that sustain young people through nights of drinking with inexpensive empanadas, pizza slices, *completos* and sandwiches.

Azul Profundo
CHILEAN $$

(Map p52; www.azulprofundo.cl; Constitución 111; mains CH$7500-13,000; ☺1-4:30pm daily, 7:30pm-12:30am Sun-Thu, 7:30pm-1:30am Fri & Sat; ⓂBaquedano) Step into this deep blue eatery – the telescope collection, maritime decor and vintage wooden bar no doubt inspired by Pablo Neruda's aesthetic – for fabulously fresh and inventive seafood. If you're up for sharing, order the delicious ceviche sampler and a round of pisco sours; the colorful (and oversized) platter might be one of the most memorable meals on your Chilean adventure.

ⓉⓄⓅ Galindo
CHILEAN $

(Map p52; www.galindo.cl; Dardignac 098; mains CH$2800-5800; ☺12:30pm-2am Sun-Thu, 12:30pm-4am Fri & Sat; ⓂBaquedano) Retro neon signs adorn the wood-backed bar at this long-running local favorite, usually packed with noisy but appreciative crowds. It's easy to see why: unlike the precious restaurants around it, Galindo's all about sizzling *parrilladas* (mixed grills) and hearty Chilean staples like *chorrillana* (french fries topped with grilled onions and meat), all washed down with freshly pulled pints or carafes of house wine.

El Caramaño
CHILEAN $$

(Map p52; http://caramano.tripod.com; Purísima 257; mains CH$3200-7500; ☺1pm-midnight; ⓂBaquedano) An extensive menu of well-prepared Chilean classics like *machas a la parmesana* (gratinée razor clams), *merluza a la trauca* (hake baked in chorizo and tomato sauce) and *oreganato* (melted oregano-dusted goat cheese) keep local families coming back here year after year. It's a reliable choice for a classy but affordable dinner.

Peperone Pizza & Wine
PIZZERIA $$

(Map p52; www.peperone.cl; Antonia López de Bello 0118; mains CH$3000-7500; ☺12:30-4:30pm & 7pm-midnight Tue-Thu, to 1am Fri & Sat, 12:30-4:30pm Sun; ⓂBaquedano) A casual, cozy eatery with mismatched vintage furniture, brightly painted walls and burning candles in the evening, Peperone is ideal for a quick bite or a glass of wine before or after touring nearby La Chascona.

BARRIO BRASIL & BARRIO YUNGAY

Peluquería Francesa
FRENCH, CHILEAN $$

(Map p54; ☎682-5243; www.boulevardlavaud.cl; Compañía de Jesús 2789; mains CH$3300-7000; ☺9am-1am Mon-Thu, to 3am Fri & Sat, 11am-5pm Sun; ⓂRicardo Cumming) One of Santiago's most unique dining experiences. The name means 'French barbershop,' and that's exactly what this elegant corner building, dating from 1868, was originally used for. Decorated with quirky antiques (all available for purchase), the building still has turn-of-the-century charm; it gets crowded on weekend evenings with hip Santiaguinos who come for the excellent French-inflected seafood dishes and funky atmosphere.

ⓉⓄⓅ El Café
CHILEAN $

(Map p54; cnr Av Brasil & Huérfanos, Barrio Brasil; set lunch CH$3200; ☺10am-midnight; ⓂCumming) Nearly as visually striking as this decorative rose-pink and white corner building is the quaint interior with old-fashioned wooden tables and vintage tiled floors. Both the indoor and sidewalk tables are inviting for morning coffee, budget-friendly lunch specials or an afternoon beer overlooking Barrio Brasil's leafy central square.

Squella Restaurant
SEAFOOD $$

(Map p54; www.squellarestaurant.cl; Av Ricardo Cumming 94; mains CH$7200-9500; ☺7pm-midnight Mon-Sat; ⓂRicardo Cumming) When you enter this minimal white eatery, your dinner may still be swimming (or crouching) in the bubbling pools that line one side of the dining room. The fresh oysters, shrimp, clams and ceviche have kept locals loyal to this seafood institution for decades.

Las Vacas Gordas
STEAKHOUSE $$

(Map p54; Cienfuegos 280; mains CH$4000-7000; ☺noon-4pm & 7pm-midnight Mon-Sat, noon-4pm Sun; ⓜCumming or Santa Ana) Steak, pork, chicken and vegetables sizzle on the giant grill at the front of the clattering main dining area, then dead-pan old-school waiters cart it over to your table. This popular steakhouse is often packed, so reserve or get there early.

Plaza Garibaldi
MEXICAN $

(Map p54; www.plazagaribaldi.cl; Moneda 2319; mains CH$3800-6200; ☺noon-4pm & 7pm-midnight Mon-Sat; ⓜCumming) From the bright walls and saloon-style doors to the tacos, quesadillas and *chimichangas* (fried burritos), Plaza Garibaldi turns out classic Mexican dishes. The food's not spicy enough to be truly authentic – this is Mexican with a Chilean touch – but it's fresh and filling, and service is friendly.

Platipus
ASIAN $

(Map p54; www.platipus.cl; Agustinas 2099, Barrio Brasil; sushi CH$2900-5900; ☺5pm-late Mon-Fri, 7pm-late Sat; ⓜCumming) Candles cast a warm glow on the exposed brick walls of this laidback sushi spot. Don't come here in a hurry, but both the sushi and the *tablas* (boards of finger food) are worth the wait. Vegetarians will find plenty to dine on here, too.

Peperone Pizza & Wine
PIZZERIA $$

(Map p54; Huérfanos 1954) Barrio Brasil branch of the Bellavista eatery that's particularly famous for empanadas.

PROVIDENCIA

🗺 Aquí Está Coco
CHILEAN $$

(Map p56; ☎410-6200; www.aquiestacoca.cl; La Concepción 236; mains CH$4000-8500; ☺1-3pm & 7-11pm Mon-Fri, 1-3pm & 8-11pm Sat, closed Feb; ☑; ⓜPedro de Valdivia) This beautifully restored mini-mansion – reconstructed with sustainable building materials – houses one of Providencia's hippest dining venues. The name, translating to 'Here's Coco,' refers to the imaginative owner who uses the space to showcase art and artifacts from his world travels (not to mention his considerable culinary talent and zeal for fine wine). The *centolla* (king crab sourced from Patagonia) is a hit every time. Highlights of Coco's self-proclaimed 'simple and honest cooking' also include scallops with coconut sauce and seared tuna from Easter Island.

Liguria
MEDITERRANEAN $$

(www.liguria.cl; mains CH$5200-8500; ☺noon-1am Mon-Sat) Av Pedro de Valdivia Norte (Map p56; Av Pedro de Valdivia 047; ⓜPedro de Valdivia); Av Providencia (Map p56; Av Providencia 1373; ⓜManuel Montt); Las Condes (Map p59; Luis Thayer Ojeda 019, Las Condes; ⓜTobalaba) A legend on the Santiago restaurant circuit, Liguria mixes equal measures of bar and bistro perfectly. Stewed rabbit or silverside in batter are chalked up on a blackboard, then dapper old-school waiters place them on the red-checked tablecloths with aplomb. Vintage adverts, Chilean memorabilia and old bottles decorate the wood-paneled inside, but it's the sidewalk tables that diners really fight over – even on weeknights you should book ahead. The Av Providencia location also features the hugely popular **Bar:Liguria** (☺open to 3am) a drinking destination in itself.

Astrid y Gastón
PERUVIAN $$$

(Map p56; ☎650-9125; www.astridygaston.com; Antonio Bellet 201; mains CH$8000-13,500; ☺1-3pm & 8pm-midnight Mon-Fri, dinner only Sat; ⓜPedro de Valdivia) The seasonally changing menu of Peruvian haute cuisine has made this one of Santiago's most critically acclaimed restaurants. The warm but expert waitstaff happily talk you through the chef's subtle, modern take on traditional ceviches, *chupes* (fish stews) and *cochinillo* (suckling pig), all beautifully presented. The barman deserves an ovation for his complex cocktails: Peruvian pisco comes with physalis juice in the Aquaymanto, for example.

Doner House
TURKISH $

(Map p56; www.donerhouse.cl; Av Providencia 1457; mains CH$1900-4200; ☺noon-10pm Mon-Fri, to 9pm Sat; ⓜManuel Montt) The doner maestro – Santiago's first purveyor of Turkish kebab – carves up a killer shawarma at this tiny eatery. Falafels and stuffed vine leaves are some of the other quick bites on hand.

Voraz Pizza
PIZZERIA $

(Map p56; www.vorazpizza.cl; Av Providencia 1321; pizzas CH$4000-12,000; ☺1-11pm Mon-Wed, 1pm-midnight Thu-Sat; ⓜManuel Montt; ☑) This hole-in-the-wall pizzeria serves great-value thin-crust pizzas and craft beers at sidewalk tables; it will happily deliver, too. An added bonus for nonmeat eaters: the pizzeria has a few tasty vegetarian options and it will also cater to vegans. Voraz recently opened a second location at Av Vitacura 2892.

El Huerto
CAFE $

(Map p56; www.elhuerto.cl; Orrego Luco 054; mains CH$4700-5900; ⊙noon-midnight Mon-Sat; Ⓜ Pedro de Valdivia; ⬚) This earthy restaurant's healthy, vegetarian-focused fare is a big hit with both hip young things and ladies who lunch. Come for egg-white omelets, strawberry smoothies, quinoa salads and wonderfully rich desserts with *café au lait*.

LAS CONDES, BARRIO EL GOLF & VITACURA

Santiago's plushest neighborhoods are home to the über-rich – and the seriously expensive restaurants and bars they frequent. You'll also see countless Starbucks locations and American-born chain restaurants; a handful of eateries stand out from the pack.

Tiramisú
PIZZERIA $$

(Map p59; www.tiramisu.cl; Isidora Goyenechea 3141, Las Condes; pizzas CH$3500-7800; ⊙12:45-4pm & 7pm-midnight; Ⓜ Tobalaba; ⬚) Bright murals, rough-hewn tables and cheerful red-checked cloths set the tone at this busy pizzeria that's perennially popular with locals. You'll spend more time choosing one of the myriad thin-crust pizzas than wolfing it down.

Café Melba
CAFE $

(Map p59; Don Carlos 2898; sandwiches CH$2900, mains CH$4000-7500; ⊙7:30am-9pm Mon-Fri, 8am-5pm Sat; Ⓜ Tobalaba; ⬚) Eggs and bacon, muffins, bagels and gigantic cups of coffee are some of the all-day breakfast offerings at this cozy cafe run by a New Zealand expat. Well-stuffed sandwiches and heartier dishes like green fish curry or pork medallions are popular with lunching local finance workers, but the specialty here is leisurely brunch – hence the steady stream of English-speaking clientele.

CasaMar
SEAFOOD $$

(off Map p59; ☑054-2112; www.restaurantcasamar. cl, in Spanish; Av Padre Hurtado 1480, Vitacura; mains CH$7900-11,900; ⊙1-3:30pm & 8-11pm Mon-Sat, lunch only Sun; Ⓜ Tobalaba) Classy, contemporary Chilean seafood and fine wines are the name of the game at this sleek Vitacura eatery. If you're willing to empty your pockets of pesos, splash out on the fabulous six-course tasting menu with wine pairing (CH$35,000).

Dominó
SANDWICHES $

(Map p59; Isidora Goyenechea 2930, Las Condes; sandwiches CH$1800-4000; ⊙8am-10pm Mon-Wed, to 11pm Thu & Fri, noon-11pm Sat; Ⓜ Tobalaba) This location of Dominó – a contemporary take on the traditional *fuente de soda* – is hopping at lunchtime with good-looking young office workers who work in the neighborhood. The cool all-white and chrome interior, plus budget-friendly sandwiches and *completos* equal stylish fast food, Chilean-style. You'll see other locations throughout the city.

ÑUÑOA

A low-profile but happening food and bar scene makes Ñuñoa a favorite night out for urbane Santiaguinos. East of Centro but well south of Providencia, it's far from the metro, but don't let that put you off: bus 505 runs along Merced and Salvador to Plaza Ñuñoa, the heart of all the action. A taxi here from Centro will cost around CH$5000.

Café de la Isla
CAFE $

(www.cafedelaisla.cl; Av Irarrázaval 3465; mains CH$2900-5500; ⊙6pm-1am Mon-Thu, to 3am Fri & Sat) This down-to-earth cafe is one of Ñuñoa's gems. The Chilean and Asian-inflected cuisine is prepared with vegetables from the cafe's garden; in the evening, the place comes alive with locals sipping fresh fruit smoothies in the garden patio or drinking wine at rustic wooden tables inside. If you can, grab a table on the dreamy candle-lit terrace.

Fuente Suiza
DINER $

(www.fuentesuiza.cl; Av Irarrázaval 3361; sandwiches CH$2400-3600; ⊙11am-midnight Mon-Fri, to 2am Fri, to 1am Sat) Dripping *lomo* (pork) sandwiches and flaky deep-fried empanadas make this simple family-run restaurant the perfect place to prepare for (or recover from) a long night of drinking.

🍷 Drinking

Cafes

Santiaguinos take their *onces* seriously – in the early evening, you're more likely to see young people having coffee and cake than celebrating happy hour with a beer. Santiago's booming cafe culture centers around JM de la Barra, a short stretch of street between Cerro Santa Lucía and the river.

Confitería Torres
BAR, CAFE $

(off Map p46; ☑688-0751; www.confiteriatorres. cl; Alameda 1570; ⊙10:30am-midnight Mon-Sat; Ⓜ Los Héroes) Even after restorations that added contemporary elegance to its appearance, Confitería Torres – one of Santiago's oldest cafes – still wears its history on its sleeve. Aging waiters attend with aplomb, chandeliers glow, and the green-and-white floor tiles are worn from use. Former president Barros Luco always ordered a steak and melted cheese sandwich here; other famous figures who downed coffee or pisco sours here include illustrious figures from Plácido Domingo to Rubén Darío.

TOP CHOICE Café Mosqueto CAFE

(Map p46; 664-0273; Mosqueto 440; 8:30am-10pm Mon-Fri, 10am-9:30pm Sat, 11am-9pm Sun; Bellas Artes) This adorable cafe is cozy inside on a rainy day – and the sidewalk tables, facing a pedestrian street, offer fantastic people-watching when the sun shines. This block (Mosqueto between Monjitas and Santo Domingo), lined with several similar cafes, is delightfully illuminated in the evening when cafe-goers sip coffee by candlelight.

Café del Museo CAFE

(Map p46; 633-2291; Lastarria 305, Plaza Mulato Gil, Lastarria; 11am-8:30pm Mon-Fri, 10am-9:30pm Sat & Sun; Bellas Artes) Adjacent to a small visual arts museum (hence the name) on one of Lastarria's quaint cobblestoned passageways, this colorful courtyard cafe does lovely cappuccino, loose-leaf tea, pastries, gourmet sandwiches and salads.

Pubs & Bars

Boy do Santiaguinos love to drink. And we're talking all-out, under-the table boozing that rivals their international counterparts. Even on weeknights, by 8pm or 9pm many bars are packed with after-work or after-school gatherings, their tables cheerfully heaving under empty bottles and beer jugs. From rowdy pubs to cozy wine bars, wherever you stay, the chances are you'll have a great watering hole nearby.

CENTRO

La Piojera BAR

(Map p46; 698-1682; Aillavilú 1030, Centro; noon-midnight Mon-Sat; Puente Cal y Canto) Saved from developers by protests from its loyal clientele – including presidents and poets – this bare-bones drinking den is the real deal. Noisy regulars pack the sticky tables, which are crammed with glass tumblers of the two house specialties: *chicha*, sweet Chilean cider, and the earth-moving (or gut-wrenching) *terremoto*, a potent mix

of wine and ice cream. Sawdust strewn on the cement floor soaks up spillage.

BARRIO LASTARRIA & BARRIO BELLAS ARTES

TOP CHOICE Bar the Clinic COCKTAIL BAR

(Map p46; Monjitas 578, Barrio Bellas Artes; Bellas Artes) This cool, quirky bar and eatery has an intellectual edge – it's the official watering hole of Chilean political magazine *The Clinic*. You'll be downing classic cocktails and gourmet pub food alongside hipster journalists in dark-rimmed glasses.

Catedral COCKTAIL BAR

(Map p46; 664-3048; www.operacatedral.cl; JM de la Barra & Merced; 12:30pm-3am Mon-Thu, 12:30pm-5am Fri & Sat; Bellas Artes) Classy Catedral has a menu that goes way beyond bar snacks – anyone for a glass of champagne with violet crème brûlée? A poised crew of professionals in their 20s and 30s love this cocktail bar's minimal two-tone couches, smooth wood paneling and mellow music. It's just one of the stylish offerings of the restaurateurs behind Opera restaurant; both are located in the same gorgeously restored corner building.

Bar Berri COCKTAIL BAR

(Map p46; 632-3190; Rosal 321, Barrio Bellas Artes; Bellas Artes) A Santiago classic for several decades, the charming, ultra-bohemian Bar Berri is furnished with an eclectic mix of antiques that channel the turn of the century. As the rotating drink list proves, the owner also knows his craft beer. Don't miss the the timeless Café Berri upstairs.

El Diablito BAR

(Map p46; 638-3512; Merced 336, Centro; Bellas Artes) Old photos and vintage household items clutter the already dark walls of this smoky den. After dark, the tiny candlelit tables seem to invite you to huddle conspiratorially into the small hours; great value *schop* (draft beer) and pisco sours are two more reasons to stay.

BELLAVISTA

In Santiago, the life and soul of the *carrete* is Barrio Bellavista. By 10pm tables inside and outside of its many bars are filled with rowdy groups of Santiaguinos giving their all to the *previa* (preclub drinking). Many of the restaurants and clubs in Bellavista also double as drinking spots.

The identical watering holes along Pío Nono are basic and ultracheap – pitchers of beer are the standard order. Both the drinks and the crowds are a bit more sophisticated along Constitución and Antonia López de Bello, both peppered with arty cocktail bars. Further west, Bombero Núñez is home to a handful of more underground bars and clubs, including some of Santiago's best gay nightlife (see boxed text, p62).

Although the bars and cafes inside **Patio Bellavista** (Map p52; ☎777-4582; www.patiobellavista.cl; Pío Nono 73; M Baquedano) are a bit bland, they're just about the only places open on Sunday nights.

Dublin PUB
(Map p52; ☎730-0526; www.dublin.cl; Constitución 58; ☺noon-midnight Sun-Thu, noon-4am Fri & Sat; M Baquedano) This lively Irish pub may not offer much in the way of local flavor – well, except for the Chilean-inspired bar food – but there is a great selection of whiskey and a happy-go-lucky crowd of young Santiaguinos and expats kicking their heels up here nearly every night of the week.

BARRIO BRASIL
This left-of-center barrio is becoming increasingly happening at night, but be aware that the quiet side streets can be sketchy after hours. Taking a taxi is advised.

Baires BAR
(Map p54; ☎697-4430; www.bairessushiclub.cl; Brasil 255; ☺12:30pm-3am Sun-Wed, to 5am Thu-Sat; M Ricardo Cumming) Technically, it's a 'sushi club,' but the nightlife at Baires is what brings in the crowds. The terrace tables fill up quickly, even on weeknights; there's an encyclopedia-sized drink list, and DJs get going upstairs on weekends.

PROVIDENCIA
Santo Remedio BAR
(Map p56; ☎235-0984; www.santoremedio.cl; Román Díaz 152; ☺6:30pm-3am Mon-Sat, from 8:30pm Sun; M Manuel Montt) Strictly speaking, this low-lighted, high-ceilinged old house is a restaurant, and an aphrodisiac one at that. But it's the bar action people really come for: powerful, well-mixed cocktails and regular live DJs keep the 20- and 30-something crowds happy.

California Cantina SPORTS BAR
(Map p56; ☎361-1056; www.californiacantina.cl; Las Urbinas 56; ☺5:30pm-2:30am Mon-Tue, from 12:30pm Wed-Fri, from 3:30pm Sat & Sun; M Los Leones) A popular new addition to the Provi-

dencia happy hour circuit is this spacious California-inspired bar with something for (almost) everyone – a dozen beers on tap, Mexican pub grub like tacos and quesadillas, terrace seating, everyday cocktail specials, *fútbol* matches on the big screen.

Phone Box Pub PUB
(Map p56; ☎235-9972; Av Providencia 1652; ☺10am-1am Mon & Tue, to 2am Wed & Thu, to 3am Fri & Sat; M Manuel Montt) Duck through the bright-red British phone booth to enter this easygoing pub that's popular with young Chileans and the expat community alike. The combination of well-pulled pints and classic pub grub (plus Latin American additions like empanadas and burritos) works perfectly.

LAS CONDES, BARRIO EL GOLF & VITACURA
Red2One COCKTAIL BAR
(Map p59; ☎770-0000; www.starwoodhotels.com; Isidora Goyenechea 3000, Las Condes; @☎; M El Golf) Look past the awkward name: the swanky rooftop bar at the W Hotel, considered the city's most exclusive watering hole, is worth the trip. The cool minimalist design and beautiful people are almost enough to distract you from the jaw-dropping view of the snow-capped Andes in the distance. Be here at sunset – if you can squeeze in.

ÑUÑOA
HBH Brewery BREWPUB
(☎204-2106; www.cervezahbh.cl; Av Irarrázaval 3176; ☺5pm-2am Mon-Fri, from 7:30pm Sat) Beer buffs and students rave about this laid-back microbrewery. As well as pouring out icy glass mugs of its own house-brewed stout and lager, HBH stocks a fantastic selection of craft beers from all over the world.

URBAN WINE TASTING

If you don't have enough time to venture into wine country, you can still do a guided tasting or even sign up for a wine class at the **Centro Desgustación de Concha y Toro** (Map p59; www.vinoscyt.com; Av Alonso de Córdova 2391; ☺9am-8pm Mon-Fri, 10am-2pm Sat) in Vitacura. It's the new urban outpost of the Concha y Toro winery (see p82) and the perfect place to stop for a sampling of Viognier after hitting the barrio's art galleries and boutiques.

⭐ Entertainment

Whether you get your kicks on the dance floor or at the soccer stadium, and whether you'd rather clap in time to strumming folksingers or at the end of three-hour operas, Santiago has plenty to keep you entertained. National dailies *El Mercurio* and *La Tercera* carry cinema, theater and classical music listings. Information and tickets for many major performances and sporting events are available through **Ticketmaster** (☎689-2000; www.ticketmaster.cl), which also has sales points in Falabella department stores and Hoyts cinemas, and **FeriaTicket** (☎592-8500; www.feriaticket.cl), which operates in Feria del Disco music stores. For the latest on clubbing, live music and nightlife check out the searchable listings on **Saborizante** (www.saborizante.com) or go straight to the source by visiting the websites or blogs of the clubs and bars themselves: those listed here update theirs regularly.

Live Music

Chile doesn't have the musical reputation of other Latin American countries. But there are some seriously good bands here – some featured at Santiago's edition of Lollapalooza (p60) and music-oriented bars are usually the best places to catch them. Save the salsa and tango for the countries that do them best: instead, your best bets in Santiago will be folksy singer-songwriters, Chilean or Argentinean indie groups, *rock nacional* (Chilean rock) upstarts, and purveyors of the most Latin of local beats, *cumbia chilombiana*. International greats also visit Chile regularly, and tickets are usually much cheaper than at home.

Bar Constitución   LIVE MUSIC
(Map p52; ☎244-4569; www.barconstitucion.cl, in Spanish; Constitución 62, Bellavista; ☺8pm-5am Mon-Sat; Ⓜ Baquedano) Bellavista's coolest nightspot hosts live bands and DJs nightly – the bar's eclectic (but infallible) tastes include electroclash, garage, nu-folk, house and more, so check the website to see if the night's program suits.

Club de Jazz   JAZZ
(☎326-5065; www.clubdejazz.cl, in Spanish; Av Alessandri 85, Ñuñoa; ☺10:30pm-3am Thu-Sat) One of Latin America's most established jazz venues – Louis Armstrong and Herbie Hancock are just two of the greats to have played here – this large wooden building hosts local

and international jazz, blues and big band performers.

La Casa en el Aire   PERFORMING ARTS
(Map p52; ☎735-6680; www.lacasaenelaire.cl, in Spanish; Antonia López de Bello 0125, Bellavista; ☺8pm-late Mon-Sun; Ⓜ Baquedano) Latin-American folk music, storytelling gatherings, film cycles and poetry readings are some of the arty events that take place nightly in this low-key old house turned bar.

Batuta   LIVE MUSIC
(www.batuta.cl, in Spanish; Jorge Washington 52, Ñuñoa; ☺10pm-3am Wed-Sat) Enthusiastic crowds jump to ska, *patchanka* (think: Manu Chau) and *cumbia chilombiana;* rockabilly and surf; tribute bands and goth rock... at Batuta, just about anything alternative goes.

Galpón Víctor Jara   LIVE MUSIC
(Map p54; ☎697-3941; Huérfanos 2146, Barrio Brasil; Ⓜ Cumming) Named in memory of 'disappeared' folk singer-songwriter and activist Víctor Jara (a Chilean revolutionary who was assumed to have been executed by the military government after publicly expressing his liberal views), this warehouselike space hosts gigs from up-and-coming local acts.

Teatro Caupolicán   LIVE MUSIC
(☎699-1556; www.teatrocaupolican.cl, in Spanish; San Diego 850; Ⓜ Parque O'Higgins) From Jarvis Cocker and Brett Anderson to the Hives, some choicest international gigs happen here. Latin American rockers who've trod the boards include far-out Mexicans Café Tacuba, and Oscar-winning Uruguayan Jorge Drexler.

Nightclubs

Don't even think about showing up at any of these places before midnight: in Santiago, if it's not all night it's not a night out. Most clubs close at about 4am or 5am, at which point those still on their feet adjourn to an after-hours to wind things up.

Blondie   CLUB
(Map p54; ☎681-7793; www.blondie.cl, in Spanish; Alameda 2879, Barrio Brasil; cover CH$3000-5000; ☺from 11pm Thu-Sat) The '80s still rule at least one floor of Blondie, while the other could have anything from goth rock and techno to Britpop or Chilean indie. A favorite with both Santiago's student and gay communities, it's usually packed.

EL HUASO ENRIQUE

To see Chileans performing their national dance, *la cueca* – a playful, handkerchief-waving ritual that imitates the courtship of a rooster and hen – you usually have to make your way to a folk festival, an Independence Day celebration or a dusty country town. But at **El Huaso Enrique** (Map p54; ☑681-5257; www.elhuasoenrique.cl; Maipú 462, Barrio Yungay; cover CH$2500-3000; Ⓜ Quinta Normal), a traditional restaurant and *cueca* venue that's been in business in Barrio Yungay for almost sixty years, you can watch proud Chileans hit the dance floor while you feast on hearty regional dishes like *pastel de choclo* (a casserole-like dish consisting of baked corn, meat and cheese). The place comes alive on weekends with live music. If you really want to get into the spirit, El Huaso Enrique also offers *cueca* lessons; check out the website for details.

Club La Feria   CLUB
(Map p52; ☑735-8433; www.clublaferia.cl; Constitución 275, Bellavista; cover CH$3000-5000; ⊙from 11pm Thu-Sat; Ⓜ Baquedano) Euphoric house and techno, an up-for-it crowd and banging DJs mean this is still the place to go for a fix of electronic music.

El Clan   CLUB
(Map p52; ☑735-3655; www.elclan.cl; Bombero Núñez 363, Bellavista; cover CH$2000-5000; ⊙from 11pm Tue-Sat; Ⓜ Baquedano) The name's short for 'El Clandestino,' a throwback from this small club's undercover days. A small crew of resident DJs keep the 20-something crowds going – expect anything from '80s to house, R&B, funk or techno.

Mito Urbano   CLUB
(Map p56; ☑235-7097; www.mitourbano.cl; Manuel Montt 350, Providencia; cover CH$4000-6000; ⊙6pm-4am Tue-Sat) At this fun-loving nightclub, disco balls cast light on the good-looking 20-, 30- and 40-somethings dancing to vintage hits and Chilean pop. Check the schedule for salsa classes, karaoke, live jazz, and other promotions that aim to bring people in before midnight.

Bar El Tunel   CLUB
(Map p46; ☑639-4914; www.bareltunel.cl; Santo Domingo 439, Centro; cover CH$2000-3500; ⊙10pm-4am Wed-Sat; Ⓜ Bellas Artes) Teenyboppers of the world unite: if you missed the '70s and '80s the first time round, this is the place to show the world your best John Travolta moves.

Theater, Dance & Classical Music

Although much of Chilean theater revolves around the sequined, tassel-toting showgirls that star in so-called *comedias musicales*, Santiago is also home to some excellent stage and ballet companies, orchestras and choirs.

Teatro Municipal   THEATER
(Map p46; ☑463-1000; www.municipal.cl, in Spanish; Agustinas 794, Centro; ⊙box office 10am-7pm Mon-Fri, 10am-2pm Sat & Sun; Ⓜ Santa Lucía) This exquisite neoclassical building is the most prestigious performing-arts venue in the city. It's home to the Ballet de Santiago and also hosts world-class opera, tango and classical music performances.

Teatro de la Universidad de Chile   THEATER
(Map p46; ☑634-5295; http://teatro.uchile.cl, in Spanish; Providencia 043, Centro; Ⓜ Baquedano) The Orquesta Sinfónica de Chile and Ballet Nacional de Chile are two high-profile companies based at this excellent theater. There is a fall season of ballet, choral, orchestral and chamber music, as well as the occasional rock gig.

Spectator Sports

Estadio Nacional   SOCCER
(National Stadium; ☑238-8102; Av Grecia 2001, Ñuñoa) On the whole, Chileans are a pretty calm lot – until they step foot in a soccer stadium. Mad screaming and dancing (or cursing, weeping and hair-tearing) accompanies international games, the most dramatic of which are against local rivals like Peru or Argentina, when 'Chi-Chi-Chi-Lay-Lay-Lay' reverberates through the Estadio Nacional. Tickets can be bought at the stadium or from the Feria del Disco. Equally impassioned are the *hinchas* (fans) of Santiago's first-division soccer teams like Colo Colo, Universidad de Chile and Universidad Católica.

Club Hípico de Santiago   HORSE RACING
(☑693-9600; www.clubhipico.cl, in Spanish; Av Blanco Encalada 2540; Ⓜ Parque O'Higgins) The

WORTH A TRIP

PERSA BÍO BÍO

Antiques, collectibles and fascinating old junk fill the cluttered stalls at this famous **flea market** (Franklin Market; ⊗9am-7pm Sat & Sun; MFranklin) between Bío Bío and Franklin. Sifting through the jumble of vintage sunglasses, antique brandy snifters, cowboy spurs, old-fashioned swimsuits and discarded books is an experience. It's also a choice spot to try some Chilean street food, from fried empanadas, tacos and grilled pork sandwiches to fresh-squeezed juices and the classic *mote con huesillo* (a sweet local snack made with dried peaches and husked wheat). Just be sure to keep one hand on your valuables while stuffing food into your mouth; pickpockets have been known to prey on unsuspecting shoppers.

main racetrack is the grand Club Hípico de Santiago, where views of the Andes compete for your attention with the action on the turf.

Shopping

Santiago may not be a world-class shopping destination, but you can still pick up interesting craft pieces and unusual clothing or housewares by young local designers. The Centro's busiest shopping streets, pedestrianized Ahumada and Huérfanos, are lined with cheap clothing, shoe and department stores. For seriously cheap clothes, head to the Korean and Palestinian immigrant area of Patronato, west of Bellavista between Patronato and Manzano. Secondhand clothes stores abound in the city (often marked by signs reading 'Ropa Europea/Americana'), especially around Providencia's Manuel Montt metro station.

The top-quality Chilean crafts you can find in Santiago include hand-woven alpaca shawls, Mapuche silver jewelry, lapis lazuli, wood and leatherwork and, occasionally, copperware. Near the entrance to Cerro Santa Lucía, look for outdoor vendors at the indigenous-focused **Centro de Exposición de Arte Indígena** (Map p46; ✆632-3668; Alameda 499, Centro; ⊗10am-6pm Mon-Sat) and the more commercial **Centro Artesanal Santa Lucía** (Map p46; cnr Carmen & Diagonal Paraguay, Centro; ⊗10am-7pm; MSanta Lucía).

Patio Bellavista   SHOPPING CENTER
(Map p52; ✆249-8700; Pío Nono 73, Bellavista; ⊗11am-10pm; MBaquedano) Posh contemporary crafts, plus leather goods, weavings and jewelry, sell at premium prices at this courtyard shopping center.

Galería Drugstore   FASHION
(Map p56; ✆490-1241; Av Providencia 2124, Providencia; ⊗10:30am-8pm Mon-Sat; MLos Leones) Head to this cool four-story independent shopping center for clothes no one back home will have – it's home to the boutiques of several tiny, up-and-coming designers, arty bookstores and cafes.

Artesanías de Chile   ARTS & CRAFTS
(off Map p52; ✆777-8643; www.artesaniasdechile. cl; Bellavista 0357, Bellavista; ⊗10am-6pm Mon-Sat; MBaquedano) Not only do this foundation's jewelry, carvings, ceramics and woolen goods sell at reasonable prices, most of what you pay goes to the artisan that made them. Look for other locations in Santiago and throughout Chile.

El Mundo del Vino   WINE
(Map p59; ✆584-1173; www.emdv.cl, in Spanish; Isidora Goyenechea 3000, Las Condes; ⊗10am-9pm; MTobalaba) This revamped location of the high-end wine chain (look for other branches throughout Santiago and Chile) features 6000 bottles from around the world – or from just a short drive away in the Colchagua Valley – at the hip W Hotel.

Portal La Dehesa   MALL
(off Map p59; ✆876-0700; www.cencosudshopping.cl/portalladehesa, in Spanish; Av La Dehesa 1445, La Barnechea; ⊗10am-9pm) The newest and poshest shopping mall, with open-air spaces and 140 shops, is a long haul from downtown.

Alto Las Condes   MALL
(✆299-6999; www.altolascondes.cl, in Spanish; Av Kennedy 9001, Las Condes; ⊗10am-10pm) As well as top-end Chilean and Argentine clothing brands, this has a branch of department store Falabella and a cinema complex. The best way to get here is to catch a bus marked

'Alto Las Condes' outside the Escuela Militar metro station.

Parque Arauco
MALL
(☎299-0500; www.parquearauco.cl, in Spanish; Av Kennedy 5413, Las Condes; ☺10am-9pm; ⓂManquehue) A huge range of local and international clothing stores make this the fashionista mall of choice. From Manquehue metro station, it's about a mile-long walk (or a quick taxi ride) northwest along Alonso de Cordova.

Kind of Blue
MUSIC
(Map p46; ☎664-4322; www.kindofblue.cl, in Spanish; Merced 323; ☺10am-10pm Sun-Thu, 10am-11pm Fri & Sat; ⓂBellas Artes) At the best music shop in town, savvy multilingual staff happily talk you through local sounds and artists, and can get hard-to-find imports in a matter of days.

Galería del Patio
BOOKS
(Map p56; Local 5, Providencia; ☺11am-2pm & 4-8pm Mon-Fri, 11am-3pm Sat; ⓂPedro de Valdivia) For Lonely Planet travel guides, used books and literature about Chile (in English).

Contrapunto
BOOKS
(www.contrapunto.cl; ☺10:30am-8pm Mon-Fri, 10:30am-2pm Sat) Centro (Map p46; ☎481-9776; Huérfanos 665, Local 1, Centro; ⓂUniversidad de Chile); Providencia (Map p56; ☎231-2947; Av Providencia 2124, Galería Drugstore, Local 010-011e, Providencia; ⓂPedro de Valdivia) Art, architecture, photography, design: if it'll look good on your coffee table, Contrapunto sells it. With other locations throughout the city, including all the major malls.

Andesgear
OUTDOOR EQUIPMENT
(Map p59; ☎245-7076; www.andesgear.cl; Helvecia 210, Las Condes; ☺10am-8pm Mon-Fri, 10:30am-2pm Sat; ⓂTobalaba) Imported climbing and high-altitude camping gear for your ongoing journey to Chilean Patagonia.

ⓘ Information
Dangers & Annoyances
Violent crime is relatively rare in Santiago. Pick-pocketing and bag-snatching, however, are on the rise, and tourists are often targets. Keep your eyes open and your bags close to you around the Plaza de Armas, Mercado Central, Cerro Santa Lucía and Cerro San Cristóbal in particular. Look around you before whipping out a digital camera; be aware that organized groups of pickpockets sometimes target drinkers along Pío Nono in Bellavista, and Barrio Brasil's smaller streets can be dodgy after dark.

Emergency
Ambulance (☎131)
Fire department (☎132)
Police (☎133)
Prefectura de Carabineros (main police station; ☎922-3660; Alameda 280, Centro)

Internet Access & Telephones
Cybercafes are everywhere: prices range from CH$400 to CH$1000 per hour. Many are part of a *centro de llamados* (public telephone center) where you can also make local and long-distance calls.

Centro de Llamados (Moneda 1118, Centro; per hr CH$600; ☺9:30am-10:30pm Mon-Fri, 10am-8pm Sat & Sun; ⓂUniversidad de Chile)
Cyber Station (www.cyberstation.cl; Av Brasil 167, Barrio Brasil; per hr CH$700; ☺1pm-11pm Mon-Sat, from 4pm Sun; ⓂCumming)

Laundry
Nearly all hotels and hostels offer laundry service; you can also drop off your clothes (expect to pay about CH$5000 per load) anywhere called '*lavandería*.' Note that self-service launderettes are uncommon in Chile.

Laundromat (☎662-1531; Amunategui 480, Centro; ⓂSanta Ana)
Lavaseco Astra (☎264-1946; Av Providencia 1604, Providencia; per load CH$4000; ⓂManuel Montt)

Maps
Tourist offices distribute an ever-changing collection of free (ie sponsored) maps of Centro and Providencia, but many lack entire streets or sights. The searchable maps at **Map City** (www.mapcity.com, in Spanish) and **EMOL** (www.mapas.emol.com) are reliable online resources.

For trekking and mountaineering information, as well as inexpensive maps and other national park publications (mostly in Spanish), visit **Conaf** (Corporación Nacional Forestal; off Map p46; ☎390-0125; www.conaf.cl, in Spanish; Bulnes 285, Centro; ☺9:30am-5:30pm Mon-Thu, 9:30am-4:30pm Fri).

Medical Services
Consultations are cheap at Santiago's public hospitals but long waits are common and English may not be spoken. For immediate medical or dental assistance, go to a *clínica* (private clinic), but expect hefty fees – insurance is practically a must.

Clínica Alemana (☎210-1111; www.alemana.cl; Av Vitacura 5951, Vitacura) One of the best – and most expensive – private hospitals in town.
Clínica Las Condes (☎210-4000; www.clinicalascondes.cl, in Spanish; Lo Fontecilla 441, Las Condes)

Clínica Universidad Católica (☎384-6000; www.clinicauc.cl, in Spanish; Lira 40, Centro; MUniversidad Católica)

Farmacia Ahumada (☎631-3005; Av Portugal 155, Centro; MUniversidad Católica) A 24-hour pharmacy.

Hospital de Urgencia Asistencia Pública (☎436-3800; Av Portugal 125, Centro; ⊙24hr; MUniversidad Católica) Santiago's main emergency room.

Hospital San Juan de Dios (☎574-2091; www. hospitalsanjuandedios.cl, in Spanish; Huérfanos 3255, Barrio Brasil; MQuinta Normal) Major public hospital.

Money

You're never far from an ATM in Santiago. Supermarkets, pharmacies, gas stations and plain old street corners are all likely locations: look for the burgundy-and-white 'Redbanc' sign.

Cambios Afex (☎688-1143; www.afex.cl; Agustinas 1050, Centro; ⊙9am-6pm Mon-Fri, 10am-2pm Sat; MUniversidad de Chile) Reliable exchange office with branches around town.

Post

FedEx (☎301-6000; Av Providencia 1951, Providencia; ⊙9am-1:30pm & 2:30-7pm; MPedro de Valdivia)

Post Office (Map p46; ☎800-267-736; www. correos.cl; Catedral 987, Plaza de Armas, Centro; ⊙8am-7pm Mon-Fri, 9am-2pm Sat; MPlaza de Armas) With offices around town.

Tourist Information

Sernatur (www.chile.travel/en.html) Airport (☎601-9320; Aeropuerto Arturo Merino Benítez at Pudahuel; ⊙8:15am-9:30pm); Providencia (Map p56; ☎731-8310; Av Providencia 1550, Providencia; ⊙8:45am-6:30pm Mon-Fri, 9am-2pm Sat, to 7pm or 8pm summer; MManuel Montt) Gives out maps, brochures and advice; reserves winery visits.

Travel Agencies

Navimag (Map p59; ☎442-3120; www.navimag. cl; Av El Bosque Norte 0440, Piso 11, Las Condes; ⊙9am-6:30pm Mon-Fri; MTobalaba) Book ahead for ferry tickets in Chilean Patagonia.

ℹ Getting There & Away

Air

Chile's main air hub for both national and domestic flights is **Aeropuerto Internacional Arturo Merino Benítez** (Pudahuel; Map p81; ☎690-1752, lost property 690-1707; www. aeropuertosantiago.cl). It's 26km west of central Santiago.

Lan (☎600-526-2000; www.lan.com), **Aerolíneas Argentinas** (☎800-610-200; www.aerolineas.com.ar) and low-cost airline **Gol** (☎1-888-0042-

0090; www.voegol.com.br) run regular domestic and regional services from here. Major international airlines that fly to Chile have offices or representatives in Santiago: see p463 for a complete list. For a list of Lan's Santiago offices and sample one-way domestic airfares from Santiago, see p467.

Bus

A bewildering number of bus companies connect Santiago to the rest of Chile, Argentina and Peru. To add to the confusion, services leave from four different terminals and ticket prices fluctuate wildly at busy times of year, and often double for *cama* (sleeper) services. The following sample *clásico* or *semi-cama* (standard) fares (approximate only) and journey times are for major destinations that are served by a variety of companies – discounts often apply so shop around. For fares to smaller destinations, see the listings under each terminal.

DESTINATION	COST (CH$)	DURATION (HR)
Antofagasta	29,300	19
Arica	40,900	30
Buenos Aires	67,745	22
Chillán	6300	5
Concepción	9900	6½
Copiapó	21,600	12
Iquique	34,400	25
La Serena	5500	7
Los Andes	2900	1½
Mendoza (Argentina)	16,000	8
Osorno	23,300	12
Pichilemu	5000	4
Pucón	16,800	11
Puerto Montt	24,600	12
San Pedro de Atacama	37,400	23
Santa Cruz	4000	4
Talca	4900	3½
Temuco	14,400	9½
Valdivia	19,100	10-11
Valparaíso	1900	2
Viña del Mar	2800	2¼

TERMINAL DE BUSES ALAMEDA

Tur Bus (☎600-660-6600; www.turbus.cl) and **Pullman Bus** (☎600-320-3200; www.pullman. cl) operate from this **terminal** (Map p46; ☎270-7500; Alameda 3750; MUniversidad de Santiago), next door to Terminal de Buses Santiago. The two companies run comfortable, punctual services to destinations all over Chile, including every 15 minutes to Valparaíso and Viña del Mar.

TERMINAL DE BUSES SANTIAGO

Santiago's largest **terminal** (☎376-1750; Alameda 3850; **M**Universidad de Santiago) is also known as Terminal Sur, and is usually manically busy. The companies operating from the large, semicovered ticket area mainly serve destinations south of Santiago, including the central coast, the Lakes District and Chiloé. A few companies also operate northbound buses.

Bus Norte (☎779-5433; www.busnortechile. cl) runs excellent-value services to Puerto Montt and Valparaíso. The modern, well-appointed buses operated by **Línea Azul** (☎481-8862; www.buseslineaazul.cl) connect Santiago with southern destinations, as do **JAC** (☎481-1678; www.jac.cl) and **Andimar** (☎779-3810; www. andimar.cl). **Inter** (☎270-7508; www.busesin ter.cl) has routes all over Chile.

Nilahué (☎778-5222; www.busesnilahue. cl) goes to Cobquecura (CH$11,000, seven hours, once daily), Termas de Chillán ski resort (CH$10,000, seven hours, twice daily), Santa Cruz (CH$5500, four hours, two hourly) and Pichilemu (CH$6000, four hours, hourly). **Pullman del Sur** (☎776-2424; www.pdelsur.cl) has similar services to Santa Cruz and Pichilemu, but is slightly more comfortable. **Condor** (☎680-6900; www.condorbus.cl) goes to Concón and Quintero (CH$4800, 2½ hours, three hourly) and to major southern cities.

International tickets are sold from booths inside the terminal. **Cata Internacional** (☎779-3660; www.catainternacional.com) has four daily services to Mendoza and Buenos Aires. **El Rápido** (☎779-0310; www.elrapidoint.com.ar) has similar but slightly cheaper services, as does **Tas Choapa** (☎490-7561; www.taschoapa.cl).

TERMINAL LOS HÉROES

Also known as Terrapuerto, this small but central **terminal** (☎420-0099; Tucapel Jiménez 21; **M**Los Héroes) is the base for a handful of companies. **Libac** (☎698-5974) runs two daily northbound services whereas **Cruz del Sur** (☎696-9324; www.busescruzdelsur.cl) has several services going south, and also sells connecting tickets to Bariloche in Argentina via Osorno (CH$28,000, 24 hours). **Ahumada International** (☎784-2512; www.busesahu mada.cl) goes three times daily to Mendoza; some services continue to Buenos Aires.

TERMINAL SAN BORJA

Services to the area around Santiago depart from this renovated **terminal** (Map p54; ☎776-0645; www.terminalsanborja.cl, in Spanish; San Borja 184; **M**Estación Central). Ticket booths are on the 2nd floor, divided by region. The most useful services from here are **Ahumada** (☎684-2516; www.busesahumada.cl) and **Pullman Bus** (☎764-5060; www.pullman.cl).

Bus services to Pomaire also leave from here: see p80.

TERMINAL PAJARITOS

Buses from Santiago to the airport and Valparaíso and Viña call in at this small **terminal** (☎250-3464; General Bonilla 5600; **M**Pajaritos). It's on Metro Línea 1, so by getting on buses here you avoid downtown traffic.

Car

Intense rush-hour traffic and high parking fees mean there's little point hiring a car to use in Santiago. However, having your own wheels is invaluable for visiting the Casablanca Valley and places of natural beauty like Cerro la Campana.

Chilean rental-car companies tend to be cheaper than big international ones, but note that they often have sky-high deductibles. Most rental companies have their own roadside assistance; alternatively the **Automóvil Club de Chile** (Acchi; ☎431-1000; www.automovilclub. cl; Av Andrés Bello 1863, Providencia) provides reciprocal assistance to members of the American Automobile Association and some other associations, but you need to stop by the office to register. Some of the companies listed below also have airport offices at Pudahuel.

Budget (☎362-3605; www.budget.cl; Av Francisco Bilbao 1439, Providencia)

Chilean (☎737-9650; www.chileanrentacar.cl; Bellavista 0183, Bellavista)

First Rent a Car (☎225-6328; www.firstrenta car.cl; Rancagua 0514, Providencia)

Hertz (☎496-1000; www.hertz.com; Av Andrés Bello 1469, Providencia)

Piamonte (☎225-2623; www.piamonte.cl; Irarrázaval 4290, Ñuñoa)

United (☎236-1483; www.united-chile.com; Padre Mariano 430, Providencia)

Train

Chile's slick interurban train system, **Empresa de Ferrocarriles del Estado** (EFE; ☎600-585-5000; www.efe.cl, in Spanish), operates out of **Estación Central** (Map p54; Alameda 3170; **M**Estación Central). Train travel is generally slightly slower and more expensive than going by bus, but wagons are well maintained and services are generally punctual.

The TerraSur rail service connects Santiago three to five times daily with Rancagua (CH$4750, one hour), Curicó (CH$4000 to CH$8000, 2¼ hours), Talca (CH$4000 to CH$8000, three hours) and Chillán (CH$8000, 5½ hours), from where there's a connecting bus to Concepción. There's a 10% discount if you book online; 1st-class tickets cost about 20% more.

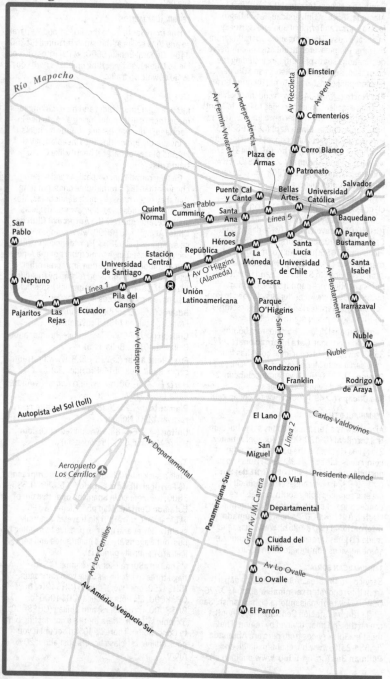

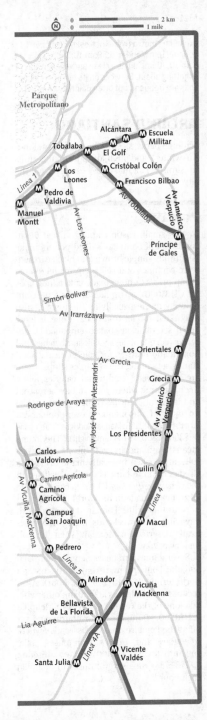

Getting Around

To/From the Airport

Two cheap, efficient bus services connect the airport with the city center: **Buses Centropuerto** (Map p54; 601-9883; www.centro puerto.cl; Manuel Rodríguez 846; one way/ round trip CH$1600/2800; every 10-15min 6am-11:30pm) and **Tur Bus Aeropuerto** (off Map p46; 607-9573; www.turbus.cl; Moneda 1523, Centro; one way/round trip CH$1700/2900; every 20min 6am-midnight). Both leave from right outside the arrivals hall, and you can buy tickets on board or from the ticket desks inside the terminal. All but the earliest buses stop at metro station Pajaritos on Line 1 – you avoid downtown traffic by transferring to the metro here. The total trip takes about 40 minutes.

A pushy mafia of 'official' taxi drivers tout their services in the arrivals hall. Although the ride to the city center should cost CH$16,000, drivers may well try to charge much more. A safer bet for private transfers is to approach the desk of **Transvip** (677-3000; www.transvip.cl) which offers fixed-price taxis (from CH$16,000) and eight-seat minibuses (from CH$6000) to the Centro. Trips to Providencia and Las Condes cost slightly more. **TurBus Aeropuerto** (607-9573; www.turbus.cl) offers similar services.

Bicycle

Santiago is flat and compact enough to get around by bike and the climate is ideal for it. Although the city still isn't particularly bike-friendly, it does have a small network of *ciclovías* (bike lanes). Check out the interactive map of bike paths and cyclist-friendly facilities at **Recicleta** (www.recicleta.cl/mapa-de-santiago -en-bicicleta), a group that promotes urban biking. Another linchpin of the local cyclist movement is **Movimiento Furiosos Ciclistas** (www.furiosos.cl, in Spanish), which organizes a Critical Mass–style bike rally the first Tuesday of each month. You can rent bikes and helmets from tour operator La Bicicleta Verde (p58).

Car & Motorcycle

To drive on any of the expressways within Santiago proper, your car must have an electronic sensor known as a TAG in the windshield – all rental cars have them. On-street parking is banned in some parts of central Santiago and metered (often by a person) in others – costs range from CH$1000 to CH$3000 per hour, depending on the area. If you're not paying a meter, you're expected to pay a similar fee to the 'parking attendant.' For more detailed information on driving and parking in Santiago, check out the helpful English-language section at **Car Rental in Chile** (www.mietwagen-in-chile.de); it will also rent you a vehicle.

Taxi

Santiago has abundant metered taxis, all black with yellow roofs. Flagfall costs CH$250, then it's CH$100 per 200m (or minute of waiting time). For longer rides – from the city center out to the airport, for example – you can sometimes negotiate flat fares. It's generally safe to hail cabs in the street, though hotels and restaurants will happily call you one, too. Most Santiago taxi drivers are honest, courteous and helpful, but a few will take roundabout routes, so try to know where you're going.

Transantiago

In 2006, sleek extra-long buses replaced the city's many competing private services when the bus and metro were united as **Transantiago** (☎800-730-073; www.transantiago.cl), a government-run public transportation system that's quick, cheap and efficient for getting around central Santiago. The Transantiago website has downloadable route maps and a point-to-point journey planner.

You'll need a *tarjeta* Bip! (a contact-free card you wave over sensors). You pay a nonrefundable CH$1350 for a card, and then 'charge' it with as much money as you want. Two people can share a card. Transantiago charges CH$580 to CH$660 during rush hour (7am to 9am and 6pm to 8pm) and CH$550 to CH$600 the rest of the time. One fare allows you two hours in the system, including multiple transfers.

Bus

Transantiago buses are a cheap and convenient way of getting around town, especially when the metro shuts down at night. Green-and-white buses operate in central Santiago or connect two areas of town. Each suburb has its own color-coded local buses and an identifying letter that precedes routes numbers (eg routes in Las Condes and Vitacura start with a C and vehicles are painted orange). Buses generally follow major roads or avenues; stops are spaced far apart and tend to coincide with metro stations. There are route maps at many stops and consulting them (or asking bus drivers) is usually more reliable than asking locals, who are still confused by new routes.

On Sundays and holidays, take advantage of the new **Circuito Cultural Santiago** (www.transantiago.cl; ☉10am-6:30pm Sun & holidays), a bus loop tour that passes by the city's main attractions (museums, cultural centers) starting at Estación Central. You use your Bip! card to pay for one regular bus fare, and the driver will give you a bracelet that allows you to board the circuit's buses as many times as you like. The buses are clearly marked 'Circuito Cultural.'

Metro

Now part of Transantiago, the city's ever-expanding **metro** (www.metrosantiago.cl; ☉6am-11pm Mon-Fri, 6:30am-10:30pm Sat, 8am-10:30pm Sun) is a clean and efficient way of getting about. Services on its five interlinking lines are frequent, but often painfully crowded.

AROUND SANTIAGO

National parks, sleepy villages, snowy slopes (in winter) and high-altitude hiking trails (in summer) all make easy escapes from the city.

Pomaire

In this small, rustic country village 68km southwest of Santiago, skilled potters make beautifully simple brown and black earthenware ceramics and sell them for incredibly cheap prices (a homemade coffee mug goes for CH$1000). A trip here makes a pleasant half-day out, especially as the town is also celebrated for its traditional Chilean food. You'll see delicious baked empanadas, *humitas* (corn tamales), steak sandwiches and homemade pastries for sale at casual food stands set among the ceramics shops; there are also several traditional eateries along the main drag where you can have a relaxed and authentic meal. Grilled meats make up most of the menu at ever-popular **La Greda** (☎831-1166; Manuel Rodríguez 251; mains CH$3000-5800; ☉10am-midnight). The name means 'clay,' and indeed, the hearty casseroles are cooked in locally made dishes. La Greda's claim to fame is that it was listed in the *Guinness Book of World Records* for the largest empanada in the world in 1995.

Note that while Pomaire is packed with day-trippers on weekends, the town is practically deserted on Monday, when the potters have a day off.

Several lines run buses between Santiago and the Pomaire area from Santiago's San Borja terminal (CH$1200, one hour). A direct bus usually leaves at 9:30am; otherwise, take one of the regular services to Melipilla (CH$1300, 30 minutes, four hourly) and get off at the Pomaire *cruce* (crossroads), where *colectivos* and *liebres* (minibuses) take you into town (CH$500). **Buses Jiménez** (☎776-5786) runs several buses to Melipilla each hour.

Around Santiago

20 km
10 miles

Cordillera de los Andes

ARGENTINA

Parque Provincial
Volcán Tupungato

Cerro Tupungato
(6570m)

Volcán
Tupungatito
(5682m)

Nevado de
los Piuquenes
(6019m)

Paso Portillo
de Piuquenes

Cerro
Marmolejo
(6108m)

Volcán
San José
(5856m)

Termas
del Plomo

Cerro
El Morado
(4490m)

Monumento
Natural
El Morado

Baños
Morales

Termas
Valle
de Colina

Región V

Cerro
Plomo
(5430m)

Santuario de
la Naturaleza
Yerba Loca

La Parva

El Colorado

Valle
Nevado

Embalse
El Yeso

Laguna
Negra

Lagunillas

Cerro San
Francisco
(4345m)

San
Gabriel

Río Volcán

Lo Valdés

El Volcán

Farellones

El Arrayán

Río Mapocho

Río Colorado

La Tinaja
(2509m)

Guayacán

San José
de Maipo

Peladeros
(3910m)

El Melocotón

Laguna del
Encañado

San Alfonso

Santuario de
la Naturaleza
Cascada de
las Ánimas

El Manzano

Cajón del
Maipo

Reserva
Nacional
Río Clarillo

Río Clarillo

Viña Aquitania

Viña Santa
Carolina

Viña Almaviva

La Florida

Puente
Alto

Isla de
Pirque

Pirque

El Principal

Viña
Santa Rita

Viña
Macul

Viña Cousiño

Viña Concha
y Toro

Alto
Jahuel

SANTIAGO

Peldehue

Colina

Río Mapocho

Panamericana

San Bernardo

Calera
de Tango

Buin

Paine

Aeropuerto Internacional
Arturo Merino Benítez
(Pudahuel)

(Toll)

Peñaflor

Talagante

Viña Dé
Martino

Isla de
Maipo

Lampa

Viña
Undurraga

Pomaire

Laguna
de Aculeo

Región
Metropolitana

Curacaví

Melipilla

Río Maipo

Reserva
Nacional
Lago Peñuelas

To Valparaíso

Región V

Casablanca

Maipo Valley Wineries

When you have had your fill of museums and plazas, head south of the city center to check out its more intoxicating sights: the wineries of the Maipo Valley, one of Chile's major wine regions. Big-bodied reds, such as Cabernet Sauvignon, Merlot, Carmenere, and Syrah – many that have notes of eucalyptus or mint – are what the valley is all about.

You can go it alone: the wineries below are within 1½ hours of the city center on public transportation. But if you'd like to hit the wine circuit with a knowledgeable guide, try the specialized tours at **Uncorked Wine Tours** (☑981-6242; www.uncorked.cl; half-/full-day tour US$135/195) – an English-speaking guide will take you to three wineries, and a lovely lunch is included. Also recommended are the personalized tours through Chip Travel (p60) and the winery bike tour with La Bicicleta Verde (p58), in which you'll be pedaling around the countryside to wineries within 10km of Santiago.

For approximate locations of wineries near Santiago, see Map p81.

◉ Sights

Viña Aquitania   WINERY
(Map p81; ☑791-4500; www.aquitania.cl; Av Consistorial 5090, Peñalolén; standard tours incl 2 reserva CH$7000, premium tours incl 3 premium CH$15,000; ⊘ by appointment only 9am-5pm Mon-Fri; Ⓜ Grecia) Set at the foot of the Andes is Santiago's most interesting winery. Aquitania works with tiny quantities and sky-high quality. From Grecia metro station (Línea 4), take bus D07 south from bus stop 6 and get off at the intersection of Av Los Presidentes and Consistorial (you need a Bip! card). Aquitania is 150m south. Note that Viña Cousiño Macul is located only 2km away.

Viña Cousiño Macul   WINERY
(Map p81; ☑351-4135; www.cousinomacul.cl; Av Quilín 7100, Peñalolén; tours incl 1 varietal & 1 reserva CH$8000; ⊘ tours 11am, noon, 3pm & 4pm Mon-Fri in English, 11am & noon Sat; Ⓜ Quilín) A pretty winery set in Santiago's urban sprawl. Most of the vineyards are now at Buin, but tours take in the production process and underground bodega, built in 1872. It's a 2.25km walk or a quick taxi ride from the metro.

Viña Almaviva   WINERY
(Map p81; ☑470-0225; www.almavivawinery. com; Av Santa Rosa 821, Paradero 45, Puente Alto;

tours incl 1 pour US$80; ⊘ by appointment only 9am-5pm Mon-Fri) This boutique vineyard runs in partnership with Baron Philippe de Rothschild. High-end tastings are available by reservation only. Bus 207 from Estación Mapocho runs past the entrance, about 1km from the winery building. It's the more sophisticated sister of **Viña Concha y Toro** (☑476-5269; www.conchaytoro. com; Virginia Subercaseaux 210, Pirque; standard tour & tasting CH$8000, sommelier-led tastings CH$17,000; ⊘10am-5pm) where you can see winemaking on a vast scale on one of the winery's mass-market tours.

Viña Santa Rita   WINERY
(Map p81; ☑362-2594; www.santarita.com; Camino Padre Hurtado 0695, Alto Jahuel) Famous for the premium Casa Real Cabernet, Santa Rita offers bike and wine tours as well as picnics. To get there, take the metro to Buin station, then take bus 5064 to the entrance of the winery.

Viña de Martino   WINERY
(Map p81; ☑819-2959; www.demartino.cl; Manuel Rodríguez 229, Isla de Maipo) The first carbon neutral winery in South America offers tastings in a Tuscan-style manor.

Viña Undurraga   WINERY
(Map p81; ☑372-2850; www.undurraga.cl; Camino a Melipilla, Km 34, Talagante) The subterranean vineyards at Undurraga date from 1885.

Cajón del Maipo

Rich greenery lines the steep, rocky walls of this stunning gorge that the Río Maipo flows through. Starting only 25km southeast of Santiago, it's popular on weekends with Santiaguinos, who come here to camp, hike, climb, cycle, raft and ski. Lots of traditional restaurants and teahouses, and a big winery, mean that overindulgence is also on the menu. Recently, a few new offerings in the Cajón del Maipo – including motorcycle tours and a venue for 'glamping' (ie glamorous camping) – have brought some buzz to the otherwise quiet region. At the time of writing, there was news that an international company was planning to build a hydroelectric station here, an event that could have serious consequences for the region's ecosystem. So take advantage of this pristine natural playground; it's an easy getaway from the capital city by car or public transportation.

Two roads wind up the Cajón on either side of the river, and join at El Melocotón, 7km before San Alfonso. The numberless road on the southern side goes through Pirque, whereas the G-25 runs along the north side past San José de Maipo and San Alfonso to Baños Morales and the Monumento Natural el Morado.

The river itself is made up of a series of mostly Class III rapids with very few calm areas – indeed, rafters are often tossed into the water. Still, it's less hazardous than when the first kayakers descended in the 1970s and found themselves facing automatic weapons as they passed the grounds of General Pinochet's estate at El Melocotón (the narrow bedrock chute here, one of the river's more entertaining rapids, is now known as 'El Pinocho,' the ex-dictator's nickname).

November to March is rafting season; ski bums and bunnies flock here June to September; and walking, horseback riding and lunching are popular year-round. Make sure you take your documents with you if you are going beyond San Gabriel (the end of the paved road and the turnoff to Baños Morales): the closeness of the Argentine border means the police run regular checks here.

PIRQUE

Although it's only just outside Santiago, Pirque has a very small-town feel to it. There's nothing small-scale or low-key about its main attraction, however: Viña Concha y Toro, Chile's largest and most industrial winery (see p82). The main road leads east from Concha y Toro up the south side of the Cajón toward San Alfonso. About 3km along it is a string of restaurants: the long-running local favorite is **La Vaquita Echá** (www.lavaquitae cha.cl; Ramón Subercaseaux 3355, Pirque; mains CH$5200-8500). It's rightly famed for its grill – steaks, ribs, fish and even wild boar all sizzle over the coals – and you might also catch some Chilean music or dancing.

RESERVA NACIONAL RÍO CLARILLO

A mix of Andean forest and scrubland make up this hilly, 100-sq-km **nature reserve** (Map p81; www.conaf.cl; adult/child CH$3000/1000; ☺8:30am-6pm) in a scenic tributary canyon of the Cajón del Maipo, 18km southeast of Pirque. It's home to abundant bird species, foxes and rodents, and the endangered Chilean iguana. Two short, clearly labeled trails start near the Conaf rangers' office, about 300m after the entrance: Quebrada Jorquera takes about half an hour, and Ali-

wen Mahuida takes 1½ hours. The rangers give advice on longer hikes along the river, but plan on starting early; camping isn't allowed here. For more information on hikes and a basic map, log onto www.pirque.com.

SAN ALFONSO & CASCADA DE LAS ANIMAS

Halfway up the Cajón del Maipo, a cluster of houses and tea rooms make up San Alfonso. It's home to the beautiful private nature reserve **Santuario de la Naturaleza Cascada de las Animas** (Map p81; ☑861-1303; www.cas cada.net; Camino al Volcán 31087), which is set up like a natural, outdoorsy theme park. Organized activities are the only way to visit it: hiking, horseback riding, rafting and ziplining are among the options. Book in advance.

The reserve takes its name from a stunning waterfall reached by the shortest walk offered (CH$4000); there are also guided half-day hikes into the hills (CH$10,000). **Horseback riding** is the real house specialty, however – indeed, the reserve is also a working ranch. Weather permitting, it offers two-hour rides (CH$20,000) and all-day trips (CH$45,000 including *asado* lunch) and overnighters (CH$160,000).

The three-hour **rafting trips** (CH$20,000) descend Class III or IV rapids, taking in some lovely gorges before ending up in San José de Maipo. They're led by experienced guides, and helmets, wetsuits and life jackets are provided. Promotions and packages often include lunch and use of the inviting swimming pool; ask ahead of time. Either way, you can use the shaded picnic facilities or have a meal at the treehouse-like restaurant perched high on a bluff over the river.

If you're into the peace and quiet, spend the night here in one of the bungalow suites at the brand-new **Cascada Lodge** (s/d with breakfast CH$60,000/80,000). The rustic-chic design features organic wood and stone fixtures, skylights, mosaic tilework and king-sized beds imported from Italy. You can also choose to stay in one of the **wood cabins** (for 3/6/8 people CH$50,000/90,000/110,000) with log fires and well-equipped kitchens, or smaller **guest rooms** (d/q CH$25,000/45,000). Alternatively, pitch your tent in the shady **campsite** (per person CH$6000-10,000).

New on the scene in 2011 was the 'glamping' (glamorous camping) experience offered by **Los Baqueanos** (☑056-9-9618-7066; www.losbaqueanos.cl; package incl meals from CH$80,000; ☎). Sleeping in the great outdoors no longer means roughing it: guests sleep in luxurious dome-shaped tents heated by solar power and comfortably furnished with cozy cots, ergonomic chairs and wi-fi access. Gourmet breakfasts and meals are prepared by the chef, while beautiful Chilean horses wait on the sidelines to take the guide and travelers on the day's excursions into the Cajón del Maipo.

The reserve runs private van transportation to and from Santiago and Valparaíso (for one/two people round-trip CH$70,000/170,000). If you'd rather save the money and use public transportation, take the Santiago metro line 4 to the Las Mercedes terminal, then hop on bus 72 (CH$550) – look for a sign in the bus window that says 'San Alfonso.' Ask the driver to drop you off at the entrance to Cascada de las Animas. The bus ride lasts about 1½ hours.

BAÑOS MORALES & MONUMENTO NATURAL EL MORADO

The G-25 continues uphill from San Alfonso – there's about 10km of tarmac, then 20km of rutted, unpaved dirt before you reach the small thermal springs of Baños Morales. You can camp here, or stay in one of the simple, wood-clad rooms at **Refugio Lo Valdés** (Refugio Alemán; ☏099-220-8525; www.refugiolovaldes.com; Ruta G-25 Km77; dm CH$15,000, d incl breakfast CH$48,000), across the Río Volcán from Baños Morales. Note that the dorm-style 'attic' accommodations do not include sheets or towels; they're designed for campers traveling with their own equipment.

Popular on weekends, the hotel boasts a stunning view over the Cajón. The on-site restaurant is renowned for its hearty meals and *onces*. The owners of Refugio Lo Valdés also run a number of excursions: excellent journeys on **horseback** (CH$14,000-30,000) can be combined with a barbecue in the mountains (from CH$30,000, including ride). They'll also arrange guides, trekking and trips to the hot springs at Termas de Colina; in winter, you can rent snowshoes (CH$10,000 per day).

Also at Baños Morales is the entrance to **Monumento Natural El Morado** (Map p81; adult/child CH$2000/1000; ☉8:30am-2:30pm Oct-Apr), a small national park. Inside, from the banks of sparkling Laguna El Morado, there are fabulous views of the San Francisco glacier and the 5000m summit of Cerro El Morado. It takes about two hours to reach the lake on the well-marked 8km trail from the Conaf post. In summer, motivated hikers

can continue to the base of Glaciar El Morado, on the lower slopes of the mountain; there are free campsites around the lake.

TERMAS VALLE DE COLINA

About 16km after the turnoff to Baños Morales, the G-25 reaches the thermal springs of **Termas Valle de Colina** (Map p81; Baños Colina; ☏239-6797; www.termasvalledecolina.cl; entrance incl camping adult/child CH$6000/3000, d without bathroom CH$30,000; ☉Oct-Feb), where hot natural pools overlook the valley. There's a well-organized campground and a basic but clean hostel; be sure to bring plenty of food supplies. The administration also offers guided hikes and one- to three-day horseback-riding expeditions.

For a real adventure, join a guided motorcycle tour of the region through **Enduro Trip** (☏56-2-229-1697; www.endurotrip.com; tours per person CH$100,000). Leaving from Santiago at 9am, these energetic guides run four standard circuits, including one that goes to Baños Morales, Termas de Colina and Glaciar El Morado. In addition to the ride itself and some excellent wildlife viewing, you'll be stopping along the way to try regional treats from empanadas to homemade bread.

⊙ Getting There & Away

To get to Pirque, take the Santiago metro to Plaza de Puente Alto, the end of line 4. Then catch a blue minibus (labeled 'Pirque' in the window) and tell the driver you want to go to Plaza Pirque or Viña Concha y Toro. Departures are frequent and the fare is CH$500. Plaza Pirque is about 4km before the entrance to RN Río Clarillo – some services continue to the park entrance.

To get to San Alfonso from Santiago, take metro line 4 to the Las Mercedes terminal, then hop onto bus 72 (CH$550) – or any bus that says 'San Alfonso' on the window. Some lines continue to Baños Morales from September to March, and there's one service a day there from April to October at 7am on weekends, returning at 5pm. Note that some bus services only go as far as San José de Maipo (CH$450, 1½ hours, four hourly) – but that will be marked clearly on the bus. These buses may also be boarded outside Bellavista La Florida metro station (Línea 5), but the journey will be shorter if you take the Santiago metro as far as Las Mercedes.

There is no public transportation to Termas Valle de Colina. However, private vans run by **Manzur Expediciones** (☏777-4284) go to the baths from Santiago's Plaza Italia, usually on Wednesday, Saturday and Sunday. **Alicia Miranda** (☏737-2844) runs similar services from Alameda.

The 93km drive from central Santiago to Baños Morales takes about two hours, and is usually doable in a regular car. Count on another 20 minutes to reach Termas Valle de Colina; depending on the state of the last stretch of road, you may need a 4WD here.

Ski Centers

Several of Chile's best ski resorts are within day-tripping (or two-day tripping) distance from Santiago. Aim to go midweek, if you can: snow-happy Santiaguinos crowd both the pistes and the roads up to the resorts on weekends.

LAGUNILLAS

The cheapest skiing to be had near Santiago is at **Lagunillas** (Map p81; ✆638-0497; www.skilagunillas.cl, in Spanish; day ski pass adult/child CH$18,000/12,000), a small resort 67km southeast of Santiago via San José de Maipo. Run by the Club Andino de Chile, it has four lifts and 13 runs; note that though the scenery is stunning, the snow here is generally not as good as at Santiago's more exclusive resorts. Club Andino runs a few small cabins here, but it's an easy day trip from Santiago.

CAJÓN DE MAPOCHO – TRES VALLES

Santiago's four most popular ski centers – Farellones/El Colorado, La Parva and Valle Nevado – are clustered in three valleys in the Mapocho river canyon, hence their collective name, Tres Valles. Although they're only 30km to 40km northeast of Santiago, the traffic-clogged road up can be slow going. All prices given here are for weekends and high season (usually early July to mid-August). Outside that time, there are hefty midweek discounts on both ski passes and hotels. Well-marked off-piste runs connect the three valleys. The predominance of drag lifts means that lines get long during the winter holidays, but otherwise crowds here are bearable. Ask about combination tickets if you're planning on skiing at multiple resorts.

Farellones & El Colorado

Just 32km from Santiago, these two **resorts** (✆398-8080; www.elcolorado.cl; Apoquindo 4900, Oficina 48, Santiago) are close enough together to be considered a single destination. The eating and after-ski scenes are scanty here, so locals tend just to come up for the day.

The cheaper of the two is the village of **Farellones** (Map p81; day ski pass CH$11,000),

Chile's first ski resort. At about 2500m, it's lower than El Colorado and its handful of runs tend to attract mainly beginner skiers, as well as tubing fans. There's more choice further up the mountain at **El Colorado** (Map p81; day ski pass adult/child CH$33,000/22,000). The 22 runs range from beginner to expert and the highest of its 18 lifts takes you 3333m above sea level.

La Parva

The most exclusive of Santiago's ski resorts, **La Parva** (Map p81; ✆in Santiago 339-8482, in La Parva 220-9530; www.laparva.cl; office Av El Bosque Norte 0177, 2nd fl, Las Condes, Santiago; day ski pass adult/child CH$35,000/25,000) is definitely oriented toward posh families rather than the powder-and-party pack. Private cottages and condos make up ski base Villa La Parva, from where 14 lifts take you to its 30 runs, the highest of which starts at 3630m above sea level. Snow permitting, there's plenty of off-piste skiing here, too. The ski between La Parva and Valle Nevado or Farellones (via Valle Olímpico) is also a favorite among more experienced skiers.

Valle Nevado

About 12km from Farellones is **Valle Nevado** (Map p81; ✆477-7700; www.vallenevado. com; Av Vitacura 5250, Oficina 304, Santiago; day ski pass adult/child CH$37,000/26,000). Modeled on European setups, Valle Nevado boasts almost 3000 hectares of skiable domain – the largest in South America. It's also the best-maintained of Santiago's resorts and has the most challenging runs. A variety of beginner runs make it good for kids, too. Thirteen chairlifts and surface lifts take you to the 27 pistes' high-altitude start points, which range from 2860m to 3670m. At the time of writing, construction on an eight-person gondola – the first of its kind in Chile – was underway. Adrenaline levels also run high here: there's a snow park, good off-piste action and heli-skiing.

In summer, the Mirador chairlift (round-trip ticket CH$10,000), transporting hikers and picnic-toting families to a 3300m peak, is open daily. Check the website for more on horseback riding excursions, rock climbing, guided trekking, children's activities and lunch with panoramic views at the mountaintop restaurant.

Valle Nevado's three hotels are expensive, yet the quality of both accommodations and service can be hit or miss. Rates at all include a ski pass and half-board. During July, only weeklong stays are available; for more flexibility, come in June, August or September.

You can ski right onto your balcony at **Hotel Valle Nevado** (Camino Farellones s/n; d incl breakfast & dinner from US$724; @ ⊠). The best-appointed option, it has a heated outdoor pool, spa, and piano bar with a huge open fire. Dinner at the hotel's Fourchette D'or restaurant goes some way to offsetting the rates. The 'budget' option skimps on luxury but not on prices: at **Hotel Tres Puntas** (Camino Farellones s/n; dm/d incl breakfast & dinner US$219/412) there's a mix of regular and dorm-style rooms, all of which are cramped but functional. Alternatively, the resort offers pleasant condo-style apartments (apt for 2/3/6 people from US$427/586/1137 per night); lift tickets and meals are not included in the room price.

The most distinguished of the resort's six restaurants is **La Fourchette D'or** (☎698-0103; Hotel Valle Nevado; mains CH$15,000-22,000; ⊙8-11pm Mon-Fri, 12:30-3:30pm & 8-11pm Sat & Sun). For a quick sandwich or snack, try the fast-food joint adjacent to the ski area at Hotel Puerta del Sol. Note that the resorts don't have supermarkets – you'll want to stock up on groceries and supplies before leaving Santiago.

❶ Getting There & Away

There is no public transportation to Santiago's ski resorts. Several private companies run regular shuttle services to the Tres Valles and Lagunillas during ski season, including the following:

KL Adventure (☎217-9101; www.kladventure.com; Augusto Mira Fernández 14248, Las Condes, Santiago; round trip to Tres Valles CH$10,000, with hotel pickup CH$22,000) The shuttle leaves at 8am and returns at 5pm.

SkiTotal (☎246-0156; www.skitotal.cl; Av Apoquindo 4900, Local 39-42, Las Condes, Santiago; round trip to Valle Nevado CH$12,000, with hotel pick-up CH$20,000-35,000) The shuttle leaves at 8am and returns at 5pm.

You can also reach Lagunillas by taking a bus to San José de Maipo (see p84) and getting a taxi for the remaining 20km.

Middle Chile

Best Places to Eat

» Café Vinilo (p98)

» Vino Bello (p115)

» La Casa de las
Empanadas (p117)

» Restaurante Miguel Torres
(p122)

» La Cocó (p98)

Best Places to Stay

» La Joya del Mar (p128)

» Yellow House (p96)

» Cabañas Guzmán Lyon
(p116)

» Hotel Santa Cruz Plaza
(p115)

» Ecobox Andino (p127)

Why Go?

There's no avoiding the sad truth: Middle Chile was at the epicenter of the February 2010 earthquake. Towns and cities like Concepción, Talca and Curicó, having suffered the hardest hit, were still recovering at the time of writing. But despite some crumbled churches, roped-off plazas and reduced lodging and dining options, things are up and running – and tourists are more than welcome; they're actually vital to continued development throughout this area of Chile. Happily, most of the main attractions here – from the picturesque port city of Valparaíso and the surf mecca of Pichilemu to lovely national parks, ski slopes, and the rolling hills of Chile's principal wine-producing region – have rebounded well from the natural disaster. Yes, some neighborhoods are still rebuilding and vineyards lost thousands of bottles from their cellars' collections, but why cry over spilled wine? After all, Middle Chile still has world-class surf breaks, excellent skiing and killer Cabernet Sauvignon.

When to Go
Valparaiso

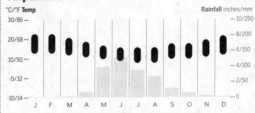

Jun–Sep
Frequent snowfall brings skiers and snowboarders to the slopes in full force.

Oct–Dec Before the summertime rush, the beach towns are calm and hotel rates are cheaper.

Jan–May Wine lovers migrate to the vineyards for the grape harvest and the festivals surrounding it.

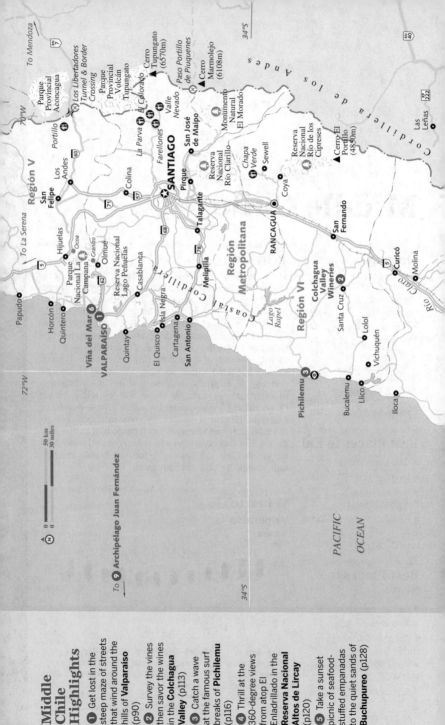

Middle Chile Highlights

1 Get lost in the steep maze of streets that wind around the hills of **Valparaíso** (p90)

2 Survey the vines then savor the wines in the **Colchagua Valley** (p113)

3 Catch a wave at the famous surf breaks of **Pichilemu** (p116)

4 Thrill at the 360-degree views from atop El Enladrillado in the **Reserva Nacional Altos de Lircay** (p120)

5 Take a sunset picnic of seafood-stuffed empanadas to the quiet sands of **Buchupureo** (p128)

Malargüe

36°S

Mendoza

Bardas
Blancas

RP
224

Paso
Pehuenche
(2553m)

Reserva Nacional
Radal Siete Tazas

4 Reserva Nacional
Altos de Lircay

Región VII

Lago
Colbún

115

Neuquén

70°W

38°S

Cordillera de los Andes

ARGENTINA

Chos-Malal

RN
40

Constitución

Río Maule TALCA

Viña Gillmore **8**

San Javier

Linares

Reserva Nacional
Federico Albert

Chanco

Reserva
Nacional
Los Ruiles

Cauquenes

Curanipe

San Carlos

Chillán

Chillán Viejo

Minas
del Prado

Volcán
Chillán
(3122m)

Nevados
de Chillán **7**

Valle Las
Trancas

Termas de
Chillán

Reserva
Nacional Ñuble

Región VIII

Coastal Cordillera

Ninhue

5 Buchupureo

Cobquecura

Penco

Tomé

Talcahuano

CONCEPCIÓN

Coronel

Lota

Salto
del Laja

Los Ángeles

Laguna
del Laja

Parque Nacional
Laguna del Laja

Paso
Pichachén

Volcán
Callaqui
(3164m)

Panamericana

180

Río Biobío

Renaico

Mulchén

Cuesta
Esperanza

Collipulli

5

To Temuco 72°W

180

Angol

Los
Sauces

Curanilahue

Parque
Nacional
Nahuelbuta

Monumento
Natural
Contulmo

Cañete

Región IX

Lebu

Isla Santa
María

38°S

36°S

6 Sun yourself
on a beach blanket
beside vacationing
Santiaguinos in **Viña
del Mar** (p102)

7 Ski through the
trees on the longest
ski slope in South
America at **Nevados
de Chillán** (p126)

8 Get a wine-based
spa treatment and
sample Cabernet
Franc at **Viña
Gillmore** (p118)

9 Relive a
castaway's Robinson
Crusoe-style
adventure in the
**Archipiélago Juan
Fernández** (p135)

❶ Getting There & Away

The Panamericana runs through or near to most of the areas covered in this chapter, all of which are less than an overnight journey from Santiago. The excellent long-distance bus services that travel up and down this highway are the quickest and cheapest way to arrive, whether you're coming from the Lakes District to the south, from Santiago or the north, or internationally via Mendoza in Argentina.

❶ Getting Around

Frequent local and long-distance buses connect all the major towns in Middle Chile to each other and to Santiago, which sits in the center of the region. Trains are also an option for travel between cities on the Panamericana between Santiago and Chillán – journeys take as long as on a bus, and are markedly more expensive, so train travel is probably only worth doing for the novelty value.

Getting to national parks and smaller towns can be trickier: snow closes some areas in winter, in others public transportation reduces to a trickle outside summer, and a few have no public transportation at all.

Having a car is invaluable for quick trips to far-flung parks and for touring wineries.

VALPARAÍSO & THE CENTRAL COAST

Only 120km northwest of Santiago lies Chile's second-most-important city, distinctive Valparaíso: cultural capital, seat of congress and a vital port. North of the city is Viña del Mar and the string of coastal towns where Santiaguinos love to holiday. A major wine region (the Casablanca Valley) and a little-known national park (La Campana) are between the coast and Santiago.

Valparaíso

☑ 032 / POP 282,500

Pablo Neruda said it best: 'Valparaíso, how absurd you are...you haven't combed your hair, you've never had time to get dressed, life has always surprised you.' But Neruda wasn't the only artist to fall for Valparaíso's unexpected charms. Poets, painters and would-be philosophers have long been drawn to Chile's – no, Latin America's – most unusual city. Along with the ever-shifting port population of sailors, dockworkers and prostitutes, they've endowed gritty and gloriously spontaneous Valparaíso with an edgy air of 'anything goes.' Add to this the spectacular faded beauty of its chaotic *cerros* (hills), a maze of steep, sinuous streets, alleys and *escaleras* (stairways) piled high with crumbling mansions, and it's clear why some visitors are spending more time here than in Santiago.

History

The sea has always defined Valparaíso and the region surrounding it. Fishing sustained the area's first inhabitants, the Chango, and no sooner had the Spanish conquistadores arrived than Valparaíso became a stop-off point for boats taking gold and other Latin American products to Spain. More seafaring looters soon followed: English and Dutch pirates, includ-

---

NAVIGATING VALPARAÍSO

Valparaíso is a city of two parts: El Plan, the congested, flat commercial district closest to the sea; and the 42 *cerros* (hills) that rise up steeply behind it. Most major thoroughfares in El Plan run east–west, parallel to the shoreline: the closest is Av Errázuriz, which merges with Av España and leads to Viña del Mar. The oldest part of town, Barrio El Puerto (the port neighborhood), is in the west of El Plan. The two main streets in the east are Independencia and Av Pedro Montt, where you'll find the bus station.

Valparaíso's hills defy even determined cartographers. Av Almirante Montt and Urriola lead from El Plan to Cerros Concepción and Alegre. From Plaza Aníbal Pinto, Cumming takes you to Cerro Cárcel; from nearby Av Ecuador, Yerbas Buenas winds up Cerro Bellavista, accessible from the other side by Ferrari. Av Alemania winds along the top of the more central *cerros*.

Valparaíso Map (www.valparaisomap.cl) is by far the best map of this notoriously hard-to-navigate city, while **Ascensores de Valparaíso** (www.ascensoresvalparaiso.org) has an interactive map of the city's old elevators. Also check out the cool online maps of the city's barrios at **Ciudad de Valparaíso** (www.ciudaddevalparaiso.cl). Look for print maps at hotels and tourist information kiosks.

ing Sir Francis Drake, who repeatedly sacked Valparaíso for gold.

The port city grew slowly at first, but boomed with the huge demand for Chilean wheat prompted by the California gold rush. The first major port of call for ships coming round Cape Horn, Valparaíso became a commercial center for the entire Pacific coast and the hub of Chile's nascent banking industry.

After Valparaíso's initial glory days, the port saw hard times in the 20th century. The 1906 earthquake destroyed most of Valparaíso's buildings, then the opening of the Panama Canal had an equally cataclysmic effect on the city's economy. Only the Chilean navy remained a constant presence.

Today Valparaíso is back on the nautical charts as a cruise-ship stop-off, and Chile's growing fruit exports have also boosted the port. More significantly, the city has been Chile's legislative capital since 1990 and was voted the cultural capital in 2003. Unesco sealed the deal by giving it World Heritage status, prompting tourism to soar.

◉ Sights & Activities

Don't take it from us, take it from Unesco: the whole of Valparaíso is a sight worth seeing. Beautiful buildings and a handful of museums, these Valparaíso has; but the most exciting thing to do here is just walking the city streets. Extra adrenaline shots come courtesy of the 15 rattling *ascensores* (funiculars) built between 1883 and 1916 that crank you up into the hills and meandering back alleys. Wherever you wander, have your camera at the ready: Valpo brings out the photographer in most people.

CERROS CONCEPCIÓN & ALEGRE

Sighing on every corner quickly becomes a habit on these two hills, whose steep cobbled streets are lined with traditional 19th-century houses with painted corrugated-iron facades that form a vivid patchwork of colors. Some of the city's best cafes and restaurants are here (though not clubs, as late-night music is banned) and new hotels and hostels open up here all the time. Lower Cerro Concepción is more touristy, whereas Cerro Alegre still has an arty air to it.

Ascensor Concepción HISTORIC SITE
(CH$250; ☺7am-10pm) The city's oldest elevator, Ascensor Concepción takes you to Paseo Gervasoni, at the lower end of Cerro Con-

cepción. Built in 1883, it originally ran on steam power.

Palacio Baburizza PALACE
(Paseo Yugoslavo s/n, Cerro Alegre) The rambling art nouveau building at the western end of Cerro Alegre is Palacio Baburizza; it houses the **Museo de Bellas Artes** (Fine Arts Museum), which was closed at the time of writing but set to reopen later in 2012. **Ascensor El Peral** (CH$100; ☺7am-8pm) runs here from just off Plaza Sotomayor. A quick way up to the eastern side of Cerro Alegre is the **Ascensor Reina Victoria** (CH$250; ☺7am-11pm), which connects Av Elias to Paseo Dimalow.

Museo Lukas MUSEUM
(☐222-1344; www.lukas.cl; Paseo Gervasoni 448, Cerro Concepción; adult/child & senior CH$1000/500; ☺10:30am-2pm & 3-6pm Tue-Sun) Local cartoonist Lukas had a sharp eye for the idiosyncrasies of Valparaíso. You need to speak Spanish to understand his sardonic political strips in the Museo Lukas, but the ink drawings of Valpo buildings speak for themselves.

CERRO CÁRCEL

FREE **Cultural Park Valparaíso (Parque Cultural Ex-Cárcel)** HISTORIC SITE
(Former Prison Cultural Park; www.excarcel.cl; Castro s/n, Cerro Cárcel) The prison that gave this hill its name was closed in 1999, but the crumbling remains of cellblocks and exercise yards, decorated with huge graffiti, functioned for years afterward as a grassroots cultural center. Protests broke out after Brazilian architect Oscar Niemeyer was

HOP ON THE BUS

Sure, you can take the creaky antique elevators or huff it uphill on foot – but there's another unforgettable way to experience some of Valparaíso's magic. The route of local bus O (labeled *micro O* or sometimes *micro 612*) carries a mix of weary locals and camera-toting tourists through the narrow alleyways and across several of the city's steep hillsides; you can board in front of Congreso Nacional, atop Cerro Alegre or at various other points throughout town. For more on Valparaíso's bus system, see p102.

Valparaíso

To Caleta El Membrillo (1.6km)

To El Mirado (500m)

Paseo 21 de Mayo

Cerro Artillería ▲

Museo Naval y Marítimo 🏛️

⊕ 17

31

◉ 1

Artillería

Av Carampangue

Cerro Arrayan ▲

Plaza Aduana (Wheelwright)

Muelle Prat

Valdivia

◉ 11

Plaza Matriz

Santo Domingo

Matriz

⊕ 51

Cerro Santo Domingo ▲

10 ✚

Plaza Echaurren

Goñi

M Hurtado

Blanco

18 ⊕

Tourist Information Kiosk ℹ️

San Francisco Carrasco

V Hugo

Merlet

Cochrane

47 ⊕

Plaza Sotomayor

⊕ 20

9 🏛️

Cerro Cordillera ▲

Castillo

Av Tomás Ramos

19 ⊕

2 ◉

Señoret

Av Brasil

Av Errázuriz

Paseo Yugoslavo

Museo de Bellas Artes

15 🏛️

16 ◉

Esmeralda

🖥️ 22

Higuera

Urriola

45

◉ **Ascensor Concepción**

Ross

50 ☆

Martinez

Papudo

⊗ 35

Lautaro Rosas

32

27 ▲

🖥️ 21

44 ⊗

14 🏛️

Cerro Alegre

52

24 🖥️

Cerro Concepción ▲

33

34 ⊗

Tourist Information Kiosk ℹ️

San Enrique

Templeman

Concepcion

48 ⊗

53

54

Plaza Anibal Pinto ▲

Monte Alegre

30

43 ⊗

39

Av Almirante Montt

46 ⊗

Cerro Panteón ▲

40 ⊗

42 ⊗

Morrison

San Galos

55

◉ 4

Cumming

41 ⊗

Estanque

🖥️ 25

29 🖥️

26 ⊗

Elias Atahualpa

37 ⊗

5 ✚

Cementerio Católico

Piramide

Bellavista

Condell

Cerro Cárcel ▲

◉ 8

Cementerio de Disidentes

◉ 6

◉ 7 ✚

Mackenna

Av Yerbas Buenas

Cerro Miraflores ▲

Cumming

Plaza Bismark

Av Equador

🖥️ 28

Bahía de Valparaíso

Blanco

Pudeto

Av Brasil

E. Ramírez

Plaza Simón Bolívar   Yungay

Molina   Chacabuco   Las Heras

Plaza Victoria

Av Pedro Montt

Lira   Edwards

Aldunate

Independencia

Carrera   Buenos Aires

Av Colón

Cerro Bellavista

Lastra

chosen (and later released from his duties) to turn the space into a huge arts center. At the time of writing, the new **Cultural Park Valparaíso**, a recycled version of the original prison now complete with a theater and artists' workshops, was set to open in 2012. Reach it by walking up Subida Cumming.

CERRO PANTEÓN

Cementerios 1 & 2   CEMETERY

(Dinamarca s/n; ⊘8am-dusk) The city's most illustrious, influential and infamous residents rest in peace in Cementerio 1, where the tombs look like ornate mini palaces. Adjoining it is Cementerio 2, including the **Cementerio de Disidentes** ('dissident cemetery') where English and European immigrants were buried. Despite the name, these departed souls weren't rabble-rousers; they were simply Protestants, and therefore not accepted at the traditional cemeteries. The views from here are worthwhile in themselves. If you're up for the walk, you can also get here by hiking up Av Ecuador.

CERRO BELLAVISTA

Artists and writers have long favored this quiet residential hill, but the steady stream of hotels and hostels opening here signal that Cerro Bellavista may well be Valpo's next big thing.

TOP CHOICE **La Sebastiana**   HISTORIC BUILDING

(✆225-6606; www.fundacionneruda.org; Ferrari 692, Cerro Bellavista; adult/child & senior CH$3000/1500; ⊘10:30am-6:50pm Tue-Sun Jan & Feb, 10:10am-6pm Tue-Sun Mar-Dec) Bellavista's most famous resident artist was Pablo Neruda, who made a point of watching Valparaíso's annual New Year's fireworks from his house at the top of the hill, La Sebastiana. Getting here involves a hefty uphill hike, and the climbing continues inside the house – you're rewarded on each floor with ever more heart-stopping views over the harbor. The best of all are from Neruda's crow's nest study. Unlike at Neruda's other houses, you can wander around La Sebastiana at will, lingering over the chaotic collection of ship's figureheads, glass, 1950s furniture and artworks by his famous friends. Just don't go behind the bright pink bar, which was reserved for Don Pablo himself.

Alongside the house, the Fundación Neruda has built the **Centro Cultural La Sebastiana**, containing a small exhibition space, cafe and souvenir shop. To get here, walk 800m uphill along Héctor Calvo from

Valparaíso

Ascensor Espíritu Santo. Alternatively, take green bus O on Serrano near Plaza Sotomayor or in El Plan, or from the plaza at the top of Templeman on Cerro Alegre and get off at the 6900 block of Av Alemania.

FREE **Museo a Cielo Abierto** MUSEUM
(Open-Air Museum; www.pucv.cl/site/pags/museo) Twenty classic, colorful murals are dotted through this *cerro's* lower streets, forming the Museo a Cielo Abierto, created between 1969 and 1973 by students from the Universidad Católica's Instituto de Arte. The

Ascensor Espíritu Santo (CH$250; ⊙7am-8:30pm) takes you from behind Plaza Victoria to the heart of this art.

CERRO ARTILLERÍA
Clear views out over the sea made this southwestern hill a strategic defense spot, hence the name.

Museo Naval y Marítimo MUSEUM
(Naval & Maritime Museum; ☎243-7651; www.museonaval.cl; Paseo 21 de Mayo 45, Cerro Artillería; adult/child CH$700/300; ⊙10am-5:30pm Tue-Sun) Cannons still stand ready outside

the Museo Naval y Marítimo. Much space is devoted to Chile's victory in the 19th-century War of the Pacific. Other exhibits include historical paintings, uniforms, ship's furniture, swords, navigating instruments and medals, all neatly displayed in exhibition rooms along one side of a large courtyard. Rattling **Ascensor Artillería** (CH$250; ⊙7am-10pm) brings you here from Plaza Aduana (Wheelwright).

CERROS BARÓN & LECHEROS

Mirador Diego Portales   LOOKOUT
(cnr Av Diego Portales & Castelar, Cerro Barón) You can see all of central Valpo's colorful hills from the Mirador Diego Portales in the east of town.

Iglesia San Francisco   CHURCH
(cnr Blanco Viel & Zañartu, Cerro Barón) Nearby to the *mirador* (lookout), the bell tower of the ornate, red-brick Iglesia San Francisco served as a landmark for approaching mariners, who gave the city its common nickname 'Pancho' (a diminutive of Francisco).

EL PLAN & EL PUERTO
Valparaíso's flat commercial zone isn't as atmospheric as the hills that rise above it, but it contains a fair few monuments.

Barrio El Puerto   NEIGHBORHOOD
In the west of El Plan, Barrio El Puerto (the port neighborhood) has the twin honors of being the oldest part of Valparaíso and the most run-down. Crumbling stone facades hint of times gone by – such as the **Mercado Puerto** (cnr Cochrane & San Martín, Puerto), a defunct food market now home to a pack of street cats.

Plaza Matriz   PLAZA
The historic heart of the city is Plaza Matriz, which is watched over by **Iglesia La Matriz**. Begun in 1837, it's the fifth church to oc-cupy this site since the construction of the original chapel in 1559. In nearby streets, luridly lit 'cabarets' (read: brothels) and liquor stores testify that port life in Valpo is still very much alive. The prime point for crane- and container-spotting here is **Muelle Prat**, along the seafront.

A more severe strain of seafarer dominates Plaza Sotomayor: the Chilean navy, whose petrol-blue **Edificio de la Comandancia Naval** (Naval Command Building) looms large on the southwestern side. In the middle of the square lies the **Monumento a los Héroes de Iquique**, a tribute to Chile's naval martyrs, who are buried in a crypt beneath it. Where Prat and Cochrane converge to become Esmeralda, the Edificio Turri narrows to the width of its namesake clock tower, the **Reloj Turri**.

Museo de Historia Natural   MUSEUM
(www.mhnv.cl; Condell 1546, El Plan) What the security guards at the Museo de Historia Natural most love to show visitors is the two-headed human baby (in formaldehyde) that was born in the city in 1915. The museum was closed for extensive restorations at the time of writing; check the website for reopening information and the new hours and ticket prices.

Congreso Nacional   HISTORIC BUILDING
(Av Pedro Montt s/n, El Plan) One of Valpo's only modern landmarks is the controversial Congreso Nacional, located in the east section of El Plan. Its roots lie in Pinochet's presidency both literally and legislatively: it was built on one of his boyhood homes and mandated by his 1980 constitution (which moved the legislature away from Santiago).

Mercado Cardonal   MARKET
(⊙6am-5pm) As colorful as Valparaíso's trademark houses – and built almost as

MIDDLE CHILE VALPARAÍSO

DON'T MISS

SENDERO BICENTENARIO

If you only do one thing in Valparaíso, this is it. Get to the bottom – or rather, the top – of the city by exploring part of the **Sendero Bicentenario**, a 30km cultural and historical route designed by local not-for-profit organization **Fundación Valparaíso**. The trail is divided into 15 themed sections and takes in parts of the port, El Plan and many of the city's lesser-known hills. From the excellent **website** (www.senderobicentenario.cl) you can download maps and English-language instructions for each section, which include all sorts of juicy details about the streets and buildings you pass. If you can't access the map online, ask around; some hotels or tourist kiosks stock print versions.

high – are the fruit and vegetable displays in the Mercado Cardonal, bordered by Yungay, Brasil, Uruguay and Rawson. Ground-floor stalls spill out onto the street, while upstairs is taken up by cheap seafood restaurants (see p98). Whole families of cats are on constant leftover-fish patrol.

Courses

Chilean Cuisine   COOKING COURSE
(☎096-621-4626;   www.cookingclasseschile.cl; meeting place at top of Ascensor Artillería; 5hr course per person CH$37,000) An energetic chef takes you to shop for ingredients at the local market, then teaches you to make pisco sours, taste local wines, and cook – then eat – a menu of Chilean classics. Check the online sample menus to get an idea: we like the seafood lesson, but great vegetarian options are also available.

Gonzalo Lara   COOKING COURSE
(☎223-0665; gonzalolarachef@yahoo.es) The madcap chef of Café Vinilo (p98) runs a similar tour that's won rave reviews from travelers; email him directly for prices and availability.

Natalis Language Center   LANGUAGE COURSE
(☎246-9936; www.natalislang.com; cnr Plaza Justicia 45, 6th fl, Oficina 602, El Plan; courses per week from CH$99,000, 3-day crash courses CH$150,000, 1-day survival Spanish CH$33,000) Has a good reputation for quick results.

☞ Tours

Many companies run whistle-stop day tours from Santiago, but most leave little time for the aimless wandering that's central to experiencing Valparaíso. One operator that runs high-quality, customizable tours of Valparaíso is **Santiago Adventures** (☎02-244-2750; www.santiagoadventures.com; Guardia Vieja 255, Oficina 403, Providencia, Santiago).

Local tour operators come and go. When you're in Valparaíso, ask at the tourist office or look for posted flyers of specialized tours tailored to specific interest areas, from antique shopping to tours of local artists' studios.

Harbor boat tours   BOAT TOUR
(from Muelle Prat; 20min tour per person from CH$1500, 1hr tour on private boat CH$12,000; ☉9:30am-6:30pm) Pass alongside giant cruise vessels or naval battleships, or spot sea lions frolicking in the harbor. Several companies operate boats – ask around for the best price.

Tours 4 Tips   WALKING TOUR
(www.tours4tips.bligoo.cl; Plaza Sotomayor 120, El Plan; ☉10am & 3pm) Just what the name says: pay-as-you-wish walking tours every morning and afternoon, no reservation required. Just show up at Plaza Sotomayor for this friendly introduction to the city.

★彡 Festivals & Events

Año Nuevo   NEW YEAR
Fantastic fireworks displays over the harbor draw hundreds of thousands of spectators to the city each December 31. Book accommodations well in advance.

🛏 Sleeping

TOP CHOICE Yellow House   B&B $
(☎233-9435;   www.theyellowhouse.cl;   Capitán Muñoz Gamero 91, Cerro Artillería; d incl breakfast CH$26,000-33,000, s/d without bathroom CH$18,000/24,000, apt CH$40,000; @🖵) Oh-my-god views over the old port and the hills really set this quiet B&B apart, and so does the friendly care lavished on guests by the Australian-Chilean couple that owns it. The cozy, pastel-painted rooms come with kettles and heaters; add the big breakfasts, kitchen, laundry, wi-fi and peaceful location on Cerro Artillería, and it's clear why the Yellow House is so popular. An adjacent apartment comes with private bathroom and fully equipped kitchen.

El Mirador   B&B $$
(☎234-5937;   www.elmiradordevalparaiso.cl;   Levarte 251, Cerro Playa Ancha; s/d/tr incl breakfast CH$15,500/36,200/51,700, apt for 2 people CH$41,300; @) Budget-minded couples and solo travelers rave about this lovely B&B. Though slightly out of the way, the beautifully tended property – a restored house with comfortable doubles, apartments with kitchenettes, accommodating hosts and a spacious terrace where you can enjoy coffee or cocktails with a view of the ocean – is tremendous value. To get here, from the Museo Naval y Maritimo, walk uphill along Playa Ancha and turn left on Levarte.

🏅 Hostal Jacaranda   HOSTEL $
(☎327-7567;   www.hostaljacaranda.blogspot.com; Urriola 636, Cerro Alegre; dm/d without bathroom from CH$6800/24,200; 🖵) Small but very welcoming – and perfectly located in a lively section of Cerro Alegre filled with small museums and cafes – this cheerful, sustainably run hostel (note the recycling efforts)

features a terrace that's romantically illuminated at night. The owners are a wealth of knowledge; if you ask, they might even show you how to make Chilean specialties like pisco sours and empanadas.

Hostal Nomades B&B **$$**

(☎327-0374; www.hostalnomades.cl; Urriola 562, Cerro Alegre; d with/without bathroom incl breakfast CH$40,000/27,000, tr without bathroom CH$40,700; ☎) In a city as bohemian and colorful as Valparaíso, where better to sleep than an artist's home? The owner of this friendly B&B is a talented painter; his large-scale works brighten the walls of an antique house that already has charm enough in its rustic wood beams and Spanish-style tiles. Though the place functions as a B&B, the communal amenities are hostel-style: guests have access to the kitchen, a TV room, luggage storage and a book exchange.

Casa Higueras BOUTIQUE HOTEL **$$$**

(☎249-7900; www.hotelcasahigueras.cl; Higuera 133, Cerro Alegre; r CH$145,200-265,370; ☎☰) Rich Santiaguinos always preferred weekending in Viña to Valpo but they've been won over by this hotel's slick rooms with dark-wood furniture and huge beds, mosaic-tiled bathrooms with big bowl sinks and the quiet living room filled with Asian sculptures and low beige sofas. It has views out over the bay, as do the lovely swimming pool, Jacuzzi and terrace, ideal for cocktails at sunset.

Hostal Morgan B&B **$$**

(☎211-4931; www.hostalmorgan.cl; Capilla 784, Cerro Alegre; d/ste incl breakfast CH$45,000/50,000; @☎) This cheery yellow B&B is a perennial travelers' favorite. The old-fashioned iron and wooden bedsteads, springy mattresses and crisp white sheets at this deliciously homey old house are perfect for sleeping in. Do try to get up for breakfast, though, which is served on country-style pine tables in a light-filled dining room.

La Nona B&B **$**

(☎618-6186; www.bblanona.com; Galos 660, Cerro Alegre; s/d incl breakfast CH$16,000/30,000; ☎) The English-speaking owners of this B&B are mad about Valpo, and love sharing insider tips with their guests. The breakfast spread is a cut above the standard, and doubles are generally spacious; the central location on Cerro Alegre is also a serious selling point.

Hostal Luna Sonrisa HOSTEL **$**

(☎273-4117; www.lunasonrisa.cl; Templeman 833, Cerro Alegre; dm/d without bathroom incl breakfast CH$7000/22,000, apt CH$49,000; ☎) Small, quiet and close to Cerro Alegre's restaurants and bars, this welcoming hostel is run by a guidebook writer, who's happy to help you plan your adventures in the city, and his wife, who runs an excellent bakery nearby. For extra privacy, ask about the independent apartment (El Nidito 1; www.elnidito.cl) on the top floor of the building.

Casa Aventura HOSTEL **$**

(☎275-5963; www.casaaventura.cl; Pasaje Gálvez 11, Cerro Concepción; dm/s/d without bathroom incl breakfast CH$8500/12,000/20,000; ☎) One of Valpo's oldest hostels. The ramshackle old house has airy, pastel-painted dorms, while doubles feature sky-high ceilings and original wooden floors. Thanks to the excellent location in the middle of the action, 1st-floor rooms can be noisy – request accommodations on the 2nd floor if possible. Breakfasts include eggs and fruit alongside the standard bread and cheese.

Puerto Natura B&B B&B **$$$**

(☎222-4405; www.puertonatura.cl; Héctor Calvo 850, Cerro Bellavista; d with/without bathroom incl breakfast CH$67,000/40,000; ☎☰) The fluffy beds and spotless, individually decorated rooms in this 1935 castle make it like staying at a very well-appointed relative's place – but so do the shared bathrooms. The owners are actually natural therapists: reiki, massages, yoga and Turkish baths are available on-site. A terraced garden filled with fruit trees is tucked away behind the house and Pablo Neruda's house, La Sebastiana, is a stone's throw away.

Hotel Ultramar BOUTIQUE HOTEL **$$$**

(☎221-0000; www.hotelultramar.com; Pérez 173, Cerro Cárcel; d/ste incl breakfast CH$72,500/88,700; ☎) Unparalleled views over the bay justify the trek to sleek Ultramar, high on Cerro Cárcel. Behind the brown-brick front it's very mod, with soaring red and white walls, black banisters and checkered floor tiles. It's a boutique-style B&B with plenty of character. Just make sure you understand which room you're booking ahead of time – there's a big difference between a spacious double with a view and a smaller room that doesn't face the ocean.

Zerohotel BOUTIQUE HOTEL $$$

(☑211-3113; www.zerohotel.com; Lautaro Rosas 343, Cerro Alegre; d overlooking street/sea incl breakfast CH$115,600/163,800; ✴🕸🛜) Sprawl under soaring ceilings on your over-sized bed then make the hardest choice of the day: where to take in the views from – the bay windows of the living room, the pool or the three-tier garden bursting with bougainvillea. The staff will arrange private guided tours of the city and deliver breakfast to your room if you like; there's a convenient 'honesty bar' where you can help yourself to a glass of Carmenere or a nightcap.

Pata Pata Hostel HOSTEL $

(☑317-3153; www.patapatahostel.com; Templeman 657, Cerro Alegre; dm/d without bathroom CH$8500/22,000; 🛜) Bright, ultrasimple dorms, cozy doubles and a quiet atmosphere with an appealing communal patio.

Hostal Caracol HOSTEL $

(☑239-5817; www.hostalcaracol.cl; Hector Calvo 371, Cerro Bellavista; dm/d incl breakfast CH$8000/28,000; 🛜) There's no skimping on details here: a wood-burning stove keeps the living room warm in winter, and dorm beds come with feather comforters, well-sprung mattresses and reading lights.

✖ Eating

CERRO CONCEPCIÓN

🍴 Bijoux CHILEAN $$

(☑322-5306; Abtao 561, Cerro Concepción; mains CH$7900; ⊙12:30pm-midnight Mon-Fri, 1pm-1am Sat, 1pm-midnight Sun; 🖉) This small but innovative new restaurant works with a simple concept: in the interest of serving fresh and seasonal cuisine, there's no menu. Instead, the chef greets you at your table to tell you about the daily catch and to discuss different Chilean-inspired dishes he could make with it, improvising according to your preferences. Dinner here is highly personalized, but the experience is far from snooty – the 'wine list' consists of exactly one bottle of red and one bottle of white.

Puerto Escondido CHILEAN $

(www.puertoescondido.cl; Papudo 424; mains CH$3500-6200) Situated in yet another of Valparaíso's quaint antique houses, this family-run eatery offers a short menu of well-made Chilean classics like *pastel de papas* (a potato casserole similar to shepherd's pie) and other homey dishes you won't find in contemporary restaurants. Come for the down-to-earth ambience as well as the food.

Café Turri SEAFOOD $$

(www.cafeturri.cl; Templeman 146; mains CH$4500-8200) Though service can be hit or miss and prices steep for what you get, Café Turri boasts unforgettable views over the harbor and ocean. Especially if you're not in a hurry, you can't go wrong by grabbing a seat on the terrace and ordering a pisco sour with steamed mussels or *palta cardenal* (avocado stuffed with shrimp).

CERRO ALEGRE

La Cocó SANDWICHES $

(www.lacoco-sangucheriaartesanal.blogspot.com; Monte Alegre 546; sandwiches CH$3800-5000; ⊙closed Mon, lunch only Sun; 🖉) Almost brand-new and already very popular with hip porteños and savvy travelers, this *sanguchería artesanal* (artisan sandwichmaker), slightly off the beaten path and run by a cool young couple, is truly a delight. Gourmet sandwiches come piled high with fresh seafood (smoked salmon with spicy chorizo is a current hit) or vegetarian-friendly toppings (try the Simona, which features goat cheese, arugula, pesto, olives and sun-dried tomatoes). Beer, wine, coffee, salads and pastries round out the creative menu, while a line-up of live music performances and poetry readings enliven the space in the evening.

Café Vinilo CHILEAN $$

(www.cafevinilo.cl; Almirante Montt 448; mains CH$5200-8500) From bakers to butchers to effortlessly hip resto-bar: the mismatched tile floor tells the story of the many incarnations of this Cerro Alegre institution. Sandwiches and chocolate-and-raspberry cake seduce during the day. Later, quirky Chilean fare takes center stage. As the last plates are licked, the namesake vinyl gets turned up and things slip into bar mode.

TOP CHOICE ⟩ Norma's CHILEAN $$

(Almirante Montt 391; set lunch $4900-6900) Don't let the name (or the nondescript entryway) throw you off: just climb the tall stairway into this cheerful, casually elegant restaurant for a surprisingly well-prepared set lunch that's friendlier on your wallet than most others in the area. The restored house still has the grand dimensions, polished wood and charming antique window frames of the original structure, and the staff here work hard to please, promptly serving up tangy pisco sours, gourmet Chilean dishes and impeccable desserts from berry cheesecake to homemade flan.

El Desayunador   BREAKFAST $
(www.eldesayunador.cl; Almirante Montt 399; breakfasts CH$2500-4800; 8:15am-8:45pm Mon-Sat, 8:30am-8pm Sun;) This charming old-school cafe – housed in an old stone building complete with vintage tile floors and rustic wooden tables – does breakfasts all day, plus sandwiches, salads, desserts, coffee and fresh-squeezed juices. Much of the menu is made with organic produce.

Viá Viá Café   FUSION $$
(www.viaviacafe.cl; Almirante Montt 217; set lunch CH$4500-5900; noon-5pm, dinner by reservation only;) If the idea of eating at a Belgian-inspired restaurant during your Chilean travels doesn't exactly reel you in, try this: Viá Viá occupies a gorgeous old art deco house, employs eco-friendly practices (note the solar-powered kitchen), offers quiet outdoor tables under the shade of leafy trees, and runs economical lunch specials on weekdays featuring rotating dishes like beer-battered fish, quinoa burritos and papaya and coconut mousse.

Pasta e Vino   ITALIAN $$
(249-6187; www.pastaevinoristorante.cl; Templeman 352; mains CH$6900-9900) The word on Pasta e Vino – credited with starting Valpo's gastro revival – has gone from 'fabulous' to 'overrated' and back to 'fabulous' again. If you want to compete with local foodies, you'll probably have to reserve ahead (you can simply fill out the online form on the website); you'll be dining on inventive pastas of the day in a sleek, intimate atmosphere with only a dozen tables.

CERRO CÁRCEL
Caruso   SEAFOOD $$
(www.caruso.cl; Av Cumming 201; mains CH$6000-7800; closed Mon) Locally caught rock- and shellfish get fresh, unpretentious treatment at Caruso. Start with the flaky filo seafood empanadas, then move on to the spicy Peruvian ceviche. Corn ice cream makes a teeth-sticking good finish.

EL PLAN & EL PUERTO
Empanadas Famosas   CHILEAN $
(Salvador Donoso 1381, El Plan; empanadas CH$1200-2000) Celebrating its 50-year an-

niversary in 2012, this classic empanada joint has hardly changed since its early days. This is the locals' pick for baked *empanadas de pino* (beef) and *mariscos* (shellfish), plus deep-fried varieties from simple *queso* (cheese) to *camarones* (shrimp), all washed down with icy beer or hearty red wine.

El Rincón de Pancho   MARKET $
(Mercado Cardonal, 2nd fl, Local 164, El Plan; mains CH$3500-5000; 9am-10pm) The best-known of many seafood stands in Mercado Cardonal, Valparaíso's main food market. Pancho does good-value fried fish, seafood stews, grilled meats and salads.

Caleta El Membrillo   SEAFOOD $
(Av Altamirano 1569, El Puerto; mains CH$2800-5200; noon-6pm Mon-Thu, open later Fri & Sat) This casual, family-friendly seafood marketplace on the waterfront is a laid-back lunch spot where you can sit outside and watch the commercial fishermen coming and going while feasting on fresh, simply prepared shrimp, fried fish and Chilean specialties.

Casino Social J Cruz   CHILEAN $
(Condell 1466, El Plan; mains CH$4500-6000) Liquid paper graffiti covers the tabletops and windows at this tiny cafe, tucked away down a narrow passageway in El Plan. Forget about menus, there's one essential dish to try: it's said that *chorrillana* (a mountain of French fries under a blanket of fried pork, onions and egg) was invented here. Folk singers serenade you into the wee hours on weekends.

Café del Poeta   CAFE $
(Plaza Aníbal Pinto 1181, El Plan; mains CH$3500-7800; 8:30am-midnight Mon-Fri, from 11am Sat & Sun;) This sweet cafe and eatery brings some sophistication to a busy central plaza in El Plan. On the menu are savory crepes, pasta and seafood; there's also sidewalk seating, a relaxing afternoon tea, wines by the glass and a collection of books about Valparaíso that guests are invited to linger over.

El Sandwich Cubano   SANDWICHES $
(O'Higgins 1224, Local 16, El Plan; sandwiches CH$1100-1600; noon-10pm Mon-Sat) Barely bigger than Fidel's handkerchief, this Cuban cafe churns out over-stuffed sandwiches. Don't get revolutionary: go for the classic *ropa vieja* (literally, 'old clothes,' a shredded beef sandwich).

TOP FIVE VALPO VIEWS

» Paseo 21 de Mayo on Cerro Artillería to survey the cranes and containers of the port.

» Plaza Bismark on Cerro Cárcel for a panoramic take of the bay.

» Mirador Diego Portales on Cerro Barón for a sweeping perspective of Valpo's colorful house-cluttered central views.

» The viewpoint at the end of Calle Merlet on Cerro Cordillera to see the rusting roofs of Barrio El Puerto and the civic buildings of Plaza Sotomayor from above.

» Paseo Atkinson on Cerro Concepción for views of typical Valpo houses during the day, and a twinkling sea of lights on the hills at night.

Drinking & Entertainment

Pajarito BAR
(www.pajaritobar.blogspot.com; Salvador Donoso 1433, El Plan) Artsy *porteños* in their 20s and 30s cram the formica tables at this laid-back, old-school bar to talk poetry and politics over beer and piscola.

Cinzano BAR
(www.barcinzano.cl; Plaza Aníbal Pinto 1182, El Plan) Drinkers, sailors and crooners have been propping themselves up on the cluttered bar here since 1896. It's now a favorite with tourists, too, who come to see tuneful old-timers knocking out tangos and boleros like there's no tomorrow.

TOP CHOICE La Piedra Feliz BAR, CLUB
(☎225-6788; www.lapiedrafeliz.cl; Av Errázuriz 1054; admission from CH$3000) Jazz, blues, tango, son, salsa, rock, drinking, dining, cinema: is there anything this massive house along the waterfront doesn't do? In the basement, DJs spin till 4am at the nightclub **La Sala**.

Bar La Playa BAR
(Serrano 567, El Puerto) It might be over 80 years old, but this traditional wood-paneled bar shows no signs of slowing down. On weekend nights, cheap pitchers of beer, powerful pisco and a friendly but rowdy atmosphere draw crowds of local students and young bohemian types.

Exodo CLUB
(www.paganoindustry.cl/exodo; Blanco 298, El Puerto; ☉9:30pm-3:30am Wed & Thu, 10pm-4:30am Fri & Sat) There's an alternative and goth twist to Exodo, a cornerstone of the Valpo gay scene. The good-value cocktails keep both gay and straight regulars returning.

El Huevo CLUB
(www.elhuevo.cl; Blanco 1386, El Plan; cover CH$1500-4000; ☉11pm-late Wed-Sat) Ask any heavily made-up 20-year-old where they're going on a Saturday night and this behemoth of a building will be their answer. For some, its shaking floors are a meat market; for others, they're dance heaven.

Máscara CLUB
(www.mascara.cl; Plaza Aníbal Pinto 1178, El Plan; cover CH$2500-3500) Music-savvy clubbers in their 20s and 30s love Máscara: the beer's cheap, there's plenty of room to move and hardly any teenyboppers. Happy hours run from 6pm to 10pm Tuesday to Friday.

Pagano CLUB
(☎223-1118; www.paganoindustry.cl; Blanco 236, El Puerto; cover varies) Die-hard clubbers both gay and straight can dance all week on Pagano's packed, sweaty floor.

Shopping

Young clothing designers, craftspeople and artists abound in Valparaíso. So do easy-come, easy-go shops selling their wares, most of which are concentrated on Cerros Concepción and Alegre: wander for a couple of hours and you'll have seen them all. Painters, photographers and fridge-magnet makers often set up stands on Pasaje Atkins and along Muelle Prat.

Taller Antiquina ACCESSORIES
(San Enrique 510, Cerro Alegre; ☉11am-8pm) Beautifully worked leather bags, belts and wallets are lovingly made on-site here.

Bazar La Pasión FASHION, JEWELRY
(www.bazarlapasion.blogspot.com; Almirante Jorge Montt 1, Cerro Concepción) A pair of designer sisters display a lovely, eco-friendly collection of clothing, accessories and antiques.

Art in Silver Workshop JEWELRY
(☎222-2963; Pasaje Templeman 8, Cerro Concepción) Silver and lapis lazuli come together in unusual designs at this small, cluttered workshop, where you can sometimes see their creator, silversmith Victor Hugo, at work.

Cummings 1 BOOKS
(www.cummings1.cl; Subida Cummings 1, Plaza Aníbal Pinto, El Plan; ⊘noon-9pm Mon, 11:30am-2pm & 4:30-9pm Tue-Sat) Latin American literature in Spanish, English, French and German.

❶ Information

Dangers & Annoyances

Petty street crime and muggings are often reported in the old port area of Valparaíso, so keep a close watch on your belongings, especially cameras and other electronics. The rest of Valparaíso is fairly safe, but stick to main streets at night and avoid sketchy *escaleras*.

Internet Access & Telephone

Many lodgings have free internet or wi-fi.
Centro de Llamados (Condell 1265, Local 19, El Plan; per hr CH$700; ⊘9:30am-9pm) One of several along this street.

Cerro@legre (Urriola 678, Cerro Alegre; per hr CH$600; ⊘10:30am-10pm Mon-Fri, to 11:30pm Sat & Sun) Popular cybercafe.

Tera Cyber (☎251-6759; www.teracyber.cl; Condell 1340; per hr CH$700; ⊘9:30am-1am Mon-Sat, from 11am Sun) This cybercafe offers flat-screen monitors and headsets.

Laundry

Lavanda Café (Av Almirante Montt 454, Cerro Alegre; per load CH$7500; ⊘9:30am-7pm Mon-Fri, 10am-2pm Sat)

Media

Ciudad de Valparaíso (www.ciudaddeval paraiso.cl) Helpful, comprehensive listings of services in the city.

El Mercurio de Valparaíso (www.mercurio valpo.cl, in Spanish) The city's main newspaper.

Valparaíso Times (www.valparaisotimes.cl) Online English-language newspaper run by the same people as the *Santiago Times*.

Medical Services

Hospital Carlos Van Buren (☎220-4000; Av Colón 2454, El Plan) Public hospital.

Money

Banco Santander (☎220-7940; Prat 882, El Plan) One of many banks with ATMs along Prat.

Inter Cambio (☎215-6290; Plaza Sotomayor 11, El Plan; ⊘9am-6pm Mon-Fri, 10am-1pm Sat)

Post

Post office (Prat 856, El Plan; ⊘9am-6pm Mon-Fri, 10am-1pm Sat)

Tourist Information

Tourist information kiosks (☎293-9262; www.ciudaddevalparaiso.cl; Condell 1490, El Plan; ⊘10am-2pm & 3-6pm Mon-Sat) Muelle Prat (opposite Plaza Sotomayor, El Plan); Plaza Aníbal Pinto (cnr O'Higgins & Plaza Aníbal Pinto, El Plan) At these small information stands, you can pick up maps and battle with other tourists for a chance to talk to the experts. Do yourself a favor and check out the revamped website ahead of time; it's truly a wealth of information.

❶ Getting There & Away

Bus

All major intercity services arrive and depart from the **Terminal Rodoviario** (☎293-9695; Av Pedro Montt 2800, El Plan), about 20 blocks east of the town center. Be aware, especially if you're arriving at night, that taxis often aren't waiting around the terminal; if you need a ride to your hotel or hostel, you might have to call one or arrange a pickup ahead of time.

Services to Santiago leave every 15 to 20 minutes with **Tur Bus** (☎221-2028; www.turbus.cl) and **Condor Bus** (☎221-2927; www.condorbus.cl), which both also go south to Puerto Montt (three each daily), Osorno (three each daily) and Temuco (three each daily). In addition, Tur Bus goes to Pucón (three daily), Concepción (five daily) and Chillán (three daily).

Tur Bus also operates to the northern cities of Iquique (twice daily), Calama (three daily) and Antofagasta (three daily). **Romani** (☎222-0662; www.romani.cl) has less frequent services on the same routes.

VALPARAÍSO'S MURALS

Wandering up and down the winding hills of Valparaíso, you'll see colorful public art everywhere, from dreamlike wall paintings of glamorous women to political graffiti-style murals splashed across garage doors. Setting a fresh precedent for the city's outdoor artwork and causing another stir in the street art scene is Chilean artist Inti, fresh off his first solo show in Paris. His large-scale mural, painted across the surface of several neighboring buildings and visible from Cerro Concepción, was unveiled in early 2012. The vibrant sideways image shows a mysterious, partially fragmented figure draped with exotic jewelry. The highlight is the awkwardly beautiful pair of feet – you'll have to see it for yourself.

You can reach Mendoza in Argentina with Tur Bus, **Cata Internacional** (☑225-7587; www.catainternacional.com), **El Rápido** (☑225-8322; www.elrapidoint.com.ar), **Ahumada** (☑221-6663; www.busesahumada.cl) and **Andesmar** (www.andesmar.com). Some buses continue to Buenos Aires. **Pullman Bus San Felipe de los Andes** (☑225-3125) and **Buses JM** (☑225-2106; www.busesjm.cl) each offer hourly services to Los Andes.

Pullman Bus Lago Peñuela (☑222-4025) leaves to Isla Negra every 15 minutes. From 12 de Febrero, just outside the terminal, **Transportes Quintay** (☑236-2669) runs *taxi colectivos* (shared taxis) every 15 minutes to Quintay.

The city transport network, **Transporte Metropolitano Valparaíso** (TMV; www.tmv.cl), has services to the beach towns north of Valparaíso and Viña del Mar. For Reñaca, take the orange 607, 601 or 605. The 601 and 605 continue to Concón. All run along Condell then Yungay.

Note that fares may increase considerably during school holidays or long weekends, and you'll pay more for the *cama* class (with fully reclining seats) on long-haul rides.

DESTINATION	COST (CH$)	DURATION (HR)
Antofagasta	33,600	15
Calama	35,300	23
Chillán	3900	8
Concepción	10,700	9
Iquique	34,700	20
Isla Negra	2600	1½
Los Andes	4500	7
Mendoza	21,200	8
Osorno	24,100	14
Pucón	16,500	12
Puerto Montt	23,800	16
Santiago	1500	1½
Temuco	15,100	11

Car

Valparaíso's steep hills and traffic-clogged streets make driving here a nightmare. However, a car is indispensable for exploring the Casablanca Valley wineries, and useful for getting to Cerro La Campana. The closest car rental agencies to Valparaíso are in Viña del Mar (p107) – if you book in advance, some will bring cars to your hotel.

ⓘ Getting Around

Walking is the best way to get about central Valparaíso and explore its *cerros* – you can cheat on the way up by taking an *ascensor* or a *taxi colectivo* (CH$500). *Colectivos* to Cerros

Concepción and Alegre line up at the bottom of Almirante Montt, while those to Cerros La Cárcel and Bellavista leave from Av Ecuador.

Countless local buses run by **TMV** (one way within El Plan CH$310, El Plan to Cerro CH$370) run along Condell and Av Pedro Montt, Av Brasil and Yungay, connecting one end of El Plan with the other. A few climb different *cerros* and continue to Viña or along the northern coast; destinations are displayed in the windshield. The city's most famous line is the 801, which uses the oldest working trolleybuses in the world. The curvy cars date to 1947 and have been declared a national monument.

The **Metro Regional de Valparaíso** (Merval; ☑252-7633; www.merval.cl) operates commuter trains every six to 12 minutes from Valparaíso's **Estación Puerto** (cnr Errázuriz & Urriola) and **Estación Bellavista** (cnr Errázuriz & Bellavista) to Viña del Mar (CH$389).

Taxis are much more expensive in Valparaíso than other Chilean cities. High-speed driving round hairpin bends on steep roads makes them more alarming, too.

If you're willing to brave the hills on a bike, you'll see several outfitters around town renting bicycles (CH$5000 per half day). For an extra CH$1000, they'll deliver to your hostel.

Viña del Mar

☑032 / POP 320,000

Clean, orderly Viña del Mar is a sharp contrast to the charming jumble of neighboring Valparaíso. Manicured boulevards lined with palm trees and beautiful expansive parks have earned it the nickname of Ciudad Jardín (Garden City). Its official name, which means 'vineyard by the sea,' stems from the area's colonial origins as the hacienda of the Carrera family. Viña remains a popular weekend and summer destination for well-to-do Santiaguinos, despite the fact that its beaches get seriously packed and the Humboldt Current causes waters chilly enough to put off most would-be swimmers. Although Chileans rave about the city, there's not much here in the way of tourist sights: consider just making it a day trip from Valparaíso.

◉ Sights & Activities

Parque Quinta Vergara   PARK
(☉7am-6pm) Nowhere is Viña's nickname of 'the garden city' better justified than at the magnificently landscaped Parque Quinta Vergara; the entrance is on Errázuriz at the south end of Libertad. It once belonged to one of the city's most illustrious families, the

Alvares-Vergaras, but when they fell on hard times they sold it to the city council. Their residence was the Venetian neo-Gothic-style Palacio Vergara, which houses an interesting collection of 17th- to 19th-century European and Chilean art at the **Museo Municipal de Bellas Artes**. Unfortunately, the museum was badly damaged in the 2010 earthquake and was closed indefinitely at the time of writing. Major concerts and the celebrated Festival Internacional de la Canción are held in the striking concrete amphitheater in the grounds.

Museo de Arqueología e Historia Francisco Fonck   MUSEUM

(☏268-6753; www.museofonck.cl; 4 Norte 784; adult/child CH$2000/300; ⊙10am-6pm Tue-Fri, 10am-2pm Sat & Sun) The original *moai* (Easter Island statues) standing guard outside the Museo de Arqueología e Historia Francisco Fonck are just a teaser of the beautifully displayed archaeological finds from Easter Island within, along with Mapuche silverwork and anthropomorphic Moche ceramics. Upstairs are old-school insect cases and a lively explanation of how head shrinking works (finished examples are included).

FREE **Castillo Wulff**   HISTORIC BUILDING

(☏226-9728; Av Marina s/n; ⊙10am-1:30pm & 3-5:30pm Tue-Sun) Pretty Castillo Wulff, built by a prominent Valparaíso businessman in the early 20th century, hangs out over the sea: pass through the art exhibitions to the tower at the back, where you can peer through the thick glass floor at the rocks and waves below.

Jardín Botánico Nacional   PARK

(National Botanical Garden; ☏267-2566; www.jardin-botanico.cl, in Spanish; Camino El Olivar s/n; adult/child CH$1200/400; ⊙10am-6:30pm) There are over 3000 plant species in the 61 hectares of parkland that comprise Chile's Jardín Botánico Nacional. It's 8km southeast of the city center; take a taxi or catch bus 203 from Viña along Calle Alvarez to Puente El Olivar, then cross the bridge and walk about 500m north to the park's entrance signs.

Beaches   BEACH

Viña's white-sand beaches stretch northward from the northern bank of the Estero Marga Marga to the suburbs of Reñaca and Concón (see boxed text, p109).

★★ Festivals & Events

Festival Internacional de la Canción   SONG (International Song Festival; www.festivaldevina.cl) At Chile's biggest music festival, Latin American pop, rock and folk stars have been drawing huge crowds since 1960.

🛌 Sleeping

Viña's hotels have a reputation for high prices but indifferent quality, despite the fact that outside summer supply really exceeds demand.

Casa Olga   B&B $$

(☏318-2972; www.casa-olga.com; 18 de Septiembre 31; d/apt incl breakfast CH$45,000/55,000; 🛜) This gorgeous boutique-style B&B, outfitted with breezy all-white decor, brand-new LCD TVs and cozy doubles with renovated private bathrooms, is practically right on the beach. It's just outside of Viña – an advantage or disadvantage depending on your travel plans – but it's close to the Recreo metro station, which connects to the center of the city in just two stops (CH$147).

Kalagen Hostel   HOSTEL $$

(☏299-1669; www.kalagenhostel.com; Av Valparaíso 618; dm/d incl breakfast CH$10,300, d with/without bathroom CH$76,600/70,400; 🛜) This cheery, recently renovated hostel contains stylish dorms and doubles with colorful linens, hard-wood floors and Asian-style paper lanterns. These are pricey hostel accommodations, even for the area, but the central location is great and the communal kitchen is inviting to use if you want to save cash on dining out.

TOP CHOICE Hotel Cap Ducal   HISTORIC HOTEL $$

(☏262-6655; www.capducal.cl; Av Marina 51; r incl breakfast CH$58,100, ste CH$68,000-87,100; ✳@) Waves batter the foundations of this iconic art deco building, which was built to resemble a ship. Spiral staircases and narrow corridors lead to irregular-shaped rooms with cruise-liner-worthy sea views (those on the 3rd floor have balconies, too). The furnishings are starting to look a bit dated, but it works with the faded grandeur theme. The seafood restaurant here is a Viña classic.

Che Lagarto Hostel   HOSTEL $

(☏262-5759; www.chelagarto.com; Portales 131; dm/d incl breakfast from CH$6250/17,200; 🛜) The huge long garden in front of Viña's first hostel means you don't have to limit your

Viña del Mar

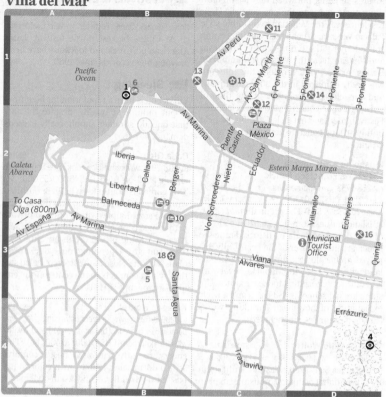

Viña del Mar

◎ Sights

🛏 Sleeping

✕ Eating

☆ Entertainment

open-air lounging to the beach. The right-on vibe stops at the door: clean but simple dorms make the place feel like a university residence.

Residencia Offenbacher-hof   B&B $$
(📞262-1483; www.offenbacher-hof.cl; Balmaceda 102; s incl breakfast CH$33,000; d CH$38,500-44,000; 🖧) There are fabulous views over

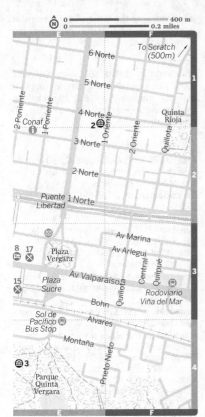

can see the sea from your bed and even the indoor pool seems to merge with the waves beyond the window. The glamorous service and style evokes the roaring twenties – most guests are won over by the welcome chocolates, marble baths, access to the rooftop spa, and a few free chips for the adjoining casino.

Hotel Monterilla
HOTEL **$$$**

(297-6950; www.monterilla.cl; 2 Norte 65; s/d CH$54,500/85,500;) The dead-plain facade is deceiving: bright artworks and engravings offset the white walls and boxy sofas in this hotel's light-filled lobby and restaurant. The tiled floors and sparse furnishings look refreshing in hot weather, but might leave you longing for some color in winter – it's best for those looking for American-style amenities over Chilean charm.

Eating

Most of Viña's cheap eats are clustered on and around busy Av Valparaíso in the town center. These include the string of *schops* (draft beer)-and-sandwich joints that fill the open-fronted 2nd floor of **Portal Álamos** (Av Valparaíso 553), a downtown shopping arcade, and crowd the 2nd-story balconies overlooking the central shopping streets.

Entremasas
CHILEAN **$**

(5 Norte 377; empanadas CH$800-1200;) Frothy pisco sours and creative empanadas – prawn and mushroom in a cheese-cilantro sauce, ground beef and chorizo with goat's cheese – make a quick and classic Viña lunch or late-afternoon snack. You'll see a few other locations in the area.

Enjoy del Mar
TOP CHOICE
CHILEAN **$$**

(www.enjoy.cl; Av Perú s/n; set lunch $7900;) A sunset drink here should be on everyone's Viña to-do list – there are panoramic views of the Pacific from its terrace above the mouth of the Marga Marga. The set lunch is a much better deal than the pricey à la carte menu at night.

Chez Gerald
SPANISH **$$**

(www.chezgerald.com; Perú 496; mains CH$7900-10,900) An old-fashioned Viña classic that's been serving up stiff drinks, hearty lasagna, seafood pasta and Spanish-influenced dishes for over 50 years. Chez Gerald is a classy spot across from the beach – in the evening, you'll enjoy great sunset views through the glass picture windows.

the sea and the city from this commanding chestnut-and-yellow clapboard house atop quiet Cerro Castillo. Sea views, newly renovated bathrooms and antique furnishings make the spacious superior rooms worth the extra.

Vista Hermosa 26
HOTEL **$$**

(266-6820; www.vistahermosa26.cl; Vista Hermosa 26; s/d/tr CH$27,000/34,000/39,000;) Polished wooden floors and a big fireplace lend stately charm to the lounge of this quiet but friendly hotel on the edge of Cerro Castillo. You get plenty of space (and plenty of towels) in the simple rooms, which have small but new bathrooms.

Hotel del Mar
LUXURY HOTEL **$$$**

(250-0800; www.enjoy.cl; cnr Av Perú & Los Héroes; r incl breakfast CH$158,000-214,200;) The view from the sleek, glass-fronted lobby of Viña's top hotel is a preview of what awaits upstairs – on many floors you

ADDRESSES

Several bridges cross the Marga Marga into the newer residential area to the north. In this part of town, most streets are identified by a number and direction, either Norte (north), Oriente (east) or Poniente (west). Av Libertad separates Ponientes from Orientes. These streets are usually written as a numeral, but are sometimes spelled out, so that 1 Norte may also appear as Uno Norte.

Samoiedo SANDWICHES $
(☎268-1382; Valparaíso 637; sandwiches CH$2500-4500) For half a century the old boys have been meeting at this traditional *confitería* (tearoom) for lunchtime feasts of steak and fries or well-stuffed sandwiches. The outdoor seating is greatly preferable to the interior, which is open to a busy shopping mall.

Panzoni ITALIAN $
(Paseo Cousiño 12-B; mains CH$3000-4800) One of the best-value eateries in central Viña, Panzoni's well-prepared Italian pastas and friendly service reel in the lunchtime diners. The location is slightly hidden on an out-of-the-way passageway.

Divino Pecado ITALIAN $$
(www.divinopecado.cl; Av San Martín 180; mains CH$6500-9900) The short but surprising menu at this intimate, candlelit Italian restaurant includes scallops au gratin, tuna carpaccio and fantastic fettuccini with lamb ragu.

Drinking & Entertainment

La Flor de Chile BAR
(www.laflordechile.cl; 8 Norte 601; ☺10pm-late) For nearly a century, Viñamarinos young and old have downed their *schops* over the closely packed tables of this gloriously old-school bar.

Casino Municipal CASINO
(☎250-0700; www.enjoy.cl/casino; Av San Martín 199) Overlooking the beach on the north side of the Marga Marga, this elegant local landmark is the place to squander your savings on slot machines, bingo, roulette and card games. Formal attire is encouraged.

Café Journal CLUB
(www.cafejournal.cl; cnr Santa Agua & Alvares; cover free-CH$3000; ☺10pm-late Wed-Sat) Elec-

tronic music is the order of the evening at this boomingly popular club, which now has three heaving dance floors

Scratch CLUB
(www.scratch.cl; Quillota 898; cover CH$2000-5000) This superclub is immensely popular with the university set and 20-something locals who dance to reggaeton and DJ-spun tunes until 5am.

Information

Afex (☎268-8102; Av Arlegui 690; ☺9am-6:30pm Mon-Fri, 9am-2pm Sat) Change cash and traveler's checks here.

Banco Santander (☎226-6917; Plaza Vergara 108) One of several banks with ATMs on the main square.

Conaf (☎232-0210; www.conaf.cl; 3 Norte 541; ☺8:30am-5:30pm Mon-Fri) Provides information on nearby parks, including Parque Nacional La Campana.

Hospital Gustavo Fricke (☎265-2200; Alvares 1532) Viña's main public hospital, located east of downtown.

Lavarápido (☎290-6263; Av Arlegui 440; per load CH$4200; ☺10am-9pm Mon-Sat)

Municipal tourist office (www.visitevinadelmar.cl) Plaza Vergara (☎226-9330; Av Arlegui 715, at Hotel O'Higgins; ☺9am-2pm & 3-7pm Mon-Fri, 10am-2pm & 3-7pm Sat & Sun); Rodoviario (☎275-2000; Av Valparaíso 1055; ☺9am-6pm) Distributes an adequate city map and a monthly events calendar.

Post office (Plaza Latorre 32; ☺9am-7pm Mon-Fri, 10am-1pm Sat)

Tecomp (Av Valparaíso 684; ☺9am-midnight Mon-Sat, 11am-9pm Sun) One of many phone centers along the street offering cheap international calls and internet access.

Tera Cyber (☎276-8091; www.teracyber.cl; Quinta 219; per hr CH$700; ☺9:30am-1am Mon-Sat, from 11am Sun) The 50 well-maintained machines at this internet cafe all have flat-screen monitors and headsets.

Getting There & Away

All long-distance services operate from the **Rodoviario Viña del Mar** (☎275-2000; www.rodoviario.cl; Valparaíso 1055), four long blocks east of Plaza Vergara. Nearly all long-distance buses to and from Valparaíso stop here; see p101 for details of services.

Several local bus lines through the TMV **Transporte Metropolitano Valparaíso** (TMV; www.tmv.cl), plus privately run line Sol del Pacífico, make frequent departures for northern coastal towns from Reñaca to Concón. To catch one, go to Plaza Vergara and the area around Viña del Mar's metro station; expect to pay between CH$1200 and CH$2200 one-way, depending on your final destination. For Reñaca, take the orange 607, 601 or 605. The 601 and 605 continue to Concón.

ℹ Getting Around

Frequent local buses run by **Transporte Metropolitano Valparaíso** (TMV; www.tmv.cl; one way CH$440) connect Viña and Valparaíso. Some routes run along the waterfront following Av Marina and Av San Martín; others run through the town center along Av España and Av Libertad. Destinations are usually displayed in the windshield. The commuter train **Metro Regional de Valparaíso** (Merval; ☎252-7633; www.merval.cl) also runs between Viña and Valpo.

In summer Viña is congested and very tricky to park in. However, a car can be very useful for touring the northern coast or the Casablanca Valley wineries. **Budget** (☎268-3420; www.budget.cl; 7 Norte 1023) is your best bet for a rental.

Casablanca Valley Wineries

A cool climate and temperatures that vary greatly from day to night have made this valley halfway between Santiago and Valparaíso one of Chile's best regions for fruity Chardonnays, Sauvignon Blancs and Pinots. Its well-organized wineries take food and wine tourism seriously, and many have on-site restaurants. There's no public transportation to any of the wineries, but in a rental car you can easily blitz four or five of them in a day – most are on or around Ruta 68. Alternatively, contact the **Ruta del Vino de Casablanca** (☎032-274-3755; www.casablancavalley.cl; Punta Arenas 46, Casablanca) for tours. Most wineries have excellent on-site restaurants and/or upscale lodgings; some of the standouts are listed below.

Note that servings at tastings tend to be generous – you can save money and sobriety by sharing them between two people.

◉ Sights & Activities

For most of these wineries, see the Map on p108.

⎡TOP⎤
⎣CHOICE⎦ Viñedos Orgánicos
Emiliana   WINERY
(☎099-9327-4019; www.emiliana.cl; Ruta 68 Km61.5; tastings from CH$6800; ⊙10am-5pm) Tastings take place in a gorgeous slate-and-wood building looking out over the vines,

grown organically using biodynamic principles. Reserve ahead for special-interest tastings like 'natural chocolates and wine' or 'organic cheese and wine.'

Viña Indómita   WINERY
(☎032-215-3900; www.indomita.cl; Ruta 68 Km6; tour incl 3 pours CH$9000; ⊙11am-5pm) There's no beating the views from these vineyards – the Hollywood-style sign on the hillside is easily spotted from afar. Indómita's top-shelf Carmenere scored an honorable mention at the recent edition of the International Wine Competition.

Viña Matetic   WINERY
(☎562-232-3134; www.matetic.com; Fundo Rosario, Lagunillas; tasting with 2 pours & tour CH$10,000; ⊙11am-3:30pm Tue-Sun) A real show-stopper of a winery: the glass, wood and steel gravity-flow winery has attracted almost as much attention as the wines. Reservations several days in advance are usually necessary; you can stay the night at La Casona, the boutique hotel on-site.

House of Morandé   WINERY
(☎032-275-4701; www.morande.cl) Featuring a fantastic restaurant, House of Morandé.

Viña Casas del Bosque   WINERY
(☎02-480-6900; www.casasdelbosque.cl) With a stunning *mirador* over the Casablanca Valley.

William Cole Vineyards   WINERY
(☎032-215-7777; www.williamcolevineyards.cl) With architecture that is inspired by old-fashioned Chilean missions, this contemporary winery is visitor-friendly. Reserve ahead if possible.

Catrala   WINERY
(☎562-243-2861; www.catrala.cl) Wine tastings include a hike through the vineyard at Catrala, which is named after an enigmatic Chilean woman who lived during the 17th century.

Viña Mar   WINERY
(☎032-275-4300; www.vinamar.cl) The striking manor at the heart of this carefully landscaped property houses the gourmet Ristorante San Marco.

Viña Veramonte   WINERY
(☎032-232-9924; www.veramonte.cl) Veramonte's Cabernets and Chardonnays win frequent 'top value' awards with Wine Spectator.

Around Valparaíso & Viña del Mar

Getting There & Around

You'll need a car to visit these wineries. Drive over from Valparaíso, or see p77 for information on car rentals from Santiago.

South of Valparaíso

QUINTAY

As the sun sets over the Pacific, the craggy rocks protecting the tiny fishing cove of **Caleta Quintay** are stained a rich pink. Several of the colorful houses clustered here are seafood restaurants. One of the best places for sundowners and garlic prawns or *centolla* (king crab) is the terrace of **Restaurant Miramar** (Costanera s/n; mains CH$5900-8500). You can see your future dinner up-close on the guided scuba dives run by **Austral Divers** (www.australdivers.cl), a PADI-certified dive company with an outpost here.

A signposted turnoff about 1.2km back down the road toward Valparaíso takes you down a 1.5km dirt road to the long, sweeping **Playa de Quintay**, one of the most unspoilt beaches in the region.

Getting There & Away

Quintay is an easy half-day trip from Valparaíso. **Transportes Quintay** (032-236-2669) operates *taxi colectivos* between just outside Valparaíso's bus terminal and Quintay's main street (from CH$1800, one hour), 500m from Caleta Quintay and 2.5km from Playa de Quintay. If you're coming by car, take Ruta 68 from Valparaíso or Viña toward Santiago; the turnoff is 18km south of Valpo, then it's another 23km to Quintay.

ISLA NEGRA

The spectacular setting on a windswept ocean headland makes it easy to understand why **Isla Negra** (035-461-284; www.fundacionneruda.org; Poeta Neruda s/n; admission by guided tour only in English/Spanish CH$3500/3000; 10am-6pm Tue-Sun, to 8pm Sat & Sun Jan-Feb) was Pablo Neruda's favorite house. Built by the poet when he became rich in the 1950s, it was stormed by soldiers just days after the 1973 military coup when Neruda was dying of cancer. Overenthusiastic commercialization gives a definite Disney-Neruda vibe to visits here: indifferent guides quick-march you through the house, and they'd rather you lingered in the gift shop than over the extraordinary collections of shells, ships in bottles, nautical instruments, colored glass and books. Despite this, the seemingly endless house (Neruda kept adding to it) and its contents are still awe-inspiring. There's no one to stop you taking your time on the terrace outside, however, where Neruda's tomb and that of his third wife, Matilde, overlook the sea. Reservations are essential in high season.

Getting There & Away

Isla Negra is an easy half-day trip from Valparaíso. **Pullman Bus Lago Peñuela** (032-222-4025) leaves from Valparaíso's bus terminal every 30 minutes (CH$3200, 1½ hours). **Pullman Bus** (600-320-3200; www.pullmanbus.com) comes here direct from Santiago's Terminal de Buses Alameda (CH$7500, 1½ hours, every 30 minutes).

Parque Nacional La Campana

Within this **national park** (033-441-342; www.conaf.cl/parques/ficha-parque_nacional_la_campana-38.html; adult/child CH$2500/1500; 9am-5:30pm Sat-Thu, 9am-4:30pm Fri) are two of the highest mountains in the coastal range, **Cerro**

IF YOU LIKE.... BEACH TOWNS

North of Viña del Mar, a beautiful road snakes along the coast, passing through a string of beach towns that hum with holidaying Chileans December through February. The beaches range from small, rocky coves to wide open sands. Towering condos overlook some, while others are scattered with rustic cottages and the huge summer houses of Chile's rich and famous.

Reñaca & Concón

Viña's high-rises merge into the multitiered apartments of Reñaca, a northern suburb with a wide, pleasant beach. Come to local landmark **Roca Oceánica**, a rocky hill looking out over the Pacific, for a sunset hike with incredible views (it's on your left, on the oceanside, as you head north from the town.) Concón, just north of Reñaca, is known for its casual and wonderfully authentic seafood restaurants. Top on the list are the crab-stuffed empanadas at **Las Deliciosas** (Av Borgoño 25370; empanadas CH$900) and evening cocktails and *machas* (razor clams) at local legend **La Gatita** (Av Borgoño 21550; mains CH$6000-8500).

Horcón

Chile's hippie movement began at the small fishing town of Horcón, on a small curving peninsula that juts out into the Pacific 28km north of Concón. Brightly painted, ramshackle buildings clutter the steep main road down to its small, rocky beach where fishing boats come and go. These days there's still a hint of peace, love and communal living – note the happy-go-lucky folks gathering on the beach with dogs, guitars, and bottles of liquor in paper bags at sunset.

Maitencillo

About 21km north of Horcón, Maitencillo's long, sandy beaches stretch for several kilometers along the coast and attract many visitors. **Escuela de Surf Maitencillo** (www.escueladesurfmaitencillo.cl; Av del Mar 1250; group class CH$15,000 per person) is a relaxed place to learn how to surf. Although the town's packed with holiday homes, it retains a pleasant low-key vibe. A favorite restaurant and bar is **La Canasta** (www.hermansen.cl; Av del Mar 592; mains CH$5900-8800) for wood-baked pizzas and – of course – fresh fish.

Cachagua

This small, laid-back town 13km north of Maitencillo sits on the northern tip of a long crescent beach. Just across the water is the **Monumento Nacional Isla de Cachagua**, a guano-stained rocky outcrop that's home to more than 2000 Humboldt penguins, as well as a colony of sea lions.

Zapallar

Santiago's elite wouldn't dream of taking their beach holidays anywhere but here, the most exclusive of Chile's coastal resorts, 2km north of Cachagua. Instead of high-rises, multimillion-dollar mansions cover the wooded hillsides leading up from the beach, which is an unspoiled arc of yellow sand in a sheltered cove. Everyone who's anyone in Zapallar makes a point of lunch at **El Chiringuito** (Caleta de Pescadores; mains CH$8200-12,400) where terrace tables look out over the rocks and pelicans fishing for their dinner.

Papudo

The northernmost town on this stretch of coast is known for its down-to-earth vibe and long, straight beach, **Playa Grande**. Papudo falls well short of paradisiacal, however: 1980s high-rises crowd the shore and the tiny town center is dusty and run-down. The coast road, Av Irarrázaval, first passes sheltered Playa Chica and then runs on to Playa Grande. The huge ultramarine dining room at **Gran Azul** (Irarrázaval 86; mains CH$4500-6800) fills up quickly in summer – classic Chilean seafood is the attraction.

For general locations of the beach towns, see opposite. To arrive at the northernmost beaches from Viña del Mar or Valparaíso, a rental car is your best bet. You can also catch a ride on a local bus (see p106) or come directly to Concón from Santiago on **Pullman del Sur** (📞02-776-2424; www.pdelsur.cl); see p76.

El Roble (2200m) and **Cerro La Campana** (1880m), which Charles Darwin climbed in 1834. Visitor numbers have risen since then, but La Campana remains relatively uncrowded despite its closeness to Santiago. It's subdivided into two main sectors: Conaf's main administration station is at **Granizo**, near Olmué, 1.5km before the southwest entrance side of the park; and there are sometimes rangers at **Ocoa**, in the north of the park.

In geological structure and vegetation, most of the park's 80 sq km resemble the dry, jagged scrubland of the mountains of Southern California. The park protects stands of the deciduous roble de Santiago (*Nothofagus obliqua*) and is known for its 20-sq-km grove of Chilean palms (*Jubaea chilensis*). There's excellent hiking to be had here: profuse wildflowers and a reliable water supply make spring the best time for a visit. Paved access roads lead to the two entrances, but there are no roads within the park.

◉ Sights & Activities

Most people come to make like Darwin and ascend Cerro La Campana: on clear days its summit affords spectacular views stretching from the Pacific to the Andean summit of Aconcagua. From the Granizo park entrance (373m above sea level), the **Sendero Andinista** climbs 1455m in only 7km – mercifully, most of the hike is in shade, and there are three water sources en route. Prior to the final vertiginous ascent you pass a granite wall with a plaque commemorating Darwin's climb. Figure at least four hours to the top and three hours back down.

The 5.5km **Sendero Los Peumos** connects the Granizo entrance to the **Sendero Amasijo**, which winds for another 7km through a palm-studded canyon to Ocoa. The whole hike takes five hours one way. The southern part of Sendero Amasijo plunges down into Cajón Grande, a canyon with deciduous forests of southern beech. From Ocoa, **Sendero La Cascada** leads 6km to **Salto de la Cortadera**, an attractive 30m waterfall that is best during the spring runoff.

🛏 Sleeping

Conaf runs two basic 23-tent **campsites** (CH$7000) with toilets, barbecue areas and cold-water showers at Granizo and Cajón Grande, further south. Backcountry camping is not permitted. In really dry weather, only a handful of campers are permitted at a time to reduce the risk of fires. You need to bring all food – and, depending on the weather, drinking water – with you.

ⓘ Getting There & Away

Ranger presence is sporadic at Ocoa, so it makes more sense to go through the Granizo entrance. Buses go regularly from Errázuriz in Valparaíso to Limache (CH$1000), from where local buses and *colectivos* continue to Olmué, and some to Granizo. Talca-based **Casa Chueca/Trekking Chile** (☑071-197-0096; www.trekkingchile.com) operates guided hiking trips (CH$30,000) to the park.

The park is accessible by car from Santiago (160km) and Viña del Mar/Valparaíso (60km). Head north from Santiago on the Panamericana (CH-5), take the turnoff to Tiltil and continue to Olmué, 4km from Granizo. From Viña and Valparaíso take the Autopista Troncal Sur (CH-62) past Quilpué and Villa Alemana to Limache, where you head east to Olmué.

ACONCAGUA VALLEY

If you arrive in Chile overland from Mendoza, the fertile Valle de Aconcagua is the first scenery you see. It's watered by the Río Aconcagua, which flows west from the highest mountain in the Americas, Cerro Aconcagua (6959m), just over the Argentine border. Scenic highway CH-60 runs the length of the valley and across the Andes to Mendoza.

Los Andes

📱034 / POP 61,000

They couldn't have chosen a better name: the mountains loom large and lovely over this foothill town. Indeed, most of Los Andes' visitors are on their way to ski the slopes at the Portillo resort near the Argentine border. But skiers aren't the only ones the Andes have inspired. Two of Chile's most famous daughters lived here: Nobel Prize–winning poet Gabriela Mistral, who taught at the school; and Santa Teresa de los Andes, who became a nun and died here. The town is a pleasant stop-off but there's not enough here to justify a visit in itself – aside from the views, Los Andes is short on sights.

◉ Sights

Museo Arqueológico   MUSEUM
(📱420-115; Av Santa Teresa 398; admission CH$1000; ☺10am-6pm Tue-Sat) The small Museo Arqueológico contains some interesting

pre-Columbian pottery displayed in dusty exhibit cases.

Museo Antiguo Monasterio del Espíritu Santo
MUSEUM

(☑421-765; Av Santa Teresa 389; adult/child CH$500/300; ⊗9am-1pm & 3-6pm Mon-Fri, 10am-6pm Sat & Sun) The award for the most unintentionally bizarre museum displays in Middle Chile goes to the Museo Antiguo Monasterio del Espíritu Santo. Mannequins in nuns' habits re-create scenes from Santa Teresa's life: she took her vows in this ex-convent then died of typhus, aged 19. Also celebrated is folk saint and preteen rebel Laura Vicuña, who willed herself to die because her widowed mother took a married lover.

🛏 Sleeping & Eating

Family-friendly restaurants line Av Santa Teresa.

Hotel Don Ambrosio
HOTEL $

(☑425-496; Freire 472; s/d incl breakfast CH$20,000/25,000; 🛜) The cheapest rooms in town won't win any style points, but they're perfectly serviceable and come with cable TV and free wi-fi. Don Ambrosio is on a quiet street two blocks from the Plaza de Armas.

Hotel Plaza
HOTEL $$

(☑402-157; www.hotelplazalosandes.cl, in Spanish; Rodríguez 368; s/d CH$28,000/32,500) With its beige bedspreads and varnished wood furnishings, there's something very 1970s about Los Andes' upmarket option (a very relative claim to fame). Rooms look out onto the car park but they're big, airy and light-filled, and have heating and cable TV. The on-site restaurant has good-value set lunch menus.

Fuente de Soda Primavera
CHILEAN $

(cnr Santa Rosa & O'Higgins; mains CH$2850-5200) The house special at this popular *fuente de soda* (soda fountain) is the delicious *completo* (hot dog) piled high with fresh toppings. Well-prepared sandwiches and Chilean staples round out a standard menu.

La Table de France
FRENCH $$$

(www.latabledefrance.cl; Camino Internacional Km3, El Sauce; mains CH$4500-12,900) Rolling countryside is the only thing between the Andes and the sweeping terrace of this French-run restaurant on a hill 3km out of town. Duck, rabbit, wild boar and even ostrich satisfy creative carnivores, while dishes such as goat's cheese gnocchi or kingklip in Carmenere cater to vegetarians. From the center of

ACONCAGUA MOUNTAIN

So you're dying to get closer to the highest peak in the Americas – but you don't have time to travel? Santiago-based outfitter **Andes Wind** (☑02-458-7411; www.andeswind.cl; day trip CH$48,000) runs day-long journeys that take you close to the summit. You'll leave your hotel by 7:30am, drive three hours and cross the border into Argentina, then hike to the Aconcagua viewpoint. A picnic lunch and bilingual guide is included; they'll also throw in snowshoes in winter. After stopping in Portillo on the way back, you'll be back in the capital city around 7:30pm, just in time for a pisco sour and a night on the town.

town, take Av Esmeralda east to General del Canto; it's a quick three-minute drive.

ℹ Information

The highway to the Argentine border (CH-60, the Carretera Internacional) runs across the north of Los Andes, where it's called Av Argentina. The bus station lies north of it, eight blocks from the town center. Esmeralda, the main commercial street, runs along the south side of the Plaza de Armas; you'll find most travelers' services here.

Banco Santander (☑421-061; O'Higgins 348; ⊗9am-2pm)

Hospital San Juan de Diós (☑490-300; www.hosla.cl; Av Argentina 315 & Hermanos Clark) Public hospital.

Municipal tourist office (☑902-525; Av Santa Teresa 333; ⊗10am-6pm Tue-Sun) Tourist office near the archaeological museum.

Post office (☑800-267-736; Av Esmeralda 387; ⊗9am-2pm & 3:30-6pm Mon-Fri, 10am-1pm Sat)

ℹ Getting There & Away

Los Andes is the last (or first) Chilean town on the route between Santiago and Mendoza in Argentina – buses pass through its **Rodoviario Internacional** (☑408-188; Av Carlos Díaz 111), eight blocks northwest of the Plaza de Armas on the northern extension of Av Santa Teresa.

Ahumada (☑421-227; www.busesahumada.cl) and **Pullman Bus** (☑425-973; www.pullman.cl) have regular services to Santiago's terminal San Borja (CH$1500 to CH$2900, 1½ hours, hourly). **El Rápido** (☑779-0310; www.elrapidoint.com.ar) goes to Mendoza (CH$21,200, six hours, five daily).

MIDDLE CHILE LOS ANDES

Portillo

Set around the spectacular alpine lake of Laguna del Inca on the Argentine border, **Portillo** (📞02-263-0606; www.skiportillo.cl; daily ski pass adult/child CH$33,000/22,000) is one of Chile's favorite ski resorts. It's not just amateurs who love its ultrasteep slopes: the US, Austrian and Italian national teams use it as a base for their summer training and the 200km/h speed barrier was first broken here. Some of its terrain is apt for novices but it's hard-core powder junkies that really thrive. Altitudes range from 2590m to 3310m on its 19 runs, the longest of which measures 3.2km. The slopes are prepared daily, apart from expert runs like Cóndor, La Garganta and Roca Jack, which are left with their natural ice pack.

Accommodations in Portillo are geared around weeklong stays. (If you're looking for something a lot cheaper, consider sleeping 70km west in Los Andes.) The most luxurious option is the **Hotel Portillo** (r per person per week incl meals & lift pass US$3350-4000), which has cozy doubles with views of the lake or valley. Bunk beds are available at the resort's other two lodging options. The **Octagon Lodge** (r per person per week incl meals & lift pass US$1800) has four-bunk rooms with bathrooms and draws a slightly older crowd, while the **Inca Lodge** (r per person per week full board US$990) has a bit more of a backpacker vibe to it. You can pay extra to have rooms to yourself at the Octagon and Inca lodges; regardless of where you stay, you can use the gym, yoga facilities, skating rink, games room, small cinema and babysitting services for free. Shops, an internet cafe and a bar and disco are also on-site. But far and away the most stand-out amenity is the spectacular heated outdoor swimming pool – the sight of bare-chested snowboarders jumping into the water against this snowy backdrop is a photo op unlike any other.

🛈 Getting There & Away

Driving to Portillo takes one to two hours from Santiago, depending on road conditions.

The ski resort (www.skiportillo.cl) runs shuttle buses (US$70 one-way) to and from Santiago airport, but only on Saturdays. **Portillo Tours & Travel** (📞263-0606; ptours@skiportillo.com) can arrange shuttle transportation for a slightly higher price other days of the week.

An alternative is provided by private ski transfers that run affordable Wednesday and Saturday shuttles from Santiago to the slopes; we like **Ski Total** (📞02-236-0156; www.skitotal. cl; Apoquindo 4900, locales 37-46, Las Condes, Santiago; one-way CH$20,000). It will also rent equipment, which will save you time once you reach Portillo.

The Santiago–Mendoza services run by **Buses Tas Choapa** (📞02-438-238) stop at Portillo – if there are seats you can catch them to Los Andes, Santiago or Mendoza.

SOUTHERN HEARTLAND

South of Santiago, squeezed between the Andes and the coastal cordillera, the central valley is Chile's fruit bowl, with a Mediterranean climate and endless orchards and vineyards – this region produces most of Chile's wine. The Andes in this sector are spectacular, with deciduous beech forests climbing their slopes and broad gravel-bedded rivers descending into the valley. Most of the large settlements here are agricultural service towns; though they're not filled with tourist sights, they make good bases for excursions to the hinterland.

The 8.8-magnitude earthquake that rocked Chile in February 2010 was particularly devastating to this region. In addition to the countless houses and offices that were destroyed in Curicó, Concepción and Chillán, historic landmarks like Talca's central market were so badly damaged that they may never reopen. The businesses that did survive suffered a chaotic period of looting and disorder; the city of Concepción had to enforce a widespread curfew for months after the quake.

Though the aftermath of the quake had a direct impact on the region's burgeoning wine tourism industry, the central valley was more or less back in business at the time of writing. There may not be as many accommodations and restaurants available to tourists, but new businesses are opening at a quick clip as the Chilean government pours money into rebuilding efforts.

History

After 7000 relatively undisturbed years, central Chile's Mapuche communities were invaded twice in quick succession, first by the Inka and then by the Spanish. Earthquakes and constant Mapuche sieges meant that early Spanish colonial cities floundered almost as often as they were founded. Eventually the Mapuche retreated south of the Río Biobío, and colonial central Chile grew,

RANCAGUA'S RODEO

Buckin' broncos in a dusty arena, real-life cowboys in leather chaps – it's the **Campeonato Nacional de Rodeo** (National Rodeo Championship; ☏221-286; www.rodeochileno.cl; Medialuna de Rancagua, cnr Av España & Germán Ibarra; admission CH$7500-12,000). Held from late March to early April in Rancagua, the championship is the culmination of Rancagua's rip-roaring annual rodeo season. At night, the Plaza de los Héroes comes alive with traditional Chilean *cueca* dancing (a playful, handkerchief-waving dance that imitates the courtship of a rooster and hen) and a colorful market of regional foods and crafts.

Rancagua is an easy day trip from Santiago. From the EFE **train station** (☏600-585-5000; www.terrasur.cl; cnr Av Estación & Carrera Pinto) there are five to seven daily Terrasur trains north to Santiago (CH$4750, one hour). From terminals in the west of town, **Tur Bus** (☏230-341; www.turbus.cl; O'Carroll 1175) and **Pullman** (☏227-756; www.pullman.cl; cnr Av Brasil & Lastarria) have hourly services to and from Santiago (CH$1500 to CH$2200, 1½ hours).

becoming a linchpin in the struggle for independence. Political change gave way to economic growth: massive irrigation projects transformed the central valleys into fertile agricultural land, and major natural resources were discovered and exploited – coal mines near Concepción, copper at Rancagua. The area was a focus of repression during the dictatorship, but since the return to democracy has been the backdrop for vociferous strikes by students and workers.

ⓘ Getting There & Away
The comfortable and easily accessible TerraSur train line (p77) connects Santiago to Chillán, stopping at all major towns and cities along the way. The prices are cheaper, and departures more frequent, through the various bus lines that serve the region.

ⓘ Getting Around
From a practical point of view, a rental car is a must for visiting wineries and far-flung national parks. It's possible to take public transportation to some destinations, though service is rarely direct – travelers should to be prepared to walk a few kilometers from where the bus drops off.

Colchagua Valley

With around 20 wineries open to the public, the Colchagua Valley is Chile's biggest and best-established wine region. Its deep loamy soils, abundant water, dry air, bright sunshine and cool nights have given rise to some of the country's best reds: Cabernet Sauvignon, Merlot and Carmenere make up most of the grapes, but top-notch Malbecs are also appearing. Note that most travel-

ers who come here to taste wine book hotel rooms in Santa Cruz.

COLCHAGUA VALLEY WINERIES
An extremely helpful resource, with a friendly office on Santa Cruz's main square, is **Ruta del Vino** (☏823-199; www.rutadelvino.cl; Plaza de Armas 298, Santa Cruz; ⏰9am-6pm Mon-Fri, 10am-6pm Sat & Sun). In addition to providing tourists with information and recommendations about the region's wineries, it offers tasting tours (CH$10,000 to CH$20,000; reservations required 48 hours before tour).

However, transportation to the wineries, which costs an arm and a leg in the Colchagua Valley, isn't included in the basic price (for a full tour with lunch and transportation, you'll be paying upwards of CH$128,500.) If you're fine sticking with the wineries closer to town, you can splash out for taxi rides. As car rental isn't available in Santa Cruz, an economical option is renting a car in Santiago and driving yourself around the wine country – even if you're planning on joining a guided tour. Having a rental car also opens up a wider range of accommodations options: family-run B&Bs and high-end boutique hotels are scattered across the wine country, including several at the wineries themselves, if you're looking to really get away from it all.

⊙ Sights & Activities
The star wineries are listed below. Reserve ahead and note that some wineries close in August.

Lapastolle/Clos Apalta Winery WINERY

(☎072-321-803; www.lapastolle.com; tour incl 2 pours CH$20,000; ⏰10:30am-5:30pm) The most exclusive setup in Colchagua, and arguably in all of Chile, produces a single premium wine from hand-picked, hand-separated grapes. You can reserve online for extras like horseback riding through the vineyard (CH$50,000).

TOP CHOICE Emiliana WINERY

(☎099-9225-5679; www.emiliana.cl; Camino Lo Moscoso s/n, Placilla; tours incl 4 pours CH$8400, tastings per pour CH$1000-2350; ⏰tours 10:30am, noon, 3:30pm & 4:30pm) Biodynamic growing techniques are explained at this ecofriendly vineyard through the 'organic & biodynamic' tour (CH$10,000). To make a day of it, add on the gourmet organic picnic (CH$28,000 for two people, including organic tour).

Viu Manent WINERY

(☎072-858-751; www.viumanent.cl; Carretera del Vino Km37; tours incl 3 pours CH$14,000; ⏰tours 10:30am, noon, 3pm & 4:30pm Tue-Sun) At this third-generation family-owned vineyard, tours involve a carriage ride through 80-year-old vineyards and an insightful visit to the winery. It's located close to Santa Cruz.

MontGras WINERY

(☎072-823-242; www.montgras.cl; Camino Isla de Yáquil s/n, Palmilla; 2/4/6 reservas tastings CH$6000/9000/12,000; ⏰tastings 10:30am-6pm Mon-Fri, 10:30am-4:30pm Sat) In addition to tastings and 'make your own wine' workshops, this friendly, award-winning winery offers horseback riding, hiking, ziplining and mountain biking, all on the vineyard.

Estampa WINERY

(☎02-202-7000; www.estampa.com) Have a picnic under a huge fig tree after a hands-on tasting.

Montes WINERY

(☎072-825-417; www.monteswines.com) Ecofriendly, high-tech wine-making and vineyards covering picturesque hillsides.

Viña Bisquertt WINERY

(☎072-821-792; www.bisquertt.cl) Famous for its La Joya Cabernet. You can stay overnight at the winery's charming Las Majadas guesthouse.

Viña Casa Silva WINERY

(☎072-710-204; www.casasilva.cl) One of Chile's oldest wineries, Casa Silva features carriage rides and a polo pitch.

SANTA CRUZ

The epicenter of Chile's winemaking and wine-touring scenes is a fairly sleepy place with a pretty main square. But the small-town vibe may be changing. At the time of writing, an elegant new Mediterranean-style resort and casino had recently opened here – walking through the center of town, you'll see well-heeled guests sunning themselves around a lagoon-style swimming pool and tasting locally produced Cabernet at a sophisticated wine bar. The wine is what they're here for, after all, as the beautiful rolling hills and vineyards around Santa Cruz remind you.

⊙ Sights & Activities

Museo de Colchagua MUSEUM

(☎821-050; www.museocolchagua.cl; Errázuriz 145; adult/child CH$5000/2000; ⏰10am-7pm) Exhibiting the impressive private collection of controversial entrepreneur and arms dealer Carlos Cardoen, this is the largest private museum in Chile. The collection includes pre-Columbian anthropomorphic ceramics from all over Latin America; weapons, religious artifacts and Mapuche silver; and a whole room of *huasos* (cowboy) gear. The new headlining exhibit here is *El Gran Rescate* (The Big Rescue), showing objects, photos and films related to the August 2010 rescue of the 33 miners trapped 700m underground in San José. In the museum courtyard, you'll find steam-driven machinery, winemaking equipment and a re-creation of Colchagua's original train station, while adjoining display rooms showcase old carriages and vintage cars.

Tren del Vino TOUR

(www.rutadelvino.cl) At the time of writing, service of the 'wine train' had been suspended indefinitely; inquire at the Ruta del Vino office for more information on whether it's running again, as it's been a traveler's favorite for years. Traditionally, the steam-train tour left from San Fernando station – you start the wine tasting on board, visit a vineyard and have lunch there, then wind up at the Colchagua museum before returning to Santiago by bus.

⚒ Festivals & Events

Fiesta de la Vendimia HARVEST FESTIVAL

Santa Cruz celebrates the grape harvest each March with the lively Fiesta de la Vendimia. Local wineries set up stands in the Plaza de Armas, a harvest queen is crowned, and there is singing and folk dancing all round.

🛏 Sleeping & Eating

Wine country is filled with beautiful B&Bs and wine lodges, many located at the wineries themselves; they're mostly high-end and geared to travelers who are getting around in their own cars.

🍴 Hotel Santa Cruz Plaza RESORT $$$

(☎209-600; www.hscp.cl; Plaza de Armas 286; s/d/ste from CH$110,000/140,000/210,000; 🅿🛜🏊👪) Pass through the archway off the main square to enter this striking new Spanish colonial-inspired resort. Stroll through the lush landscaping to a lagoon-style swimming pool, classy *vinoteca*, a pair of gourmet restaurants (recommended and open to the public), a spa and, of course, the brand-new Casino Colchagua. Guest rooms are large and impeccable, furnished with wooden beds from Peru and glowing lamps made by local artisans. Added benefits include solar energy-powered heat pumps and an innovative kids' center, ideal for traveling families.

Hostal D'Vid B&B $

(☎821-269; www.dvid.cl; Alberto Edwards 205; s/d incl breakfast without bathroom CH$17,000/25,000, d/f with bathroom CH$38,000/55,000; 🅿🛜🏊👪) This quiet, centrally located B&B has small but contemporary rooms, comfortable new beds and flat-screen TVs. A lovely continental breakfast is served by the garden and pool.

Casa Silva HISTORIC HOTEL $$$

(☎710-204; www.casasilva.cl; Hijuela Norte s/n, San Fernando; d incl breakfast from CH$120,000) Maple trees shade the stone-tiled courtyard, complete with fountain, at the heart of this 100-year-old house on the edge of a vineyard, near Ruta 5 Km132. The sumptuous rooms ooze old-world style with their padded fabric wall-coverings, old prints, and antique wardrobes and bedsteads (many are four-posters).

Vino Bello ITALIAN $$

(www.vinobello.cl; Barreales s/n; mains CH$4600-7800) It's just 1km out of town, but this warm Italian restaurant really makes you feel like you're in the heart of wine country – especially when you're sipping a glass of Carmenere on the gorgeous patio at sunset or dining by candlelight on homemade gnocchi, thin-crust pizzas and baked Brie with pears. From Plaza de Armas, take Nicolas Palacios, passing the Laura Hartwig vineyards; you'll see the entrance to Vino Bello on the left.

WORTH A TRIP

LOLOL

Sleepy **Lolol**, 23km southeast of Santa Cruz, makes a picture-perfect side trip from Santa Cruz. Walk past the beautifully preserved colonial houses with wooden columns and terracotta roofs before stepping into the **Museo Artesanía Chilena** (Los Aromos 95; adult/child CH$2000/1000). This new and smartly managed folk art museum shows thousands of pieces of Chilean rural artwork – from ceramics to textiles to cowboy spurs – many were collecting dust in the Universidad Católica de Chile's storage for decades. It's a worthwhile new cultural attraction for Lolol and all of central Chile.

179 Sandwich Bar SANDWICHES, BAR $

(www.bar179.cl; Besoain 179; sandwiches CH$3400-5900) Gourmet sandwiches and excellent wines by the glass bring in a small lunch crowd to this stylish space just above Plaza de Armas. At night, the bar comes alive with glowing blue lights, DJ lineups and creative, potent cocktails.

La Casita de Barreales PERUVIAN $$

(www.lacasitadebarreales.cl; Barreales s/n; mains CH$5600-8500) Local foodies adore the subtle ceviches and *chaufas* (Chinese-style fried rice) at this warmly lit adobe house. It's a gourmet take on Peruvian food, with prices to match.

ℹ Information

BancoEstado (☎745-874; Besoain 24; ⊙9am-2pm Mon-Fri)

Cibermanía (☎821-527; Av Errázuriz 559; per hr CH$500; ⊙11am-10pm) One of several internet cafes on the main avenue.

Post office (☎800-267-736; Besoain 96; ⊙9am-2pm & 3-6pm Mon-Fri, 10am-1pm Sat)

ℹ Getting There & Away

Long-distance buses operate from the open-air **Terminal de Buses Santa Cruz** (Rafael Casanova 478), about four blocks west of the Plaza de Armas. **Buses Nilahué** (☎825-582; www.busesnilahue.cl) and other lines offer two hourly departures from Santa Cruz to Pichilemu (CH$4000, 3½ hours), San Fernando (CH$1000, 30 minutes) and Santiago (CH$7000, four hours).

To get to Lolol or Curicó (CH$800 to CH$1200), look for the fleet of local minibuses;

they're usually waiting to fill up with passengers at the parking lot adjacent from the main terminal.

Pichilemu

☑072 / POP 12,500

Wave gods and goddesses brave the icy waters of Chile's unofficial surf capital year-round, while mere beach-going mortals fill its long black sands December through March. All but the major streets here are still unpaved, which lends a down-to-earth, almost ramshackle air to the town. Its wealthy early-20th-century founder, Agustín Ross Edwards, had quite a different image in mind: an upmarket beach resort based on an outcrop overlooking the sands.

Pichilemu's laid-back vibe, great waves and surprisingly energetic summer nightlife make it easy to see why it's so popular with visiting board-riders.

🏃 Sights & Activities

Beaches

The westernmost part of Pichi juts out into the sea, forming **La Puntilla**, the closest surfing spot to town. Fronting the town center to the northeast is calm **Playa Principal** (main beach), while south is the longer and rougher **Infiernillo**, known for its more dangerous waves and fast tow. The best surfing in the area is at **Punta de Lobos**, 6km south of Pichi proper, which you need to drive or hitchhike to.

Surfing

Lobos del Pacífico   SURFING

(☑098- 461-3634; www.lobosdelpacifico.cl; Av Costanera 720; full-day board hire CH$8000-5000, 2hr classes CH$12,000) You can hire boards, wetsuits (a must) and take classes with internationally certified instructors at Lobos del Pacífico at Infiernillo. It's also said to be the best board repair shop in Pichi.

Escuela de Surf Manzana 54   SURFING

(☑099-574-5984; www.manzana54.cl; Av Costanera s/n; full-day board & gear hire CH$7000-8000, 2hr classes CH$10,000) Another reliable surf school, on La Puntilla beach, where conditions are good for beginners.

Discover Surf Trips   SURFING

(www.discoversurftrips.cl; per week incl meals & accommodations US$1600) If you're looking to explore several surf breaks in the area and have some extra cash to spend, consider

booking a weeklong guided surf tour through the region. Discover Surf runs a recommended circuit of hard-to-reach beaches including Matanzas and Puertecillo, both north of Pichilemu. Note that rates are considerably cheaper if you get a few friends to go.

Horseback Riding

Always fantasized about galloping along the beach on horseback? You're in luck. When the weather's not too hot in Pichilemu, you'll see a small group of beautiful horses – saddled up and ready to ride – on the northern end of the main beach, near the lake. At the time of writing, it was easy to negotiate a lovely guided hour-long ride (CH$4000 to CH$6000) that goes past the lake, through the forest and returns along the oceanfront.

🛏 Sleeping

Reserve well ahead during summer, and inquire about discounts during winter and fall.

Cabañas Guzmán Lyon   BUNGALOW $$

(☑841-068; www.cabanasguzmanlyon.cl; San Antonio 48; 2-person cabins incl breakfast CH$45,500; 🛜🏊) This rambling cliff-top resort, comprised of a series of white clapboard cottages, feels stuck in the 1950s. But the privileged views over the ocean and lake are stunning from the private patio off the front of each bungalow, where your breakfast will be served each morning. Extras like in-room refrigerators and a pretty pool, also offering beautiful views, make up for other little details, like the fact that the wi-fi signal isn't strong enough to reach half the cottages.

Hotel Chile España   HOTEL $$

(☑841-270; www.chileespana.cl, in Spanish; Av Ortúzar 255; s/d/tr incl breakfast CH$30,000/40,000/60,000; @) Once a popular surfer hangout, this central budget hotel now caters largely to older travelers. If you're not looking to join the party with other surfers at a youth hostel, score a room here; the Spanish-style building, with its leafy central patio, wooden shutters and antique interior, is utterly charming.

Pichilemu Surf Hostal   HOSTEL $$

(☑842-350; www.pichilemusurfhostal.com; Eugenio D Lyra 167; dm/d CH$11,200/39,700) Attic-style lookouts with incredible sea views top all the rooms at this unusually designed clapboard hostel opposite Infiernillo beach. Each has firm beds, pale linens and huge framed photos of the nearby waves. You get expert wave advice from the windsurfing Dutch owner,

Marcel. Note that the accommodations are expensive for a hostel – but you are, after all, on a relatively remote stretch of sand.

Posada Punta de Lobos LODGE $$$
(☎099-8154-1106; www.posadapuntadelobos.cl; s/d incl breakfast CH$60,000/75,000, 4-/10-person cabins CH$90,000/120,000) Pines and eucalypts surround the boxy, modular structures of this self-styled surf lodge, set 1km from the turnoff to Punta de Lobos. Rooms are earthy – think pine-paneled walls and slate-tiled bathrooms – but not entirely tranquil, due to thin partitions.

✗ Eating & Drinking

In this town, most drinking and revelry happens at the surf hostels down on the beach, though you'll also see plenty of locals kicking back with a beer at small, down-to-earth bars around town.

La Casa de las Empanadas CHILEAN $
(Aníbal Pinto 268; empanadas CH$1200-1900) Just look for all the surfers eating out of brown paper bags at the wooden benches outside: this cheerful takeaway counter does killer gourmet empanadas. The seafood versions, like *machas y queso* (razor clams and cheese) are to die for.

Restaurant Los Colchaguinos CHILEAN $
(Aníbal Pinto 298; empanadas & pailas CH$900-2500; ⏰noon-3pm & 7:30-11pm Mon-Sat, noon-3pm Sun) Big, dripping empanadas are the star attraction at this small, family-run hole-in-the-wall, which also makes rich, homey *paila marina* (seafood stew).

El Puente Holandés SEAFOOD $$
(☎842-350; Costanera Eugenio Díaz Lira 167; mains CH$3500-6900; ⏰9am-11pm) An arching wooden bridge leads from the Costanera into this high-ceilinged bar and restaurant on Infiernillo beach, run by the same owners as Pichilemu Surf Hostal. It does simple seafood dishes well – grilled sea bass or clam and prawn ravioli, for example – or you can nurse a beer and some empanadas on the terrace.

El Alero CHILEAN $
(Av Ross 427; mains CH$3400-5800) This simple family-run restaurant does inexpensive Chilean classics like *paila marina* and grilled fish – but the real draw is the gorgeous ocean view from the hilltop picture windows. Come for lunch to appreciate it during daylight.

Donde Pinpón CHILEAN $
(Av Ross 9; mains CH$3000-5500) The menu runs to steak, fried fish and seafood stews, but that's more than enough to keep local families returning to this friendly, low-key restaurant whose long windowed front looks out onto the main drag.

☆ Entertainment

Disco 127 CLUB
(Av Angel Gaete 217; ⏰10pm-late Thu-Sat Mar-Dec, 10pm-late daily Jan & Feb) Most travelers' stories of derring-do in Pichilemu feature at least one 'and then I collapsed on the dance floor' moment at this rowdy club.

❶ Information

BancoEstado (☎745-650; Errázuriz 397; ⏰9am-2pm Mon-Fri) ATM and currency exchange.

Oficina de Información Turística (☎841-017; www.pichilemu.cl; Municipalidad, Av Angel Gaete 365; ⏰9am-6pm) Basic information about accommodations and events is available from this office within the main municipal building.

Post office (☎800-267-736; Av Ortúzar 568; ⏰9:30am-4pm Mon-Fri, 9:30am-noon Sat)

Surfnet (☎841-324; Aníbal Pinto 105; per hr CH$600; ⏰9am-11:30pm Mon-Sun) One of several cybercafes in town offering cheap phone calls and internet access.

❶ Getting There & Away

The **Terminal de Buses** (☎841-709; cnr Av Millaco & Los Alerces) is in the southwestern section of Pichilemu – the closest stop to the town center is the corner of Santa María and Ortúzar. From the terminal there are frequent services to Santa Cruz (CH$3000, three hours), San Fernando (CH$4000, 3½ hours) and Santiago (CH$5500, four hours) with **Buses Nilahué** (☎842-138; 842-042; www.busesnilahue.cl;

Aníbal Pinto 301) and **Pullman del Sur** (☑843-008; wwwpdelsur.cl; Aníbal Pinto 213, Local A) – you can buy tickets at the downtown offices. Change at San Fernando for buses or trains south. If you're going to Santiago, make sure to ask for a bus that goes through Melipilla; though it bumps along country roads for miles, it's a newer, more direct service that gets you into Santiago in less than four hours.

Maule Valley

The Maule Valley, a hugely significant wine-producing region for Chile, is responsible for much of the country's export wine; the specialty here is full-bodied Cabernet Sauvignon. The area was at the epicenter of the February 2010 earthquake – one winery reported losing its 80,000-bottle collection, and countless vineyard workers were left homeless, while the nearby city of Talca lost its historic marketplace, hospital and museum. Needless to say, tourist activity has been down, but the wine industry has largely recovered, thanks in part to some inspired community efforts.

Apart from wine, many visitors use Talca as a base for exploring the wineries and the nearby Reserva Nacional Altos de Lircay. Ask for the free *Región del Maule* booklet for great information (in English) on recommended treks, local tips and a guide to flora and fauna of the region.

MAULE VALLEY WINERIES

You can visit many of the vineyards independently or through one of the tours run by the **Ruta del Vino** (☑08-157-9951; www.valledelmaule.cl; Plaza Cienfuegos 1 Sur & 4 Oriente, Talca; ☺9am-6:30pm Mon-Fri). More than a dozen wineries are associated with the Ruta del Vino, including the following standouts (see Map p120 for locations).

◉ Sights & Activities

Viña Balduzzi
WINERY

(☑073-322-138; www.balduzziwines.cl; Av Balmaceda 1189, San Javier; tours CH$5000-7000; ☺9am-6pm Mon-Sat) A visitor-friendly fourth-generation winery surrounded by spacious gardens and well-kept colonial buildings. Unlike at many other wineries, no reservation is required. Balduzzi is also one of the few wineries that's easy to reach by public transportation. From the bus terminal in Talca, look for a bus labeled 'San Javier Directo' (CH$750), which drops passengers off near the winery.

Via Wines
WINERY

(☑071-415-511; www.viawines.com; Fundo Las Chilcas s/n; tours CH$10,500-18,000, tastings CH$11,500-19,000; ☺9am-5pm Mon-Sat, tours & tastings by reservation) One of Chile's first certifiably sustainable wineries, Via Wines turns out delicious Sauvignon Blanc and Syrah. Visitor-friendly programs include the organic winery tour and the 'Vino, Arte y Sabores' tour (CH$60,000 to CH$94,500 per person including lunch) that takes guests to meet local artisans before serving four Reserva selections.

Viña Gillmore
WINERY

(☑073-197-5539; www.gillmore.cl; Camino Constitución Km20; ☺9am-5pm Mon-Sat) There's more to do at this boutique winery than sip and swirl (though their Cabernet Franc is indeed fantastic). The winery, which is converting to an organic system, also features beautiful hiking trails and a spa offering various wine-based therapies.

Viña J Bouchon
WINERY

(☑073-972-708; www.jbouchon.cl; Evaristo Lillo 178, Of. 21, Las Condes; ☺9am-6pm Mon-Sat) Located 30km from Constitución, this sustainable winery offers horseback riding and other outdoor activities, plus a beautiful inn for overnight stays.

Casa Donoso
WINERY

(☑071-341-400; www.casadonoso.cl; Fundo La Oriental, Camino a Palmira Km3.5; ☺8am- 6pm Mon-Fri) A traditionally run vineyard set around a colonial homestead. At the time of writing, the winery was still recovering from the earthquake and hadn't reopened for tours and tastings, but check for updates. Located 30km from Constitución, this sustainable winery offers horseback riding and other outdoor activities, plus a beautiful inn for overnight stays.

TALCA
☑071 / POP 199,000

Founded in 1690, Talca was once considered one of the country's principal cities; Chile's 1818 declaration of independence was signed here. These days, it's mainly known as a convenient base for exploring the gorgeous Reserva Nacional Altos de Lircay and the Maule Valley wineries. Parts of Talca were badly damaged in the 2010 earthquake, but the city is on the mend. You'll find a decent range of traveler's services, including dining and lodging options, plus lovely views of the Andes when you're strolling down the sun-baked pedestrian thoroughfare at midday.

🛏 Sleeping & Eating

Cabañas Stella Bordestero
BUNGALOW $

(☑235-545; www.turismostella.cl; 4 Poniente 1183; s/d/tr/q CH$18,000/25,000/36,000/42,000; ❄🛜🌊) Four blocks from the Plaza de Armas but a world apart, these clapboard cabins are surrounded by a leafy garden with a swimming pool, deck chairs and swings. The owners been just as thorough inside: these pretty bungalows have firm beds, cable TV and small decks where you can relax with a glass of wine in the evening.

Hostal Casa Chueca
HOSTEL $$

(☑197-0096, 099-419-0625; www.trekkingchile. com/casachueca; Viña Andrea s/n, Sector Alto Lircay; dm incl breakfast CH$9500-12,000, d CH$39,000; 🛜🌊🛁) Gardens looking over the Río Lircay surround the rustic cabins at the German-run Casa Chueca. It's in the countryside outside Talca, but the hostel has become a destination in its own right for fans of the great outdoors – the knowledgeable owners can help you plan trekking and horseback riding adventures in the nearby Parque Nacional Altos de Lircay. They'll also arrange wine tastings, Spanish lessons, even a kid-friendly treasure hunt. Call first from Talca terminal (or contact the hostel ahead of time with your arrival time), then take the Taxutal 'A' micro toward San Valentín to the last stop, where you'll be picked up.

Hostal Maea
HOSTEL $

(☑210-910; www.hostalmaea.cl; 1 Sur 1080; d with/ without bathroom from CH$15,000/10,000; 🛜) This basic but welcoming hostel mixes 1950s-style decor with a slightly institutional atmosphere – the place feels like it was once an office building. The breezy twin rooms are a steal, though, and the location just off Talca's pedestrian promenade is ideal.

La Buena Carne
CHILEAN, STEAKHOUSE $

(cnr 6 Oriente & 1 Norte; mains CH$3000-5500) This cozy, contemporary steakhouse offers friendly service, a fantastic central location, and a menu of gigantic steak sandwiches, wine by the glass, classic Chilean platters and even well-prepared Peruvian ceviche. In the evenings, locals come to drink beer and watch *fútbol*.

Tierra & Fuego
STEAKHOUSE $$

(www.tierrafuego.cl; 10 Oriente 1261; mains CH$4800-8000; ⊙noon-11:30pm) One of Talca's classiest dining options is this low-lit steakhouse complete with a romantic poolside terrace and a private wine cellar. Sushi and seafood round out the menu, but we'd stick with sizzling cuts of beef or lamb from the *parrilla* (grill) paired with a glass or two of Cabernet. Pisco hours are CH$1000 at the 7pm to 9:30pm happy hour.

Las Viejas Cochinas
CHILEAN $

(☑221-749; www.lasviejascochinas.cl; Rivera Poniente; mains CH$4200-10,000; ⊙noon-midnight) One of Talca's most popular restaurants is a huge, clattering, low-roofed canteen out of town alongside the Río Claro. Dour waiters take forever to bring out the house specialty, *pollo mariscal* (chicken in a brandy and seafood sauce), but it's worth the wait and big enough to share. To get there, leave town heading west along Av Bernardo O'Higgins, cross the Río Claro bridge, keep right, then stay right at the fork in the road.

Rossini
CAFE $

(cnr 1 Norte & 3 Oriente; set lunch CH$3300; 🛜) This central, contemporary cafe is a great place to catch up on emails over coffee or grab a quick lunch.

Centro Alemán
SANDWICHES $

(1 Sur 1330, Local 21-26; sandwiches CH$1800-4200) Delicious pork sandwiches and sidewalk seating.

Cafetería La Papa
CAFE $

(1 Sur 1271; snacks CH$800) Strong espressos and homemade cakes are the perfect pick-me-up if you overindulged in the local vintage the night before.

Pirandello
PIZZERIA $

(5 Oriente 1186; pizzas CH$5000) Cheap meals, cheap pisco sours, cheap everything.

ℹ Information

BancoEstado (☑345-201; 1 Sur 971; ⊙9am-2pm) One of many ATMs along 1 Sur.

Cibernautus Internet Café (5 Oriente 1058; per hr CH$600; ⊙9am-9pm Mon-Fri)

Conaf (☑228-029; 3 Sur 564; ⊙9am-1pm & 2-5:30pm Mon-Fri) Limited information about nearby national parks.

Hospital Regional (☑242-406; www.hospital detalca.cl; 1 Norte) Busy public hospital on the corner of 13 Oriente.

Post office (☑800-267-736; 1 Oriente 1150; ⊙9am-6pm Mon-Fri, 9am-noon Sat) Inside a large building off Plaza de Armas.

Sernatur (☑233-669; www.chile.travel/en.html; 1 Oriente 1150; ⊙8:30am-5:30pm Mon-Fri) An exceptionally helpful, English-speaking staff offer travelers advice on accommodations and activities as well as money-saving tips in Talca.

MIDDLE CHILE MAULE VALLEY

ⓘ Getting There & Away

BUS

Most companies use the **Terminal de Buses de Talca** (☏243-366; 2 Sur 1920, cnr 12 Oriente), 11 blocks east of the Plaza de Armas. **Talca, París y Londres** (☏261-000; www.busestalcapari sylondres.cl) has hourly buses to Santiago. So does **Buses Linatal** (☏242-759; www.linatal.cl), which also has 11 southbound buses daily. **Buses Línea Azul** (☏613-670; www.buseslineaazul.cl) has hourly buses south to Chillán. **Buses Vilches** (☏235-327) has five daily buses to Vilches Alto, gateway to the Reserva Nacional Altos de Lircay. To get to Villa Cultural Huilquilemu, take a bus to San Clemente and ask to be let off at Ruta del Vino (CH$500, 10 minutes).

Tur Bus (☏265-715; www.turbus.cl; 3 Sur 1960) has hourly buses to Santiago and six buses south to Puerto Montt, stopping at Chillán, Los Angeles, Temuco, Osorno and other cities on the Panamericana. Other companies operating with similar services include **Pullman del Sur** (☏264-787; www.pdelsur.cl) and **Pullman Bus** (☏244-039; www.pullman.cl).

DESTINATION	COST (CH$)	DURATION (HR)
Chillán	3500	3
Osorno	11,200	11
Puerto Montt	14,700	12
Santiago	3200	3
Temuco	5300	6
Valparaíso/ Viña del Mar	7500	6
Vilches	1400	1½

TRAIN

From the EFE **train station** (☏226-254; 11 Oriente 1000) there are eight trains a day to Santiago (CH$4000 to CH$8000, 2¾ hours) and south to Chillán (CH$9500, two hours).

Around Talca
VILLA CULTURAL HUILQUILEMU
Once an important *fundo* (farm), this complex of restored 19th-century buildings is a cultural landmark and a wonderful example of colonial architecture. It was damaged in the 2010 earthquake and the museum (containing folk art, religious tableaux, and the basin where local hero Bernardo O'Higgins was baptized) was forced to close. At the time of writing, the space had opened for special events and festivals, and it's worth a trip to check out the building's old adobe walls and the surrounding gardens filled

Around Curicó & Talca

with sequoias, araucarias, magnolias, palms and oaks. Ask at Talca's Ruta del Vino (p118) office for more information. It's located 7km east of Talca; all buses to San Clemente from Talca's bus station pass Huilquilemu.

Reserva Nacional Altos de Lircay
The range of challenging hikes at this well-organized, easily accessible **national park** (www.altosdelircay.cl; adult/child CH $3500/600; ☉8:30am-5:30pm) will leave you as short of breath as the fabulous views. Its 121 sq km are made up of a mix of high-Andean steppes and deciduous forest – notably seven species of *Nothofagus* (southern beech) and *Austrocedrus chilensis,* a native conifer – which is home to a large population of tricahues and other native parrots. Pudú deer, Patagonian foxes and pampas cats also live here, though sightings are uncommon.

About 2km before the park entrance, Conaf runs the **Centro de Información Ambiental**, which has displays on local natural and cultural history (the area has seen four sequential indigenous occupations). You pay admission and register for camping and trekking at the **Administración**, about 500m after the entrance.

🏃 Activities
Hiking
The helpful team of Conaf rangers who run the park give detailed advice about hiking and camping within it, and distribute photocopied maps of the area. Arguably the best hike in the whole of Middle Chile, the **Sendero Enladrillado** takes you to the top of a 2300m basalt plateau. The trail starts with a two-hour stretch east along the Sendero de Chile, then a signposted right-hand fork climbs steeply through dense forest for about an hour before leveling off. You eventually emerge onto the dead-flat platform of **El Enladrillado** – many people think it's a UFO-landing ground. To the west you can see the flat-topped crater of the **Volcán Descabezado** (literally, 'headless volcano') and next to it the sharp peak of **Cerro Azul**. The 10km trek takes about four hours up and three down. There are two or three potable springs before the trail emerges above the tree line, but carry as much water as possible.

The **Sendero Laguna** also follows the Sendero de Chile for an hour before forking right into a steep, three-hour uphill stretch to the gorgeous **Laguna del Alto**, a mountain-ringed lake at 2000m above sea level. Plan on three hours there and back, or you can continue for two hours on a trail leading northwest to El Enladrillado – the round-trip takes eight hours.

A gentler three-hour hike along the Sendero de Chile takes you from the Administración to the **Mirador del Valle Venado**, which has views over the Volcán Descabezado and the Río Claro Valley. A trail continues southeast from here (still along the Sendero de Chile) through a long gorge, before arriving at Río Claro, 15km (six hours) from the Administración, where there's a small refuge. Another 5km (three hours) further on is Valle del Venado, where camping is permitted. It's a two-day trip.

Longer hikes in and around the park include the seven-day **Circuito de los Cóndores**, for which it's advisable to carry topographic maps or hire a guide. Another such offering is the loop across the drainage of the Río Claro to exit at Reserva Nacional Radal Siete Tazas (p123).

Respected hiking guides and operators in the area include:

Casa Chueca/Trekking Chile   HIKING, GUIDES
With tours run by an expert German hiker, including a full-day hike to El Enladrillado (CH$33,000); based at Hostal Casa Chueca (see p119).

**Costa y
Cumbre Tours**   HIKING, HORSEBACK RIDING
(☎99-435-766; www.costaycumbretours.cl) Runs horseback riding and trekking excursions; provides camping equipment.

Horseback Riding
If you want a taste of the wilderness without getting chafed feet, you could always let a beast of burden take the strain. Several Vilches residents rent horses from near the park entrance (horse/guide per day CH$10,000/15,000).

🛏 Sleeping
Camping Antahuara   CAMPGROUND
(campsites per person CH$2500 & one-off site fee CH$8000) Conaf runs the excellent Camping Antahuara about 500m beyond the Administración, next to Río Lircay. It's accessible by car and has electricity, hot water, flush toilets and garbage collection. There are two *campings primitivos* (designated camping areas with no facilities) which are respectively one-hour and 2½-hour hikes east from the Administración along the Sendero de Chile.

Hostería de Vilches   CABIN
(☎9-826-7046; www.hosteriadevilches.cl; Camino Vilches Alto Km22, San Clemente; 2-person cabin from CH$50,000; 🏊) You can stay just outside the park but keep the back-to-nature vibe at Hostería de Vilches where adorable private cabins overlook well-tended gardens and a pair of swimming pools. The hearty homemade cuisine (dinner CH$7500), laid-back atmosphere and inviting hot tub are a godsend after a day of trekking.

❶ Getting There & Away
Buses Vilches goes from the **Terminal de Buses de Talca** (☎071-243-366; 2 Sur 1920, Talca) to Vilches Alto (CH$1400, two hours), a scattering of houses about 3km below the Centro de Información Ambiental and 5km from the Administración of the Reserva Nacional Altos de

Lircay. Buses leave Talca daily at 7:15am, 10am, noon, 1pm and 4:55pm from March to December, and there are 10 services daily in January and February.

It takes about 1½ hours to drive to the reserve from Talca. Take road 115 through San Clemente; 38km from Talca is the left-hand turnoff to Vilches, another 25km further on.

Curicó

📞075 / POP 244,053

'Nice plaza' is about as much as most locals have to say about Curicó. They're right: some 60 towering palm trees ring the square, while the inside is decorated with cedars, monkey puzzles, a striking early-20th-century wrought-iron bandstand and a wooden statue of the Mapuche chief Toqui Lautaro. (Fun fact: Curicó means 'black water' in Mapuche.) Luckily, the postcard-pretty plaza was mostly untouched by the 2010 earthquake. The rest of the town didn't fare as well – according to BBC reports, up to 90% of the older buildings in Curicó's historic center fell. Despite the recent hardship, Curicó still bursts into life for the **Festival de la Vendimia** (Wine Harvest Festival), which lasts three days in early fall.

Most travelers use Curicó as a base for exploring the stunning Reserva Nacional Radal Siete Tazas.

Sleeping & Eating

Hotel Prat   HOSTEL $
(📞311-069; hotelpratcurico.cl; Peña 427; s/d incl breakfast CH$24,000/34,000, s without bathroom CH$13,000; 📶) A rambling old building painted in acid colors houses Curicó's cheapest digs. The kitchen and in-room cable TV make it popular with exchange students, but beware that there's no heating and most rooms open straight onto the patio.

Hostal Viñedos   B&B $
(📞326-785; www.hostalvinedos.cl; Chacabuco 645; s/d incl breakfast from CH$28,000/38,000; 📶🅿️) Rooms at this modern, wine-themed B&B are named after different grapes – the ones at the front are lighter. Whether you've been drinking or not, the huge bouncy beds are a godsend.

Hotel Raíces   BUSINESS HOTEL $$
(📞543-440; www.hotelraices.cl; Carmen 727; s/d incl breakfast CH$49,000/58,000) Under new ownership and with a fresher look, this contemporary hotel – often filled by

businesspeople in the wine industry – has slate floors, a sleek wine bar and a glass-encased cafe that is drenched with sunlight. Guest rooms, though somewhat generic, feature large plasma TVs and comfortable beds where you can relax after drinking Cabernet all day.

Restaurante Miguel Torres   CHILEAN $$$
(📞242-9360; www.migueltorres.cl; Panamericana Sur Km195; mains CH$8100-13,400) Set amid rolling vineyards, this high-end eatery does gourmet versions of Chilean classics – and every dish is listed with a recommended wine pairing (olive ravioli stuffed with smoked salmon and blue cheese, paired with Santa Digna rosé? *Si, por favor.*) Wines by the glass, gorgeous desserts and a grand set lunch menu all add to the country-chic appeal. It's just south of town off Hwy 5.

El Rincón Che   SANDWICHES $
(Carmen 485; mains CH$3500-5200) A laid-back spot near Plaza Talca for sandwiches and microbrews.

ℹ️ Information

Banco Santander (📞311-585; Estado 356; ⏰9am-2pm Mon-Fri) One of many banks with ATMs around the Plaza de Armas.

Centro de Llamados (📞314-426; Prat 588; ⏰9am-9pm Mon-Sat, 10am-2pm Sun)

Post office (📞800-277-736; Carmen 556; ⏰9am-6pm Mon-Fri, 9am-12:30pm Sat)

Tourist office (📞543-027; www.turismocurico.cl; Yungay 620)

ℹ️ Getting There & Away

Bus

Most Curicó buses arrive and leave from the **Terminal de Buses** (cnr Prat & Maipú), near the train station five blocks west of the Plaza de Armas. From here **Andimar** (📞312-000; www.andimar.cl) and **Pullman del Sur** (📞328-090; www.pdelsur.cl) have frequent services to Santiago (CH$2000 to CH$3200, 2½ hours, every 30 minutes).

To get to Parque Nacional Las Siete Tazas, catch a bus to Molina (CH$500, 35 minutes, every five minutes) with **Aquelarre** (📞314-307) from the Terminal de Buses Rurales, opposite the main bus terminal. From Molina there are frequent services to the park in January and February, and one daily service to Radal, 9km before the park proper, the rest of the year. For more information, see p123.

Tur Bus (📞312-115; www.turbus.cl; Av Manso de Velasco 0106) has its own terminal that is located southeast of town. From here, services leave to Santiago (CH$2900, 2½ hours, three daily) and Valparaíso (CH$10,000, 4½ hours, one daily), and also south to Osorno (CH$5900, 10 hours, four daily), Puerto Montt (CH$7200, 12 hours, two daily) and Valdivia (CH$8600, 11 hours, two daily). Tur Bus also goes to Talca (CH$900 to CH$2100, 1¼ hours, every 15 minutes).

Train

EFE passenger trains between Santiago and Chillán stop at Curicó's **train station** (☎600-585-5000; www.terrasur.cl; Maipú 657), five blocks west along Prat from the Plaza de Armas, near the bus station. There are seven trains a day to Santiago (CH$4000 to CH$8000, 2¼ hours) and Chillán (CH$8000, 2½ hours), with connections from there to Concepción.

Reserva Nacional Radal Siete Tazas

The upper basin of the Río Claro marks the beginning of the ecological transition between the drought-tolerant Mediterranean vegetation to the north and the moist evergreen forests to the south. Here, 78km southeast of Curicó along a narrow gravel road, lies the **Reserva Nacional Radal Siete Tazas** (☎09-168-7820; www.conaf.cl, www.sietetazas.cl; adult/child CH$4000/600; ☺8:30am-8pm Dec-Feb, to 5:30pm Mar-Nov).

Conaf's main post is at the **Parque Inglés** sector, 9km beyond the park entrance at Radal, but there are two interesting stopoffs between the two points. The **Velo de la Novia** (literally, 'the bridal veil') is a 40m waterfall which you can see from a small roadside viewing point 2.6km from Radal. Another 4.4km on is the car park and Conaf ranger hut (usually only used in summer) that mark the access point for the 400m trail to the **Siete Tazas** (literally, 'seven cups'), a breathtaking series of seven waterfalls and pools carved out of black basalt rock by the Río Claro. From here, another short trail leads to a viewpoint for the **Salto la Leona**, a waterfall that drops more than 50m from a narrow gorge to the main channel of the Río Claro.

Two well-marked hiking trails loop from Camping Los Robles at Parque Inglés: the 1km **Sendero el Coigüe** and 7km **Sendero Los Chiquillanes**, which has great views of the Valle del Indio (plan on about four hours in total). The first segment of this trail is part of the **Sendero de Chile** (www.senderodechile.cl), which continues to El Bolsón, where there is a refuge, and Valle del Indio. From here you can trek across the drainage of the Río Claro to Reserva Nacional Altos de Lircay, taking about two days: the route is unsigned and crosses private land, so either do it with a guide or get detailed information from Conaf and carry a topographical map, compass and adequate supplies.

☞ Tours

Casa Chueca/
Trekking Chile   GUIDED TREK
(☎071-197-0097; www.trekkingchile.com) Offers one-day guided excursions to Siete Tazas from Talca.

🛏 Sleeping & Eating

Conaf runs two cold-water **campsites** (☎075-228-029; campsites per person CH$1500) at the Parque Inglés: Camping Rocas Basálticas and Camping Parque Inglés. Both get very busy during summer.

Camping Los Robles   CAMPGROUND $
(☎075-228-029; 6-person campsites CH$8000) There's hot water and barbecue areas at this privately run campsite. Bring food supplies with you – there's a big supermarket opposite the bus station in Molina.

Valle de las Catas   CAMPGROUND $$
(☎099-168-7820; www.sietetazas.cl; Camino Privado s/n; campsites for 2/4/6 people CH$12,000/20,000/30,000, cabins for 2/4/6 people CH$35,000/40,000/45,000) This well-organized camping and cabin complex will help you organize kayaking and mountain biking excursions.

❶ Getting There & Away

During January and February Buses Hernández operates frequent services from Molina (Maipú CH$1735) to the Parque Inglés sector of the park (CH$1800, 2½ hours, eight daily). From March to December there is one daily bus to Radal (CH$2000, two hours, daily at 5pm), 10km down the hill from Parque Inglés.

To drive to Radal Siete Tazas, take the Panamericana south of Curicó then turn off to Molina. Leave Molina to the south on paved road K-25 toward Cumpeo, 25km further on, where the road turns to gravel. From here, it's a bumpy 39km more to Radal, and another 10km to Parque Inglés.

Chillán

📞042 / POP 180,197

Earthquakes have battered Chillán throughout its turbulent history; the 2010 earthquake was yet another hit. While this perpetually rebuilding city isn't especially interesting, it is a gateway to some of the loveliest landscapes in Middle Chile.

◉ Sights

Catedral de Chillán
CHURCH

(cnr Av Libertad & Arauco; ⊙10am-6pm Mon-Sat, 10am-2pm Sun) On the northeast corner of Chillán's main square stands the stark, modernist Catedral de Chillán. Built in 1941, its soaring semi-oval form is made of a series of earthquake-resistant giant arches. The 36m-high cross next to it commemorates the thousands of Chillán residents who died in the 1939 earthquake.

Escuela México
MONUMENT

(Av O'Higgins 250; donations welcome; ⊙10am-1:30pm & 2-6pm Mon-Fri, 10am-6pm Sat & Sun) In response to the devastation that the 1939 quake caused, the Mexican government donated the Escuela México to Chillán. At Pablo Neruda's request, Mexican muralists David Alfaro Siqueiros and Xavier Guerrero decorated the school's library and stairwell, respectively, with fiercely symbolic murals, now set within an otherwise normal working school.

⌐TOP⌐ Mercado de Chillán
CHOICE
MARKET

(⊙9am-6pm) The city's main market is split into two sections on either side of Maipón between Isabel Riquelme and 5 de Abril. On the north side is a covered section known as the **Mercado Central**, which contains cheap eateries and butchers' stands festooned with strings of the *longaniza* (a spicy salami-type sausage) that Chillán is famous for throughout Chile. The open-air stalls of **La Feria de Chillán** (Plaza de la Merced) are crammed with a colorful mix of fresh produce and local arts and crafts. Especially good are ceramics from the nearby village of Quinchamalí, but you'll also see rawhide and leatherwork, basketry, weavings and the typical straw hats called *chupallas*.

⏃ Sleeping

Chillán's hotels fill up very rapidly during the ski season so try to book ahead.

Hotel Bavaria
GUESTHOUSE $

(📞217-235; www.hotelbavaria.cl; 18 de Septiembre 648; d incl breakfast CH$20,000-30,000; 🛜) This cozy house, which now operates as a small hotel, has tidy doubles with twin beds, TVs and private bathrooms. The downstairs living area has homey charm; unfortunately, a faint smoky smell hangs in the air.

Hostal Canadá
GUESTHOUSE $

(📞234-515; hostalcanada269chile@gmail.com; Av Libertad 269; s/d CH$7000/14,000) Spending a night in this no-nonsense mother-and-daughter setup is like staying in their apartment – fraying floral sheets, worn carpets, lumpy pillows and all. To their credit, the owners keep the shared bathrooms spotless. Other budget places line the same block, but are more like men's boarding houses: Hostal Canadá is a better bet for solo female travelers.

Hotel Las Terrazas Express
HOTEL $$$

(📞437-000; www.lasterrazas.cl; Constitución 663; s/d incl breakfast CH$48,00/61,000; @🛜) An airy light-filled lobby and friendly staff greet you at this small hotel half a block from the Plaza de Armas – as do a welcome cocktail, a buffet breakfast and complimentary parking.

✗ Eating & Drinking

Cocinerías del Mercado Central
MARKET $

(Maipón btwn 5 de Abril & Isabel Riquelme; set lunches CH$1800-2800; ⊙8am-6pm Mon-Sat) The dinky eateries at the market specialize in local classics such as *chupe* (a rich fish stew) or *paila marina*. The *longaniza* adorning the surrounding butchers' stalls also appears regularly in the grease-slicked but filling fare.

Fuego Divino
STEAKHOUSE $$

(📞430-988; www.fuegodivino.cl; Gamero 980; mains CH$5500-7800) Stylish restaurants are thin on the ground in Chillán – perhaps that's why the gleaming black tables here are always booked up at weekends. Or maybe it's because the expertly barbecued prime cuts of Temuco beef taste so delicious.

Arcoiris Vegetariano
VEGETARIAN $

(El Roble 525; mains CH$2500-5200; ⊙9am-6:30pm Mon-Sat; 🛜) A good vegetarian restaurant in provincial Chile? We'll take it. Filling lentil-and-bulgur-style set lunches are served at the back, while a cafe upfront does sandwiches and cakes, all to the tune of wind-chime and whale music.

Chillán

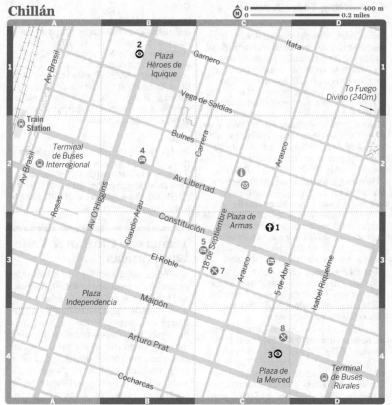

Santos Pecadores COCKTAIL BAR
(www.santospecadores.cl; Av Vicente Méndez 275; ⊙8:30pm-late Tue-Sat; ☏) Chillanejos with plenty of dash and cash pour into this chichi red-walled bar northeast of the city center for sushi, ceviche and lots and lots of cocktails. DJs keep things going till late at weekends.

❶ Information

Look for internet cafes, call centers, laundromats and other travelers' services along pedestrianized Arauco.

BancoEstado (☏455-291; Constitución 500; ⊙9am-2pm Mon-Fri) One of many ATMs on this street.

Hospital Herminda Martín (☏208-221; Francisco Ramírez 10) Public hospital on the corner of Av Argentina.

Post office (☏800-267-736; Av Libertad 501; ⊙8:30am-6:30pm Mon-Fri, 9am-12:45pm Sat)

Sernatur (☏223-272; www.chile.travel/en. html; 18 de Septiembre 455; ⊙8:30am-1:30pm & 3-6pm Mon-Fri) Friendly staff provide city maps and information on accommodations and transport.

MIDDLE CHILE TERMAS DE CHILLÁN & VALLE LAS TRANCAS

❶ Getting There & Away

Bus

Chillán has two long-distance bus stations. The most central is **Terminal de Buses Interregional** (✆221-014; Constitución 01), five blocks west of the Plaza de Armas on the corner of Rosas. From here, **Tur Bus** (✆248-327; www.turbus.cl) has services to Santiago (hourly), some of which stop in Talca and other cities along the Panamericana. Tur Bus also goes direct to Valparaíso and south to Temuco, Osorno, Valdivia and Puerto Montt (seven daily). There are similar services to Santiago with **Línea Azul** (✆211-192; www.buseslineaazul.cl), which also goes to Los Angeles (10 daily), Angol (two daily) and Concepción (every 15 minutes).

Other long-distance carriers use the **Terminal María Teresa** (✆272-149; O'Higgins 010), north of Av Ecuador. These include **Buses Jota Be** (✆423-230), which makes daily journeys to Salto del Laja and has direct services to Los Angeles (hourly). **Pullman Bus** (✆272-178; www.pullmanbus.cl) runs north to Calama, Antofagasta and Arica (five daily), and south to Puerto Montt (five daily).

Sol del Pacífico (✆272-177) also goes to Santiago, Viña and Valparaíso. Other companies covering the Panamericana include **Buses Jac** (✆273-581) and **Condor** (✆270-264), traveling between Temuco and Santiago.

Local and regional services leave from the **Terminal de Buses Rurales** (✆423-814; Maipón 890). **Rembus** (✆229-377) takes you to Valle Las Trancas (six to seven daily); the 7:50am and 1:20pm buses continue to Valle Hermoso on Fridays, Saturdays and Sundays. **Vía Itata** (www.busesviaitata.cl) operates routes to Ninhué (10 daily) and Cobquecura (four daily), while **Turbus** goes to Quirihue (three daily) with connections to surf hangout Buchupureo.

DESTINATION	COST (CH$)	DURATION (HR)
Angol	1400	2¼
Cobquecura	1800	2¾
Concepción	1700	1½
Los Angeles	2600	1½
Osorno	7200	8
Puerto Montt	7300	9
Quirihue	1500	1
Santiago	5100	6
Talca	3500	3
Temuco	3300	5
Termas de Chillán	2200	1½
Valdivia	6800	6
Valparaíso	8700	8
Valle Los Trancas	1500	1¼

Car

Driving makes it possible to cram in lots of national park action or quick day trips up the mountain to Termas de Chillán. Local rental companies include **Rent-a-car** (✆212-243; www.rentacares.com; 18 de Septiembre 380) and **EcaRent** (✆229-262; www.ecarent.cl; Av Brasil, Oficina 3) at the train station. Rates at both start at about CH$23,000 a day. Note that if the mountain roads are slippery you may need to hire wheel chains, too.

Train

The EFE TerraSur line runs from the **train station** (✆222-424; www.terrasur.cl; cnr Avs Brasil & Libertad) to Santiago (CH$8000, 4½ hours, three daily), stopping along the way at Talca (CH$8000, 1¾ hours) and Curicó (CH$8000, 3¼ hours), among other places.

Termas de Chillán & Valle Las Trancas

A winding road leads from Chillán 80km up into the mountains to Valle Las Trancas and the Termas de Chillán. Chilean powder-fiends flock to these slopes in winter, when bumper-to-bumper traffic is common at the top. The pace is less manic the rest of the year, when the valleys turn a luscious green and are perfect for hiking, climbing and horseback riding, or just lazing around and drinking in the views. Despite the hikers that come out on summer weekends, the place is almost dead on a weekday in summer – bring your own picnic and don't count on hotels being open. Note that there aren't ATMs around most of these accommodations; you'll want to bring cash from Chillán.

❍ Sights & Activities

Nevados de Chillán Ski Center   SKIING
(✆600-626-3300;   www.nevadosdechillan.com; day ski pass adult/child CH$30,000/20,000) The southern slopes of the 3122m Volcán Chillán are the stunning setting of this ski mecca. Unusually for Chile's ski resorts, many of its 30 runs track through forest, and there's a good mix of options for beginner and more experienced skiers. Superlatives abound here: they've got the longest piste in South America (13km Las Tres Marías), the longest chairlift and some of the biggest and best off-piste offerings. Since 2008 a snow park has been added, too. The season can start as early as mid-May and usually runs to mid-October – locals swear that great snow, emp-

ty slopes and discounted ski passes make the beginning of October one of the best times to come. In summer, there's hiking, horseback riding, climbing, canyoning and bike rental; check the website for full offerings. If money's no object, stay on-site at the **Hotel Nevados de Chillán** (d incl breakfast & dinner CH$118,000-149,000; ☒), where warm thermal waters fill an outdoor pool surrounded by snow.

Valle Hermoso OUTDOORS
(adult/child CH$4500/2500) A turnoff halfway between Valle Las Trancas and the ski center takes you to this leafy recreational area. Most people come here for the **thermal springs** (☺9am-5pm) – sheltered inside a wooden house, they're open year-round. Ziplines, climbing walls and horseback riding provide extra action in summer, when you can stay at the small **campsite** (per tent CH$21,000). There's also a basic minimarket and fast-food restaurant.

🛏 Sleeping & Eating

Accommodations on the mountain divide into two camps. The posh hotels in Termas de Chillán, at the top of the road, get you closest to the slopes. Prices are much lower, however, if you stay in the cabins, hostels and lodges downhill at Valle Las Trancas. There's also slightly more variety for dining and après-ski, but note that businesses are fairly spread out along the mountain road – unless you're willing to get in the car, you'll probably be having breakfast and dinner at your hotel or hostel. Note that most places have huge low-season discounts.

📷 **Ecobox Andino** BOUTIQUE HOTEL **$$$**
(☎042-423-134; www.ecoboxandino.cl; Camino a Shangri-Lá Km0.2; cabins 2-5 people from CH$100,000; ☒) Perhaps the hippest, most unique lodgings in Middle Chile. It's hard to guess these impeccably decorated cabins were once shipping containers – bright geometric patterns cover the outside walls; inside, modern furnishings are offset by handicrafts. Wooden decks overlook the tree-filled garden through which paths wind to the pool.

Riding Chile Hostal & Restaurant HOSTEL **$**
(☎042-835-120, 07-779-197; www.ridingchile.com; Ruta 55, Camino Termas de Chillán Km73; dm/d without bathroom incl breakfast CH$10,000/20,000; 🛜☒) This wooden lodge at the foot of the mountains offers simple

accommodations. The real draw is the relative proximity to the slopes (in comparison with most hostels here, which are further down the hill), plus a small swimming pool and an appealing cafe and restaurant on the wooden terrace.

Chil'in Hostería & Restaurante HOSTEL **$**
(☎042-247-075; www.chil-in.com; Ruta 55, Camino Termas de Chillán Km72; dm/d without bathroom CH$10,000/25,000; @🛜) At this ski lodge–style hostel, rooms are simple but clean, and several have mezzanines for squeezing more people in. The cozy living room has a log fire and wi-fi, while out front French owner Gregory serves up delicious thin-crust pizzas loaded down with toppings.

📷 **MI Lodge** LODGE **$$$**
(☎099-9623-0412; www.milodge.com; Camino a Shangri-Lá; s/d incl breakfast CH$50,000/90,000; @☒) This eco-friendly lodge has plenty to offer: rustic-chic furnishings, a fire crackling in the middle of a beautifully designed glass-and-wood-walled French restaurant (specializing in crepes and open to the public), the snowboarding owners giving expert advice on the ski scene, and hiking and horseback riding expeditions in summer. The canopy zipline is particularly recommended by past guests. If all that's not enough, you also get unobstructed views from the deck-rimmed pool and outdoor hot tubs.

Restaurante El Tren CHILEAN **$$**
(Camino Termas de Chillán Km73; mains CH$4500-6800) The snug dining room of the classy El Tren is, in fact, an antique English train car. There's a good wine list, Chilean staples and a wooden terrace with lovely views of the snow-capped mountains.

Snow Pub PUB **$**
(www.snowpub.cl; Camino Termas de Chillán Km71.5; mains CH$3200-5000) For years the après-ski in Valle Las Trancas has centered on this feel-good bar, which gets packed with revelers in high season.

❶ Getting There & Away

From Chillán's Terminal de Buses Rurales, **Rembus** (☎042-229-377; www.busesrembus.cl) has buses to Valle Las Trancas (CH$1800, 1¼ hours) at approximately 7:50am, 8:50am, 10:15am, 11:15am, 12:40pm, 1:20pm, 3:10pm, 5pm, 5:50pm and 7:20pm Monday to Saturday (times may vary slightly with the season). All but the last departure also run on Sundays. On

Fridays and weekends, some services continue to Valle Hermoso (CH$3000, 1½ hours) – if that's your final destination from Chillán, ask ahead of time which buses will take you all the way. From Santiago's Terminal Sur there are two direct services to Valle Las Trancas (CH$14,000, seven hours, 6:50am and 2:55pm) with **Buses Nilahué** (☑in Santiago 02-778-5222, in Chillán 042-270-569; www.busesnilahue.cl). In winter there are shuttle buses from Valle Las Trancas up to the ski center. Hitchhiking up is also possible.

Coastal Towns

Quiet beaches come with rural surroundings in the remote coastal towns northwest of Chillán. The area's perfect for long lazy walks along the sand, and there's good, low-key surfing for those who want the waves without the parties.

COBQUECURA

A quiet little town with picturesque houses and dry walls made from local slate – a few too many that crumbled to pieces in the 2010 earthquake – Cobquecura has a long, wide beach with wild surf. The sands fill up in early February when Cobquecura hosts the Campeonato Nacional de Surf y Body Board. A deep baying sound resonates from a rock formation 50m offshore: known as the **Piedra de la Lobería**, it's home to a large colony of sunbathing sea lions. Follow the coast road 5km north and back to the beach and you reach the exquisite **Iglesia de Piedra** (Church of Stone), a massive monolith containing huge caves that open to the sea. The light inside the caves is mysterious – Cobquecura's pre-Hispanic inhabitants held ritual gatherings inside the stone, and it now contains an image of the Virgin Mary.

From Chillán's Terminal de Buses Rurales, **Via Itata** (☑042-211-196; www.busesviaitata.cl) has buses to Cobquecura (CH$2200, 2½ hours) continuing on to Buchupureo (CH$2500). Note that there are several daily departures during summer, but in the off-season there's only one bus, leaving at 7:30am from Chillán. **Nilahué** (☑02-778-5222; www.busesnilahue.cl) operates a direct bus from Santiago's Terminal Sur to Cobquecura (CH$11,000, seven hours, once daily).

BUCHUPUREO

Perhaps the most magical spot along Middle Chile's coastline, this tranquil farming village 13km north of Cobquecura along a dirt road is becoming increasingly popular with surfers; it's officially giving Pichilemu a run for its money. Steep slopes covered with lush greenery surround the settlement, lending it a tropical air. Indeed, papayas are a major crop, as are potatoes, which many claim are the best in the country. Despite growing interest from tourists, the pace of life is slow here: oxen pulling carts are still a common sight. It's also a famous fishing spot – *corvina* (sea bass) apparently jump onto any hook dangled off the beach.

Dunes and scrubland separate the beach from the main road, which runs parallel to the shore before looping through the small town center to the beach. A couple of wooden walkways also connect the road and the sand.

🛌 Sleeping & Eating

La Joya del Mar　　　　　RESORT $$$
(☑042-197-1733; www.lajoyadelmar.com; 2-/4-person villas incl breakfast CH$95,000/115,000; 🛜🐕) With their springy white beds, stylish bathrooms and open decks with panoramic views of the Pacific, these villas are so perfect a honeymoon spot they're worth getting married for. Rich tropical plants overhang the terraces, and the pool seems to merge with the view of the sea. The vibe spills over into the airy, glass-fronted restaurant (mains CH$5200 to CH$9800, open noon to 10pm), where locally grown ingredients play a big role in the creative pizzas, salads and sandwiches. A sunset cocktail here is a must.

Ayekán Aldea Turística　　CAMPGROUND $$
(☑9-988-5986; www.turismoayekan.cl; campsites CH$15,000, 4-/6-/8-person cabins CH$40,000/60,000/70,000) In summer you can pitch your tent at one of 20 campsites in a pretty clearing at the bottom of a eucalypt-lined drive, close to the beach. A wooden barnlike building contains a restaurant serving cheap homemade food, and there's also a cabin for rent.

**Cabañas Mirador
de Magdalena**　　　　　BUNGALOW $$
(☑042-197-1890; www.miradormagdalena.com; La Boca s/n; 4-person cabin from CH$38,000) Perched on stilts beside the river delta at the entrance to Buchupureo, these all-wood cabins have incredible sea views. The cabins are simple but clean, clustered around a lush garden with a walkway straight to the beach.

ⓘ Getting There & Away

From Chillán's Terminal de Buses Rurales, **Via Itata** (✆042-211-196; www.busesviaitata.cl) has a few daily buses to Buchupureo (CH$2500, three hours) during high season. It's your best bet for making a connection to other destinations.

Concepción

✆041 / POP 221,163 / 12M

Sadly, 'Conce' was yet another city terribly damaged in the February 2010 earthquake; it was also ravaged by looting and lawlessness during the aftershocks. But unlike some of its central Chilean neighbors, Concepción is very important to Chile's economy – specifically because of its manufacturing industry, port facilities and nearby coal deposits. Chileans consider Concepción a socialist hotbed – mainly because of the intellectual influences of its dozen or so universities.

Concepción sits on the north bank of the Río Biobío, Chile's only significant navigable waterway, about 10km from the river's mouth. Hills block the city's expansion to the south and east, so Concepción's urban sprawl is moving rapidly in the opposite direction, toward Talcahuano, 15km to the northwest.

History

In 1551 Pedro de Valdivia founded the original city of Concepción north of where it is today, near Penco (indeed, Conce's inhabitants are still known as Penquistas). Over the next few centuries the city was repeatedly besieged during the Spanish-Mapuche war, attacked by British and Dutch pirates and devastated by earthquakes in 1730 and 1751. But the colonizing residents stuck to their guns, and Concepción eventually became one of the Spanish empire's southernmost fortified outposts.

After independence, Concepción's isolation from Santiago, coupled with the presence of lignite (brown coal) near Lota, a coastal town south of Concepción, fomented an autonomous industrial tradition. The export of wheat for the California gold-rush market further spurred the area's economic growth.

During the early 1970s the city was a bulwark of support for Marxist President Salvador Allende and his Unidad Popular party, and it suffered more than other regions under the military dictatorship of 1973 to 1990.

◉ Sights

FREE **La Casa del Arte** MUSEUM
(✆224-2567; cnr Chacabuco & Paicaví, Barrio Universitario; ☉10am-6pm Tue-Fri, 10am-5pm Sat, 10am-2pm Sun) The massive, fiercely political mural *La Presencia de América Latina* is the highlight of the university art museum La Casa del Arte. It's by Mexican artist Jorge González Camarena, a protégé of muralist legend José Clemente Orozco, and celebrates Latin America's indigenous peoples and independence from colonial and imperial powers. For more socially minded artwork, take a stroll around the campus and check out the vibrant public murals covering nearly every wall.

Parque Ecuador PARK
(Av Lamas) The museum is a few blocks south of the city center within Parque Ecuador, a narrow stretch of well-maintained urban parkland which runs along the foot of **Cerro Caracol** – walk up one of the two access roads (continuations of Caupolicán and Tucapel) to a viewpoint with great views of Concepción.

🛏 Sleeping

Most of Concepción's hotel guests are here on business. The constantly high demand they create means lodgings here tend to be expensive for what they are.

Hotel Boutique Antiyal MOTEL $$
(✆221-8623; antiyalhltda@hotmail.com; d CH$40,000; ☎) These friendly family-run lodgings – think of the place as a 'boutique motel' – contain a long line of comfortable guest rooms with down comforters, wood paneling and cable TV. It's a short walk to the city center and several large supermarkets.

Hotel Alborada BOUTIQUE HOTEL $$
(✆291-1121; www.hotelalborada.cl; Barros Arana 457; d incl breakfast CH$56,800; ☎) A surprisingly stylish addition to Concepción's hotel scene is this centrally located, coolly minimalist hotel. The public spaces – outfitted with all-white furnishings, glass and mirrors – are sleeker than the guest rooms themselves, which are spacious and comfortable, but standard.

Hostal Bianca HOSTEL $
(✆225-2103; www.hostalbianca.cl; Salas 643-C; s/d incl breakfast CH$21,600/29,600, without bathroom CH$15,000/25,000; ☎) Conce's best budget

hotel has bright, newly renovated – if rather small – rooms with firm beds and cable TV.

Eating & Drinking

Penquistas have an almost religious obsession with *onces* (afternoon tea), so there's great coffee and moreish cakes and pastries to be had all over town. For inexpensive ethnic food (Japanese, pizza, gyros, tacos, you name it) and free-flowing beer and pisco, head down to the university area around Plaza Perú. There are more late-night eats and nightlife around Plaza España, in the neighborhood known as Barrio Estación.

Café Rometsch   CAFE $
(274-7040; Barros Arana 685; ☺8:30am-8:30pm) Delicious cakes and gelato, classy sidewalk tables on the plaza – need we say more?

TOP CHOICE Deli House   CHILEAN $
(www.delihouse.cl; Av Diagonal Pedro Aguirre Cerda 12-34; mains CH$3500-4800; 🛜) These leafy sidewalk tables are a relaxed place to kick back for coffee, sandwiches, gourmet pizza or happy hour while watching the bohemian university set pass by.

Fina Estampa   PERUVIAN $$
(Angol 289; mains CH$4900-7500) Starched tablecloths, fiercely folded napkins and deferential bow-tied waiters bring old-time elegance to this Peruvian restaurant. Ceviches, *ají de gallina* (chicken in a spicy yellow-pepper sauce) and other classics are perfectly executed, as is grilled seasonal fish.

Chela's   DINER $
(Barros Arana 405; mains CH$2000-3500) The TV blares in this cheap, corner cafe, which serves up mountainous portions of *chorrillana* (a pile of fries and onions with bits of sausage) and steaks that are perfect for throwing cholesterol counts to the wind.

Information

BancoEstado (905-200; O'Higgins 486; ☺9am-2pm Mon-Fri) One of many banks with ATMs near Plaza Independencia.

Conaf (262-4000; www.conaf.cl; Barros Arana 215; ☺8:30am-1pm & 2:30-5:30pm Mon-Fri) Limited information on nearby national parks and reserves.

Hospital Regional (220-8500; cnr San Martín & Av Roosevelt) Public hospital.

Matrix (279-0460; Caupolicán 346; per hr CH$600; ☺9:30am-11pm Mon-Sat) Fast internet and cheap calls.

Post office (800-267-7736; cnr O'Higgins & Colo Colo; ☺8:30am-7pm Mon-Fri, 8:30am-1pm Sat)

Sernatur (02-741-4145; www.chile.travel/en.html; Aníbal Pinto 460; ☺8:30am-8pm Jan & Feb, 8:30am-1pm & 3-6pm Mon-Fri Mar-Dec) Provides brochures, but little else.

Getting There & Away

Bus

Concepción has two long-distance bus terminals. Most companies use the **Terminal de Buses Collao** (274-9000; Tegualda 860), 3km east of central Concepción. From outside the terminal, grab a taxi into town. Some companies also use the separate **Terminal Chillancito** (231-5036; Camilo Henríquez 2565), northeast along the extension of Bulnes.

There are dozens of daily services to Santiago with companies including **Eme Bus** (232-0094), **Pullman Bus** (232-0309; www.pullmanbus.cl), **Nilahué** (231-0489; www.busesnilahue.cl) and **Tur Bus** (231-5555; www.turbus.cl; Tucapel 530), which also goes to Valparaíso and south to Temuco, Valdivia and Puerto Montt.

Línea Azul (286-1179; www.buseslineaazul.cl) goes to Chillán (half-hourly). **Buses Jota Be** (286-1533; www.busesjotabe.cl) connects Conce with Los Angeles (25 daily); some stop at the Salto del Laja. **Buses Biobío** (231-5554; www.busesbiobio.cl) has similar services and also goes to Angol (10 daily).

For services south along the coast, try **Jota Ewert** (285-5587; downtown ticket office Lincoyán 557).

DESTINATION	COST (CH$)	DURATION (HR)
Angol	4000	2½
Chillán	3500	2
Los Angeles	4500	2
Lota	700	30min
Puerto Montt	18,000	7
Santiago	15,000	6½
Talcahuano	500	30min
Temuco	15,000	4
Valdivia	12,000	6
Valparaíso/Viña del Mar	18,000	8

Car

A car can be useful for exploring the national parks south of Concepción. **Hertz** (279-7461;

www.autorentas.cl; Av Arturo Prat 248) has an office downtown.

Train

There are no direct trains to Concepción, but you can buy combination bus-train tickets to Santiago (CH$12,000, 6¼ hours, five daily) from **EFE** (☑286-8008; www.terrasur.cl; cnr Freire & Av Padre Hurtado) in Barrio Estación. You transfer to the train at Chillán, so direct buses, though they take slightly longer, are an easier (and cheaper) option.

Salto del Laja

Halfway between Los Angeles and Chillán, the Río Laja plunges nearly 50m over a steep escarpment to form a horseshoe-shaped **waterfall**. Some have dubbed the sight a miniature Iguazú Falls when it's full, but the comparison is far-fetched. Still, there are great views from where the road bridges the Río Laja. This road is the old Pan-American Hwy, but a new Ruta 5 bypass to the west means that only a few buses between Chillán and Los Angeles detour through here. A cluster of tacky souvenir stands and competing restaurants are evidence of the

Salto del Laja's popularity with Chileans on road trips or outings from nearby cities.

To linger longer at Salto del Laja, check into **Los Manantiales** (☑043-314-275; www.losmanantiales.saltosdellaja.com; Variante Salto del Laja Km480; campsite CH$12,000-16,000, s/d incl breakfast CH$21,000/30,000; ☒), a popular budget hotel whose large restaurant has spectacular views over the falls. The wood-paneled rooms are spacious and clean, and the decor of the whole complex seems gloriously unchanged since the 1970s. There's also camping if you happen to be traveling with a tent. Regardless of what the signs at the entrance say, it's a good 15-minute walk along the winding access road.

If Los Manantiales is booked out with tour groups, try **Hotel Salto del Laja** (☑043-321-706; www.saltodellaja.cl; Ruta 5 Sur, Km480; s/d incl breakfast from US$80/100; ☏☒), across the street, where many rooms have fireplaces and sweeping waterfall views. The terrace restaurant is open to the public if you're just stopping by to check out the falls.

With its gorgeous rural setting, 15km south of Salto del Laja, the German-run **Residencial El Rincón** (☑099-9082-3168; www.elrinconchile.cl; s/d CH$30,000/37,000, without

WORTH A TRIP

LOTA

Concepción's exponential industrial and economic growth owes much to the huge offshore coal deposits discovered south of the city along the so-called Costa del Carbón (Coal Coast). The hilly coastal town of Lota spiraled into poverty when the mines closed in 1997, ending up with some of the most deprived shantytowns in the country. However, it has now reinvented itself as a tourist destination and makes an interesting half-day out from Concepción.

The star attraction is the **Mina Chiflón del Diablo** (Devil's Whistle Mine; ☑041-287-1549; www.lotasorprendente.cl; tours adult/child CH$5000/4500; ☉10:30am-7:30pm), a naturally ventilated undersea mine that operated between 1884 and 1976. Ex-coal miners now work as guides on well-organized 45-minute tours that take you through a series of galleries and tunnels to a coal face some 50m under the sea. Before clambering into the rattling metal cage-elevator that takes you down, you're kitted out with safety gear. You can also visit the **Pueblito Minero**, painstaking recreations of typical miners' houses built for the Chilean movie Sub Terra (Underground), which was filmed here. Admission to the mine includes entrance to the stunning 14-hectare **Parque Botánico Isidora Cousiño** down the road. Paths wind through the mix of manicured flower beds, small ponds and wilder woodland to a lighthouse on a tip of land jutting out into the sea. To the right, an abandoned mineshaft and slag heap form stark industrial contrasts to the park's cultivated beauty.

To reach Lota from Concepción, catch a bus labeled 'Coronel-Lota' (CH$800, 30 minutes, every 15 minutes). Ask the driver to drop you at the Iglesia Parroquial, then follow the signs downhill to the mine. At the time of writing, the microbus line was on strike and service had been temporarily suspended. Ask at Concepción's bus terminal for the latest.

bathroom CH$19,000/27,000) is a relaxing place to take time out from traveling. The lodge has cozy, all-wood rooms and does fabulous homemade breakfasts and dinners (three-course dinner CH$16,000). The owners also lead hiking and horseback-riding excursions. Get off southbound buses at the Perales/Los Olivos exit of the Panamericana (Km494), also known as Cruce La Mona (tell the driver and he'll stop for you). Signs point the 2km to the lodge; if you call or email ahead of time, the owners will pick you up here for free.

Many of the services run by **Buses Jota Be** (☑in Concepción 041-286-1533; www.buses jotabe.cl) between Los Angeles and Concepción or Chillán stop at Salto del Laja. Timetables change frequently, so always confirm the time of the next bus through to make sure you don't get stranded – and be sure to tell the driver that you want to be dropped off at Salta del Laja, or he might barrel right by your stop.

Parque Nacional Laguna del Laja

Some 93km east of Los Angeles lies the 116-sq-km **Parque Nacional Laguna del Laja** (☑043-321-086; www.conaf.cl; adult/child CH$1200/600; ☺8:30am-8pm Dec-Apr, to 6:30pm May-Nov). Within the park is the **Volcán Antuco** (2985m), whose strikingly symmetrical flat-topped cone lies ahead of you on the drive up. Lava from this volcano dammed the **Río Laja**, creating the lake from which the park takes its name. The lava fields immediately around the lake form an eerie lunar landscape. Although the volcano may seem quiet, it is not extinct: volcanic activity was last recorded about 70 years ago.

The park protects the mountain cypress (*Austrocedrus chilensis*) and the monkey-puzzle tree, as well as other uncommon tree species. Mammals are rare, though puma, fox and viscacha have been sighted. Nearly 50 bird species inhabit the area, including the Andean condor.

There's a small Conaf post at **Los Pangües**, the park entrance, where you sign in. From here, a winding road takes you to the park headquarters at **Chacay**, 3km on.

◎ Sights & Activities

As well as hiking, you can drive through parts of the park: there's 6km of uphill hairpin bends between Chacay and the start of the lava-edged Laguna del Laja. The road then winds alongside the lake for 28km until it reaches the red army hut at Los Barros, from where 4WD vehicles can continue to the Argentine border (closed April through September).

Chacay   HIKING
Chacay is the starting point for several well-marked hiking trails. On the left-hand side of the road is the easy 1½-hour trail to two small but stunning waterfalls, the **Salto de Las Chilcas** (the point where the underground Río Laja emerges) and the **Salto del Torbellino**.

A 10km section of the Sendero de Chile leaves from the right-hand side of the road and goes to **Laguna del Laja**. Nearby is the starting point for **Sendero Los Coigües**, a 2.5km hike to a spot with fabulous views of Volcán Antuco.

Sendero Sierra Velluda   HIKING
The park's star trek is the three-day Sendero Sierra Velluda circuit, named for the hanging glacier you pass along the way. It winds around Volcán Antuco, passing waterfalls and lava fields; condors are also a common sight. Conaf rangers provide detailed instructions and information about all these hikes.

Club de Esqui de los Angeles   SKIING
(☑043-322-651; www.skiantuco.cl; day ski pass adult/child CH$19,000/12,000) In winter, the Club de Esqui de los Angeles operates two drag-lifts and a small restaurant on the slopes near Chacay, known as the Cancha de Ski Antuco.

🛏 Sleeping

Lagunillas   CAMPGROUND **$**
(☑043-321-086; campsites CH$10,000, 6-person cabins CH$30,000) You can camp inside the park at Lagunillas, 2km from the park entrance, where there are 22 sites with electricity, showers and toilets. Basic cabins with hot water and electricity are also for rent. Reserve ahead by emailing altosdellaja@gmail.com.

❶ Getting There & Away

Departing from Los Angeles' Terminal de Buses Rurales, local buses go through Antuco to the village of El Abanico, 11km from the entrance to Parque Nacional Laguna del Laja (CH$1600, 1½ hours, seven daily). The last bus back to Los Angeles leaves Abanico at 5:30pm, except on Sundays, when the last bus leaves at 7:15pm.

Note that here's no public transportation between Abanico and the park. It takes about 1½ hours to walk this stretch, and another half-hour to reach the Lagunillas campsite. Hitchhiking is technically possible, but vehicles are a rare sight. If you're driving, you'll need 4WD and chains to negotiate this road between May and September.

Los Angeles

☏043 / POP 169,929

A useful base for visiting Parque Nacional Laguna del Laja, Los Angeles is an otherwise unprepossessing agricultural and industrial service center 110km south of Chillán.

◉ Sights

FREE **Museo de la Alta Frontera**   MUSEUM

(☏408-643; Colón 121, 2nd fl, Plaza de Armas) Though it was closed at the time of writing, it's worth checking to see if you can get into this museum that was built to celebrate the city's 250th birthday in 1989. An extraordinary collection of Mapuche silverwork is the star exhibit; masks and headdresses, textiles and ceramics are among the other pieces on display.

🛏 Sleeping & Eating

A string of *residenciales* (budget accommodations) line Caupolicán west of the Plaza de Armas. Despite appearances, they're not particularly cheap and mostly function as men's boarding houses, so women travelers might not feel comfortable there. You'll see plenty of casual cafes and teahouses serving inexpensive sandwiches and cakes around the busy *centro*.

Hotel Dikran   HOTEL **$$**

(☏230-030; www.hoteldikran.cl; Almagro 393; s/d incl breakfast CH$31,500/42,000; ❄️🐾) Wicker furniture, wooden floors and ocher- or butter-colored walls give this friendly hotel a warm, homey feel.

Hotel del Centro   HOTEL **$$**

(☏236-961; www.hoteldelcentro.cl; Lautaro 579; s/d incl breakfast CH$36,900/46,800) Though this hotel underwent extensive renovations in 2010, it's still more traditional than stylish – but with colorful paintings on the walls, flat-screen TVs in the rooms and a convenient continental breakfast, it's fine for an overnight stop.

Four Points Sheraton   BUSINESS HOTEL **$$$**

(☏406-400; www.starwoodhotels.com; Colo Colo 565; r incl breakfast CH$68,800; 🐾📶) This spiffy new business hotel is the place to be if you need to recharge your batteries with North American–style amenities: there's a beautiful swimming pool, fitness center and spa, plus a cocktail bar in the lobby that's open to the public.

Solcito   CHILEAN **$**

(www.solcito.cl; Villagrán 300; mains CH$2800-4500; ⊙9am-midnight Mon-Sat, noon-7pm Sun) Tables in the front half of this bright restaurant on the corner of Lautaro are scattered with newspapers, coffees and hot chocolates during the day, and icy *schops* at night. At the back, simple but flavorful grilled steaks or fish are served – soccer games on TV are the soundtrack.

ⓘ Information

BancoEstado (☏455-450; Colón 140) Has an ATM and changes dollars.

Ciber Plus Internet (☏345-710; Colo Colo 451, Local 1; per hr CH$550; ⊙9:30am-midnight)

Hospital Los Angeles (☏409-600; Ricardo Vicuña 160) Public hospital.

Lavandería Matic (☏348-015; Almagro 748; per kg CH$1000; ⊙9am-1pm & 3-6:30pm Mon-Sat)

Post office (800-276-7736; Caupolicán 464; ⊙9am-7pm Mon-Fri, 9am-1pm Sat)

Sernatur (☏317-107; www.chile.travel/en.html; Caupolicán 450, 3rd fl, Oficina 6; ⊙9am-5:30pm Mon-Fri)

ⓘ Getting There & Away

Bus

Long-distance buses leave from two adjacent bus terminals on Av Sor Vicenta, the continuation of Villagrán, on the northeast outskirts of town.

Pullman Bus (☏363-053) and **Tur Bus** (☏600-660-6600; www.turbus.cl) leave from the **Tur Bus terminal** (☏363-136; Av Sor Vicenta 2061). Both have numerous daily departures to Santiago (CH$8000, 6½ hours), most of which stop at Talca, Curicó and Rancagua. Over 20 daily services head south to Temuco (CH$4300, two hours), Osorno (CH$8100, 5½ hours) and Puerto Montt (CH$9300, seven hours).

All other services use the next-door **Terminal Santa María** (☏363-035; Av Sor Vicenta 2051). From here **Buses Jota Be** (☏533-181; www.busesjotabe.cl) runs buses to Concepción (CH$2400, two hours, every 30 minutes) and

Angol (CH$1000, 1½ hours, hourly), the gateway to Parque Nacional Nahuelbuta. Some buses to Chillán (CH$2600, 1¾ hours, hourly) pass by Salto del Laja (CH$2000, 45 minutes). **Buses Bio Bio** (534-699; www.busesbiobio.cl) operates along the same routes slightly less frequently.

Local bus routes operate out of the **Terminal de Buses Rurales** (Terminal Santa Rita; 313-232; Villagrán 501), on the corner of Rengo. To get to Parque Nacional Laguna del Laja, see p132.

Car

As there's no public transportation right up to the entrance of Parque Nacional Laguna del Laja, a rental car can be useful, especially for one- or two-day visits. **Interbruna** (313-812; www.interbruna.cl; Caupolicán 350) is one of a few agencies that rents cars; expect to pay around CH$32,000 per day for a compact car and CH$60,000 for a 4WD truck.

Angol

045 / POP 56,204

It was seventh time lucky for Angol, which was razed to the ground on six separate occasions during the conflict between the Mapuche and the conquistadores. Despite its turbulent history, Angol is a small, sleepy town with little to do, but it provides the best access into mountainous Parque Nacional Nahuelbuta, a forest reserve that protects the largest remaining coastal stands of araucaria pines, or monkey-puzzle trees.

The town Angol straddles the Río Vergara, an upper tributary of the Biobío formed by the confluence of the Ríos Picoiquén and Rehue. The city's older core lies west of the river and centers on the attractive Plaza de Armas with a fountain adorned by four gloriously poised marble statues that represent Europe, Asia, the Americas and Africa; and huge, shady trees and well-kept flower beds.

✲ Festivals & Events

Brotes de Chile MUSIC
One of Chile's biggest folk festivals takes place in the second week of January and includes traditional dances, food and crafts.

🛏 Sleeping & Eating

Hotel Angol HOTEL $
(719-036; Lautaro 176; d incl breakfast CH$28,000;) These 15 simple, centrally located rooms come with private bathrooms and cable TV. Breakfast is served downstairs at the Café de la Rueda, which is open to the public.

Duhatao BOUTIQUE HOTEL $$
(714-320; www.hotelduhatao.cl; Arturo Prat 420; s/d incl breakfast CH$36,00/43,500;) Here's a surprise: there's a design hotel in Angol. The Duhatao blends clean modern lines with local crafts and colors – the springy beds have headboards made from old gate posts and hand-woven throws, and bathrooms have big bowl sinks. A slick restaurant and bar are on-site.

Sparlatto Pizza PIZZERIA $
(Lautaro 418; mains CH$3500-5200) This bustling little restaurant on the plaza serves steak sandwiches, salads, Chilean comfort food and pizza; in the evening it fills up with a younger, beer-drinking crowd.

🛈 Information

BancoEstado (945-900; Chorillos 390) ATM and currency exchange.

Hospital Angol (551-048; Ilabaca 752) Public hospital.

Municipal tourist office (990-840; Glorieta Plaza de las Siete Fundaciones; ⊙8:30am-5:20pm Mon-Fri Mar-Dec, 8am-8pm daily Jan & Feb) In the middle of the plaza.

Post office (800-276-7736; Lautaro 202; ⊙9am-1pm & 3-6:30pm Mon-Fri, 9am-12:30pm Sat)

🛈 Getting There & Away

Most long-distance bus services leave from Angol's **Terminal Rodoviario** (Bonilla 428), a 10-minute walk from the Plaza de Armas. To get to the center of town, turn left from the main exit and walk four blocks along José Luis Osorio to Bulevar O'Higgins, the main road, where you turn right and cross the bridge.

Several companies run multiple daily services north to Santiago (CH$9300 to CH$11,200, eight hours), including **Pullman JC** (716-866), **Línea Azul** (715-867; www.buseslineaazul.cl) and **Tur Bus** (711-655; www.turbus.cl) also stopping at Chillán (CH$2500, 3¼ hours, two daily) and Talca (CH$7500, five hours, two daily). **Buses Jota Be** (712-262; www.busesjotabe.cl) has buses to Los Angeles (CH$3600, one hour, 22 daily) and also travels to Concepción (CH$3200, 2½ hours, every 30 minutes).

Leaving from its own terminal, **Buses Bio Bio** (465-387; www.busesbiobio.cl; Caupolicán 98) serves Los Angeles (CH$1000, one hour, 11 daily) and Concepción (CH$3500, 2½ hours, 25 daily).

Local and regional services leave from the **Terminal de Buses Rurales** (712-021; Ilabaca

422), including buses to Parque Nacional Nahuelbuta.

Parque Nacional Nahuelbuta

Between Angol and the Pacific, the coast range rises to 1550m within the 68 sq km **Parque Nacional Nahuelbuta** (www.conaf.cl; adult/child CH$4500/2000; ☉8:30am-8pm), one of the last non-Andean refuges of araucaria, or monkey-puzzle trees. In summer, other interesting plant life includes 16 varieties of orchids and two carnivorous plant species. Various species of *Nothofagus* (southern beech) are common here, and the Magellanic woodpeckers that typically inhabit them make for great birdwatching. Rare mammals such as pumas, Darwin's fox and the miniature Chilean deer known as the pudú also live in the park. According to some, it's a prime location for UFO spotting, too.

The dirt road between Angol and Cañete runs through the park. Conaf maintains the park headquarters and information center at **Pehuenco**, roughly halfway between the two park entrances, which are sometimes staffed by rangers, too. There are no shops or restaurants within Nahuelbuta, so bring your own supplies. The park enjoys warm, dry summers, but is usually snow-covered during winter. November to April is the best time to visit.

☉ Sights & Activities

Some 30km of roads and 15km of footpaths crisscross the park, so you can tour by car and on foot. Several marked **hiking** trails start at Pehuenco. The most popular is an easy 4.5km walk through pehuén forests to the 1379m granite outcrop of **Cerro Piedra del Águila** (literally, 'eagle rock'), which has fabulous views from the Andes to the Pacific. To the southeast you can see the entire string of Andean volcanoes – from Antuco, east of Chillán, to Villarrica and Lanín, east of Pucón. You can loop back to Pehuenco via the valley of the Estero Cabrería to the south: the trail starts beneath the west side of the outcrop and the whole hike takes about three hours. Alternatively, you can reach Piedra del Águila by walking 800m from the end of a shorter approach accessible by car. Another trail leads 5km north from Pehuenco to **Cerro Anay**, a 1450m hill with similar views. It's an easy three-hour

walk past wildflower beds and huge stands of araucarias.

🛏 Sleeping

Camping Pehuenco   CAMPGROUND **$**
(6-person campsites CH$12,000) Next to the park headquarters, 5.5km from the entrance on the Angol side of the park. There are 11 campsites in shady forest clearings with picnic tables, and basic bathrooms with flush toilets and cold showers.

❶ Getting There & Away

Several local bus lines, including **Buses Carrasco** (☑045-715-287), **Buses Nahuelbuta** (☑045-715-611) and **Buses Moncada** (☑045-712-021) depart Angol at 6:45am and 4pm for Vegas Blanca (CH$1700, 1½ hours), 7km from the eastern park entrance and 12.5km from the park headquarters at Pehuenco. Some lines go on Monday, Wednesday and Friday, others on alternate days. All leave from Angol's **Terminal de Buses Rural** (cnr Ilabaca & Lautaro), and return from Vegas Blancas at 9am and 6pm (confirm these times so you don't get stranded). In January and February the morning service usually continues to the park entrance. Motorists with low-clearance vehicles may find the steep and dusty road difficult in spots, and you need a 4WD and chains June through August.

Mountain bikers generally need to dismount and walk at least part of the way up; note that water is hard to find along the way. However, local buses to Vegas Blancas are generally happy to carry bikes, so cycling from there is an alternative.

ARCHIPIÉLAGO JUAN FERNÁNDEZ

Although these remote islands are 667km west of Valparaíso, they are considered part of Valparaíso region; the archipelago was originally discovered by a sailor making his way from Peru to Valparaíso. This chain of small volcanic islands is also the place where castaway Alexander Selkirk (inspiration for Daniel Defoe's *Robinson Crusoe*) whittled away lost years scampering after goats and scanning the horizon for ships. Once an anonymous waypoint for pirates, sealers and war ships, the archipelago was later declared both a national park and an Unesco Biosphere Reserve.

This Pacific outpost has made headlines in recent times for two major tragedies: first, the islands' infrastructure was badly

Archipiélago Juan Fernández

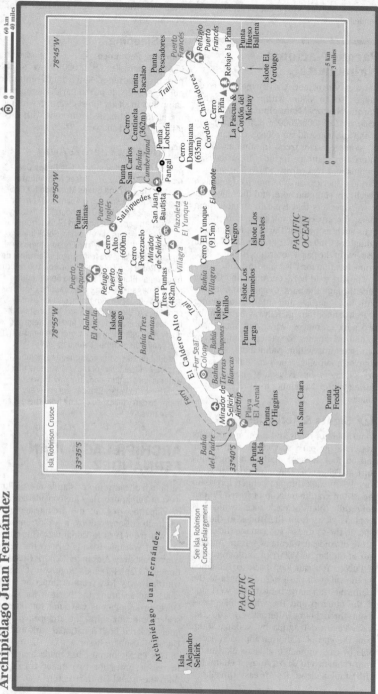

damaged in the tsunami following the 2010 earthquake, prompting action from a charity foundation, Desafío Levantemos Chile (Together We Pick Up Chile) intent on rebuilding after the disaster. And in September 2011, a group of prominent Chilean TV journalists and crew from the morning program *Buenos Días a Todos* boarded a plane to the islands to film a segment on the reconstruction efforts. The plane crashed near Robinson Crusoe Island, killing all 21 passengers, shocking the Chilean public and sending the islands into a further tailspin. At the time of writing, the islands were still recovering. Though the area may well emerge as a world-class diving destination in years to come, travel to the archipelago is still considered a sensitive issue. Check out www.comunajuanfernandez.cl (in Spanish) for the latest.

History

In November 1574, Portuguese mariner Juan Fernández veered off course between Peru and Valparaíso and discovered these islands that now bear his name. In following centuries the islands proved a popular stop-off for ships skirting around the Humboldt Current. Pirates sought refuge in the few bays – hunting feral goats and planting gardens to stock future visits – and traffic increased with sealers.

After the turn of the 18th century, one island played a notorious role in Chile's independence struggle, as Spanish authorities exiled 42 criollo patriots to damp caves above San Juan Bautista after the disastrous Battle of Rancagua in 1814. The patriots in exile included Juan Egaña and Manuel de Salas, figures from the Chilean elite who would not quickly forget their cave-dwelling days.

Chile established a permanent settlement in 1877. For many years the island remained a nearly escape-proof political prison for the newly independent country. Later during WWI it again played a memorable historic role, as the British naval vessels *Glasgow* and *Orama* confronted the German cruiser *Dresden* at Bahía Cumberland.

SELKIRK: THE QUINTESSENTIAL CASTAWAY

The archipelago's claim to fame is Scotsman Alexander Selkirk, who spent four years and four months marooned on Masatierra after requesting to be put ashore. He had had a dispute with the captain of the privateer *Cinque Ports* in 1704 over the seaworthiness of the vessel (the ship was rotting). Abandonment was tantamount to a death sentence for most castaways, who soon starved or shot themselves, but Selkirk adapted to his new home and endured, despite his desperate isolation.

Although the Spaniards vigorously opposed privateers in their domains, their foresight made Selkirk's survival possible. Thanks to them, unlike many small islands, Masatierra had abundant water and goats. Disdaining fish, Selkirk tracked these feral animals, devoured their meat and dressed himself in their skins. He crippled and tamed some for their company and easy hunting. Sea lions, feral cats and rats – the latter two European introductions – were among his other companions. Selkirk would often climb to a lookout above Bahía Cumberland (Cumberland Bay) in hope of spotting a vessel on the horizon, but not until 1708 did his savior, Commander Woodes Rogers of the British privateers *Duke* and *Duchess,* arrive with famed privateer William Dampier as his pilot. Rogers recalled his first meeting with Selkirk when the ship's men returned from shore. He called him 'a man Cloth'd in Goat-Skins, who look'd wilder than the first Owners of them.'

After signing on with Rogers and returning to Scotland, Selkirk became a celebrity and the inspiration for a rag-tag army of reality shows, theme park rides and great literature alike. Daniel Defoe's classic *Robinson Crusoe* is thought to be inspired by Selkirk. Other worthy reads include Captain Woodes Rogers' *A Cruising Voyage Round the World,* by Selkirk's rescuer, *Robinson Crusoe's Island* (1969) by Ralph Lee Woodward and Nobel Prize winner JM Coetzee's revisionist novel *Foe* (1986).

Traditional biography was cast away when British writer Diane Souhami made a portrait of the man through the place. Her take, *Selkirk's Island,* won the 2001 Whitbread Biography Award. While in the archipelago researching, Souhami became intrigued with the way the island pared down modern life, leaving what was essential. Souhami noted how Selkirk's relationship to the island he once cursed changed post-rescue. 'He started calling it "my beautiful island,"' said Souhami. 'It became the major relationship in his life.'

Geography & Climate

Adrift in the open Pacific Ocean, the Juan Fernández archipelago consists of Isla Robinson Crusoe; tiny Isla Santa Clara (known to early privateers as Goat Island), just 3km off the main island's southern tip; and Isla Alejandro Selkirk, another 170km away from the continent.

The islands' land areas are very small, but their topography is extraordinarily rugged; geologically, the entire archipelago is a group of emergent peaks of the submarine mountain range known as the Juan Fernández Ridge, which goes east–west for more than 400km at the southern end of the Chile Basin.

The archipelago is far enough from the continent for subtropical water masses to moderate the chilly sub-Antarctic waters of the Humboldt Current, which flows northward along the Chilean coast. The climate is distinctly Mediterranean, with clearly defined warm, dry summers and cooler, wet winters.

Wildlife

ANIMALS

The only native mammal, the Juan Fernández fur seal, inhabits the seas and shores of Isla Robinson Crusoe and Isla Santa Clara. Of 11 endemic bird species, the most eye-catching is the Juan Fernández hummingbird *(Sephanoides fernandensis)*. Only about 700 hummingbirds survive, feeding off the striking Juan Fernández cabbage that grows in many parts of San Juan Bautista, but the birds do best in native forest.

PLANTS

The archipelago is considered a unique eco-region with plants that slowly evolved in isolation, adapting to local environmental niches; today, the greatest concentration of native flora survives in sectors where goats can neither penetrate nor completely dominate.

Vegetation spans an extraordinary range of geographic affinities, from the Andes and sub-Antarctic Magallanes to Hawaii and New Zealand. Of 87 genera of plants on the islands, 16 are endemic, found nowhere else on earth; of 140 native plant species, 101 are endemic. These plants survive in three major communities: the evergreen rainforest, the evergreen heath and the herbaceous steppe. Perhaps the most striking vegetation, however, is the dense understory of climbing vines and the towering endemic

tree ferns *Dicksonia berteroana* and *Thyrsopteris elegans*.

❶ Getting There & Away

From Santiago, two airlines operate flights to Juan Fernández. There are usually several daily flights between September and April, with fewer departures the rest of the year. The 2¼-hour flight takes 10 to 20 passengers; note that climate is a major factor with flight schedules and foul weather on the island can provoke last-minute departure changes and cancellations.

Flights depart from Santiago's Aeródromo Tobalaba in the eastern residential neighborhood of La Reina. To get there take the metro to Principe de Gales and hail a taxi (CH$3500) to the nearby hangar. Upon arrival to the island, passengers take a one-hour boat taxi (usually included in the airfare) to the pier of San Juan Bautista. Return flights require a minimum number of passengers to depart, so keep travel arrangements flexible enough to allow for a few extra days on the island. Consult the airlines for prices, but count on paying upwards of CH$350,000 round-trip.

ATA (☑02-234-3389; www.aerolineasata.cl; Larraín Alcalde s/n)

Lassa (☑02-273-4354; www.aerolassa.cl; Larraín Alcalde s/n)

❶ Getting Around

With only a few kilometers of roads in San Juan Bautista and steep peaks that bookend the valleys, boating is the best way to get around. To arrange a water taxi, ask around at the Municipalidad across from the plaza.

San Juan Bautista

☑032 / POP 600

The sole town on Isla Robinson Crusoe, San Juan Bautista (St John the Baptist) is the proverbial sleepy fishing village, down to the lobster catchers in knitted caps, and dusty stores that run out of cheese and beer before the provisions ship arrives. The village's steep hills are strewn with lush gardens and modest cottages with paths leading into horse pastures and wooded hiking trails. Sadly, the town's landmark lighthouse and cemetery were destroyed in the earthquake.

◎ Sights

San Juan is the organizational and departure point for all of the islands' main activities, including fishing, hiking, boat tours of the islands, diving and tours of the local sights.

Fuerte Santa Bárbara   MONUMENT
Built in 1749 to discourage incursions by pirates, these Spanish fortifications were reconstructed in 1974. To get there, follow the path from Cuevas de los Patriotas, or climb directly from the plaza via Subida El Castillo. The track continues to Mirador de Selkirk.

Cuevas de los Patriotas   CAVE
Up a short footpath from Larraín Alcalde and illuminated at night, these damp caverns sheltered Juan Egaña, Manuel de Salas and 40 other patriots exiled for several years during Chile's independence movement after their defeat in the Battle of Rancagua in 1814.

🏃 Activities

Getting into the water around Robinson Crusoe is like slipping into a great abyss: this idiosyncratic ecosystem hosts world-class scuba diving. Moray eel, flounder, lobster and enormous schools of yellowtail troll the clear waters. But the biggest attraction is the playful Juan Fernández fur seal (*Arctocephalus philippii*).

☞ Tours

The Conaf kiosk on the plaza has a list of registered guides and tour schedules.

Endémica Expediciones   DIVING, FISHING
(☎032-275-1003; www.endemica.com; Larraín Alcalde 399b) Multilingual and cutting-edge, this excellent agency offers scuba diving, hiking, kayaking, fishing and snorkeling trips. Recommended are day trips to lobstering grounds with artisan fisherfolk. The owner is set to reopen the renowned Hostal Pez Volador; check the website for updates.

Festivals & Events

Rodeo de Villagra   RODEO
Held at the end of January or early February, this is an island-wide rodeo festival with more cattle than you can possibly imagine live out here.

Fiesta de San Pedro   RELIGIOUS
The patron saint of fishermen is honored on June 29 with decorated boats making a procession at sea.

Fiesta de Aniversario   HISTORICAL
On Día de la Isla, held on November 22, a celebration commemorates the day Portuguese sailor Juan Fernández discovered the archipelago in 1574. Festivities include a regatta and a 13km foot race from Punta de Isla to Bahía Cumberland.

San Juan Bautista

San Juan Bautista

◉ Sights

◉ Activities, Courses & Tours

🛏 Sleeping

🛏 Sleeping & Eating

Local businesses have been in flux since the tsunami. The municipal website (comunajuanfernandez.cl, in Spanish) lists a dozen basic lodging options that are open and receiving visitors. Since restaurants are few, most guests take half-board (dinner and breakfast); lodging rates quoted here include half-board. Full board is usually available on request. Reserve ahead when dining out, especially for groups or when requesting a specific dish.

Residencial Mirador de Selkirk
GUESTHOUSE $$

(☑275-1028, 988-457-024; mfernandeziana@hotmail.com; Pasaje del Castillo 251; r per person incl breakfast CH$30,000; @) High on the hillside, this family home has three snug rooms and a sprawling deck overlooking the bay (where you recover your breath from the hike up). Señora Julia serves up fantastic meals (CH$5000). Foodies shouldn't miss her lobster empanadas or seafood *parol* (stew).

Hostería Petit Breulh
GUESTHOUSE $$

(☑275-1107; crusoeppetithotmail.com; Vicente González 80; r per person CH$22,500; @) Bedside minibars, dark leather, massage showers and cable TV nurture a haven for would-be playboys that relish a few pelts on the wall (think 1980s). Yet, meals (CH$6000) are showstoppers – think ceviche with capers and zucchini stuffed with fresh fish and baked under bubbling cheese. Nonguests should make reservations.

Refugio Naútico
BOUTIQUE HOTEL $$$

(☑974-835-014; www.islarobinsoncrusoe.cl, in Spanish; Carrera Pinto 280; s/d/tr incl breakfast CH$55,000/100,000/135,000; @) This waterfront refuge is stylin' with kitchen competence and all the comforts of home. Its bright terraced rooms are plenty private but the real treat is the living area brimming with books, DVDs and music – perfect for that rainy day, or for your post-meal coma. Kayak rentals, hiking and dive trips are available through the onsite PADI-certified dive center. Credit cards are accepted.

📷 Crusoe Island Lodge
LUXURY HOTEL $$$

(☑562-432-6800; www.crusoeislandlodge.com; s/d incl breakfast from $US244/406; 🔊📶) *Travel & Leisure* has already featured this stylish new ecolodge with 15 rustic-chic rooms and suites overlooking Pangal Bay. In addition to a small spa and a gourmet restaurant specializing in fresh lobster and golden crab, the lodge arranges birdwatching, trekking, historical tours and fishing excursions.

Baron de Rodt
CHILEAN $$

(☑994-402-007; La Polvera 353; mains CH$5000-8500) Try *la vidriolaza*, a tasty sandwich.

ℹ Information

There are no banks or money changers on the island, so bring all the pesos you need, preferably in small bills. Credit cards are rarely accepted, though some tour operators or hotels will take US dollars or euros, at poor rates.

Several kiosks have public telephones, although international rates are prohibitively expensive.

Centro Información al Turista (Vicente González; ⊙8am-12:30pm & 2-6pm Mon-Fri, 8am-12:30pm & 2-4:30pm Sat & Sun) At the top of Vicente González, this large open hall has photo displays, a meeting room, and detailed information on the park and the history of the islands, all with decent English translations.

Conaf (Larraín Alcalde; ⊙8am-6pm Mon-Fri, 9am-6pm Sat & Sun) This small kiosk near the plaza collects park admission and distributes leaflets with decent maps. For information on visiting any part of the park outside the immediate environs of San Juan Bautista, it's advisable to contact Conaf in advance.

Conaf administrative office (☑275-1004, 275-1022; Vicente González) Located next door to Centro Información al Turista. Ask for a tour of the next door plant nursery, where more than 40 endemic species are cultivated and the saplings are later replanted in the park and given to locals to plant around the town.

Post office (⊙9am-6pm Mon-Fri, 9am-12pm Sat) On the south side of the plaza.

Posta de Salud (☑275-1067; Vicente González) A government medical clinic, just below the entrance to Conaf's grounds.

Parque Nacional Archipiélago Juan Fernández

This **national park** (www.conaf.cl; adult/child CH$3000/800) covers the entire archipelago, a total of 93 sq km, though the township of San Juan Bautista and the airstrip are de-facto exclusions. In an effort to control access to the most fragile areas of the park, Conaf requires many of the hikes to be organized and led by local registered guides. A list of the guides with pricing information is posted at the kiosk near the plaza, where you should register before taking any self-guided hike. Day hikes for a group of six people cost

CH$15,000 to CH$30,000. Still, a number of areas are accessible without guides. Another way to see the park is by boat. Local tour operators can arrange trips to see fur seal colonies at different points around the island. Camping is possible only in organized campsites, each with a one-night limit.

Self-guided Hiking Trails

MIRADOR DE SELKIRK
Perhaps the most rewarding and stunning hike on the island is to Selkirk's *mirador* above San Juan Bautista, where he would look for ships appearing on the horizon. The 3km walk, gaining 565m in elevation, takes about 1½ hours of steady walking but rewards the climber with views of both sides of the island.

VILLAGRA TO LA PUNTA DE ISLA
Beyond Selkirk's overlook, the trail continues on the south side, taking one hour to reach **Villagra** (4.8km), where there are campsites. From here the wide trail skirts the southern cliffs to **La Punta de Isla** (13km; approximately four hours) and the airstrip, where there is also camping available. En route is **Bahía Tierras Blancas**, the island's main breeding colony of Juan Fernández fur seals. This scenic and reasonably challenging hike takes in a significant part of the island and is an excellent way to enjoy its serenity.

PLAZOLETA EL YUNQUE
Plazoleta El Yunque is a tranquil forest clearing with bathrooms, water and picnic areas at the base of the 915m-high Cerro El Yunque (The Anvil). You will pass the crumbled foundation of the home of a German survivor of the *Dresden* who once homesteaded here. He was known as the 'German Robinson.'

CENTINELA
Cerro Centinela (362m) holds the ruins of the first radio station on the island, which was established in 1909. The 3km hike is accessed from Pangal.

SALSIPUEDES
At the top of La Pólvora, a trail zigzags through eucalyptus groves, then endemic ferns, then thickets of murtilla to reach the ridge Salsipuedes, which translates to 'Leave if you can.'

To arrange a **guided hike**, contact any of the island's travel agencies.

PUERTO INGLÉS & PUERTO VAQUERÍA
The 2.3km trail to Puerto Inglés starts at Salsipuedes and continues down a very precarious ridge to the beach area, where there is a reconstruction of Selkirk's shelter.

VILLAGRA TO CERRO NEGRO
From Villagra guided hikes go to the base of Cerro El Yunque and Cerro Negro (3.5km).

PUERTO FRANCÉS
Located on the eastern shore of the island, Puerto Francés was a haven for French privateers, whose presence motivated Spain to erect a series of fortifications in 1779, the ruins of which are all but gone. From Cerro Centinela, a 6.4km trail reaches the port where there are five campsites, a *refugio*, running water and a bathroom.

Isla Alejandro Selkirk

If Robinson Crusoe falls short of castaway ambience, search out Isla Alejandro Selkirk. Hard to reach and rarely visited by foreigners, the island lies 181km west of Robinson Crusoe. It's a seasonal lobstering base for 25 families from Crusoe who, when not fishing, can be found playing soccer, fixing boats or going on Crusoe-esque hunts for feral goats. More mountainous than Crusoe, Selkirk's highest point in the archipelago is 1650m Cerro Los Inocentes. Islanders are welcoming to respectful visitors, but you should plan to camp and bring provisions. Make sure to settle your return trip in advance, or you may be putting in some time as an island exile.

Norte Grande

Best Places to Eat

» El Tercer Ojito (p168)
» La Casona (p184)
» Mata-Rangi (p151)
» Blanco (p184)

Best Places to Stay

» Mirador El Buey (p149)
» Terrace Lodge & Cafe (p158)
» Tierra Atacama Hotel & Spa (p181)
» La Casona 1920 (p167)

Why Go?

Devil dusters zoom wantonly through sun-scorched Norte Grande with its undulating curves of rock and stone, Andean lagoons, snow-capped volcanoes, salt flats and sensuously perforated coastline. Famous as much for its hilltop observatories as its massive copper mines, those vast, uninhabited spaces touch the soul and the imagination. Norte Grande's star attraction is the tiny adobe village of San Pedro de Atacama, just a day trip away from the world's highest geyser field and some astounding desert formations.

But there's more to Norte Grande than San Pedro. Go for lung-bursting, jaw-dropping adventure near the mountain village of Putre in the high-altitude reserve of Parque Nacional Lauca or further afield to Salar de Surire. Spend a week perfecting your tan on the beaches outlying Iquique and Arica, or make your own adventure in the lost ghost towns and hard-sprung mining centers that make this region unique.

When to Go
Iquique

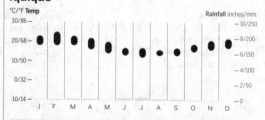

Jan–Feb Vacationers hit the coast and some highland spots become impossible to reach.

Sep–Oct The altiplano has solid weather and European summer visitors have gone home.

Jul–Aug Best for highland destinations (though it gets bitterly cold at night) and for hard-core surfing.

Dangers & Annoyances

Northern Chile is a very safe place all in all. In the rough-and-tumble mining towns like Calama, however, women may get unwelcomed leers and whistles, and should be careful walking alone at night. Many of the low-budget hotels in the region are now full-time residences of visiting miners, which may make for an unpleasant situation for single female travelers.

The currents on the beaches can be quite strong, meaning good surf, but less-than-ideal swimming. Signs saying *'no apta para bañarse'* (not suitable for swimming) are posted on most beaches that have strong currents.

You should drive with your lights on during the day (and at night), and use caution when you see *zona de derrumbes* (rock-fall zone) signs.

Another thing to keep in mind is that there are still a few land mines in the desert around San Pedro, even in the touristy Valle de la Luna, and especially in the areas close to Peru. These were put down by the Pinochet dictatorship during tensions with Peru in the 1970s. In the most recent incident, the border between the two countries was shut down for a few days in February 2012, because the heavy rains dislodged some land mines and floated them onto the Panamericana. While you're unlikely to step on one, you may want to think twice before heading out to remote border areas by yourself.

ⓘ Getting There & Around

If you are taking a car to Peru or Bolivia, check with the consulate about the latest required forms. The border at Chacalluta is open from 8am to midnight (Chilean time) and 24 hours from Friday to Saturday. Be sure to bring extra gas, water and antifreeze. If heading north to Peru, you'll pass through the Complejo Fronterizo Santa Rosa at Tacna, open 7am to 11pm (Peru time), and 24 hours Friday to Saturday.

The easiest way to get around Norte Grande is by rental car, which you can arrange in major cities. Buses run frequently, offering top-notch service to nearly everywhere you'll want to go. Tour agencies run trips to the hard-to-reach national parks. While it's very expensive, you can fly to all of Norte Grande's major cities.

Arica

♩058 / POP 185.268

The pace of Arica is simply delightful. It's warm and sunny year-round, there's a cool pedestrian mall to flip-flop around come sunset and decent brown-sugar beaches are just a short walk from the town center. Top this off with some kick-ass surf breaks and a cool cliff-top War of the Pacific battlefield at El Morro, and you may just stay another day or two before you head up to nearby Parque Nacional Lauca or take an afternoon off from 'beach duty' to visit the Azapa Valley, home to some of the world's oldest known mummies.

History

Pre-Hispanic peoples have roamed this area for millennia. Arica itself was the terminus of an important trade route where coastal peoples exchanged fish, cotton and maize for the potatoes, wool and charqui (jerky) from the people of the precordillera and altiplano.

With the arrival of the Spanish in the early 16th century Arica became the port for the bonanza silver mine at Potosí, located in present-day Bolivia. As part of independent Peru, the city's 19th-century development lagged behind the frenzied activity in the nitrate mines further south. Following the dramatic battle over Arica's towering El Morro in the War of the Pacific, the city became de facto Chilean territory, an arrangement formalized in 1929.

⊙ Sights

Lording over the city is the dramatic headland, El Morro de Arica, a major battle site during the War of the Pacific. At the foot of El Morro are the manicured gardens of Plaza Vicuña Mackenna.

Museo de Sitio Colón 10   MUSEUM

(Colón 10; adult/child CH$2000/1000; ⊙10am-7pm Tue-Sun Jan-Feb, 10am-6pm Tue-Sun Mar-Dec) See the 32 excavated Chinchorro mummies in situ at this tiny museum below El Morro. They were discovered when an architect bought this former private home with the intention of converting it into a hotel. You can gape at the glass-protected bodies as they were found, in the sand below the floors, in different positions, complete with their funerary bundles, skins and feathers of marine fowl. There are a few infants, with red-painted mud masks. Go up the wooden ramp for a better vantage point of the mummies and then check the great view of the city from the covered terrace.

El Morro de Arica   HILL

This imposing coffee-colored shoulder of rock looms 110m over the city. It makes a great place to get your bearings, with vulture-eye views of the city, port and Pacific

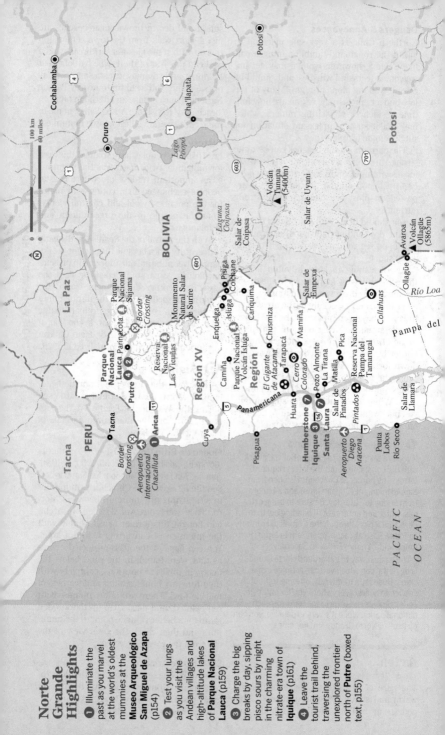

Norte Grande Highlights

1 Illuminate the past as you marvel at the world's oldest mummies at the **Museo Arqueológico San Miguel de Azapa** (p154)

2 Test your lungs as you visit the Andean villages and high-altitude lakes of **Parque Nacional Lauca** (p159)

3 Charge the big breaks by day, sipping pisco sours by night in the charming nitrate-era town of **Iquique** (p161)

4 Leave the tourist trail behind, traversing the unexplored frontier north of **Putre** (boxed text, p155)

5 Spot llama and vicuña on the way to the highest geyser field in the world El Tatio Geysers (p189)

6 Go sand-boarding in the Death Valley, just outside San Pedro de Atacama (p181)

7 Ponder the past as you wander through the spooky ghost towns of Humberstone and Santa Laura (p170)

La Quiaca

Jujuy

San Antonio de los Cobres

Salta

Payogasta

Cafayate

Salar de Olaroz

Laguna Colorada

Reserva Nacional de Fauna Andina Eduardo Avaroa

Portezuelo del Cajón

El Tatio Geysers

Volcán Licancábur (5916m)

San Pedro de Atacama

Toconao

Reserva Nacional Los Flamencos

Reserva Nacional Los Flamencos

Salar de Arizaro

ARGENTINA

Catamarca

Socompa

Border Crossing

Volcán Socompa (6051m)

Salar de Atacama

Valle de la Luna

Chiu Chiu

Amarugal

Quillagua

Chuquicamata

Coya

Calama

Sierra Gorda

Oficina Chacabuco

Baquedano

Panamericana

Región de Antofagasta (II)

Atacama Desert

Salar Punta Negra

Volcán Llullaillaco (6720m)

Región III

Tocopilla

Gatico

Cobija

María Elena

Pedro de Valdivia

Cordillera de la Costa

Monumento Natural La Portada

Reserva Nacional La Chimba

Mejillones

Aeropuerto Cerro Moreno

Bolsico

Juan López

Antofagasta

Mano del Desierto

Observatorio Cerro Paranal

Reserva Nacional Paposo

Paposo

Taltal

Las Tórtolas

Cifuncho

Parque Nacional Pan de Azúcar

Tropic of Capricorn

Arica

PACIFIC
OCEAN

Parque
Brasil

22

Av Máximo Lira

Pedro Montt

Prat

Estación Ferrocarril
Arica-La Paz

Plazoleta
Estación

Parque
General
Baquedano

Mercado
Colón

12

14

Colón

18 de Septiembre

Baquedano

Sernatur

1

6

24 17

5

Maipú

Plaza Vicuña
Mackenna

Plaza
Colón

18

25

8

20 27

13

19 16

3

28

Av Comandante San Martin

Bolognesi

Iglesia
San
Marcos

Mercado
Central

21 de Mayo

2

Sotomayor

El Morro
de Arica

Museo de Sitio
Colón 10

15

9

Trail

San Marcos

Yungay

El Morro

10

26

4

21

Ocean. This lofty headland was the site of a crucial battle in 1880, a year into the War of the Pacific, when the Chilean army assaulted and took El Morro from Peruvian forces in under an hour. The hilltop is accessible by car or taxi (CH$4000 round trip with a 30-minute wait), or by a steep footpath from the south end of Calle Colón. The story of El Morro is told step by step in the flag-waving **Museo Histórico y de Armas** (admission CH$600; ☉9am-5pm), which has information in Spanish and English.

Iglesia San Marcos
CHURCH

(Plaza Colón; admission free; ☉mass 8:30am Mon-Fri, 8pm Sat, 10am-noon & 8pm Sun) This Gothic-style church has a threefold claim to fame. First, it was designed by celebrated Parisian engineer Alexandre Gustave Eiffel, before his success with the Eiffel Tower. Second, it was prefabricated in Eiffel's Paris shop in the 1870s (at the order of the Peruvian president) then shipped right around the world

to be assembled on site. Still more curious is the construction itself: the entire church is made of stamped and molded cast iron, coated with paint.

FREE **Ex-Aduana de Arica** HISTORIC BUILDING
(☉8:30am-8pm daily Jan & Feb, 8:30am-5:30pm Mon-Thu & 8:30am-4:30pm Fri Mar-Dec) Eiffel designed this former customs house. Also prefabricated in Paris, it was assembled on site in 1874, with walls made of blocks and bricks stacked between metallic supports. Restored as the city's cultural center, it hosts a smattering of exhibitions and has an impressive 32-step wrought-iron spiral staircase.

🏃 Activities
Beaches

Surfers, swimmers and sunbathers can all find their niche along Arica's plentiful beaches. The Pacific is warm enough to bathe comfortably here, although there

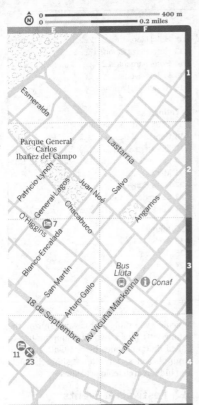

Beaches are also strung along the Panamericana Norte for 19km to the Peruvian border; these beaches are longer and rougher, but cleaner. The enormous **Playa Chinchorro**, 2km north of downtown, is veritable playland: a long wide beach strung with overpriced restaurants, ice-cream shops and, in holiday seasons, jet-ski rentals. The sea is a bit on the rough side but fine for experienced swimmers. The water here turns somewhat silty in February.

Playa Las Machas, a few kilometers north, is a surfers' haunt. Take bus 12 or 14 from 18 de Septiembre; get off on the corner of Av Antartica and Av España.

Surfing

The secret's out: Arica's reputation for terrific tubes has spread worldwide. It now hosts high-profile championships and tempts surfing film crews to the area. July sees the biggest breaks. As well as Playa Las Machas, expert surfers also hit the towering waves of El Gringo and El Buey at Isla de Alacrán, an expert point break south of Club de Yates.

You can get board shorts and other threads at **Solari Surf Shop** (233-773; 21 de Mayo 160).

Courses

Academia de Artes y Lenguas   LANGUAGE COURSE

(258-645; www.spanishinchile.blogspot.com; 21 de Mayo 483, 3rd fl) Offers Spanish courses (CH$6000 per hour or CH$162,000 for 30 hours) and occasional music lessons.

Tours

Several agencies in Arica offer anything from shopping day trips to Tacna to half-day visits to the Azapa Valley. The most popular tour takes in Parque Nacional Lauca (CH$20,000 for day trips, CH$70,000 to CH$100,000 for two days with lodging); note that many agencies don't go to Lauca on Mondays. While most people do it as a whirlwind day trip, it's better to devote at least two days to acclimatize properly.

Other available tours take in less-known altiplano destinations and precordillera villages. Four-day circuits to Lauca, Surire and Isluga are also available, with a drop-off in Iquique at the end (from CH$180,000).

The agencies listed offer the usual roster of tours (except Chinchorro) but each has its specialty. Prices vary according to the number of participants.

are strong ocean currents that make some beaches more dangerous for swimming than others. The mirrorlike waters of sheltered Playa La Lisera are the safest place to take young children swimming.

The most frequented beaches are south of town, along Av Comandante San Martín, where there are several sheltered coves and seaside restaurants. The closest is **Playa El Laucho**, a 20-minute walk away, followed by decidedly prettier **Playa La Lisera**, 2km south of downtown, with change rooms and showers. Both have only gentle surf and are worthy spots for swimming and lounging alike. Nearby, rougher **Playa Brava** is suitable for sunbathing only.

About 9km south of town, past a pungent fish-meal processing plant, is **Playa Corazones**, with wild camping and a kiosk. Just past the beach a trail leads to caves, cormorant colonies, tunnels and a sea-lion colony. Hire a cab or bike it here.

Arica

Raíces Andinas   GUIDED TOUR

(📞233-305; www.raicesandinas.com; Héroes del Morro 632) A well-run outfit recommended for encouraging better understanding of the local people. It specializes in trips of two or more days, and offers expeditions to Sajama in Bolivia via Lauca as well as adventures into Salar de Uyuni. It has a few bikes for rent (CH$7000 per day).

Suma Inti   GUIDED TOUR

(📞225-685; www.sumainti.cl; Gonzalo Cerda 1366) A little Aymara-run outfit which focuses on ancestral traditions; tours often feature rituals involving coca leaves and chants. Can also arrange longer treks and climbing expeditions.

Ruta Andina   GUIDED TOUR

(📞252-676; www.rutaandina.com; Bolognesi 362) The more interesting jaunts (two-day minimum) tackle the 'mission route' of the precordillera villages; you can trek, bike or go by 4x4. The longer trips to the undiscovered north, where the owner hails from, focus on cultural encounters and hidden spots. It also rents bikes (CH$10,000 per day) and sells bus tickets to Arequipa, Cusco and Lima.

Chinchorro Expediciones   BOAT TRIP

(📞233-404; chinchorroexpediciones@gmail.com; Muelle Pesquero) This specialist in marine expeditions offers three-hour sea safaris (with a picnic, swimming and kayaking) from the fishing jetty plus a two-day camping trip to Caleta de Camarones by 4x4, with hikes to virgin beaches, forgotten fishing hamlets and hidden archaeological sites.

🎉 Festivals & Events

Carnaval Andino con La Fuerza del Sol   CARNIVAL

Visitors in late January-early February witness blaring brass bands and dancing by traditional *comparsas* groups. The festival draws around 15,000 spectators during a three-day weekend, mostly happening on Av Comandante San Martín near El Morro.

Concurso Nacional de Cueca   DANCE

A folkloric dance festival in the Azapa Valley held each June.

Semana Ariqueña   FESTIVAL

Arica week is held in early June.

🛏 Sleeping

Taxi drivers earn commission from some *residenciales* (budget accommodations) and hotels; avoid these. Free camping is possible in the north sector of Playa Las Machas and at dark-sand, no-shade Playa Corazones, 8km south at the end of Av Comandante San Martín, with dirty, crowded sites; bring water.

Arica Surfhouse
HOSTEL $

(☎312-213; www.aricasurfhouse.cl; O'Higgins 661; dm per person CH$9500, s/d CH$20,000/27,000, without bathroom CH$14,000/23,000; @🖥) Doubling as Arica's surfer central, this is one of Arica's top hostels, with a variety of clean rooms, complimentary breakfast with real coffee, a great open-air communal area, 24-hour hot water and laundry service. There's a shuttle service to the beaches in winter months and they'll hook you up with surf classes and equipment rental.

Sunny Days
HOSTEL $

(☎241-038; www.sunny-days-arica.cl; Tomas Aravena 161; dm CH$9000, r per person incl breakfast with/without bathroom CH$10,000/12,000; P@🖥) A hop and a skip from the bus terminals in an alleyway behind Chinchorro beach, this supremely welcoming hostel is lovingly run by a helpful Kiwi-Chilean couple who live on site. Laundry, storage, bike rental, use of two communal kitchens and loads of info are all available. Rates include an 'all you can eat' breakfast at one big table. It's cash only.

TOP CHOICE Mirador El Buey
GUESTHOUSE $$

(☎325-530; www.miradorelbuey.cl; Punta del Este 605; s/d/ste CH$20,000/40,000/50,000;

P@🖥) The coolest beachside option, this whitewashed Med-style house sits on the residential hillside above La Lisera beach. It's for surfers with style, with hardwood floors, gorgeous terraces, sparkling kitchens, sweeping ocean views and a communal rooftop terrace with hammocks. There's surf equipment rental, surf classes, tow-in sessions, bike rental... You can rent a whole floor (sleeps up to eight) for CH$100,000.

Casa Beltrán
HOTEL $$

(☎257-898; www.hotelcasabeltran.cl; Sotomayor 266; s/d CH$50,000/60,000; P@🖥) Arica's only true boutique hotel, this sleek city center charmer inside an old *casona* comes with 17 well-designed rooms with dark hardwood floors and all the upscale trimmings. Some rooms have balconies. The gourmet restaurant (closed Sundays) serves *almuerzos* (set lunches) and afternoon tea overlooking a leafy patio. The 4th-floor terrace has great views of El Morro.

Hostal Jardín del Sol
HOSTEL $

(☎232-795; www.hostaljardindelsol.cl; Sotomayor 848; s/d incl breakfast CH$11,000/$22,000; @🖥) It's been here for ages but still lives up to its reputation as one of Arica's best hostels,

NORTE GRANDE ARICA

10 STEPS TO A CHINCHORRO MUMMY

The Chinchorro mummies are the oldest known artificially preserved bodies in the world, predating their Egyptian counterparts by more than two millennia. They were created by small groups that fished and hunted along the coast of southern Peru and northern Chile from around 7000 BC. The mummification process was remarkably elaborate for such a simple culture. While the order and methods evolved over the millennia, the earliest mummies were made more or less by doing the following:

» dismembering the corpse's head, limbs and skin

» removing the brain by splitting the skull or drawing it through the base

» taking out other internal organs

» drying the body with hot stones or flames

» repacking the body with sticks, reeds, clay and camelid fur

» reassembling parts, perhaps sewing them together with cactus spines

» slathering the body with thick paste made from ash

» replacing the skin, patched with sea-lion hide

» attaching a wig of human hair and clay mask

» painting the mummy with black manganese (or, in later years, red ochre)

Several hundred Chinchorro mummies have now been discovered; all ages are represented and there's no evidence to suggest that mummification was reserved for a special few. Interestingly, some mummies were repeatedly repainted, suggesting that the Chinchorro kept and possibly displayed them for long periods before eventual burial. Millennia later, the conquistadores were appalled by a similar Inka practice, in which mummified ancestors were dressed up and paraded in religious celebrations.

HISTORY OF NORTE GRANDE

Despite its distance from Santiago, Norte Grande has always played a strong role in Chile's political and economic arenas, thanks mostly to the vast mineral wealth sitting just below the rocky surface. And even with its extreme desert aridity, it has sustained humans for many thousands of years.

The earliest culture to leave its mark was the Chinchorro, famous for its extraordinary burial practices. Coastal Chango peoples also fished from inflatable sealskin canoes and hunted guanaco here in pre-Columbian times. Far into the desert, irrigated agricultural practices adopted from the Tiwanaku culture, which had its power center near Lake Titicaca in present-day Bolivia, sustained the Atacameño people who lived in oases near Calama and San Pedro de Atacama. These cultures – along with the Inka, who enjoyed a brief reign here from 1470 till the time of conquest – left impressive fortresses, agricultural terraces and huge stylized designs or geoglyphs on hillsides. Representations of llama trains still decorate the same valleys that served as pre-Columbian pack routes from cordillera to coast.

The indigenous populations were largely subdued during the conquest, which took place in the later part of the 16th century, with the Spaniards implementing the *encomienda* system, by which the Crown granted individual Spaniards rights to indigenous labor and tribute, and establishing ports in the coastal towns of Arica, Pisagua and Iquique. But pockets of independent Changos remained, and the area wasn't substantially resettled until large deposits of 'white gold' – nitrate (saltpeter) – brought the first boom to the region in the 1810s.

Interestingly, this part of the country was not actually considered Chilean until the late 19th century. It was claimed rather by Peru and Bolivia. However, that all changed with the pivotal War of the Pacific (1879–84), which was provoked by treaty disputes, the presence of thousands of Chilean workers who were in Bolivian mines, and Bolivian attempts to increase the taxation on mineral exports. Within the next five years, Chile had taken control of the staggeringly important land, which was rich in copper and nitrate.

However, Chileans were not the only ones to reap the benefits. Foreign prospectors had been sniffing around for some time, and moved quickly to capitalize on Chilean land gains. Beneficiaries included British speculator John Thomas North, who went on to take control of the railroads and more or less dominate the region's postwar economy.

The nitrate boom was uniquely explosive here. Nitrate *oficinas* (company towns) such as Humberstone, also known as the *salitreras,* flourished in the early 20th century and became bubbles of energy and profit in the lifeless desert. Large port cities such as Antofagasta and Iquique also began to flourish. However, the swift rise of the industry would be followed by a sharp fall. New petroleum-based fertilizers were devised in Europe and the nitrate-mining industry withered, exposing Chile's crippling dependence upon its revenue.

The nitrate bust drove the nation to near bankruptcy, and scores of 19th- and 20th-century nitrate ghost towns now pockmark both sides of the Panamericana. Luckily for Chile, Norte Grande had another trump card up its sleeve – copper. Vast veins of this valuable resource sprang to the country's rescue and still keep it afloat today, especially with copper prices soaring. One of the world's largest open-pit copper mines, at Chuquicamata, is just one of many vast mines honeycombing the region. But with the boom came a slew of unique, modern problems, including environmental degradation, higher prices, overcrowding and pollution.

The region's rich pickings have at times acted as a kind of political smokescreen; the steady flow of revenue allowed Chilean politicians to postpone dealing with major social and political issues until well into the 20th century.

Militant trade unions also first developed in the north, during the late 19th and early 20th century, and introduced a powerful new factor into Chilean politics.

with small but spotless rooms, fans included. Guests mingle on the leafy patio, the upstairs terrace, in the shared kitchen and the lounge room. There's a book exchange and lots of tourist info.

Hotel Samaña HOTEL $$

(☏255-453; www.hotelsamana.cl, in Spanish; Maipú 271; s/d CH$33,000/36,500; P@☎) This sparkling new hotel smack at the heart of Arica's commercial center has well-appointed rooms set around a sunny central courtyard, each with cable TV and spacious bathroom. Rooms get remarkably hot, but luckily come equipped with fans.

Hotel Savona HOTEL $$

(☏231-000; www.hotelsavona.cl, in Spanish; Yungay 380; s/d CH$25,500/36,000; P@☎☀) This snowy-white hotel at the foot of El Morro has a concertina-style front and an attractive inner patio with bougainvillea blooms and a pill-shaped pool. The classic-style rooms are a bit clunky but well equipped. Those overlooking the pool can get noisy.

Hotel Inti-Jaya HOTEL $$

(☏230-536; www.hotelintijaya.cl; 21 de Mayo 850; s/d CH$19,350/32,500; P✲@☎) Behind its glass-fronted facade, this over-the-top hotel hides intricate wood-carvings, oversized mirrors, polished stone, statues and potted plants. Rooms are well equipped, with safes and a toiletry kit (for CH$3000). Check out the views from the 4th-floor terrace. Cash only.

Hotel Arica HOTEL $$$

(☏254-540; www.panamericanahoteles.cl; Av Comandante San Martín 599; s/d CH$95,000/112,000, cabin for 2 CH$130,000; P✲@☎☀) This large-scale oceanfront resort offers a range of rooms, including cabins overlooking the ocean, plus all four-star trappings. It's south of the center by Playa El Laucho. Request a room with an ocean view and check for web-only specials.

Hostelling International Doña Inés HOSTEL $

(☏248-108; hiarica@hostelling.cl; Pasaje Manuel Rojas 2864; dm incl breakfast CH$7800-8500, d CH$16,500-18,500; @☎) Run by the unofficial nightlife king of Arica, this hostel doubles as a hip hang-out, with graffiti-covered walls, a patio with foosball, breakfast till noon and weekly barbecues and clubbing. It's a 20-minute walk from the bus station. Paragliding tours available.

Hostal Huanta-Jaya HOSTEL $

(☏314-605; hostal.huanta.jaya@gmail.com; 21 de Mayo 660; s/d CH$12,000/20,000; ☎) The pleasant, clean and spacious, if a bit dark, rooms are reached via a long hallway lined with African-themed artwork. There's a small shared lounge and dining room, where breakfast is served (CH$1500 extra).

Hotel Plaza Colón HOTEL $

(☏232-125; www.hotelplazacolon.cl, in Spanish; San Marcos 261; s/d CH$24,000/30,000; P@☎) The superb position facing Iglesia San Marcos and El Morro make up for the stale rooms, though some have lots of light and fab vistas (ask to see a few).

Hotel Mar Azul HOTEL $

(☏256-272; www.hotelmarazul.cl, in Spanish; Colón 665; s/d CH$15,000/20,000; ☎☀) The flag-fronted Mar Azul at the heart of town has an all-white interior, an alluring little outdoor pool, cable TV, breakfast till 11am and massages on request.

Residencial Arica GUESTHOUSE $

(☏255-399; 18 de Septiembre 466; d CH$12,000, s/d without bathroom CH$6000/9000; ☎) Clean and central, this friendly joint is a good bet for budget hunters, with nine cheerful rooms boasting TVs and fans but spongy beds.

✖ Eating

Mata-Rangi SEAFOOD $

(Muelle Pesquero; set menu CH$3800-4800, mains CH$3500-4500; ☉lunch only) Superb seafood is served at this adorable spot hanging over the harbor by the fishing jetty. A wooden shack-style place packed with wind chimes, it has a breezy dining room and a small terrace above the ocean. Get here early to grab a seat or be prepared to wait.

Zumería CAFE $

(Sotomayor 193; snacks CH$750-900; ☉closed dinner & Sun) Grab a freshly squeezed fruit juice or smoothie, a healthy wrap or sandwich and delicious homemade cake at this tiny take-out spot. Great for breakfast, picnic on the beach or a quick lunch on the small counter.

El Arriero PARRILLA $$

(21 de Mayo 385; mains CH$4000-9100; ☉closed Sun) This old-school eatery is perfect for red-blooded carnivores who don't mind waiting for an old-fashioned *parrillada* (a mixture of grilled meats). Expect gracious service and an aging steakhouse atmosphere.

Boulevard Vereda Bolognesi CAFETERIA $

(Bolognesi 340; ⊘closed Sun) Hip little shopping mall with a clutch of cool cafes, restaurants and bars. Choose between a salad bar, a Peruvian joint, an Italian trattoria or a sushi bar, and eat on the central patio. There's real espresso, too.

Salon de Te 890 PIZZERIA $

(21 de Mayo 890; pizzas CH$2700-3600; ⊘closed Sun) Come to this cheerful teahouse for the great pizzas and cakes served in a pair of pastel-colored rooms with hardwood floors. Don't miss the signature Siete Sabores cake.

Cafe del Mar CAFETERIA $

(21 de Mayo 260; mains CH$2550-4200; ⊘closed Sun) It's more about the location than the food – although the menu is quite big – at this buzzy cafe, worth a bite at its sidewalk tables, great for people-watching.

Maracuyá SEAFOOD $$

(Av Comandante San Martín 0321; mains CH$6000-11,000) To treat yourself to a superb seafood meal complete with bow-tie service and sea view, head to this villa-style restaurant next to Playa El Laucho.

La Bomba CHILEAN $

(Colón 357; set lunch menu CH$2800, mains CH$2000-5000) Hang out with the locals at this unassuming eatery inside the fire station. It serves cheap Chilean mainstays in fit-for-firemen portions.

🍷 Drinking

Take time out over a hot coffee or a chilled Escudo in one of a dozen streetside cafes strung along the 21 de Mayo pedestrian strip. At night, seek out the bars along Bolognesi between 21 de Mayo and Plaza Colón.

Así Sea Club BAR

(San Marcos 251; ⊘closed Sun) This swank hideaway inside a rambling historic townhouse has a set of sleek rooms featuring original detail, and a back patio. It serves delicious lunches on weekdays (CH$2800) and on weekend nights, a menu of *tablas* (shared plates; CH$3900 to CH$7500), cocktails and all-Chilean wines, paired with loungey tunes.

Naif BAR

(Colón 342) Food served by the kilo during the day and a smoky atmosphere with loud music and a young crowd keep this cavern-

ous place going at all times. There's live music on weekends, and DJs on some week nights.

Barrabás BAR

(Av Comandante San Martín 222) Head to this newly opened spot right on the ocean for sunset cocktails on the banquettes with dazzling views of crashing waves below. There's food during the day (mains CH$5100 to CH$8500) and talk of bringing in DJs.

Vieja Habana BAR

(21 de Mayo 487) Has salsa and bachata classes on weeknights (CH$2000) to get those gringo hips shaking, and functions as a lively *salsoteca* (salsa club) on weekends.

☆ Entertainment

Some of the hippest bars and discos are strung along Playa Chinchorro, including **Soho** (cover with drink CH$6000-8000; ⊘closed Sun), the city's most happening disco, and the attached pub **Drake** (cover with drink CH$6000-8000; ⊘closed Sun), both of which get a variety of DJs as well as live salsa and rock bands. Steps from these two is **Bar Previa** (Av Buenos Aires 160), which has a large terrace with live music shows and karaoke nights and stays open seven days a week; if you spend more than CH$5000 in drinks, you get free entry to Soho.

🛍 Shopping

A part-kitsch, part-crafts artisans' market is strung along Pasaje Bolognesi, a narrow passageway running from Plaza Colón.

Poblado Artesanal MARKET

(Hualles 2825; ⊘10:30am-1:30pm & 3:30-7pm Tue-Sun) On the outskirts of Arica, near the Panamericana Sur, is this full-on shopping experience: a mock altiplano village filled with serious craft shops and studios, selling everything from ceramic originals to finely tuned musical instruments. The village even has its own church, a replica of the one in Parinacota, complete with copies of its fascinating murals. *Taxis colectivos* (shared taxis) 7 and 8 pass near the entrance, as do buses 7, 8 and 9.

ℹ Information

Dangers & Annoyances

While Arica is a very safe city, it has a reputation for pickpockets. Be especially cautious at bus terminals and beaches.

Internet Access

Several internet cafes can be found on and around 21 de Mayo and Bolognesi; most charge CH$400 per hour.

Medical Services

Hospital Dr Juan Noé (☎232-242; 18 de Septiembre 1000)

Pharmacy (cnr Colón & 18 de Septiembre)

Money

There are numerous 24-hour ATMs as well as *casas de cambio,* which change US dollars, Peruvian, Bolivian and Argentine currency, and euros, along the pedestrian mall (21 de Mayo).

Telephone

The mall is lined with public payphones and phone centers are found throughout the city.

Post

Post office (Prat 305) On a walkway between Pedro Montt and Prat.

Tourist Information

Conaf (☎201-200; tarapaca@conaf.cl; Av Vicuña Mackenna 820; ⊙8:30am-5:35pm Mon-Fri) This outlet carries some useful information about Región I (Tarapacá) national parks. To get there, take *micro* 9 or *colectivos* 7, 2 or 23 from downtown (*micro* CH$350, *colectivo* CH$500).

Sernatur (☎252-054; infoarica@sernatur.cl; San Marcos 101; ⊙9am-8pm Mon-Fri, 10am-2pm Sat Jan-Feb, 9am-7pm Mar-Dec) Friendly service with some brochures on Tarapacá and other Chilean regions.

① Getting There & Away

From Arica, travelers can head north across the Peruvian border to Tacna and Lima, south toward Santiago or east to Bolivia.

Air

Aeropuerto Internacional Chacalluta is 18km north of Arica, near the Peruvian border. Santiago-bound passengers should sit on the left side of the plane for awesome views of the Andes and the interminable brownness of the Atacama Desert.

Lan (☎600-526-2000; www.lan.com; Arturo Prat 391) has direct daily flights to Santiago (CH$223,000, 2½ hours) and to Iquique (CH$31,500, 50 minutes).

Sky (☎600-600-2828; www.skyairline.cl, in Spanish; 21 de Mayo 356) has less frequent flights to Santiago (around CH$85,200), Calama (CH$51,500) and Iquique (CH$19,600). It also flies to Arequipa (CH$52,000) on Thursdays and Sundays and to La Paz daily (CH$71,200).

Bus

Arica has two main bus terminals. **Terminal Rodoviario de Arica** (Terminal de Buses; ☎241-390; Diego Portales 948) houses most companies traveling south to destinations in Chile. Next door, **Terminal Internacional de Buses** (☎248-709; Diego Portales 1002) handles international and some regional destinations. The area is notorious for petty thievery, so be sure to keep an eye on your luggage at all times. To reach the terminals, take *colectivo* 8 from Maipú or San Marcos; a taxi costs between CH$1500 and CH$2000.

More than a dozen companies have offices in Terminal Rodoviario de Arica, and ply destinations toward the south, from Iquique to Santiago. Some major ones are **Buses Pullman Santa Rosa** (☎241-029), **Buses Zembrano** (☎248-672), **Flota Barrios** (☎223-587), **Pullman Bus** (☎241-972), **Pullman Carmelita** (☎241-591), **Pullman San Andrés** (☎242-971), **Ramos Cholele** (☎221-029) and **Tur Bus** (☎222-217).

A schedule board inside the terminal helps you find your bus (but it's not always accurate). Buses on Sunday run less often.

Some of the standard destinations and fares are shown here.

DESTINATION	COST (CH$)	DURATION (HR)
Antofagasta	16,000	10
Calama	16,000	9
Copiapó	18,000	18
Iquique	7000	4
La Paz, Bolivia	8000	9
La Serena	25,000	23
Santiago	30,000	27

Bus Lluta (cnr Chacabuco & Av Vicuña Mackenna) goes to Poconchile and Lluta four to five times daily (CH$900 to CH$2000, one hour).

Buses La Paloma (☎222-710; Germán Riesco 2071) travels to the Belén precordillera villages of Socoroma on Wednesday and Saturday (CH$3500), Belén on Tuesday and Friday (CH$3500), leaving Arica at 7am and returning at 1pm, and to Putre daily (CH$3500) at 7am, returning at 2pm. La Paloma also goes to Codpa on Monday, Wednesday and Friday at 8am (CH$2500, three hours), returning at 5pm. It's recommended you take a taxi to this area when leaving early in the morning.

Transportes Gutierréz (☎229-338; Esteban Ríos 2140) also has buses to Putre on Wednesday and Friday at 7:30am and Sunday at 8pm (CH$3500, three hours).

For Parinacota (CH$5000) and Parque Nacional Lauca, look for **Trans Cali Internacional** (☎261-068; Oficina 15) in the international terminal. Trips depart daily at 9:15am.

To get to Tacna, Peru, **Adsubliata** (☑263-526) buses leave the international terminal every half-hour (CH$2000); *colectivos* charge CH$3500. No produce is allowed across the border.

To get to La Paz, Bolivia (around CH$8000, nine hours), the comfiest and fastest service is with **Chile Bus** (☑260-505), but cheaper buses are available with **Trans Cali Internacional** (☑261-068) and **Trans Salvador** (☑246-064) in the international bus terminal. Buses on this route will drop passengers at Parque Nacional Lauca, but expect to pay full fare to La Paz.

Buses Géminis (☑351-465), in the main terminal, goes to Salta and Jujuy in Argentina via Calama and San Pedro de Atacama (CH$42,000) on Monday, Thursday and Saturday at 10pm.

Train

Trains to Tacna (CH$1900, 1½ hours) depart from **Estación Ferrocarril Arica-Tacna** (☑097-633-2896; Av Máximo Lira 791) at 9am, Monday to Saturday.

❶ Getting Around

To/From the Airport

Aeropuerto Internacional Chacalluta (☑211-116) is 18km north of Arica. Shared taxis charge CH$3500 to the airport. In town, call **Radio Taxi Aeropuerto Chacalluta** (☑254-812; Patricio Lynch 371). **Arica Service** (☑314-031) runs airport shuttles (CH$3000 per person). **Radio Taxi service** (☑259-000) – if you don't like sharing your cab – charges CH$7000.

Bicycle

You can rent mountain bikes from several tour agencies and hostels in town.

Bus & Taxi

Local buses (*micros*) and shared taxis (*colectivos*) connect downtown with the main bus terminal. *Taxis colectivos* are faster and more frequent, costing CH$500 per person. Destinations are clearly marked on an illuminated sign atop the cab. *Micros* run to major destinations, and cost CH$400 per person. **Radio Taxi service** (☑259-000) – if you don't like sharing your cab – is between CH$1500 and CH$1800, depending on your destination.

Car

Rental cars are available, starting at around CH$22,000 per day. The two locals are cheaper than the chains.

Cactus Rent a Car (☑257-430; cactusrent@hotmail.com; General Lagos 666)

Europcar (☑258-911) At the airport

Hertz (☑231-487; Baquedano 999)

Klasse (☑254-498; www.klasserentacar.cl; Av General Velásquez 762, Local 25)

Around Arica

AZAPA VALLEY

Some of the world's oldest known mummies reside in the Azapa Valley's superb **Museo Arqueológico San Miguel de Azapa** (adult/child CH$2000/1000; ☉10am-7pm Jan & Feb, 10am-6pm Mar-Dec). Set in a lush garden dotted with tall palm trees, the museum has two sections. The original exhibition hall displays a large assemblage of exhibits from 7000 BC right up to the Spanish invasion, from dioramas, baskets and masks to pottery, panflutes and an enormous 18th-century olive press. Well-written booklets in several languages are available to carry around this section. Past the outdoor 'petroglyph park' is the new hall in a modern concrete building backed by mountains and olive groves. Inside is a swank permanent exhibit dedicated to Chinchorro mummies, with display cases featuring tools, clothing and adornments used in the process as well as infant mummies, a few skulls and lifesize figures of Chinchorro peoples.

Once you've taken in the mummies, pop over to the cute **Machakuna cafe** (☑098-684-7577; sandwiches CH$800-2500) across the road, which serves *almuerzos* (set lunches) for CH$2300 as well as natural juices, coffee and sandwiches. The owner can arrange horseback rides into the valley and to the beach, from CH$15,000. Arrange at least a day ahead.

The museum is 12km east of Arica. From Parque General Carlos Ibáñez del Campo in Arica, at the corner of Chacabuco and Patricio Lynch, yellow *colectivos* charge CH$1000 (one way) to the front gate of the museum.

Chile 11 Highway

About 10km north of Arica, the Panamericana intersects paved Chile 11, which ushers traffic east up the valley of the Río Lluta to Poconchile and on to Putre and Parque Nacional Lauca. The road features a clutch of worthy stops, if you want to break up the journey. Note that this heavily trafficked winding route toward La Paz, Bolivia, gets about 500 trucks per day.

A short distance inland from the intersection of the Panamericana and Chile 11, you'll see the pre-Columbian **Lluta geoglyphs**, also known as the Gigantes de Lluta. These are sprinkled along an otherwise barren slope of the southern Lluta Valley; markers indicate when to pull over and squint toward the hillsides. The diverse figures include a frog, an eagle, llamas and the occasional human. These delightful geoglyphs recall the importance of pre-Columbian pack trains on the route to Tiwanaku.

In the village of Poconchile, along a gravel road that runs for 1km along train tracks from the marked turnoff of Chile 11 is a slightly surreal Hare Krishna ashram called **Eco Truly** (📞096-875-0732; www.ecotrulyarica.cl, in Spanish; Sector Linderos, Km29; campsites per person CH$4000, r incl breakfast CH$8000). It's a nice spot to stop for vegetarian lunch (CH$4000, served 1pm to 3:30pm) or a sugar-free pie, or stay on for a few days of simplified relaxation. If you spend part of the day helping out with errands, you get free food and discounted lodging. Free yoga classes are held on Monday, Wednesday and Friday mornings; they do temazcal (sweat lodge) rituals last weekend of the month.

There's little proselytizing going on – though residents are happy to share their religious and spiritual views – and the funky conical 'truly' rooms are made with local and recycled materials. To get to Poconchile, 35km from Arica, take Bus Lluta to the end of the line at the police checkpoint. *Taxis colectivos* charge around CH$2000 from outside Arica's international bus terminal; you'll have to wait for it to fill up.

The road begins to climb steadily here so it's wise to stop by the roadside **Posada Pueblo Taki** (Km88; campsites per person with a loaf of homemade bread & coca tea CH$7000), where artsy owners Andrea and Alexis serve delicious herbal teas that will help you adjust to the altitude, and check your oxygen levels and heart pressure. They've raised and home-schooled their six children in their wind- and solar-powered home at 3166m, and now run a nonprofit that focuses on the Andean world and offbeat guided tours that highlight the area's hidden spots (CH$6000

NORTE GRANDE CHILE 11 HIGHWAY

WORTH A TRIP

THE NEW FRONTIER IN THE ANDEAN FOOTHILLS

There's a new frontier for adventurous travelers who want to get off the beaten path near Arica: a string of isolated villages that necklaces the Andean foothills. A series of rough gravel roads connects these pretty traditional hamlets in the precordillera, including **Belén**, **Saxamar**, **Tignamar** and **Codpa**. Highlights include colonial churches, ancient agricultural terraces and *pukarás* (pre-Hispanic fortifications). There's been a recent effort to develop heritage tourism in this Andean region; the project is being promoted as the 'mission route.' This has been headed up by **Fundación Altiplano** (www.fundacionaltiplano.cl), a foundation that is trying to promote sustainable development of these nearly forgotten Andean communities.

For travelers with vehicles (note that a 4x4 is highly recommended, if not imperative) this spectacular route is a great way to get from Codpa to Putre, or vice versa. Make sure you get a good road map and don't attempt this journey during the winter season (December through March), since rivers run amok due to heavy rains and often wash the roads away.

Accommodations and eating options in these villages are limited to a few simple *hospedajes* (budget accommodations); ask around when you arrive and you'll likely find someone willing to host you in their home. The fertile oasis of the Codpa valley is home to the area's best place to overnight, **Codpa Valley Lodge** (www.codpavalleylodge.cl; d incl breakfast CH$60,000;🐾), run by Azimut 360. This solar energy–powered hideaway (there's electricity only two hours nightly) has cozy rustic rooms with private patios set around a swimming pool, and a good restaurant. The lodge offers a variety of tours, including a scenic two-day overland to Putre through the precordillera, which includes a night in Putre, takes in Lauca and Surire the following day and returns to the lodge on the second night. It costs CH$255,000, based on two people; the price goes down with more participants. Make sure you try the sweet dessert wine called *pintatani*, which is produced only in the Codpa valley.

La Paloma in Arica has departures for Belen and Codpa several times per week; see (p153) for transportation details. It's not possible, however, to make a loop through all of the villages on public transportation.

Chile 11 & Parque Nacional Lauca

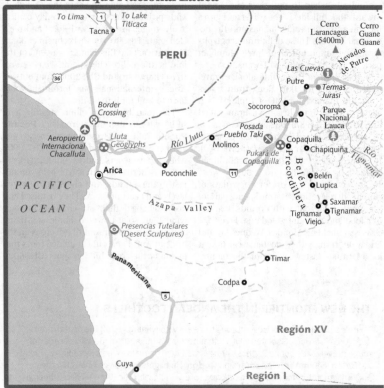

per hour). Stop for delicious freshly baked bread, hot drinks and a chat with this fascinating couple.

Teetering on the brink of a spectacular chasm 1.5km beyond the *posada* (inn) is 12th-century fortress **Pukará de Copaquilla** (admission free), built to protect pre-Columbian farmlands below and once home to 500 people. Peering over the canyon's edge will reward with views of the abandoned terraces and forbidding mountains all around. There's a great echo, too. At around 10am, you can sometimes see condors flying above the fortress.

Beyond Copaquilla, paved Chile 11 climbs steadily through the precordillera toward the altiplano proper. If you're driving, the Aymara farming village of **Socoroma** on the colonial pack route between Arica and Potosí is worth a quick detour. To see its cobbled streets, a 17th-century church that's currently being restored, bits of colonial remains and terraced hills of oregano, take the serpentine road that descends from Chile 11 for 4.5km.

Putre

📍 058 / POP 1977

Pocket-sized Putre is an appealing Aymara village perched precariously on a hillside in the precordillera at a dizzying elevation of 3530m. Just 150km from Arica, it serves as an ideal acclimatization stop en route to the elevated Parque Nacional Lauca on the altiplano. As such, this languid mountain village now hosts a number of hostels and tour agencies.

Originally a 16th-century *reducción* (Spanish settlement to facilitate control of the native population), the village retains houses with late-colonial elements. In the surrounding hills local farmers raise alfalfa for llamas, sheep and cattle on extensive

stone-faced agricultural terraces of even greater antiquity.

☞ Tours

Tours to Parque Nacional Lauca aren't necessarily cheaper than from Arica but will give you more time to acclimatize to the altitude. At the time of research, there were serious roadworks en route to and inside the park, part of the new Corredor Oceanico route that will connect Brazil to Chile via Bolivia. This has had an impact on visits to the park, as most day trips involved long waits at road blocks.

Other destinations reachable from Putre include Salar de Surire, Parque Nacional Volcán Isluga and the little-explored northern wilderness toward the border with Peru. The latter, with spectacular areas such as the canyons of Quebrada de Allane and the multicolored mountains of Suriplaza, is becoming the new frontier for explorer types, so get there before everyone else discovers it.

Note that things seriously wind down in Putre from mid-December through February, which is the rainy season. Some areas become inaccessible, roads get washed away and many agencies work by request only. Before jumping on the bus from Arica during this time of year, call one of the agencies in Putre (they only check their email sporadically) to arrange things ahead of your arrival. Otherwise you may find yourself waiting a couple of days to find a tour.

Before booking a tour, ask what kind of vehicle they use, whether the guide speaks English (which is rare) and if they carry oxygen. These are all factors that can make or break your trip.

Alto Andino Nature Tours   BIRDWATCHING
(☏099-890-7291;   www.birdingaltoandino.com; Baquedano 299) Alaskan biologist Barbara Knapton offers customized birdwatching, wildflower and natural-history excursions in either English or Spanish. Make reservations well in advance. She joins clients in their car as a guide, or otherwise has to rent a vehicle.

Terrace Lodge & Tours   GUIDED TOUR
(☏584-275; www.terracelodge.com; Circunvalación 25) Flavio of Terrace Lodge is not only a fountain of info but runs a range of excellently guided tours, which take you away from the crowds and to some hidden spots, both in the immediate area around Putre as well as further up north.

Tour Andino   ADVENTURE TOUR
(☏099-011-0702; www.tourandino.com; Baquedano 340) A one-man show run by local guide, Justino Jirón. While he does the usual roster of tours – which get mixed reviews – his specialty is treks into the surrounding mountains and volcano climbs.

Cali Tours   GUIDED TOUR
(☏098-536-1242; www.calitours.cl; Baquedano 399) Specialist in adventure tours and treks, this outfit also rents mountain bikes (CH$12,000 per day) and cars (from CH$50,000 for a small one), and sells bus tickets to La Paz (daily departures at 11:30am, six hours, CH$7000 to CH$20,000 depending on the season).

Mayuru Tours   GUIDED TOUR
(☏098-844-6568; www.mayurutour.com; Baquedano 411) Another local outfit that will arrange

anything from treks to the ancient wall paintings of Wilacabrani to two-day ventures into Isluga via Surire.

Festivals & Events

Carnaval
CARNIVAL

Visitors get dragged into the fun during Putre's Carnaval in February. Scores of balloon-bombs filled with flour are pelted around, not to mention clouds of *chaya* (multicolored paper dots). Two noncompetitive groups, the older *banda* and younger *tarqueada*, provide the music. The event ends with the burning of the *momo*, a figure symbolizing the frivolity of Carnaval.

Feria Regional
FAIR

Held in November; music and dancing are accompanied by dozens of stalls selling crafts, regional produce and tasty local dishes.

Sleeping

At the time of research, a couple of the otherwise solid budget options were booked through 2013 by miners and road workers. During Putre's high season, July through October, book well in advance.

TOP CHOICE Terrace Lodge & Cafe
LODGE $$

(☎584-275; www.terracelodge.com; Circunvalación 25; d/tr CH$30,000/37,000; ℗@🖙) A friendly pair of multilingual Italian expats runs this hideaway with five rustic-chic rooms. Units are small but well-heated, with mountain views through tiny long windows, down duvets and all-day hot water. Free breakfast is served till 9am in the cafe, which also whips up real Italian espressos and cappuccinos. Look for the sign as you enter town. It's also the only place in town that accepts plastic. Book way ahead. The owner also runs tours.

Hotel Q'antati
HOTEL $$

(☎228-916; reservashotelqantati@vtr.net; Hijuela 208; d CH$48,000; ℗) The favorite of tour groups, this Aymara-run hotel is Putre's most upscale and priciest option, with 24-hour hot showers, firm beds, heated doubles with unheated large bathrooms and a fancy living room with a fireplace. Get rooms 8, 9 or 10 for best views. It's behind the army barracks on the edge of town.

Hotel Kukuli
HOTEL $

(☎099-161-4709; reservashotelkukuli@gmail.com; off Baquedano; s/d CH$20,000/30,000; ℗🖙) Kukuli is a decent choice on the main strip, with spotless rooms sporting either a small terrace or a sunny alcove but, regrettably, no heating. If the hotel seems closed, inquire in the owner's store at Baquedano 301.

Hostal Cali
HOSTEL $

(☎318-456; contacto@calitours.com; Baquedano s/n; s/d CH$15,000/24,000, d without bathroom $18,000; ℗@🖙) This family-run spot with 12 rooms is a good bet for budget-busters. The hot gas-heated showers are a godsend, and you can request a heater for about CH$4000 extra. It offers tour services, too.

Residencial La Paloma
GUESTHOUSE $

(☎099-197-9319; lapalomaputre@hotmail.com; O'Higgins 353; r per person with/without bathroom CH$6000/8000; ℗) Putre's most established *residencial* and restaurant slots nine rooms around two concrete courtyards. It has hot showers (morning and evening only) and noisy rooms. Enter from the back on Baquedano or through the restaurant.

Eating

Residencial La Paloma has a decent restaurant, which serves simple breakfasts and lunches.

Cantaverdi
INTERNATIONAL $

(Arturo Perez Canto 339; set lunch CH$4000, mains CH$4500-6500; ☉lunch & dinner) Two rustic rooms with contemporary artwork and a fireplace right off the main plaza. The menu features a few Andean staple dishes as well as crowd-pleasers like sandwiches, pizzas, *tablas* and empanadas.

Rosamel
CHILEAN $

(Latorre 400; set meal CH$3500) Rub shoulders with a mixed bunch of locals and road workers in this modest restaurant serving set meals under fluorescent lights. It opens for breakfast (from CH$1000) as early as 5am.

Kuchu Marka
CHILEAN $

(Baquedano 351; set lunch CH$3500, set dinner CH$5500; ☉lunch & dinner) Colorful and cozy Kuchu Marka dishes out tasty local staples like alpaca steaks as well as a range of vegetarian options and drinks.

Information

BancoEstado (Arturo Prat 301) Putre's only bank, off the main plaza, has a 24-hour ATM, which – note – doesn't accept some Visa cards. It changes US cash and euros but it's wise to bring sufficient cash with you from Arica.

Centro de Llamadas & Internet Campanani (Baquedano 500; ☺9am-10pm) Call home or get online.

Hospital (Baquedano 261) This 24-hour clinic will give you oxygen if the dizzying altitude gets to you.

Oficina de Información Turística (☎594-897; imputre@entelchile.net; Latorre s/n; ☺10am-1pm & 2-5:45pm Mon, 8:30am-1pm & 2-5:45pm Tue-Fri) A handy resource on the plaza, although it has no town maps and opens only sporadically.

❶ Getting There & Away

Putre is 150km east of Arica via paved Chile 11, the international highway to Bolivia. **Buses La Paloma** (☎222-710; Germán Riesco 2071) serves Putre daily, departing Arica at 7am, returning at 2pm (CH$3500). Buy return tickets at Hotel Kukuli.

Transportes Gutierréz (☎229-338; Esteban Ríos 2140) also runs from Arica to Putre on Wednesday and Friday at 7:30am and Sunday at 8pm (CH$3500, three hours). From Putre, buses leave for Arica on Wednesday and Friday at 5pm.

Buses to Parinacota, in Parque Nacional Lauca, pass the turnoff to Putre, which is 5km from the main highway.

Parque Nacional Lauca

It's not just the exaggerated altitude (between 3000m and 6300m above sea level) that leaves visitors to this national park breathless. Lauca is home to some breathtaking altiplano scenery, snow-sprinkled volcanoes, sparkling lakes and isolated hot springs. It also shelters pretty highland villages and a huge variety of wildlife. The nimble-footed vicuña (see boxed text, p161) and the rabbitlike viscacha are the star attractions, but you're also likely to see other South American camelids and a variety of bird species (there are more than 150 species in the park, including the occasional condor and fast-footed rhea).

Lauca's most spectacular feature is the glistening Lago Chungará, one of the world's highest lakes and particularly abundant with bird life. Looming over it is the impossibly perfect cone of Volcán Parinacota, a dormant volcano with a twin brother, Volcán Pomerape, just across the border. These pristine white-capped volcanoes could almost be painted onto the landscape, but the ominous Volcán Guallatire puffs up dark fumes a short distance to the south.

Situated 160km northeast of Arica, near the Bolivian border, Parque Nacional Lauca, comprising 1380 sq km of altiplano, is a Unesco Biosphere Reserve rich in wildlife. It nuzzles close to two more protected areas, the Reserva Nacional Las Vicuñas and Monumento Natural Salar de Surire. Once part of the park, they now constitute technically separate units but are still managed by Conaf. A trip that combines these parks is well worth the extra time and energy.

Rainfall and vegetation increase with altitude and distance from the coast; it can snow in the park during the summer rainy season, known as *invierno boliviano* (Bolivian winter), when heavy fog often covers the precordillera approaches to the park.

Dangers & Annoyances

Take it easy at first: the park's altitude is mostly well above 4000m and overexertion is a big no-no until you've had a few days to adapt. Eat and drink moderately; have mainly light food and no fizzy drinks or (little) alcohol. If you suffer anyway, try a cup of tea made from the common Aymara herbal remedy *chachacoma, rica rica* or *mate de coca*. Keep water at your side, as the throat desiccates rapidly in the arid climate and you lose lots of liquids, and definitely wear sunblock and a wide-brim hat – tropical rays are brutal at this elevation.

◉ Sights & Activities

Most agencies will cover the following highlights. Lauca's crown jewel, the glittering **Lago Chungará** (4517m above sea level), is a shallow body of water formed by lava flows damming the snowmelt stream from Volcán Parinacota (6350m), a beautiful snow-capped cone that rises immediately to the north. Now sadly shallow, but still picturesque (although crisscrossed by power lines which spoil the photo ops), **Laguna Cotacotani** sparkles at the foot of sprawling lava flows and cinder cones. The lake has been partially drained by the national electricity company but you will still see diverse bird life along its shores and scattered groves of queñoa *(Polylepis tarapacana)*, one of the world's highest-elevation trees.

Tours include a wander around beautiful **Parinacota**, a tiny Aymara village of whitewashed adobe and stone streets. If you're lucky, the guide will procure the key for the town's undisputed gem, its 17th-century **colonial church** (donations welcome) reconstructed in 1789. Inside is a glorious display of surrealistic murals by artists from the Cuzco school: think Hieronymus Bosch in a hurry. Look for a small table tethered down like a dog; local legend tells how this little critter once escaped, walked through town and stopped in front of someone's house; the next day, that man died. At the park's western entrance, **Las Cuevas** has a viewing point, marked by a sculpture resembling *zampoña* (panpipes) balanced on a garish staircase.

Some (but not all) tours will include a quick dip in **Termas Jurasi** (adult/child CH$2000/1000), a pretty cluster of thermal and mud baths huddled amid rocky scenery 11km northeast of Putre.

 Tours

Many agencies offer one-day blitzes from sea-level Arica to 4517m Lago Chungará in Parque Nacional Lauca – a surefire method to get *soroche* (altitude sickness). These tours cost from CH$20,000 (including a late lunch in Putre) and leave around 7:30am, returning about 8:30pm. Verify whether the operator carries oxygen on the bus, as many people become very sick at high altitudes. Avoid overeating, smoking and alcohol consumption the day before and while you are on your tour. Tours that include at least a night in Putre are a wiser option, allowing more time to acclimatize.

 Information

The park is administered from the *refugio* (rustic shelter) at Parinacota. Otherwise, rangers at the Las Cuevas entrance and at Lago Chungará are sometimes available for consultation; posts are, in theory, staffed from around 9am to 12:30pm then 1pm to 5:30pm. If you prefer to visit the park independently, you'll need a car with extra supplies of gas, lots of flexibility and a laid-back attitude. Inquire with Conaf about hikes and lodgings (the latter mainly basic options for the hardcore).

Getting There & Away

Parque Nacional Lauca straddles Chile 11, the paved Arica–La Paz highway; the trip from Arica takes just under three hours. There are several buses from Arica. Other bus companies with daily service to La Paz, Bolivia will drop you off in the park, but you might have to pay the full fare.

Agencies in Arica and Putre offer tours. Renting a car will provide access to the park's remoter sites such as Guallatire, Caquena and beyond into the Salar de Surire (the latter only with a high-clearance vehicle, since you'll ford several watercourses, and not during the rainy season). Carry extra fuel in cans; most rental agencies will provide them. Do not forget warm clothing and sleeping gear, and take time to acclimatize.

South of Parque Nacional Lauca

More than 20,000 wild vicuña are thought to roam the sparsely inhabited 2100 sq km of the off-the-beaten-path **Reserva Nacional Las Vicuñas**, directly south of Lauca and surrounded by sky-hugging volcanoes. Formed to provide a protective zone for Lauca, the reserve is facing environmental degradation with the Vilacollo mining company winning approval in August 2007 to explore for mineral resources in the reserve. At the base of smoking Volcán Guallatire, 60km from Parinacota via a roundabout route, the village of **Guallatire** features a 17th-century church and a couple of no-frills lodging options. Bring a warm sleeping bag.

Visiting nearby **Monumento Natural Salar de Surire** is a surefire way to see huge herds of roaming vicuña, pockets of cuddly viscacha, as well the occasional ungainly ñandú (the ostrichlike rhea). But the star attraction of this isolated 113-sq-km salt flat is the flamingo; three species, including the rare James flamingo, come to nest in the sprawling salt lake. The best time to see them is from December to April. Situated 126km from Putre, the reserve was formed in 1983, when the government chopped up Parque Nacional Lauca. In 1989, the outgoing dictatorship gave 45.6 sq km to mining company Quiborax. There is no public transportation and lodging is possible only at a simple *refugio* (rustic shelter); reserve with Conaf in Arica. Camping is possible beside Polloquere's tempting thermal baths, but there are no toilet facilities and it's bitterly exposed to the elements.

Although most visitors return to Putre, it's possible to make a southerly circuit through Parque Nacional Volcán Isluga and back to Arica via Camiña or Huara. Always consult Conaf or the police first. This route is particularly iffy during the summer rainy season.

Most agencies in Arica and Putre offer two- to four-day circuits that take in these two reserves and drop you off either back in Arica or in Iquique.

VICUÑA RESURGENCE: AN ENVIRONMENTAL SUCCESS STORY

Back in Inka times vast herds of vicuña, numbering in the millions, roamed the altiplano from here all the way to southern Ecuador. But overpredation and habitat loss have sorely depleted the herds over the years, and in the 1970s barely a thousand vicuña were left in northern Chile. Today, there are more than 25,000 in the region and several hundred thousand throughout the Andes: an environmental success story that seems to only be getting better.

Unlike the alpaca or llama, the vicuña has never been domesticated. These shy fellows just don't seem to want to mate in captivity. So conservationists had to figure out a way to protect them, while still providing an economically viable trade for local Aymara who for centuries have relied on vicuña for their valuable meat and fur. Initially, species-protection measures were put in place, but even its endangered status could not save the vicuña, whose buttery wool is used to make shawls that cost hundreds (if not thousands) of US dollars. In the 1990s, they started to catch the vicuña live, shear them on the spot, and then release them back in the wild. This innovative program has allowed for continued cultivation of vicuña wool, while providing a deterrent to poachers: a shorn vicuña is essentially worthless. These measures, combined with larger national parks and greater protection, mean that herds of these beautiful, elegant creatures may again trundle across the vast expanses of the high Andes.

Iquique

📞057 / POP 216,419

Barefoot surfers, paragliding pros, casino snobs and frenzied merchants all cross paths in the rather disarming city of Iquique. Located in a golden crescent of coastline, this city is counted among Chile's premier beach resorts, with a glitzy casino, beachfront boardwalk and more activities (from paragliding to sand-boarding) than any sane person can take on in a week. The big draw here is the swaths of pitch-perfect beach, which offer some of the best surfing around.

Refurbished Georgian-style architecture from the 19th-century mining boom is well preserved, and the Baquedano pedestrian strip sports charming wooden sidewalks. Iquique's main claim, however, is its duty-free status, with a chaotic duty-free shopping zone *(zona franca)*, which uses the ominous-looking sandy hills behind the town as an outlandish nighttime billboard.

The city, 1853km north of Santiago and 315km south of Arica, is squeezed between the ocean and the desolate brown coastal range rising abruptly some 600m behind it.

History

The lifeless pampas around Iquique is peppered with the geoglyphs of ancient indigenous groups (see p172 and p171), and the shelf where the city now lies was frequented by the coastal Chango peoples. However, the Iquique area was first put on the map during the colonial era, when the Huantajaya silver mine was discovered.

During the 19th century, narrow-gauge railways shipped minerals and nitrates through Iquique. Mining barons built opulent mansions, piped in water from the distant cordillera and imported topsoil for lavish gardens. Downtown Iquique reflects this 19th-century nitrate boom, and the corroding shells of nearby ghost towns such as Humberstone and Santa Laura whisper of the source of this wealth.

After the nitrate bust, Iquique reinvented itself primarily as a fishing port, shipping more fish meal than any other port in the world. However, it was the establishment of the *zona franca* in 1975 that made this one of Chile's most prosperous cities.

⊙ Sights

The good ol' nitrate days are evident throughout Iquique's center, focused on Plaza Prat and Av Baquedano, an attractive pedestrian mall that lies just to the south lined with Georgian-style balustraded buildings dating from 1880 to 1930.

Museo Corbeta Esmeralda　　　MUSEUM
(www.museoesmeralda.cl, in Spanish; Paseo Almirante Lynch; admission CH$3000; ⊙10am-1pm & 2-6pm Tue-Sun) This replica of sunken *Esmeralda,* a plucky little Chilean corvette that challenged ironclad Peruvian warships in the War of the Pacific, is Iquique's new pride and glory. The original ship was captained

Iquique

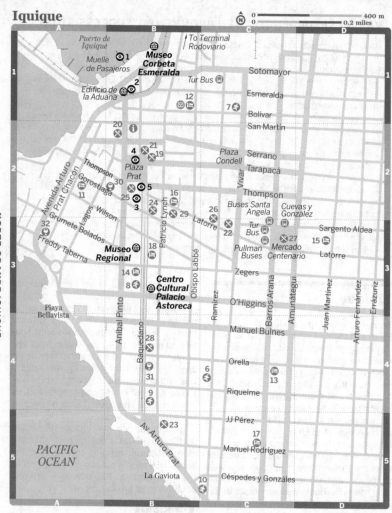

NORTE GRANDE IQUIQUE

by Arturo Prat (1848–79), whose name now graces a hundred street maps, plazas and institutions. Guided tours (reserve ahead for a tour in English), complete with piped-in sounds, take you inside the staff quarters, past the orange-lit engine, and onto the ship's deck where you are shown a techy video explaining how the cannons shot at the Peruvians. Book ahead or come on Sunday when it is first-come, first-served.

Plaza Prat
PLAZA

The city's 19th-century swagger is hard to miss on Iquique's central square. Pride of

place goes to the **Torre Reloj** (1877) clock tower, seemingly baked and sugar-frosted rather than built. Jumping fountains line the walkway south to the marble-stepped **Teatro Municipal**, a neoclassical building that has been hosting opera and theater since 1890. A handsomely restored **tram** sits outside and occasionally jerks its way down Av Baquedano in the high season.

FREE Centro Cultural Palacio Astoreca
HISTORIC BUILDING

(O'Higgins 350; ☉10am-1pm & 4-7pm Mon-Fri, 11am-2pm Sat) Originally built for a nitrate

Iquique

NORTE GRANDE IQUIQUE

tycoon, this 1904 Georgian-style mansion is now a cultural center, which exhibits contemporary work produced by local artists. It has a fantastic interior of opulent rooms with elaborate woodwork and high ceilings, massive chandeliers, a gigantic billiard table and balconies.

Casino Español　　　　HISTORIC BUILDING
The prize for the showiest building in Iquique goes to this Moorish-style place from 1904, on the plaza's northeast corner. The gaudily tiled creation is now a club and restaurant, but staff are surprisingly tolerant of travelers taking a quick whirl around the fanciful interior, which features murals and paintings of Don Quixote.

Museo Regional　　　　MUSEUM
(Baquedano 951; admission CH$1500; ◷9am-5:30pm Tue-Fri, 9:30am-6pm Sat winter, plus 10am-2pm Sun summer) Iquique's former courthouse now hosts the catch-all regional museum, which earnestly recreates a traditional adobe altiplano village and also exhibits masked Chinchorro mummies and elongated skulls. Photographs explore Iquique's urban beginnings, and a fascinating display dissects the nitrate industry.

FREE **Museo Naval**　　　　MUSEUM
(Esmeralda 250; ◷10am-1pm & 3-6pm Tue-Sat, 11am-2pm Sun) Take in the artifacts salvaged from the sunken *Esmeralda* at this small museum inside the haughty colonial-style customs house, built in 1871 when Iquique was still Peruvian territory. Peru incarcerated prisoners here during the War of the Pacific, and the building would later see battle in the Chilean civil war of 1891.

🏃 Activities

Beaches
Iquique's main beaches are south of downtown, off which **Playa Cavancha**, from the corner of Avs Arturo Prat and Amunátegui, is the most popular. It's pleasant for swimming but sometimes gets crowded. There are also some decent surf breaks along its rocky northern parts, and a playground for children. In summer, the kiosk run by the municipal tourist office dishes out useful info.

Further south, crashing waves and rip currents at scenic **Playa Brava** make it dangerous for swimming, but there's plenty of space to sunbathe. Toward the hills, look for the massive dunes of Cerro Dragón, which looks like a set for a science-fiction movie.

WORTH A TRIP

POIGNANT PISAGUA

The ghosts of Pisagua's past permeate every aspect of life in this isolated coastal village, located 120km north of Iquique. Not much more than a ghost of its former self, when it was one of Chile's largest 19th-century nitrate ports, today it is home to some 250 people who make their living harvesting *huiro* (algae) and *mariscos* (shellfish). A penal colony where Pinochet cut his teeth as an army captain, the town would acquire its true notoriety shortly afterward when it became a prison camp for Pinochet's military dictatorship (1973–89). After the return to democracy, the discovery of numerous unmarked mass graves in the local cemetery caused an international scandal.

There is a spooky magic and lyricism to Pisagua, which crouches like a wounded tiger on a narrow shelf below a near-vertical rock face. History buffs will be greatly rewarded for the detour with the sight of its abandoned nitrate-era mansions and tales of grand balls and woeful sorrows.

Visit the **Teatro Municipal**, a once-lavish, now crumbling theater with a broad stage, opera-style boxes and peeling murals of cherubim on the ceiling. Ask for the key at the library next door, which is open Monday to Friday 10am to 3pm and 4pm to 7pm. Just beyond the police station, the **abandoned train station** recalls the time when Pisagua was the northern terminus of El Longino, the longitudinal railway that connected the nitrate mines with the ports of the Norte Grande. Pisagua's most sobering site is its old **cemetery** 3km north of town, spread over a lonely hillside that slips suddenly into the ocean. Here, vultures guard over a gaping pit beneath the rock face, where a notorious mass grave of victims of the Pinochet dictatorship was discovered. A poignant memorial plaque quotes Neruda, 'Although the tracks may touch this site for a thousand years, they will not cover the blood of those who fell here.' Beyond the cemetery, the road continues for 3.5km to **Pisagua Vieja**, with a handful of adobe ruins, a pre-Columbian cemetery and a broad sandy beach.

If you want to stay, do so at **Hostal La Roca** (☎057-731-502; caterine.saldana@gmail.com; s/d/tr incl breakfast CH$20,000/24,000/26,000; P@🛜), a quirky little place perched on a rocky rise overlooking the Pacific. Run by a friendly historian and her husband, it offers four charming rooms, two of which have ocean views. The *señora* speaks French and some English, and will cook up seafood dinners upon request. Note that use of wi-fi costs extra.

Pisagua is 40km west of the Panamericana by a paved but potholed road from a turnoff 85km south of the police checkpoint at Cuya, and 47km north of Huara. There is no public transportation to the town.

Taxis colectivos run to Playa Brava from downtown – look for the destination on the sign atop the cab. There are scores of sandy beaches further south, but you'll need to rent a car or bike, or take a taxi.

Surfing

An army of wetsuited warriors is always to be found dripping its way along Iquique's coastal road. Surfing and body-boarding are best in winter, when swells come from the north, but they're possible year-round. There's less competition for early morning breaks at Playa Cavancha. **Playa Huaiquique**, on the southern outskirts of town, is also an exhilarating choice but the sea is warmer further north near Arica. One of Chile's biggest surf events takes place in Iquique on 21 May, a championship called Héroes de Mayo.

Vertical   SURFING
(www.verticalst.cl, in Spanish; Av Arturo Prat 580) This is Iquique's surfer central, which sells and rents equipment. Wetsuit and board will set you back CH$10,000 for two hours; one or the other only costs CH$7000. Private lessons start at CH$20,000 for 1½ hours, and it runs surf trips outside the city. There's a cafe on site and a sushi bar. Vertical also offers **sand-boarding** trips to Cerro Dragón, which cost CH$25,000 for three hours and typically depart to catch the sunset.

Paragliding

Go jump off a cliff…and fly! That's the message you'll get from Iquique's many *parapente* (paragliding) fanatics. The city's unique geography, with its steep coastal escarpment, rising air currents and the soft, extensive dunes of Cerro Dragón, makes it one of the best places for paragliding in South America. It's theoretically possible to glide all the way to Tocopilla, 240km south – but that's not for novices. Bring along a windbreaker, sunblock and guts.

Altazor   EXTREME SPORTS

(☎380-110; www.altazor.cl; Flight Park, Vía 6, Manzana A, Sitio 3, Bajo Molle) Located 500m south of Universidad del Mar (south of Iquique's center) offers paragliding courses (CH$40,000 per day, including equipment and transportation). An introductory tandem flight costs CH$35,000; two-week courses are also available, as is accommodations at their cozy

hostel (s/d CH$15,000/18,000, without bathroom CH$10,000/12,000). Experienced paragliders can rent equipment or have their own repaired. Owners Philip and Marlene speak German, English, Portuguese and French.

Puro Vuelo   EXTREME SPORTS

(☎311-127; www.purovuelo.cl; Baquedano 1440) Another well-run outfit that specializes in paragliding, it charges CH$35,000 for a tandem flight, with photos included. As with most paragliding jaunts in Iquique, this includes pickup at your hotel, brief instruction and about 30 minutes of flying time. The best time for jumping off is between 10am and 11am, when the winds are low. You land on either Playa Cavancha or Playa Brava. Prices drop by some CH$5000 in low season, between April and November.

THE DAKAR DOES SOUTH AMERICA

When French racer Thierry Sabine got lost on his motorbike in the desert of Libya back in 1977 and miraculously returned to France in one piece, little did he know that his misadventure would spawn the world's most famous off-road race. So inspired was he that he went on to create a rally that would kick off in Paris, pass through Algiers and continue via the grasslands and deserts of Africa, eventually ending in Dakar, Senegal. And so the storied Paris–Dakar was born. With its catchy motto: 'A challenge for those who go. A dream for those who stay behind,' the rally soon started to attract amateur and professional riders from all corners of the globe.

Over the next 30 years, the Dakar passed through 27 host countries in Africa and Europe. Until 2008, when four French citizens and three Mauritanian soldiers were killed in terrorist attacks in Mauritania. The rally, up against its biggest challenge in history, was called off. But the pause was brief: the Dakar simply switched continents and in 2009 the first race entirely off African soil was held in Argentina and Chile. In just a few years since, the historic event has taken firm root in South America, traversing the continent annually from Buenos Aires through Chile, through the world's driest desert, and back to Argentina's capital. Its third edition in 2011 attracted no less than 5 million spectators, of those 1.5 million just in Chile.

In 2012, the Dakar made history again. Peru joined the pair of host countries for the first time and the rally now connected the oceans. The 2012 edition kicked off in Argentina's Atlantic city of Mar de Plata, passing through the Atacama, before moving north to Peru for the final stages. The awards ceremony was held in Lima on the Pacific side of the continent, making it a coast-to-coast escapade.

The 2012 edition broke a record: entries increased by 15% from 2011 and 465 vehicles competed in the four categories – motorcycles, quads, cars and trucks. The competitors from over 50 countries crossed over 9000km through Argentina, Chile and Peru. In this most demanding of endurance events, they pitted against each other and against the rough terrain of giant sand dunes, mud, camel grass and rocks. Chile hosted Stages 7 through 10 of the 14-stage rally, with spectator zones set up in Vallenar, Copiapó, Antofagasta, Iquique and Arica.

Tragedy is part of the Dakar repertoire, too, with fatal accidents occurring annually. In 2012, a rider from Argentina died after a crash during the first stage and two spectators crashed with their ultra-light aircraft. But the Dakar is here to stay. By now, it's a staple of the South American summer. The brand has become so strong in Chile in such a short time that travel agencies are now selling 'The Dakar route' trips.

For more info, check out the official website: www.dakar.com.

Boat Rides

Boat Tours
BOAT RIDES

(adult/child CH$3000/2000, minimum 11 passengers) For nautical adventures, try the hourlong boat tours from Iquique's 1901 passenger pier just west of the Aduana, which pass by the commemorative buoy marking the spot where the *Esmeralda* sank and also approach a colony of sea lions.

Nautitour
BOAT RIDES

(adult/child CH$3000/2000, minimum 10 passengers) You could also hop on a boat ride of the bay, departing next to Museo Esmeralda. Nautitour has larger boats equipped with bathrooms and a cafe. There are two departures daily, at 2:30pm and 6pm, and also a three-hour sunset trip to Playa Cavancha and back for CH$10,000, with a cocktail included.

⚓ Courses

Academia de Idiomas del Norte
LANGUAGE COURSE

(☑411-827; www.languages.cl; Ramírez 1345) The Swiss-run Academia de Idiomas del Norte provides Spanish-language instruction. Classes are small (one to four students) and cost CH$252,000 to CH$317,000 per week, depending on intensity.

☞ Tours

Public transportation to many surrounding attractions is tricky, so tours are worth considering. In summer, agencies set up streetside tables on Prat and along Baquedano, hawking their most popular offerings. Among these is a day trip, which runs daily in summer season, to the oasis towns of Pica, La Tirana and Matilla, taking in the nitrate ruins at Humberstone and Santa Laura en route (CH$20,000 to CH$28,000). Other options, although running less regularly, include an excursion to the hot springs of Mamiña (from CH$30,000), a history-themed day trip to the Gigante de Atacama and Pisagua (from CH$27,000) and four-hour city tours (from CH$12,000).

From March onwards, as the weather in the altiplano improves, more adventurous off-road tours become available, such as to stunning multicolored lagoons near Camiña (CH$80,000 per day, CH$110,000 for a two-day jaunt) and to Parque Nacional Volcán Isluga (CH$45,000). Note that these often require a five-person minimum.

If you have more time and cash, it's worth booking a three-day jaunt into the altiplano that takes in Isluga, Salar de Surire, Las Vicuñas and Lauca, finishing in Arica or returning late to Iquique.

Civet Adventure
MOUNTAIN BIKING

(☑428-483; www.civet-adventure.cl; Bolívar 684) Organizes small, all-equipped 4WD, buggy or bicycle adventure tours to altiplano destinations for three or more days, as well as camping and land-sailing trips in the Atacama. German and English spoken.

OC Travel
GUIDED TOUR

(☑573-260; www.octravel.cl, in Spanish; Luis Uribe 445, Oficina 2H) Offers most of the major tours, including the popular day trip to Pica, which takes in Humberstone and Santa Laura. Also offers diving excursions (CH$35,000) at Playa Blanca and biking jaunts that take in the city and the beaches ($35,000 for six hours).

Magical Tour Chile
GUIDED TOUR

(☑217-290; www.magicaltour.tk, in Spanish; Baquedano 1035) This is the only agency that runs creepy nocturnal tours of the *salitreras*, departing at 8pm and getting you back into town at around 2:30am. They depart a couple of times per week and cost $21,000 per person, but there's a 10-person minimum.

Ferrocarril TransAtacama
TRAIN TOUR

(☑02-620-9620; www.transatacama.com) Hop on a newly renovated historic train that runs the old 19th-century nitrate route from Iquique through the desert, passing the *salitreras* and going all the way to Pintados and back. It departs on Saturdays (but check beforehand as the schedule may change) and costs CH$35,000, with lunch and a bilingual guide.

Llamatrekking
CULTURAL TOUR

(☑097-709-6864; www.llamatrekking.cl) Soft treks to surrounding attractions focused on Aymara traditions of the altiplano, ranging from day trips to nearby villages to seven-day llama caravans.

Show Travel
ADVENTURE TOUR

(☑099-382-7212; www.showtravel.cl, in Spanish) In addition to the usual roster of tours, this is a good bet for active trips to places off the beaten track, like the El Huarango eco-camp near La Tirana.

🛏 Sleeping

Taxi drivers earn commission from some *residenciales* and hotels; be firm in your decision or consider walking. The beachfront has a Holiday Inn Express and a Radisson, if you're craving a little dependable chain action.

La Casona 1920 — HOSTEL $

(☑413-000; www.casonahostel.com; Barros Arana 1585; dm per person incl breakfast CH$6000-8000, d incl breakfast CH$20,000; @🛜) Iquique's place to be, this cool and colorful hostel inside an old *casona* has four- to nine-bed dorms and a few doubles, some with balconies over the street, others overlooking the back patio. There's a shared kitchen, a pool table, lockers, multilingual staff, weekly sushi parties with live DJs, poker nights, salsa classes, movie nights... and free breakfast.

Jham Hotel — HOTEL $$

(☑549-134; www.hoteljham.cl; Latorre 426; s CH$31,000-34,000, d CH$39,000-47,000; P🛜) It is admittedly kitschy, with its dark-pink wall paint, but this well-appointed business hotel features spacious, bright and superclean rooms (a few with Jacuzzis) and a small leafy patio in the back. It has another building across the street, if all is booked.

Hotel Barros Arana — HOTEL $$

(☑412-840; www.hotelbarrosarana.cl; Barros Arana 1302; s CH$36,500-45,000, d CH$46,500-55,000; P@🛜🏊) The inner courtyard and sunchair-fringed pool make this hotel a pleasant place to recharge your batteries. Standard rooms are tidy but a little stale and stingy on space, with tiny tubs; the bigger superior rooms showcase natural light and some even have ocean views.

Backpacker's Hostel Iquique — HOSTEL $

(☑320-223; www.hosteliquique.cl; Amunátegui 2075; members dm/s/d CH$6000/9500/18,000, nonmembers CH$6500/10,000/19,000; @🛜) Iquique's best hostel for beach bunnies, sitting steps from Cavancha and with a sociable 'surfer dude' vibe. There's a lounge, shared kitchen, hammocks, Ping-Pong, laundry, weekly barbecues, surf classes, sand-boarding and free breakfast. Two doubles have private bathrooms (CH$19,000).

Sunfish Hotel — HOTEL $$$

(☑541-000; www.sunfish.cl; Amunátegui 1990; s/d CH$80,000/85,000; P🌐@🛜🏊) This luxe option in a bright-blue high-rise just behind Playa Cavancha has a full spectrum of four-star facilities, including a business center, a sushi restaurant and a rooftop pool. Most rooms come with balconies. For best vistas, get one on the top two floors.

Hotel Terrado Suites — HOTEL $$$

(☑363-900; www.terrado.cl; Los Rieles 126; d CH$115,700-155,500; P🌐@🛜🏊) Lording it over Playa Cavancha, this lofty five-star hotel has every luxury, including two restaurants, a bar, three swimming pools, both outdoor and indoor, sauna and gym. Smaller rooms have city views; bigger, pricier rooms look out to sea.

Hotel de La Plaza — HOTEL $

(☑417-172; Baquedano 1025; s/d CH$18,000/ 30,000; 🛜) One of the best deals in its category, this Georgian-style building fronts onto the pedestrian strip. There is a welcoming lobby with a big skylight; rooms with cable TVs come arranged around a patio with a supertall tree.

Hostal Casa Blanca — HOSTEL $

(☑420-007; www.hostalcasablanca.cl, in Spanish; Gorostiaga 127-129; s/d incl breakfast CH$17,000/ 26,000; 🛜) This congenial guesthouse is tucked away down a nondescript street a stone's throw from the plaza. It's a sedate spot with a set of spacious clean rooms, kindly service and a palette of simple pastel shades.

YMCA — HOSTEL $

(☑415-551; reservas@ymcaiquique.com; Baquedano 964; r per person CH$10,000; 🛜) They took an elegant *casona* and wedged the works of a YMCA in the interior. Rooms have bunk beds and clean bathrooms but can get noisy. Salsa and bachata classes are downstairs on some nights.

Hostal Catedral — HOSTEL $

(☑391-296; Obispo Labbé 253; s/d incl breakfast CH$18,000/28,000, without bathroom per person CH$12,000; 🛜) Homey place opposite the city's main church, handy for early or late Tur Bus connections. Has stuffy but adequate rooms – the clean baths are a godsend – and scattered fake and real plants.

Hotel Santa Laura — HOTEL $

(☑474-238; hotelsantalaura@hotmail.com; Juan Martínez 849; d/tr CH$30,000/35,000; 🛜) An ambitious 80-room hotel, Santa Laura tries hard with friendly service and a cozy interior. It's overpriced for what you get (no breakfast and dark rooms) and the surrounding area is a bit rough.

🍴 Eating

For the cheapest and fastest place to fill out, head to Mercado Centenario, a boxy market on Barros Arana. Note that many restaurants close on Sundays; a few below remain open.

El Tercer Ojito
INTERNATIONAL $$

(Patricio Lynch 1420; set weekday lunch CH$3900, mains CH$5200-8900; ⊘closed all day Mon & dinner Sun; ✈) Recognizable by the huge lump of quartz outside, this laid-back restaurant serves great vegetarian and carnivore-friendly dishes. Its globally inspired repertoire includes Peruvian dishes, Thai curries and occasional sushi. A pleasant bamboo-covered patio sports cacti and murals.

Ruta del Gigante
CHILEAN $$

(Baquedano 1288; mains CH$6500-13,500) Savor Andean fusion cuisine, featuring dishes like llama stroganoff and charqui-stuffed eggplant, in this altiplano-themed restaurant with Andean tablecloths and bagpipes. Coca bread is served for free.

Club Croata
CHILEAN $

(Plaza Prat 310; set lunch CH$3700; ⊘lunch, closed Sun) Plaza-side restaurant with arched windows, Croatian coats of arms and a clutch of tables outside. It has the best fixed-price lunch on the square – you get three courses plus a drink.

Skorpios
CHILEAN $

(Latorre 433; set lunch CH$2500; ⊘lunch only Mon-Sat) Look for the green Café Express sign, walk through the hallway and you'll find this rickety little spot with antique furniture, serving home-cooked lunches to a loyal crowd of locals.

El Viejo Clipper
INTERNATIONAL $$

(Baquedano 796; set lunch CH$3500, mains CH$3200-12,000) Service is spotty at best but this Baquedano favorite packs 'em in for its delicious brick-oven pizzas and a wide range of international mainstays, from *tablas* and tapas to Thai chicken.

Cioccolata
CAFE $

(Aníbal Pinto 487; set menu CH$4150, sandwiches CH$1400-4100; ⊘closed Sun) Proof positive that Chileans do enjoy a decent espresso, this classy coffee shop is usually crammed with people. It offers filling breakfasts and lunches, plus sandwiches, scrumptious cakes and waffles.

La Protectora
CHILEAN $$

(Thompson 207; set lunch CH$3900, mains CH$4000-7000; ⊘lunch & dinner, lunch only Sun & Tue) Old world atmosphere reigns at this

grand always bustling restaurant fronting onto the plaza; the building, the Sociedad Protectora de Empleados de Tarapacá, hosted one of Chile's first trade unions.

Doña Lucy
CAFE $

(Vivar 855; sandwiches CH$1200-3400, cakes CH$1700; ⊘closed Sun) Locals pile into this fussy little cafe for its ambrosial cream cakes, equally creamy cappuccinos, ice cream and freshly squeezed juices. Tables spill onto the hedged courtyard behind.

M.Koo
SWEETS $

(Latorre 600; snacks from CH$700) Colorful corner shop famous for its crumbly *chumbeques* (sweet regional biscuits), the recipe for which is guarded zealously. It also sells snacks like *humitas* (corn tamales) and empanadas.

Casino Español
INTERNATIONAL $$

(Plaza Prat 584; mains CH$4500-9500; ⊘closed lunch Sun) Expect over-the-top decor – stained glass, checked tiles, suits of armor and all – and an internationally minded menu of à la carte dishes.

⬤ Drinking & Entertainment

Iquique has a fun-filled nightlife, with a few boho resto-bars in the center and clubs and pubs lining the seafront south of town.

Lobby Resto Bar
BAR

(Gorostiaga 142; ⊘closed Sun) Sweet resto-bar with a boho vibe, Lobby has four small rooms and a loungey back patio. Come for great cocktails – try the *raspirinha*, with raspberry vodka and berries, the sushi bar, DJ-spun tunes on weekends, great-for-sharing *tablas* and happy hour nightly.

La Mona Stereo
BAR

(Gorostiaga 123; ⊘Thu, Fri & Sat evening) Chill out with a cool pisco or bourbon in the two dimly lit rooms and a palm tree–filled back patio of this sleek resto-bar. Food is great, too, as is the choice of music.

Mi Otra Casa
BAR

(Baquedano 1334; ⊘closed Sun) Laid-back artsy bar at the far end of Baquedano, with an interior full of mismatched objects and a range of different events, from poetry readings to live music.

Pub Britania
PUB

(Av Arturo Prat 1092) It may be cheesy but this three-floor faux medieval fort on the oceanfront buzzes with activity nightly – from karaoke and salsa to tango dancing and live music.

Shopping

Created in 1975, Iquique's **zona franca** (Zofri; ⊙11am-9pm Mon-Sat) is a massive monument to uncontrolled consumption. The entire region of Tarapacá is a duty-free zone, but its nucleus is this shopping center for imported electronics, clothing, automobiles and almost anything else. If you want to shop, take any northbound *colectivo* from downtown.

 Information

There are many ATMs downtown and at the *zona franca*. Several *cambios* exchange foreign currency and traveler's checks.

Iquique's city center is jam-packed with internet cafes, which charge around CH$500 per hour.

Hospital Regional Dr Torres Galdames (⌨395-555; Av Héroes de la Concepción 502) Ten blocks east of Plaza Condell.

Municipal tourist info kiosks (⊙10am-2pm & 3-7pm summer only) Superfriendly and knowledgeable staff dish out bilingual info and brochures at the two seasonal kiosks, one by the Museo Corbeta Esmeralda and another on Playa Cavancha.

Post office (Bolívar 458)

Sernatur (⌨419-241; infoiquique@sernatur.cl; Aníbal Pinto 436; ⊙10am-8pm Mon-Sat, 10am-3pm Sun summer, 9am-5pm Mon-Thu, 9am-4:30pm Fri rest of the year) This office has tourist information, free city maps and brochures.

 Getting There & Away

Air

The local airport, **Aeropuerto Diego Aracena** (⌨410-787), is 41km south of downtown via Ruta 1.

Lan (⌨600-526-2000; www.lan.cl; Aníbal Pinto 699; ⊙9am-1:30pm & 4-8pm Mon-Fri, 9:30am-1pm Sat) flies daily to Arica (CH$31,500, 50 minutes), Antofagasta (CH$47,500, 50 minutes) and Santiago (CH$220,000, 2½ hours). It also has four weekly flights to La Paz, Bolivia (around CH$192,000, 1½ hours). Prices are cheaper the further ahead you book.

Sky (⌨600-600-2828; www.skyairline.cl; Tarapacá 530) also goes to Arica (CH$19,700, two daily), Antofagasta (CH$27,800, two daily), Santiago (CH$83,900, four daily) and other destinations in the south of Chile.

Bus

The main bus station, **Terminal Rodoviario** (⌨427-100), is at the north end of Patricio Lynch. Most major bus companies, as well as a few local ones, also have offices clustered around the Mercado Centenario, mainly along Barros Arana. Services north and south are frequent, but most southbound services use Ruta 1, the coastal highway to Tocopilla (for connections to Calama) and Antofagasta (for Panamericana connections to Copiapó, La Serena and Santiago).

Several major bus companies travel north to Arica and south as far as Santiago:

Expreso Norte (⌨573-693; www.expreso norte.cl, in Spanish) Mercado Centenario (Barros Arana 881).

Pullman (⌨429-852; www.pullman.cl, in Spanish) Mercado Centenario (Barros Arana 825).

Ramos Cholele (⌨471-628; www.ramoscholele.cl, in Spanish) Mercado Centenario (Barros Arana 851).

Tur Bus (⌨420-634; www.turbus.cl, in Spanish) Mercado Centenario (Barros Arana 869); Plaza Condell (Esmeralda 594).

Sample fares are as follows:

DESTINATION	COST (CH$)	DURATION (HR)
Antofagasta	10,000	6
Arica	7000	4
Calama	10,000	6
Copiapó	22,000	14
La Serena	28,000	18
Santiago	35,000	24

To get to Pica, try one of the agencies on Barros Arana, between Zegers and Latorre. **Chacón** (Barros Arana 957) has several departures daily to Pica (about CH$2500) as does **Agencia Barreda** (⌨411-425; Barros Arana 965) next door, which also goes to La Tirana (CH$2000) and Humberstone (CH$1900). **Santa Angela** (⌨423-751; Barros Arana 971) also travels to Pica for CH$2500.

Tamarugal (⌨419-288; Barros Arana 897-B) has daily *colectivo* minibuses for Mamiña (CH$4000).

To get to La Paz, Bolivia, try **Paraiso** (⌨318-821; Juan Martínez 220), which has 8:30pm departures Monday to Friday (CH$7000, 17 hours) or **Lujan** (⌨326-955; Esmeralda 999) which has two daily departures (11am and 8:30pm) from Monday to Friday (CH$7000, 12 hours).

The easiest way to get to Peru is by going first to Arica (CH$7000), then hooking up with an international bus there.

 Getting Around

Colectivos are the easiest way to get around town. Destinations are clearly marked on an illuminated sign on top of the cab.

To/From the Airport

Iquique's **Aeropuerto Diego Aracena** (☎461-200) is 41km south on Ruta 1. Minibus transfer to your hotel costs CH$5500; there are a few stands at the airport. Alternatively, shared taxis charge CH$7000 per person; private cabs cost CH$15,000. Try **Taxis Aeropuerto** (☎419-004; cnr Gorostiaga & Baquedano) just off the plaza, or **AG Taxis** (☎413-368; Aníbal Pinto s/n).

Bicycle

Paseando en Bici (☎099-033-1906; bicicletas. baquedano@hotmail.com; Baquedano 1440) rents double and single bikes for CH$2000 (1½ hours) to CH$6000 (eight hours). Ring the bell outside the wooden door.

Iquique Biking (www.iquiquebiking.cl) Offers interesting biking tours around the city.

Car

Cars cost from CH$25,000 per day; Procar had the lowest rates at the time of writing. Local agencies often require an international driver's license. The following rental vehicles also have stands at the airport:

Econorent Car Rental (☎417-091; Hernán Fuenzalida 1058)

Europcar (☎416-332; Manuel Bulnes 542)

Hertz (☎510-432; Aníbal Pinto 1303)

Procar (☎413-470; Serrano 796)

East of Iquique

☑057

Ghost towns punctuate the desert as you travel inland from Iquique; they're eerie remnants of once-flourishing mining colonies that gathered the Atacama's white gold – nitrate. Along the way you'll also pass pre-Hispanic geoglyphs, recalling the presence of humans centuries before. Further inland the barren landscape yields up several picturesque hot-spring villages, while the high altiplano is home to some knockout scenery and a unique pastoral culture.

HUMBERSTONE & SANTA LAURA

The influence and wealth of the nitrate boom whisper through the deserted ghost town of **Humberstone** (www.museodelsalitre. cl, in Spanish; adult/child CH$2000/500; ⊙9am-7pm). Established in 1872 as La Palma, this mining town once fizzed with an energy, culture and ingenuity that peaked in the 1940s. However, the development of synthetic nitrates forced the closure of the *oficina* by 1960; 3000 workers lost their jobs and the town dwindled to a forlorn shell of itself.

HALFWAY STOPS ALONG THE COAST

The distances between destinations in Norte Grande can be overwhelming and the drives dusty and boring. So if you're making your way up or down by car and need to break up the journey, here are two pit stops that will come in handy for refueling your car, filling your stomach and getting some rest.

Halfway house between Antofagasta and Iquique, **Tocopilla** is an ugly port for the remaining nitrate *oficinas* of Pedro de Valdivia and María Elena, which offers a chance to break the long journey along a desolate stretch of coast. It sits off Ruta 1, the paved highway between Iquique and Tocopilla which has largely superseded the older Panamericana for southbound travelers. The town has a handful of lodging options although they are often booked up by miners; the best-value is **Hotel Galvarino** (☎055-813-585; www.hotelgalvarino.cl; 21 de Mayo 2182; s/d CH$28,000/32,000; P🖙) with pleasant rooms on the northern end of the town's main drag. For a filling good-quality meal, try **El Trebol** (Bolívar 1345), which serves set menu dinners for CH$4500 in two cheerful dining rooms just up the main strip.

The only settlement of any size on the long thirsty haul from Chañaral to Antofagasta, the fishing port of **Taltal** is a surprisingly neat little town. For such a small place, it has a palpable pride in its heritage with elegantly manicured plazas and lovely period architecture from its nitrate export heyday (when its population was 20,000). Still, there isn't much to see or do here, except have a stroll, a meal and a good night's sleep. You can fill up at **Club Social Taltal** (Torreblanca 162; mains CH$5500-9000), an old-school dining room just one block west of the plaza. Around since 1893, it's got high ceilings, grumpy service and good seafood. Around the town's most adorable place to stay is **Hotel Mi Tampi** (☎055-613-605; www.hotelmitampi.cl; O'Higgins 138; s/d CH$24,000/29,000; P🖙), where spacious rooms with firm beds and TVs come around a cheerful leafy patio.

The grand theater (rumored to be haunted, like a lot of the town's other buildings) that once presented international starlets; the swimming pool made of cast iron scavenged from a shipwreck; the ballroom, where scores of young *pampinos* (those living or working in desert nitrate-mining towns) first caught the eye of their sweethearts; schools; tennis and basketball courts; a busy market; and a hotel frequented by industry big-shots: all now lie quiet and emptied of life.

Some buildings are restored, but others are crumbling; take care when exploring interiors. At the west end of town, the electrical power plant still stands, along with the remains of the narrow-gauge railway to the older Oficina Santa Laura.

Although designated a historical monument in 1970, Humberstone fell prey to vandalism and unauthorized salvage. However, the site's fortunes were boosted in 2002, when it was acquired by a nonprofit association of *pampinos* (Corporación Museo del Salitre) that set about patching up the decrepit structures. In July 2005 the site was designated a Unesco World Heritage site. Admission includes a free leaflet in English or Spanish.

The skeletal remains of **Oficina Santa Laura** (admission free), 2km away, are a half-hour walk southwest across the highway. Even more atmospheric than Humberstone, it's worth the walk so that you can snoop around the haunting small museum with creaky floors and a series of rooms with old machinery, dusty dresses and heaps of old shoes. Like in Humberstone, ghost stories abound; visitors have heard children's crying and felt strange presences following them around.

ⓘ Getting There & Away

Humberstone is an easy day trip from Iquique. It sits less than 1km off the Panamericana, about 45km due east of the city. Any eastbound bus from Iquique will drop you off there, and it is easy to catch a return bus (CH$1500, 40 minutes). You can also catch any *colectivo* that goes to Pozo Almonte from the Mercado Central area for CH$2000 to CH$2300; try **Taxi Pampa y Mar** (cnr Barros Arana & Sargento Aldea) or **Taxi Chubasco** (cnr Amunátegui & Sargento Aldea). Tours are available from Iquique.

Wear closed shoes and take food, sunblock, water and a camera, since it's easy to spend hours exploring the town. Early morning is best, although afternoon breezes often moderate the midday heat.

EL GIGANTE DE ATACAMA

It's the biggest archaeological representation of a human in the world – a gargantuan 86m high – and yet little is really known about the 'Giant of the Atacama.' Reclining on the isolated west slope of Cerro Unita 14km east of Huara, the geoglyph is thought to represent a powerful shaman. Experts estimate that the giant dates from around AD 900. Don't climb the slope, as it damages the site.

The Huara–Colchane road, the main Iquique–Bolivia route, is paved; only the very short stretch (about 1km) from the paved road to the hill itself crosses unpaved desert. The isolated site is 80km from Iquique; the best way to visit is to rent a car or taxi, or take a tour.

PARQUE NACIONAL VOLCÁN ISLUGA

If you want to get off the beaten track, this isolated national park richly rewards the effort. Dominated by the malevolently smoking Volcán Isluga, the park is dotted with tiny pastoral villages that house just a few hardy families or, at times, nobody at all. The park's namesake village, **Isluga**, is itself uninhabited. It functions as a *pueblo ritual* (ceremonial village), where scattered migrational families converge for religious events that center on its picture-perfect 17th-century adobe church. Hot springs can be found 2km from the village of **Enquelga**.

Parque Nacional Volcán Isluga's 1750 sq km contain similar flora and fauna to those of Parque Nacional Lauca, but it is far less visited. The park is 250km from Iquique and 13km west of **Colchane**, a small village on the Bolivian border.

From Isluga it's a bouncy but beautiful off-road trip to the stunning **Monumento Natural Salar de Surire** and **Parque Nacional Lauca**, finishing up down in Arica. Inquire about the state of the roads first, especially in the summer rainy season, and do not attempt the trip without a high-clearance vehicle, extra petrol and antifreeze. Several tour agencies in Arica and Iquique offer this trip.

🛏 Sleeping

Chilly little Colchane, 3730m above sea level, is the easiest base for travelers.

Hotel Isluga   HOTEL $

(☏527-668; www.hotelisluga.cl; Teniente González s/n, Colchane; s without bathroom CH$16,000, d $20,000-36,000) The nicest place to stay in the area, this little hotel has comfy rooms, although they tend to get cold at night. It also organizes tours to nearby attractions.

Hostal Camino del Inca
HOSTEL **$**

(☎098-446-3586; Teniente González s/n, Colchane; r per person CH$13,500, without bathroom CH$10,500) Run by a local family, it has two floors of sparse but clean rooms, with hot showers. It gets bitterly cold, so bring a sleeping bag, and a flashlight, because electricity is cut at midnight. Rates include breakfast and dinner.

Refugio Enquelga
HUT **$**

(Enquelga; dm CH$5500) Try this basic eight-bed *refugio* in Enquelga, if you're in a pinch. You can book ahead in Arica's Conaf office.

❶ Getting There & Away

The road to Colchane is paved, but the park itself is crisscrossed by myriad dirt tracks. Several daily buses (fewer on Sundays) that depart Iquique, 251km away, pass Colchane on their way to Oruro (CH$6000, eight hours, plus more for border passing); try **Lujan** (☎326-955; Esmeralda 999), which has 12:30pm and 9pm departures from Monday to Saturday.

At Colchane it's also possible to cross the border and catch a truck or bus to the city of Oruro, in Bolivia.

MAMIÑA
☎057 / POP 429

Upon arrival, Mamiña appears to be a dusty desert village surrounded by parched precordillera. However, the valley floor below is home to famously pungent hot springs, around which a small sleepy resort has shaped itself. The baths, particularly popular with local miners, are the only reason to come here, which you can easily do on a day trip from Iquique.

The village huddles into upper and lower sectors, the former clustered around the rocky outcrop where the 1632 **Iglesia de San Marcos** stands, while the latter lies low in the valley, where the hot springs are. 'Resort facilities' include **Barros Chinos** (admission CH$2000; ⊙9am-5pm) where mud treatments are available and **Baños de Ipla** (⊙8am-2pm & 3-9pm), where CH$2000 buys you a soak in tiny (dirty) tubs.

Note that there is no bank so bring enough cash with you. Nights can get very chilly here.

🛏 Sleeping & Eating

Termas de Mamiña
HOTEL **$$$**

(☎574-635; www.termasdemamina.cl; Sulumpa 85; s incl full board CH$35,000-45,000, d incl full board

CH$60,000-80,000; ⓟ🛜🛁) Perched just above the valley floor, this recently renovated hotel and spa have 'executive' and 'superior' rooms, the latter with balconies and Jacuzzis sporting views of the valley. The cheaper standard rooms are mostly booked solid by visiting miners. There's a hot-springs pool, massage services and a good restaurant.

Hotel Los Cardenales
HOTEL **$$**

(☎575-642; hotelloscardenales2009@yahoo.cl; r per person incl full board CH$35,000; ⓟ🛜🛁) Sloping down a hillside, this pleasant place has a large covered pool fed by spring waters and rooms with TVs and oversized tubs that pipe in the curative waters.

❶ Getting There & Away

Mamiña is 73km east of Pozo Almonte. Buses and *taxis colectivos* from Iquique stop in the plaza opposite the church. To get here from Iquique, catch one of the **Tamarugal** (☎419-288; Barros Arana 897-B) *colectivo* minibuses (CH$4000), which has daily departures at 8am, returning from Mamiña at 6pm.

LA TIRANA

Curly-horned devils prance, a sea of short skirts swirls, a galaxy of sequins twinkles, and scores of drum-and-brass bands thump out rousing rhythms during La Tirana's **Virgin of Carmen festival**. Chile's most spectacular religious event, the fiesta takes place in mid-July. For 10 days, as many as 230,000 pilgrims overrun the tiny village (permanent population 1300) to pay homage to the Virgin in a Carnaval-like atmosphere of costumed dancing.

The village, 72km from Iquique at the north end of the Salar de Pintados, is famed as the final resting place of a notorious Inka princess (see boxed text, opposite), and is home to an important religious shrine. The **Santuario de La Tirana** consists of a broad ceremonial plaza graced by one of the country's most unusual, even eccentric, churches.

Although several restaurants surround the plaza, there are no accommodations.

PINTADOS

No less than 420 geoglyphs decorate the hills like giant pre-Columbian doodles at **Pintados** (adult/child CH$2000/free; ⊙10am-4pm), 45km south of Pozo Almonte. Geometrical designs include intriguing ladders, circles and arrows, and depictions of humans include vivid scenes of hunting in canoes and women giving birth. Animal and alienlike figures also roam the hillsides, which have a

173

THE TYRANT PRINCESS

The village of La Tirana is named after a bloodthirsty tale from the era of the conquistadores. It's said that an Inka princess was forced to accompany Diego de Almagro on his foray into Chile in 1535. The young miss gave him the slip at Pica, where she assembled a band of loyal Inka warriors eager for revenge. They promptly set about exterminating as many Spaniards as they could, as well as any indigenous people who had been baptized. Thus she earned the title La Tirana – The Tyrant.

However, her fearful image took a fatal blow in 1544, when her followers captured a Portuguese miner fighting for the Spanish. According to the legend, this pale-skinned soldier left the ferocious princess weak at the knees; and she provoked a major scandal by shielding him from execution. However, that was nothing compared to her followers' fury when she converted to her lover's Catholic faith: moments after her baptism, the pair was killed by a storm of arrows.

Ten years later, a traveling evangelist discovered a cross in the woods, supposedly marking the lovers' grave, and built a chapel. This structure was eventually replaced by a larger building, and the legend of La Tirana has flourished ever since.

NORTE GRANDE PICA

2km trail skirting their base; walk or drive it to scan the figures.

These enigmatic geoglyphs are thought to have served as signposts to nomadic peoples: marking trade routes and meeting points, indicating the presence of water, identifying ethnic groups and expressing religious meaning. Most date from between AD 500 and AD 1450.

A derelict nitrate rail yard of ruined buildings and rusting rolling stock, Pintados lies 4.5km west of the Panamericana via a gravel road, nearly opposite the eastward turnoff to Pica.

Pica

📞057 / POP 6178

The friendly and laid-back desert oasis of Pica appears as a painter's splotch of green on a lifeless brown canvas. It boasts lush fruit groves and is justly famous for its limes, a key ingredient in any decent pisco sour. Visitors come here to cool off in the attractive but overcrowded freshwater pool and to slurp on the plethora of fresh fruit drinks.

Pica's main attraction is **Cocha Resbaladero** (admission CH$2000; ⊘8am-8:30pm) at the upper end of General Ibáñez. Encircled by cool rock, hanging vegetation and a watery cave, it makes a terrific spot to beat the desert heat but gets crowded with vacationing families and screaming children in summer months.

We recommend visiting Pica on a day trip from Iquique but should you want to stay,

a couple of lodging and eating options are available.

🛏 Sleeping & Eating

There are numerous roadside eateries on the road to the Resbaladero. All offer decent food; pick the ambience you like best.

Hostal Cafe Suizo HOSTEL $
(📞741-551; Ibáñez 210; s/d CH$16,000/20,000; 🅿🛜) Just 100m west of the Resbaladero, this is a sweet little guesthouse run by an elderly Danish-Swiss couple, with a handful of sprucely kept rooms around a leafy little patio behind a white-picket-fenced facade. Breakfasts are served, from CH$1800.

Alfajores Rah SWEETS $
(Balmaceda; alfajores CH$100) Visit the counter of this ramshackle little shop opposite the church for the best *alfajores* (crackers sandwiching sweetened condensed milk, and rolled in shredded coconut) and local honey.

El Gato Rapido CHILEAN $
(Esmeralda 255; mains CH$2500-7500) Simple eatery close to the main plaza, with good-value set lunches (although they tend to sell out early) as well as sandwiches and meaty mains.

ℹ Information

A tiny **tourist office** (📞741-841; Balmaceda 203; ⊘8:30am-2pm & 3:30-6:30pm Mon-Fri, 9am-2:30pm & 4-7pm Sat & Sun summer, weekdays only winter), just a few blocks east of the plaza, offers information on the area's highlights although little English is spoken.

❶ Getting There & Away

Only 42km from La Tirana by paved road, Pica is served by buses and tours operating from Iquique.

Calama

📞055 / POP 138,402

It may appear drab and gritty but Calama (elevation 2250m) happens to be the pride and joy of northern Chile, an economic powerhouse that pumps truckloads of copper money into the Chilean economy year on year. And while it holds little attraction for visitors – most people will only stop here for the night (if they have to) on their way to the lala-land of San Pedro de Atacama – there is a visceral appeal to this mining town that definitely goes that extra mile in 'keeping it real.'

Everywhere are reminders of the precious metal: copper statues, copper wall-etchings and reliefs, and even a copper-plated spire on the cathedral. In 2004 the city also inherited a wave of copper refugees when the entire population of polluted mining town Chuquicamata relocated here.

The city's short history is inextricably tied to that of Chuquicamata. It's a measure of Calama's relative youth that it did not acquire its cathedral until 1906 – until then, it was ecclesiastically subordinate to tiny Chiu Chiu.

Calama sits on the north bank of the Río Loa. Though the city has sprawled with the influx of laborers from Chuquicamata, its central core is still pedestrian-friendly. Calle Ramírez begins in an attractive pedestrian mall leading to the shady Plaza 23 de Marzo, which bristles with market stalls and pigeons.

🛏 Sleeping

Prices are grossly inflated in Calama, as most hotels cater to workers at the town's lucrative copper mines. Book ahead, especially if you want to stay on a weekday.

Hotel L&S
HOTEL $$
(📞361-113; www.lyshotel.cl; Vicuña Mackenna 1819; s CH$34,000, d CH$36,000-44,000; 🅿@🛜) This is Calama's best-value choice, a sleek 'business-lite' hotel with a fresh modern look and light-filled interiors. Sparkling-clean rooms with a beige color theme feature light-wood furniture and heating. Make sure you ask for *'convenio,'* the special price for foreigners.

Hotel El Mirador
HOTEL $$
(📞340-329; www.hotelmirador.cl; Sotomayor 2064; s/d CH$43,000/48,000; 🅿🛜) This historic hotel fronted by an octagonal tower has colonial-style rooms with a pleasant grandmotherly vibe and small bathrooms, all set around a sun-splashed patio. The sitting room comes complete with historic photos of Calama. Note that it only accepts cash.

Hostería Calama
HOTEL $$$
(📞341-511; www.hosteriacalama.cl; Latorre 1521; s/d CH$64,000/73,000; 🅿@🛜🏊) This top hotel features spacious carpeted rooms decked out in a classic style, some with leafy views. It has all the conveniences of an upscale hotel, including a gym, restaurant, a patio and a small swimming pool by the parking lot.

Hostal Abaroa
HOSTEL $
(📞941-025; Abaroa 2128; s/d CH$16,000/32,000, without bathroom per person CH$10,000; 🛜) The best buy in its category, this friendly new hostel a couple of blocks from the plaza has bright clean rooms along a back patio, and a convenient location for bus departures. Breakfast and lunch are available.

Hostal Nativo
HOSTEL $$
(📞846-331; www.nativo.cl, in Spanish; Sotomayor 2215; s/d incl breakfast CH$25,000/39,000, without bathroom CH$15,000/27,000; 🛜) Location is the best thing about this little crash pad with somewhat gloomy rooms, as it sits a stone's throw from the main square. Plus rates include breakfast.

Hotel Atenas
HOTEL $
(📞342-666; inmobiliariacalama@yahoo.com; Ramírez 1961; s/d CH$15,000/20,000; 🛜) A dark warren of rooms right off the pedestrian mall, the Atenas is the best of Calama's rock-bottom choices, with spacious clean bathrooms and a good location.

🍴 Eating

Club Croata
CHILEAN $$
(Abaroa 1869; mains CH$5000-8500, set lunch CH$3000-5500) Decorated with the Croatian coat of arms outside, this restaurant on the main plaza serves Chilean favorites, including *pastel de choclo* (maize casserole). It's one of the best traditionally styled eateries in town.

Café Viena
DINER $
(Abaroa 2023; mains CH$1300-5500) This downhome diner with a wide choice of simple dishes also whips up fast food like sand-

wiches, pizzas and hot dogs. It does takeout and stays open till 2am.

Barlovento   CHILEAN $$
(Av Granaderos 2034; mains CH$5000-7000; ☉closed Sun) With *peña* (live folkloric performances) on Fridays and Saturdays (CH$5000 cover), this simple restaurant is a nice place to go for dancing or a meaty meal.

Brooklyn   RESTAURANT, BAR $
(Vicuña Mackenna 1973; mains CH$2800-6000; ☉closed Sun) Come for *schop* (draft beer) and *tablas* to this two-story spot with an earthy vibe. It also serves cheap set-menu lunches and stays open late.

Mercado Central   MARKET $
(Latorre; set meals CH$2200-2500) For quick filling eats, take advantage of the *cocinerías* (greasy spoons) in this busy little market between Ramírez and Vargas.

ℹ Information

Several banks with ATMs are to be found in the city center, some of which also change currency.

There are pay phones and call centers all along Calama's pedestrian strip, and internet shops (about CH$400 per hour) throughout the pedestrian mall and the streets around it.

Hospital Carlos Cisterna (☎655-700; Av Granaderos 2253) Five blocks north of Plaza 23 de Marzo.

Oficina Municipal de Información Turística (☎096-679-7253; infoturismo@calamacultural.cl; Latorre 1689; ☉8am-1pm & 2-6pm Mon-Fri) The tourist office has cordial, helpful staff and can sign you up for a Chuqui tour.

ℹ Getting There & Away

Air

Lan (☎600-526-2000; Latorre 1726) flies to Santiago (CH$223,000) several times daily. **Sky** (☎600-600-2828; Latorre 1499) has flights to Santiago (from CH$102,000).

Bus

Bus companies are scattered throughout the town but mostly concentrated along Av Balmaceda and Antofagasta. Those with services northbound and southbound on the Panamericana include:

Condor Bus/Flota Barrios (☎345-883; www.condorbus.cl, in Spanish; Av Balmaceda 1852)

Expreso Norte (☎347-250; www.expreso norte.cl, in Spanish; Balmaceda 1902)

Géminis (☎892-050; www.geminis.cl, in Spanish; Antofagasta 2239) To Salta and Arica only.

Pullman Bus (☎341-282; www.pullmanbus.cl, in Spanish; Balmaceda 4155)

Tur Bus (☎688-812; www.turbus.cl, in Spanish; Ramírez 1850) For tickets only – departures are from the terminal at Granaderos 3048.

DESTINATION	COST (CH$)	DURATION (HR)
Antofagasta	4000	3
Arica	14,000	6
Iquique	14,000	6½
La Serena	22,800	14
Santiago	30,000	22

Tur Bus provides regular services to San Pedro de Atacama (CH$2600, one hour). **Buses Frontera** (☎824-269; Antofagasta 2046) also has buses to San Pedro (CH$2200, 1½ hours) as does **Buses Atacama 2000** (☎316-664; Abaroa 2106) for a few cents less.

International buses are invariably full, so reserve as far in advance as possible. To get to Uyuni, Bolivia (CH$14,000, nine hours) via Ollagüe (CH$7000, three hours), ask at Frontera and Buses Atacama 2000; services go only several times per week so buy ahead.

Service to Salta and Jujuy, Argentina, is provided by Pullman on Monday, Wednesday and Friday mornings at 8am (CH$32,000, 12 hours), and by Géminis on Tuesday, Friday and Sunday at 8:30am (CH$32,000). Buy tickets in advance during the high summer season.

ℹ Getting Around

Aeropuerto El Loa (☎312-348) is a short cab ride south of Calama (CH$3000). Minibus transfers cost CH$2500 per person to drop you at your hotel. Taxis (CH$25,000 to CH$35,000) will drive tourists to San Pedro de Atacama but it's cheaper to arrange for a transfer ahead of time (CH$10,000 to CH$12,000); try **City Express** (☎099-816-2091) or **Transfer Lincancabur** (☎543-426).

Car-rental agencies include **Hertz** (☎341-380; Av Granaderos 1416) and **Avis** (☎563-152; calama@avischile.cl; Aeropuerto El Loa); daily rates start at CH$28,500.

Fill up the tank in Calama, as the lone gas station in San Pedro charges a fortune. To visit the geysers at El Tatio, rent a 4WD or pickup truck; ordinary cars lack sufficient clearance for the area's rugged roads and river fords.

Chuquicamata

Slag heaps as big as mountains, a chasm deeper than the deepest lake in the USA, and trucks the size of houses: these are some

CHUQUI THROUGH THE EYES OF CHE

Over 50 years ago, when it was already a mine of monstrous proportions, Chuquicamata was visited by a youthful Ernesto 'Che' Guevara. The future revolutionary and his traveling buddy Alberto Granado were midway through their iconic trip across South America, immortalized in Che's *Motorcycle Diaries*. An encounter with a communist during his journey to Chuqui is generally acknowledged as a turning point in Che's emergent politics. So it's especially interesting to read his subsequent memories of the mine itself (then in gringo hands). In one vivid paragraph, the wandering medical student writes of such mines: '...spiced as they would be with the inevitable human lives – the lives of the poor, unsung heroes of this battle, who die miserably in one of the thousand traps set by nature to defend its treasures, when all they want is to earn their daily bread.'

In a footnote to this much-analyzed encounter, the 'blond, efficient and arrogant managers' gruffly told the travelers that Chuquicamata 'isn't a tourist town.' Well, these days it receives around 40,000 visitors per year.

of the mind-boggling dimensions that bring visitors to gawp into the mine of Chuquicamata (or just Chuqui). This awesome abyss, gouged from the desert earth 16km north of Calama, is one of the world's largest open-pit copper mines.

Chuqui was also, until quite recently, the world's largest single supplier of copper (a title just snatched by Mina Escondida, 170km southeast of Antofagasta), producing a startling 630,000 tonnes annually. It's largely thanks to Chuqui, then, that Chile is the world's greatest copper producer. In total, copper accounts for around one-third of Chilean exports. And with the price of copper shooting up in recent years (courtesy of huge demand in China and India) its importance to the Chilean economy is hard to overestimate.

The mine, which employs 20,000 workers, spews up a perpetual plume of dust visible for many miles in the cloudless desert, but then everything here dwarfs the human scale. The elliptical pit measures an incredible 8 million sq meters and has a depth of up to 1250m. Most of the 'tour' is spent simply gazing into its depths and clambering around an enormous mining truck with tires more than 3m high; information is minimal, although the bilingual guide answers questions.

Chuquicamata was once integrated with a well-ordered company town, but environmental problems and copper reserves beneath the town forced the entire population to relocate to Calama by 2007. The 'city of Chiquicamata' is not much more than a ghost town these days.

History

Prospectors first hit the jackpot at Chuquicamata in 1911. However, they were soon muscled out by the big boys, otherwise known as the US Anaconda Copper Mining Company, from Montana. In the blink of an eye, the company created a fully functioning mining town, with rudimentary housing, schools, cinemas, shops and a hospital, although labor unrest became rife and resentment toward the corporation snowballed. By the 1960s Chile's three largest mines (all run by Anaconda) accounted for more than 80% of Chile's copper production, 60% of total exports and 80% of tax revenues. Despite coughing up elevated taxes, Anaconda was a sitting duck for the champions of nationalization.

During the government of President Eduardo Frei Montalva in the late 1960s, Chile gained a majority shareholding in the Chilean assets of Anaconda and Kennecott. In 1971 Congress approved the full nationalization of the industry. After 1973 the military junta agreed to compensate companies for loss of assets, but retained ownership through the Corporación del Cobre de Chile (Codelco).

Tours

Codelco MINE TOURS
(322-122; visitas@codelco.cl; cnr Avs Granaderos & Central Sur, Calama; bookings 9am-5pm Mon-Fri) Arrange visits through Codelco by phone or email, or ask Calama's tourist office to make the reservation. Tours run from Monday to Friday, in both English and Spanish. Report to the Oficina on the corner of Avs Granaderos and Central Sur in the north of

the city, 15 minutes before your tour; bring identification and make a voluntary donation. Tours are limited to 40, but they occasionally add a second bus. Demand is high in January and February, so book at least a week ahead.

The two-hour tour begins at 1:30pm. Wear sturdy footwear (no sandals), long pants and long sleeves.

ℹ Getting There & Away

From Calama, Codelco has a free shuttle that picks people up at their Oficina. You must be there at 1:15pm. To get to the pickup point, take a taxi colectivo (CH$600, 15 minutes) – look for 5, 65, 11 or 17 – from Latorre, or hop on the micro D (CH$400).

San Pedro de Atacama

📞 055 / POP 4969

They say the high quantities of quartz and copper in the region gives their people positive energy, and the good vibes of northern Chile's number-one tourist draw, San Pedro de Atacama (elevation 2438m), are sky high.

The popularity of this adobe precordillera oasis stems from its position in the heart of some of northern Chile's most spectacular scenery. A short drive away lies the country's largest salt flat, its edges crinkled by volcanoes (symmetrical Licancábur, at 5916m, looms closest to the village). Here too are fields of steaming geysers, a host of otherworldly rock formations and weird layer-cake landscapes.

San Pedro itself, 106km southeast of Calama via paved Chile 23, seems hardly big enough to absorb the hordes of travelers that arrive; it's little more than a handful of picturesque adobe streets clustering around a pretty tree-lined plaza and postcard-perfect church. However, the last decade has seen a proliferation of guesthouses, upscale resorts, restaurants, internet cafes and tour agencies wedging their way into its dusty streets, and turning the town into a kind of highland adobe-Disneyland.

And sure enough, San Pedro suffers from the classic drawbacks of any tourist honey pot: high costs, irritating restaurant touts and lackadaisical tour agencies. However, the town has an addictively relaxed atmosphere and an enormous array of tours that can hook travelers for weeks. And at the end of every trip, there's the comfort of a creamy cappuccino, a posh meal and a soft bed waiting in San Pedro.

History

San Pedro was once a pre-Columbian pit stop on the trading route from the highlands to the coast. It was visited by Pedro de Valdivia in 1540, and the town later became a major stop on early-20th-century cattle drives from Argentina to the nitrate oficinas of the desert.

Locals, the Atacameño people, still practice irrigated farming in the ayllus (a-ee-oos; small indigenous communities). Many still farm on terraces over a thousand years old.

◉ Sights

The village itself is small and compact, with almost everything of interest within easy strolling distance of the plaza. Many buildings now have street numbers, although many still do without.

Museo Gustavo Le Paige   MUSEUM
(Gustavo Le Paige 380; adult/student CH$2500/1000; ☺9am-6pm Mon-Fri, 10am-6pm Sat & Sun) Even if museums aren't your thing, make an exception for San Pedro's superb Museo Gustavo Le Paige. The Atacama is nirvana for archaeologists because of its nearly rainless environment, which preserves artifacts for millennia. And so this octagonal museum is packed with such fascinating finds as well-preserved ceramics and textiles, and an extraordinary collection of shamanic paraphernalia for preparing, ingesting and smoking hallucinogenic plants.

Detailed English and Spanish explanations follow the region's evolution through the earliest cultures to the Inka conquest and the Spanish invasion. No opportunity is lost to link information with surrounding

RESPONSIBLE TOURISM

High season brings thousands of tourists to tiny San Pedro. Residents, especially the indigenous Atacameño peoples, are sensitive to the overwhelming presence of outsiders. Make a special effort to behave appropriately and blend in as best you can; avoid wearing highly revealing clothes in town (save those bikinis for the hot springs), remove hats while visiting churches and consider wearing long pants. And don't take photographs of the people without asking for their permission first.

Water is scarce (obviously), so refrain from long soaks in the shower.

San Pedro de Atacama

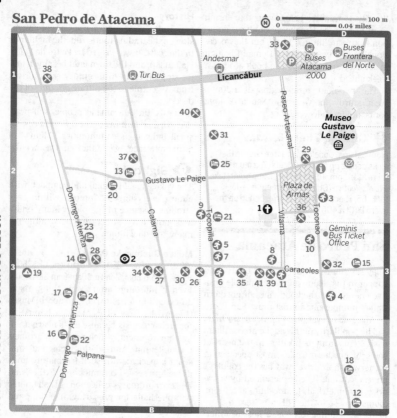

archaeological sites, including Pukará de Quitor and Aldea de Tulor.

The credit for this excellent museum goes principally to the Belgian priest and amateur archaeologist after whom it is named. Father Gustavo Le Paige arrived as a priest in San Pedro in 1955, and dedicated the next 35 years of his life to collecting ancient artifacts from the area. His statue now stands outside and a small exhibit is dedicated to him within.

There are 45-minute guided tours a few times daily Tuesday to Sunday (CH$1800), in various languages. Temporary exhibits in the back section change every few months.

Iglesia San Pedro

CHURCH

(admission free; Plaza de Armas) The sugar-white Iglesia San Pedro is a delightful little colonial church built with indigenous or artisanal materials – chunky adobe walls and roof, a ceiling made from *cardón* (cactus wood) resembling shriveled tire tracks and, in lieu of nails, hefty leather straps. The church dates from the 17th century, though its present walls were built in 1745, and the bell tower was added in 1890.

☞ Tours

A bewildering array of tours is on offer. Activities can be as leisurely or hardcore as you please: from nodding off in hot volcanic springs to bombing down steep trails on mountain bikes; from musing over the remains of ancient civilizations to sweating up active volcanoes; and from surfing down giant sand dunes to stargazing in the cloudless desert nights.

Unfortunately, the quality of some tours has become somewhat lax, and travelers complain of operators who cancel abruptly or run unsafe vehicles. Tour leaders are often merely drivers rather than trained guides. Agencies often contract out to independent drivers, many of whom work

San Pedro de Atacama

for different companies, so the quality of your driver – or guide, for that matter – can depend on the luck of the draw. That said, don't unfairly dismiss local Spanish-speaking drivers. Many of them are very courteous and knowledgeable, and they can provide a valuable insider's viewpoint.

You may find that the agency you paid is not the same agency that picks you up. Some agencies offer tours in English, German or Dutch, but these tours may require advance notice or extra payment. Competition keeps prices down, and operators come and go.

The tourist information office has a helpful, entertaining and occasionally terrifying book of complaints on various tour agencies; the problem is that nearly every agency is featured and, by the time you read about unlicensed or drunken drivers over the passes to Bolivia, you may decide to do nothing but write postcards from the safety of your hostel, which would be a tragic mistake in such a beautiful area. Nevertheless, when choosing an operator, ask lots of questions, talk to other travelers, trust your judgment and try to be flexible.

At last count, there were 48 tour agencies in town. While recommending any of them is a can of worms, let's just say that the following two boast the most recent stamp of approval by Sernatur:

Desert Adventure (☑851-067; www.desertad venture.cl; Caracoles s/n)

Terra Extreme (☑851-274; www.terraextreme. cl; Toconao s/n)

Standard Tours

The following are the standard best-selling tours offered by most agencies in San Pedro. Note that entrance fees are not included in the tour prices.

Altiplano lakes   GUIDED TOUR
(CH$10,000-25,000, entrance fees CH$5000-7000) Leaves San Pedro between 7am and 8am to see flamingos at Laguna Chaxa in the Salar de Atacama, then moves on to the town of Socaire, Lagunas Miñiques and Miscanti, Toconao and the Quebrada de Jere, returning between 4pm and 7pm.

El Tatio geysers   GUIDED TOUR
(CH$18,000-20,000, entrance fees CH$5000) This hugely popular tour leaves San Pedro at

WORTH A TRIP

EXCURSION TO UYUNI, BOLIVIA

Colorful altiplano lakes, weird rock playgrounds worthy of Salvador Dalí, flamingos, volcanoes and, most famously of all, the blindingly white salt flat of Uyuni: these are some of the rewards for taking an excursion into Bolivia northeast of San Pedro de Atacama. However, be warned that this is no cozy ride in the country, and for every five travelers that gush about Uyuni being the highlight of their trip, there is another declaring it a waking nightmare.

The standard trips take three days, crossing the Bolivian border at Hito Cajón, passing Laguna Colorada and continuing to the Salar de Uyuni before ending in the town of Uyuni. The going rate of CH$75,000 includes transportation in crowded 4WD jeeps, basic and often teeth-chatteringly cold accommodations, plus food; an extra CH$15,000 to CH$23,000 will get you back to San Pedro on the fourth day (some tour operators drive through the third night). Bring drinks and snacks, warm clothes and a sleeping bag. Travelers clear Chilean immigration at San Pedro and Bolivian immigration on arrival at Uyuni. Note that entrance fees to Bolivian parks are charged extra, and amount to approximately CH$16,000.

None of the agencies offering this trip get consistently glowing reports. **Cordillera Traveler** (☑851-291; www.cordilleratraveller.com; Toconao 447-B & Tocopilla 429-B) gets the best feedback from travelers.

4am in order to see the surreal sight of the geysers at sunrise, returning between noon and 1pm. Most tours include thermal baths and breakfast.

Valle de la Luna
GUIDED TOUR

(CH$8000-10,000, entrance fees CH$2000) Leaves San Pedro mid-afternoon to catch the sunset over the valley, returning early evening. Includes visits to Valle de la Luna, Valle de la Muerte and Tres Marías.

Tulor and Pukará de Quitor
GUIDED TOUR

(around CH$15,000, entrance fees CH$8000) Half-day archaeological tours take in this pair of pre-Columbian ruins (departures between 8am and 9am, returning between 1pm and 3pm).

Less Standard Tours

Other available tours include a full-day excursion that takes in the Tatio geysers in the morning and continues on to the pueblos of **Caspana** and **Chiu Chiu**, then the **Pukará de Lasana**, finishing in Calama (a good tour to do before your flight the next day), or returning to San Pedro.

A few other tours are becoming increasingly popular, such as jaunts to **Laguna Cejar** and **Ojos de Salar** (you can swim in both, and in Cejar you can float just like in the Dead Sea), to **Valle del Arcoiris** with its rainbowlike multicolored rock formations and **Salar de Tara**. The last is one of the most spectacular, if back-breaking, trips

from San Pedro, which involves a round-trip journey of 200km, to altitudes of 4300m.

Note that the above tours don't leave as regularly and have a higher price tag than the bestsellers.

Trekking & Biking

Around San Pedro rise immense volcanoes, a few of them active, and begging to be climbed. If climbing isn't your cup of tea, consider a more active trekking or biking trip to the usual suspects in the area, such as Valle de la Luna. Bikes are available for rent at several agencies and hotels around town, for about CH$6000 per day; try **Km O** (Caracoles 282B).

Vulcano Expediciones
ADVENTURE SPORTS

(☑851-023; www.vulcanochile.com; Caracoles 317) Runs treks to volcanoes and mountains, including day climbs to Sairecabur (5971m; CH$90,000), Lascar (5592m; CH$90,000) and Tocco (5604m; CH$70,000). Longer climbs take in Licancábur and Llullaillaco. It also runs downhill bike rides (from CH$35,000 for two hours) and motorbike tours (from $91,000 for half day).

CosmoAndino Expediciones
HIKING

(☑851-069; www.cosmoandino.cl; Caracoles 259) This well-established operation specializes in trekking excursions to nearby highlights; expect to pay more than for a standard tour but you'll also get more 'quality time in the Atacama,' as their motto claims.

Azimut 360 ADVENTURE SPORTS
(02-235-1519; www.azimut360.com) Although it doesn't have an office in town, Santiago-based Azimut 360 still has its experts on the ground and remains one of the top choices for climbing and trekking tours. For information and bookings, call the office in Santiago.

Horseback Riding
Rancho La Herradura HORSEBACK RIDING
(851-956; www.atacamahorseadventure.com; Tocopilla 406) Sightseeing from the saddle is available from several places, including Rancho La Herradura. Tours vary from two hours for CH$14,000 to epic 10-day treks with camping. English-, German- and French-speaking guides are available.

Sand-boarding
Jumping on a sand-board and sliding down enormous sand dunes is the most popular of the adrenaline-pumping activities around San Pedro. This happens in Valle de la Muerte, where 150m-high dunes make perfect terrain.

Atacama Inca Tour SAND-BOARDING
(851-034; www.sandboardsanpedro.com; Toconao 421-A) While several agencies offer sand-boarding, many actually sell tours for Atacama Inca Tour, our top pick for their pro boards and experienced instructors. Standard trips, for CH$10,000, depart either at 9am and return at noon or leave at 4pm, returning at 7pm. They involve a two-hour class, plus you get a DVD with a video clip of your escapade.

It also offers sand-boarding followed by a short trek in Valle de la Luna and a pisco at sunset for CH$15,000. Its latest offering is the night sand-board party (10:30pm till 1:30am), with spotlights for the dune, massive speakers and a DJ.

Once you've got the hang of it, you can hire boards directly from several agencies in town, including Vulcano; it costs CH$4000 for half a day.

★ Festivals & Events
Fiesta de Nuestra Señora de la Candelaria RELIGIOUS
In early February, San Pedro celebrates with religious dances.

Carnaval CARNIVAL
Takes place in February or March, depending on the date of Easter.

Fiesta de San Pedro y San Pablo RELIGIOUS
June 29 has the locals celebrating with folk dancing, Mass, a procession of statues, a rodeo and modern dancing that gets rowdy by midnight.

Fiesta de Santa Rosa de Lima RELIGIOUS
This traditional religious festival takes place on August 30.

🛏 Sleeping
While San Pedro has a dizzying choice of places to stay – 98 at our last count – don't expect to find many rock-bottom options. Prices are inflated as a result of San Pedro's status as the tourist hub of the north. Note that some budget places request that solo travelers share a room in the busy summer period.

Exclusively midrange hotels are in short supply at this backpackers' haven, but many hostels in the budget category have midrange rooms at the ready. Top-range hotels have sprouted all around San Pedro, though many are outside the center.

Hotel Terrantai HOTEL $$$
(851-045; www.terrantai.com; Tocopilla 411; d CH$100,000-110,000; P🛱🌊) This is arguably the most intimate and central of San Pedro's upscale hotels. The key is in the architecture: high, narrow passageways made from smooth rocks from the Río Loa lead guests to the elegant rooms with Andean textiles and ceiling fans. Slightly pricier superior rooms have more space, light and nicer views. There's a bamboo-shaded sculpture garden out back as well as a dip pool and a bar.

Hotel Kimal HOTEL $$$
(851-030; www.kimal.cl; Domingo Atienza 452; s/d CH$99,000/111,000; @🛱🌊) Rustic chic dominates this small but leafy villagelike hotel complex; closely knit one-story buildings with individually decked out rooms are built with simple adobe bricks and topped by cane roofs. There is also a cute circular pool and a good regional restaurant. Its new **Poblado Kimal** (s/d CH$85,000/95,000) across the road has cabin-style rooms in the shape of a coca leaf, each with a small terrace. The Poblado is often booked by tour groups.

Tierra Atacama Hotel & Spa HOTEL $$$
(555-976; www.tierraatacama.com; Séquitor s/n; s/d US$350/420; P@🛱🌊) All the luxe perks paired with heaps of style await those who stay at this resort-style hideaway 20 minutes

out of town. Stone-floored rooms showcase an organic minimalist look, outdoor showers and terraces that sport wow vistas of Licancábur. There's a spa as well as a restaurant. Choose a stay (single/double US$1290/2100 for two nights), with all food, drinks and tours thrown in, or go for just B&B.

Hostal Sonchek   HOSTEL $$
(☎851-112; www.hostalsonchek.cl; Gustavo Le Paige 170; s without bathroom CH$11,000, d with/without bathroom CH$34,000/18,000; P🖥) Thatched roofs and adobe walls characterize the carpeted rooms at this lovely hostel. It's centered on a small courtyard, and there's a shared kitchen, luggage storage and a small garden out back with Ping Pong and a few hammocks. The common bathrooms with solar-heated showers are some of the cleanest in town. English and French spoken.

Hostal La Ruca   HOSTEL $$
(☎851-568; www.larucahostal.cl; Toconao 513; dm per person CH$10,000, s/d CH$35,000/42,000; P@🖥) A nice touch of rustic style – think colorful Andean bedspreads and tapestries – graces the rooms of this sweet hostel with tiny but clean bathrooms, a sunny patio with hammocks and a shared kitchen, all presided over by friendly staff who speak English and some German. Breakfast is available, as are transfers from/to Calama.

Hostal Quinta Adela   HOSTEL $$
(☎851-272; quintaadela@gmail.com; Toconao 624; s incl breakfast CH$30,000, d incl breakfast CH$35,000-45,000; P@🖥) This friendly family-run place, just a quick walk from town, has seven character-filled rooms (each with its own individual style), a shady terrace and is situated alongside a sprawling orchard with hammocks. There's luggage storage and they're flexible with check-in and check-out. Rates include breakfast.

Katarpe Hostal   HOSTEL $$
(☎851-033; katarpe@galeon.com; Domingo Atienza 441; s/d CH$32,000/40,000, d without bathroom CH$25,000; P🖥) Great location just off Caracoles, a range of reasonable-size rooms, crisp sheets and decent beds make this a good if unexciting choice. Rooms are arranged around a couple of patios, one featuring long wooden tables. There's a laundry service, too, and the staff is accommodating.

Hotel Tulor   HOTEL $$$
(☎851-027; www.tulorchile.cl; Domingo Atienza 523; s CH$90,000-120,000, d CH$105,000-135,000;

P🖥✈) Built and run by a resident archaeologist, using a circular design inspired by the Aldea de Tulor site, the Tulor isn't as charming as the neighboring Kimal, but has nice tasteful rooms. More spacious units in the superior section, connected by leafy boardwalks, have small terraces.

Hostal Edén Atacameño   HOSTEL $
(☎851-154; hostaleden@gmail.com; Toconao 592; s without bathroom CH$10,000, d with/without bathroom CH$40,000/20,000; P@🖥) This is a laid-back hostel with rooms around a couple of sociable, hammock-strung patios with plentiful seating. Guests can use the kitchen, and there's laundry service and luggage storage. The shared bathrooms are clean; breakfast is included for rooms with private bathrooms.

Hotel Takha Takha   HOTEL $$
(☎851-038; www.takhatakha.cl; Caracoles 101-A; campsite per person CH$10,500, s CH$40,000-44,000, d CH$47,500-65,000, s/d without bathroom CH$16,000/31,500; P🖥✈) A popular catch-all outfit with decent campsites, plain budget rooms and spotless midrange accommodations set around a sprawling flowery garden with a swimming pool. Rates for rooms with private bathrooms include breakfast.

Hostal Candelaria   HOSTEL $
(☎851-284; Candelaria 170, El Carmen; dm per person $8000, d with/without bathroom CH$35,000/30,000; P🖥) Skip the tourist buzz of the center and head to the workaday neighborhood of El Carmen, to this family-run spot with a leafy patio, cozy and clean rooms and a shared kitchen. To get here, follow the road by the parking lot marked 'Vilama, Guatin and Puritama,' past the cemetery to the right, for 700m.

Hotel Don Sebastián   HOTEL $$
(☎851-972; www.donsebastian.cl; Domingo Atienza 140; s/d CH$40,000/54,000, cabins CH$64,000; P@🖥) Solid midrange option a hop and a skip from town, with well-appointed heated rooms and a handful of cabins with kitchenettes. There are nice shared areas, but it can get busy with tour groups.

Hostal Lickana   HOSTEL $$
(☎851-940; www.lickanahostal.cl; Caracoles 140; s/d incl breakfast CH$32,000/38,000; P🖥) Just off the main drag, this strip hotel has super-clean rooms with big closets, colorful bedspreads and straw-covered front patios.

What it lacks is the common-area ambience of other hostels.

Hotel Tambillo
HOTEL $$

(☎851-078; www.hoteltambillo.cl; Gustavo Le Paige 159; s & d CH$45,000, tr CH$55,000; P☎) The small plain rooms with tiny tubs at this centrally located hotel are strung along an inner breezeway and a shady courtyard. They'll give you a fan, if you ask.

Hostelling International
HOSTEL $

(☎564-683; hostelsanpedro@hotmail.com; Caracoles 360; members incl breakfast dm/d CH$7000/20,000, nonmembers CH$9000/23,000, d CH$33,000/36,000; ☎) This convivial spot offers dorms – with some bunks nearly 3m up – and a few private doubles around a small patio. Services include shared kitchen, lockers, and they'll book tours.

Residencial Vilacoyo
GUESTHOUSE $

(☎851-006; vilacoyo@sanpedroatacama.com; Tocopilla 387; per person CH$8000; P) A no-frills but friendly *residencial* with a snug gravel patio hung with hammocks, a kitchen and luggage storage. The shared showers only have hot water between 7am and 10pm.

Hotel Licancábur
HOSTEL $

(☎851-007; Toconao 495; s/d CH$16,000/35,000, without bathroom CH$12,000/20,000; ☎) You won't find any trimmings at this last resort kind of place, recommended if all else fails. Rooms with private bathroom include breakfast, and there's a laundry service.

Camping Los Perales
CAMPGROUND $

(☎851-114; campinglosperales@hotmail.com; Tocopilla 481; campsite per person CH$4000; P) Sprawling site with basic facilities, including kitchen access and hot showers.

DESERT STARGAZING

The flats of Chajnantor plateau, at 5000m of altitude 40km east of San Pedro de Atacama, host the most ambitious radio telescope that the world has ever seen. The Atacama Large Millimeter/submillimeter Array (ALMA; meaning 'soul' in Spanish) consists of 66 enormous antennae, most of them with a diameter of around 12m. Once finished in 2013, this field of interstellar 'ears' will simulate a telescope an astonishing 16km in diameter and make it possible to pick up objects in space as much as 100 times fainter than those currently detected. It is also slated to open a visitor center in 2013; for up-to-the-minute info, see www.almaobservatory.org.

This is just the latest of northern Chile's cutting-edge astronomical facilities. Climatic conditions in the Atacama Desert make it an ideal location for stargazing. This is not only thanks to cloudless desert nights, but also the predictable winds that blow steadily in from the Pacific Ocean, causing minimal turbulence – a crucial requirement for observatories to achieve optimal image quality.

Other major facilities in northern Chile include the European Southern Observatory (ESO) at Cerro Paranal (p192). Norte Chico has Observatorio Interamericano Cerro Tololo (see boxed text, p213) and the nearby Cerro El Pachón. Another ESO site is at La Silla (which also has free visits open to the public each Saturday at 1:30pm, except in July and August; see www.eso.org/public/teles-instr/lasilla.html), while the Carnegie Institution's Observatorio Las Campanas is just north of La Silla.

If all that whets your appetite for astronomy, consider taking a Tour of the Night Sky from San Pedro. French astronomer Alain Maury ferries travelers into the desert, far from intrusive light contamination, where they can enjoy the stars in all their glory. He owns several chunky telescopes through which visitors can gawk at galaxies, nebulae, planets and more. Shooting stars are guaranteed. Reserve a place at **Servicios Astronómicos Maury y Compañía** (☎055-851-935; www.spaceobs.com; Caracoles 166; 2½hr tours CH$18,000). Tours leave nightly starting at 7:30pm in winter, and 9pm and midnight in summer (except around the full moon). Tours are available in Spanish, English and French. Bring warm clothes as it can get very cold in the desert at night.

The new kid of the star-gazing block in San Pedro is **Ahlarkapin** (☎099-579-7816; www.ahlarkapin.cl), which offers more personalized observation tours (12 people maximum) with a focus on Andean cosmology. The two-hour tours (in Spanish and English) run nightly at 9:30pm in summer (earlier in winter) and cost CH$15,000/10,000 for adults/children.

✗ Eating & Drinking

A word of warning: while San Pedro restaurants offer welcome variety, especially for vegetarians, it comes with an elevated price tag. Touristy places have touts offering 10% off or a free drink (make sure you get it).

To best avoid San Pedro's skyrocketing prices, follow the locals out to the town periphery, such as the eateries along Licancábur, where a set lunch goes for CH$3500 to CH$4000. Your best bet for really cheap is the food stalls by the parking lot on the northern edge of town, which serve simple set lunches of *cazuela,* mains and dessert (for around CH$2000), and all-day empanadas for snacking.

TOP CHOICE La Casona
CHILEAN $$
(Caracoles 195; set lunch CH$6000-7000, mains CH$6000-8900; ⊘closed lunch Tue) A high-ceilinged dining room with dark wood paneling and an adobe fireplace in the middle, the classic La Casona serves up sizzling *parrilladas* and Chilean staples like *pastel de choclo.* Stays open till 1am and has a long list of Chilean wines.

Cafe Peregrino
CAFETERIA $
(Gustavo Le Paige 348; breakfast from CH$3000, snacks CH$2500-4300;🛜) The loveliest cafe in town, overlooking the plaza from a few alfresco benches strategically placed for people-watching. Inside are only four tables. Food-wise, you'll find pizzas, salads, sandwiches and nice cakes and pastries. And, yes, real espressos and cappuccinos!

Salon de Te O2
CAFE $
(Caracoles 295; breakfast from CH$2250, snacks CH$2100-4300) Early morning breakfasts (from 7am), great quiches, juicy meat sandwiches and lovely tarts are the highlights of this colorful cafe run by a French-Chilean couple. You can while away the afternoon on the shady back patio – there's free wi-fi.

Blanco
INTERNATIONAL $$
(Caracoles 195b; mains CH$6800-7900; ⊘dinner only, closed Tue) The hippest eatery in town, this all-white adobe-clad restaurant has fishtank windows, a terrace with a fireplace out back, a good range of dishes and a buzzy vibe. Set menus are a good deal, for CH$6000 to CH$7000, with a drink.

Las Delicias de Carmen
CHILEAN $$
(Calama 370b; mains CH$3000-8000; ✎) Great breakfasts, delicious cakes and empana-

das, brick-oven pizzas (choose your own toppings) and different dishes daily are churned out at this light-flooded restaurant with leafy views. It shares its terrace with Hostal Sonchek next door.

Adobe
INTERNATIONAL $$
(Caracoles 211; mains CH$6000-8900; ⊘closed lunch Wed) Popular with travelers for its studied rusticity, rock-art decor, benchlike seating and smoky fire in the alfresco dining room. Adobe serves tasty but pricey dishes like mushroom quinoa risotto and is a good spot for a drink.

Cafe Esquina
CAFETERIA $
(Caracoles 160; mains CH$3000-4500; ⊘closed Wed or Thu) This laid-back little corner cafe serves natural juices, empanadas, sandwiches, pizzas and quesadillas. It tends to be quieter and has lower prices than other spots on the strip. Grab one of the tree-shaded streetside tables.

Ckunna
INTERNATIONAL $$
(Tocopilla 359; set meal CH$7000, mains CH$6000-9000; ⊘lunch & dinner) Come for the homemade pastas and the fusion of altiplano and Mediterranean fare served inside an old school building a stroll from the main strip. There's a welcoming bar and a terrace with a bonfire out back.

La Estaka
INTERNATIONAL $$
(Caracoles 259b; mains CH$8900; ⊘closed lunch Thu; ✎) A lively gathering point late into the night, with sloping wooden beams, a fireplace and colorful wall art. La Estaka comes recommended for its risottos, a wide range of soups and salads, and a decent wine list.

Todo Natural
INTERNATIONAL $$
(Caracoles 271; set meal CH$7000, mains CH$4500-8000; ✎) Healthy offerings on the lengthy menu include whole-wheat sandwiches and good salads in this cute cafe with a tunnel-shaped straw roof-covered courtyard. The service is erratic but the food decent, and there's happy hour.

Casa de Piedra
PIZZA $$
(Caracoles 225; pizzas from CH$3500, mains CH$4800-9000; ⊘closed Mon) Thin-crust pizza steals the show at this main drag eatery, with homemade tomato sauce and Gouda cheese; you just add the toppings, CH$800 per pop.

La Plaza
INTERNATIONAL $$
(Plaza de Armas 315b; set meal CH$5000, mains CH$5500-8500) Pretty cheap eats of the usual

'sandwich, pizza, pasta' variety, especially considering its bees-knees location right on the plaza. Sit plaza-side under the arcades or on the inner patio.

Quitor   CHILEAN $
(Licancábur 154; set meals CH$6000, mains CH$4000-5000) Locals, Chilean tourists and gringos alike frequent this two-room eatery, next to the bus stop, for its simple but filling meals, breakfasts and an efficient get-it-on-the-table attitude.

Tahira   CHILEAN $
(Tocopilla 372; CH$2000-3500) Another down-to-earth cafe where the locals outnumber the gringos, Tahira serves up no-frills mainstays that are satisfying, and barbecues on weekends.

Export   BAR $
(Toconao 441; mains CH$5500-8200; ⊙lunch & dinner) Food is not the forte and neither is the service at this funky spot with white adobe walls and a roaring fire. Best come for post-dinner drinks, with occasional live DJs.

☆ Entertainment

While San Pedro's small community welcomes tourism, it draws the line at late-night revelers. Establishments that sell only alcohol have been outlawed, no alcohol is sold after 1am, police have cracked down on public drinking *and* local lawmakers recently banned nocturnal dancing in downtown San Pedro. The night is also cut short by travelers with early tours: after all, waking up for a 4am jaunt to El Tatio is enough of a headache *without* a hangover!

All that said, all is not lost for lovers of nightlife; a very cozy bar-cum-restaurant scene predominates here, with travelers swapping stories around open fires and making the most of abundant happy hours. And there's a well-kept public secret: rave-like parties in the desert occur on a regular basis although they aren't advertised due to police crackdowns. It's all word of mouth so ask around town to see what's happening and where.

🛍 Shopping

The shaded Paseo Artesanal, a poker-straight alley squeezing north from the plaza, is the place to hunt down novel *cardón* carvings, llama and alpaca woolens and other curious trinkets. More artisanal outlets are strewn throughout town.

ℹ Information

There are only two ATMs in town (one on Caracoles and Vilama and the other opposite the museum) but they do not always have money, so bring a big wad of cash, just in case. Many establishments take plastic, but some prefer the real stuff. Several money changers are found around town, especially along Toconao, but don't expect good exchange rates.

Half a dozen internet cafes (CH$800 per hour) dot Caracoles, and many accommodations offer access; there's also free wi-fi on the main plaza.

Oficina de Información Turística (📞851-420; sanpedrodeatacama@gmail.com; cnr Toconao & Gustavo Le Paige; ⊙9am-9pm) Helpful tourist office offering advice and doling out town maps and brochures. Check out the annual book of comments for up-to-date traveler feedback on tour agencies, hostels, restaurants, transportation providers and more.

Post office (Gustavo Le Paige 365)
Posta Médica (📞851-010; Toconao s/n) The local clinic, on the plaza.

ℹ Getting There & Away

Travelers to and from Argentina and Bolivia clear immigration with the Policía Internacional, customs and agricultural inspections, just east of town. **Buses Atacama 2000** (Licancábur) has regular departures to Calama (CH$2500, three daily), where you can connect to their Uyuni bus. **Buses Frontera del Norte** (Licancábur) goes to Calama (five daily) as well as Arica (CH$17,150) and Iquique (CH$14,000), departing at 8pm every night.

Tur Bus (📞851-549; Licancábur 294) has hourly buses to Calama (CH$2900), from where you can connect to all major destinations in Chile such as Santiago (CH$32,000, 22 hours), Arica (CH$14,000, nine hours) and Iquique (CH$10,000, six hours).

Andesmar (www.andesmar.com; Licancábur s/n) serves Salta and Jujuy, Argentina, leaving at 9:30am on Tuesday, Wednesday, Friday and Sunday (CH$30,000, 16 hours with border time). **Géminis** (📞892-049; Toconao 428) also goes to Salta (CH$32,000, 12 hours) on Tuesday and Sunday at 9:30am and on Friday at 8:30am.

Several agencies in town offer transfer services to Calama airport, which cost around CH$15,000 per person; try **Desert Adventure** (📞851-067; Caracoles s/n).

ℹ Getting Around

Mountain bikes are a terrific way to steam around San Pedro. However, to ensure that only calories are burned, be sure to carry water and sunblock. Several agencies and hostels rent mountain bikes, for the current going rate of

CH$6000 per day. Some agencies will give out photocopied maps to guide your forays.

Around San Pedro de Atacama

Most attractions are beyond walking distance from town, and public transportation is limited. Options include renting a car (in Calama), hiring a bike or taking a tour. Luckily, vigorous competition among numerous operators keeps tours reasonably priced. Also, consider staying the night in the remote villages and attractions you visit. By spreading the tourist trail, you help create a more sustainable future for the people of the region.

Dominating a curvy promontory over the Río San Pedro, the crumbling 12th-century **Pukará de Quitor** (adult & student CH$3000; ⊘9am-7:30pm Jun-Aug, 9am-6pm Sep-May) was one of the last bastions against Pedro de Valdivia and the Spanish in northern Chile. The indigenous forces fought bravely but were overcome and many were promptly beheaded. A hundred defensive enclosures hug the slopes here, like big stone bird's nests. The hilltop commands an impressive view of the entire oasis. The fort is just 3km northwest

Around Calama & San Pedro de Atacama

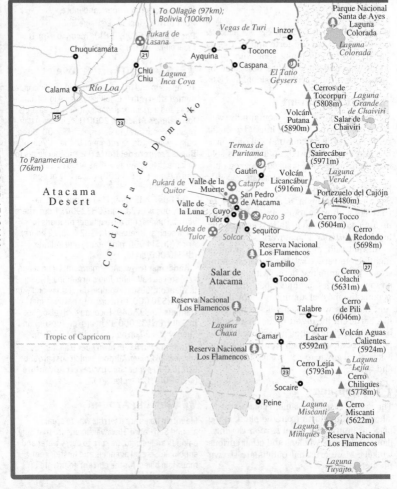

of San Pedro, and easily accessible on foot, by bike or by vehicle.

Circular adobe structures huddle together like muddy bubble-wrap in the ruins of **Tulor** (admission CH$5000), the oldest excavated village in the region. It's an interesting diversion 11km southwest of San Pedro; however, you'll have to take a tour, drive along sandy tracks or mountain-bike it.

The idyllic **Termas de Puritama** (admission CH$12,000, CH$7000 on weekdays 2:30-6pm) puddle together in a box canyon 34km north of San Pedro, en route to El Tatio. Maintained by the Explora company, it has changing rooms on site. Few tours stop here because of the hefty admission charged, but taxis will take you from San Pedro. The springs are a 20-minute walk from the parking lot. The temperature of the springs is about 33°C, and there are several falls and pools. Bring food, water and sunblock.

You can also go swimming at **Pozo 3** (admission CH$3000; ⊙9am-7pm), 3km east of San Pedro off the road to Paso Jama. The swimming pool here is well kept, and there are changing rooms. Gas-heads can rent ATVs, and you can camp for around CH$5000 per person, though you are better off camping in one of the spots closer to town.

Reserva Nacional Los Flamencos

This sprawling reserve encompasses seven geographically distinct sectors south, east and west of San Pedro de Atacama, and encloses many of the area's top attractions.

Conaf maintains a **Centro de Información Ambiental** (⊙10am-1pm & 2:30-4:30pm, in theory) at the *ayllu* of Solcor, which is located 2km past San Pedro de Atacama's customs and immigration post on the road to Toconao.

VALLE DE LA LUNA

Watching the sun set from the exquisite **Valley of the Moon** (adult/student CH$2000/1500; ⊙dawn-dusk) is an unforgettable experience. As you sit atop a giant sand dune, panting from the exertion of climbing it, drinking in spectacular views and watching the sun slip below the horizon, a beautiful transformation occurs: the distant ring of volcanoes, rippling Cordillera de la Sal and surreal lunar landscapes of the valley, are suddenly suffused with intense purples, pinks and golds.

The Valle de la Luna is named after its lunarlike landforms eroded by eons of flood and wind. It's found 15km west of San Pedro de Atacama at the northern end of the Cordillera de la Sal and forms part of Reserva Nacional Los Flamencos.

The valley is San Pedro's most popular and cheapest organized tour; trips typically depart about 4pm, leaving good time to explore before sunset. If you want to avoid dozens of tourist vans, all making the same stops, pick an alternative time. Some hardy souls come here at dawn to sidestep the sunset crowds.

Mountain biking is a great way to get here, but keep to the roads and trails, and make sure you take a flashlight if you're staying for the sunset. If driving, you can leave the highway to explore the dirt roads and box canyons to the north; take care not to get stuck in the sand. Park only on the shoulder or at other designated areas – do not tear up the fragile desert with tire tracks.

Note that camping is not permitted. The area is now being administrated by the Atacameño people, and these are their ancestral grounds and sacred space, so be considerate and clean up your trash.

LAGUNA CHAXA

The jagged crust of the **Salar de Atacama** looks for all the world like God went crazy with a stippling brush. But in the midst of these rough lifeless crystals is an oasis of activity: the pungent **Laguna Chaxa** (admission CH$5000), 65km from San Pedro, the reserve's most easily accessible flamingo breeding site. Three of the five known species (James, Chilean and Andean) can be spotted at this salt lake, as well as plovers,

coots and ducks: bring zoom lenses and snappy reflexes. Sunrise is feeding time for the birds and is the best time to see them. The lagoon is also gorgeous at sunset.

LAGUNAS MISCANTI & MIÑIQUES

Shimmery high-altitude lakes dot the altiplano and make for long but worthwhile excursions from San Pedro. From a junction 3km south of the oasis town of **Toconao**, where some tours stop to take in the distinctive church made of volcanic rock and the nearby **Quebrada de Jere** (admission CH$2000), Ruta 23 heads 46km south toward the village of **Socaire**, which has a pretty colonial church with a cactus-wood ceiling, and a remarkable density of Inkan terraces.

The road then climbs 18km to an eastbound turnoff leading to the glittery-blue sweet-water lakes, **Miñiques** and **Miscanti** (admission CH$2500), watched over by snowtouched volcanoes. The smaller Laguna Miñiques is the largest breeding site for the horned coot on the western side of the Andes, and visitors are kept at bay when the

---

WORTH A TRIP

THE UPPER LOA & ITS TRIBUTARIES

A string of typically Andean villages and ancient forts fleck the difficult terrain to the north of San Pedro de Atacama and east of Calama. A few tour operators from San Pedro visit these villages after the early morning spectacle of watching the El Tatio geysers – taking passes as high as 4800m and jiggling along some tight switchbacks.

From the geysers it's 46km along some switchbacks to highland idyll **Caspana**, as delightful as it is surprising. Nestled in its namesake valley, the 'new' village is built into the rocky escarpment, while the 'old' town teeters on the edge of a high plateau above. It's exactly what an Andean village is supposed to look like – verdant terraces, thatched roofs, the colonial **Iglesia de San Lucas** and a small archaeological **museum**. Do not drink the tap water here.

At this point you could head north to **Ayquina**, an agricultural village, and the nearby thermal springs **Vegas de Turi**, and then east to tiny **Toconce**.

However, most tours now take the road west from Caspana, taking the turnoff northwest via **Laguna Inca Coya** (also known as Laguna Chiu Chiu), a perfectly round oasis, 80m deep according to an expedition led by Jacques Cousteau. A legend claims it was filled by the tears of the jilted lover of Inka Tupac Yupanqui.

From here the dirt road continues west to a junction, where you can turn north to Chiu Chiu and the 12th-century **Pukará de Lasana**, an extensive fortress built into the salmon-pink volcanic rock of the valley. Its husk is pockmarked with defensive nooks and occasional petroglyphs. A touristy restaurant sits alongside.

On the trip back to Chiu Chiu, take time to appreciate the enigmatic petroglyphs that smother the valley, some in plain view and some hiding behind hefty boulders.

Chiu Chiu itself is just 33km from Calama via paved Ruta 21. It's difficult to overestimate the significance of its chunky little **Iglesia de San Francisco** (a national monument and thought to be Chile's oldest church, built in 1540). Peek inside at the cactuswood ceiling and take a stroll around the sandcastle-like whitewashed exterior.

Several companies in San Pedro de Atacama offer organized tours to this area.

birds are breeding. Conaf and the local community from Socaire maintain a lakeside **cabin** (per person CH$20,000) on Miscanti, where you can stay. Rejoining Ruta 23 about 15km south of the turnoff, the road heads eastward past more salt lakes, including **Laguna Tuyajto**, to the Argentine border at Paso de Lago Sico (4079m).

Socaire is 100km from San Pedro, and the *lagunas* are 110km distant at 4300m.

El Tatio Geysers

Visiting the world-famous El Tatio at dawn is like walking through a gigantic steam bath, ringed by volcanoes and fed by 64 gurgling geysers and a hundred gassy fumaroles. Swirling columns of steam envelop onlookers in a Dantesque vision, and the soundtrack of bubbling, spurting and hissing sounds like a field of merrily boiling kettles. The experience does not *feel* like bathtime, however: unless it's bathtime in the arctic. Most visitors find themselves wishing the geysers would spread their heat more efficiently during the freezing dawn.

At 4300m above sea level, El Tatio is the world's highest geyser field. The sight of its steaming fumaroles in the azure clarity of the altiplano is unforgettable, and the mineral structures that form as the boiling water evaporates are strikingly beautiful. As dawn wears on, shafts of sunlight crown the surrounding volcanoes and illuminate the writhing steam. Plans have been in the works for several years to create a thermo-electric plant here, but at the time of writing the Tatio geysers were still free to shoot their steam skyward.

ⓘ Information

The geysers are 95km north of San Pedro de Atacama. Administration of the geysers was handed over to indigenous Atacameño people in 2004. You'll need to stop to pay the entrance fee (CH$5000) at the site's administrative kiosk, about 2km before the geysers.

Tours, priced around CH$20,000, leave at the forbidding hour of 4am to reach the geysers by 6am, the best time to see them. Almost every tour agency in San Pedro offers this tour, so hundreds of sleepy-eyed tourists stumble from minibuses at the appointed hour. After about 8:30am, the winds disperse the steam, although most tours leave by that time so you can enjoy the large thermal pool in virtual privacy. Watch your step – in some places, visitors have fallen through the thin crust into underlying pools of scalding water and suffered severe burns. Dress

in layers: it's toe-numbingly cold at sunbreak but you'll bake in the van on the way back down.

ⓘ Getting There & Away

Tours from San Pedro include breakfast, often with cartons of milk and fresh eggs boiled in geyser pools.

If driving, leave San Pedro no later than 4am to reach the geysers by sunrise. The route north is signed from San Pedro, but some drivers prefer to follow tour minibuses in the dark (the bus drivers do not appreciate this, however). Do not attempt this rough road, which has some difficult stream fords, without a high-clearance pickup or jeep, preferably one with 4WD.

If you rented a vehicle in Calama, consider returning via the picturesque villages of Caspana and Chiu Chiu rather than via San Pedro. Some tours from Calama and San Pedro take this route as well.

Antofagasta

📞055 / POP 296,905

Chile's second-largest city is a rough-and-ready jumble of one-way streets, modern mall culture and work-wearied urbanites. As such, this sprawling port city tends not to tickle the fancy of passing travelers, who often choose to leapfrog over Antofagasta en route north to San Pedro de Atacama or south to Copiapó. And leapfrog they may as well.

However, the city is not all high-rise concrete and gridlocked streets. The old-fashioned plaza is a pleasure to kick back in, and evidence of the golden nitrate era can be found in the wooden-fronted Victorian and Georgian buildings of the coastal Barrio Histórico. Ancient spindly *muelles* (piers) molder picturesquely along the grubby guano-stained port.

The port here handles most of the minerals from the Atacama, especially the copper from Chuquicamata, and is still a major import-export node for Bolivia, which lost the region to Chile during the War of the Pacific.

◉ Sights

Plaza Colón PLAZA
The British community left a visible imprint on Antofagasta's beautiful 19th-century Plaza Colón, which sports rushing fountains amid its palms, mimosas and bougainvilleas. The cute **Torre Reloj** is a replica of London's Big Ben; its chimes even have a baby Big Ben ring to them, and tiled British and Chilean flags intertwine on its trunk.

Barrio Histórico NEIGHBORHOOD

British flavour prevails in the 19th-century Barrio Histórico, between the plaza and the old port, where handsome Victorian and Georgian buildings still stand. On Bolívar, the bottle green-colored **train station** (1887) is the restored terminus of the Antofagasta–La Paz railway. It's closed to the public but you can see several old engines and British-style telephone boxes through the western railings.

Museo Regional MUSEUM

(Av Balmaceda & Bolívar; adult/child CH$600/300; ☺9am-5pm Tue-Fri, 11am-2pm Sat & Sun) The former Aduana (customs house) now houses this two-floor museum, which contains well-presented displays on natural history, and prehistoric and cultural development. Artifacts include a deformed skull, early colonial tidbits and paraphernalia from the nitrate era, including toys fashioned from tin cans.

Resguardo Marítimo HISTORIC BUILDING

This handsome chocolate-colored building with wooden balustrades, built in 1910 as the coast guard, sits at the entrance to the decrepit **Muelle Salitrero** (Nitrate Pier), where locals defy danger signs and fish for crabs. A wrought-iron passageway links it to the former **Gobernación Marítima**.

Terminal Pesquero MARKET

A few blubbery male sea lions, snorting loudly and occasionally snapping at unwary pelicans, circle hopefully below Antofagasta's busy fish market, just north of the Port Authority.

Monumento Natural La Portada LOOKOUT

While not in Antofagasta proper, but rather 25km north of the city, this enormous offshore arch – the centerpiece of a 31-hectare protected zone – is the most spectacular of the area's sights. Topped by marine sediments and supported by a sturdy volcanic base, the stack has been eroded into a natural arch by the stormy Pacific. It's situated on a short westbound lateral off the highway; there are picnic tables, a restaurant, a small Conaf-managed **museum** (admission free; ☺Tue-Sun 10am-6pm) and cliff-top views over surrounding beaches. Take *micro* 129 from Antofagasta's Terminal Pesquero to the junction at La Portada, and then catch the connection (these run in the busy summer season only) or walk 3km west.

🛌 Sleeping

Antofagasta's lodging options are problematic. The budget hostels are no great shakes, many catering to visiting miners and to the surrounding red-light district that spreads around the city center. Midrange properties are mostly overpriced for what you get, and top-end options are mainly limited to chains. Note that weekdays tend to get busy with visiting miners; it's easier to nab a well-priced room on weekends.

Hotel Paola HOTEL $$

(☎268-989; www.hotelpaola.cl; Matta 2469; s/d CH$37,700/50,000; P☎) By far the most stylish choice in the center, the lovely Paola opened recently with its white marble hallway, a contempo look, an inner patio on the 3rd floor and five floors of rooms featuring hardwood floors, fans, flat-screen TVs, fridges and ample closet space. Note that a single room is big enough to accommodate two, plus it runs great weekend discounts.

Hotel Ancla Inn HOTEL $$

(☎224-814; www.anclainn.cl; Baquedano 516; s/d CH$28,000/35,500; P☎) Central location, friendly staff and well-equipped rooms make this a good choice, behind a funny chaletlike facade. The standard rooms are often booked up by miners Monday through Wednesday, when only executive units on top three floors remain. These cost CH$6000 but come with wi-fi, fridges and more space.

Hotel Antofagasta HOTEL $$$

(☎228-811; www.hotelantofagasta.cl; Balmaceda 2575; d CH$67,400-89,700; P@☎≋) Part of the Panamericana Hoteles chain, this five-star mammoth in the old harbor has great ocean views from the lobby, well-appointed rooms (those with ocean vistas are pricier) and all the luxe trimmings. It gets packed on weekdays but often runs great weekend promotions.

Hotel San Marcos HOTEL $

(☎226-303; hsanmarcos@terra.cl; Latorre 2946; s/d CH$21,000/29,500; P☎) The furniture is worn-out, the rooms that overlook the street are quite noisy and the fluorescent lights are not too cozy, but this hotel on the edge of the city center offers decent value for the price and has very friendly service. If you don't need a receipt, you'll get a CH$3000 discount off the room.

Hotel Diego de Almagro HOTEL **$$**
(☎268-331; www.dahoteles.com; Condell 2624; s/d CH$45,300/55,400; @🖥🛜) This chain hotel's liberal use of faux armor, coats of arms and black ironwork succeeds in giving it character. The central location is a blessing and a curse: street-facing rooms get ringside seats over the buskers below. The hotel also has a more upscale offering south of town; check online for specials.

Marsal Hotel HOTEL **$$**
(☎268-063; www.marsalhotel.cl, in Spanish; Arturo Prat 867; s/d CH$35,000/42,000; 🅿🛜) This stony-faced establishment with a wannabe-classic look in the lobby has spacious if soulless rooms with small bathrooms; expect cable TV, fridge, large mirrored wardrobes and, off some rooms, balconies.

Hotel Costa Marfil HOTEL **$**
(☎283-590; www.hotelcostamarfil.cl; Arturo Prat 950; s CH$20,400-25,400, d CH$25,400-28,500; 🅿@🛜) The blazing neon light might get to you, but the rooms in this large hotel block are acceptable. Don't go for the dark standard units that face the noisy inner hallway; upgrade to a bigger executive room, which comes with natural light.

Hotel Frontera HOTEL **$**
(☎281-219; Bolívar 558; s/d CH$17,000/22,000, without bathroom CH$12,000/17,000; 🛜) Behind the modern-looking front is a set of basic but decently clean rooms, each complete with a cable TV. No breakfast is included or available but at least there's wi-fi.

Camping Rucamóvil CAMPGROUND **$**
(☎262-358; Km11; campsite per person CH$4000) A fairly well-equipped site south of town with an ocean view from its terrace and family cabins (CH$25,000, up to four people). Take *micro* 102 from Mercado Central and ask to be dropped off at Cruce Roca Roja.

🍴 Eating & Drinking

Perched on the north end of the old port, **Terminal Pesquero** is host to over 20 stalls that peddle tasty fresh shellfish; get there by early afternoon, before all the fish are sold. More fish, as well as meat, vegetables and fruity fare, is available at the attractive old **Mercado Central** (JS Ossa), which is located between Maipú and Uribe.

Cafe del Sol CHILEAN **$$**
(Esmeralda 2013; mains CH$7000-8000; ⊘closed Sun) On weekend nights, this ramshackle corner resto-bar comes alive with live Andean music and dancing (CH$3000 cover after 11pm). Other nights, it serves a good range of mains in the cozy wooden interior with dim lighting. Plus it does a good set lunch for CH$2500.

Macao RESTAURANT, BAR **$$**
(Av República de Croacia 155; mains CH$7800-14,000) Come to this trendy beachfront spot on Playa Balneario for the Polynesian-style decor, complete with lanterns and sand floors, great palm tree-fringed views of the city, innovative mains, nice cocktails and live DJ tunes.

El Arriero PARRILLA **$$**
(Condell 264; mains CH$3800-12,000; ⊘closed dinner Sun) Meat is the specialty at this rustic dining room decked out with arches, dried hanging hams and a fountain in the middle. Full of old-fashioned charm, it serves huge portions of mainly meaty dishes. The *parrillada* for two (CH$15,500) is a feast.

Bongo DINER **$**
(Baquedano 743; set menu CH$2100-2900, mains CH$1400-3900; ⊘closed Sun) Buzzy eatery with thick-cushioned booths, a tidy mezzanine above and a good 'n' greasy menu for those times when only a draft beer and burger will do. Place your order at the counter and pay before you sit down.

Don Pollo FAST FOOD **$**
(JS Ossa 2594; chicken from CH$1500; ⊘lunch & dinner) Cheap, cheerful and usually crowded, Don Pollo has plastic tables huddled around a grass-hut patio. Locals come in droves for the succulent chicken.

Che Ignacio PUB **$$**
(Antonino Toro 982; mains CH$5900-9800; ⊘closed Sun) This European-style bar with patio seating has a meat-focused pub menu and lots of men who come to watch sports on TV.

ℹ Information

Numerous ATMs are located downtown. Internet cafes around the center offer access for CH$500 per hour.

Conaf (☎383-320; Av Argentina 2510; ⊘8:30am-1:30pm & 3-5:30pm Mon-Thu, 8:30am-1:30pm & 3-4:15pm Fri) For information on the region's natural attractions.

Hospital Regional (☎656-551; Av Argentina 1964)

Sernatur (☎451-818; infoantofagasta@sernatur.cl; Arturo Prat 384; ⊘8:30am-7pm

Mon-Fri, 8:30am-2pm Sat Jan-Mar, 8:30am-5:30pm Mon-Fri Apr-Dec) The city tourist office, conveniently located by the plaza, gives out a generous amount of brochures.

❶ Getting There & Away

Air

Lan (☑600-526-2000; www.lanchile.com; Arturo Prat 445) has several daily flights to Santiago (CH$220,000, two hours), as well as direct daily flights to Iquique (CH$47,500, one hour) and La Serena (CH$132,500, 1½ hours).

Sky (☑600-600-2828; www.skyairline. cl; General Velasquez 890, Local 3) also flies to Iquique (CH$27,800, two daily), Arica (CH$52,800, one daily), Copiapó (CH$80,500, one daily via La Serena) and Santiago (CH$86,200, six daily), with connections to the south.

Bus

The new **Terminal de Buses Cardenal Carlos Oviedo** (Av Pedro Aguirre Cerda 5750) serves most inter-city destinations. A few bus companies still operate also out of their own terminals near downtown, mainly along Latorre. Locally based companies use the **Terminal de Buses Evaristo Montt** (Riquelme 513), also known as the Terminal de Buses Rurales.

Nearly all northbound services now use coastal Ruta 1, via Tocopilla, en route to Iquique and Arica.

Buses Romani (☑226-974; www.busesromani. cl, in Spanish; Latorre 3055)

Condor/Flota Barrios (☑223-442; www. flotabarrios.cl, in Spanish; Av Pedro Aguirre Cerda 5336)

Pullman Bus (☑224-976; www.pullman.cl, in Spanish; Latorre 2805)

Tur Bus (☑220-240; www.turbus.cl, in Spanish; Latorre 2751)

DESTINATION	COST (CH$)	DURATION(HR)
Arica	19,400	9
Calama	5000	3
Copiapó	24,000	9
Iquique	17,000	6
La Serena	24,800	12
Santiago	34,400	18

❶ Getting Around

To/From the Airport

Antofagasta's Aeropuerto Cerro Moreno is 25km north of the city. Private taxis cost CH$13,000; try calling **Gran Via** (☑240-505).

Car

Avis (☑563-140; www.avis.cl, in Spanish; Baquedano 364)

First (☑225-777; www.firstrentacar.cl, in Spanish; Bolívar 623)

South of Antofagasta

The Panamericana south of Antofagasta continues its trip through the dry Atacama Desert, where water, people and tourist attractions are scarce.

MANO DEL DESIERTO

A towering **granite hand**, its oddly tapering fingers outstretched in a mock salute, breaks through the desert crust about 45km south of the junction of the Panamericana and Ruta 28. This curious *mano del desierto* was built in 1992 by sculptor Mario Irarrázaval. Bus travelers should look to the west side of the highway.

OBSERVATORIO CERRO PARANAL

In the world of high-powered telescopes, where rival institutes jostle to claim the 'biggest,' 'most powerful' or 'most technologically advanced' specimens, Paranal is right up there with the big boys. This groundbreaking observatory has a Very Large Telescope (VLT) consisting of an array of four 8.2m telescopes – for a time at least, the most powerful optical array in the world. The **Cerro Paranal observatory** (☑055-435-100; www. eso.org) is run by the European Southern Observatory (ESO), and is so futuristic-looking that portions of the James Bond flick, *Quantum of Solace,* were filmed here. There's a hotel for scientists on site, which looks like it is built underground; you'll enter the foliage-filled lobby as part of the tour. The observatory complex is situated on Cerro Paranal at 2664m above sea level, 120km south of Antofagasta; a lateral leaves the Panamericana just north of the Mano del Desierto (assuming you're heading south). The drive from Antofagasta takes about two hours.

The fascinating free visits are allowed on Saturdays, at 9:30am and at 1:30pm. You must show up half an hour early; tours last three hours. You'll need to schedule months in advance, and you'll also need your own vehicle to get there. Call or check the observatory's website for details and updates.

Norte Chico

Best Places to Eat

» Chaski (p216)

» Coral de Bahía (p198)

» Donde Martita Solar
Kitchen (p216)

» Legado (p201)

Best Places to Stay

» Hotel La Casona (p200)

» Hostal El Punto (p209)

» Hacienda Los Andes
(p221)

» El Tesoro de Elqui (p218)

Why Go?

Caught between the ocean and the Andes, Chile's Norte
Chico (Little North), is unique unto itself. La Serena, a coastal colonial capital and the region's largest city, is a must-see
for anybody visiting. From there, move on to the mystical
Elqui Valley, the verdant home to Chile's pisco producers,
new-age communes and cutting-edge observatories. Further north are some amazing national parks, a trendy little beach hideaway, and kilometers of uncharted coastline
just waiting for you to set up camp or charge out for an
afternoon surf. Wildlife lovers won't want to miss the playful penguins of Reserva Nacional Pingüino de Humboldt
and Parque Nacional Pan de Azúcar. And high in the Andes,
the seldom-visited Parque Nacional Nevado Tres Cruces is
a great place to spot vicuña and flamingos. Despite its diminutive moniker, the Little North is just a bit bigger than
most people thought.

When to Go

La Serena

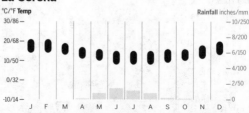

Jan–Feb Chileans
on vacation storm
the beaches,
making hotel op-
tions scarcer and
sights crowded.

Jul–Aug Tem-
peratures drop
dramatically at
night but days are
hot and blissfully
free of crowds.

Sep–Nov Catch
the storied sight
of the flowering
desert, best in
Parque Nacional
Llanos de Challe.

Norte Chico Highlights

1 Lounge around Norte Chico's coolest little beach town, the pretty **Bahía Inglesa** (p197)

2 Learn just how potent the little pisco grape can be as you hop through villages of the groovy **Elqui Valley** (p214)

3 Take in starry southern skies at one of many **observatories** dotting Norte Chico (p213)

4 Get lost on your way to the high-Andean lagoons of **Parque Nacional Nevado Tres Cruces** (p202)

5 Hop on a boat to the penguin colonies at **Reserva Nacional Pingüino de Humboldt** (p205)

6 Bop through the colonial center of **La Serena** (p206), then head to the beach for surf, sun and sand

7 Find your own way as you pioneer campsites and surf spots in the beachfront **Parque Nacional Pan de Azúcar** (p195)

❶ Getting Around

The Panamericana wiggles its way along Norte Chico's coastline, making it easy to reach by car or bus. There are also busy domestic airports near La Serena and Copiapó. Turning off the Panamericana can quickly feel like venturing into the outback as gravel and dirt roads deteriorate rapidly and public transportation quickly dwindles. As a result, getting to many out-of-the-way national parks and attractions can be tricky without taking a tour or having your own wheels; in some cases only high-clearance pickup trucks or 4WDs will do.

Parque Nacional Pan de Azúcar

An abundance of white sandy beaches, sheltered coves and stony headlands line the desert coastline 30km north of Chañaral. Chañaral itself is a cheerless mining and fishing port set among the rugged headlands of the Sierra de las Animas and offers little appeal to the traveler; it's best used only as the gateway for the park.

It's the wildlife that brings most international travelers to Pan de Azúcar, which straddles the border between Regiónes II and III. That's because the cool Humboldt Current supports a variety of marine life. Star of the show is the endangered Humboldt penguin, which nests on an offshore island. Here you'll also spot slippery marine otters and rowdy sea lions, as well as scores of pelicans and cormorants.

At higher elevations, moisture from the *camanchaca* (thick fog) nurtures a unique collection of more than 20 species of cacti and succulents. Further inland, guanacos (wild camelid related to llamas) are a common sight and wild foxes will approach you in hope of scraps.

The 437-sq-km park's altitude ranges from sea level to 900m. There are great coastal campsites, which get busy in summer.

◉ Sights & Activities

Isla Pan de Azúcar   ISLAND

The subtriangular-shaped 'Sugarloaf' Island, or Isla Pan de Azúcar, lies a tantalizingly short distance offshore, its base often shrouded by *camanchaca* at twilight. It is home to about 2000 Humboldt penguins, as well as other birds, otters and sea lions. The island is a restricted area, but local fishers approach the 100-hectare island by boat for up-close-and-personal views.

Launches charge CH$5000 per person (with a 10-person minimum) from Caleta Pan de Azúcar; in the low season, you could end up forking out as much as CH$50,000. Round trips take 1½ hours, and run from 10am to 6pm in summer, and to 4pm in winter. You'll have to sign up at the bay kiosk and wait for the next tour. Note that it is more difficult to round up enough people during the week; prepare to wait longer or pay more.

Trails   HIKING

There are five trails in the park. The most popular is the 2.5km **El Mirador**; en route you will see sea cacti, guanaco and chilla fox. Next up is **Las Lomitas**, an easy 4km trail with minimal slope; look out for the black-hooded sierra finch. You can also walk the 1.5km coastal path that goes from Pan de Azúcar harbor to Playa Piqueros.

☞ Tours

Etty Tour   GUIDED TOUR

(🖉481-733) Does guided tours (in Spanish) to Isla Pan de Azúcar from Chañaral for about CH$40,000 (up to five people) for half a day or CH$20,000 if the guide joins you in your own car. The owner can also hook you up with taxi transfers. In the high season these cost between CH$4000 and CH$5000 per person.

🛏 Sleeping & Eating

Camping is available at Playa Piqueros, Playa El Soldado and Caleta Pan de Azúcar. The most basic facilities start at CH$2000 per person. Caleta also has two privately owned campsites. You can guerrilla (free) camp on an arching spit of white sand called El Refugio, 14km north of Chañaral.

There are three restaurants in Caleta Pan de Azúcar, which all charge about CH$4500 for a dish of fish with sides; try the friendly El Changuito at the end of the bay.

Pan de Azúcar Lodge   LODGE $

(www.pandeazucarlodge.cl; 2-person campsite CH$15,000) The best camp is run by the ecological Pan de Azúcar Lodge. It has two sites, one on Playa Piqueros and another on El Soldado, both with bathrooms, hot water, solar energy and activities (in summer) like yoga, treks and various workshops. The lodge also has five **beach cabins** (2/3 people CH$45,000/60,000) and an outdoor spa.

ℹ️ Information

One kilometer south of Caleta Pan de Azúcar, Conaf's **Environmental Information Center** (Playa Piqueros; ⊙8:30am-12:30pm & 2-6pm) has exhibits on the park's flora and fauna, and a cactarium. It also has a brochure in English, with explanations and a trails map. There is a Conaf checkpoint at Km15 on the southern entrance road from Chañaral, where you pay the CH$4000 fee. Make sure you hold on to your ticket, as you'll be asked to present it at different trailheads.

ℹ️ Getting There & Away

Pan de Azúcar is 30km north of Chañaral by a well-maintained paved road. Most people reach it by tour or transfer from Caldera/Bahía Inglesa or Copiapó.

If you are driving from the north, there are two minor park entrances off the Panamericana – one at Km1014 (connecting to Route C-112) and another at Km968 (connecting to Route C-110).

Caldera

📱052 / POP 13,734

Year-round sun, some great beaches around town and abundant seafood make Caldera – once the second-biggest port during the 19th-century mining boom – and its sister resort at nearby Bahía Inglesa Región III's most popular seaside retreats. While Caldera is hugely popular with vacationing Chileans, most foreign visitors fall in love with neighboring Bahía Inglesa for its crop of great little hotels and restaurants and its laid-back vibe. If you're on a budget, it's cheaper to stay in Caldera by night and spend your days on Bahía's beach.

Caldera is on the south shore of the Bahía de Caldera, 75km west of Copiapó and just west of the Panamericana. Av Diego de Almeyda continues south as Av Carvallo to Bahía Inglesa. The action centers around the large plaza, from where the pedestrian mall on Gana leads you to the brown-sand beach.

👁️ Sights

Casa Tornini   MUSEUM
(www.casatornini.cl; Paseo Gana 210; admission CH$2000; 6 tours daily in Spanish, English & German during summer) This red neoclassical mansion from the early 1890s, once owned by a family of Italian immigrants, is the town's newest attraction. The guided tours take in six period rooms, with historical items and original furniture, plus two spaces that host temporary photo and art exhibits.

Plaza Carlos Condell   PLAZA
This pretty plaza-cum-playground presides over the town center. Its highlight is the chocolate-and-cream 19th-century **Iglesia San Vicente** (1862) and its Gothic tower.

FREE **Centro Cultural**
Estación Caldera   HISTORIC BUILDING
(⊙10am-2pm & 4-7pm Tue-Sun) Built in 1850, this distinctive building on the north side of the jetty was the terminus for South America's first railroad. Today it houses a gorgeously airy exhibition space with wooden beams, sometimes used for festivals and various events, and a **paleontology museum** (admission CH$600).

Muelle Pesquero   HISTORIC BUILDING
Down by the seafront, Caldera's colorful fishing jetty teems with hungry pelicans, colorful little boats and knife-wielding *señoras* busily gutting and frying the catch.

👉 Tours

The town's beach is slightly contaminated with gasoline from the nearby dock. You are better off taking a short day trip to Bahía Inglesa or further afield to Playa La Virgen. There's a 7km bike trail from Caldera to Bahía Inglesa.

La Ruta del Ostion   BIKE, VAN TOUR
(patricio.covarrubias@gmail.com; Montt 274) Run by friendly Patricio. Has bikes for rent (CH$5000 to CH$7000 per day, CH$4000 for drop-off in Bahía Inglesa) and offers van tours to Pan de Azúcar (CH$90,000) and Playa La Virgen (CH$70,000), based on four people.

Geoturismo Chile   BIKE, VAN TOUR
(www.geoturismo-chile.cl) Doesn't have a physical address; offers similar prices to La Ruta del Ostion.

Trimaran Ecotour   BOAT TOUR
(adult/child CH$2000/1500) You can take a one-hour boat tour to the lighthouse, spotting penguins and sea lions en route. Trimaran Ecotour has a kiosk on the jetty; it runs four tours daily (12:30pm, 2pm, 3:30pm and 5:30pm) during the summer, and on weekends only otherwise.

🛏️ Sleeping

Hotel Costa Fosil   HOTEL $$
(📱316-451; www.jandy.cl, in Spanish; Gallo 560; s/d CH$29,800/38,900; 🅿🛜) This ship lookalike is the town's best-value hotel as well as

its most central, just half a block from the plaza. Its 23 pleasant rooms are set around a breezy patio and there's a small sun-drenched terrace upstairs.

Hotel Montecarlo
HOTEL $$

(315-388; www.hotel-montecarlo.cl, in Spanish; Av Carvallo 627; s/d CH$34,500/39,500; P) Behind the modern facade of this two-floor hotel hides a leafy patio complete with cart-wheels, vines and trickling fountains. The service is warm and professional and the 34 spotless rooms have TVs.

Residencial Millaray
GUESTHOUSE $

(315-528; Cousiño 331; d without bathroom CH$25,000; P) This ramshackle but friend-ly family home opposite the plaza offers a handful of simple rooms. The same family has two hotels nearby, **Hotel Millaray II** (Gallo 300; d/tr CH$40,000/45,000; P) and **Hotel Montriri** (Tocornal 371; d/tr CH$40,000/45,000; P); rooms have TV but not much charm.

Hotel Terrasol
HOTEL $$

(319-885; hotelterrasolcaldera@gmail.com; Gallo 370; d/tr CH$30,000/45,000; P) A decent choice for its laid-back atmosphere, family vibe and acceptable rooms. There's a funky back patio complete with AstroTurf.

Eating

For the cheapest seafood, head to the Ter-minal Pesquero behind the old train sta-tion. The food stands here serve up simple fish dishes with sides from CH$3000, which you can enjoy on a wraparound seaside ter-race. Outside the market are several stands serving seafood empanadas (turnovers) and fried fish sandwiches.

For more interesting restaurants, head over to Bahía Inglesa.

Il Piron di Oro
SEAFOOD $$

(Cousiño 218; mains CH$5000-8000) This no-frills locals' favorite just up from the harbor serves up simple decor, a couple of sidewalk tables and sizable portions of mostly sea-food, and some fusion options like oyster and shrimp burritos. It gets packed with families for lunch.

Cafe Museo
CAFE $

(Edwards 479a; cakes CH$1000-2200, sandwiches CH$1200) Head to this cute little cafe with old posters and newspaper clips, adjacent to Casa Tornini, for its delicious cakes, sand-wiches and real espressos on six wooden tables inside and a couple on the sidewalk.

Miramar
SEAFOOD $$

(Gana 090; mains CH$6000-9950) A posh pink restaurant on the seafront, with lots of win-dows offering beach and harbor views and dependable seafood mainstays.

Drinking

Pepe's
BAR

(Pasaje Bombero Alfaro 340; to 4am) This buzzy bar, just behind the western side of the plaza, has DJs on weekends, live music, theater performances, plus cocktails and seafood bites.

Information

Centro Telefonica (Cousiño 329; 9am-10pm) For international calling.
Oficina de Turismo (316-076; 9am-10pm Sun-Thu, 9am-midnight Fri & Sat summer, 9am-2pm & 4-7pm Mon-Sat rest of year) The friendly tourist kiosk, on the northwest side of the Plaza de Armas, offers a wealth of brochures although staff speak limited English.

Getting There & Around

Private taxis to Aeropuerto Desierto de Ata-cama, 20km to the south, cost CH$5000. The **Pullman** (315-227; cnr Gallo & Cousiño) and **Tur Bus** (317-399; Gana 241) terminals, about five blocks southeast of the plaza, offer services to Copiapó (CH$2000, one hour), Antofagasta (CH$15,000 to CH$22,700, six hours) and Santiago (CH$20,000 to CH$29,400, 12 hours). Buses and taxi colectivos (shared taxis) run between Caldera and Bahía Inglesa for CH$500 and CH$900 respectively.

Bahía Inglesa
052

A short distance south of Caldera is the sweet little seaside resort of Bahía Inglesa. With rocky outcrops scudding out of the crystal waters, this is the place to come for a spot of beachside fun. It has become one of the north's most popular vacation spots, with a trendy feel and a long white-sand beach. There's a nice beachfront promenade peppered with shops, restaurants and arti-sanal ice-cream stands, and a cool Mediter-ranean feel. Bahía Inglesa gets going late in the morning so don't expect much to be open if you're an early riser.

Bahía Inglesa takes its name from the British pirates who took refuge here in the 17th century; there are legends of their treasure still being hidden somewhere in these parts.

VIRGIN SLICE OF BEACH PARADISE

Until just a couple of years ago, the stunning **Playa La Virgen** (☎052-216-524; www.playalavirgen.cl, in Spanish), 46km south of Bahía Inglesa along a lovely coastal road, was a well-guarded treasure of few in-the-know Chileans. While the secret is now out, it's worth a day trip or a couple of days' stay at this little sliver of sandy paradise. In January the parasol-dotted beach does get packed with a young party crowd and in February with families.

You can head there with one of the tour agencies in Caldera or Bahía Inglesa or arrange your own minivan transport. If you have your own wheels, note that the road is rough (but doable with a regular car) and that it costs CH$6000 to park by the reception, unless you're renting one of the cabins. To avoid the fee, park at the top and walk downhill for 10 minutes to the crescent-shaped beach.

Kayaks are for rent on the beach (CH$3000 for a single, CH$6000 for a double).

For accommodations, two-person cabins start at CH$50,000 in high season; it's CH$65,000 for one with a kitchen. A campsite (no electricity) for six people costs CH$36,000. The pricey restaurant-bar, earthy **Turqueza** (mains CH$7500-9900), has sandy floors, a thatched roof, straw chairs and a terrace with panoramic ocean views.

🏃 Activities

A popular pastime in Bahía Inglesa is **windsurfing**, though equipment is not available for hire.

Morro Ballena　　　WATER SPORTS
(www.morroballena.cl, in Spanish) Has a kiosk at the far end of the beach, below Coral de Bahía. It offers two-hour boat trips to El Morro island across the way (CH$50,000 for six people), one-hour kayaking jaunts (CH$15,000 for two) and one-hour snorkeling trips (from CH$15,000). It rents kayaks, too (from CH$2000 for 30 minutes) and snorkeling equipment (CH$12,000 for two hours). There are a few tables on the sand where you can have natural juices and live scallops (from CH$2000 per pop).

Caldera Tour Atacama　　VAN TOURS
(www.calderatouratacama.cl; Av El Morro 610b) Next to Domo Bahía Inglesa hotel. Arranges excursions and day trips (CH$20,000 to CG$30,000, with a six-person minimum) to nearby beaches, like Playa La Virgen, as well as to Pan de Azúcar and the San José mine near Copiapó. At the time of writing it was getting bikes for rent.

Nautica La Rada　　　SAILING
(☎099-684-64032; antonioabelli@hotmail.com) For a worthwhile splurge, book a sailing trip with Nautica La Rada, run by seawolf Antonio and his sons. The shortest one (from CH$25,000 per person, with a two-person minimum, raw food snacks and drinks included) takes you to El Morro; you'll see

humpback whales if luck strikes. To rent the sailboat for a day costs CH$250,000 with all meals included. You can even live it up and do a two-day sail to Playa La Virgen.

🛏 Sleeping & Eating

Coral de Bahía　　　HOTEL $$
(☎319-160; www.coraldebahia.cl, in Spanish; Av El Morro 564; d CH$50,000-70,000, ste CH$80,000; 🅿🛜) Eleven lovely rooms upstairs, some with balconies and sweeping ocean views at the far end of the beach. This hotel gets booked up in summer, when it accepts either seven-night advance reservations or walk-ins. The beachfront **restaurant** (mains CH$6500-11,000) downstairs has a nice terrace, and dishes up delectable seafood with a twist. Asian, African and Mediterranean influences inspire the menu.

Nautel　　　GUESTHOUSE $$
(☎09-7849-9030; www.nautel.cl, in Spanish; Copiapó 549; d incl breakfast CH$55,000-65,000, tr incl breakfast CH$75,000, cabin CH$120,000; 🅿🛜) Stylish boutique-y guesthouse on a street just up from the Domo hotel, and a few steps to the right. The modern building has six earth-toned doubles (four with ocean view) and there's an adorable four-person wooden cabin on the beachfront. The open-air kitchen and living space are a boon if you want to mingle, and there's direct access to the beach. Service can be spotty, though.

Hotel Rocas de Bahía　　HOTEL $$$
(☎316-005; www.rocasdebahia.cl, in Spanish; El Morro 888; r/tr CH$89,300/105,900; 🅿@🛜🏊)

The town's swankiest hotel is this sparkling-white five-floor maze that shoots up the cliff overlooking the bay. All the rooms have balconies and lots of natural light; about half come with ocean views. The small pool on the 4th floor has stretching vistas.

Domo Bahía Inglesa　　　　　HOTEL $$
(www.domobahiainglesa.cl; Av El Morro 610; d/tr CH$42,000/52,000; 🛜) The two five-person concrete domes come with bathrooms and wooden interiors. Prices drop considerably out of summer season. Reserve by email. The **restaurant** (mains CH$5400-9900; 🛜) in a huge dome facing the seafront has an open-air terrace and stays open late.

Camping Playa Las Machas　CAMPGROUND $
(📞315-424; Playa Las Machas; campsites up to 6 people CH$18,700, cabañas CH$25,420-43,320) A big exposed campsite on sandy land overlooking Bahía Inglesa, this is a good camping spot but overpriced during summer. Enter from the road to Ruta 5 south of town. Some cabins share bathroom facilities with the campsite.

El Plateao　　　　　INTERNATIONAL $$
(Av El Morro 756; mains CH$6000-8500) Beachfront views and a funky bohemian vibe are trademarks at this buzzing two-floor bar and restaurant, which serves a global mix of favorites, from Thai curries to Italian risottos. The views are more impressive than the food.

Punto de Referencia　　　　FUSION $$
(Miramar 182; mains CH$6500-8000) Chic choice tucked inside a side street right next to Domo, it specializes in sushi and sashimi (from CH$2500) served on light-colored wooden tables inside and a small terrace up front.

Naturalia　　　　　PIZZERIA $
(pizzas CH$2900-3900) Next door to Punto de Referencia, and sharing the same terrace, this simple eatery churns out pizzas, empanadas and freshly squeezed juices.

Catalina Amenabar　　　　CAFE $
(cakes CH$1200-2100; 🕙noon-9:30pm) This seafront cafe has delicious cakes, espressos and teas, to take away or enjoy on one small table, if you're lucky enough to snag it.

ℹ Information

There is no money exchange or an ATM in Bahía Inglesa. The nearest ATM is in Caldera so stock up before you come here.

Caldera Tour Atacama has internet access (CH$1000 per hour).

The small **oficina de turismo** (🕙10am-9pm Mon-Fri, 11am-9pm Sat & Sun summer, 10am-6pm daily rest of year), right on the seafront, is staffed with young enthusiastic Chileans who happily shell out useful phone numbers as well as info about secret beaches and spots in the area.

ℹ Getting There & Away

Most transit is out of neighboring Caldera. You can get there by *colectivo* for CH$900 or arrange a transfer by minivan for a little less; the tourist office has phone numbers. In summer months *colectivos* get packed at the end of the day so you may have to wait a while. Minivans charge about CH$10,000 per person to get to Playa La Virgen, with a three- or four-person minimum.

Copiapó

📞052 / POP 129,090

Powerful men wrangle through the bars and strip clubs of this perfectly pleasant mining town. But like most places on the frontier, there's a certain edgy visceral attraction to it all. With its pleasing climate, a leafy main plaza and many historic buildings, you may find yourself oddly comfortable amid the milling miners and down-to-business pace of Copiapó. This said, it's not really worth stopping here for too long unless you want to make a foray into the remote mountains near the Argentine border, especially the breathtaking Parque Nacional Nevado Tres Cruces, Laguna Verde and Ojos del Salado, the highest active volcano in the world.

The town, nestling in the narrow valley floor on the north bank of Río Copiapó, does earn some kudos for being the site of several historical firsts: South America's first railroad (completed in 1852) ran from here to Caldera; here, too, appeared the nation's first telegraph and telephone lines, and Chile's first gas works. All came on the back of the 18th-century gold boom and the rush to cash in on silver discovered at neighboring Chañarcillo in 1832. Today it's mainly copper that keeps the miners and beer-hall gals in the green. In fact, the town is booming as of late; some 150,000 people have come to take advantage of multimillion-dollar investments in mining, expected to keep the town thriving for the next 15 years.

◉ Sights

Copiapó's mining heyday is evident throughout its town center. Shaded by century-old pepper trees, Plaza Prat, which marks the city's historical center, is graced by several buildings from the early mining era, not least the elegant **Iglesia Catedral**, with its three-tiered bell tower and neoclassical design.

Museo Mineralógico   MUSEUM
(cnr Colipí & Rodríguez; adult/child CH$500/200; ⊙10am-1pm & 3:30-7pm Mon-Fri, 10am-1pm Sat) This must-see museum literally dazzles. A tribute to the raw materials to which the city owes its existence, it displays a kaleidoscopic collection of more than 2300 samples, some as delicate as coral, others bright as neon under fluorescent light.

Museo Regional de Atacama   MUSEUM
(Atacama 98; adult/child CH$600/300, Sun admission free; ⊙2-5:45pm Mon, 9am-5:45pm Tue-Fri, 10am-12:45pm & 3-5:45pm Sat, 10am-12:45pm Sun & holidays) Built in the 1840s by industrial moguls and radical politicians, the Matta family, this national monument is worth a snoop for the architecture and the piecemeal museum with indigenous artifacts and a mock mine made of fiberglass.

FREE **Museo Minero de Tierra Amarilla**   MUSEUM
(www.museominerodetierraamarilla.cl, in Spanish; ⊙8am-5pm Mon-Fri, 9am-1pm Sat & Sun) To find out more about the region's geology, head 18km east of town to this new private museum near the village of Tierra Amarilla. Surrounded by working mines, the restored 200-year-old *quincho* (traditional mudhouse) features eight rooms exhibiting fossils, volcanic rocks, meteorites, minerals and oxidated rare stones. Catch a yellow *colectivo* from the corner of Chacabuco and Chañarcillo (CH$900).

☞ Tours

Copiapó is the gateway for trips to highland destinations, such as Parque Nacional Nevado Tres Cruces and Ojos del Salado, and the coastline highlights like Bahía Inglesa and Parque Nacional Pan de Azúcar. Sandduning with a 4WD in the desert just outside town is another thrilling option. Guided tours to the surrounding mines are just getting started in the area; ask at the Sernatur office.

Puna de Atacama   GUIDED TOUR
(☎099-051-3202; www.punadeatacama.com; O'Higgins 21) Ercio Mettifogo Rendic offers fun customized tours to surrounding highlights as well as lots of secret spots in the desert and the mountains.

Atacama Chile   GUIDED TOUR
(☎211-191; www.atacamachile.com; Maipú 580, Local C) Offers all the standard trips to attractions around town and beyond.

Aventurismo Expediciones   ADVENTURE TOUR
(☎09-599-2184; www.aventurismo.cl; Atacama 240) This agency has the concession on Ojos del Salado climbs.

★★ Festivals & Events

Copiapó celebrates its own creation on December 8. August 10 is **Día del Minero** (Miner's Day).

Fiesta de la Candelaria   RELIGIOUS
The first Sunday of February sees this festival celebrated at the Iglesia de la Candelaria at Los Carrera and Figueroa, 2km east of Plaza Prat. The Virgin of the Candelaria is said to protect miners – hence her celebrity in the region.

⌨ Sleeping

Hotels and *residenciales* (budget accommodations) get booked up by visiting miners during the week and prices are generally inflated, year-round.

TOP CHOICE **Hotel La Casona**   HOTEL $$
(☎217-277; www.lacasonahotel.cl; O'Higgins 150; s/d from CH$43,000/49,000; ℗@⊚) There's airiness and charm to this wonderfully homey 12-room hotel a 10-minute walk west of the plaza, boasting a series of leafy patios and bilingual owners. All room categories have a country-casual feel, hardwood floors and cable TVs. The restaurant serves delicious dinners.

Hotel Montecatini   HOTEL $$
(☎211-363; www.hotelmontecatini.cl; Infante 766; s/d standard CH$22,000/30,000, superior CH$30,000/37,000; ℗⊚☀) It is worth the extra expense for the spacious superior rooms along a tranquil verdant courtyard. The older units are out of date. The pool may or may not have water. Note that the hotel is located right by Copiapó's unofficial red-light district.

Hotel Chagall
HOTEL $$$

(☑352-900; www.chagall.cl; O'Higgins 760; d CH$69,000-79,000; ᴘ@⊛⬛) This four-star business property just off Plaza Prat has a swanky spotlit lobby, a full set of facilities and plush rooms, the more expensive ones equipped with air-conditioning.

Hotel del Sol
HOTEL $

(☑215-672; Rodríguez 550; s/d CH$22,000/28,000; ᴘ⊛) Cheerful yellow-painted hotel with a string of simple but clean rooms at a good price, just a short walk from the plaza.

Residencial Benbow
GUESTHOUSE $

(☑217-634; Rodríguez 541; s/d CH$12,000 /16,000, without bathroom CH$7000/14,000; ⊛) Its location a few steps from the plaza is the reason to stay at this basic guesthouse with a set of dark rooms. The adjacent restaurant serves decent food.

✗ Eating & Drinking

Restaurants in Copiapó are pricey. At night, women come out to entertain miners, and ladies of the night roam the streets just off the main plaza.

Legado
INTERNATIONAL $$

(O'Higgins 12; mains CH$6950-17,450; ⊙dinner only, closed Sun) The town's most innovative restaurant, with a series of small cheerful rooms and interesting meats like crocodile and Wagyu beef. Great wine list, too, with some 1200 Chilean wines.

Don Elias
CHILEAN $

(☑364-146; Los Carrera 421; mains CH$2800-7700; ⊙closed Sun dinner) A downmarket canteen with bright lights and a blaring TV, it churns out excellent-value *almuerzos* (set lunches) and à la carte dinners.

Cafelatte
RESTAURANT, BAR $$

(O'Higgins 857; mains CH$5440-9590; ⊙closed Sun) Cozy resto-bar a few blocks from the square serving the usual suspects, from pizzas and pastas to salads and sandwiches, and a happy hour daily.

Tololo Pampa
BAR $

(Atacama 291; ⊙closed Sun & Mon) A happening boho joint with a series of artsy colorful rooms and an open-air back patio with rough-hewn furniture and an outdoor fireplace. Come for drinks and late-night snacks (CH$4000 to CH$5500).

Café Colombia
CAFE $

(Colipí A101; ⊛) Right on the main plaza by Mall Plaza Real, this is a good choice for real coffee and snacks. Great people-watching from the sidewalk tables.

❶ Information

Numerous ATMs are located at banks around the plaza. There's a *cambio* (money exchange) on the 1st floor of Mall Plaza Real.

Internet cafes charge around CH$500 and can be found all over the center.

Conaf (☑213-404; Juan Martínez 55; ⊙8:30am-5:30pm Mon-Thu, to 4:30pm Fri) Has information on regional parks, including brochures in English about Pan de Azúcar.

Hospital San José (☑212-023; Los Carrera 1320; ⊙24hr)

Post office (Los Carrera 691) Behind the Sernatur office.

Sernatur (☑212-838; www.chile.travel/ en.html; Los Carrera 691; ⊙9am-8pm daily summer, 9am-7pm Mon-Fri, 9am-3pm Sat rest of the year) The well-run tourist office on the main plaza gives out a wealth of materials and information in English.

❶ Getting There & Away

Air

The Aeropuerto Desierto de Atacama is about 50km west of Copiapó.

Lan (☑600-526-2000; Mall Plaza Real, Colipí 484, Local A-102) Flies daily to Santiago (CH$166,500, 1½ hours).

PAL Airlines (☑524-603; www.palair.cl; O'Higgins 106, Local F, Edificio Plaza Real) Flies to Antofagasta three times per week (CH$53,000, one hour) and to Santiago daily (CH$53,000, 1½ hours).

Sky Airline (☑214-640; www.skyairline.cl; Colipí 526) Flies to Antofagasta twice weekly (CH$48,000, one hour), La Serena on weekdays (CH$38,000, one hour) and to Santiago daily (CH$62,000, 1½ hours).

Bus & Taxi Colectivo

Bus companies are scattered through Copiapó's southern quarter. Virtually all north–south buses stop here, as do many bound for the interior. **Pullman Bus** (☑212-977; Colipí 109) has a large terminal and a central **ticket office** (cnr Chacabuco & Chañarcillo). **Tur Bus** (☑213-724; Chañarcillo 650) also has a terminal and a **ticket office** (Colipí 510) downtown. Other companies include **Expreso Norte** (☑231-176; Chañarcillo 655), **Buses Libac** (☑212-237; Chañarcillo 655) and **Flota Barrios** (☑213-645; Chañarcillo 631), all located in a common terminal on Chañarcillo.

Note that many buses to northern desert destinations leave at night.

Standard destinations and common fares are shown in the following table:

DESTINATION	COST (CH$)	DURATION (HR)
Antofagasta	16,000-28,000	8
Arica	25,000-33,100	16
Calama	18,000-29,000	10
Iquique	22,100-30,900	15
La Serena	7800-13,300	5
Santiago	18,000-26,000	11
Vallenar	4500-6300	2

Colectivos take passengers to Caldera (CH$3500, one hour) from the terminal on Chacabuco. **Buses Casther** (☎218-889; Buena Esperanza 557) also go to Caldera for CH$2200.

ℹ️ Getting Around

To/From the Airport

Private taxis to the Aeropuerto Desierto de Atacama cost CH$25,000; try **Radio Taxi San Francisco** (☎218-788). There's also **Transfer Casther** (☎235-891), which ferries new arrivals to town (CH$6000, 40 minutes). Buses and *taxi colectivos* plowing between Copiapó and Caldera may agree to drop you at the junction, from where it's a straightforward 300m walk to the airport.

Car

Copiapó's car-hire agencies include **Hertz** (☎214-562; Av Copayapu 173), **Avis** (☎524-591; Rómulo Peña 102) and **Budget** (☎216-272; Ramón Freire 050); all three can also be found at the airport. Another Chilean option is **Rodaggio** (☎212-153; www.rodaggio.cl, in Spanish; Colipí 127), which has unlimited mileage rates for a small car starting at CH$21,420 per day, with the 19% IVA (the value-adding tax, or VAT) included. Pickup trucks and 4WDs cost at least CH$77,350 per day.

Parque Nacional Nevado Tres Cruces

Hard-to-reach **Parque Nacional Nevado Tres Cruces** (adult/child 6-12yr CH$4000/1500) has all the rugged beauty and a fraction of the tourists of more famous high-altitude parks further north. Apart from pristine peaks and first-rate climbing challenges, the park shields some wonderful wildlife: flamingos spend the summer here; large herds of vicuñas and guanacos roam the slopes; the lakes are home to giant and horned coots, Andean geese and gulls; and even the occasional condor and puma are spotted.

The 591-sq-km park is separated into two sectors of the high Andes along the international highway to Argentina via Paso de San Francisco. The larger **Sector Laguna Santa Rosa** comprises 470 sq km surrounding its namesake lake at 3700m, and includes the dirty-white salt-flat Salar de Maricunga to the north. There's a basic shelter on the south side of the lake; by the time you read this there should be another, much nicer option, a lodge managed by Puna de Atacama.

The considerably smaller **Sector Laguna del Negro Francisco** surrounds a lake of the same name. The shallow waters here are ideal for the 8000 birds that summer here, including Andean flamingos, Chilean flamingos and few rare James flamingos. The highest quantity of birds is present from December through February. Conaf runs the **Refugio Laguna del Negro Francisco** (per person per night CH$10,000) here, cozy with beds, cooking facilities, electricity, flush toilets and hot showers. Bring your own bed linen, drinking water and cooking gas.

ℹ️ Getting There & Away

It's easy to get lost on your way to the national park and there is no public transportation to get you here so we recommend taking a tour from Copiapó. If you do decide to attempt it by car, a high-clearance 4WD is highly recommended, as well as a satellite phone and a really good map.

Sector Laguna Santa Rosa is 146km east of Copiapó via Ruta 31 and another (nameless) road up the scenic Quebrada de Paipote. Sector Laguna del Negro Francisco is another 81km south via a rambling road that drops into the Río Astaburuaga valley.

Ojos del Salado

Located just outside the park boundaries, 6893m-high Ojos del Salado is Chile's highest peak (69m below South America's highest peak, Aconcagua in Argentina) and the highest active volcano in the world; its most recent eruptions were in 1937 and 1956.

The mountain can be climbed between November and March. While some people try to climb it in eight days, this is not ad-

LOS 33

For 121 years, the San José mine 45km north of Copiapó went about its business of digging for gold and copper deep in the Atacama Desert. Then in the afternoon of 5 August, 2010, a major cave-in trapped 33 of its workers 700m underground. Suddenly, San José was in the spotlight and Los 33, as the buried miners became known, became unlikely superstars of one of the most televised rescue efforts in human history.

Less than six months before this incident, Chile had gone through the 2010 earthquake and the subsequent tsunami. With sympathy levels running high, the eyes of the nation were on the plight of the miners and their families. Under immense pressure, the government took over the rescue from the mine owners. The venture, at an estimated cost of US$20 million, involved international drilling rig teams, experts from NASA and several multinationals. On 13 October, 2010, in a televised finale that lasted nearly 24 hours and drew an estimated viewing audience of one billion from around the world, the last of the 33 men was hoisted up to freedom through a narrow shaft, and a sign was held up for the TV cameras reading: 'Misión cumplida Chile' (Mission accomplished Chile).

While they were trapped, the ordeal of Los 33 became a round-the-clock soap opera. At one point, a buried man had a wife and a lover waiting for him above. After 69 days in the pitch-dark depths of the earth, the 33 men resurfaced to find themselves in the spotlight. The next thing: they were cheered on by football fans at the Wembley, jetted off to all-expenses-paid trips to Disneyland, showered with gifts and money and flown to New York to be interviewed by David Letterman. In summer 2011, it was announced that Los 33 had gone Hollywood by selling film rights to their story to producer Michael Medavoy of Black Swan fame.

But the dark side of unsought fame caught up with the miners. With the public drama over, the men faced a set of medical and psychological issues. A year after the event, most of were struggling to find work; at the time of writing, only two of the 33 had returned to work in the mines.

The miners' story, a symbol of survival against all odds, has inspired many. Meanwhile, the Fenix 2, the oxygen-enriched capsule daubed in red, white and blue, the colours of Chile's flag, that hauled each of the 33 miners up to safety, is doing museum rounds. For a definitive account of the rescue, read Jonathan Franklin's bestselling book 33 Men.

NORTE CHICO HUASCO VALLEY

visable. Only 25% of people attempting to reach the peak actually get there, and that's not because it's a technical climb – only the last 50m or so requires skill. It's because people don't take time to acclimatize slowly, so be wiser and allow 12 days for the climb.

Expeditions typically spend nights in four shelters en route to the peak. They start at the spectacular turquoise lake **Laguna Verde** (elevation 4342m), about 65km beyond Laguna Santa Rosa, which glows like liquid kryptonite – brighter even than the intense blue of the sky. There's a frigid campsite beside the lake, as well as shallow thermal baths in which to heat frozen toes.

Further up, at 4540m, climbers stay at Refugio Claudio Lucero. The next one up, at 5100m, is the Universidad de Atacama, managed Refugio Atacama. The determined climbers reach Refugio Tejos (5833m), from where it's just the peak.

Aventurismo Expediciones (p200) is the only agency allowed to take people up; (US$160 for the expedition). Because Ojos del Salado straddles the border, climbers must get authorization from Chile's Dirección de Fronteras y Límites (Difrol; see p29), which oversees border-area activities. Permission can be granted on its website.

For more information on the park, stop by the Conaf or Sernatur offices in Copiapó.

Huasco Valley

A lush thumb of greenery snaking its way down from the Andes, the fertile valley of the Río Huasco, roughly midway between Copiapó and La Serena, is famous for its plump olives, pisco and a deliciously sweet wine known as *pajarete*. However, the region's other claim to fame – mining – is now threatening this agricultural oasis.

High up in the Andes, Canadian mining conglomerate Barrick Gold has recently started a mining operation along the Argentinean border to exploit the massive Pascua Lama deposits, which are thought to be the world's largest untapped source of gold. The project has long been disputed by local farmers and environmentalists from both Chile and Argentina. Since it began in October 2009, Río Alto del Carmen has been polluted with chemical residues and glaciers have been affected. Chilean environmental authorities began a probe into the Pascua Lama project, with a threat of fines or even revoking the concession. But for now, Pascua Lama is still going, with Barrick Gold announcing production in mid-2012. To learn more about this issue, and the indigenous Diaguita community's struggle to protect their ancestral land, see *Cry of the Andes* documentary.

VALLENAR
051 / POP 48,040

The valley's principal town, Vallenar, is a bucolic settlement that runs at a soothingly slow pace. Strange as it seems, its name is a corruption of Ballinagh – an Irish town and home to the region's colonial governor, Ambrosio O'Higgins. After serious earthquake damage in 1922, Vallenar was rebuilt with wood instead of adobe, but the city's buildings still rest on unconsolidated sediments.

Though there is little to do in town other than stroll around the central plaza, it's a good jumping-off point for visits to Parque Nacional Llanos de Challe and a place to break the journey if driving or heading up north.

Motorists often bypass Vallenar because Puente Huasco (Huasco Bridge), which spans the valley, does not drop into the town itself. At the bridge's southern end, the Vallenar-Huasco Hwy leads east then branches across the river. Semipedestrian Prat has a wide sidewalk with a single automobile lane, east of Plaza O'Higgins. Everything is within walking distance from here.

Sleeping & Eating

Hotel Puerto de Vega
HOTEL $$$
(613-870; www.puertodevega.cl; Ramírez 201; s/d from CH$53,400/64,200; P@🖵🌊) Just one block north of the bus station, this swank villa has a clutch of beautifully kept rooms, personable service and a leafy patio. The superior rooms with cool hardwoods, modern

lines and leather headboards are well worth the extra money.

Hostal Real Quillahue
HOSTEL $
(619-992; pedroprokurica@yahoo.com; Plaza 70; s/d CH$16,000/27,000, without bathroom CH$14,000/24,000; P🖵) Located right on the south side of the plaza, this freshly painted blue building has 11 rather boring and noisy rooms with decent beds and TVs. Rates include a modest breakfast.

Hotel Takia
HOTEL $$
(613-819; hotel_takia@yahoo.es; Prat 600; s/d CH$25,000/44,000; P🖵) Somebody really loves pink in this business-style hotel one block west of the plaza. The large bland rooms come with cable TV and most have balconies.

Hotel Cecil
HOTEL $$
(349-650; Prat 1059; s/d CH$30,000/38,000; P🖵) Sister hotel to Hotel Takia, further down along Prat and past the plaza, Hotel Cecil offers more soul and value in the cabin-style rooms, a verdant patio and a pool that sometimes has water.

Nativo
TOP CHOICE CHILEAN $$
(Ramírez 1387; mains CH$5200-13,000; ⊘closed Sun; 🖵) On a leafy block a 10-minute walk from the plaza, this stylish bar and restaurant offers up earthy decor of wood and adobe, snacks, and pizzas with unusual toppings like river shrimp and charqui (jerky). Stays open late, has set lunch menus, a nice sunny patio and a dome lounge in the back.

El Comilon
SANDWICHES $
(sandwiches CH$1000-3200; ⊘closed lunch Sun) This corner sandwich store on the western side of the plaza, across from the hostel, buzzes with locals and stays open late on weekends.

Il Bocatto
ITALIAN $$
(Prat 750; mains CH$3200-7950) Pair your meal with plaza views at this pleasant Italian restaurant beside the church, which serves pizzas, sandwiches and mainstays on wooden tables.

ℹ Information

Banks with ATMs, a post office, internet shops and long-distance telephone offices are all available around the plaza.

ℹ Getting There & Away

Vallenar's **Terminal de Buses** (cnr Prat & Av Matta) is at the west end of town, some 500km

THE FLOWERING DESERT

In some years a brief but astonishing transformation takes place in Norte Chico's barren desert. If there has been sufficiently heavy rainfall, the parched land erupts into a multicolored carpet of wildflowers – turning a would-be backdrop from *Lawrence of Arabia* into something better resembling a meadow scene from *Bambi*.

This exquisite but ephemeral phenomenon is appropriately dubbed the *desierto florido*, the 'flowering desert.' It occurs between late July and September in wetter years when dormant wildflower seeds can be coaxed into sprouting. Many of the flowers are endangered species, most notably the endemic *garra de león* (lion's claw, one of Chile's rarest and most beautiful flowers). Even driving along the Panamericana near Vallenar you may spot clumps of the delicate white or purple *suspiro de campo* (sigh of the field), mauve, purple or white *pata de Guanaco* (Guanaco's hoof) and yellow *corona de fraile* (monk's crown) coloring the roadside.

Llanos de Challe is one of the best places to see this phenomenon, although the region's erratic rainfall patterns make it difficult to predict the best sites in any given year.

west of Plaza de Armas. **Pullman** (☑619-587; cnr Atacama & Prat) is right next door, while **Tur Bus** (☑611-738) is opposite the main bus terminal; both have extensive north- and south-bound routes. Destinations include Santiago (CH$8500, nine hours), La Serena (CH$5000, three hours), Copiapó (CH$4000, two hours) and Antofagasta (CH$16,000, 10 hours).

Parque Nacional Llanos de Challe

This isolated **national park** (adult/child 6-12yr CH$4000/1500) hugs the desert coastline 40km north of Huasco. It generally sees little through-traffic, except in those years when the *desierto florido* bursts into bloom (see boxed text, above). There is also an interesting selection of cacti, flighty guanacos and canny foxes.

The park is accessible only by private vehicle. It consists of a coastal sector south of Carrizal Bajo around Punta Los Pozos, where there is a small and basic **campground** (campsites per person CH$4000, showers per 3min CH$800), and an inland sector along the Quebrada Carrizal, 15km southeast of Carrizal Bajo. Campers should bring plenty of water, as there is none on-site, and warm clothes during the winter. You can also try to guerrilla (free) camp at Playa Blanca near the park's entrance for free. There are good beach breaks along the coast here: good news for surfers, bad news for swimmers.

From Huasco, take the decaying asphalt road along the coast north from the nearby farming village of Huasco Bajo. Alternatively, a reasonable dirt road leaves the Panamericana 40km north of Vallenar.

Reserva Nacional Pingüino de Humboldt

Pods of bottle-nosed dolphins play in the waters of this **national reserve** (adult/child 5-15yr CH$2500/1000), while slinky sea otters slide off boulders and penguins waddle along the rocky shoreline – keeping their distance from sprawling sea-lion colonies. The 888-hectare reserve embraces three offshore islands on the border between Regiónes III and IV, and makes one of the best excursions in Norte Chico. The reserve takes its name from the Humboldt penguin, which nests on rocky Isla Choros.

Humboldt penguins breed along the Peruvian and Chilean coasts. The International Union for the Conservation of Nature and Natural Resources lists them as a 'vulnerable species,' with an estimated population of around 12,000 breeding pairs. Overfishing and the exploitation of guano were the primary causes for the penguin's decline, and experts say that if new conservation measures are not put in place, the species could well become extinct in the next few decades.

While noise and pollution from boats visiting the area is affecting local marine life, it is really Isla Damas – the only place where boats can land – that is suffering the most. Local biologists are reporting that the number of birds that call the island home has significantly dropped in recent years. The island was originally supposed to have a maximum visitation of 60 people per day. But these days, it seems that hundreds of tourists are flocking to the island daily. If you do decide to visit the park, you may consider skipping an excursion to Isla Damas altogether. If you visit the island, you should definitely keep to the established paths.

◉ Sights

At Punta de Choros boats ply the route to Isla Damas for CH\$8000, which lies 5.6km away from the shore. This 60-hectare metamorphic outcrop capped by a low granite summit has two snowy-white beaches with crystal-clear water: **Playa La Poza**, where boats land, and the fine-sand **Playa Tijeras**, a 1km walk away. Visitors are required to pay the visitor fee at a Conaf stand located at the Isla Damas dock and are only allowed to stay on the island for one hour.

Hired boats also pass Isla Choros but landing is not permitted here. On the circuit around the island, you're likely to see pods of bottle-nosed dolphins that splash alongside the boat, a large sea-lion colony, groups of otters and Humboldt penguins, and massive rookeries of cormorants, gulls and boobies.

Isla Chañaral, the largest and most northerly of the three islands comprising the reserve, is less easily accessible but most protected and least crowded. Its access point is the scenic coastal village of Caleta Chañaral de Aceituno, where boats take people to the island for about CH\$80,000 (based on 10 people) between 9am and 4pm. There are a couple of campgrounds and a simple eatery.

Bad weather and high waves can occasionally prevent boat trips: call the **Conaf station** (☑099-544-3052; www.conaf.cl; in Spanish; Caleta San Agustín; ⊘8:30am-5:30pm) to check conditions before leaving. Note that tickets for boat trips are only sold till 2pm.

From a turnoff on the Panamericana, about 87km north of La Serena, a rough gravel road passes through Los Choros, an oasis of olive trees that was one of Spain's earliest (1605) settlements in the area, and continues to Punta de Choros (123km from La Serena, about two hours by car). Caleta Chañaral de Aceituno is another 25km to the north.

🏃 Activities

Explora Sub   DIVING
(☑099-279-6723; www.explorasub.cl; 1-tank dive with rental CH\$50,000) Arranges diving trips near Isla Damas. You'll find it 200m south of the Punta de Choros dock.

🛏 Sleeping & Eating

There are numerous homes offering both camping (around CH\$1500 per person) and

cabañas (beginning at CH\$20,000) along the main road and in Caleta San Agustín, which also has food stands serving fish sandwiches and seafood empanadas.

Explora Sub   CABIN \$\$
(www.explorasub.cl; for 6 people CH\$60,000; P🐾🛜🛁) This cute group of cabins, 200m south of the Punta de Choros dock, looks out onto the sea. Each has a double room, bunkbed room and a kitchen and living area. It offers free kayaks for guests.

Eneyde   SEAFOOD \$\$
(Punta de Choros plaza; mains CH\$4500-8500; ⊘open daily to 7pm) This requisite post-trip lunch spot has pleasant outdoor seating that looks onto the town's main 'plaza.' It has a changing menu of locally caught seafood.

❶ Getting There & Away

The park is best reached from La Serena. **Profetur** (☑51-255-199) offers bus service to and from La Serena (CH\$4000, two hours). Buses depart from close to the police station and the school; the last bus leaves at 7pm. La Serena-based travel agencies also offer tours. Unfortunately, the one-way 123km distance means transit time is long.

La Serena

☑051 / POP 160,148

Chile's second-oldest city and the thriving capital of Región IV, La Serena is doubly blessed with some beautiful architecture and a long golden shoreline, making it a kind of thinking-person's beach resort. The city absorbs hoards of Chilean holidaymakers in January and February, though it is fairly peaceful outside the summer rush. Sauntering through downtown La Serena reveals dignified stone churches, tree-shaded avenues and some pretty plazas. Some of the city's architecture is from the colonial era, but most of it is actually neocolonial – the product of Serena-born president Gabriel González Videla's 'Plan Serena' of the late 1940s.

La Serena also has numerous attractions in the surrounding countryside, with pretty villages and pisco vineyards aplenty, as well as international astronomical observatories that take advantage of the region's exceptional atmospheric conditions and clear skies.

History

Encomendero Juan Bohón, the lieutenant of Pedro de Valdivia, founded La Serena in

1544, but the town was promptly destroyed and Bohón killed in a Diaguita uprising. His successor, Francisco de Aguirre, refounded the city in 1549, but a century later poor old La Serena was razed once more, this time by British pirate Sharpe in 1680. Following Chilean independence, the city grew fat on silver and copper, supported by agriculture in the Elqui Valley. Silver discoveries were so significant that the government created an independent mint in the city.

◉ Sights

Plaza de Armas
PLAZA

La Serena has 29 churches to its credit, many beautiful stone creations in neoclassical or eclectic styles; a bunch of the prettiest can be found on or near the Plaza de Armas. On the east side, the handsome neoclassical **Iglesia Catedral** dates from 1844; it has a small museum of religious art. Just to its north are the bluff facades of the **Municipalidad** – pop your head inside to check out photos of the city's past – and **Tribunales** (Law Courts; cnr Prat & Los Carrera), built as a result of González Videla's Plan Serena.

Museo Histórico Casa Gabriel González Videla
MUSEUM

(Matta 495; adult/child CH$600/300; ☺10am-6pm Mon-Fri, to 1pm Sat) Although richly stocked with general historical artifacts, this two-story museum in an 18th-century mansion concentrates on one of La Serena's best-known (and most controversial) sons. González Videla was Chile's president from 1946 to 1952. Ever the cunning politician, he took power with communist support but then promptly outlawed the party, driving poet Pablo Neruda out of the Senate and into exile. The reverent exhibits omit such episodes, but pop upstairs for the historical displays and changing modern-art exhibits.

Beaches
BEACH

A swath of wide sandy beaches stretches from La Serena's nonfunctional lighthouse right to Coquimbo: there are so many that you could visit a different beach every day for a two-week vacation. Unfortunately, strong rip currents make some unsuitable for swimming – but good for surfing. Safe swimming beaches generally start south of Cuatro Esquinas. Those between the west end of Av Francisco de Aguirre and Cuatro Esquinas (ie closer to town) are friskier and generally dangerous for bathers. Look for the signs 'Playa Apta' (meaning beach safe

for swimming) and 'Playa No Apta' (meaning beach not safe for swimming).

For quick beach access, take either bus Liserco or *colectivos* running between La Serena and Coquimbo, and get off at Peñuelas and Cuatro Esquinas, a block from the beach. During January and February direct buses (CH$400) head down Av Francisco de Aguirre to Playa El Faro. During the remainder of the year, you'll have to take a *colectivo* (CH$500) or do the 3km walk to the lighthouse from town.

Museo Arqueológico
MUSEUM

(cnr Cordovez & Cienfuegos; adult/child CH$600/300, Sun free; ☺9:30am-5:50pm Tue-Fri, 10am-1pm & 4-7pm Sat, 10am-1pm Sun) Inside a crescent-shaped building with a leafy patio, the museum makes an ambitious attempt to corral Chile's pre-Columbian past. Its highlights include an Atacameña mummy, a hefty 2.5m-high *moai* (large anthropomorphic statue) from Easter Island and interesting Diaguita artifacts that include a dinghy made from sea-lion hide.

The Museo Histórico Casa Gabriel González Videla and Museo Arqueológico share admission – entry to one is valid for the other.

Iglesia San Francisco
CHURCH

(Balmaceda 640) The granddaddy of all La Serena's churches is a colonial marvel, two blocks southeast of the plaza, and built in the early 1600s. It's a stone construction, with a tower and fancy baroque facade.

Parque Japones Kokoro No Niwa
PARK

(adult/child 5-12yr CH$1000/300; ☺10am-8pm summer, to 6pm rest of year) With its trickling brooks, drifting swans and neatly manicured rock gardens, this Japanese garden makes a good escape from the city bustle.

🖈 Activities

A bike path runs all the way to Coquimbo; **Vicamawi** (✆227-939; Vicente Zorrilla 990) rents bikes for CH$6000 per day.

Other popular activities include **sailing** (buddy up to a yacht-club member), **surfing** (hit Playa El Faro with local body-boarders) and **windsurfing** (keep an eye on swimmers within 200m of the beach or you'll run afoul of the Gobernación Marítima). Playa Totoralillo, south of Coquimbo, is rated highly for its surf breaks and windsurfing potential. **Poisson** (✆099-138-2383; Av del Mar 1001) rents surfboards for CH$5000 per hour.

 NORTE CHICO LA SERENA

La Serena

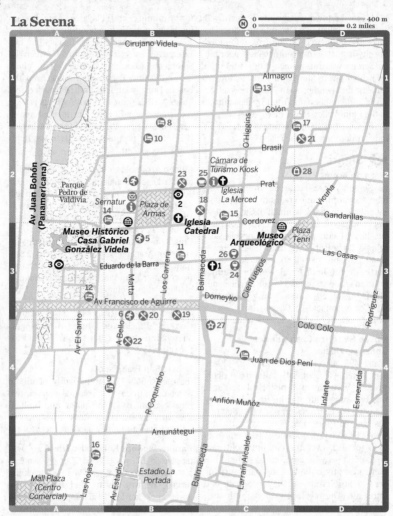

Courses

La Serena School   LANGUAGE COURSE
(☎211-487; www.laserenaschool.cl; Rodríguez 450) This institution offers Spanish courses (CH$24,000 for 2½ hours of instruction with a minimum of 10 classes) and homestays (CH$105,000 per week with breakfast and dinner).

Tours

Agencies offer a wealth of excursions, ranging from national park visits to nighttime astronomical trips, and pisco-tasting tours to new-age jaunts in UFO central, Cochiguaz. Traditional excursions include half-day city tours (from CH$5000), full-day trips through the Elqui Valley (CH$20,000 to CH$25,000), Parque Nacional Bosques de Fray Jorge and Valle del Encanto (CH$30,000 to CH$35,000), and Parque Nacional Pingüino de Humboldt (CH$32,000 to CH$35,000). Agencies also provide excursions to the observatories, mainly going out to Mamalluca (CH$16,000 to CH$18,000). If there is a demand, they will also do trips to Andacollo as well as treks to mines (the so-called Ruta del Quarzo) that are located

La Serena

nearby. The minimum number of passengers ranges from two to six.

Tembeta Tours CULTURAL TOUR
(☎215-553; www.tembeta.cl, in Spanish) Sign up for a walking city tour; these cost CH$5000 per person and depart daily if at least two people sign up.

Elqui Valley Tour GUIDED TOUR
(☎214-846; www.goelqui.com; Matta 367) Daily departures to Elqui Valley, with a discount if you take a day trip plus a night visit to Mamalluca.

Nomade Experience GUIDED TOUR
(☎217-925; Matta 510, Oficina 4) All the usual tour suspects through the surrounding area, running with a five-person minimum requirement.

Talinay Adventure Expeditions ADVENTURE TOUR
(☎218-658; www.talinaychile.com; Av Francisco de Aguirre 301) Good choice for adventure tours, from kayaking, mountain biking and horseback riding to diving, trekking and rock climbing.

Festivals & Events

Jornadas Musicales de La Serena MUSIC
In early January this traditional festival sees a series of musical events.

Feria Internacional del Libro de La Serena BOOK FAIR
Brings prominent Chilean authors to the historical museum in early February.

Artisan's fair CRAFTS
In the second fortnight of February this fair is held in the historical museum.

Sleeping

La Serena gets booked up fast in January and February and some hotels won't accept one-night stays.

TOP CHOICE **Hostal El Hibisco** HOSTEL $
(☎211-407; hostalelhibisco@hotmail.com; Juan de Dios Pení 636; r per person CH$7000; P ☜) A familial atmosphere prevails at this cheerful guesthouse. It offers a dozen wooden-floored clean rooms with shared facilities (one with private bath is CH$9000), free laundry and breakfast with homemade

jams. The friendly owner serves brunch on weekends (CH$5000), and other meals on request. There's bike rental, and a communal kitchen.

Hostal El Punto   HOSTEL $

(☏228-474; www.punto.de; Andrés Bello 979; s incl breakfast CH$14,000-24,000, d incl breakfast CH$26,000-30,000, dm/s/d without bathroom CH$8000/15,000/17,000; P@🖥) This is La Serena's top-notch choice with a wide range of rooms, a bunch of sunny terraces, bright mosaics, flower gardens and tree-trunk tables. The staff speak German and English, and provide travel tips, tours, bike rental, nice cakes, laundry, book exchange…you name it. It's so great and popular in fact that you'll want to book months ahead, especially in high season.

Hostal Tierra Diaguita   HOSTEL $

(☏216-608; www.fogoncasatamaya.cl; Eduardo de la Barra 440; d CH$28,000, without bathroom CH$24,000; 🖥) Inside a colonial house, this friendly place has well-kept rooms in the main building and add-ons in the back reached through the verdant garden. Guests can use the shared kitchen and the lovely patio. Free perks include breakfast and luggage storage. There's a loft-style room for four in the back (CH$48,000) and one double has a balcony. The sign out front says 'Casa Tamaya.'

Maria's Casa   GUESTHOUSE $

(☏229-282; www.hostalmariacasa.cl; Las Rojas 18; r per person CH$9000; 🖥) The cottage-style rooms at this family-run spot are simple and cozy. There's a garden in the back, where you can camp (CH$3500 per person). Other backpacker-friendly amenities include well-scrubbed shared bathrooms, a quaint country kitchen with free tea and coffee, laundry service and bike rental.

Hotel del Cid   HOTEL $$

(☏212-692; www.hoteldelcid.cl; O'Higgins 138; s/d CH$40,000/45,000; P@🖥) A dependable midrange option, this pleasant hotel has rooms with classic flair around a colonial-style patio and a set of more modern units in the extension out back. It's all paired with very friendly service.

Hotel Cristobal Colón   HOTEL $$

(☏224-656; www.hotelcristobalcolon.cl, in Spanish; Colón 371; s/d CH$30,000/40,000; P🖥) Recently renovated, this quiet boutique wannabe in a colonial building comes with a series of snug rooms, an upstairs terrace with nice views, and a restaurant on-site.

Hotel Francisco de Aguirre   HOTEL $$$

(☏222-991; www.dahoteles.com, in Spanish; Cordovez 210; s/d CH$76,000/91,000; P@🖥🏊) This large hotel's imposing neocolonial frontage faces Iglesia Santo Domingo, the bells of which often wake late risers. Rooms range in size; the superior ones are pricier. There's a gym and sauna.

Hotel Londres   HOTEL $$

(☏219-066; www.hotellondres.cl, in Spanish; Cordovez 550; s/d CH$32,000/42,000; P🖥) Besides having a great location, this little business-style hotel features classic rooms with a bit of chintz, but firm beds and spacious bathrooms. Rooms in the front are noisier but also lighter.

Hotel Costa Real   HOTEL $$$

(☏221-010; www.costareal.cl, in Spanish; Francisco de Aguirre 170; s/d CH$82,000/88,000; P@🖥🏊) For the best comforts central La Serena can offer, head to this flashy five-star hotel, with a conical turret, an upscale international restaurant, sizable rooms and a small pool.

Hotel Campanario del Mar   HOTEL $$$

(☏245-516; www.hotelcampanario.cl, in Spanish; Avenida del Mar 4600; d/ste CH$80,800/97,460; P🖥) Our top pick among La Serena's beach-front properties, this four-star hotel comes with 14 rooms with kitchenettes, some showcasing direct ocean views.

Hostal Matta   HOSTEL $

(☏210-014; www.hostalmatta.cl, in Spanish; Matta 234; s/d CH$20,000/24,000, without bathroom CH$16,000/20,000; @🖥) Ten decently clean rooms with TVs, quite a cheerful vibe, a big full kitchen and friendly owners. There's a small terrace in the back and breakfast is served for CH$1500.

Residencial Suiza   GUESTHOUSE $

(☏625-214; hostalsuiza@gmail.com; Cienfuegos 250; s/d CH$15,000/20,000; P🖥) If all else fails, get one of the basic rooms with private baths at this rock-bottom spot. The owner speaks English and some German. If all are booked, check out the slightly pricier and nicer Residencial Croata next door.

🍴 Eating

For those wanting to self-cater, there are several markets in town. Some have food stalls, others offer good options to make your own picnic lunch. The biggest is Mercado La Recova on the corner of Cienfuegos and Cantournet, which has a string of cheap restaurants upstairs. Supermarkets are all over town.

El Nuevo Peregrino RESTAURANT, BAR $
(Andrés Bello 886; mains CH$3200-3800; ⊘closed Sat lunch & all day Sun) This cool little corner restaurant and bar serves up down-home mainstays and sandwiches in a series of colorful rooms, and stays open late on weekends, when the music gets loud and cocktails and wine flow.

Donde El Guatón PARRILLA $$
(Brasil 750; mains CH$2900-8900) El Guatón prepares sizzling *parrilladas* (grilled meats) right before your hungry eyes. The characterful dining area is hung with flowers and chandeliers made from old bicycle wheels. The weekday set lunch menu is great value at CH$3500.

Casona del 900 PARRILLA $$
(Av Francisco de Aguirre 431-443; mains CH$3900-9000; ⊘closed Sun) Inside an old beer factory, this high-ceilinged steakhouse with a

---

WORTH A TRIP

CHECK OUT QUIRKY COQUIMBO

The rough-and-tumble port of Coquimbo next door to La Serena has been undergoing something of a revolution in recent years. Clinging to the rocky hills of Península Coquimbo, the town was long written off as La Serena's ugly cousin, but it has blossomed into the area's up-and-coming spot for nightlife. On top of its nighttime buzz, it's worth a trip for a wander around its beautifully restored 19th-century Barrio Inglés (English Quarter) and a visit to the fishing jetty for some fresh seafood. Despite its slow and steady gentrification, Coquimbo remains a gritty working port.

For a dizzying view of the bay and out to La Serena, climb atop **Cruz del Tercer Milenio** (Cross of the Third Millennium; www.cruzdeltercermilenio.cl, in Spanish; Cerro El Vigía; admission CH$2000; ⊘8:30am-9:30pm; P), reaching for the sky above Coquimbo. A surreal mix between a holy pilgrimage site and theme park, this whopping 93m-high concrete cross contains a museum (largely devoted to the late Pope John Paul II), praying rooms and an elevator ride to the top. The first level is free.

Hour-long **boat tours** (CH$15; ⊘11am-8pm) of the harbor depart regularly from Av Costanera in January and February, weekends only in winter.

If you decide to swap the colonial charms of La Serena for the grit of Coquimbo, the best place to stay, if slightly overpriced, is **Hostal Nomade** (☎315-665; www.hostal nomade.cl; Regimiento Coquimbo 5; r per person CH$15,000, d CH$35,000; P🖧) inside a rambling old mansion on a hillside with views out to the port. This quirky place houses several high-ceilinged living rooms complete with odds and ends from the 19th century, a full kitchen, large garden area with hammocks, and dorm rooms. Freebies include breakfast, a welcome pisco sour and laundry services. Homemade meals and tours are available. Hostelling International members get a 10% discount.

The Terminal Pesquero (Fish Market), located along the bay, offers a wealth of cheap fish options so head here for lunch. For dinner, check out the 2nd-floor **La Barceloneta** (Aldunate 726; mains CH$6000-7200), a Mediterranean-flavored resto-bar with a dark red interior.

The **Casa de la Cultura y Turismo** (☎313-204; Av Costanera 701; ⊘8:30am-5:30pm) houses a small exhibition hall and the town library. You may be able to get some tourist information here.

Most of the nightlife action is along Aldunate, heading northwest from the Plaza in Barrio Inglés, and below on Costanera. This entire area, stretching for several blocks, is chock-full with bars and clubs, which get going on weekends. Weeknights in Coquimbo can be pretty quiet although the small strip between Aldunate and Costanera, called Ramon Freire, is likely to have a couple of bars open. Places in Coquimbo seem to come and go so we won't recommend any in particular. Wander around the area and you're bound to find plenty of action.

Coquimbo's bus terminal is between Borgoño and Alcalde. Many local buses and *colectivos* also link the two cities (bus CH$500, *colectivo* CH$800, private taxi CH$6000 to CH$10,000).

glassed-in garden oozes ambience and packs in meat-loving locals for its great-value barbecues (CH$16,900 for two, with wine).

Daniela II
CHILEAN $

(Av Francisco de Aguirre 335; snacks CH$1500, mains CH$2500-7500; ☺closed dinner Sat) Cheerful local favorite serving hearty portions of Chilean comfort food. It gets packed at lunchtime, when set menus start at CH$1500.

Rapsodia
INTERNATIONAL $$

(Prat 470; mains CH$5800-8900; ☺closed dinner Sat & all day Sun) With several side rooms looking onto the inner courtyard with a giant palm tree, this old *casona* serves up a variety of well-prepared snacks and dishes, and live music on some nights.

La Tabla
SEAFOOD $$

(Avenida del Mar 3200; mains CH$4200-7900) The nicest of the beachfront restaurants, with great views out toward Coquimbo, fairly innovative dishes, a range of light snacks and a terrace right on the beach.

Café Colonial
INTERNATIONAL $

(Balmaceda 475; mains CH$3000-7000) This buzzy tourist-friendly restaurant serves up anything from breakfasts and burgers to pizzas and pancakes. It's used to accommodating kids, vegetarians and non-Spanish speakers. Grab a sidewalk table.

Drinking & Entertainment

The happening part of town is the area around the corner of Eduardo de la Barra and O'Higgins, where you'll find boho student crowds. Nightclubs sparkle along the seafront, past the lighthouse and all the way to Barrio Inglés in Coquimbo; they're especially hot during summer.

Coffee Express
CAFE

(Prat 492) Oversized glass-and-plastic coated coffee shop serving java and offering 2-for-1 drinks from 4pm daily.

Caseron
LIVE MUSIC

(Balmaceda 824) This seedy-looking bar in a 130-year-old house hosts regular acts, including jazz on Thursdays and Latin rhythms on weekends.

Tacuba
BAR

(Eduardo de la Barra 589) This darkly lit small corner tavern plays contemporary rock and pop and draws in a slightly older crowd for its low-key vibe.

Boicot
BAR

(cnr Eduardo de la Barra & O'Higgins) Stay out late drinking on the interior patio at this popular student hangout with occasional live music.

Information

Banks with ATMs are readily available in the blocks around Plaza de Armas. There are several money exchange shops on Balmaceda, between Cordobez and Prat.

There are numerous internet joints around town, most charging around CH$600 per hour. To boot, most hotels offer wi-fi.

Hospital Juan de Diós (☎333-424; Balmaceda 916; ☺24hr) The emergency entrance is at the corner of Larraín Alcalde and Anfión Muñóz.

Post office (cnr Matta & Prat)

Sernatur (☎225-199; www.turismoregion decoquimbo.cl; Matta 461; ☺9am-8pm summer, 9am-6pm Mon-Fri, 10am-2pm Sat winter) Excellent tourist info shelled out from this office by Plaza de Armas. During the summer, the municipal tourist office runs an information kiosk by Iglesia La Merced and another in the lighthouse by the beach.

Getting There & Away

Air

La Serena's **Aeropuerto La Florida** (☎271-870) is 6km east of downtown along Ruta 41. **Lan** (☎600-526-2000; Balmaceda 406) flies daily to Santiago (CH$112,000, one hour) and to Antofagasta (CH$132,500, 1½ hours). There's another Lan office with longer hours in Mall Plaza.

Bus

La Serena's **Terminal de Buses** (☎224-573; cnr Amunátegui & Av El Santo), which lies just southwest of the center, has dozens of carriers plying the Panamericana from Santiago north to Arica, including **Tur Bus** (☎219-828; www.turbus.cl, in Spanish; Balmaceda 437) and **Pullman Bus** (☎218-879; www.pullman.cl, in Spanish; Eduardo de la Barra 435).

Typical destinations and fares:

DESTINATION	COST (CH$)	DURATION (HR)
Antofagasta	22,000	12
Arica	32,000	23
Calama	24,000	14
Copiapó	9000	5
Iquique	29,000	19
Santiago	10,000	6
Vallenar	5500	3

To get to Vicuña (CH$2000, 1½ hours), Ovalle (CH$2500, two hours), Montegrande (CH$3500, two hours) or Pisco Elqui (CH$3500, 2½ hours), try **Via Elqui** (☎312-422; cnr Juan de Dios Peñí & Esmeralda). You can even do Elqui Valley as a day trip; the first bus to Vicuña departs at 6:40am and the last returns at 9pm.

For Argentine destinations, **Covalle Bus** (☎213-127; Infante 538) travels to Men-doza (CH$30,000, 12 hours) and San Juan (CH$30,000, 18 hours) via the Libertadores pass every Sunday, leaving at 11pm.

Taxi Colectivo

A large number of regional destinations are frequently and rapidly served by *taxi colectivo*. *Colectivos* to Coquimbo (CH$800, 15 minutes) leave from Av Francisco de Aguirre between Balmaceda and Los Carrera.

THE BEST OF STARGAZING IN NORTE CHICO

The star of the stargazing show, the purpose-built **Observatorio Cerro Mamalluca** (☎051-670-330; www.mamalluca.org; adult/child CH$4500/2000), 9km northeast of Vicuña, is Elqui Valley's biggest attraction. So big, in fact, that you're likely to share the tour with hordes of other tourists, all looking for their chance to goggle at distant galaxies, star clusters and nebulae through a 30cm telescope.

Bilingual guided two-hour tours take place nightly at 8:30pm and 10:30pm in summer and at 6:30pm and 8:30pm in winter. The cheesy Cosmo Visión Andina tour (in Spanish only) includes presentations and music but no access to the telescopes – so you're better off booking the basic astronomy tour. Moonless nights are best for observing distant stars so check out the lunar calendar beforehand, and bring a warm sweater.

Make reservations through the office at Av Gabriela Mistral 260 in Vicuña; advance booking is recommended. There is no public transportation, but a minivan takes visitors from the Vicuña office (reserve in advance; per person CH$1500). Some La Serena tour agencies arrange trips, or you can hire a taxi in Vicuña. Vehicles go by convoy to the site, which is otherwise difficult to find.

Like Mamalluca, the shiny hilltop **Observatorio Collowara** (☎051-432-964; www.collowara.cl; adult/child/senior CH$3500/1500/2500) in Andacollo is built for tourists; no serious interstellar research is conducted here. Two-hour tours run in summer at 9pm, 10:30pm and midnight; in winter they run at 7pm, 9:30pm and 10:30pm. The facility boasts three viewing platforms and a 40cm telescope – slightly larger than that at Mamalluca. There are also three smaller telescopes available, so you won't have to wait for long. There are plenty of accommodations in Andacollo, 54km from La Serena and connected by bus (CH$2000, 1½ hours) and *colectivo* (CH$2500, one hour).

The latest on the observatory front is **Observatorio del Pangue** (☎051-412-584; www.observatoriodelpangue.blogspot.com; with transportation CH$16,000), 17km south of Vicuña, run by three enthusiastic French and Chilean astronomers. The two-hour tours (in English, French and Spanish) that leave nightly – unless there's a full moon – at 8:30pm (and on demand at 10:30pm) offer pure observation, with a 10-person maximum.

Probing the mysteries of stars billions of miles into the past is all in a night's work at the futuristic **Observatorio Interamericano Cerro Tololo** (☎051-205-200; www.ctio.noao.edu), which sits at 2200m atop its hill. And while visitors can't stargaze through its monstrous telescopes (even the astronomers don't do that as the telescopes first feed data into computer monitors), a daytime tour of the facilities is still an enlightening experience. Operated by the Tucson-based Association of Universities for Research in Astronomy (AURA; a group of about 25 institutions, including the Universidad de Chile), Tololo has an enormous 4m telescope. Free bilingual tours take place on Saturday only. Make reservations at least one month ahead in high season. Two-hour tours are held at 9am and 1pm. There is no public transportation so rent a car or taxi, or arrange to come with a tour operator (even then you *still* must make your own reservations with the observatory).

For professionally guided astronomy tours, contact **Astronomy Adventures** (☎051-477-918; www.astronomyadventures.cl), a La Serena–based outfit that arranges customized stargazing experiences all around Chile.

❶ Getting Around

Private taxis to Aeropuerto La Florida, 5km east of downtown on Ruta 41, cost CH$5000; try **Turismo Nielsen** (⌂097-659-9341; www. turismonielsen.cl). Alternatively, **She Transfer** (⌂295-058) provides door-to-door minibus transfer for CH$2000.

Women traveling alone should be wary of taxi drivers in La Serena; sexual assaults have been reported. Only take company cabs.

For car hire, try **Avis** (⌂271-509) at the airport, **Hertz** (⌂226-171; Av Francisco de Aguirre 0225) or **Econorent** (⌂220-113; Av Francisco de Aguirre 0135).

Elqui Valley

The heart of Chilean pisco production, the Elqui Valley is carpeted with a broad cover of striated green. Famous for its futuristic observatories, seekers of cosmic energies, frequent UFO sightings, poet Gabriela Mistral and quaint villages, this is a truly enchanting – and enchanted – area, and one of the must-visit places in Norte Chico.

VICUÑA

⌂051 / POP 24,010

The spirit of Gabriela Mistral's somnambulist poetry seeps from every pore of snoozy little Vicuña. Just 62km east of La Serena, this is the easiest base from which to delve deeper into the Elqui Valley. The town itself, with its low-key plaza, lyrical air and compact dwellings, is worth a visit for a day or two before you head out into the countryside to indulge in the nearby solar kitchens (where the sun cooks the food), and the fresh avocados, papayas and other fruits grown in the region – not to mention the famous grapes that are distilled into Chile's potent grape-brandy pisco.

On the north bank of the Río Elqui, across a bridge from Ruta 41, Vicuña has a geometric plan centered on the Plaza de Armas.

◉ Sights

Two of Vicuña's big attractions, Planta Pisco Capel (p214) and Observatorio Cerro Mamalluca (p213), are just outside town. The town itself offers a clutch of sights.

Museo Gabriela Mistral   MUSEUM
(Av Gabriela Mistral 759; adult/child & senior CH$600/300; ⊙10am-7pm Mon-Fri, 10:30am-7pm Sat, 10am-6pm Sun Jan & Feb, 10am-5:45pm Mon-Fri, 10:30am-6pm Sat, 10am-1pm Sun Mar-Dec) The town's landmark Museo Gabriela Mistral, between Riquelme and Baquedano, is a tan-

gible eulogy to one of Chile's most famous literary figures. Gabriela Mistral was born Lucila Godoy Alcayaga in 1889 in Vicuña. The museum charts her life (in Spanish only), from a replica of her adobe birthplace to her Nobel Prize, and has a clutch of busts making her seem a particularly strict schoolmarm. Her family tree indicates Spanish, indigenous and African ancestry.

Plaza de Armas   PLAZA
A sinister portrait of Gabriela Mistral gazes blankly up at the sky from a watery pit in the center of this leafy square. Just off the plaza's western edge, the **Torre Bauer** (1905) is a rusty-colored clock tower resembling a toy castle; it was built by a former German mayor and brought over from Germany.

**Casa Solar de
los Madariaga**   HISTORIC BUILDING
(Av Gabriela Mistral 683; adult/child CH$800/free; ⊙10am-8pm Wed-Mon Dec-Feb, 11am-5:30pm Wed-Mon Mar-Nov) Dating from 1875, and looking good for it, the adobe mansion with a few leafy patios contains furnishings and artifacts from an influential family who made its money exporting chinchilla. Two of the rooms are available for rent (see opposite).

**Museo Entomológico y
de Historia Natural**   MUSEUM
(Chacabuco 334; adult/child CH$600/300; ⊙10:30am-9pm summer, 10:30am-1:30pm & 3:30-7pm rest of year) Crawling with color and antennae, this museum specializes in insects and kaleidoscopic butterflies, but also has fossils, stuffed birds and invertebrates.

Inti Runa   OBSERVATORY
(⌂099-968-8577; Chacabuco 240; tours CH$6000; ⊙closed Jun-Aug) The German owner of this sun observatory claims he has two of the world's biggest solar telescopes. He keeps them in his lovely *casona,* and offers one-hour 'tours.' Basically, he talks while you look at the sun through the telescope. He also offers on-site nighttime observation, which includes a 90-minute video.

Cerro de la Virgen   HILL
The dusty hike up Cerro de la Virgen, just north of town, offers vast panoramas of the entire Elqui Valley, but it's hot and exposed – bring water. The summit is less than an hour's walk from the Plaza de Armas.

Planta Pisco Capel   PISQUERIA
(www.centroturisticocapel.cl; admission CH$1500; ⊙10am-7pm Jan & Feb, to 5pm Mar-Dec), Located

20-minutes walk from town, here you can take a 45-minute bilingual tour of the facilities, which include an on-site museum and serving of a few skimpy samples. Capel distils pisco at this facility and has its only bottling plant here, with 36 million bottles per year shipped to imbibers across Chile and abroad. In addition to pisco, the swanky sales room offers *pajarete,* the region's lipsmacking dessert wine. To get here, head southeast of town and across the bridge, then turn left.

🏃 Activities

Vicuña is a great base if you want to devote more time to exploring Elqui Valley. Not only is it the gateway to two great observatories (see boxed text, p213) but also offers bike rides into the surrounding countryside, trips to remote mountains around Paso del Agua Negra (in summer only) and horseback jaunts. There is even kitesurfing on the Puclaro reservoir, 10km away along the road to La Serena; **KiteSurf Puclaro** (www.kitepark.cl) offers classes. The owner of Chaski restaurant does bike tours (from CH$15,000, three hours) focusing on indigenous culture and visits to *pisquerias* (pisco producers).

Elki Magic   ADVENTURE SPORTS
(☎097-459-8357; www.elkimagic.com; Av Gabriela Mistral 472) Run by an enthusiastic Chilean-French couple, this agency offers guided downhill bike jaunts (from CH$10,000), horseback riding (CH$6000 per hour), one-day van tours to valley highlights (from CH$30,000, with lunch in the solar kitchens) and to the lagoons near Argentina (from CH$35,000). They also rent bikes (CH$6500 per day) and can supply you with a map of the 16km trail around the surrounding villages.

✨ Festivals & Events

Carnaval Elquino   CARNAVAL
Vicuña holds its annual grape harvest festival, Carnaval Elquino, in mid-January; it ends February 22, the anniversary of the city's founding, with activities including live music and folkloric dancing.

🛏 Sleeping

Casa Solar de los Madariaga   GUESTHOUSE **$$**
(☎411-220; mitzi.diaz@hotmail.com; Av Gabriela Mistral 683; d CH$30,000; P@🎧) The friendly old couple who run the museum recently converted two of the gorgeous colonial-style

rooms into quiet lodgings. Each comes with original antique furniture, brand-new private bathroom, beds dressed in Egyptian cotton and access to verdant patios. Breakfast features avocados and other fresh fruit from the garden.

Hostal Valle Hermoso   HOSTEL **$**
(☎411-206; www.hostalvallehermoso.com; Av Gabriela Mistral 706; s/d CH$14,000/25,000; P🎧) Great lodging choice with eight airy and immaculately clean rooms around a sundrenched patio inside an old adobe *casona* with Oregon pine beams and walnut floors. Staff is warm and friendly and ambience laid-back – as if staying with old friends.

Hostal Aldea del Elqui   HOSTEL **$$**
(☎543-069; www.hostalaldeadelelqui.cl, in Spanish; Av Gabriela Mistral 197; s/d CH$20,000/35,000; P🎧🏊) Another of the *casonas* converted into accommodations, this friendly hostel has well-kept rooms with good beds and TVs, some on the 2nd floor of a newer adjacent building. There's a tranquil garden with a small pool, swings and a gazebo. The breakfast is quite generous, too.

Hostal Donde Rita   HOSTEL **$**
(☎419-611; www.hostaldonderita.com; Condell 443; d CH$27,000, s/d without bathroom CH$12,500/25,000; P🎧) A motherly hostess who speaks German presides over this private home with a pool and four cozy rooms, one with its own bath. There's breakfast with homemade jam and fresh coffee, a shared kitchen, a small wooden *quincho* (barbecue house) out back and a solar kitchen should you wish to try sun-cooking.

Hostería Vicuña   HOTEL **$$**
(☎411-301; Sargento Aldea 101; s/d/tr CH$40,000/54,000/69,000; P🎧🏊👤) Its floral rooms leave a bit to be desired for the price, but the gardens have warm vine-touched patios with gazebos, sentinel palm trees and swinging chairs, a big pool area (available to nonguests for CH$4000 per day) and a tennis court. The hotel's main claim to fame is that Gabriela Mistral spent a night in room No 1 on her last trip to Chile in 1954.

Residencial La Elquina   GUESTHOUSE **$**
(☎411-317; www.laelquina.tk, in Spanish; O'Higgins 65; campsites per person CH$4000, s/d CH$12,000/24,000, without bathroom CH$8000/16,000; P🎧) A veil of flowering vines and citrus trees welcomes visitors to this humble, but cozy family-run *residen-*

NORTE CHICO ELQUI VALLEY

cial. The rooms are well worn but clean and with TVs, there's a small shared kitchen and a garden to camp in out back.

Hotel Halley HOTEL **$$**
(☑412-070; www.turismohalley.cl, in Spanish; Av Gabriela Mistral 542; d/tr CH$39,000/55,000; P☞☎) This breezy old mansion with creaking wooden floors has rooms with chintzy decor (think lots of lace, old radios and crosses), some with nice views onto the street. There is a swimming pool and ping-pong table out back.

Eating & Drinking

TOP CHOICE Chaski CHILEAN **$$**
(O'Higgins 159; mains CH$6500-7500; ☉closed Tue low season) This tiny outdoor restaurant run by a Diaguita couple offers up Elqui Valley's most innovative dining. Local ingredients, like quinoa, goat and amaranth, are prepared with a twist, and doused in fragrant Andean herbs. Drinks include great pisco cocktails, a local artisanal beer called Guayacan and organic wines. Inquire about their great biking tours, with the accent on the indigenous culture.

Donde Martita Solar Kitchen CHILEAN **$**
(Villaseca village; menu with wine CH$5000-7000; ☉lunch only, closed Mon low season) Don't miss lunch at this restaurant 5km out of town in the village of Villaseca, where a group of women back in 2000 discovered a groundbreaking way to cook with sun rays instead of hard-to-find firewood. At this best of Villaseca's solar kitchen restaurants, service is slow, but the food that comes out of the solar ovens is deliciously tasty and paired with lovely vineyard views.

Paraiso del Elqui CHILEAN **$$**
(Chacabuco 237; mains CH$4100-7500; ☉lunch & dinner; ✏) Recently opened by a professional chef, this cozy spot with a backyard, two small dining rooms and tables on the patio serves up regional specialties, no less than 306 kinds of empanadas and good-value *almuerzos*. Vegetarian offerings are also good.

Halley CHILEAN **$$**
(Av Gabriela Mistral 404; mains CH$2900-9900; ☉lunch & dinner) A spacious colonial-style restaurant with a thatched ceiling over the patio, a couple of interior dining rooms and scattered handicrafts. This locals' favorite is recommended for typical Chilean food, including roast *cabrito* (goat) and plentiful salads.

Mistik Coffee CAFE **$**
(Chacabuco 237; ☉breakfast & lunch) A new-age theme prevails at this airy, colorful cafe run by dynamic Carmen Gloria – think wind chimes, incense sticks and bookshelves lined with spiritual texts. Great for healthy lunches, sandwiches, natural juices, teas and espressos.

Club Social de Elqui CHILEAN **$$**
(Av Gabriela Mistral 445; mains CH$4800-9800) Enthusiastic waiters usher passing travelers into this upmarket courtyard restaurant, or into its posh side rooms that are laden with linen and candlesticks. The food is well prepared, though rather bland, and mainly focused on Chilean mainstays.

Yo y Soledad BAR
(Carrera 320; ☉9pm to late) Fight off those lonely bugs at the town's popular bar. The fireplace on chilly winter nights makes it a popular spot to hole up.

ⓘ Information

There is a bank on the main plaza, which changes US dollars. The city center also has three ATMs.

There are several internet cafes that are located near the central plaza, which charge around CH$500 per hour; most double as calling centers.

Hospital San Juan de Dios (☑333-141; cnr Independencia & Prat; ☉24hr) Located a few blocks north of Plaza de Armas.

Oficina de Información Turística (☑670-307; San Martín 275; ☉8:30am-8pm Jan & Feb, 8:30am-5:30pm Mon-Fri, 9am-6pm Sat, 9am-2pm Sun Mar-Dec) Gather a bit of info on the town's past and present at the municipal tourist office.

ⓘ Getting There & Away

From Vicuña, eastbound Ruta 41 leads over the Andes to Argentina. A rugged, dusty and bumpy (though passable in a regular car) secondary road leads south to Hurtado and back down to Ovalle.

The **bus terminal** (cnr Prat & O'Higgins) has frequent buses that travel to La Serena (CH$1800, one hour), Coquimbo (CH$1800, 1¼ hours), Pisco Elqui (CH$1200, 50 minutes) and Montegrande (CH$1200, 40 minutes). Expresso Norte has a twice-daily service to Santiago (CH$10,000 to CH$12,000, seven hours). There's a wider choice of destinations in La Serena.

SOUR RELATIONS OVER PISCO

Chileans celebrate the ubiquitous pisco sour – a tangy cocktail made from a type of grape brandy called pisco – as their national tipple. But mention this to a Peruvian and you risk having your drink thrown in your face. The trouble is, the Peruvians also claim pisco as their national beverage, and the bitter row over the liquor's rightful origin has been intensifying for decades.

Local legend tells how back in the 1930s the former Chilean president Gabriel González Videla personally changed the village of La Unión's original name to Pisco Elqui to undermine Peruvian claims of having originated the beverage. Meanwhile, Peru points to its own colonial port named Pisco in a grape-growing valley of the same name. The Peruvians have a strong historical case for appellation, if only because it was there that the Spaniards first introduced vineyards, and historical records demonstrate that the drink was consumed in Peru as early as 1613.

But Chileans argue that pisco has also been produced in Chile for centuries and claim that its pisco is of superior quality. They also point out that Chile produces, imbibes and exports vastly more pisco than Peru, and thus claim to have popularized the drink.

After years of acrimony Peru scored a partial victory in 2005 when it received a favorable enactment by World Intellectual Property Organization (WIPO). But the legal wrangling looks set to continue for some time yet.

Located inside the bus terminal complex is the **Terminal de Taxis Colectivos** (cnr Prat & O'Higgins), which has fast *taxi colectivos* that run to La Serena (CH$2000, 50 minutes) as well as Pisco Elqui (CH$2000, 50 minutes) via Montegrande.

MONTEGRANDE
051

This skinny roadside village is the former home of the internationally renowned poet Gabriela Mistral (see p438), who is a Nobel Prize winner and national icon. Her burial site, found on a nearby hillside, is the destination of many Chilean and literary pilgrims. Mistral received her primary schooling at the Casa Escuela y el Correo, where there is a humble **museum** (admission CH$300; 10am-7pm Dec-Feb, 10am-1pm & 3-6pm Tue-Sun Mar-Nov) dedicated to the poet, with a reconstructed schoolroom and dorm.

Stop by **Casa de la Cultura Gabriela Mistral** (www.montegabriela.cl, in Spanish; admission free, guided tour CH$1000; 9am-1pm & 2-7pm Mon-Fri). On the main road through town, it's a cultural center and women's cooperative that conducts textile and art workshops with underemployed women from the area. There's a library for children on-site, free internet (tip if you use it) and gorgeous handmade crafts on sale, made on-site by the women.

There's a short **trail** leading down to the river just north of the Hotel Las Pleyades. It makes for a nice afternoon excursion – be sure to bring a swimsuit.

Set in an old adobe *casona,* the gorgeously rustic **Hotel Las Pleyades** (451-107; monica.baltra@gmail.com; Montegrande s/n; d CH$50,000; P) is a boutique five-room hotel hideaway which offers nice touches such as cane roofs, leafy views, a shared kitchen and an outdoor plunge swimming pool with mountain views.

Mesón del Fraile (mains CH$5200-9100; closed Mon & Tue in low season), opposite Casa Escuela y el Correo, is worth stopping at for pizzas with local goat cheese, stewed *cabrito* and great pisco sour. For the town's best *mote con huesillos,* a traditional dessert, stop at Los Paltos on Montegrande's plaza.

Local buses provide regular service from Vicuña (CH$700, 40 minutes).

PISCO ELQUI
051

Renamed to publicize the area's most famous product, the former village of La Unión is a laid-back hideaway in the upper drainage area of the Río Claro, a tributary of the Elqui. It has become the area's most popular backpacker draw in recent years, and while it can get overcrowded, it's well worth a couple of days' stay. The architecture is rustic minimalism, but with a hint of bucolic elegance that harkens to a Tuscan village.

⊙ Sights

Distileria Pisco Mistral   DISTILLERY
(www.piscomistral.cl; O'Higgins 746; tours
CH$6000; ⊙noon-7:30pm Jan & Feb, 10:30am-6pm
Tue-Sun Mar-Dec) The star attraction is the Dis-
tileria Pisco Mistral, which produces the premium Mistral brand of pisco. The hour-long
'museum' tour gives you glimpses of the dis-
tillation process and includes a free tasting
of two piscos and a drink at the adjacent restaurant, which hosts occasional live music.

🏃 Activities

Pisco Elqui may be small in size but it's big
in terms of tours and activities you can do in
and around the valley. These include guided
treks (CH$5000 to CH$8000), horseback
riding trips (from CH$6000 per hour, and
more for multiday trips into the mountains),
mountain-bike excursions (CH$12,000 to
CH$18,000), stargazing trips (CH$14,000 to
CH$22,000) as well as canopy adventures
(CH$16,000 to CH$22,000).

The following agencies offer the above:
Paralelo 30 Aventura (☑099-036-2957; Prat
s/n; www.turismoparalelo30aventura.blogspot.com,
in Spanish), **Turismo Migrantes** (☑451-917;
www.turismomigrantes.cl; O'Higgins s/n) and
Elqui Expediciones (☑098-379-7999; www.
elquiexpediciones.cl; O'Higgins s/n).

Bikes can be rented in several places
around town for around CH$1500 per hour
or CH$7000 per day. Turismo Migrantes
also rents motorbikes (from CH$25,000 for
half a day).

🛏 Sleeping

El Tesoro de Elqui   HOTEL $$
(☑451-069; www.tesoro-elqui.cl; Prat s/n; dm
CH$9500, d CH$32,000-42,000, tr CH$39,000-
52,000; ℗🔊🏊) Up the hill from the center
plaza, this tranquil oasis dotted with lemon
trees, lush gardens and flowering vines has
10 wooden bungalows with terraces. There
is a restaurant which serves great coffee and
cake. You can even get a massage or have
your aura cleaned in the cabin by the swimming pool's 'beach.' It also offers motorbike
tours, car rental and tours to secret hot
springs and other sites in the area.

Refugio Misterios de Elqui   CABIN $$$
(☑451-126; www.misteriosdeelqui.cl, in Spanish;
Prat s/n; cabins for 2 CH$65,000; ℗🔊🏊) Pisco
Elqui's most luxe choice, sitting on the edge
of town on the road to Alcoguaz, with seven
cabins set around lush gardens that slope
down toward the swimming pool and the

valley below. Cabins come with stylish decor,
such as headboards made of recycled train
tracks, wooden beams, cool tile floors and
terraces. There's minigolf on-site, a restaurant and massages on request.

Hostal Triskel   HOSTEL $
(☑099-419-8680; www.hostaltriskel.cl, in Spanish; Baquedano s/n; r without bathroom per person
CH$10,000; 🔊) Up the hill from the town,
this lovely adobe and wood house has seven
stylish and clean rooms with four shared
bathrooms and a shared kitchen. A giant fig
tree provides shade for the patio and there's
a fruit orchard with lots of nooks, crannies
and hammocks, plus bikes for rent and laundry services, all presided over by the friendly
live-in owner.

Elqui Domos   HOTEL $$$
(☑097-709-2879; www.elquidomos.cl; Prat s/n;
domes & cabins CH$85,000; ℗🔊) This 'astro-
lodge' lies 3.5km (a 45-minute walk) north of
town, on the road toward Alcoguaz, and has
seven two-story domes with canvas ceilings
that open up to the night skies. The four
wooden cabins have panoramic valley views
and upstairs terraces. The restaurant serves
lunch and dinner, and the lodge will arrange
anything from yoga classes to reflexology,
tarot readings and horseback rides.

Hostal San Pedro   HOSTEL $
(☑451-061; ecohostalsanpedro@hotmail.com;
Prat s/n; r without bathroom per person CH$9000;
@🏊) The rooms at this cozy hostel full of
wind chimes are clean and simple, and there
is a small pool in the back with a view of
the entire valley arching down below. Guests
share kitchen facilities, a cool living room
and a garden.

Hotel Elqui   HOTEL $
(☑451-130; www.hotelelqui.cl; O'Higgins s/n; r
without bathroom per person CH$10,000; @🔊🏊)
Simple rooms, a big thatched restaurant and
creaky floors, all in an airy wooden house
steps from the plaza. There are three pools
in the back. Don't be fooled by the Hotel
Valle Azul sign outside – it's a leftover from a
soap opera that was recently shot here.

Refugio del Angel   CAMPGROUND $
(☑451-292; refugiodelangel@gmail.com; campsites
per person CH$5000, day-use CH$2500) This
idyllic spot by the river comes complete
with swimming holes, bathrooms and a little
shop. The turnoff is 200m south of the plaza
on Manuel Rodríguez.

✕ Eating & Drinking

Most restaurants in Pisco Elqui double as bars, and stay open until 2am or 3am.

El Rumor   RESTAURANT, BAR $

(O'Higgins s/n) This jazzy resto-bar on the main road into town serves up great lunches (CH$4000) and giant sandwiches (CH$3500 to CH$4500) and, come night, 15 varieties of pisco cocktails. There's a Moroccan vibe to this tiny colorful spot that buzzes late into the night to a loungey soundtrack and occasional strumming of guitars in the lovely garden with a firepit.

El Durmiente Elquino   RESTAURANT, BAR $

(Carrera s/n; mains CH$3500-5500) Sample the tasty tapas, pizzas and interesting mains, like quinoa risotto, in the all-natural interior of this resto-bar full of wood, bamboo, clay and pebbles. Sip an artisanal beer or organic wine on the small patio out back, with nice mountain views.

Rustika   RESTAURANT, BAR $

(Carrera s/n) Across the street from El Durmiente, Rustika's outdoor section by a gurgling brook serves natural juices, pizzas and artisanal chocolates during the day. The cozy restaurant-bar section opens for dinner and remains buzzing till 3am.

Los Jugos   RESTAURANT, BAR $$

(Plaza s/n; mains CH$2900-8100) Come here for the views of the plaza, delicious natural juices, a good range of salads and pizzas and cocktails at night. Otherwise, the food is passable.

ℹ Information

Note that Pisco Elqui doesn't have an ATM or a bank so make sure to bring enough cash with you. It also has no gas station so fill up before leaving Vicuña.

ℹ Getting There & Away

Frequent buses go to Pisco Elqui (CH$700, 50 minutes) from Vicuña, and vice versa.

COCHIGUAZ
🖉051

New-age capital of northern Chile, the secluded valley of Cochiguaz is accredited with an extraordinary concentration of cosmic vibes, a vortex of powerful energies, much-publicized UFO sightings and formidable healing powers. But you needn't be a

---

WORTH A TRIP

EXPLORING THE ELQUI VALLEY

The first point of interest on the drive from Vicuña, at Km14.5 just before Montegrande, at an altitude of 1080m, is the **Cavas del Valle winery** (🖉051-451-352; www.cavasdelvalle.cl; ⊙10am-8pm summer, to 7pm rest of year). Opened in 2004, this little boutique bucks the trend by serving actual wine, rather than pisco. The *cosecha otoñal* dessert wine, made of pink muscatel grapes, alone is worth the stop. A quick tour of the facilities, with a tasting of three wines, is free, although you are encouraged to purchase a bottle.

An artisanal *pisqueria* established in 1868, located 3km south of Pisco Elqui, **Fundo Los Nichos** (www.fundolosnichos.cl) still produces pisco the old-fashioned way. Its four guided tours (CH$1000; in Spanish only; at 12:30pm, 1:30pm, 4:30pm and 5:30pm daily in summer) include a visit to the facilities and a tasting of three piscos. Or just stop by between 11am and 7pm for a free tasting; bottles start at CH$3200.

Drive on from here and you'll reach **Horcón artisanal market** (⊙noon-8:30pm) in the valley of its namesake village, worth a browse for its wealth of gorgeous handmade arts and crafts, local all-natural food and cosmetic products, all sold out of bamboo stalls. At the center of the market is a small stone amphitheater, which occasionally hosts live music. It's a feast of colors, dream catchers, wind chimes, knit dresses and jewelry. You can even do a mud therapy treatment by the river (look for the Magiterra stand) or simply have a swim.

From here, the paved road turns into a dusty dirt track leading to the adorable village of **Alcoguaz**, 14km beyond Pisco Elqui. Note its yellow and red wooden church and, if you wish to stay, move on to **Casona Distante** (www.casonadistante.cl; d/tr CH$50,000/70,000; 🅿🐕), a big wooden 1930s farmhouse beautifully restored into a rustic eight-room ecolodge with a swimming pool, riverside trails, a small observatory and a split-level restaurant. Rates include mountain-bike use; massages and horseback rides can be arranged for an extra fee.

believer to enjoy the beautiful valley, which is also the jumping-off point for hiking and horseback rides in the backcountry. It sometimes snows here in the winter, so bring warm clothes.

The village is presided over by the hippy-kitsch **El Alma Zen** (☎099-047-3861; refugiocochiguaz@gmail.com; Km11; domes/d CH$25,000/35,000), which serves up conveyor belt spirituality. While it – paradoxically – lacks soul and service, it does have a full-service spa (book an aura cleaning), a restaurant (which doesn't open until10:30am and charges CH$2500 for breakfast and CH$6000 for lunch or dinner), a small shop, two swimming pools and six concrete domes with shared bath in a eucalyptus forest down by the river. Nonguests can enjoy the grounds for CH$7000 per day.

The town's latest attraction is **Observatorio Cancana** (www.cancana.cl, in Spanish) by the owners of El Alma Zen, located right across the road. They shuttle people in for the nightly two-hour tours with observation (at 9:30pm and 11:30pm in summer, 30 minutes earlier in winter). Tours happen pending a six-person minimum, at CH$6000.

Camping Cochiguaz (☎451-154; cabanas chanarblanco@gmail.com; campsites per person CH$5000) has some labyrinthine campgrounds in a tall forest down by the river. It's 19km from Montegrande at the end of a tortuous dirt track. It also offers horseback riding trips.

Hummingbirds flit around the hammock-filled gardens of **Casa del Agua** (☎321-371; www.casadelagua.cl, in Spanish; 2-person cabins CH$60,000; P), a pretty cabin complex 13km north of Montegrande, perched delicately along the banks of the Río Cochiguaz. There's a restaurant, two pools and nine swimming holes, mountain-bike hire, a labyrinth, a meditation cave and walking paths. It also offers tours and massages.

At the time of writing, there was no public transportation to Cochiguaz so the only way to get there is with your own wheels or by hitching a ride from Montegrande.

PASO DEL AGUA NEGRA

A spectacular rollercoaster of a road crosses the mountains into Argentina, 185km east of Vicuña. At an ear-popping 4765m above sea level, it's one of the highest Andean passes between Chile and Argentina. It's also one of the best areas to see the frozen snow formations known as *penitentes*, so called because they resemble lines of monks

garbed in tunics. There are also accessible glaciers on both the Chilean and Argentinean sides.

From Vicuña, Ruta 41 climbs along the Río Turbio to the Chilean customs and immigration post at Juntas del Toro. It continues south along the turquoise reservoir known as La Laguna before switch-backing steeply northeast to Agua Negra. The road leads to the hot-springs resort of Termas de Pismanta in Argentina, and to the provincial capital San Juan.

Once mined by the Argentine military during tensions over the Beagle Channel in 1978, the route is usually open to vehicular traffic from mid-November to mid-March or April, and cyclists enjoy the challenge of this steep, difficult route. The road is passable for any passenger vehicle in good condition.

There is no public transportation but agencies in Vicuña and Pisco Elqui offer trips.

Limarí Valley
☑053

The unassuming market town of **Ovalle** on the north bank of the Río Limarí is the capital of the prosperous agricultural province of Limarí. This workaday place is more famous for its surrounding attractions than its own modest charms so we recommend you use it only as the gateway to places further afield and perhaps a stop for lunch.

Should you decide to do so, try **D'Oscar** (Miguel Aguirre 292; mains CH$4800-8500) on the southeast corner of the main plaza, a cafeteria-style place that buzzes with locals and dishes out the usual spectrum of dishes – sandwiches, pizzas and pastas.

If you have your own transportation you can make a loop from La Serena to Vicuña, Hurtado and Ovalle. The 43km gravel road from Vicuña to Hurtado is usually manageable in a regular car, but a 4WD or high-clearance vehicle would be less hair-raising. The drive is through beautiful, sometimes steep, desert scenery with cacti, multicolored rocks and views of hilltop observatories. Public transportation from Ovalle goes as far as Hurtado, but there is no direct connection to Vicuña.

VALLE DEL ENCANTO

An intriguing gallery of pre-Colombian rock art can be found at **Monumento Arqueológico Valle del Encanto** (adult/child CH$500/300; ☺8:15am-8:30pm summer, to 7pm winter), a rocky tributary canyon of the Río Limarí 19km west of Ovalle. An array of petroglyphs and pictographs depict dancing stick-men, alienlike figures with antennae and characters sporting spectacular head-dresses. The valley rocks are also riddled with holes called *tacitas,* which were used as mortars to grind ceremonial plants and food.

The figures mostly date to the El Molle culture, which inhabited the area from the 2nd to the 7th century AD. The rock art is best viewed around noon when shadows are fewer, but it can be very hot at that time of day.

The friendly wardens are often happy to accompany guests around the site on quiet days. A more leisurely walk around all the three sectors takes 1½ hours. Both picnicking and camping are possible. Bring water, although there is potable water in the canyon itself.

To get here, take any westbound bus out of Ovalle and disembark at the highway marker; Valle del Encanto is an easy 5km walk along a gravel road, but with luck someone will offer you a lift.

TERMAS DE SOCOS

After a grueling day in the desert it's blissful to sink into the steamy thermal baths or a refreshingly cool swimming pool at Termas de Socos, a tiny spring hidden 1.5km off the Panamericana at Km370. Here you can indulge in saunas (CH$7000), Jacuzzis (CH$5900) and massages (CH$15,000). Private tubs cost CH$3900 for a half-hour soak; access to the public swimming pool also costs CH$3900 for nonguests. Spring water is bottled on-site.

The **Hotel Termas Socos** (☎198-2505; www.termasocos.cl; s/d CH$41,000/75,800; ᴾ⊠) is an unexpected delight. It is guarded by tall eucalyptus, surrounded by lush foliage and isolated amid arid hills. Its room rates include a piping-hot private bath and access to the pool. Slightly pricier rooms on the lower level have patios and TVs. All-inclusive rates are available.

Camping Termas de Socos (☎631-490; www.campingtermassocos.cl, in Spanish; campsites per person CH$5000, cabins per person CH$8000; ⊠☗) is a pleasant gravel-and-sand campsite with its own pool and baths, though they are less swanky than those in the neighboring hotel. There's only partial shade but it has a good games room and playground. Non-

guests can use the pool and picnic area for CH$3900, have a dip in the thermal waters for CH$3500 and rent bikes for CH$1200 per hour.

Río Hurtado Valley

☑053

The least explored of Norte Chico's valleys, this verdant region is crisscrossed with curvy roads, hillside hamlets and endless vineyards, all enveloped by barren mountains rising on all sides. It's the type of place where you won't see anyone for kilometers on end, and then a man on horseback will trot along its dusty roads.

By far the nicest place to stay, overlooking the lush banks of Río Hurtado, is **Hacienda Los Andes** (☎691-822; www.haciendalosandes.com; campsites per person CH$5000, s/d incl breakfast from CH$36,000/54,000; ᴾ), a gorgeously rambling hideaway that offers skinny dipping in a cool highland river, dozy afternoons spent in a hammock and other ways to disconnect. It also has horseback trips (from CH$60,000 for three hours) during the day and even at night, as well as 4WD jaunts to nearby attractions (from CH$60,000). Free activities include scenic walks on the marked trails that dot the property. The latest addition is a small observatory, where you can observe the night skies for CH$7500.

To get here, take one of the buses from Ovalle to Hurtado (CH$1800, between noon and 4pm); return buses leave early morning only (around 7am). The hacienda is 6km before Hurtado, just before the bridge. It can provide a pick-up service from Ovalle (CH$28,000 per car), La Serena (CH$38,000) and Vicuña (CH$50,000). The hacienda is 46km from Vicuña via a gravel mountain road (best tackled with a 4WD), and 75km from Ovalle (the road is paved as far as Pichasca).

In nearby Hurtado, if budget is a concern, try **Tambo del Limarí** (☎691-854; Caupolicán 027; r per person CH$10,000) on the main drag, which has three immaculate rooms (one of which has a private bathroom) decorated with iron bedstands and light comforters above the *dueña's* (female owner's) home. She'll also prepare simple meals upon request for CH$3000 per pop, which is a boon since the only restaurant in town is mostly closed.

Parque Nacional Bosques de Fray Jorge

The last thing you'd expect to stumble across in a cactus-riddled semidesert would be lush cloud forest of the type found around Valdivia, 1205km south. But that's exactly what you'll find at **Parque Nacional Bosques de Fray Jorge** (adult/child CH$2500/1000; ⊙9am-6pm, last access at 4:30pm), a smear of green squeezed between the ocean and the desert.

The puzzle of how this pocket of verdant Valdivian cloud forest came to exist in this parched environment is answered by the daily blanket of moist *camanchaca* that rolls in from the Pacific Ocean. Come around noon and you'll witness this white cushion of clouds cloaking the sea and progressively swallowing the forest's base, giving the impression that you could be on top of the world – when you're only really 600m above the sea. That said, the best time to appreciate the forest's ecology is early morning, when condensation from the fog leaves the plants dripping with moisture.

Patches of green inland suggest that the forest was once far more extensive. Of Fray Jorge's 100 sq km, there remain only 400 hectares of its truly unique vegetation – enough, though, to make it a Unesco World Biosphere Reserve. Some scientists believe this relict vegetation is evidence of dramatic climate change, but others argue that humans are responsible for the forest's destruction, using it for fuel, farming and timber.

Scant mammals include skunks and sea otters, as well as two species of fox. There are also some 80 bird species; small hawks sit atop the cacti while eagles wheel high above in search of prey.

The park is named after the first recorded European visitor, a Franciscan priest named Fray Jorge, in 1672.

🏃 Activities

In the late afternoon the rising *camanchaca* moistens the dense vegetation at **Sendero El Bosque**, a 1km trail that runs along the ridge above the ocean. The trail is at the end of the 27km-long road from the Panamericana. The last segment of the road is very steep, rough and dusty.

ℹ Information

Fray Jorge's gated road may be locked outside opening hours. The Centro de Información has piecemeal displays about 1km past the entrance; admission is paid here. The park is only open for day use; no camping is allowed.

ℹ Getting There & Away

Take a westward lateral off the Panamericana, at Km387, about 20km north of the Ovalle junction. There's no public transportation but several agencies in La Serena offer tours. The park is a six-hour drive from Santiago.

Sur Chico

Includes »

Best Places to Eat

» Fogón del Leñador (p278)

» Hostería de la Colina (p235)

» Cocina Mapuche Mapu Lyagl (p248)

» Tradiciones Zuny (p228)

Best Places to Stay

» Refugio Tinquilco (p247)

» Refugio Cochamó (p273)

» La Montaña Magica (p255)

» Hotel Antumalal (p240)

Why Go?

The Chilean south begins here. The regions of La Araucanía, Los Ríos and the Lakes District jar travelers with their menacing ice-topped volcanoes; its glacial lakes that look like melted Chinese jade; and roaring rivers running through old growth forests and villages inhabited by the indomitable Mapuche people. Though not as rugged or as challenging as Patagonia – call it Patagonia Lite – it is home to seven spectacular national parks, many harboring perfectly conical volcanoes (like Volcán Osorno, which stands sentinel over the entire area) and has become a magnetic draw for both outdoor adventure enthusiasts and devil-may-care thrillseekers. Peppered about sprawling workhorse travel hubs like Temuco, Valdivia, Osorno and Puerto Montt, you'll find charming lake and mountain hamlets, rich in architecture, culture and, most obviously, stunning backdrops of national parks and nature reserves, each one like an Ansel Adams photograph brought to life in cinematic color.

When to Go
Puerto Montt

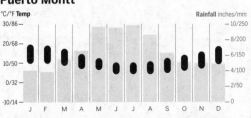

Jan–Feb Summer in this weathered region brings less rain, but you'll still need a raincoat.	**Nov–Mar** Navimag ferry high season: spectacular Patagonian sunsets and glaciers.

Jan One of the most crowded months for summiting Volcán Villarrica but also the sunniest skies.

Sur Chico Highlights

1 Visit one of the most beautiful places in the world you've probably never heard of on an *etnoturismo* jaunt to **Caleta Condor** (boxed text, p257)

2 Trek the otherworldly landscapes of La Araucanía's volcanically altered national parks: **Reserva Nacional Malalcahuello-Nalcas** (p233) and **Parque Nacional Conguillío** (p231)

3 Shred Andean powder driving your own dogsled on a majestic seven-day Andean crossing with **Aurora Austral Patagonia Husky** (p235)

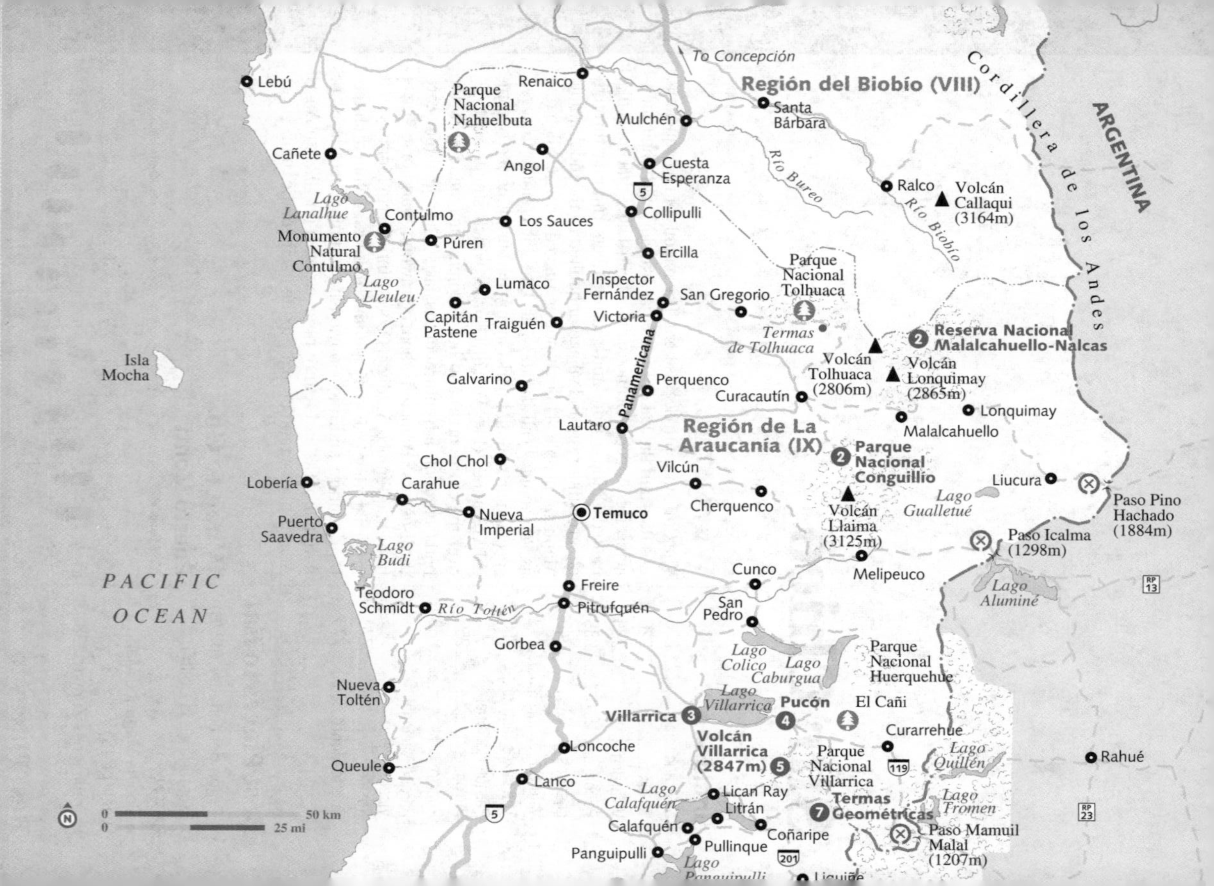

ARGENTINA

Cordillera de los Andes

Región del Biobío (VIII)

Región de La Araucanía (IX)

PACIFIC OCEAN

Isla Mocha

50 km
25 mi

ARGENTINA

Río Negro

Región de Los Ríos (XV)

Región de Los Lagos (X)
(Lakes District)

Panamericana

❹ Push your adrenaline to the limits every day of the week in **Pucón** (p238) and **Puerto Varas** (p263)

❺ Glaciate down **Volcán Villarrica** (p244) after summiting its fuming crater

❻ Hike or horse trek deep into the Río Cochamó Valley to the granite playground at impossibly gorgeous **La Junta** (p273)

❼ Burn a day at the romantic and spectacular **Termas Geométricas** (boxed text, p246)

❽ Sleep in a fairy-tale hotel inside **Huilo-Huilo Reserva Natural Biosfera** (boxed text, p255)

① Caleta Condor

History

As the Spanish conquistadores pushed their way south from present-day Santiago, they were motivated by stories of precious metals and the possibility of a large, docile indigenous workforce. The land of La Araucanía and the Lakes District would be the ideal territory to continue the imperial dream. Or maybe not. The Mapuche waged one of the fiercest and most successful defenses against the European invaders anywhere in the Americas, and the Spanish were not able to settle south of the Río Biobío until the mid- to late 19th century.

Germans were recruited to settle the Lakes District, leaving their mark on architecture, food, manufacturing and dairy farming. Today millions of national and international tourists, plus wealthy Santiago refugees looking for country homes, are doing more than anybody to continue to tame and colonize the once wild lands. Real-estate prices are skyrocketing and the several hundred thousand remaining Mapuche are being pushed further and further into the countryside. Tourism, logging and salmon farming – despite a near-collapse in the late 2000s (see boxed text, p275) – are driving the future of the region.

In 2007, the Lakes District was subdivided and Chile's 14th region, Los Ríos, was created with Valdivia as its capital, returning to the city the power it had held up until 1974, when the military junta deemed it second class during a regional restructuring and stripped it of its designation as an administrative capital.

❶ Getting There & Away

Most visitors enter this region by bus or train from Santiago. All of the major cities also have airports. By the time you get to Puerto Montt you are pretty far from Santiago and the short flight will save you a lot of time on the bus. Puerto Montt is also the ferry terminus for the Patagonian ferries, the most popular of which takes travelers back and forth to Puerto Natales (see boxed text, p280).

❶ Getting Around

La Araucanía, Los Ríos and the Lakes District have an excellent network of buses: big buses, minibuses, vans, minivans and pretty much anything else that you can imagine. Bus transportation is the easiest and most low-maintenance way to get around. To get to some of the smaller and more remote towns, it may be necessary to backtrack to the closest city in order to find the correct bus. The roads are generally accessible for rental cars. There are taxis and occasionally *colectivos* (shared taxis) within all of the larger towns that cannot be covered on foot.

LA ARAUCANÍA

Temuco

📞 045 / POP 259,102

With its leafy, palm-filled plaza, its pleasant Mercado Municipal and its intrinsic link to Mapuche culture, Temuco is the most palatable of all Sur Chico's blue-collar cities to visit. The city is the former home of Pablo Neruda, one of most influential poets of the 20th century, who once called it the Wild West. It is also the regional transit hub, with steady transportation to Santiago and connections to everywhere in Sur Chico and beyond.

◉ Sights & Activities

Museo Regional de La Araucanía MUSEUM
(www.museoregionallaaraucania.cl; Av Alemania 084; adult/child CH$600/300; ⊙9:30am-5:30pm Tue-Fri, 11am-5pm Sat, 11am-2pm Sun) Housed in a handsome frontier-style building dating from 1924, this small but vibrant regional museum has permanent exhibits recounting the history of the Araucanían peoples before, during and since the Spanish invasion in its newly renovated basement collection, including an impressive Mapuche dugout canoe. A ground-floor gallery caters to temporary exhibitions. Along with the museum at Huilo-Huilo (see boxed text, p255), this is the region's best, though an extensive renovation could only manage signage in Spanish and Mapudungun.

Buses 1, 9 and 7 run along Av Alemania, but the route is also reasonable walking distance from the *centro*.

**Monumento Natural
Cerro Ñielol** HISTORIC SITE
(📞298-222; Calle Prat; adult/child CH$1200/600; ⊙8am-7pm) Cerro Ñielol is a hill that sits among some 90 hectares of native forest – a little forested oasis in the city. Chile's national flower, the copihue *(Lapageria rosea)*, grows here in abundance, flowering from March to July. Cerro Ñielol is also of historical importance, since it was here in 1881, at the tree-shaded site known as La Patagua, that Mapuche leaders ceded land to the colonists to found Temuco. Whether or not the actual papers were signed on the hill is up

for debate. The park has picnic sites, a small lagoon, footpaths and an environmental information center.

🛏 Sleeping

Temuco is not fundamentally a tourist town, and therefore lodging can be a bit tricky. Budget options around the train station and Feria Pinto are inexpensive and downright dirty. The neighborhood between the Plaza de Armas and the university has higher-quality budget options and is more secure at night for women.

Hospedaje Tribu Piren GUESTHOUSE $
(☑985-711; www.tribupiren.cl; Prat 69; r per person after/before 6pm CH$10,000/12,000; P🐕@📶) The young English-speaking owner at this traveler's *hospedaje* (budget accommodation) makes this a great choice for foreigners. Everything is clean and polished, and rooms, some of which open out onto a small terrace, offer cable TV and central heating. Alvaro, the owner, also guides snow-sport tours in the winter. If you're nice, he'll even make you Brazilian *café coado* (filtered through a cloth). Definitely your best bet in Temuco proper.

Adela y Helmut GUESTHOUSE $
(☑098-258-2230; www.adelayhelmut.com; Faja 16,000 Km5 N; dm CH$7000-9000, r from CH$23,000; P🐕) If a gritty, working-class city isn't your thing, make your way out to this backpacker favorite on a small farm 48km from town on the road to Parque Nacional Conguillío. Solar-heated water, small kitchens in the apartments and outstanding views to still-smoldering Volcán Llaima are highlights, as are the Suabian treats from the kitchen such as *Hefezopf* sweetbread. It also rents bikes and offers horseback riding. For the CH$7000 dorm rate, you must show up of your own volition, which means legging it the 4.5km from the main road.

Hostal Pewman Ruka GUESTHOUSE $$
(☑594-245; www.pewmanruka.cl; Francia 245; s/d/tr CH$25,000/34,000/43,000; P@📶) A friendly, kind of pricey guesthouse off Av Alemania with a small, bright courtyard, simple rooms

THE INDOMITABLE MAPUCHE

Chile's largest indigenous group, the Mapuche (*che* meaning 'people' and *mapu* meaning 'of the land'), is the first and only indigenous nation on the continent whose sovereignty and independence was legally recognized, but they have exhausted generations in fighting to keep it that way.

The Mapuche first successfully fought off the marauding Inka empire, only to take on a sustained 300-year attack by the Spanish empire. They used the Río Biobío as a natural frontier and resisted colonization until the 19th century. It was the longest and hardest-fought indigenous defense in the Americas. By its end, the nation's once vast territory of 100,000 sq km was reduced to a mere 5000 sq km of *reducciones* (settlements).

The Mapuche signed the Treaty of Killin with the colonizing Spaniards in 1641 (the document solidified the territorial autonomy of the Mapuche and 28 others over two centuries of diplomatic relations). Yet, in the late 1800s, the Chilean and Argentine military massacred an estimated 100,000 Mapuche. From 1965 to 1973, land reform improved the situation for the Mapuche, but the military coup of 1973 reversed many of these gains. Between the restoration of democracy in 1989 and 2012, the Mapuche people made limited progress in their continuing fight for reparations and the return of their lands. However, most of the court rulings granting them land were effectively overturned by powerful business interests.

Various human rights organizations, as well as the Special Rapporteur of the UN, have widely reported the imposition of assimilation policies, and protests in Temuco are nearly a daily affair. It's not uncommon for tourists, filmmakers and foreign journalists to be harassed by police, arrested and/or deported after being seen among Mapuche communities where there exist ongoing land-dispute conflicts. In 2010 a series of hunger strikes were organized by Mapuche leaders in response to the Chilean government's efforts to prosecute some of the Mapuche community's more violent wings, such as the Coordinadora Arauco-Malleco (CAM). The government has accused it of using occupation, death threats and arson as tactics in the ongoing dispute.

Temuco

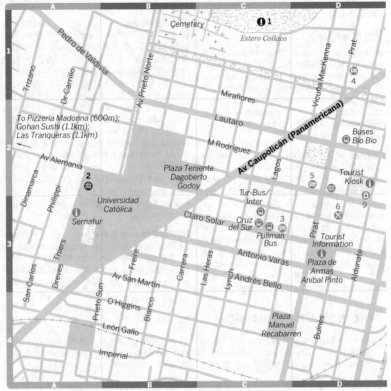

and a well-appointed living room – all with the advantage of being within walking distance of the best restaurants and nightlife.

Hospedaje Klickmann GUESTHOUSE $
(☎748-292; claudiz_7@hotmail.com; Claro Solar 647; r per person with/without bathroom CH$14,500 /11,800; P@🛜) This clean and friendly *hospedaje* is barely a hiccup from several bus companies.

Hotel RP HOTEL $$
(☎977-7777; www.hotelrp.cl; Portales 779; r week/ weekend CH$65,400/47,588; P@🛜) Not as trendy as the lobby would have you believe, but a decent top-end place with run-of-the-mill chain-hotel rooms and friendly service.

✖ Eating & Drinking

Most of the choice restaurants and bars are along Av Alemania on Temuco's west side. The cheapest eats can be had at the dynamic Feria Pinto, where vendors churn out *ca-*

zuelas (stews), *sopapillas con queso* (traditional fried dough with cheese), empanadas, seafood stews and other tasty dishes.

TOP CHOICE Tradiciones Zuny CHILEAN $
(Tucapel 1374; meals CH$1700-3300; ☯breakfast & lunch Mon-Sat) Temuco's best-kept secret is an underground local's haunt specializing in the fresh, simple food of the countryside served out of an indigenous-themed home. It's hard to find, not helped by the fact that the front entrance says 'Restaurante Las Acacias' instead of its real name, but the cheap, Chilean-Mapuche fusion is worth it (look for the Indian-themed graffitied wall). A typical menu here might include salad, beef *cazuela* with pumpkin, bread with a smoky hot sauce, avocado juice (try it!), and a super interesting quinoa and raspberry dessert, all for around CH$3100. You're welcome.

0   400 m
0   0.2 miles

To Terminal
Rodoviano
(400m)

Conaf

Tucapel
8

Janequeo

Patzke

Av A Pinto

Nar-Bus

Bilbao

Terminal
de Buses
Rurales

Buses
JAC

Av Balmaceda

General Mackenna

General Cruz

Zenteno

Matta

Feria
Pinto

7

Estación de
Ferrocarril

Diego Portales

Manuel Montt

Av Barros Arana

Temuco

& dinner) Temuco's top choice for pizza and pasta is a bustling (especially on Sunday) checker-tableclothed spot where the specialty is *Tricotta* (ravioli three ways).

🔒 Shopping

Temuco is great for Mapuche woolen goods (ponchos, blankets and pullovers), pottery and musical instruments, such as *zampoñas* (panpipes) or drums. The best spot in town is the Mercado Municipal.

TOP CHOICE Fundación Chol-Chol ARTS & CRAFTS, HOMEWARES
(☏614-007; www.cholchol.org; Camino Temuco a Imperial Km16; ⊙9am-5:30pm) The most responsible spot to buy Mapuche gear is located 16km out of town. This nonprofit, Fair Trade organization works with 600 rural Mapuche women to offer top-quality weavings and textiles made entirely by hand. Throw rugs, wall hangings, bags, shawls – nothing is cheap, but everything is simply gorgeous. To get here, take any bus toward the towns of Nueva Imperial, Carahue or Puerto Saavedra from the rural bus terminal and ask to be let off at the Fundación.

❶ Information

Keep an eye out for pickpockets at in *centro*, especially Mercado Municipal and Feria Pinto. Snatch-and-grab thievery has also been reported on the Cerro Ñielol hike.

ATMs and exchange houses are plentiful all around Plaza de Armas Aníbal Pinto.

Gohan Sushi JAPANESE $$
(www.gohan.cl; Hochstetter 401; rolls CH$2950-4650; ⊙lunch & dinner Mon-Sat; 🛜) It was only a matter of time before Gohan got too big for its downtown britches and moved out to Av Alemania with the rest of the trendsetters. Still, this innovative sushi spot gets the job done with an extensive list of funky rolls and shrimp dishes. If you stay within these walls, Temuco suddenly starts to feel a little *Temucool*. Prices drop on Mondays and lunch Tuesday to Thursday.

Confiteria Central CAFE $
(Bulnes 442; mains CH$2600-5950; ⊙breakfast, lunch & dinner; 🛜) Coffee, tea, breakfast, sweets, gooey ham-and-cheese sandwiches and other meals are the staples at this classic spot, pleasing *temuquenses* since 1948.

Pizzería Madonna ITALIAN $$
(www.madonnapizza.com; Alemania 660; pizzas CH$4400-9700, pasta CH$6400-7800; ⊙lunch

Conaf (☎298-100; Bilbao 931, 2nd fl) Mainly administrative offices, but has maps of the regional parks in the adjacent building (Pasilla D, 2nd floor).

Hospital Hernán Henríquez Aravena (☎212-525; Manuel Montt 115; ◷24hr) Six blocks west and one block north of Plaza de Armas Aníbal Pinto.

Post office (cnr Diego Portales & Prat)

Sernatur (☎312-857; Thiers 539; ◷8:30am-8:30pm Mon-Sat, 10am-2pm Sun Dec-Feb, 9am-2pm & 3-5:30pm Mon-Thu, 9am-2pm & 3-4:30pm Fri Mar-Nov) Near the Museo Regional.

Tourist kiosk Mercado Municipal (☎973-628; ◷8am-8pm Mon-Sat, 9am-4pm Sun); Plaza de Armas Aníbal Pinto (☎720-777; ◷9am-7pm Mon-Fri, to 6pm Sun) On Sunday, only the Mercado branch is open.

❶ Getting There & Away

Air

Aeropuerto Maquehue is 6km south of town, just west of the Panamericana. **Lan** (☎600-526-2000; www.lan.com; Bulnes 687; ◷9am-1:30pm & 3-6:30pm) flies to Santiago (from CH$152,500). **Sky Airlines** (☎777-300; www.skyairline.cl; Bulnes 677; ◷9am-2pm & 3-7:30pm Mon-Fri, 9:30am-1:30pm Sat) flies for considerably less one way to Santiago (from CH$48,400) and Concepción (from CH$20,700).

Bus

Temuco is a major bus hub. Long-haul bus services run from the **Terminal Rodoviario** (☎225-005; Pérez Rosales 1609), located at the northern approach to town. Companies have ticket offices around downtown. Times and frequencies vary throughout the year, with fewer buses in winter.

Bus lines serving main cities located along the Panamericana include: **Tur-Bus/Inter** (☎234-349; cnr Lagos & Manuel Montt) and **Pullman Bus** (☎212-137; Claro Solar 611), both of which offer frequent services to Santiago and the latter to Valparaíso/Viña del Mar; **Cruz del Sur** (☎730-320), which is set up at at two locations at Claro Solar 599 and Manuel Montt 290, which also serves the island of Chiloé and Bariloche via Osorno; and **Igi Llaima/Nar-Bus** (☎407-777; Balmaceda 995), which also heads over to Argentina.

The **Terminal de Buses Rurales** (☎210-494; Av Aníbal Pinto 32) serves local and regional destinations. Nar-Bus goes to Melipeuco (CH$1700, two hours) seven times daily as well as having one daily direct departure to Parque Nacional Conguillío itself (CH$3000, three hours, Monday to Saturday 10:30am).

Buses JAC (☎465-465; cnr Av Balmaceda & Aldunate), with its own terminal, offers the most frequent service to Villarrica and Pucón, plus services to Santiago, Lican Ray and Coñaripe.

Buses Bio Bio (☎465-351; www.busesbiobio. cl; Lautaro 854) operates frequent services to Angol, Los Angeles, Concepción and Curacautín, as well as Lonquimay.

Sample travel times and costs are as follows (prices fluctuate with the quality of the bus/ classes):

DESTINATION	COST (CH$)	DURATION (HR)
Castro	10,500	9
Chillán	6500	4
Concepción	7000-8300	4½
Curacautín	3400	2
Osorno	4500-10,500	4
Pucón	2500-4800	2
Puerto Montt	6000-12,300	5
Santiago	15,000-51,000	9
Valdivia	3000-3400	3
Valparaíso/Viña del Mar	19,000	10
Villarrica	1400	1½
Zapala & Neuquén (Ar)	15,000-30,000	7½-12
San Martín de Los Andes (Ar)	12,000	6½

❶ Getting Around

Colectivo 11P goes from downtown (Claro Solar) to the bus terminal (CH$450 to CH$600). A taxi from *centro* should cost CH$2500. For those who want to go straight to the airport, many long-haul buses coming into town can drop you at the Cruce del Aeropuerto, from where you can catch a taxi for CH$4000, the same price it costs from *centro*. Car rental is from **Europcar** (☎232-715; cnr Diego Portales & Vicuña Mac-Kenna) and **Avis** (☎456-280; San Martín 755). Both also have branches at the airport.

Parque Nacional Tolhuaca

As the early-morning mist burns off from the surrounding hill country, gaggles of parrots can sometimes be spotted lingering on the dusty road that leads to the 64-sq-km **Parque Nacional Tolhuaca** (adult/child CH$3500/1500) – a clear indication you're on the road less traveled. One of the park system's best-kept secrets, mainly because it's harder to get to than nearby Conguillío, Tolhuaca is located northeast of Temuco, on the north bank of the Río Malleco. The park offers trekking over elevation changes from 850m around Laguna Malleco to 1830m on the summit of Cerro Colomahuida; the 2806m Volcán Tolhuaca is beyond the park's southeast boundaries.

The park's best hike goes to **Laguna Verde** (one way two hours, 4km), reached via a trailhead about 5km east of Laguna Malleco on the road to Termas de Tolhuaca; it's named for its greenish waters and verdant circumference flanked by lush araucaria (monkey puzzle tree) and lenga. The trail crosses the Río Malleco and passes several waterfalls. A shorter trip is to **Salto de Malleco** (one way one hour, 1.7km), a 49m waterfall.

Easily accessed from the eastern sector of the park and located 33km north of Curacautín, the rustic complex at **Termas de Tolhuaca** (☎045-881-211; www.termasdetolhuaca.cl; Curacautín office at Calama 240; day use adult/child CH$8000/6000) has some steaming baths in natural outdoor settings. Rooms at **Hotel Termas de Tolhuaca** (r per person CH$52,000) include full board.

You can stay at **Camping Inalaufquén** (campsites CH$8000), which is located on the southeastern shore of Laguna Malleco. It has secluded woodsy sites, including running water, firepits, picnic tables and toilets with cold showers that could use a little elbow grease. For more information on the park or camping, contact Conaf in Temuco (see p229).

❶ Getting There & Away

There is no direct public transportation from Temuco to the park. From Victoria, buses leave every weekday for San Gregorio, from where it's a 19km walk to the campground at Laguna Malleco. The other option is a taxi from Curacautín for CH$20,000.

Parque Nacional Conguillío

Llaima means 'Blood Veins' in Mapudungun and that is exactly what tourists who were visiting **Parque Nacional Conguillío** (www.parquenacionalconguillio.com; adult/child CH$4500/2500), and its towering Volcán Llaima (3125m), saw on New Year's Day 2008. As the centerpiece of this Unesco Biosphere Reserve, it is one of Chile's most active volcanoes. Since 1640 Llaima has experienced 35 violent eruptions. Eruptions as recently as 2008 spewed fiery lava 300m into the air and created a 20km-long plume of billowing smoke that forced Chile's National Forestry Corporation (Conaf) to evacuate 43 trapped tourists as well as 11 of its own employees from the park; and an additional 40 people when a second eruption occurred. In other words, this monster likes to cough up blood.

Despite the fire spitting, this wonderful park, which was created in 1950 primarily to preserve the araucaria and 608 sq km of alpine lakes, deep canyons and native forests, is open. The gray-brown magma that has accumulated over the years is to blame for the dramatic vistas and eerie lunarscape atmosphere – at its most dramatic, perhaps, in late April when the leaves are in full autumn bloom.

You can access Parque Nacional Conguillío from three directions. The first, and shortest (80km), is directly east of Temuco via Vilcún and Cherquenco; this accesses the ski resorts at Sector Los Paraguas, but doesn't access (by road, anyway) the campgrounds, main visitor center and trailheads. All of those are best reached by taking the more northern route from Temuco via Curacautín (120km). The park's southern entrance, also 120km from Temuco, is accessed via Melipeuco. From here a road heads north through the park to the northern entrance, also accessing the trailheads and campgrounds.

🏃 Activities

Hiking

The 2008 eruption coughed up lava to the southeast into Sector Cherquenco, sparing all of the park's designated trails. One of Chile's finest short hikes, the **Sierra Nevada trail** (one way three hours, 7km) to the base of the Sierra Nevada, leaves from the small parking lot at Playa Linda, at the east end of Laguna Conguillío. Climbing steadily northeast through dense coigüe forests, the trail passes a pair of lake overlooks; from the second and more scenic overlook, you can see solid stands of araucarias beginning to supplant coigües on the ridge top.

Conaf discourages all but the most experienced hikers from going north on the **Travesía Río Blanco** (one way five hours, 5km), an excursion detailed in Lonely Planet's *Trekking in the Patagonian Andes*.

Near the visitors center, the **Sendero Araucarias** (45 minutes, 0.8km) meanders through a verdant rainforest. At Laguna Verde, a short trail goes to La Ensenada, a peaceful beach area. The **Cañadon Truful-Truful trail** (30 minutes, 0.8km) passes through the canyon, where the colorful strata, exposed by the rushing waters of Río Truful-Truful, are a record of Llaima's numerous eruptions. The nearby **Los Vertientes trail** (30 minutes, 0.8km) leads to an opening among rushing springs.

Climbing

Experienced climbers can tackle Volcán Llaima from **Sector Los Paraguas** on the west side of the park, where there is a *refugio* (rustic shelter) on the road from Cherquenco, or from Captrén on the north side. Although you do not need a climbing permit, you must stop by Conaf's Centro de Información Ambiental for equipment inspection.

Skiing

Centro de Ski Las Araucarias   SKIING
(☏045-239-999; www.skiaraucarias.cl; Temuco; half-/full-day lift tickets CH$ 19,000/22,000) Sector Los Paraguas has just three ski runs, but is a tranquil and scenic area to enjoy a day on the slopes. Ski and snowboard rental costs CH$15,000 per day.

🛏 Sleeping

TOP
CHOICE **La Baita**   CABIN $
(☏099-733-2442;   www.labaitaconguillio.cl; s/d CH$48,000/60,000, cabañas 4/6 people CH$60,000/70,000; P🐾) Spaced amid pristine forest, this is an ecotourism project just outside the park's southern boundary. It's home to six attractive cabins with slow-burning furnaces, turbine-powered electricity and hot water; an extremely cozy, incense-scented lodge and restaurant with 15 rooms complete with granite showers and design-forward sinks; and a pleasant massage room, outdoor hot tub and sauna. Rates at the lodge include breakfast; otherwise the Chilean-Italian restaurant with Mapuche touches runs CH$14,000 extra for half-board. It is owned by adorable, hippie-esque, former singer Isabel Correa, who entertains guests over organic wines each evening. Yoga, mountain bikes, kayaks and trekking are all at the ready. La Baita is located 15km from Melipeuco and 60km from Curacautín.

Cabañas Conguillío   CABIN $
(☏02-588-4035; cabañas 3/7 people CH$50,000/ 75,000) On the southwest end of the lake, are very well equipped. There's a small store (open from mid-December to early March).

Centro de Ski Las Araucarias has four options right on the mountain: The newest, **Edificio Araucarias** (apt 4/6 people CH$90,000/110,000), has a cozy living room and bar area; and there's **Edificio Llaima** (q apt CH$60,000), **Refugio Pehuén** (dm CH$12,000, d without bathroom CH$13,000) and **Refugio Los Paraguas** (dm CH$10,000, ste CH$60,000). If you are staying in the dorms, you may need to provide your own sleeping bag. Contact the ski center for bookings.

Conaf operates five **campgrounds** (campsites CH$18,000) inside the park including around the south shore of Lago Conguillío and the northwest shore of Laguna Captrén, including a special camping sector set aside for backpackers (campsites CH$5000). in season, the park also operates two solar-run **domes** (CH$50,000) with a double bed and sofa on Lago Conguillío. A five-star, architecturally intriguing lakeside lodge was projected when we came through

ℹ Information

Conaf's **Centro de Información Ambiental** (Laguna Conguillío; ⊙8:30am-9:30pm) offers a variety of programs mainly in the summer (January and February), including slideshows and ecology talks, hikes to the Sierra Nevada and outings for children. Good trail maps with basic topographic information and trail descriptions are available here.

ℹ Getting There & Away

To reach Sector Los Paraguas, **Vogabus** (☏045-910-134), at Temuco's Terminal de Buses Rurales, runs hourly to Cherquenco (CH$1400, 1½ hours) from 8am to 6:30pm Monday to Saturday, from where it's a 17km walk or hitchhike to the ski lodge at Los Paraguas.

For the northern entrance at Laguna Captrén, **Buses Flota Erbuc** (☏045-272-204) has regular service from Curacautín (CH$3400, two hours), where a shuttle (CH$500) runs to the park border at Guardería Captrén twice a day (6am and 6pm). **Buses Curacautín Express** (☏045-258-125) offers the same shuttle at the same times Monday to Friday only. In winter the bus will go as far as conditions allow. Both options leave you with a 2km walk to the park entrance. The only other option is a taxi for CH$30,000.

For the southern entrance at Truful-Truful, **Nar-Bus** (☎045-211-611; www.narbus.cl) in Temuco runs six buses daily to Melipeuco (CH$1300, two hours), where the tourism office can help arrange transport to the park.

Curacautín

☎045 / POP 16,995

Curacautín is the northern gateway to Parque Nacional Conguillío. There are more services here in Melipeuco and a pleasant step-up in traveler accommodations has leveled the playing field a bit, though you'll still be happier if you base yourself along the road to Lonquimay, a more central location for the area's three parks.

If you sleep here, the price is right at **Hostal Epu Pewen** (☎881-793; Manuel Rodríguez 705; dm CH$7000, d CH$22,000; [P][☺][@][☎]), run by a half-Mapuche couple. It's superclean and comfortable for the price and features all sorts of Mapuche touches, like bathroom and wall tiles patterned with *kultrün* (ceremonial drums). English is spoken and all park treks and activities can be organized. **Hostal Rayén** (☎099-001-4421; Manuel Rodríguez 104; r per person with/without bathroom CH$12,000/8000; [P][☺]) isn't the nicest or the quietest, but hospitality speaks volumes. A step up but with a similar family atmosphere is the kitschy **Dream's House** (☎881-462; Iquique 115; r per person with/without breakfast CH$12,000/10,000; [P][@][☎]).

The helpful **tourist office** (☎464-858; Manuel Rodríguez s/n; ☺8:30am-9pm Jan-Feb, 8:30am-6:30pm Mon-Sat, 9:30am-2pm Sun Mar-Dec) has brochures and information on the park and accommodations in town.

The **bus terminal** (cnr Arica & Manuel Rodríguez) is directly on the highway to Lonquimay. **Buses Bio Bio** (☎881-123; www.busesbiobio.cl) heads to Temuco via Victoria (CH$4300, six daily) and four times daily via Lautaro (CH$3000). **Buses Curacautín Express** (☎258-125) goes to Temuco all day long via Lautaro (CH$1200, 1½ hours). For transportation details to Parque Nacional Conguillío, see opposite. **Tur-Bus/Inter** (☎881-596; Serrano 101) has a few direct buses per day to Santiago (CH$21,100 to CH$23,500). You can also try **Jet Sur** (☎099-486-9156), which goes nightly at 9pm for considerably less (CH$10,000 to CH$15,000).

For accommodations on the road to Lonquimay, **Buses Flota Erbuc** (☎272-204) goes to Malalcahuello six times daily and can drop you anywhere along the route (CH$700).

Reserva Nacional Malalcahuello-Nalcas

The jewel of northern Araucanía's national parks, **Reserva Nacional Malalcahuello-Nalcas** (adult/child CH$1000/500) is a combined reserve of 303 sq km just north of the town of Malalcahuello, en route to Lonquimay, and extends almost to the border of Parque Nacional Tolhuaca. Though off the main park circuit, Malalcahuello-Nalcas offers one of the most dramatic landscapes in all of Sur Chico, a charcoal desertscape of ash and sand that looks like the Sahara with a nicotine addiction.

◉ Sights & Activities

Though not an ambitious hike, the trek to **Cráter Navidad** (two hours, 1.5km), which last blew on Christmas Day 1988, takes in this otherworldly atmosphere – not unlike Mars with its desolate red hues reflecting off the soils of magma and ash – and the magnificent backdrop of Volcán Lonquimay, Volcán Tolhuaca and Volcán Callaqui off in the distance.

The most easily accessible trail is **Piedra Santa** (five hours, 7.5km), which is the beginning stretch of the longer Laguna Blanca trail. From Piedra Santa, **El Raleo** (two hours, 3.5km) branches off and leads through coigüe forest and introduced pine. The trail starts near the small Conaf **information center** (097-488-5816; Camino Internacional Km82) near the road to the hamlet of Malalcahuello along the highway to Lonquimay. Wild camping is permissible along the trails.

Nalcas' western boundary abuts Volcán Tolhuaca, while Volcán Lonquimay marks the division between the two reserves. In Nalcas, **Sendero Tolhuaca** (one way 24 hours, 40km) is accessible only from **Sendero Laguna Blanca** (one way two days, 40km), which traverses the western flank of Volcán Lonquimay and ends in a spectacular aquamarine lake at the foot of Volcán Tolhuaca outside the park's western boundary. There is a great view of both volcanoes. An old logging road connects the trail west to Termas de Tolhuaca and Laguna Verde in Parque Nacional Tolhuaca (the trails may be hard to find; guides are recommended).

Centro de Montaña Corralco (☑02-202-9325; www.corralco.com; half-/full-day lift tickets CH$18,000/23,000) has better skiing than in Conguillío, with numerous runs and prettier scenery. A brand-new lodge has also just been built. To get here, the turnoff is 2km east of Malalcahuello on the road to Lonquimay, where a good gravel road takes you the remaining 9km up the mountain. Rentals here run CH$16,000.

🛏 Sleeping

There are two great sleeping options for travelers, both on the road to Lonquimay, which is otherwise lined with waterfalls and hot springs.

Andenrose
LODGE **$$**

(☑099-869-1700; www.andenrose.com; Camino Internacional Km68.5; s/d from CH$25,000/33,000; [P][⊖][☎]) The Bavarian-styled Andenrose, on the rushing and kayakable Río Cautín, is built from organic woods and is full of exposed brick and southern German hospitality (the enthusiastic owner is quite the firecracker). The nightly three-course meals are serious business (hope for veal goulash/späetzle pairing) and there's a rich breakfast. They also arrange excellent horseback riding, jeep tours and excursions in the area.

Suizandina
LODGE **$$**

(☑197-3725; www.suizandina.com; Camino Internacional Km83; campsite per person CH$6000, dm CH$13,000, s/d/tr from CH$29,000/41,000/49,000; [P][@][☎]) The slightly more upscale Suizandina was originally founded by a young Swiss family and recently sold to a hospitable Swiss-Chilean couple who have maintained the eternally Swiss vibe (same owners as EcoHostel in Santiago). Cleanliness is next to godliness in the roomy lodgings (fantastic bathrooms), the best of which for travelers are the cheaper offerings in the separate Casa de Huéspedes, which share a common kitchen. The bathrooms for campers, located in the main house, are surely the nicest in Sur Chico. It's well stocked with wine and mini-küchens (sweet, German-style cakes) to go and the menu goes all out with excellent Swiss specialties like *rösti* (hashbrowns), fondue and raclette (melted Swiss cheese). There's a new emphasis on massages and horseback riding as the new owner is a physiotherapist horse lover; and all treks can be organized.

❶ Getting There & Away

Heading east of Malalcahuello the road passes through the narrow, one-way 4527m Túnel Las Raíces, a converted railway tunnel from 1930 that emerges into the drainage of the upper Biobío and has sealed its place in history as the longest tunnel in South America. The road eventually reaches 1884m Paso Pino Hachado, a border crossing that leads to the Argentine cities of Zapala and Neuquén.

Malalcahuello-Nalcas is best accessed on a tour or by taxi from Curacautín – the road through the parks requires a 4WD.

Melipeuco

☑045 / POP 4980

Melipeuco, the southern gateway to Parque Nacional Conguillío, is 90km east of Temuco via Cunco. If you're looking to base yourself nearer the park than Temuco, this is a good spot for day trips, though you're better off going all the way to truly absorb the otherworldly atmosphere of Conguillío.

To get out and about, **Andes White** (☑099-460-9720; www.andeswhite.com; Pedro Aguirre Cerda 702) is a great new upstart agency run by two enthusiastic outdoorsmen. Line up climbs of Volcán Llaima (CH$75,000), visits to the caldera and glacier at Sollipulli (CH$50,000) and day trips into the park (CH$35,000) here.

Antü Mahuida Excursiones (☑098-806-4743; www.antu-mahuida.com; Pedro Aguirre Cerda 702) takes folks to the park for CH$18,000 per person.

Top choice to bed down is **Hostal Sendero Andes** (☑581-306; www.senderoaventuras andes.cl; Pedro Aguirre Cerda 384; r per person with/without bathroom CH$22,000/16,000; [P][⊖][@][☎]), a friendly hostel with bilingual staff. The inviting bar and restaurant feels like a mountain lodge, while the simple rooms upstairs are more typical of small-town Sur Chico. **Hospedaje Icalma** (☑099-280-8210; hospeda jeicalmademelipeuco@gmail.com; Pedro Aguirre Cerda 729; r per person CH$12,000; [P][⊖][@]) is a decent choice with a few basic rooms.

Melipueco has a few restaurants and a helpful **tourist office** (☑581-062; Pedro Aguirre Cerda s/n; ⊙8:30am-1pm & 2-6pm Mon-Fri, 10am-2pm Sat, 3-8pm Sun).

From Temuco's Terminal de Buses Rurales, Nar-Bus has seven buses daily Monday to Saturday to Melipeuco (CH$1700), less on Sunday, and one direct departure Monday to Saturday to the park entrance itself (CH$3000, three hours).

Villarrica

📞 045 / POP 39,727

Unlike Pucón, its wild neighbor across wind-swept Lago Villarrica, Villarrica is a real living, breathing Chilean town. While not as charming, it's more down to earth than Pucón, lacks the bedlam associated with package tour caravans, and has more reasonable prices and a faded-resort glory that attracts travelers of a certain lax disposition.

The new *costanera* (lakeshore road), rebuilt after the 2010 Concepción earthquake, makes for a nice walk and Villarrica's grassy lawn-cum-beach is more pleasant than it sounds. Considering you can book all the same activities here as Pucón, it makes for an agreeable alternative if that's what you're looking for.

◉ Sights & Activities

Museo Histórico y Arqueológico   MUSEUM
(Av Pedro de Valdivia 1050; admission CH$300; ⊙9am-1pm & 3-7:30pm Mon-Fri) Mapuche artifacts (including jewelry, musical instruments and roughly hewn wooden masks) are the focus of the Museo Histórico y Arqueológico, alongside the tourist office. It was closed for renovation during the time of our research – a mini-tornado had torn its roof off!

TOP CHOICE **Aurora Austral**
Patagonia Husky   DOG SLEDDING
(📞098-901-4518; www.auroraaustral.com; Camino Villarrica-Panguipulli Km19.5) Located about 19km from Villarrica on the road to Lican Ray is this German-run husky farm, where you'll find over 50 of the cutest Siberian and Alaskan huskies you ever did see, ready to take you on the ride of your life. In winter, there are day trips (CH$60,000) and a seriously awe-inspiring seven-day Andean crossing (CH$1,950,000). In summer, there are 6km rides with a barbecue (CH$30,000) and husky trekking on Volcán Villarrica (CH$45,000). True dog lovers can sleep out here as well in three extremely nice cabins (CH$30,000 to CH$60,000).

✱ Festivals & Events

Muestra Cultural Mapuche   CULTURAL
The annual Muestra Cultural Mapuche, in January and February, has exhibits of local artisans, indigenous music and ritual dance.

🛏 Sleeping

More than half a dozen campgrounds can be found along the road between Villarrica and Pucón.

🍴 Hostería de la Colina   INN $$
(📞411-503; www.hosteriadelacolina.com; Las Colinas 115; s/d from CH$30,000/47,000, ste CH$67,000; P🐕☀@🖥) This smart *hostería* (inn) and restaurant is set on meticulously manicured and lush grounds on a hill with stupendous views just southwest of town. The US-expat owners are some of the few in the area who understand true hospitality (and gardening). Rooms in the main house are classically inclined while the two independent suites offer more privacy and contemporary decor. Little afternoon surprises include snacks of smoked salmon or free-range European elk salami.

La Torre Suiza   HOSTEL $
(📞411-213; www.torresuiza.com; Bilbao 969; dm CH$8500, s/d/tr from CH$15,000/20,000/27,000; P@🖥) This charming wooden chalet and traveler staple offers a fully equipped kitchen, laundry, multilingual book exchange, mountain-bike rental, lots of area information and all the traveler camaraderie you are seeking. There was talk of a possible change in ownership at the time of writing.

Hostería Hue-quimey   GUESTHOUSE $$
(📞411-462; www.huequemay.cl; Valentin Letelier 1030; r from CH$40,000; P🐕☀@🖥) Hue-quimey is rife with newly renovated character, from its dollhouse exterior to the subtle African artwork done by the new German-French owners, who came over from Cameroon. The front-facing rooms take full advantage of the views that put Villarrica on the map, and the 2nd-floor offers small terraces as well. The bay windows on the lower floor and the large upstairs windows illuminate the rooms on sunny days.

Hostal Don Juan   INN $
(📞411-833; www.hostaldonjuan.cl; General Körner 770; s/d CH$20,000/31,000, without bathroom CH$14,000/24,000; P@🖥) Don Juan wins travelers over with its numerous distractions: a game room, a large *fogón* (outdoor oven) which was designed by the friendly owner, a multi-use room that includes a kitchen and shower – it's all here. There are also fabulous volcano views from some rooms on the 2nd floor.

Villarrica

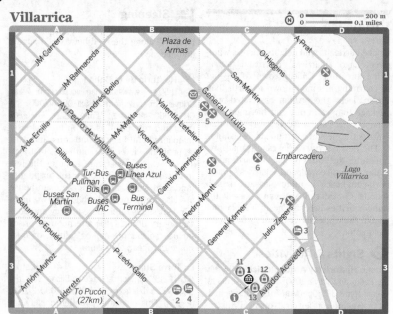

✗ Eating

There are a few atmospheric food stalls in the back of Centro Cultural Mapuche serving up Mapuche cuisine and other cheap and hearty fare for CH$900 to CH$3500.

Hostería de la Colina
CHILEAN, INTERNATIONAL $$

(☑411-503; www.hosteriadelacolina.com; Las Colinas 115; mains CH$5500-7900; ⊘lunch & dinner; 🛜) This excellent restaurant, worth trying even if you're not staying at the *hostería*, does Chilean and international comfort food that is *comida* (food) cut from a different cloth. The limited seasonal, daily changing menu often includes standouts like Aztec soup, a mean veggie lasagna, excellent hormone-free elk and hazelnut-crusted trout; and meals here almost always end with a sampling of any number of the 12 flavors of homemade ice cream. Worth the drive up to right your culinary wrong.

TOP CHOICE The Travellers
INTERNATIONAL $

(www.thetravellers.cl; Valentin Letelier 753; mains CH$3950-8500; ⊘breakfast, lunch & dinner-late; 🛜) Chinese, Mexican, Thai, Indian, Italian – it's a passport for your palette at this resto-bar that is ground zero for foreigners.

A makeover marries classic album covers and postcards from *amigos* the world over with a modern motif and a new expansive terrace. German and English traveler advice is available, and so are discounted cocktails at the lengthy happy hour (6pm to 9:30pm; try a towering mojito). Bottom line: it's in all the guidebooks for good reason – if you've spent considerable time in Chile, a dish like the awesome Thai chicken curry (a mismatch of red and Penang styles) is salvation. The awesome cocktails and *enchuladas* (draft beer, Tabasco, lime and salt) are gravy.

TOP CHOICE Huerto Azul
DESSERTS $

(www.huertoazul.cl; Henríquez 341; items CH$690-1900; ⊘breakfast, lunch & dinner) Blindingly blue, this fabulous gourmet store/ice-cream parlor dares you to walk in without stumbling out in a sugar coma. Artisanal marmalades and chutneys, eg fig with *merkén* (Mapuche spice-smoked chili) and onion with merlot, line the walls; an extensive line of housemade Belgian chocolate bars (decadent!) line the display case; and locals line the outside for Italian-style gelato, also made on the premises (try the antioxidant-laced *maqui*, the world's new *açaí*).

Villarrica

El Sabio PIZZERIA $

(www.elsabio.cl; Zegers 393; pizzas CH$3900-8900;
⊙lunch & dinner; closed Mon Mar-Dec; 🛜) A friendly Argentine couple runs the show here, creating fantastic, uncut oblong pizzas served on
small cutting boards. Forget everything you
thought you knew about pizza in Chile.

Fuego Patagón STEAKHOUSE $

(cnr Pedro Montt & Prat; steaks CH$4950-6900;
⊙lunch & dinner Jan-Feb, closed Mon Mar-Dec)
You'll find satisfying *carne*-to-cost benefit at
this quiet neighborhood steakhouse tucked
away from the hubbub. It was the juici-
est *lomo vetado* (sirloin) we found under
CH$5000, and the spicy green salsa that
comes with your *sopapillas* will jumpstart
your dormant tastebuds.

Caramel CAFE $

(Urrutia 837; items CH$850-3000; ⊙breakfast,
lunch & dinner Mon-Sat Dec-Feb) Simple Swiss-
run cafe serving great espresso (with mini-
artisanal donuts) and interesting paninis.

Café Bar 2001 CAFE $

(Camilo Henríquez 379; mains CH$2750-5600;
⊙breakfast, lunch & dinner) The breakfast special here for CH$2700 nabs you küchen,
toast, juice and coffee, though it doesn't
open until 9am. There is also a decent selection of rarer microbrews and an extensive
coffee menu.

🛍 Shopping

Surrounding the tourist office, there is a
high concentration of *artesanías* (handicrafts). The **Pueblito Artesanal** (cnr Acevedo
& Pedro de Valdivia; ⊙10:30am-8pm), the **Feria
Artesanal** (Acevedo 565; ⊙10am-midnight Jan-
Feb) and the **Centro Cultural Mapuche**
(⊙10am-11pm) have all the typical tourist
wares, the most interesting of which are the
Mapuche figures carved from laurel wood
and raulí wood bowls.

ℹ Information

Banks with ATMs and internet are plentiful,
especially near the corner of Pedro Montt and Av
Pedro de Valdivia.

Banco de Chile (cnr Pedro Montt & Av Pedro
de Valdivia)

Hospital Villarrica (San Martín 460; ⊙24hr)

Oficina de Turismo (📞206-619; www.visitvil
larrica.cl; Av Pedro de Valdivia 1070; ⊙8am-
11pm Jan-Feb, 9am-1pm & 2:30-6pm Mar-Dec)
Municipal office that has helpful staff and
provides many brochures.

Post office (Anfión Muñoz 315)

ℹ Getting There & Around

Villarrica has a main **bus terminal** (Av Pedro
de Valdivia 621), though a few companies have
separate offices nearby. Long-distance fares
are similar to those from Temuco (an hour
away), which has more choices for southbound
travel.

Buses JAC (📞467-775; Bilbao 610) goes to
Pucón every 20 minutes, Temuco every 20 minutes and Lican Ray (CH$700, 40 minutes) and
Coñaripe (CH$1100) every 30 minutes. From the
main terminal, **Buses Vipu-Ray** (📞096-835-
5798) goes to Pucón every five minutes. **Buses
Coñaripe** (📞097-265-8183) departs throughout the day to Lican Ray (CH$700) and Coñaripe
(CH$1000). **Condor** (📞413-436) goes to Viña
del Mar/Valparaíso at 8:30am daily.

Tur-Bus (📞413-652; Anfión Muñoz 657),
Pullman Bus (📞414-217; cnr Anfión Muñoz &
Bilbao) and Buses JAC offer the most frequent
services to Santiago. The latter also departs several times daily to Valdivia, Temuco and Puerto
Montt. **Buses Línea Azul** (📞416-667; www.
buseslineaazul.cl; Muñoz 647) most frequently
services Middle Chile.

For Argentine destinations, **Igi Llaima** (📞412-
733), in the main terminal, leaves at 9am Monday to Saturday and 11:30am Sunday for San
Martín de los Andes, Zapala and Neuquén, via
Paso Mamuil Malal. **Buses San Martín** (📞411-
584; Pedro León Gallo 599) does the same route
Tuesday to Sunday at 10am.

SUR CHICO VILLARRICA

Sample bus fares from Villarrica (prices fluctuate with the quality of the bus/classes):

DESTINATION	COST (CH$)	DURATION (HR)
Chillán	12,000	6
Concepción	10,500	6
Los Angeles	8000	4
Pucón	800	¾
Puerto Montt	8300	5
San Martín de los Andes (Ar)	12,000	5
Santiago	20,000-64,500	10
Temuco	1800	1
Valdivia	3900	2½
Viña del Mar/Valparaíso	24,900-38,500	15

Pucón

045 / POP 16.970

Pucón is firmly positioned on the global map as a mecca for adventure sports, its setting on beautiful Lago Villarrica under the smoldering eye of the volcano of the same name sealing its fate as a world-class destination for adrenaline junkies. Once a summer playground for the rich, Pucón is now a year-round adventure machine catering to all incomes, especially in February (a time to avoid, if possible), when it is absolutely overrun. The town receives alternating floods of package tourists, Santiago holidaymakers, novice Brazilian snowboarders, adventure-seeking backpackers, new age spiritualists and mellowed-out ex-activists turned eco-pioneers.

While the popularity and international feel can be off-putting for some, Pucón boasts the best small-town tourism infrastructure south of Costa Rica. That means quality accommodations, efficient tourism agencies, hundreds of activities and excursions, vegetarian restaurants, falafel, microbrews, and hundreds of expat residents from the world over.

Like every other place in the region, the crowds do trickle in winter and skiing and snowboarding become the focus. In summer, if you're not hiking it, jumping off of it, riding it or climbing it, you'll likely find yourself planted on Pucón's gorgeous black-sand beach, tucked behind the Gran Hotel Pucón – blink and you'll swear you're in the tropics!

Activities

It's easy to overdose on adrenaline before actually doing any activity in Pucón – the wealth of adventure operators lining Av O'Higgins and the bounty of activities on offer in and around Pucón can easily overwhelm. For a list of recommended agencies, see opposite. The standards, climbing Villarrica and rafting Río Trancura, are offered by many, but consider some of the other activities – those that allow you to appreciate the area away from the masses, such as horseback riding, renting a bike, snowshoeing or exploring some of the smaller nature reserves on foot. In addition to what we have focused on here, there's canopying, skydiving, paragliding, motocross, hydrospeed – you name it.

Horseback Riding

There are a few spectacular options for horse treks in this region. Most rides take in various environments and may include stopovers so riders can meet with local *huasos* (cowboys) or Mapuche communities. Half- and full-day rides hover around CH$18,000 to CH$42,000 depending on the grade of difficulty and number of people going. Recommended agencies all offer excursions for first-time riders too.

Mountain Biking

Mountain bikes can be rented all over town. Daily rental prices are negotiable but shouldn't be more than CH$7000 unless it is a brand-new bike with full suspension.

The most popular route is the Ojos de Caburgua Loop. Take the turnoff to the airfield about 4km east of town and across Río Trancura. It's a dustbowl in summer, though, and tends to irritate all but the most hard-core riders. Extensions off the same route include the Lago Caburgua to Río Liucura Loop and the full Río Trancura Loop.

Two other popular trails that are close to town are Correntoso and Alto Palguín Chinay (to the Palguín hot springs). Any bike-rental agencies will be able to give you more details and should provide a decent trail map.

Rafting & Kayaking

Pucón is known for both its river sports and the quality of the rafting and kayaking infrastructure. Most of the larger travel agencies run rafting trips. For recommended agencies, see opposite. The rivers near Pucón and their corresponding rapids classifications are: the Lower Trancura (III), the Upper

Trancura (IV), Liucura (II–III), The Puesco Run (V) and Maichín (IV–V). When negotiating a rafting or kayaking trip, recognize that the stated trip durations often include transportation, not just the time spent on the water. Prices can range from CH$12,000 to CH$28,000 depending on the season, the number of people per raft or kayaking trip, the company and the level of challenge. Many of the rivers are swollen in the winter and closed for most sports, although it is still possible to raft or kayak in some. If you have a half-day to kill before a bus ride, consider the No-Carbon paddling experience (CH$7500) dreamed up by Aguaventura and ¡école! to help save the Trancura River Delta from a proposed development.

Rock Climbing

Cerduo, at the foot of Volcán Villarrica, offers 15 different climbing routes ranging from 5.8 to 5.12d for those looking for more serious climbing. There's sport climbing as well as traditional and you will be surrounded by native forest. For more intense and physically demanding climbing, head to pristine Las Peinetas near the Argentine border, where climbs consist of five to six pitches and can last up to 12 hours. It is a three-hour hike in to where the climbing commences. For experienced and certified guides, check out Summit Chile below, where, in addition to advanced options, owner Claudio Retamal has opened up two routes at Cerduo for all skill levels.

☞ Tours

Most of the tour operators are on Av O'Higgins or within a half block. Prices are similar throughout, but quality of service can vary. In summer, seasonal operators pop up on all corners, but are not as established as those listed below – you are strategically advised to stick to these for most activities.

TOP CHOICE **Aguaventura**　　CLIMBING, OUTDOORS
(☑444-246; www.aguaventura.com; Palguín 336) This friendly French-owned agency is your one-stop shop, offering highly skilled guides for the volcano (beer after!); and also specializing in snow sports and kayaking, but can book it all. It also rents everything for the mountain, water and snow; and book flights/ferries, too.

Summit Chile　　CLIMBING, ROCK CLIMBING
(☑443-259; www.summitchile.org; Urrutia 585) Started by internationally certified Claudio

Retamal, a former Chilean climbing champion and the most experienced guide on the volcano. He can also take you up the other volcanoes – Lanín, Llaima and Lonquimay – as well as rock climbing, throwing in some geology and natural history along the way. Advanced/backcountry skiers should ask about skiing *up* Villarrica.

Kayak Pucón　　KAYAKING
(☑099-716-2347; www.kayakpucon.net; Av O'Higgins 211) This well-regarded kayak operator offers three-day kayak courses (CH$150,000) as well as multiday expeditions for more experienced kayakers. Half-day ducky (single-man inflatable boats) tours on Class III rapids are a good option for those with less kayak experience (CH$20,000).

🌿 **Elementos**　　CULTURAL TOURS
(☑441-750; www.elementos-chile.com; Caupolicán 243) A good bet for *etnotourism,* offering day trips delving deeper into Mapuche culture, including cooking lessons with Mapuche chefs, visits to an organic honey/natural-cosmetic farm and a meet and greet with Mapuche medicine men; with a few waterfalls and Andean lagoons thrown in.

Canyoning Pucón　　CAYONING
(☑099-294-6913; www.canyoningpucon.cl) The recommended agency for canyoning offers half-day trips for CH$39,000 to Pillan (November and December) and Nevados (January to March) canyons.

Huepilmalal Centro Ecuestre　　HORSEBACK RIDING
(☑099-643-2673; www.huepilmalal.cl; Km27 Camino Pucón-Huife) This reputable equestrian center uses pure Chilean bred *caballos* (horses) for its half-day to multiday treks in the Cañi cordillera. It's run by a charming couple with over 40 years' experience in Europe and South America.

Politur　　RAFTING
(☑441-373; www.politur.cl; Av O'Higgins 635) Avoid for the volcano, but is the go-to agency for rafting.

⌖ Sleeping

While Pucón has plenty of places to stay, prices are higher than in other cities (even for the budget options). In the low season, rates are about 20% less. Reservations are absolutely necessary in advance in January and February, but aren't a problem in

Pucón

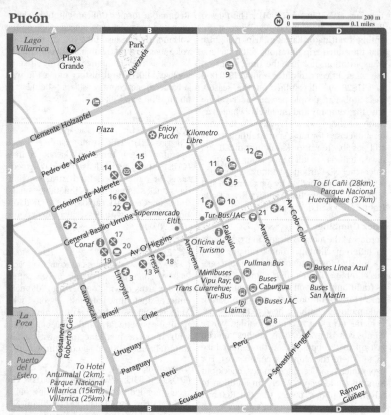

the winter. Note that due to the nature of early-rise tourism here, breakfast is often not included.

Hotel Antumalal
BOUTIQUE HOTEL $$$

(☎441-011; www.antumalal.com; Km2; r from CH$176,000; P@🛜🏊) This testament to Bauhaus architecture on the road to Villarrica is built into a cliffside above the lake. From its tree-bark lamps to araucaria-clad walls, it instills a sense of location while all the while being wildly and wonderfully out of place. Its huge slanting windows give unbeatable views of Lago Villarrica from the swanky common areas and all the minimalist rooms offer fireplaces and some have fern- and moss-covered raw rock for the internal walls. The restaurant does advanced Chilean cuisine (and a ridiculously famous hot chocolate mousse), with many ingredients plucked right from the organic vegetable patch, just a drop in the bucket of the property's 12 hectares of gardens.

TOP CHOICE iécole!
HOSTEL $

(☎441-675; www.ecole.cl; General Basilio Urrutia 592; dm with/without bedding CH$10,000/7000, d/tr CH$30,000/38,000, d/tr without bathroom CH$20,000/25,000; P@🛜) The ecoconscious iécole! is a travel experience in itself. It's a meeting point for conscientious travelers and a tranquil and artsy hangout that has long been Pucón's most interesting place to stay. Rooms are small, clean and comfortable, but walls are thin and voices carry within the leafy grounds, so it's not a wild party hostel. The excellent vegetarian restaurant is one of Chile's best (mains CH$3900 to CH$4500) and is as much an attraction as the lodging. There are concerns that it is losing some of its vibe of international camaraderie, and a few general touch-ups are needed (spotty wi-fi, leaking faucets), but these guys were preaching sustainability, conservation and eco-everything nearly two decades before anyone else in Chile.

Pucón

Bambu Lodge   B&B **$**
(☎096-802-9145; www.bambulodge.com; Camino a Volcán Km4.2; s/d CH$40,000/50,000; P@) For those looking to stay away from the madness but still enjoy all that Pucón has to offer, or perhaps those who are traveling a bit more romantically but are still budget-conscious, this discerning four-room B&B in a woodsy spot on the road to the volcano is a wonderful find. The French owner has imported much of his decor from Morocco, and service is as personalized as possible: it's just Guillaume and his Chilean girlfriend, Beatriz, tending to your solitude. A taxi from town is CH$5000.

The Tree House   HOSTEL **$**
(☎444-679; www.treehousechile.cl; Urrutia 660; dm from CH$8000, d with/without bathroom CH$30,000/20,000; P☎) This cozy hostel is run by a British-Chilean tag team of former tour leaders for English-based outfitter Journey Latin America. Orthopedic mattresses, individual lockers, British fire alarms, central heating and yes, a tree house (no, sorry, you can't sleep in it) are pluses, but the real leg up here is that most of the shared dormitories have no more than four beds, some of them even have two, so it's more intimate and private without having to spring for a private room.

La Tetera   GUESTHOUSE **$$**
(☎464-126; www.tetera.cl; Urrutia 580; s/d CH$35,500/39,000, without bathroom CH$27,500/31,000; P☎@☎) As Villarrica is to Pucón, La Tetera is to its famous neighbor iécole! This German-Austrian effort has a lot to offer, though, with a small range of inviting and well-heated rooms that have indigenous touches, all run and cleaned with spirited Germanic efficiency. Prices include an excellent breakfast.

La Bicicleta   HOSTEL **$**
(☎444-583; labibicletapucon@gmail.com; Palguín; dm CH$13,000, d CH$36,000, s/d without bathroom CH$14,000/26,000; ☎@☎) Run by a friendly *Chileno* from Viña del Mar, this subtlety stylish spot gets great reviews from travelers. There is a bar (with Stella on tap) and a restaurant in the front (guests can claim a 10% discount) and a great outdoor patio that is located upstairs, only rivaled by a spacious streetside deck that is attached to one of the private rooms. José, the owner, is an immediately likable dude, who rents mountain bikes, and just so happens to have the most beautiful Weimaraner that you have ever met.

Gran Hotel Pucón   HISTORIC HOTEL **$$$**
(☎913-300; www.granhotelpucon.com; Clemente Holzapfel 190; s/d incl breakfast from CH$160,000/184,000; P@☎☎) You can just picture Pucón's gorgeous black-sand beach that was once teeming with ladies bathing in caps and skirts at this aged 1936 relic – the whole thing looks like an unearthed B&W photo from the '20s. Now owned by the Enjoy casino folks, who have failed to capitalize on much of this days-of-yore charm (duct taping the earthquake-damaged floors doesn't quite cut it), but there are some upsides: 5th-floor standard rooms have stupendous views and the back patio, pool and lawn area is a caught-in-time glimpse of throwback days. Best option for families.

SUR CHICO PUCÓN

Hospedaje Victor
GUESTHOUSE $

(☎443-525; www.pucon.com/victor; Palguín 705; dm CH$10,000, r CH$25,000; ❀@⊛) Victor stands out for cleanliness and a warm atmosphere, ensured by several wood-burning stoves. It offers kitchen access, big TVs and two kitchens for guest use.

Hostel Etnico
HOSTEL $

(☎442-305; www.etnicohostel.com; Colo Colo 36; dm from CH$8000, r with/without bathroom CH$40,000/24,000; ❀@⊛✉) In a former monastery that now feels more like an American university fraternity house, this good-time hostel is notable for its huge backyard and pool area.

✕ Eating

Pucón is the undisputable king of culinary variety in southern Chile. Fresia is the town's Restaurant Row.

Trawen
CHILEAN, FUSION $

(Av O'Higgins 311; mains CH$3900-8900; ⊙breakfast, lunch & dinner; ⊛♪) This time-honored favorite does some of Pucón's best gastronomic work for the price, boasting innovative flavor combinations and fresh-baked everything. Highlights include home-style breakfasts, venison with green tomato chutney, Antarctic krill empanadas, seafood risotto with *merkén* and a veggie sandwich on crunchy homemade bread. Waiters are happy to make recommendations. Creative types tend to congregate here as well.

La Maga
STEAKHOUSE $$

(www.lamagapucon.cl; Gerónimo de Alderete 276; steak CH$8900-10,900; ⊙lunch & dinner Tue-Sun) There is a *parrilla* (steakhouse) for every budget in Pucón, but this Uruguayan steakhouse stands out for its *bife de chorizo* (steak) and house-cut fries. It's not the cheapest, but this was second only to Fogón del Leñador in Puerto Montt for Sur Chico's best steak. The only things missing are proper napkins and some decent steak knives.

Viva Perú
PERUVIAN $

(www.vivaperudeli.cl; Lincoyán 372; mains CH$5900-8900; ⊙lunch & dinner Tue-Sun; ⊛) This intimate Peruvian restaurant does all the classics and does them well: *ceviche* (raw fish and onions marinated in citrus juices and spices), *tiradito* (onion-free *ceviche*), *chicharónes* (deep-fried pork rinds) and *ají de gallina* (creamy chicken stew with cheese, peppers and peanuts) – even Peru's famous Chinese fusion *chifa* dishes.

Pledge your allegiance for the chaser: pisco sours come with Peruvian or Chilean pisco. Do not confuse this with the Peruvian place on the corner; keep on walking.

Pizza Cala
PIZZERIA $$

(Lincoyán 361; pizzas CH$3200-12,000; ⊙lunch & dinner; ⊛) The best pizza in town is spit from a massive 1300-brick oven by an Argentine-American pizza maker who grows his own fresh basil. In winter, it's the only warm restaurant in town. A plan to expand to Villarrica was keeping the owner busy when we came through.

Mora
JAPANESE $$

(www.morasushibar.cl; Fresia 236; rolls CH$3150-7900; ⊙lunch & dinner) If you could swallow a Jamiroquai track, it would likely taste like this funky sushi spot looks, all dressed up in retro fuchsia, violet and orange against a white clapboard background that sort of feels like the Caribbean. The sushi rolls are really solid, if not borderline too big for a mouthful.

Latitude 39°
AMERICAN $

(Gerónimo de Alderete 324-2; mains CH$3400-4900; ⊙breakfast, lunch & dinner) California transplant owners filling a gringo niche – juicy American-style burgers, fat breakfast burritos, veggie tacos, BLTs, chili – but consistency has been an issue.

Huerto Azul
DESSERTS $

(O'Higgins 291) Smaller, less frenzied branch of the Villarrica gourmet store and ice-cream parlor.

⬤ Drinking & Entertainment

The bar scene in Pucón, like Puerto Varas, changes more often than a baby's diapers and most spots last just about as long. You can also head to the Enjoy Pucón Casino, which has several bars and restaurants within it.

Mama's & Tapas
BAR, CLUB

(Av O'Higgins 597; cocktails CH$4000-5500; ⊙6pm-late) Known simply as 'Mama's,' this is the most popular place to go out in Pucón and has proved its staying power. Recent renovations have expanded the outdoor patio, trendied up the inside and added a club in the back on weekends. The resident DJ, an acoustic engineer, spins everything from indie rock to old-school hip-hop in an all-wood wall and ceiling space designed to make sure your brain is sonically seized by what he spins. There is a CH$5000 cover to get into the club, but this cost includes one drink.

Newen
BAR

(Fresia 248) Notable for the town's best microbrew, made from *piñones,* the nut of the araucaria tree. Chase it with a wild boar burger!

Café de la P
CAFE

(www.cafedelap.com; cnr Lincoyán & Av O'Higgins; coffee CH$1300-2900; ⊘breakfast, lunch & dinner; ⊚) Great coffeehouse.

🛍 Shopping

🎁 Siempreverde
BEAUTY, MARKET

(www.siempreverdepucon.cl; Gerónimo de Alderete 324; ⊘to midnight Jan-Feb, to 7pm Mon-Sat Mar-Dec) One of Chile's first eco-shops, Siempreverde stocks natural/organic cosmetics, feminine hygiene products, artisan chocolate and loads more enviromentally friendly feel-good stuff.

ⓘ Information

Petty theft is on the rise in Pucón, especially in the areas around the beach. Bikes and backpacks are the biggest targets, but you can't leave anything in your vehicle overnight, either. Use prudence.

You can expect a better exchange rate on cash in Temuco. There are several banks with ATMs up and down Av O'Higgins.

Chile Pucón (www.chile-pucon.com) Complete coverage, non-advertising-generated.

Conaf (☑443-781; Lincoyán 336) The best-equipped Conaf in the region.

Hospital San Francisco (www.hospsanfrancisco.cl; Uruguay 325; ⊘24hr)

Oficina de Turismo (☑293-002; cnr Av O'Higgins & Palguín; ⊘8:30am-10pm Dec-Feb, to 7pm Mar-Nov) Has stacks of brochures and usually an English speaker on staff.

Post office (Fresia 183)

Supermercado Eltit (Av O'Higgins 336; ⊘8:30am-10pm) Changes US cash and has an ATM.

ⓘ Getting There & Away

Air

In summer only, both **Lan** (☑600-526-2000; CH$74,900) and **Sky Airlines** (☑600-600-2828; cnr Gerónimo de Alderete & Ansorena) offer flights to and from Pucón – these run twice per week.

Bus

Bus transportation to and from Santiago is best with **Tur-Bus** (☑443-934; Av O'Higgins 910) east of town and **Pullman Bus** (☑443-331; Palguín 555) in the center. **Buses JAC** (☑990-885; cnr Uruguay & Palguín) goes to Puerto Montt. For Temuco, Buses JAC goes every 20 minutes. For Valdivia, JAC has seven daily buses. From the same station, **Minibuses Vipu-Ray** (☑096-835-5798) and **Trans Curarrehue** (☑089-528-4958; Palguín 550) have continuous services to Villarrica and Curarrehue. Buses JAC and **Buses Caburgua** (☑098-038-9047; Palguín 555) have service to Parque Nacional Huerquehue (CH$1000, 45 minutes), Termas Los Pozones and Termas Peumayen. In summer **Buses Línea Azul** (☑443-513; Colo Colo 580) has direct service to Viña del Mar while Valparaíso is serviced by Pullman buses once daily at 7:50pm.

To get to San Martín de los Andes, Argentina, **Buses San Martín** (☑443-595; Av Colo Colo 612) offers departures Tuesday to Sunday at 10:30am stopping in Junín on the way. **Igi Llaima** (☑444-762; cnr Palguín & Uruguay) goes Monday to Saturday at 9:45am and Sunday at 12:15pm.

Some sample travel times and costs are as follows (prices fluctuate with the quality of the bus/classes):

DESTINATION	COST (CH$)	DURATION (HR)
Curarrehue	800	¾
Puerto Montt	9800	5
San Martín de los Andes (Ar)	12,000	5
Santiago	18,000-64,500	9½
Temuco	2700	1
Valdivia	3500	3
Valparaíso	15,000-25,000	12½
Villarrica	800	½
Viña del Mar	28,000	13

ⓘ Getting Around

Pucón itself is very walkable. A number of travel agencies rent cars and prices can be competitive, especially in the low season, though prices tend to climb on weekends. **Pucón Rent a Car** (☑443-052; www.puconrentacar.cl; Av Colo Colo 340; per weekday from CH$25,000) is recommended. If you want to dump the car in Puerto Montt, **Kilometro Libre** (☑099-218-7307; Gerónimo de Alderete 480) is one of the few that will let you – at a hardly-worth-it price of CH$90,000.

SUR CHICO PUCÓN

Around Pucón

Parque Nacional Villarrica

Parque Nacional Villarrica is one of the most popular parks in the country because of its glorious mix of volcanoes and lakes. Its proximity to Pucón, with all of the town's tourism infrastructure, also makes Villarrica an unusually accessible park for everyone from bus-trippers to climbers, skiers and hardcore hikers.

The highlights of the 630-sq-km park are the three volcanoes: 2847m Villarrica, 2360m Quetrupillán and, along the Argentine border, a section of 3747m Lanín. (The rest of Lanín is protected in an equally impressive park in Argentina, from where it may be climbed.)

🏃 Activities

Climbing

The hike up to the smoking, sometimes lava-spitting crater of Volcán Villarrica is a popular full-day excursion (around CH$35,000 to CH$50,000 not including the chairlift fee of CH$6000), leaving Pucón between 4am and 7am depending on the season. You do not need prior mountaineering experience, but it's no Sunday stroll and can challenge even seasoned trekkers. Conditions are most difficult in fall when snow levels are depleted. It is important to use reliable equipment and choose an outfitter whose guides are properly trained (see boxed text, opposite). Note that bad weather may delay organized ascents for days. Climbs are sometimes cancelled altogether or may be required to turn back partway. Check cancellation policies carefully, but know that less reputable operators may take you partway up on days when they know the weather won't hold, just so they don't have to return the money as per your agreement.

Experienced mountaineers may prefer to take a taxi or bus to the ski area and tackle the volcano without a tour. Most folks ride the ski lift to the top of Chair 5 and start from there. Ascents without a tour group are officially discouraged and should only be done by two or more experienced hikers under clear conditions. Solo climbers must have a mountaineering license and obtain permission from Conaf in Pucón before setting out for the park, as well as pay a CH$4000 volcano-ascension fee (already included in group tour prices). Obligatory gear includes crampons, ice pick and helmet and can be rented for around CH$7000 if you don't have your own. It is also possible to ski down from June to December.

Hiking

The most accessible sector of the park, Rucapillán, is directly south of Pucón along a well-maintained road and takes in the most popular hikes up and around Volcán Villarrica.

The trail **Challupen Chinay** (23km, 12 hours) rounds the volcano's southern side, crossing through a variety of scenery to end at the entrance to the Quetrupillán sector. This sector is easily accessed via the road that goes to Termas de Palguín. However, if you plan to continue through to Coñaripe, the road south through the park requires a high-clearance 4WD even in good weather. A 32km combination of hikes, with a couple of camping areas, links to the Puesco sector, near the Argentine border, where there is public transportation back to Curarrehue and Pucón (or you can make connections to carry on to Argentina).

Those traversing the volcano (as opposed to climbing it) will be charged a CH$8000 fee.

Skiing

Ski Pucón
SKIING

(☎441-901; www.skipucon.cl; Pucón office at Enjoy Tour at Gran Hotel Pucón, Clemente Holzapfel 190, Pucón; full-day lift ticket adult/child CH$25,000/19,000; ☺Jul-Sep) Ski Pucón is not on a par with Valle Nevado, Termas de Chillán, Portillo or the other resorts to the north, but it is the most developed ski area in La Araucanía and the Lakes District. Plus, where else do you get to ski on a live, smoking volcano? The views from the mid-mountain lodge almost single-handedly make the lift ticket worth the price. It can get alternately windy or cloudy and shuts down with some frequency.

The ski area is mainly for beginners, with a bit of steeper terrain for intermediates. However, skiing out of bounds just to the left or right of the lifts offers a range of more challenging options for experienced skiers and snowboarders.

The weather at the ski area tends to be different from the town of Pucón. Look at how the smoke from the crater is blowing to gauge how windy it will be. Rentals are available on the mountain, but are less expensive (and often better quality) in town. Almost every agency and a number of hotels send minivans (from CH$7000 to CH$9500) up to the base lodge.

Runs are sometimes open until October, snow conditions permitting.

ℹ Getting There & Away

Taxis to the volcano base (CH$18,000), your own car or a tour are the only ways to get to the park (although fit mountain bikers can make it too).

SAFETY ON VOLCÁN VILLARRICA

Summiting Volcán Villarrica is far and away the number-one excursion in Pucón, and, by all means, do it! But reaching the summit is never a guarantee and if the weather turns, responsible agencies will always turn back, no questions asked. Others press on and the consequences have been fatal. Researching the last edition of the book, we witnessed a tourist tumble 30m down the snow, only to be stopped by rocks; while researching this edition, two tourists were killed and two seriously injured after similar falls. Crampons and ice axes are required on the snow and it can be treacherous and frightening at times. Some 15,000 people per year climb the volcano, which some local experts say is far too many.

Moral of the story: summiting this roaring monster is a truly unforgettable experience, but choosing your agency wisely is key. Fundamentally, you will get what you pay for and it is worth spending CH$5000 to CH$10,000 more for safety, insurance and to not be treated like part of a cattle drive to the top. If you have any doubts about commitment to safety, walk on. And don't hesitate to peruse the tourist complaint book on offer at the Oficina de Turismo (p243) in Pucón.

BEST HOT SPRINGS IN LA ARAUCANÍA & LOS RÍOS

If all that climbing, trekking, paddling and cycling have left your bones rattled and your muscles begging for mercy – you're in luck. Pucón's environs are sitting on one of the world's biggest natural Jacuzzis. Hot springs are as common as adventure outfitters around here, but these three are our favorites.

Termas Geométricas (www.termasgeometricas.cl; adult/child 10am-1pm CH$14,000/7000, 1-11pm CH$16,000/8000; ⏰10am-10pm Jan-Feb, 11am-8pm Mar-Dec) For couples and design aficionados, this Asian-inspired, red-planked maze of 17 beautiful slate hot springs set upon a verdant canyon over a rushing stream is the top choice. It's simply gorgeous. There are two waterfalls and three cold plunge pools to cool off and a cafe heated by *fogón* (outdoor oven) and stocked with natural chicken soup and real coffee. If it weren't for the Spanish, you'd think this was Kyoto. It's located 15km north of Coñaripe. Transport is available from Conaripe and other towns around the lake . Note you will need a 4WD if you are driving yourself – the road can get nasty.

Termas Peumayen (☎045-197-0060; www.termaspeumayen.cl; day use adult/child CH$8000/600; P@🞰) This outstanding newcomer carved from copious amounts of cypress wood is home to some of the nicest *termas* you can sleep at, offering three comfortable lodge rooms (from CH$58,000) and four riverside *cabañas* (CH$104,000). The best springs are two riverside pools in a beautiful outdoor setting on the banks of the Río Liucura. The real coup, however, is the restaurant. Basque country chef Michel Moutrousteguy offers a Mapuche-infused French menu (mains CH$6500 to CH$14,500) that's worth stopping in for even if you don't plan on getting wet. Standouts include a savory lamb shank with sage sauce that's cooked for five hours and served with *quinoa roja* ratatouille from the beautiful organic herb garden, and the Magellanic crab, shrimp and four-herb *chupe* (seafood casserole). Peumayan is reachable by car or from Pucón several times daily with **Buses Caburgua** (☎098-038-9047; Palguín 555, Pucón).

Termas Los Pozones (Km37; day use adult/child CH$4000/2000, night use adult/child CH$5000/3000; ⏰11am-6am) The most popular *termas* (hot springs) to visit from Pucón has six natural stone pools with a variety of temperatures spaced along the rushing Río Liucura. It's open nearly 24 hours but gets crowded so come during nighttime hours (8pm to 6am). It can be a fun spot – people sneak alcohol in the pools even though it's prohibited – so don't count on a place to meditate. Transportation from Pucón (CH$12,000) is included in the admission price, but it's reachable on public transportation as well. Keep an eye on your valuables.

Río Liucura Valley

Heading east out of Pucón, the wishbone road splits into two valleys – 24km to the north you will find Lago Caburgua and its wonderful Playa Blanca, as well as the waterfall-heavy Ojos del Caburgua, as highlights of the Río Caburgua Valley; to the northeast, the Camino Pucón-Huife road leads to myriad hot springs, El Cañi nature sanctuary and views of the silver-ribbon Río Liucura that cuts through this richly verdant valley. Both roads eventually link back up with the road that goes to to Parque Nacional Huerquehue.

The nature sanctuary **El Cañi** (Km21; admission with/without guide CH$10,000/3000) is proof that concerned citizens can make a difference and affect conservation of old-growth forests. When logging interests threatened the area in 1991, Fundación Lahuen, a small cluster of concerned folks with start-up funding from Ancient Forests International, formed to purchase the land and develop a drop-dead-gorgeous park with an emphasis on education and scientific research. This success story is now a reserve that protects some 500 hectares of ancient araucaria forest, all of which has been turned over and now successfully maintained by a local guide association, **Cañe Guides Group** (☎098-373-928; santuariocani@gmail.com).

A **hiking trail** (9km, three hours) ascends the steep terrain (the first 3km very steep) of lenga and araucaria to arrive at Laguna Negra. On clear days the lookout – another 40 minutes – allows for spectacular views of the area's volcanoes. In winter, when the underbrush is covered in snow, the area is particularly gorgeous. All hikers must go with a guide except in summer when the trail is easier to find. An alternative route, which detours around the steepest part, starts along the road to Coilaco; a guide is required. Camping is also now available (CH$3000).

Arrangements to visit El Cañi can be made at iécole! (p240) or Aguaventura (p239) in Pucón or at the entrance to the park. Alternatively, **Buses Caburga** (098-038-9047; Uruguay 540, Pucón) can drop you at the park entrance – it has services several times per day.

Parque Nacional Huerquehue

Startling aquamarine lakes surrounded by verdant old-growth forests ensure wonderful **Parque Nacional Huerquehue** (adult/child CH$4500/2500) is one of the shining stars of the south and a standout in the Chilean chain of national parks. The 125-sq-km preserve, founded in 1912, is awash with rivers and waterfalls, alpine lakes and araucaria forests, and a long list of interesting creatures, including the pudú (the world's smallest deer) and arañas pollitos (tarantula-like spiders that come out in the fall). The trails here are well marked and maintained and warrant multiple days of exploration, but a day trip from Pucón, about 35km to the southwest, is a must for those in a bigger hurry. Stop off at Conaf's **Centro de Informaciones Ambientales** (096-157-4809; 10:30am-2:30pm & 4:30-7:30pm) at the entrance for hiking maps and park info.

The **Los Lagos trail** (round trip four hours, 7km) switchbacks from 700m to 1300m through dense lenga forests with rushing waterfalls, then enters solid stands of araucaria surrounding a cluster of pristine and placid lakes. Most hikers turn back at Lago Verde and Laguna el Toro, the largest of the cluster, but continuing on to the lookout at **Mirador Renahue** will give hikers their just rewards with a spectacular view into their canyon. At Laguna Huerquehue, the trail **Los Huerquenes** (two days) continues north then east to cross the park and access **Termas de San Sebastián** (02-196-8546; www.termassansebastian.cl; Río Blanco; campsites per person CH$5000, cabins

for 2/5 CH$35,000/50,000), just east of the park boundary. You'll need to call ahead all months outside summer so they know to buy food (the phone listed is an on-property satellite phone with a Santiago area code). From there a gravel road connects to the north end of Lago Caburgua and Cunco.

Refugio Tinquilco (09-539-2728; www.tinquilco.cl; campsites CH$12,000, dm with/without bedding CH$12,000/10,000, d with/without bathroom CH$31,900/25,900; closed Jun-Aug;), on private property at the Lago Verde trailhead 2km past the park entrance, is a luxe two-story lodge offering much more than a bed and a meal in a quiet place to get away from it all – it's an experience. After hiking, be sure to submit yourself to the addictive forest sauna/plunge-pool treatment (CH$10,000). Your host, Patricio, turns out hearty home-style Chilean cuisine with welcome touches, such as French-press coffee and an extensive wine list, and is a helluva guy to share a bottle of Carménère with. He also produces an invaluable field guide to the park that is leaps and bounds beyond anything published by Conaf. Designed by an architect, a writer, an engineer and an Emmy-nominated documentary filmmaker, it's the kind of place people lose themselves for a week; and lost souls find their way. Breakfast is included; lunch or dinner is CH$6500.

Camping accommodations are at the Conaf-managed 22-site **Lago Tinquilco** (campsites CH$10,000) and at **Renahue** (campsites CH$10,000) on the Los Huerquenes trail. There are also a few private options in the vicinity of Tinquilco, where you can also park your car for CH$1000.

Buses Caburgua (098-038-9047; Uruguay 540, Pucón) has regular services that run to and from Pucón three times a day (CH$2000, one hour) through the summer, less in winter; purchase tickets in advance. Most agencies and outfitters offer organized excursions.

Currarehue

045 / POP 5615

The Mapuche stronghold of Curarrehue, which is located 40km west of the Argentine border, isn't much to look at, but it has begun a slow rise to fame for its excellent museum and wealth of *etnoturismo* opportunities. The small pueblo counts 80% of the population as Mapuche and is the last town of note before the border with Argentina. There is a small **tourism office** (☑197-1587; ☺9:30am-8:30pm Dec 15-Mar 15) with helpful brochures.

Aldea Intercultural Trawupeyüm (Héroes de la Concepción 21; adult/child CH$1000/500; ☺10am-8pm Dec-Mar, to 6pm Apr-Nov) is a sparse but interesting museum of Mapuche culture housed in a modern interpretation of a mountain *ruka,* a traditional circular Mapuche dwelling oriented to the east.

Curarrehue's real attraction is **Cocina Mapuche Mapu Lyagl** (☑098-788-7188; anita.epulef@gmail.com; Camino al Curarrehue; ☺lunch & dinner;☑), where Mapuche chef Anita Epulef turns seasonal ingredients into adventurous vegetarian Mapuche tasting menus for CH$4800. You can sample such indigenous delicacies as *Mullokiñ* (bean puree rolled in quinoa), sautéed *Piñoñes,* the nut of the araucaria tree (in season only!), and roasted corn bread with an array of salsas – all excellent and unique. For those with extra time, she also offers half-day cooking courses. You'll find her on the right-hand side of the main road just before the town entrance.

Patragon (☑099-441-5769; www.patragon. cl) offers fascinating tours in the area that include Mapuche cooking classes and lunch in a traditional *ruka.*

There's a great new option for overnighting in a massive *ruka.* **Ruka Ngen** (☑099-568-2968; www.turismorukangen.cl; s/d/tr CH$17,000/24,000/33,000; ☑)

Lican Ray

☑045 / POP 2600

Of all the towns in the municipality, Lican Ray (meaning 'flower among the stones' in Mapudungun) is the prettiest for its location on the lovely north shore of island-studded Lago Calafquén. Just 30km south of Villarrica, this bathing resort is home to a long black-sand beach and ash-strewn roads. The town itself is tiny and organized around its only paved street, Av General Urrutia, which has most of the cabins, restaurants, cafes and artisan markets. In the low season Lican Ray all but closes down.

🛏 Sleeping & Eating

Within 5km on either side of Lican Ray are lakeside campgrounds. The more expensive side is the road toward Coñaripe, with sites ranging between CH$8000 and CH$18,000. More modest sites on the road toward Villarrica are between CH$2000 and CH$3500. The camping and a number of the hotels shut down in winter.

Hostal Hofmann   B&B $$
(☑431-109; carmenhofmann@gmail.com; Camino Coñaripe 100; s/d CH$35,000/37,000; ℗☺@) This attractive wooden home offers down comforters, strong hot showers and a filling breakfast, including excellent küchen. Try to get the upstairs room, which has a bigger, wooden-walled bathroom and feels a little more woodsy. English and German are spoken.

Hospedaje Victor's Playa   GUESTHOUSE $
(☑983-467; Puñulef 120; s/d/tr CH$20,000/30,000/40,000; ℗) Right on Playa Grande, this creaky, 100-year-old wooden home is overpriced, but remains the best budget option. There's fat küchen (Swiss ancestry here) and Victor is a real character – who knows, maybe 30 years ago when he started this *hospedaje,* the beach *was* his.

The Ñaños   CHILEAN $
(☑431-026; Av General Urrutia 105; mains CH$3450-6500; ☺lunch & dinner) This is a popular eating spot with a great outdoor patio and deck, serving local staples such as steaming-hot *cazuela* and memorable baked empanadas.

Frutos del Parador   CHILEAN $
(www.frutosdelparador.cl; Av General Urrutia 455-B; ☺9am-11pm Jan-Feb) Great spot for artisanal jams, marmalades, honey and freshly baked whole-wheat bread.

❶ Information

The **Oficina de Turismo** (☑431-516; Calle Esmeralda 426; ☺8am-11pm Jan-Feb, 9am-12:30pm & 2-6pm Mon-Fri Mar-Dec), across from Plaza de Armas, distributes maps and brochures and has a list of accommodations.

❶ Getting There & Away

Buses JAC (☑431-616; Marichanquín 240) travels frequently to Villarrica (CH$700 to CH$900, 30 minutes) and Coñaripe (CH$600, 30 minutes). There is also one bus to Santiago daily year-round, three in summer (CH$24,700 to CH$40,300).

Panguipulli (CH$1000, one hour) is serviced hourly per day by local minibus on the plaza across from JAC.

LOS RÍOS

Valdivia

📞 063 / POP 139,505

Valdivia was crowned the capital of Chile's newest Región XIV (Los Ríos) in 2007 after years of defection talk surrounding its inclusion in the Lakes District despite its geographical, historical and cultural differences. It is the most important university town in southern Chile and, as such, offers a strong emphasis on the arts, student prices at many hostels, restaurants and bars, and a refreshing dose of youthful energy.

With its German effervescence and subtle cafe culture, Valdivia is also one of the more attractive cities in the region due to its scenic location at the confluence of the Calle Calle, Cau Cau and Cruces rivers, but, truth be told, Germanic heritage is way more present in Puerto Varas or Puerto Octay.

◉ Sights & Activities

Av Costanera Arturo Prat (known simply as Prat) is a major focus of activity, but the most important public buildings are on Plaza de la República. To the west, the Puente Pedro de Valdivia crosses the river to Isla Teja, a leafy suburb that is the site of the Universidad Austral.

TOP
CHOICE **Cervecería Kunstmann**   BREWERY
(www.lacerveceria.cl; Ruta T-350 950; pitchers CH$6750-6950, mains CH$4750-7400; ⊙noon-midnight) On Isla Teja at Km5 on the road to Niebla, you'll find the south's best large-scale brewery. Tours leave hourly from 1pm to 8pm (CH$5000) and include a takeaway glass mug and a 300mL sampling of the Torobayo unfiltered, available only here, straight from the tank. Unless you're a beer-history nut, the cost of the tour is better spent on sampling your way through the 10 beers on offer here, chased with hearty German fare that includes lots of pork chops, späetzle, sauerkraut and apple sauce. There isn't a German in sight, and it's nearly overflowing with tourists and tour buses, but you could do worse than drinking away an afternoon here. Bus 20 from Carampague to Isla Teja (CH$625) can drop you off – a good idea even if you have wheels.

Museo Histórico y Antropológico   MUSEUM
(Los Laureles 47; admission CH$1300; ⊙10am-8pm Dec 15-Mar 15, to 6pm Mar 16-Dec 14) Housed in a fine riverfront mansion on Isla Teja, this museum is one of Chile's finest. It features a large, well-labeled collection from pre-Columbian times to the present, with particularly fine displays of Mapuche Indian artifacts and household items from early German settlements. On the same grounds, you'll find the sparse **Museo de Arte Contemporáneo** and, in a neighboring mansion, the science and nature-oriented **RA Philippi Museo de la Exploración**.

Feria Fluvial   MARKET
(Av Costanera Arturo Prat s/n; ⊙7am-3:30pm) The lively riverside market south of the Valdivia bridge, where vendors sell fresh fish, meat and produce. Waterfront sea lions have discovered the Promised Land here – a place where they can float around all day and let tourists and fishmongers throw them scraps from the daily catch. To get closer to the sea lions, walk up the Costanera another 200m.

Parque Saval   PARK
Parque Saval on Isla Teja has a riverside beach and a pleasant trail that follows the shoreline of Laguna de los Lotos, covered with lily pads. It's a good place for birdwatching.

Torreón del Barro   TOWER
(Av Costanera Arturo Prat s/n) A couple of turrets can be seen around town: east of the bus terminal, the Torreón del Barro is from a Spanish fort built in 1774, while the **Torreón de los Canelos** (cnr Yerbas Buenas & General Lagos) dates from the 17th century.

🕝 Tours

Valdivia's main and traditional tourist attraction is the boat cruises (CH$18,000, 6½ hours) that ply the rivers to visit the different forts (see p255). Each tour says it's different, but most take the same route, stopping at Corral and Isla Mancera for 45 minutes to one hour each, and all include lunch and *onces* (afternoon tea). Outfitters include the **Reina Sofia** (📞207-120), which departs from Puerto Fluvial at the base of Calle Arauco once per day at 1:30pm.

⭐ Festivals & Events

Bierfest/Oktoberfest   BEER
Kunstmann-organized suds festival every January; newly inaugurated Oktoberfest in Parque Saval.

Noche de Valdivia   CULTURAL
The largest happening is Noche de Valdivia, on the third Saturday in February, which features decorated riverboats and fireworks.

SUR CHICO VALDIVIA

Valdivia

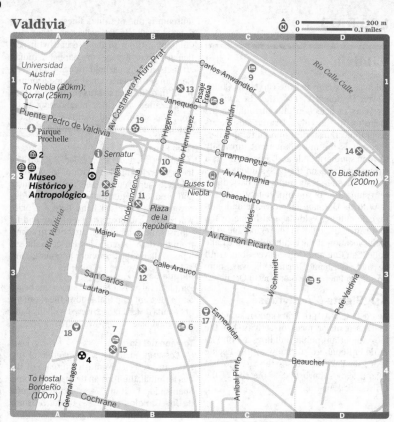

🛏 Sleeping

For most of the year students from the Universidad Austral monopolize the cheapest lodging, but many of these same places vigorously court travelers during summer. There are cheaper, dingier *hospedajes* near the bus terminal along Av Ramón Picarte and Carlos Anwandter.

Airesbuenos Hostel   HOSTEL $
(☎222-202; www.airesbuenos.cl; Garcia Reyes 550; dm CH$9000, s/d CH$18,000/25,000; ☻@🛜) A new American owner has put this long-standing traveler mainstay that's a five-minute walk to the river and bus station through the eco-ringer. Buzzwords now thrown about here include recycling, permaculture and compost. Besides the sustainable makeover, you'll find comfy, colorful dorm rooms and simple, well-done private rooms (though the shower tubs are cramped and can be slippery). But all things considered, this is your requisite nomad home away from home.

Hostel Bosque Nativo   HOSTEL $
(☎433-782; www.hostelnativo.cl; Pasaje Fresia 290; dm CH$8000, s/d CH$18,000/25000, without bathroom CH$16,000/20,000; P☻@🛜) This excellent and cozy hostel, run by a sustainable forestry management NGO, is a wooden den of comfort hidden away down a gravel lane in a residential neighborhood a short walk from the bus station. The lack of English means you forgo the camaraderie of Airesbuenos, but the potential here is palpable.

Hotel Encanto del Río   HOTEL $$
(☎225-740; Av Costanera Arturo Prat; s/d CH$45,000/59,000; P☻@🛜) This midrange hotel is along a quieter and trendier stretch of the river. It's laden with indigenous weavings and Botero reprints on the walls, giving it some extra character, and the feeling

Valdivia

you're sleeping in someone's home with the services of a hotel. River-view rooms have small patios that look straight across the Río Calle Calle...to a factory. Three new floors, some with air-conditioning and Jacuzzi tubs, lead us to wonder if this intimacy will be harder to maintain.

Hostal Torreón   HISTORIC HOTEL **$**
(📞213-069; hostaltorreon@gmail.com; Pérez Rosales 783; s/d CH$20,000/30,000, without bathroom CH$15,000/25,000; 🅿🖥@🛜) This creaky old mansion tucked away off the street prides itself on uneven flooring – it's survived two massive earthquakes! – and is the best non-hostel budget option for the price. The antique-laden common areas are a nod to the house's lengthy past (and a comfy lounge for a bevy of cats) while 2nd-floor rooms offer more light and less dampness than the basement options. No breakfast.

Hostal BordeRío   GUESTHOUSE **$$**
(📞214-069; www.borderiovaldivia.cl; Camilo Henríquez 746; s/d CH$30,000/35,000; 🅿@🛜) Well-equipped with a sunny breakfast nook, large bathrooms, colorful bedspreads and even loveseats in most of the rooms. It has also taken over a historic house at General Lagos 1036, spruced it up and given it the same name.

✕ Eating

Isla Teja across the river from the city is the latest ubertrendy neighborhood for restaurants. Most of the hot spots on Esmeralda also serve good food, so you can settle in for the evening.

TOP CHOICE La Última Frontera   CAFE **$**
(Pérez Rosales 787; sandwiches CH$2600-3900; 🕐lunch & dinner Mon-Sat; 🍴) You'll find one-stop traveler nirvana at this bohemian cafe with a vibe unmatched in Valdivia and likely the whole of Sur Chico. Hidden away in a restored mansion, here you'll find creative sandwiches, fresh juices and a substantial artisanal draft beer list day and night courtesy of the town's hip artistic front. Lose yourself in one of the art-saturated rooms or knock back a cold one on the new patio and deck.

Entrelagos   CAFE **$**
(Pérez Rosales 640; sandwiches CH$2570-5190, cakes CH$1930-2110; 🕐lunch & dinner) This classic *salón de té* (tea house) is where Valdivians talk about you behind your back over delicious *café cortados* (espresso with milk), cakes, sandwiches and crepes. Hearty set menus and toasted sandwiches draw those looking for something more filling (or perhaps just escapists – the Parisian-style seating couldn't be more un-Chilean). The *chocolatería* next door, also a must, stirs Willy Wonka–level frenzy when it opens.

Café Moro   CHILEAN **$**
(Paseo Libertad 174; sandwiches CH$1400-3500; 🕐breakfast, lunch & dinner Mon-Sat; 🛜) What first appears as a likely tourist trap – due to its location off the square on a pedestrianized alley to the water – emerges as an excellent (though smoker-friendly) spot for a supervalue set-menu lunch (CH$2700). It draws an age-defying and eclectic mix of intellectual hipsters and WWF think-tank scientists from SECS, Valdivia's Centro de Estudios Científicos.

SUR CHICO VALDIVIA

THE LAKES OF LOS RÍOS

Chile's Región XIV may be named for its rivers, but it wasn't shortchanged on beautiful lakes, either. While not as heavily visited as those in Los Lagos, there are some gems here as well, and they're a good bet if you'd rather holiday with Chileans than fellow countrymen.

Lago Ranco

When it comes to southern Chilean lakes, Lago Ranco, 124km from Valdivia, is a true sleeper: though not heavily visited or well-known outside Chile, it's a glistening sapphire hideaway bound by lush mountains and peppered with verdant islands. For whatever reason, tourism hasn't dug in its heels here yet, so it's great if you want to escape the crowds and get away with your best friend's spouse or hunker down to finish that screenplay, but bad if you want to eat or sleep well while you're doing it. In one circuit around this cerulean lake you can enjoy majestic views of the Andes, simple working towns, high-end fishing resorts and Mapuche communities. On the north shore of Lago Ranco, 102km from Valdivia via Paillaco, Futrono is a dusty old town with a frontier feel. It is the main service center for the lake and the Mapuche community on Isla Huapi. The **Oficina de Turismo** (☑063-482-636; www.turismofutrono.cl; O'Higgins & Balmaceda; ⊙8am-9pm Dec-Feb, 8:30am-5:20pm Mon-Fri Mar-Nov) in Futrono is at the western approach to town and can help arrange boat passage to Isla Huapi and to hot springs, *agroturismo* (farm stays) and community stays at Lago Maihue, and horse treks, among other excursions. The staff are very eager to help. Same goes for the helpful **tourist office** (☑063-491-348; www.lagoranco.cl; cnr Av Concepción & Linares; ⊙10am-7pm Dec-Feb) in Lago Ranco.

There is regular bus service daily to both Futrono and Lago Ranco from Valdivia (CH$2000 and CH$2500, 2½ hours) and to Lago Ranco from Osorno (CH$2000, two hours), but you could also catch a bus to the town of Río Bueno and transfer there. From Lago Ranco's rural bus station on La Serena, buses go to Llifén (CH$1400) at 11:40am, noon and 9pm, continuing to Futrono. From the Tur-Bus station on Temuco, you can catch buses for Santiago (CH$26,100, 13 hours) once per day at 8:30pm as well as Río Bueno (CH$1400, 45 minutes), Valdivia (CH$3500, 2½ hours) and Temuco (CH$5300, five hours) daily. Only the western edge of the lake is currently not accessible by bus. The crossing at Puerto Lapi is manually operated by a barge run on demand.

Lago Panguipulli

At the northwest end of Lago Panguipulli, the town of **Panguipulli** is a quiet spot with awkward beach access, a lively main street and a totally odd Swiss-style church founded by Capuchin monks. You won't starve here – there are also a surprising number of restaurants. Most travelers come here just to make transportation connections, as the town is severely overpriced due to a combination of high demand and low supply. As a result, it has become a playground for the upwardly mobile – without the quality. The **tourist office** (☑063-310-435; ⊙9am-9pm), across from Plaza Arturo Prat, has lots of listings for the area and helpful staff. The regular assortment of traveler services can be found up and down the main road, Martínez de Rozsa, leading toward the lake.

Little more than two streets at the east end of Lago Panguipulli, the cute hamlet **Choshuenco** has a sweeping beach with views that are a study in serenity, with crystal

La Parrilla de Thor ARGENTINE, STEAKHOUSE **$$**
(Av Costanera Arturo Prat 653; steaks CH$8200-10,200; ⊙lunch & dinner; 🛜) A waft of cedar and *asado* (barbecue) greets diners at this Argentine steakhouse on the Costanera. The *bife de chorizo* here is solid, but the lack of Malbec or housemade *chimichurri* (Argentine steak sauce made with oil, herbs and spices) means it's just that and nothing more.

La Calesa PERUVIAN **$**
(O'Higgins 160; mains CH$6400-7900; ⊙lunch & dinner Tue-Sat, lunch Sun) This restaurant serves Peruvian staples, such as garlic-roasted chicken and *lomo saltado* (stir-fried beef with spices, onions, tomatoes and potatoes). The pisco sours are memorable as is the *suspiro,* a Peruvian dessert made from *manjar* (Chilean milk caramel) and meringue and laced with pisco.

waters and rolling hills of green. It's a relaxing base for hikes, or a good place to rest before or after the Lago Pirihueico crossing between here and Argentina.

Panguipulli's main **Terminal de Buses** (Gabriela Mistral 100), at the corner of Diego Portales, has regular departures from Monday to Saturday to Liquiñe (CH$2500, 2½ hours), Coñaripe (CH$1000, 1¼ hours) and Lican Ray (CH$1000, 45 minutes); to Choshuenco (CH$1500, one hour), Neltume (CH$2000, 1½ hours) and Puerto Fuy (CH$2200, two hours) seven times daily; and to Valdivia (CH$2900, 2½ hours), Temuco (CH$2500, 2½ hours) and Santiago (CH$19,000, 11 hours). Buses from Panguipulli to Puerto Fuy (two hours) pass through Choshuenco and return to Panguipulli early the following morning.

Lago Calafquén

Some 82% of this gorgeous lake sits in Los Ríos and Coñaripe (only the bit around Lican Ray falls in La Araucanía) in the shadow of one of Chile's most active volcanoes (Villarrica), and it's the most popular and liveliest lake town in the region. Its black-sand beaches and easy access to a number of the smaller hot springs – 14 in all – attract the summer crowds and it's a far more pleasant spot to stay than Liquiñe if you're looking to sooth your aching muscles in a little *agua caliente* (warm water). At the east end of Coñaripe, the main drag, Av Guido Beck Ramberga, intersects Ruta 201, the international highway to Junín de los Andes in Argentina; the westbound fork leads to Panguipulli and the southeast to Termas de Coñaripe, Termas Geométricas (see boxed text, p246; the area's finest), Liquiñe and the border crossing at Paso Carirriñe. The road heading north of Coñaripe leads to a number of rustic hot springs and the southern boundary of Parque Nacional Villarrica. A small **tourist kiosk** (☑063-317-378; Plaza de Armas; ☺9:30am-9pm Dec-Mar) is helpful and friendly.

In Coñaripe, the nicest spot to stay is **Hotel Elizabeth** (☑063-317-279; www.hotel elizabeth.cl; Beck de Ramberga 496; s/d CH$28,000/40,000; P ⊖ @ ☎), with well-appointed, colorful rooms (some with narrow showers), but popularity has gotten the best of it: prices have risen disproportionally for the region. It is also the best restaurant, serving beers in iced mugs. Behind the plaza, **Hostal Chumay** (☑099-744-8835; www.lagocalafquen.com; Las Tepas 201; d/tr CH$25,000/30,000, s/d without bathroom CH$15,000/20,000; P ⊖ @ ☎) is another good choice, for simple rooms, central heating, a renovated restaurant and convenience to the in-house adventure outfitter, which organizes glacial trekking, mountain-bike tours, transportation to hot springs and new winter activities (ice climbing, randonee skiing). It also rents mountain bikes. The bottom-end budget choice is **Hospedaje Calafquén** (☑098-128-1731; Beck de Ramberga 761; r per person CH$6000; P); its dead-simple rooms and borderline-scary bathrooms have one saving grace: a cozy, well-lit courtyard in its restaurant that is absolutely crammed with plants, a very inviting spot to hang out and have a beer while you're on the road.

Buses JAC (☑063-317-241; Beck de Ramberga) has several buses daily from Villarrica (CH$1100, one hour) to Coñaripe via Lican Ray (CH$600, 30 minutes; see p237). There is also one bus to Santiago daily (CH$24,000 to CH$40,300, 12 hours). A block away at the main terminal, there are several daily departures to Valdivia (CH$2500, 2½ hours), Liquiñe (CH$1500, 1½ hours) and Panguipulli (CH$1000, one hour).

Gohan Sushi JAPANESE $$
(Saelzar 20; rolls CH$2950-4650; ☺lunch & dinner Mon-Sat; ☎) Valdivia's best sushi anchors the newfound trendiness on Isla Teja.

Café Hausmann DINER $
(☑213-878; O'Higgins 394; mains CH$1850-8000; ☺breakfast, lunch & dinner Mon-Sat) This classic is family owned, serving up the best *cruditos* (carpaccio on toast), strudel and küchen.

For inexpensive seafood visit any of the several restaurants at the Mercado Central. Specialties include *choritos al ajillo* (mussels in garlic and chilies). Try La Estrella (3rd floor).

🍷 Drinking & Entertainment

The main concentration of nightlife is on Esmeralda – take your pick. Portal Valdivia, the city's glitzy new casino complex, is also an option with its glamy discoteque, called the XS Club.

Santo Pecado
BAR

(Yungay 745; 🛜) Funky lounge chairs and banquettes keep this red-hued restaurant-bar ubertrendy. There is good food (such missing-in-action culinary flavors as camembert, leeks and a monster *tortilla española* are found here; mains CH\$4200-6500; open lunch and dinner Monday to Saturday) and, weather-permitting, unstoppable river views from its waterfront back patio.

Clover
BAR

(Esmeralda 691) If serving *one* Irish beer (Guinness by the bottle) an Irish pub makes, we're James Joyce, but this is nevertheless a very popular spot to sample the bevy of Valdivian microbrews on tap (Kunstmann, Cuello, Bunder) and bottled (Duerde, Selva Fria).

ⓘ Information

Downtown ATMs are abundant.

Banco de Chile (Libertad & Henríquez)

Clínica Alemana (www.alemana.cl; Beauchef 765; ⊙24hr) Better, faster and closer than the public hospital; accepts many travel-insurance policies.

Información Turística (📞220-498; ⊙8am-10pm) At the bus terminal.

Police (📞563-085; Beauchef 1025)

Post office (O'Higgins 575)

Sernatur (📞239-060; Costanera Arturo Prat s/n; ⊙9am-9pm Dec-Feb, hours vary Mar-Nov) Located on the riverfront and provides very helpful advice.

ⓘ Getting There & Away

Air

Aeropuerto Pichoy is situated 32km from Valdivia on Ruta 5. **Lan** (📞246-494; www.lan.com; Maipú 271) flies to Santiago twice per day from CH\$104,100. **Sky Airlines** (📞216-280; www.skyairline.cl; Walter Schmidt 303) departs for Santiago (from CH\$151,500) and Concepción (from CH\$29,000) on Sundays throughout January and February only (returning every Thursday).

Bus

Valdivia's centrally located **Terminal de Buses** (Anfión Muñoz 360), along the northeast side of the *costanera* at Anfión Muñoz has frequent buses to destinations on or near the Panamericana between Puerto Montt and Santiago. Companies include **Tur-Bus** (📞212-430), **Tas-Choapa** (📞313-124), **Andesmar** (📞224-665), **Bus Norte**

(📞212-800), **Igi Llaima** (📞213-542), **Pullman** (📞204-669), **Pirihueico** (📞218-609), **San Martín** (📞251-062) and **Cruz del Sur** (📞213-840), which services the island of Chiloé as well as elsewhere.

Regional bus carriers include Pirihueico to Panguipulli; **Bus Futrono** (📞202-225) to Futrono; and **Buses JAC** (📞212-925) to Villarica, Pucón and Temuco. Ruta 5 goes to Lago Ranco. In order to get to Niebla, bus 20 leaves every 10 minutes.

Andesmar goes to Bariloche, Argentina direct daily at 8:45am on Monday, Tuesday, Thursday and Saturday; a few other bus services also leave from Osorno. San Martín buses go to San Martín de los Andes Wednesday, Friday and Sunday at 7:30am. To get to Neuquén, try Andesmar on Monday, Tuesday, Thursday and Saturday at 8:45am.

Some sample travel times and costs are as follows (prices fluctuate with the quality of the bus/classes):

DESTINATION	COST (CH\$)	DURATION (HR)
Bariloche (Ar)	13,000	7
Castro	8500	7
Futrono	5000	2
Lago Ranco	3500	2
Neuquén (Ar)	19,000-26,500	12
Osorno	3200-3600	1¾
Panguipulli	2900	2¼
Pucón	4200	3
Puerto Montt	5000-8400	3½
San Martín de los Andes (Ar)	12,000-13,000	8
Santiago	21,500-58,000	11
Temuco	4300-12,100	2½
Valparaíso	14,000-65,800	12
Villarica	3900	2¼
Viña del Mar	29,200-65,800	12

ⓘ Getting Around

To and from the airport, **Transfer Aeropuerto Valdivia** (📞225-533) provides an on-demand minibus service (CH\$3000). A taxi costs CH\$13,000. For car rental, try **Hertz** (📞218-316; Av Ramón Picarte 640).

From the bus terminal, any bus marked 'Plaza' will take you to Plaza de la República. There are also *colectivos* around town.

HUILO-HUILO RESERVA NATURAL BIOSFERA

The mostly paved road from Lago Pirihueico, 101km east of Valdivia and 80km south of Villarrica, to Puerto Fuy parallels the scenic Río Huilo Huilo, which tumbles and falls through awe-inspiring scenery to the impressive **Huilo-Huilo Reserva Natural Biosfera** (☑02-334-4565; www.huilohuilo.cl; excursions CH$2500-55,000). This conservation project, begun in 2000, encompasses 1000 sq km of private land that has been developed for low-impact ecotourism and falls within a much larger Unesco biosphere reserve. There is a wealth of excursions, a new museum and microbrewery and a bevy of lodging for all budgets, including three spectacularly insane hotels. The beautiful reserve, owned and managed by Fundación Huilo-Huilo, is especially well-known for its endemic species, including the Darwin's frog, pudú, *monito del monte* (little mountain monkey), 111 species of birds, 35 species of ferns (second only to Archipiélago Juan Fernández) and, most importantly, the endangered huemal (South Andean deer), which is being reproduced here by the Fundación with startling success.

The reserve offers numerous outdoor adventures (trekking, climbing, mountain biking, horseback riding, rafting, kayaking and ice trekking) but you need a guide to enter everywhere but the stunning 37m **Salto de Huilo Huilo**. Nonguests can arrange guides at the **Centro de Excursiones** (☺9am-8pm) inside La Montaña Magica. The new stone-domed **Museo de Volcanes** (admission CH$2000; ☺8am-6pm Mon-Fri, 10am-6pm Sat & Sun) is Sur Chico's most impressive archeological museum, covering native Chilean indigenous cultures, including one of the best Mapuche ornament collections in existence as well as an impressive lantern, padlock and iron collection. The top floors of the museum, due for completion within five years, will be dedicated to volcanoes.

La Montaña Mágica (☑063-672-020; s/d CH$119,000/160,000; P☺@☎) is a Frodo-approved spire with a fountain spewing from the top and full of kitschy furniture and supernatural design touches. The less-intimate **Hotel Baobab** (☑063-672-020; s/d CH$122,480/165,000; P☺@) is a Gaudí-inspired inverted cone suspended in the treetops with a restaurant serving international and Chilean cuisine with indigenous touches. The new mushroom-inspired **Fungi Lodge**, which will also connect to Baobab and Montaña Magica, should be open by the time you read this. Prices were undecided at the time of writing. Rates above include breakfast (full meal plan is an additional CH$18,900).

Nearby, the new and exclusive **Nawelpi Lodge** (s/d all-inclusive CH$290,000/580,000; P☺☎) offers 12 expansive cabins with luxurious furnishings, volcanic slate fireplaces and outstanding terraces overlooking the Río Fuy. The private experience here includes a dedicated lodge and rates include all meals, excursions, open bar and transfers to/from Temuco or Valdivia. More down-to-earth accommodations in the park include **Camping Huilo-Huilo** (camping 1-2 tents CH$17,980), with electricity, nice bathrooms with hot water and thermal bathtubs carved from the wooden patio deck (per half hour CH$4000); or the **Canopy Village** (cabañas 2/6 people CH$30,000/60,000) with raised cabins connected by a wooden walkway, a kitchen for guest use and outstanding views of Volcán Mocho.

From Puerto Fuy, the ferry **Hua-Hum** (☑063-197-1585; www.barcazas.cl) carries passengers and vehicles to and from Puerto Pirihueico (1½ hours) year-round once daily in each direction. Automobiles cost CH$12,000 to CH$15,000, pedestrians pay CH$1000 and bicycles CH$2000. The *Hua-Hum* can only fit 24 vehicles, so make reservations.

Around Valdivia

The 81-hectare **Parque Punta Curiñanco**, 35km northwest of Valdivia in Curiñanco, is a unique piece of Valdivian rainforest featuring four types of subforest within its boundaries. It's great for hiking and there are spectacular ocean views and a long, beautiful beach. Keep an eye out for the Darwin's frogs; they look conspicuously like an autumn leaf. To get here from Valdivia, grab a bus marked Curiñanco to the left of the bridge to Isla Teja (on the Valdivia side). The entrance to the park is hidden behind two private properties. The second is a little house where a man will open the gate to the park.

Southwest of Valdivia, where the Río Valdivia and the Río Tornagaleones join the Pacific, lie the 17th-century Spanish fortifications at **Corral**, **Niebla** and **Isla Mancera**. Largest and most intact is the **Castillo de Corral**, consisting of the Castillo San Sebastián de la Cruz (1645), the gun emplacements of the Batería de la Argolla (1764) and the Batería de la Cortina (1767). **Fuerte Castillo de Amargos**, a half-hour walk north of Corral, lurks on a crag above a small fishing village.

Located on the north side of the river, **Fuerte Niebla** (1645) allowed Spanish forces to catch potential invaders in a crossfire. The broken ramparts of **Castillo de la Pura y Limpia Concepción de Monfort de Lemus** (1671) are the oldest remaining ruins. Isla Mancera's **Castillo San Pedro de Alcántara** (1645) guarded the confluence of the Valdivia and the Tornagaleones, and later it became the residence of the military governor.

Niebla itself makes for a fine day trip – the coastal town emits a northern California beach-town vibe and is an easy escape from Valdivia.

The tours that leave from Puerto Fluvial in Valdivia would like you to believe they are the only way to get to the fortifications, but there's a much more economic alternative: *colectivos* (leaving from the corner of Chacabuco and Yungay; CH$700) or microbus (CH$500). From Niebla, ferries go back and forth to Corral every 20 minutes or so from 7am to 1pm (CH$625). Smaller boats ply the waters to Isla Mancera every 20 minutes (CH$800).

THE LAKES DISTRICT

The Lakes District, named for its myriad glacial lakes that dot a countryside otherwise characterized by looming, snow-capped volcanoes, otherworldly national parks and serene lakeside villages, is one of Chile's most picturesque regions. Outdoor adventurers congregate around pretty Puerto Varas, the region's most touristy town and the jumping-off point for most of the area's attractions, be it horseback riding or rock climbing in the Cochamó Valley, lake lingering around Lagos Llanquihue, Puyehue or Todos los Santos, or flashpacking through any number of impressive national parks.

Osorno

📖 064

Osorno (the city, not the volcano) is a bustling place and the commercial engine for the surrounding agricultural zone. Though it's an important transportation hub on the route between Puerto Montt and Santiago and the Hulliche communities of the Osorno coast (see the boxed text, opposite), most visitors spend little time here.

🛏 Sleeping

Hostal Vermont   HOSTEL $
(📞247-030; www.hostalvermont.cl; Toribio Medina 2020; dm CH$8000, s/d without bathroom CH$12,000/22,000; 🅿@🛜) Osorno's first decent hostel, run by a bilingual snowboarder who took *We Bought a Zoo* to heart: two cats (Hazelnut and Lauchín), a dog (Juno), a rabbit (Conejo) and three ducks (Anakin, Luke Skywalker and Leia) call this backpacker crashpad home as well. It's everything you want in a hostel: friendly, clean, well-equipped (and some things you don't: creaky old floors mixed with rowdiness means it gets sleep-depriving loud). From the bus station, walk two blocks south to Juan MacKenna, five blocks east to Buenos Aires and one and a half blocks south to Toribio Medina.

Hotel Villa Eduviges   HOTEL $$
(📞235-023; www.hoteleduviges.cl; Eduviges 856; s/d/tr from CH$20,000/30,000/45,000; 🅿@🛜) Midrange Eduviges is one of the few hotels in Región X that allows singles to sleep in a room with a double bed without paying for a double. The relaxed setting in a residential area south of the bus terminal bodes well, with spacious rooms, private bathrooms, tranquil gardens and kind management.

Hostal Rayenco   GUESTHOUSE $
(📞236-285; www.hostalrayenco.cl; Freire 309; s without bathroom CH$18,000, d CH$30,000; 🅿😊@🛜) For a few extra pesos over the budget options, you'll be extra comfortable at this family-run guesthouse, with a nice living room and breakfast area (remember eggs?) and central heating.

🍴 Eating

You'll find plenty to eat along the main drag, Juan McKenna, in the blocks east and west of Plaza de Armas.

HUILLICHE HOLIDAY

The indigenous Huilliche communities of Osorno's gorgeous coast are sitting on an *etno-turismo* gold mine and have only just started to realize it. Fresh off an idea planted by a decade of sustainable tourism research by the WWF (World Wildlife Fund), these off-the-beaten-path communities are beginning to embrace visitors. You can immerse yourself in their way of life over multiday trips that involve some of Chile's most stunning beaches, Valdivian forest treks, and sleeping in rural homes around San Juan de la Costa and **Territorío Mapa Lahual** (www.mapulahual.cl), an indigenous protected zone that stretches south into Río Negro province as well.

In San Juan de la Costa, a series of five magnificent *caletas* (bays) are accessible by car and could be visited as day trips from around Osorno for those short on time. **Bahía Mansa**, **Pucatrihue**, and **Maicolpué** are villages where dolphins and sea lions practically swim to shore and women scramble about wild and rugged beaches collecting *luga* and *cochayuyo*, two types of seaweed that help fuel the local economy. On either side are the two best *caletas*, **Manzano**, 20km north of Bahía Mansa, and **Tril-Tril**, 7km south of Bahía Mansa.

Going deeper requires more logistics and planning, but the rewards are spectacular. **Caleta Condor**, part of Territorio Mapa Lahual and accessible only by a two-hour boat ride (or two-day trek) from Bahía Mansa or a nine-hour 4WD/trekking/boat combo from Río Negro, is an impossibly gorgeous bay completely out of bounds – communication with the outside world here is via FM radio! If the weather is clear, arriving here is miraculous: as you enter via the scenic and translucent Río Cholcuaco from the Pacific, you are greeted with an idyllic combination of nature (moss-strewn thatches of land that line the river like wild putting greens, flush with horses and seabirds, backed by hillsides peppered with beautiful luma and arrayán trees) and nurture (10 families call this piece of paradise home on a permanent basis, and most have a bed waiting for you). It all culminates at the river's end on a sandbar strip of out-of-place *tropicália* that separates the river beach and the ocean beach.

If you just want to sleep in a breathtaking spot, you can make your own way to Caleta Condor. Boat trips can be arranged in San Juan de la Costa. Try **Paseos Náuticos Lafken Mapu Lahual** (☑097-871-6874; maitecbg@gmail.com; per 8 people CH$170,000). The best homestay option, with an elevated position affording spectacular views, is **Hospedaje Don Florentín** (r with/without breakfast CH$8000/6000, meals CH$3500). But if you want to truly experience all that a visit here has to offer, you'll need to arrange a tour. **Mawidan** (☑099-689-2053; www.mawidan.com) has the best relationships with local communities and the best logistical support, but does not speak English and is new to tourism. **Renacer** (☑098-838-4892; www.renacerexpediciones.com) is more experienced in tourism and has English infra-structure, but doesn't yet have as good a relationship with the local communities.

It is feasible to make your way to the coast and use the excellent Argentine-run **Hostería Miller** (☑064-197-5360; www.hosteriamiller.com; s/d without bathroom CH$20,000/30,000, tr CH$40,000; ℗) in Maicolpué as a base. Here you can sip on Don Rubén's pisco sours while ogling Peale's dolphins right from your window. From Osorno, minibuses depart every 30 minutes (less in winter) to Bahía Mansa, Pucatrihue and Maicolpué (CH$1500, 1½ hours) from the **Feria LibreRáhue** (cnr Chillán & Temuco, Osorno).

❶ Getting There & Away

Air

Aeropuerto Carlos Hott Siebert (Cañal Bajo) is 7km east of downtown, across the Panamericana via Av Buschmann. **Lan** (☑600-526-2000; Eleuterio Ramírez 802) flies twice daily to Santiago (from CH$151,000). An airport taxi is CH$5000.

Bus

Long-distance and Argentine-bound buses use the **main bus terminal** (Errázuriz 1400), near Angulo.

Bus companies include **Pullman Bus** (☑310-529; www.pullman.cl), **Tas-Choapa** (☑233-933; www.taschoapa.cl), **JAC** (☑553-300; www.jac.cl), **Tur-Bus** (☑201-526; www.turbus.cl), **Tal Norte** (☑236-076), **Inter** (☑324-160), **Igi Llaima** (☑234-371; www.igillaima.cl), **Bus Norte** (☑233-933; www.busnortechile.cl), **Queilen Bus** (☑233-633; www.queilenbus.cl), **Turibús** (☑232-777) and **Cruz del Sur** (☑232-777; www.busescruzdelsur.cl).

Most services going north on the Panamericana start in Puerto Montt, departing about every

BEER PARADISE FOUND

If you're within 100km of Osorno and a beer lover, you'll want to readjust your itinerary to visit **Armin Cervecería** (☎064-970-106; Ruta 215, Km12, Osorno; beer CH$1200-2000; ⊙lunch & dinner Mon-Sat), the South's best and most interesting artisanal brewery, located 12km outside of Osorno on Ruta 215 toward Entre Lagos and the border with Argentina. In a clandestine location hidden behind a tall wall of Japanese cedars (said to be coming down when the road is widened), Bavarian transplant Armin Schmid brews stunning Märzen, Bock and Doppelbock in a private home and serves them in a wonderful makeshift frontyard *biergarten*. There is requisite German food *(bratwurst, leberkäse)* and surprisingly good thin-crust pizzas. The trouble is, it's terribly hard to find (we get the feeling that's the idea).

To find it, head out on Ruta 215 from Osorno. Once you pass the small village of Las Lumas, be on the lookout for a sign on the south side of the road that reads, 'Iglesia del Señor Apostolica Las Lumas.' Exactly 350m past this sign on the same side of the road is the small unmarked gravel entrance road. *¡Salud!*

hour, with mainly overnight service to Santiago. Buses to destinations in Argentina and Chilean Patagonia, such as Coyhaique, Punta Arenas and Puerto Natales, go via Ruta 215 and Paso Cardenal Antonio Samoré.

Try Quellen Bus for Coyhaique, and Pullman or Cruz del Sur for Punta Arenas. Igi Llaima goes to Zapala and Neuquén on weekdays via Temuco, while Cruz del Sur, Tas-Choapa and **Via Bariloche** (☎253-633; www.viabariloche.com.ar) have daily service to Bariloche. **Ruta 5** (☎317-040) goes to Lago Ranco (CH$2000). Many but not all of these services also originate in Puerto Montt; for more details, see p280.

Sample travel times and fares follow (prices fluctuate with the quality of the bus/classes):

DESTINATION	COST (CH$)	DURATION (HR)
Ancud	5500	4½
Bariloche (Ar)	14,000-17,000	5
Concepción	15,000	8
Coyhaique	25,000	17
Pucón	8000	4
Puerto Montt	2000	1½
Punta Arenas	40,000-45,000	28
Santiago	24,100-43,000	12
Temuco	5200	3-5
Valdivia	3300	2
Valparaíso/Viña del Mar	30,500-45,000	16
Zapala-Neuquén (Ar)	14,000-18,000	17

Also from the main bus terminal is a service to Río Bueno, with connections to Lago Ranco and to Panguipulli (via Valdivia), and many trips daily to places around Lago Llanquihue at the foot of Volcán Osorno. Other local and regional destinations leave from the **Terminal Mercado Municipal** (cnr Errázuriz & Arturo Prat) behind the Mercado Municipal. **Buses Barria** (☎201-306; www.busesbarria.cl) goes to Entre Lagos (CH$1400, 45 minutes) from behind the northwest corner of the market, while **Expreso Lago Puyehue** (☎243-919) goes to Termas Puyehue/Aguas Calientes (CH$2200, 1½ hours) and Anticura (CH$6000, 1½ hours) from behind the northeast corner.

To get to the Huilliche communities of San Juan de la Costa (CH$1500, 1½ hours) – Bahía Mansa, Pucatrihue and Maicolpué – minibuses depart every 30 minutes (less in winter) from the **Feria Libre Ráhue** (cnr Chillán & Temuco). Catch *colectivo* 101 heading east on Los Carrera (CH$400) or take a taxi (CH$2000).

Entre Lagos

☎064 / POP 3,358

Entre Lagos is a slow-paced lakeside town 50km east of Osorno on Ruta 215, on the southwest shore of Lago Puyehue. It's a tranquil alternative to Osorno, especially if you're on your way to Parque Nacional Puyehue embarking on the Puyehue traverse from El Caulle. It's also the first town of significance after crossing the border on the road from Bariloche. The town is split into two; the western entrance is more commercial (with the post office, ATM and gas station), and the eastern entrance leads to lodging choices and the beach.

If you opt to hang around here, get in touch with new upstart agency **Always Green Tour** (📞371-452; www.agtour.cl; cnr Ruta 215 & Lord Cochrane), which does kayaking on Lago Puyehue and Lago Rupanco (from CH$15,000), fly-fishing in kayaks and catarafts on the Río Ráhue (CH$175,000; with a riverside barbecue), horseback riding to Termas de Rupanco and a new excursion to see the effects of recent eruptions that takes in several locations, including the Atacama-like Cerro Mirador (CH$25,000). The agency is a partnership between a few good options in the area, including French-run El Taique Lodge in Alto Puyehue and the Chilean-Spanish owner's own Hostal Los Juntas on Lago Puyehue.

You will feel like a thief in the new rooms at longtime favorite **Hospedaje Panorama** (📞371-398; General Lagos 687; r per person CH$10,000; 🅿🛜), an absolute steal at these prices. Things aren't so cozy when the owner is away in Argentina, but the pillow-top beds are snug and there is an excellent breakfast on offer. the first person to get up must seek out staff for hot water.

Camping No Me Olvides (📞371-633; www.nomeolvides.cl; campsite per person CH$5000, cabins 2/6 people CH$30,000/40,000), located 6km east of town on Ruta 215, is a top-notch camping ground which has large garden sites that are divided by pruned hedges underneath plum and apple trees. It offers abundant firewood, excellent showers and a restaurant.

In summer several restaurant stalls set up shop along O'Higgins, serving snacks and heftier meals.

Buses between Osorno and Aguas Calientes (CH$2200) stop in town in a parking lot on O'Higgins between Ramirez and Rodríguez every half-hour. There is also continuous service to and from Osorno (CH$1400).

Parque Nacional Puyehue

Volcán Puyehue, 2240m tall, blew its top the day after the earthquake in 1960, turning a large chunk of dense, humid evergreen forest into a stark landscape of sand dunes and lava rivers. **Parque Nacional Puyehue** (www.parquepuyehue.cl) protects 1070 sq km of this contrasting environment, and it is one of the more 'developed' of the country's national parks, with a ski resort and several hot-spring resorts within its boundaries.

There are also several hikes that explore more pristine areas of the national park. Aguas Calientes is the main sector of the park, with the hot-springs resort and Conaf's **Centro de Información Ambiental** (Aguas Calientes; 🕘9am-1pm & 2:30-7pm), which houses an informative display on Puyehue's natural history and geomorphology.

The park's western border is about 75km east of Osorno via the paved Ruta 215, which continues through the park, following the course of the Río Golgol to the Argentine border.

Buses and *colectivos* from Osorno's Mercado Municipal go to Termas de Puyehue, Aguas Calientes, Anticura and Chilean customs and immigration at Pajaritos. Any bus heading to Anticura can drop off trekkers at El Caulle. In winter there may be a shuttle to the ski lodge at Antillanca; contact the Club Andino Osorno. Otherwise, you'll need to arrange your own transportation.

AGUAS CALIENTES

An unassuming **hot-springs resort** (day use CH$3600-9600), Aguas Calientes is overrun with Chilean families and gets crowded in the summer months. On offer are typical spa services, individual tubs, a very hot indoor pool and a large shallow cement pool by the side of the river. However, you can access the free **Pocitos Termas** 80m across the Colgante bridge from the Conaf parking lot. Another way to get your heart rate up is to hike the enjoyable **Sendero El Pionero**, a steep 1800m nature trail that ends with splendid views of Lago Puyehue, the valley of the Río Golgol and Volcán Puyehue.

Cabañas Aguas Calientes (📞064-236-988; www.termasaguascalientes.cl; Ruta 215, Km4 Camino Antillanca; 4-/10-person cabins

SUR CHICO PARQUE NACIONAL PUYEHUE

COUGHING UP CORDÓN CAULLE

In 2011 the Puyehue-Cordón Caulle volcanic complex further altered the landscape, with the Cordón Caulle fissure erupting and forcing the evacuation of 600 people in the surrounding areas. The ash cloud severely disrupted tourism in nearby Bariloche and forced the closure at one time or another of the airport there as well as those in Buenos Aires, Mendoza and Montevideo. At the time of writing, the volcano was still erupting.

Parque Nacional Puyehue

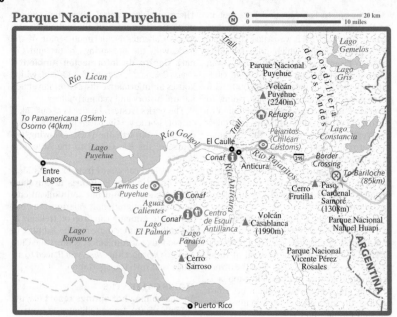

CH$115,000/222,000; P@🛜🏊) is the only lodging option. Its A-frame cabins are stacked up along the hillside like a miniature well-planned village, and they are remarkably comfortable, with plush beds, full kitchens, hot showers and wood stoves. Rates include spa facilities and a filling breakfast.

ANTILLANCA

On the southwest slope of Volcán Casablanca (1990m), **Centro de Esquí Antillanca** (✆064-612-070; www.skiantillanca.cl; office at O'Higgins 1073, Osorno) is a popular beginner/ intermediate ski resort, just 18km from Aguas Calientes. It has a friendly, small-resort ambience, but is not challenging for the more advanced skier. The road up to the resort twists and turns through scenic areas and past glassy lakes. During the no-snow months, Antillanca is rather soulless, and the resort's appeal rests with its trails, especially the walk or drive (per vehicle CH$4000) to the crater lookout, where you can drink in a spectacular view of the surrounding mountain range. The ski season runs from early June to late October; full-day lift tickets cost CH$20,500 and rentals CH$24,000. The ski area has five surface lifts and 460m of vertical drop. For details on ski packages contact

the **Club Andino Osorno** (✆064-242-010; O'Higgins 1073, Osorno).

Hotel Antillanca (✆064-612-070; s/d in refugio CH$35,280/50,400, in hotel CH$78,750/ 110,250; P@🛜🏊) is outrageously overpriced, but its typical ski-resort trimmings (gym, sauna, disco, boutique and shops) are the only option unless you're going to ski down to Aguas Calientes. The cheaper *refugio* rooms, though older and smaller, offer the same quality as the hotel. Rates include breakfast and prices level off in summer.

ANTICURA

Anticura, on Ruta 215, 17km northwest of the Aguas Calientes turnoff, is the best base for exploring the more remote sectors of the park. **Patagonia Expeditions** (✆099-104-8061; www.anticurachile.cl), co-run by a young, enthusiastic climber from Osorno, now has the concession on Centro Turístico Anticura, which has reopened after a three-year hiatus. Short hikes from the visitors center include **Salto de Princesa**, **Salto del Indio** – where, according to legend, a lone Mapuche hid to escape *encomienda* (colonial labor system) service in a nearby Spanish gold mine) – and **Repucura**, which ends back up on Ruta 215 (buses come careening down the highway; walk on the opposite side). There's also a 4km steep hike up to a lookout point. Excursions from here include climbing Volcán Casablanca (1990m; CH$35,000) and Volcán Puyehue (2240m; CH$50,000) and there's now a restaurant serving three meals a day (meals CH$3500). Conaf is planning a Cordón Caulle eruption exhibition here (see boxed text, p259).

Patagonia Expeditions has touched-up **Camping Catrué** (camping CH$3500, dm CH$9000, cabañas for 2/4/6 people CH$40,000/ 45,000/48,000), which now offers 15 woodsy sites with tree-trunk picnic tables, electricity and bathrooms with hot water. Cabins have been refurnished and are fully equipped, two of which have been converted into dorms.

EL CAULLE

Two kilometers west of Anticura, the privately owned **El Caulle** (☑099-920-3180; www.elcaulle.com; 1-time fee CH$10,000) is the southern entrance for the trek across the magnificently desolate plateau at the western base of Volcán Puyehue. While officially within park boundaries, the access land is privately owned. The admission fee is steep, but funds are used to maintain the *refugio* and the trails, to put up signs and to provide emergency assistance. Trekkers can stash any extra gear at the entrance. The **Puyehue Traverse** (three to four days) and the **Ruta de los Americanos** (six to eight days) are the most popular routes. El Caulle is signed on Ruta 215 as a restaurant.

Puerto Octay

☑064 / POP 11,540

Cute and quaint, Puerto Octay (ock-tie) isn't heavily visited, but is actually one of the more charming towns on Lago Llanquihue and a good escape from more touristy towns to the south. The tranquil streets, perched on a hillside above the lake, yield interesting 1800s German settler architectural treasures around every turn, making for a nice tour of historic homes and buildings and giving the town a supremely sedate and picturesque colonial air. It is the oldest town on the lake settled by Germans.

⊙ Sights

Historical Homes   ARCHITECTURE

A visit to Puerto Octay is really about appreciating the beautiful historic German architecture around town. Some of our favorite buildings include Casa Wulf No 2 (1926), Ho-

tel Haase (1894) and Casa Werner (1910). A map is available from the tourist office.

Museo de Puerto Octay   MUSEUM

(www.museopuertoctay.cl; Independencia 591, 2nd fl; ⊙10am-1pm & 3-7pm) A small but well-done museum inside the historic 1920 Casa Niklitschek telling the story of Puerto Octay via antiques.

🛏 Sleeping & Eating

TOP CHOICE **Zapato Amarillo**   GUESTHOUSE $

(☑210-787; www.zapatoamarillo.cl; dm CH$10,000, s/d CH$25,000/36,000, without bathroom CH$15,000/30,000; P❄@☞) Nestled on a small farm, approximately 2km north of town toward Osorno, you'll find an octagonal dorm house with two impeccably clean bathrooms as well as three separate buildings housing farmhand-chic rooms. Slow Food dinners are CH$7000, and the kitchen results are miraculous, including breakfast – you won't eat better than this for the price (highlights include smoked pork *cazuela,* fresh salmon, cheese fondue). The hospitable Chilean-Swiss owners help insure this spot as a traveler favorite for all ages. A new scooter for rent means you can hop between lake towns for the day (CH$25,000).

Hotel Centinela   GUESTHOUSE $$$

(☑391-326; www.hotelcentinela.cl; Península de Centinela; r with lake/forest view CH$95,000/ 82,000, cabins 2/6 people CH$80,000/110,000; P@☞☒) There is a bit of a *Shining* element to this isolated and restored 1913 German

> **WORTH A TRIP**
>
> ## PUERTO FONCK
>
> If Chile was tropical and the black beach at **Puerto Fonck** was white, these would be sought-after sands indeed. Instead, this hidden beach, tucked away down a long gravel road 22km east of Puerto Octay on the road from Puerto Varas, only caters to a few Chileans in the know. On a clear summer day, the dramatic volcano views over a tranquil bay make it a splendid beach to kill a day around the lake.
>
> Access is by 4WD or foot only. Any Puerto Varas/Puerto Octay-bound bus can drop you off at the turnoff. From there, you'll have to leg it the last 2.5km to the beach.

SUR CHICO PUERTO OCTAY

chalet, situated at the end of a quiet and secluded peninsula. The disappointing and sparse rooms aren't as inviting as the handsome dark alerce (Patagonian cypress) wood structure itself, but the plush beds insure getting up to explore this romantic option won't be easy. It's walking distance from a popular beach.

Hotel Haase HISTORIC GUESTHOUSE $
(☑391-302; www.hotelhaase.cl; Pedro Montt 344; d CH$25,000, without bathroom CH$12,000; P@⛱🐾⛵) Get good value for history in this 1894 home, where simple but clean rooms surround a large, creaky wooden-floored living room. The popular restaurant is a good bet in town (mains CH$2800 to CH$5000).

TOP⟩
CHOICE **Rancho**
Espantapájaros CHILEAN, BUFFET $$$
(buffet CH$13,000; ☉lunch & dinner Nov-Feb, lunch Sun-Thu, dinner Fri & Sat Mar-Oct) The most famous restaurant on the lake is 7km outside Puerto Octay on the road to Frutillar, and packs in the crowds for the main attraction, succulent *jabalí* (wild boar, fatty but fantastic) cooked on 3.5m spits across a giant *fogón* behind the buffet. It's all-you-can-eat, includes a juice, wine or beer, and everything is excellent.

❶ Information

Puerto Octay's **tourist office** (cnr Balmaceda & Pedro Montt; ☉8:30am-2pm) isn't very helpful. A better bet is the information **kiosk** (cnr San Agustín & German Wulf) in front of the church, run by a town native just for the love, but he told us he is closing indefinitely. Worth a shot.

❶ Getting There & Away

Puerto Octay's **bus terminal** (cnr Balmaceda & Esperanza) has regular service to Osorno (CH$1300), Frutillar (CH$900), Puerto Varas (CH$1400) and Puerto Montt (CH$1600).

Frutillar

☑065 / POP 14,551
Frutillar is an enchanting lakeside retreat right up the coastline of Lago Llanquihue from Puerto Varas. There is an attractive pier, a long, drawn-out lakeside beach and, above all, quaint German architecture and küchen aplenty. Though the Germanness of this town can sometimes feel forced and too touristy compared to Puerto Octay, it remains a serene spot that makes for a pleas-

ant alternative to staying in more chaotic Puerto Varas.

Sights

Museo Histórico Alemán MUSEUM
(www.museosaustral.cl; cnr Pérez Rosales & Prat; adult/child CH$2000/500; ☉9am-7:30pm Jan-Feb, to 6pm Mar-Dec) The Museo Histórico Colonial Alemán was built with assistance from Germany and is managed by the Universidad Austral. It features nearly perfect reconstructions of a water-powered mill, a blacksmith's house, a farmhouse and belfry set among manicured gardens. It is considered the best museum on German colonialism in the region.

Teatro del LagoSur ARTS CENTER
(www.teatrodellago.cl; Av Philippi 1000) This amazing 12-years-in-the-making, US$25-million world-class performing arts center opened in 2010, and has single-handedly put Frutillar on the global cultural map. The striking copper-roofed structure is a thing of beauty itself, flanked against the lake with postcard views of four volcanoes. Inside, it houses a state-of-the-art 1178-seat concert hall – acoustically insured by beautiful beechwood walls – and a second 278-seat amphitheater as well as a restaurant and lakeside cafe (sandwiches CH$2500 to CH$3500). It currently hosts a wealth of cultural events, including the music festival, and attracts internationally known orchestras and artists in all genres. Check the website for what's on during your visit.

🎭 Festivals & Events

Semana Musical de Frutillar MUSIC
(www.semanasmusicales.cl) For 10 days from late January to early February (usually January 27 through February 4) the Semana Musical de Frutillar showcases a variety of musical styles, from chamber music to jazz, with informal daytime shows and more formal evening performances from 8pm to 10pm.

🛏 Sleeping & Eating

Budget options are scarce in Frutillar, which caters more to mature travelers.

Hotel Ayacara BOUTIQUE HOTEL $$$
(☑421-550; www.hotelayacara.cl; Av Philippi 1215; s/d CH$75,000/94,000; P⊛@⛱) Streams of light flow through the inviting living areas, and upstairs front-facing rooms get a spec-

tacular volcano view in this remodeled 1910 house turned eight-room boutique hotel.

Hotel Kaffee Bauerhaus HISTORIC HOTEL **$$**
(☑420-003; Av Philippi 663; r from CH$55,000; P☺@☎) This restored 1918 colonial home is a classic choice with its tearoom decor and historic feel, right on the water.

TOP CHOICE **Se Cocina** CHILEAN **$$$**
(☑08-972-8195; www.secocina.cl; Km2 a Quebrada Honda; ☺dinner Tue-Thu, lunch & dinner Sat, lunch Sun) Se Cocina is hit or miss, but even when it misses, this beautiful 1850s farmstead 2km from Frutillar remains the lake's only surefire foodie destination and one of Sur Chico's most interesting restaurants. The daily changing menu marries *Nueva Chilena* cuisine with a modern atmosphere housed inside a historically protected farm. Each day, there are a few choices of appetizer, main and dessert, all priced separately (three courses are CH$21,500) and it wouldn't be outrageous to see sous-chefs run from the open kitchen to the organic garden and grab some greens during service. The housemade artisanal beer justifies the trip alone. Reservations essential – hours have been historically erratic.

Lavanda Casa de Té TEAHOUSE **$$**
(☑09-269-1684; www.lavandacasadete.cl; Km1.5 a Quebrada Honda; menu CH$10,500; ☺lunch) On a lavender farm just outside town, this is a lakeside favorite for tea, gourmet lavender products and farm-fresh lunches. Make a reservation and ignore the decor.

❶ Information

The town's **tourist information** (☑421-261, ext 154; cnr O'Higgins & Av Philippi; ☺9am-1pm & 2-5:30pm) is near the town pier.

❶ Getting There & Around

Minibuses to Puerto Varas (CH$900) and Puerto Montt (CH$1300) leave from a small parking lot on Pedro Montt near Av Philippi. Everything else leaves from Frutillar Alto. **Cruz del Sur** (☑451-552; Alessandri 52) has the most frequent services to Osorno (CH$1200), Valdivia (CH$3500), Temuco (CH$3500) and Santiago (CH$23,000 to CH$35,000) plus four daily departures to Chiloé (CH$5000 to CH$6300) and one daily departure for Bariloche (CH$14,000, two on Thursday and Sunday). **Tur-Bus** (☑421-810; Christiana y Misonera) goes to many of the same cities. At the Alessandri terminal, Thaebus goes to Puerto Octay, Puerto Varas and Puerto Montt.

Puerto Varas
☑065 / POP 32,216

Two menacing, snowcapped volcanoes, Osorno and Calbuco, stand sentinel over picturesque Puerto Varas and its scenic Lago Llanquihue like soldiers of adventure, allowing only those on a high-octane quest to pass. Just 23km from Puerto Montt but worlds apart in charm, scenery and options for the traveler, Puerto Varas has been touted in the past as the 'next Pucón,' but unlike its kindred spirit to the north, Puerto Varas has been able to better manage its rise as a go-to destination for outdoor adventure sports, and, as a result, avoids some of the tourist-package onslaught that besieges Pucón.

There is great access to water sports here – kayaking and canyoning in particular – as well as climbing, fishing, hiking and even skiing. While Puerto Varas gets packed in the summer, it receives many more independent travelers than Pucón. It basically shuts down in the winter except for a few hearty skiers and mountaineers.

With all of the conveniences of Puerto Montt just a short trip away, Puerto Varas is a top choice for an extended stay and also makes a good base for exploring the region. Some find it too touristy, but its juxtaposition of German heritage and contemporary Chilean adrenaline is both beautiful and addictive.

☉ Sights

Puerto Varas' well-maintained German colonial architecture gives the town a distinctive middle-European ambience.

Iglesia del Sagrado Corazón CHURCH
(cnr San Francisco & Verbo Divino) The imposing and colorful 1915 Iglesia del Sagrado Corazón, overlooking downtown from a promontory, is based on the Marienkirche of the Black Forest, Germany.

Paseo Patrimonial ARCHITECTURE
Other notable constructions are private houses from the early 20th century. Grab a city map at the tourist information office, which highlights the Paseo Patrimonial, a suggested walking tour of 10 different houses classified as Monumentos Nacionales. Several of these houses serve as *hospedajes,* including the 1941–42 **Casa Schwerter** (Del Carmen 873), the 1930 **Casa Hitschfeld** (Arturo Prat 107) and the 1930 **Casa Wetzel** (O'Higgins 608).

Puerto Varas

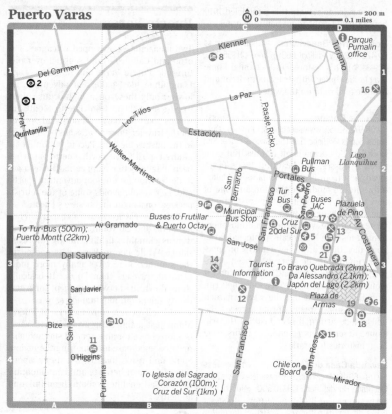

🏃 Activities

Nearby lakes, mountains, rivers and fjords provide a variety of activities. For information on climbing and skiing on Volcán Osorno, see p270. Plans are also in place to expand the *ciclovia* (bike lane) on Lago Llanquihue. It currently goes from Puerto Varas to Km12 (ruta a Ensenada) and, by 2013, a path to Ensenada should be completed.

Rafting, Canyoning & Kayaking

Opportunities abound for rafting and kayaking. Río Petrohué's blue waters churn up Class III and IV rapids. Half-day rafting trips run around CH$25,000 (5½ hours total, two hours river time). All-day kayaking on Lago Todos Los Santos is about CH$55,000.

Pachamagua   RAFTING, CANYONING
(☏542-080; www.pachamagua.com; Del Rosario 1111) Pachamagua is the canyoning specialist, highly professional and truly pioneering the sport in the area. Its half-day trip on the

Río Blanco is the area's don't-miss if you are fit and unafraid – it ends spectacularly with a rappel down the 34m Río Blanco waterfall followed by a final jump through the falls.

Ko'Kayak   RAFTING, CANYONING
(☏233-004; www.kokayak.cl; San Pedro 210) A long-standing favorite for rafting, offering half-day rafting trips go for CH$30,000 with two departures daily, full-day/two-day sea kayaking for CH$65,000/150,000 and half-day canyoning (CH$35,000).

Al Sur   RAFTING, KAYAKING
(☏232-300; www.alsurexpeditions.com; cnr Aconcagua & Imperial) Al Sur specializes in rafting and also does high-end, multiday kayaking trips within the fjords of Parque Pumalín.

Fly-Fishing

There are loads of places to cast a line, but knowing just where the best spots are will require some local knowledge.

Puerto Varas

Gray Fly Fishing   FISHING
(☎310-734; www.grayfly.com; San José 192; ⊙closed Sun) Gray Fly Fishing, the local Orvis rep, runs half-day trips on the Río Maullin for around CH$60,000 per person (not including equipment) and can set you up at more remote, high-end fishing lodges as well.

Tres Ríos Lodge   FISHING
(☎715-710; www.tresrioslodge.com) For custom programs to all fly-fishing destinations in the Lakes District as far as La Junta, full-day float trips and road trips into remote Patagonia, call John Joy at Tres Ríos Lodge, who also runs the Tradicion Austral B+B in town.

Horse Trekking
The best spot for a horse trek is the Río Cochamó Valley.

⊘ Campo Aventura   HORSEBACK RIDING
(☎099-289-4318; www.campoaventura.cl) Campo Aventura offers single-day to multiday treks,

often in conjunction with some hiking, rafting or kayaking. The most popular is a three-day jaunt that traverses the valley from its riverside lodge to its mountain lodge in the Río Cochamó Valley with as much emphasis on a cultural experience as the nature. All its guides, including three gaucho (cowboy) horse guides and a full-time trekking guide from the USA, are trained in Wilderness First Responder (WFR). English and German are spoken.

☞ Tours
Easy day tours include Puerto Montt/Puerto Varas (CH$13,000), Frutillar/Llanquihue (CH$13,000), Puello/Saltos de Petrohué (CH$30,000), Volcán Osorno (CH$16,000) and around the lake. Day tours to Chiloé are also offered, but most of your tour is spent in transportation and you do not get a quality experience of the island.

⊘ Secret Patagonia   ECOTOUR, OUTDOORS
(☎232-921; www.secretpatagonia.travel; San Pedro 311) This eco-sensitive collective marries three smaller outfitters, La Comarca, Miralejos and OpenTravel, which specialize in dramatic and custom-tailored adventure trips to less explored areas of the Río Puelo Valley, Cochamó Valley and beyond, along with Mitico Puelo Lodge on Lago Tagua-Tagua and the new Parque Tagua-Tagua nearby. Highlights include hiking in Cochamó Valley, extensive mountain-bike trips, remote French retreats on Isla Las Bandurrias in Lago Las Rocas and multiday horseback-riding/cultural farmstay trips between Argentina and Chile. Groups are never more than 12 strong and everyone here is dedicated to giving travelers a unique off-the-beaten-path experience while keeping their carbon footprint at bay.

TurisTour   OUTDOORS, GUIDED TOUR
(☎228-440; www.turistour.cl; Del Salvador 72) This agency runs the Cruce Andino crossing to/from Argentina (see boxed text, p269) as well as excursions through the region.

☆☆ Festivals & Events
The city celebrates its 1854 founding in the last week of January and the first week of February.

🛏 Sleeping
Puerto Varas is well equipped with beds for all budgets, and many places can also book

all the adventures in the area. *Hospedajes* fill up fast in January and February, so make sure you make a reservation.

For camping or calmer accommodations, head around the lake or to Ensenada.

Casa Azul
HOSTEL $

[TOP CHOICE] (☎232-904; www.casaazul.net; Manzanal 66; dm CH$9000, d CH$27,000, s/d without bathroom CH$15,000/20,000; ☜@?) It's hard to find fault with this impeccably kept German-Chilean operation in a quieter residential neighborhood just off downtown: the superbly tranquil garden and koi pond – with bonsai trees – immediately calm your nerves, anyway. Rooms are spacious, in excellent condition and there's an expansive guest kitchen and common area with cool furniture fashioned from tree branches and artisan central heating throughout. Some say there are too many rules (men should pee sitting down?), but it's all for maintaining staunch German efficiency and cleanliness – hard to complain about that. Breakfast is an extra CH$3000.

The Guest House
GUESTHOUSE $$$

(☎231-521; www.vicki-johnson.com/guesthouse; O'Higgins 608; s/d CH$40,000/45,000; P☜@?) In the historic Casa Wetzel, this art nouveau–era home caters to baby boomers with backpacks: it's simply but tastefully decorated with antiques, snug beds and beautifully restored alerce doors. Breakfast here is legendary (rightfully so, the owner is the town's gourmand) and there's a lush garden and patio area to enjoy a glass of wine and light meals in the evening.

Margouya 2 Patagonia
HOSTEL $

(☎237-695; www.margouya2.com; Purisima 681; dm CH$8000, d CH$25,000 , s/d without bathroom CH$14,000/19,000; ☜@?) This spacious and historic 1932 home on the town's list of Patrimonial Heritage sites is the nicest hostel in town, offering quieter and much larger rooms and bathrooms for the same price as the more central Casa Margouya. It also has its own in-house Spanish school and tour agency for activities in the area and bikes for rent at half the price of town. Only three dorms beds are available, but if you arrive first, you can snag the double. No breakfast.

Hostel Melmac Patagonia
HOSTEL $

(☎230-863; www.melmacpatagonia.com; Walker Martínez 561; dm CH$8000-9000, s/d CH$25,000/ 29,000, without bathroom CH$15,000/20,000;

P☜@?) Though the kitschy website sells it as intergalactic silliness, this good hostel is quite down to earth once inside. Alfonso, the friendly Argentine-Colombian owner, can pull you a draft homebrew from his beer fridge, which goes down nicely in the back garden. It's also the only hostel we have ever stumbled across that will prep a relaxing bath (with salts!) for you after a day of hiking; and one of the few that charges solo travelers a single price for a private room. There's also a 50% off breakfast deal with Caffé El Barrista.

Casa Kalfu
B&B $$

(☎751-261; www.casakalfu.cl; Tronador 1134; s/d CH$50,000/55,000; P☜@?) Since the name Casa Azul was already taken, the Chilean-Argentine couple that runs this excellent midrange choice opted for Kalfu, the Mapudungun word for blue, instead. And what a big, bright, beautiful blue it is. The home is a renovated '40s chalet that now holds 14 rooms, simply and minimally decorated with large *oveja* (natural wool) wall hangings by renowned local artist Kika Xicota. The owners are very hands-on, giving it a more personal feel than many others in town, and the house is perched just high enough for lake views from its pleasant terrace.

Compass del Sur
B&B $

(☎232-044; www.compassdelsur.cl; Klenner 467; camping CH$8000, dm/s/d CH$10,000/24,000/ 28,000; P☜@?) This charming colonial house with Scandinavian touches sits above the main area of town near the park and is accessed by a staired walking street. It has comfortable beds and extrastrength showers that please the flashpacker crowd that dominate the scene here. Basic breakfast is included but travelers can spring for muesli with yogurt or eggs for CH$600 to CH$800 extra.

Casa Margouya
HOSTEL $

(☎237-640; www.margouya.com; Santa Rosa 318; dm CH$9000-9500, s/d without bathroom CH$15,000-22,000; @?) This French-owned, excellently located hostel is smaller than average and fosters a friendly communal vibe between its guests (it's vaguely hippie) as a result.

✖ Eating

The dining scene is second only to Pucón in Sur Chico but only the strong survive winter, so restaurant turnover is high. The resto-bar craze is on overdrive here. Fancier spots tend to congregate on the *costanera,* both north and south of the *centro.*

TOP CHOICE **Caffé El Barrista** CAFE $
(www.elbarista.cl; Walker Martínez 211; mains CH$2700-4200; ☺breakfast, lunch & dinner) This Italian-style, Palestinian-Chilean coffeehouse serves the best brew in this chapter, bar none, and draws a healthy lunch crowd for excellent CH$5000 menus and a selection of tasty sandwiches. As evening wears on, it draws a hostel-owner/tour-operator crowd, who come for extensive lines of Chilean microbrews and strong mojitos, which are emptied repeatedly until the crowd heads across the street to Garage. Best in show.

La Gringa AMERICAN $
(Imperial 605; www.lagringapostres.wordpress.com; mains CH$3000-5000; ☺lunch & dinner Feb, breakfast, lunch & dinner Mar-Jan) Evoking the rainy-day cafes of the American Pacific Northwest, this charming spot run by an adorable Seattleite dishes up scrumptious muffins and baked goods, creative sandwiches (pulled pork with coffee glaze), salads (chipotle potato salad with bacon and blue cheese) and beautiful CH$5000 lunch menus. Naomi sources locally and organic where possible, and it all goes down so very nicely inside the historic Casa Bechthold.

La Marca STEAKHOUSE $$
(www.lamarca.cl; Santa Rosa 539; steaks CH$7900-8900; ☺lunch & dinner) At long last Puerto Varas has a spot for devout carnivores to delight in serious slabs of perfectly grilled beef. You won't find any obnoxious *rancho* decor here – it's all very subtle and stylish, with just 12 tables. The small filet (250g) carries some heft and is seasoned just enough. There's also the ever-popular *lomo vetado,* ox and Wagyu and a classy list of sides. Order a bottle of reasonably priced Carménère and make it a night.

Miraolas CHILEAN $$
(Santa Rosa 40; mains CH$6200-10,800; ☺lunch & dinner Mon-Sat) For an intimate dinner with lake and Calbuco views, head to this Basque-leaning seafooder with an innovative menu that skews far more complex than average. Highlights include a divine *pimentos del piqullo* (crab-stuffed peppers), a simple and elegant house fish preparation and an outstanding take on ubiquitous *merkén* mashed potatoes.

Café Dane's CAFE $
(Del Salvador 441; mains CH$1350-6300; ☺breakfast, lunch & dinner) This local favorite sums up the hybrid history of the region within its walls: küchen and empanadas, Alpen architecture and Spanish menus, *apfelstrudel* (apple strudel) and *pastel de choclo* (maize casserole). It's one of the few open early on Sunday. Try the *empanada de horno* (beef, egg, onions and olives; CH$2100).

Japón del Lago JAPANESE $$
(www.japondellago.cl; cnr Vicente Pérez Rosales & Freire; rolls CH$2000-4800; ☺lunch & dinner; 🛜) A bit of a trek down the *costanera* southeast of town, this is the requisite sushi joint with loads of rolls with the requisite cream cheese. Besides that irritating detail, it does good work for reasonable prices with lake views.

Da Alessandro PIZZERIA $$
(www.daalessandro.com; Vicente Pérez Rosales 1290; pizzas CH$5750-12,100; ☺lunch & dinner) You'll find decent thin-crust pizzas here in this legitimately Italian pizzeria on the *costanera.* There's a wealth of fresh pastas and gnocchi, too.

Donde El Gordito CHILEAN, SEAFOOD $
(San Bernardo 560; mains CH$5000-7500; ☺lunch & dinner, closed Jun) This down to earth local's favorite is a great seafood spot in the Mercado Municipal. It does wonderful things with crab sauce. It's rich, but excellent.

🍷 Drinking

Garage BAR
(Walker Martínez 220) Garage, attached to the Copec gas station, caters to an artsy, alternative crowd, staying up later than it should and hosting everything from impromptu jazz sessions to all-out Colombian *cumbia* shakedowns. It's a longtime staple kept alive by expats' devotion to it and is one of the town's only true bars.

Bravo Quebrara BAR, LOUNGE
(www.bravocabrera.cl; Vicente Pérez Rosales 1071; ☺closed Sun) Along the *costanera,* this fashionable resto-bar, named after a Patagonian Robin Hood who stole beef from the rich and threw barbecues for the poor, is where you'll find upper-class local color sipping on trendy cocktails mixed by real bartenders. It's a great place to escape the tourist throngs while throwing back a spicy ginger martini and watching how the other half of PV lives. A late-night taxi back to *centro* costs CH$1500.

Shopping

TOP CHOICE **Vicki Johnson**   CHOCOLATE
(www.vicki-johnson.com; Santa Rosa 318) Anyone who tries the ginger or *miel de ulmo/* Chilean hazelnut chocolates here would be hard-pressed to argue against this being Chile's best artisanal chocolate. There is also a wealth of high-end rauli-wood kitchen utensils, jewelry, chutneys, olive oils and other tasty take-home treats.

**Fundación
Artesanías de Chile**   HANDICRAFTS
(Del Salvador 109; ⊙9am-9pm Dec-Mar) A not-for-profit foundation offering beautiful Mapuche textiles as well as high-quality jewelry and ceramics from all over southern Chile.

Lippi   CLOTHING
(San Francisco 333) Because you need to outfit yourself in outdoor-adventure gear and it's cooler back home if your gear is Chilean.

ℹ Information

Internet is widely available in the *centro*.
Banco de Chile (cnr Del Salvador & Santa Rosa)
Chile on Board (☎237-206; Santa Rose 632) Booking for Navimag and Naveira Austral in Puerto Varas.
Clínica Alemana (www.alemanapv.cl; Otto Bader 810; ⊙24hr)
Parque Pumalín office (☎250-079; www.pumalinpark.org; Klenner 299; ⊙closed Sat & Sun) Though the park is found in Northern Patagonia, this is the official tourism office for Parque Pumalín (p310).
Police (☎765-105; San Francisco 241)
Post office (San José 242)
Tourist office (☎361-194; www.puertovaras-chile.cl; Del Salvador 320) Helpful, with brochures and free maps of the area.

ℹ Getting There & Around

Air

Lan (☎600-526-2000; Av Gramado 560; ⊙closed Sun) and **Sky Airlines** (☎234-252; San Bernardo 430; ⊙closed Sun) keep offices in town but fly from Puerto Montt.

From the Puerto Montt airport, taxis cost approximately CH$15,000.

Bus

Most long-distance bus services from Puerto Varas originate in Puerto Montt; for fares and duration information see p281. Buses leave from three terminals, one for Cruz del Sur and its affiliates 1km from town at San Francisco 1317; the Tur-Bus station at just outside *centro* on Del Salvador s/n, which also serves JAC, Condor and Tas-Choapa; and Pullman's station in town. Most companies sell tickets through their individual offices around downtown. For Osorno, Valdivia and Temuco, **Cruz del Sur** (☎236-969; Walker Martínez 230) has several departures daily from the terminal at San Francisco 1317; it also goes to Chiloé several times per day and Punta Arenas on Tuesday, Thursday and Saturday. For Santiago, Cruz Del Sur, **Tur-Bus** (☎234-163; San Pedro 210) and **Pullman Bus** (☎234-626; Portales 18) offer the most services. **JAC** (☎383-800; San Pedro 251) goes to Temuco and five times daily to Pucón. For Viña del Mar and Valparaíso, Tur-Bus has a nightly bus at 9pm.

For Bariloche (Argentina), Cruz del Sur goes daily at 8:50am and again at 11:15am on Thursday and Sunday only. Tur-Bus goes at 8:45am daily. For information on the bus-boat combination to Bariloche, see boxed text, opposite.

Long-distance bus fares from Puerto Varas (prices fluctuate with the quality of the bus/classes):

DESTINATION	COST (CH$)	DURATION (HR)
Ancud	4300	2½
Bariloche (Ar)	13,000	6
Castro	5700	4½
Osorno	1700-1900	1¼
Pucón	9100	5½
Punta Arenas	44,000	22
Santiago	20,000-46,100	12
Temuco	5700-12,800	6
Valdivia	4000-6500	3½
Viña del Mar/Valparaíso	24,900-38,500	15

Minibuses

Minibuses to and from Ensenada, Petrohué, Puerto Montt, Cochamó and Río Puelo all leave from a small stop near the corner of Walker Martínez and San Bernardo. For Frutillar and Puerto Octay, buses depart from a small stop on Av Gramado near San Bernardo.

Regional minibus fares from Puerto Varas:

DESTINATION	COST (CH$)	DURATION (HR)
Cochamó	2000	3
Ensenada	1200	1
Frutillar	900	½
Petrohué	2000	1½
Puerto Montt	800	¼
Río Puelo	2500	1½

THROUGH THE ANDES

Why plod through a line at a boring bureaucratic border crossing when you can make your way from Puerto Varas through the majestic lakes and mountains of the Pérez Rosales Pass to Bariloche, Argentina? The trip is a series of buses and boats from one breathtaking view to the next including the Saltos del Petrohué (waterfalls), Lago Todos Los Santos and Volcán Osorno.

Although you can make the trip section by section and spend time in the small scenic towns of Petrohué or Peulla, most travelers do it in a straight shot. **Cruce Andino** (www.crucedelagos.cl) runs the trip and can be contacted via its agency arm, TurisTour, at the main office in Puerto Varas (p265) or Puerto Montt (p280). Reservations for the whole excursion must be made at least a day in advance; however, if you're only going as far as Peulla, tickets may be purchased at the Petrohué dock. The total fare is approximately CH$140,000 although there are seasonal discounts and pricing for students and seniors and a backpacker price (CH$49,000) if you are willing to walk the land portions. Two things worth noting: the package-tour crowd largely dominates this trip; and prices increase an astounding US$50 every two years regardless of any corresponding relation to improved facilities or services.

There are daily departures throughout the year, but the 12-hour trip requires a mandatory overnight in Peulla in winter (May to August). Consider bringing your own food for the first part of the trip, as some feel meals aboard the catamaran to Peulla and in Peulla are expensive and dull.

SECTION	TRANSPORTATION	DURATION (HR)
Puerto Varas-Petrohué	bus	1½
Petrohué-Peulla	boat	2
Peulla-Puerto Frías	bus	2
Puerto Frías-Puerto Alegre	boat	½
Puerto Alegre-Puerto Blest	bus	¼
Puerto Blest-Puerto Pañuelo	boat	1
Puerto Pañuelo-Bariloche	bus	1

If you do decide to break up the journey, Peulla, after the stunning catamaran ride across emerald Lago Todas Los Santos from Petrohué, is tucked into a gorgeous valley rife with tall, grassy junquillo (a grassy weed that sure does pretty up the place) and is best appreciated after the package-tourist hordes have continued on. The town has been on the tourist map since 1907 and one family built almost of its infrastructure – the owners of TurisTour, who also own both hotels.

Ensenada

☑ 065 / POP 1250

Rustic Ensenada, 45km along a picturesque shore-hugging road from Puerto Varas, is really nothing more than a few restaurants, *hospedajes* and adventure outfitters, but for those looking for more outdoors, less hardwood floors, it's a nice natural setting in full view of three majestic beasts: Volcán Osorno, Volcán Calbuco and Volcán Puntiagudo. Staying here over Puerto Varas has a few advantages: if you plan to climb or ski Osorno, you can save an hour of sleep by overnighting here (and if the weather turns, you won't have come quite as far for nothing). Volcán Calbuco is also within striking distance – just to the south of Ensenada. And between them is the breathtaking Parque Nacional Vicente Pérez Rosales, the entrance of which sits just outside town.

🛏 Sleeping

Casa Ko   B&B $

(☑097-703-6477; www.casako.com; dm CH$12,000, d CH$38,000, s/d without bathroom CH$18,000/32,000; [P][❄][@][✿]) A young and artsy French couple run this cultured choice, completely renovated and homey for this price range. Artists are invited annually in exchange for leaving behind a creation, so the six-room home is filled with random creative goodness and a throwback vibe – all under the nose of super Osorno and Calbuco views. Home-cooked dinners served family-style are CH$9500.

Escala II   GUESTHOUSE **$**
(☑098-435-5677; Ruta 225, Km40; r per person CH$15,000) This friendly budget spot emphasizes upkeep and offers rooms that are positioned to have one volcanic view or another. Rates include breakfast and dinner and the four-course lunch costs an extra CH$6000. We tried the trout – it is the best deal in Ensenada.

❶ Getting There & Away

Minibuses frequently shuttle between Ensenada and Puerto Varas (CH$1200, 50 minutes). There is no public transportation between Ensenada and Las Cascadas, a distance of 22km on the road to Puerto Octay.

Parque Nacional Vicente Pérez Rosales

In this park of celestial lakes and soaring volcanoes, Lago Todos Los Santos and Volcán Osorno may be the standouts but they're actually just part of a crowd. One lake leads to the next and volcanoes dominate the skyline on all sides of this storied pass through the Andes range. The needlepoint of Volcán Puntiagudo (2493m) lurks to the north and craggy Monte Tronador (3491m) marks the Argentine border to the east. From the higher levels you can see where lava flows pinched off rivers and lakes, detouring them into new bodies of water.

Established in 1926, the 2510-sq-km Pérez Rosales was Chile's first national park, but its history goes back much further. In pre-Columbian times Mapuche traveled the 'Camino de Vuriloche,' a major trans-Andean route they managed to conceal from the Spaniards for more than a century after the 1599 uprising. Jesuit missionaries traveled from Chiloé, continuing up the Estero de Reloncaví and crossing the pass south of Tronador to Lago Nahuel Huapi, avoiding the riskiest crossings of the region's lakes and rivers.

The park is open year-round, depending on weather conditions. There is a Conaf **visitor center** (☑065-212-036; ☺9am-1pm & 2-6pm) for basic info at the entrance to the park but by the time you read this, it should

have moved a few hundred meters inside the park to Laguna Verde.

VOLCÁN OSORNO

Volcán Osorno, only rivaled by Volcán Villarrica, is a perfect conical peak towering above azure glacial lakes. It retains its idyllic shape due to the 40 craters around its base – it's there that the volcano's eruptions have taken place, never at the top. You can spend a day trekking under its nose for around CH$40,000 from Puerto Varas, but if you want to summit the volcano, plan on CH$150,000 for groups of up to three people (including snow and ice-climbing gear) and a full day starting at 5am. The trip is technical and not for the unfit. If the weather turns and the trip is aborted before leaving, agencies will refund the cost. Once you reach the snow, there is no refund regardless of cancellation due to weather. Trips up Volcán Calbuco (2003m), the region's most active volcano, cost CH$140,000 per person for two people. All the outfitters more or less hire the same guides. Contact Puerto Montt–based **Trekka Patagonia** (☑065-256-760; www.trekka.cl).

Independent climbers must obtain Conaf permission, providing detailed personal qualifications as well as lists of equipment and intended routes.

Centro de Ski y Montaña Volcán Osorno (☑065-566-624; www.volcanosorno.com; half-/full-day lift tickets CH$15,000/18,000) has two lifts for skiing and sightseeing and has recently undergone an expansion of its restaurant and rental shop. It has ski and snowboard rentals and food services on the mountain year-round. Options have expanded in summer: you can take the ski lift up for impossibly scenic views for CH$9000 (1500m) or CH$12,000 (1700m); or, come down a little faster, either by newly added zip lines (CH$16,000 to CH$19,000) or on a mountain bike (CH$18,000).

Just downhill from the ski slopes, the rustic **Refugio Teski** (☑065-566-622; www.teski.cl; dm CH$15,000, d CH$35,000; ☺year-round) offers unparalleled access to the mountain. Though simple, it's actually a spectacular spot to stay as you can have the outstanding views of Lago Llanquihue and the surrounding mountains all to yourself once the tourist buses depart in the late afternoon. Rent out a mountainside hot tub (CH$35,000 for three hours, including a pisco sour), take advantage of two-for-one happy-hour drinks at sunset and make a night of it. If you have a

Parque Nacional Vicente Pérez Rosales

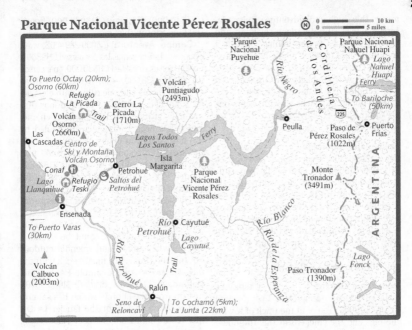

sleeping bag, you can sleep in a dorm bed for CH$15,000.

To get to the ski area and the *refugio,* take the Ensenada–Puerto Octay road to a signpost about 3km from Ensenada and continue driving 10km up the lateral. It's well worth your money renting a car and driving up the paved road, taking in spectacular views flanked by Osorno on one side, Calbuco on the other and Lago Llanquihue down below. There are no transportation services to or from the slopes for anyone except for package-tour buyers.

PETROHUÉ

People may come for the ferry cruise to Peulla, but Petrohué's majestic lakeside setting and serenity tend to convince visitors to stay a little longer. It's only 20 minutes from Ensenada down a reasonable ash road, so it has similar advantages in an infinitesimally prettier locale.

⊙ Sights & Activities

Expediciones Petrohué (☎065-212-025; www.petrohue.com; ⊕9am-6:30pm Sep-Jun) arranges climbing, rafting and canyoning excursions and has kayaks right on the lake for CH$3500 per hour. Trips to **Isla Margarita**, a wooded island with a small interior lagoon, cost CH$35,000 for up to four in a small fishing boat or CH$6000 each with TurisTour (p280) with three daily departures that operate between December and March only.

From the woodsy **Conaf campground** (campsites 1-5 persons CH$7000) just beyond the parking area, a dirt track leads to **Playa Larga**, a long black-sand beach much better than the one near the hotel. From the beach, **Sendero Los Alerces** heads west to meet up with **Sendero La Picada**, which climbs past Paso Desolación and continues on to Refugio La Picada on the volcano's north side. Alternatively, follow Los Alerces back to the hotel. Six kilometers southwest of Petrohué, the **Saltos del Petrohué** (admission CH$1600) is a rushing, frothing waterfall raging through a narrow volcanic rock canyon carved by lava. Anyone wondering why the rafting trips don't start from the lake will find the answer here, although experienced kayakers have been known to take it on.

If coming for a day trip, consider bringing food from Puerto Varas.

⏚ Sleeping & Eating

Petrohué Hotel & Cabañas LODGE $$$
(☎065-212-025; www.petrohue.com; s/d from CH$109,000/149,000, cabins for 4 people CH$140,000; 🅿😊@🛜🏊) In a gorgeous stone and wood-gabled building replete with a

tower, this high-end adventure lodge deserves a visit. Its abundant skylights and the roaring fires in the lounge make it a romantic place to relax, read a book or cuddle up. The rooms, rich in wood, have beds piled high with blankets and are scattered with candles. The restaurant is open to the general public and packages with excursions are offered. The equally luxe *cabañas* sit on the lakeshore.

Hospedaje Esmeralda   GUESTHOUSE $
(☎096-225-6230; campsite/r per person CH$5000/10,000) Like mother, like son – this wooden lodge on stilts is a nearly upscale budget option run by the son of matriarch Küschel, who owns the cheaper *hospedaje* a few hundred meters down the shore. There's a beautiful breakfast room (add CH$2500) with broad windows sucking up the lake views. If you call ahead, they will transport you from the dock for free.

Hospedaje Küschel   GUESTHOUSE $
(☎099-875-3566; campsites/r per person CH$4000/8000) You're in the thick of it with the pigs and the chickens at this run-down farmhouse across the lake (reached by boat at the dock for CH$500, though they may try to charge as much as CH$2000), but the old woman here is good-hearted and you are situated right on the lake (from where your startlingly good home-smoked trout dinner comes). Breakfast is included but dinner or lunch runs at CH$5000.

❶ Getting There & Away
Minibuses run from Puerto Varas to Petrohué (CH$2000) throughout the year. For details on the boat trip across the lake to Peulla, see the boxed text, p269.

Cochamó

☎065 / POP 4366
The Chilote-style, alerce-shingled **Iglesia Parroquial María Inmaculada** stands picturesque and proud against a backdrop of milky-blue water along the road to Cochamó, forming one of the most stunning spots throughout the region and the gateway to the upper Río Cochamó Valley.

The **municipal office** (☎350-271) in town provides a very useful Cochamó hiking map and brochure.

French-run **Southern Trips** (☎098-407-2559; www.southern-trips.com; Pueblo Hundido), on the main road, offers five-hour

(CH$40,000) to 11-day (CH$960,000) horse-trekking trips in the area.

Campo Aventura (☎099-289-4318; www.campoaventura.cl; campsites per person CH$3000, r per person incl breakfast CH$30,000, r per person full board CH$38,000; ☺☎) sleeps 15 in three splendid rooms and one cabin with electricity, a kitchen and indoor and outdoor dining areas at its riverside camp at Cochamó, which has been completely overhauled by the new American owner, a former foreign newspaper correspondent. Here you'll find lovely meals (breakfast and lunch CH$5000, dinner CH$8000) as well as a beautiful camping area at the river's edge.

The best spot in town proper is **Hospedaje Maura** (☎099-334-9213; www.experiencepatagonia.cl; J Molina 77; r per person CH$15,000), with charming owners, good beds and a snug new restaurant and splendid outdoor hot tub and sauna. For meals, stick with the *hospedajes*, or try the simple **Restaurant Reloncaví** (Av Catedral; mains CH$1000-4500), just up from the church, which has salmon and *merluza* (hake); or the fancier **La Ollita** (Calle Principal s/n; mains CH$1500-9000), on the main road above town, which serves up whatever's fresh that day with views of Volcán Yates from its mini-terrace.

There are four daily bus departures to and from Puerto Montt (CH$2000), stopping in Puerto Varas and Ensenada and continuing on to Puelo.

Río Cochamó Valley

With its impressive granite domes rising above the verdant rainforest and colossal alerce trees dominating the forest, some tout the spectacular Río Cochamó Valley as the Chilean Yosemite. It's near here where the glacial waters of the Lakes District give way to the saltwaters of the 80km Estero de Reloncaví, a fjord that forms the gateway to Northern Patagonia. The region's popularity is growing fast, especially with the rock climbers – each year new climbing routes and trails open with more adrenaline junkies clambering around the valley to reach them. The area is indeed a beautiful spot worthy of multiple days and tourism has not yet overwhelmed the area, so go now before it *does* turn into Yosemite.

To reach the valley, the route follows a 19th-century log road built for oxcarts, which carried seafood to Argentina and beef back to Chile. You can trek in, or hire horses.

The road to the trailhead begins just before the bridge to Campo Aventura, but most folks grab a taxi or drive themselves this first 7km to the trailhead (you can park at the last house on the right for CH$1000).

LA JUNTA

From Cochamó, a splendid 12km trek that goes through the deep Valdivian rainforest and along the Río Cochamó brings you to La Junta, an impressive valley situated under the watch of massive granite domes jutting from the top of the surrounding mountains. Unless they build a road here, it should remain a gorgeous and serene spot and nearly everyone who goes up for a day wishes they had allotted more time to enjoy the supreme scenery and outstanding trekking. In January, the *tábanos* (horseflies) can be relentless.

Secret Patagonia in Puerto Varas (p265) runs three- to eight-day treks (CH$300,000 to CH$795,000 per person including meals, lodging and load horses). It can take you up to the 900m viewpoint at Arco Iris through three types of native forest, with wine and cheese to boot.

At La Junta you'll find the impressive **Refugio Cochamó** (☎097-719-0906; www. cochamo.com; campsites per person CH$2500, dm CH$9000, d without bathroom CH$31,000), a fantastic gringo-Argentine climber-run cabin and camping with solar showers, water straight from the Trinadad waterfall, homemade pizza (CH$7000) and its very own homebrew, Tábano Pale Ale! It's open from October to April. To reach it, you must cross the river via a rudimentary but effective pulley system.

Also fantastic is **Campo Aventura Mountain Lodge** (☎099-289-4318; www.cam poaventura.cl; campsites per person CH$3000, dm CH$10,000, r per person full board CH$38,000; ☺), run by the most established outfitter in the area, Campo Aventura (p265). The candlelit converted farmhouse on 80 hectares has four bedrooms and a four-bed bunkhouse, wood-fired showers and a dining room with a central woodstove. A new sundeck has superb Arco Iris views and the caretakers are a delightful Chilean couple who pamper guests with mountain hospitality and hearty home-cooked food – pork and lamb *asados*, chicken and lentil *cazuelas* and the like. Nice touches like wine, homemade bread and filtered coffee are available, as is a full-time trekking guide.

Río Puelo

The road from Cochamó continues along the Estero de Reloncaví another 31km through to Río Puelo, a little hamlet that's bound for growth as a new land-lake route into Argentina develops. Under the watchful eye of Volcán Yates and the jade-hued Río Puelo, it's a serene and photogenic spot that makes for a great base for exploration further afield into the Río Puelo Valley.

Sleeping & Eating

Most decent accommodations are in Puelo Alto, 2km east of the center.

TOP CHOICE/ **Domo Camp** HUT $$
(☎099-138-2310; www.andespatagonia.cl; Puelo Alto; r 2/4 people CH$35,000/55,000; ℗☺@☎) These geodesic domes connected by planks through native forest are one of the most interesting places to stay in Región X. Each has its own fireplace for warmth, and cozy mattresses and sleeping bags are provided. There's a soothing outdoor hot tub on the premises. The only downside is that it's a long and uncomfortable haul to the showers – robes and headlamps are provided, but slippers are not, so your feet take a beating.

Camping Río Puelo CAMPGROUND $
(☎099-744-7861; Puelo Alto; campsites per person CH$4500, r per person CH$11,500; ℗@) The bathrooms are makeshift but nice on the inside at this basic campground with lovely Andes views. The owner is very friendly and he has a well-equipped *cabaña* that functions as a *hospedaje* when it's not rented. Call ahead.

Restaurant Tique CHILEAN $$
(Puelo Alto; mains CH$4600-7000; ☺breakfast, lunch & dinner; ☎) Located at the Domo Camp, this is the best spot to eat in town. Coca runs a rustic kitchen but the meals are home prepared and excellent.

Information

Head to the plaza **tourist office** (☎350-271; Santiago Bueras s/n; ☺8:30am-noon & 3-5:30pm Mon-Fri) for options on local treks, rustic family lodgings and guides.

Getting There & Away

There are four daily departures to and from Puerto Montt (CH$3500, four hours), stopping in Puerto Varas, Ensenada and Cochamó. From

SUR CHICO RÍO PUELO

PARQUE TAGUA-TAGUA

Carved out of virgin Valdivian rainforest 15km east of Puelo, **Parque Tagua-Tagua** (☎02-588-4036; www.parquetaguatague.cl; adult/child CH$4500/2500) is southern Chile's latest park. A private initiative funded by Universidad Mayor in Santiago and managed by Secret Patagonia in Puerto Varas (p265), the park preserves 3000 hectares of previously unseen alerce forest along with two lakes, Lago Alerce and Lago Quetra, bounded by granite mountains. Trekking and fly-fishing are big draws here, as is birdwatching and the chance of spotting pudú (small deer), puma and condors. There are three basic but well-made alerce *refugios* (rustic shelters) with bathrooms and wood-burning stoves in the park, built along its 16km of trails that traverse rivers via well-built wooden bridges. It's all very high-tech as well – iPod Touches are available for rent (CH$15,000 per day), and can be used to read Quick Response (QR) codes throughout the park.

To get here, catch the once-a-day Lago Tagua-Tagua–bound bus from Puerto Montt (7:45am) or Puerto Varas (8:20am), which meets the ferry at the edge of Lago Tagua-Tagua. Make sure you have called ahead to park officials, who will meet you on the other side of the Tagua-Tagua ferry crossing for the final 10-minute boat ride to the park.

the village, the road continues inland to Punta Canelo on Lago Tagua-Tagua, where a ferry service (cars CH$6500, pedestrians CH$1000) crosses the lake to the road's extension, which parallels the river to Llanada Grande. If you have wheels, show up an hour before departure to get in line.

Río Puelo Valley

☎065 / POP 500

Like a country lass of modest origins, the Río Puelo Valley remains unfazed by that massive industry called tourism, offering a few homespun adventures. It has become a hotbed of ecotourism of late, mainly due to the proposed dam at El Portón near Llanada Grande, which would flood most of the valley (see boxed text, p332). Locals are turning to tourism as a means of halting the plans. Fishing, trekking and horseback riding are king here and each offers days of satiating adventures in the area.

LLANADA GRANDE & BEYOND

After the lake crossing at Tagua-Tagua, the gravel road continues by mountainsides peppered with patches of dead coigüe trees (killed by fire but tragically pretty) and lands still traversed by gaucho families on horseback. This is Llanada Grande – you are now off the grid. A system of pioneer homes and rustic B&Bs is in place for travelers here (inquire at Campo Eggers), making your treks and horseback rides feel a little less touristy, a little more cultural. The road is being slowly forged all the way to Argentina, though Argentina has no plans to continue

it on their side. Most treks start in Llanada Grande and take different routes along the valley, including unforgettable jaunts to Lago Azul and Argentina. Hard-core hikers should seek out the amicable services of Lolo Escobar for an extraordinary five-day round-trip to the Ventisquero Glacier near Segundo Corral, the last Chilean settlement in the valley. If you fancy fishing, call on Reiner Grellich, a reputable fishing guide who also has cabins on Lago Verde (Blanca from Campo Eggers can radio both, but call with advance notice).

Camping Oro Verde (☎098-171-1859; playaoroverde1@gmail.com; campsites CH$6000-8000; ☺Dec-Mar), located on the soft sands of the southern shore of glassy Lago Totoral. An invaluable choice is **Campo Eggers** (☎02-196-9212; agroturelsalto@gmail.com; r per person without bathroom CH$25,000; [P][wifi]), in an impeccably clean and sensibly furnished log home owned by Blanca Eggers, who can set up accommodations in pioneer homes and B&Bs all the way to Lago Puelo in Argentina. Breakfast, *onces* and dinner (and wine!) are included and often involve traditional lamb or wild-boar *asado*. The animal-packed farm's postcard setting in front of the 1200m El Salto waterfall is a destination in itself, but it can be boring if it's not a full house.

Posada Martín Pescador (☎099-884-6555; www.posadamartinpescador.cl; r CH$39,500) is a two-room B&B-style fishing and birdwatching lodge with hearty food and what is perhaps the most idyllic dining table in the region – over the water on Lago Totoral. Lunch and dinner is CH$9000 extra or

CH$15,000 for both, but you'd gladly pay triple that when you see where it's served.

The same bus to Río Puelo continues on to the ferry at Punta Canelo on the north side of Lago Tagua-Tagua, where boats leave twice a day (9am and 1pm). At Puerto Maldonado on the south side, a minibus will be waiting to carry you on to Llanada Grande (CH$2000). To return, ferries leave Puerto Maldonado twice a day (noon and 4:30pm).

Puerto Montt

♪065 / POP 168,242

Say what you will about Puerto Montt (locals certainly don't hold back, with *Muerto Montt,* meaning 'Dead Montt,' topping the list), but if you choose to visit southern Chile's ominous volcanoes, its celestial glacial lakes and its mountainous national

parks, you will most likely be visiting the capital of the Lakes District and the region's commercial and transportation hub.

Puerto Montt's most redeeming quality is that of its plethora of exit points: be it by plane, ferry, bus or rental car, you can make a quick and virtually painless getaway to a near-endless inventory of memorable locales. Otherwise, travelers have occasionally become endeared of the unpolished working-class Chilean atmosphere here.

⊙ Sights

Puerto Montt doesn't offer much for lingering – it's really a large transit town.

FREE **Casa del Arte Diego Rivera**   GALLERY
(www.culturapuertomontt.cl; Quillota 116; ⊙9am-1pm & 3-6:30pm Mon-Fri) A joint Mexican-Chilean project finished in 1964, the upstairs Sala

---

SALMON SETBACK

Salmon was first imported to Chile about a century ago. It wasn't until the mid-1980s that salmon farming in submerged cages was developed on a massive scale. Nowadays Chile is the world's second-largest producer of salmon, right on the tail of Norway. Puerto Montt is the epicenter of the farming and exportation industry, where, in the late 2000s, billions of dollars in investment were pushing the farming operations further south into Patagonia as far as the Strait of Magellan and the industry was expected to double in size and growth by 2020, overtaking Norway. By 2006 salmon was Chile's third-largest export (behind copper and molybdenum) and the future looked endlessly bright. Then the bottom dropped out.

Coupled with the global recession, Chile's salmon industry was hit hard with a sudden outbreak of Infectious Salmon Anemia (ISA), first detected in 2007 at a Norwegian-owned farm, with disastrous consequences. Between 2005 and 2010, annual Atlantic salmon production dropped from 400,000 to 100,000 tonnes; 26,000 jobs in Puerto Montt and around were lost (along with nearly US$3 billion) and many players in the salmon service industry went bankrupt. Chile found itself in complete salmon panic – an increase in crime in Puerto Montt and the doubling of suicide rates didn't help matters. But there *had been* signs. Veritable mountains of organic waste from extra food and salmon feces had led to substantial contamination and depletion of other types of fish; and sanitation issues and pen overcrowding were serious industry concerns for many years.

Environmentalists, including the Chilean environmental organization **Oceana** (http://americadelsur.oceana.org) and Doug Tompkins (owner of Parque Pumalín; p310), have expressed their concerns about the negative effects of the salmon industry directly to the Chilean government. **Fundación Terram** (www.terram.cl), which closely monitors the industry, has published reports over a range of topics from working conditions to environmental damage.

By 2012 salmon was making a comeback, with production levels on the rise, mainly thanks to an insatiable emerging market in Brazil, which overtook the USA to become the world's second-largest global consumer of farmed Chilean salmon behind Japan in 2010.

As an aside, it should be noted that all the quality salmon in Chile is exported, so if it's on menus in country, it's probably one of two scenarios: it's downgraded (ie defective or not fit for export) or 'wild,' which just really means it has escaped from a farm. Proceed at your own risk.

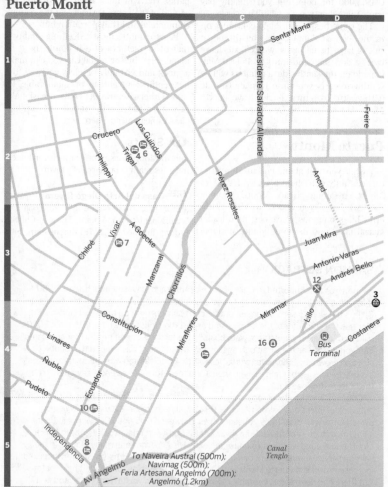

Hardy Wistuba specializes in works by local artists, sculptors and photographers. Also houses a small cafe and an excellent boutique.

Museo Juan Pablo II   MUSEUM
(Av Diego Portales 997, 2nd fl; admission CH$500; ☺9am-6pm Mon-Fri) Puerto Montt's waterfront museum was closed, graffitied and seemingly left for dead at the time of writing, but it's sworn to reopen. If it does, expect displays on natural history, archaeology, the island of Chiloé, maritime history and weapons, religious iconography, German colonization and local urbanism.

Iglesia Catedral   CHURCH
(Urmeneta s/n) Built entirely of alerce in 1856, this church, located on the Plaza de Armas, is the town's oldest building, and one of its few attractive ones.

🛏 Sleeping

Puerto Montt is a business town and port rather than a destination in itself and most travelers spend little more than one night here as a transportation hub. Most of the budget places listed are within a few blocks of the bus station. If arriving at night, stay alert; petty thievery isn't uncommon.

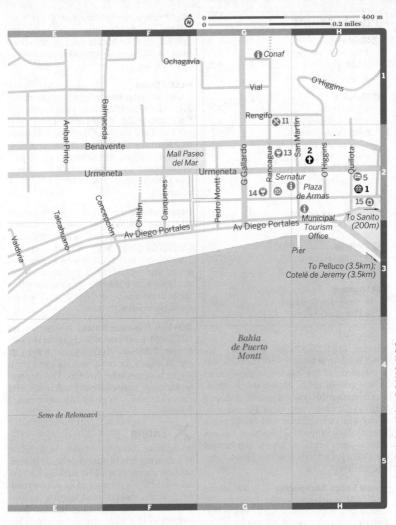

Map labels:

0 — 400 m
0 — 0.2 miles

Ochagavía

Conaf

Vial

O'Higgins

Balmaceda

Anibal Pinto

Rengifo

11

Benavente

San Martín

Mall Paseo del Mar

13

Rancagua

2

O'Higgins

Quillota

5

Urmeneta

Urmeneta

G Gallardo

Sernatur

1

Concepción

Chillán

Cauquenes

Pedro Montt

14

Plaza de Armas

15

Talcahuano

Av Diego Portales

Av Diego Portales

Municipal Tourism Office

To Sanito (200m)

Valdivia

Pier

To Pelluco (3.5km);
Cotelé de Jeremy (3.5km)

Bahía
de Puerto
Montt

Seno de Reloncaví

TOP CHOICE Tren del Sur   DESIGN HOTEL $$

(☎343-939; www.trendelsur.cl; Santa Teresa 643; s/d from CH$28,900/37,900; PⓅ🅿@🛜) A steal for the price, this boutique hotel in the old neighborhood of Modelo is full of furniture (headboards, wardrobes) fashioned from rescued railway trestles. The lobby is high style and cozy and adheres to feng shui. The 17 rooms, a step down from the high-design common areas, offer private bathroom and central heating and are entered from a sky-lit hallway. The new Slow Food seafood restaurant is excellent.

Casa Perla   GUESTHOUSE $

(☎262-104; www.casaperla.com; Trigal 312; camp-sites per person CH$6000, dm CH$9000, d without bathroom CH$20,000; ⊜@🛜) This welcoming family home's matriarch, Perla, and her family, will have you feeling like a sibling. English and German are spoken. All bathrooms are shared and guests can use the kitchen, where Perla makes jam on the wood-burning stove. It's hard to find without a map, so consider a taxi from the bus station (CH$2000).

Hospedaje Vista al Mar   GUESTHOUSE $

(☎255-625; www.hospedajevistaalmar.unlugar. com; Vihar 1337; s/d CH$15,000/28,000, without

Puerto Montt

◎ Sights

🛏 Sleeping

✴ Eating

☕ Drinking

🛍 Shopping

bathroom CH$12,000/25,000; P🍴@📶) Another family-run favorite with travelers, this is the nicest of the residential guesthouses at this end of town, decked out in great-condition hardwoods with spick-and-span bathrooms, rooms with cable TV and wonderful bay views. Eliana and family are a gaggle of sweethearts – helpful to the nth degree – and breakfast goes a step beyond for Chile: yogurt, whole-wheat breads, eggs and the like.

House Rocco Backpacker　GUESTHOUSE $
(✆272-897; www.hospedajerocco.cl; Pudeto 233; dm/s/d CH$12,000/20,000/25,000; @📶) This Chilean-American traveler's mainstay five blocks from the Navimag has a large sunny kitchen, warm wooden walls and floors and feather duvets. Home-cooked breakfasts of sweet crepes with *manjar* and real coffee are pluses.

Hostal Vista Hermosa　GUESTHOUSE $
(✆319-600; www.hostalvistahermosa.cl; Miramar 1486; r per person with/without breakfast CH$11,000/9000; P🍴@📶) A quick but uphill walk from the bus terminal, Vista Hermosa has comfortable budget rooms with cable TV. Room No 1 boasts fantastic views of the sea and Volcán Calbuco – and a sorely mis-

placed gray office building, too. To get here, exit the bus station north on Calle Lillo and turn left on Calle Miramar across the street from Santa Isabel supermarket and ascend to the end.

Hostal Suizo　GUESTHOUSE $
(✆262-640; roelckers@yahoo.es; Independencia 231; s/d CH$15,000/25,000, without bathroom CH$10,000/18,000; P🍴@📶) Judged on charisma and character alone, the junkyard charm of this artistic abode wins all the accolades, but the in-house artist/owner can be particular about who stays, though it's a lovely spot at these prices, laced with her excellent paintings.

Hospedaje Corina　GUESTHOUSE $
(✆273-948; www.hospedajecorina.cl; Los Guindos 329; d CH$26,000, s/d without bathroom CH$15,000/20,000; P📶) Behind Perla on Los Guindos is Corina's newest *hospedajes,* where she will smother you with grand-motherly love inside the large, gated white home in extremely good condition. There's a rooftop garden with views.

Don Luis Business Hotel　BUSINESS HOTEL $$$
(✆259-001; www.hoteldonluis.cl; Quillota 146; s/d/tr from CH$67,000/71,000/84,000; P@📶) A stylish choice for those seeking extra comfort or business hotel facilities. There's a restaurant, bar, business center and sauna, and caters to those who give a flip about casual Fridays.

✴ Eating

Along busy, diesel-fume-laden Av Angelmó is a dizzying mix of streetside stalls (selling artifacts, heaps of smoked mussels, *cochayuyo* – edible sea plant – and mysterious trinkets), crafts markets and touristy seafood restaurants with croaking waiters beckoning you to a table. Enjoy the frenzy, but keep on going. The best-quality crafts and food are found at the end of the road at the picturesque fishing port of Angelmó, about 3km west of downtown. It is easily reached by frequent local buses and *colectivos.*

TOP CHOICE Fogón del Leñador　STEAKHOUSE $$
(www.fogon.cl; Rancagua 245; mains CH$6000-9500; ⊙lunch & dinner) The menu at the best *parrilla* in Sur Chico states that all meat takes a minimum of 40 minutes to cook. That says it all, really, and it isn't exaggerating. *Sopapillas* are served with four house-made sauces, all of which are just as tasty

on the superior filet. Bonus points for the single-serving, Fair Trade bottles of red for solo carnivores. It lacks the intimacy of Cotelé, but you won't soon forget this steak.

Cotelé de Jeremy
STEAKHOUSE $$$
(☑278-000; www.cotele.cl; Juan Soler Manfredini 1661, Pelluco; steak per kilo CH$19,500; ⊘lunch & dinner Mon-Sat) Historically known as Fogón de Cotelé or just Cotelé, this *quincho* (barbecue hut) steakhouse has had a rough go of late: the long-standing owner, a meticulous grillman with Picasso-level focus, suffered a tragic fall and had to sell off his carnivorous empire. An amicable South African continues the tradition in this intimate spot with just seven tables surrounding an open hearth. Fortunately, he had the good sense to maintain former staff, who methodically slow-cook three choices: sirloin, filet and ribeye, cut and priced by kilo. In Pelluco, it can be easily reached by buses from the terminal marked Chamiza (CH$350) or taxi (CH$3000). Reservations are a good idea, especially Thursday through Sunday.

Sanito
CHILEAN $
(www.sanito.cl; Copiapó 66; menu CH$3000; ⊘lunch & dinner; ☎♪) Puerto Montt's best bet for healthy and homey food, served up fresh daily in an artistic atmosphere that feels more Los Angeles than Chile. Each day, there's a soup, salad or entrée menu (includes juice and coffee/tea) as well as à la carte salads and sandwiches, all coming along with a funky soundtrack that bounces from Arcade Fire to '70s soul.

El Apa
SEAFOOD $
(Angelmó, Local 5-6; mains CH$3500-5950; ⊘lunch & dinner) Don't be overwhelmed by the numerous *palafito* (houses mounted on stilts along the water's edge) stall restaurants in Angelmó, this is the one you care about. Run by a mute chef, it gets packed in by locals for its monster *curanto* (CH$4500) and other superportioned fresh, seafood favorites.

Santa Isabel
SUPERMARKET
(Diego Portales 1040) Navimag provisions, across from bus terminal. Also try Bigger next door.

🍷 Drinking

There are several low-rent spots for a drink around the plaza, a good selection around the corner of Benavente and Rancagua, and an all-out booze-fest in nearby Pelluco.

Boule Bar
BAR
(Benavente 435; ⊘closed Sun) Old *Rolling Stone* covers and other musical propaganda dot this multiroomed bar lit with candles and featuring several tables and a bar rack made from tree bark. It's a good spot to carry on late into the evening with a crowd that appreciates a smart soundtrack.

Sherlock
CAFE, BAR
(Antonio Varas 452; ⊘lunch & dinner; ☎) It doesn't take much investigation to find out that Sherlock is one of the better places to hang out in town. Based on the fact that Detective Holmes was supposed to have paid a visit to Puerto Montt, this cafe/bar has a touch more style than the cookie-cutter competition and live music most nights of the week.

🛍 Shopping

This being a regular stopover for tourists and cruise ships, the Feria Artesanal Angelmó is wall-to-wall with souvenir stands along Av Angelmó selling crafts from throughout the country and an amazing amount of stuff (some junk, some decent) from more northerly countries. Also try the labyrinthine waterfront market Pueblito de Melipulli, opposite the bus terminal. Gear up at **Mall Paseo Costanera** (www.mallpaseodelmar.cl; Lllapel 10), which includes Colombia and Andesgear shops, just southeast of Plaza de Armas.

ℹ Information

Consulates
Argentine Consulate (☑253-996; Pedro Montt 160, 6th fl; ⊘9am-1pm Mon-Fri)

Emergency
Police (☑765-162; cnr Gallardo & Amunategui; ⊘24hr)

Medical Services
Hospital Regional (Seminario s/n; ⊘24hr) Near the intersection with Décima Región.

Money
There are more banks along Antonio Varas near Plaza de Armas than there are in Switzerland.
Afex (Av Diego Portales 516) Money exchange.

Post
Post office (Rancagua 126) One block west of the plaza.

Tourist Information
Conaf (☑486-118; Ochagaviá 458) Can provide details on nearby national parks.

THE NAVIMAG EXPERIENCE: THE GOOD, THE BAD & THE UGLY

Back in the prehistoric Patagonian travel days of the 1980s and early '90s, travelers had to beg and swindle just to stow away on the rusty cargo freighters that plied the waters between Puerto Montt and Puerto Natales. No regular passenger ferries were installed as tourism to the region increased, but the Navimag shipping company caught on and decided to dedicate a section of their boats to passenger transportation. So, these days, you can have that same experience of stowing away on a freighter – sometimes packed with 18-wheelers, drunken truck drivers and cattle – but you can make a reservation on your smartphone and click away hundreds of dollars for your bunk.

If you are looking for a cruise, check out *Skorpios* (p282) or *Mare Australis* (p301). The Navimag is a quirky travel experience that comes with the good, the bad and the ugly. If you like to try different experiences and are adventurous it just might be the highlight of your trip.

The Good

The Japanese-built, Patagonian-adapted cargo boat takes you through days of uninhabited fjords, close encounters with glaciers and views of surreal orange sunsets over the Pacific. It passes through Aisén's maze of narrow channels, navigates narrow passages like the White Channel (a tight, 80m passage that's quite a challenge for the 24km-wide ship) and the Angostura Inglesa (the ship seems to graze the shoreline on both sides) and stops at the impossibly remote Puerto Edén, a small fishing port and the last outpost of the region's Qawashqar Indians. To the south, the channels become narrower, the snowy peaks get closer and hundreds of waterfalls tumble from glacial valleys to the water's edge. Along the way, you might spot minke and Humboldt whales, a variety of birds, a long-abandoned sea-level shipwreck and South American sea lions.

Beyond the stellar scenery, the trip has become a unique bonding experience for independently minded travelers (the common areas are like UN break rooms – 23 nationalities on our trip). Strangers become tight friends after numerous bottles of wine, round after round of pointless card games, sympathizing about queasy stomachs, deck-top soccer matches, late-night dance parties and plans to meet up in Torres del Paine. Even though the ship's common spaces are bare and not particularly comfortable, the crew does a yeoman's job of trying to entertain with karaoke, slide shows, music, English-language movies and video games for the kiddies.

Municipal tourism office (☏223-027; Antonio Varas 415; ◷8:15am-9pm) More eager to help than Sernatur, with plenty of national-park info. It's on the plaza.

Sernatur (☏254-580; ◷8:30am-1pm & 2:30-5pm Mon-Fri) On the west side of Plaza de Armas.

Travel Agencies

TurisTour (☏228-600; www.turistour.com; Antonio Varas 216, Edificio Torre del Puerto, 9th fl; ◷closed Sun) For the Cruce de Lagos bus-ferry combo trip to Argentina, and excursions throughout the region.

ⓘ Getting There & Away

Air

Lan (☏600-526-2000; O'Higgins 167, Local 1-B) flies four times daily to Punta Arenas (one-way fares from CH$148,000), twice daily to Balmaceda/Coyhaique (one-way fares from

CH$112,000) and up to nine times daily to Santiago (one-way fares from CH$183,000).

Sky Airlines (☏437-555; www.skyairline.cl; cnr San Martín & Benavente) flies to Punta Arenas twice daily (one-way fares from CH$63,144) and four times to Santiago (one-way fares from CH$61,644) – considerably cheaper fares than Lan.

For Chaitén, **Aerocord** (☏262-300; www.aerocord.cl; Aeródromo La Paloma) flies Beechcraft and Twin Otters Monday, Wednesday and Friday at 4pm; Tuesday, Thursday and Saturday at 1pm (CH$40,000). **Pewen Services Aéreos** (☏224-000; www.pewenchile.com; Pedro Montt 65, Of 607) also flies Monday to Saturday (CH$42,000) and offers charters for up to nine passengers for CH$600,000 with a week's notice.

Bus – Regional

Puerto Montt's newly madeover, drastically improved waterfront **bus terminal** (☏283-000;

Life on board is cramped, but beds are surprisingly cozy, hovering somewhere between 1st class on an Indian train and mid-level rock-band tour bus for comfort level. Those who book into C class can expect very little space or privacy, just a curtain separating you and a hallway, while those who spring for BB get private rooms (though cramped if full) while AAA affords a private dining room, separate menus and larger rooms. Breakfast leaves something to be desired (instant coffee, *pan típico*, bowls of eggs and uninspired cold cuts). Coffee is predictably foul, but the bar sells machine cappuccinos, which are a step up for CH$1000. Lunch and dinner can be hit or miss, but sophisticated dishes like roasted hake with lemon cream sauce occasionally find their way into the cafeteria-style meal plan. Cocktails are made with glacial ice!

The Bad

If the weather is poor, your views are limited and you will spend much of your time watching movies or drinking in the dining area. If the weather is worse, you can spend a day or so pitching back and forth on rough seas and fighting to hold down your lunch. If the weather is worse than that your trip can be delayed (for days) prior to departure and you can even be delayed en route if the Golfo de Penas (on the open Pacific) is too rough to cross. Cancellations altogether are not infrequent. Either way, it's windy and cold, summer included.

In the winter the boat can have less than a dozen passengers, which can be fine or can really detract from the social experience. In the heart of summer, it is often so full that people are packed on top of each other and must dine in shifts. A very crowded boat can make the cramped downstairs dorm rooms seem less bearable.

For anxious travelers, the trip can become tedious by the third day. There is no internet on board and only very sporadic mobile signals throughout the trip.

The Ugly

During the winter, when there are fewer passengers and more cargo, hundreds of head of cattle are kept on the top and middle decks in open-top trucks. They are packed together so tightly that not all animals can keep their feet on the ground and after a day or two the stench of 300 cattle can be tough on your nose – especially if you are already seasick.

However, as you should know by now, no valuable travel experience comes without a dose of hardship. If you have the time, a journey with Navimag will not only change the way that you see and understand Chilean Patagonia, it will also add depth to your entire trip.

SUR CHICO PUERTO MONTT

cnr Av Diego Portales & Lillo) is the main transportation hub for the region, and it gets busy and chaotic – watch your belongings or leave them with the *custodia* (per 24 hours CH$500 to CH$1000) while sorting out travel plans. In summer trips to Punta Arenas and Bariloche can sell out, so book in advance.

Regional minibuses, including Puerto Varas (CH$800, 25 minutes), Frutillar (CH$1300, one hour) and Puerto Octay (CH$1600, two hours), leave frequently from the northern front of the terminal. Buses leave for the villages of Ralún (CH$1500, two hours) and Cochamó (CH$2000, 2½ hours) four times daily, and all carry on to Río Puelo (CH$3500).

Bus – Long-Distance

Bus companies, all with offices at the bus terminal, include **Cruz del Sur** (☎483-127; www.busescruzdelsur.cl), with frequent services to Chiloé; **Tur-Bus/Tas-Choapa** (☎259-320; www.

turbus.cl), with daily service to Valparaíso/Viña del Mar; **Igi Llaima** (☎254-519; www.igillaima.cl); and **Pullman Bus** (☎254-399; www.pullman.cl). All of these services go to Santiago, stopping at various cities along the way; **Buses Fierro** (☎289-024; www.busesfierro.cl) has an 8:15pm 'direct' service that only stops in Osorno. For long-haul trips to Punta Arenas via Argentina, try Cruz del Sur, Pullman Bus or **Queilen Bus** (☎253-468; www.queilenbus.cl), all of which go a few times per week, with the latter stopping in Coyhaique.

For Bariloche, Argentina, Cruz del Sur, Tur-Bus/Tas-Choapa, **Via Bariloche** (☎253-841; www.viabariloche.com.ar) and **Andesmar** (☎280-999; www.andesmar.com) go daily via the Cardenal Samoré pass east of Osorno. For information on the popular bus-boat combination trip to Bariloche, see the boxed text, p269.

Kemelbus (☎253-530; www.kemelbus.cl) has a 10am daily departure to Chaitán and Parque

Pumalín (CH$14,000); otherwise catch more frequent buses to Hornopiren (CH$4000, four hours) and switch there.

Some sample travel times and costs are as follows (prices fluctuate with the quality of the bus/classes):

DESTINATION	COST (CH$)	DURATION (HR)
Ancud	4000	2½
Bariloche (Ar)	13,000-15,000	6
Castro	5100	4
Chaitán	14,000	9½
Concepción	15,000-16,700	10
Coyhaique	25,000	24
Osorno	1500-1600	1½
Pucón	9100	5½
Punta Arenas	40,000-55,000	30
Quellón	7000	6
Santiago	18,000-26,000	12-14
Temuco	6000-7200	5
Valdivia	4700	3½
Valparaíso/Viña del Mar	31,600	15
Villarrica	8300	5

Boat

Puerto Montt is the main departure port for Patagonia. At the Terminal de Transbordadores, you can find ticket offices and waiting lounges for both **Navimag** (☏432-360; www.navimag.com; Angelmó 1735) and **Naviera Austral** (☏270-430; www.navieraustral.cl; Angelmó 1673), housed inside the same building. Both companies are primarily commercial transporters, so don't expect thread counts and Dom Pérignon.

The most popular trip is Navimag's ferry *Evangelistas*, which sails on Friday from Puerto Montt to Puerto Natales and back on Friday (boarding Thursday evening). It is a popular three-night journey through Chile's fjords; book passage at Navimag offices in Santiago, Puerto Montt, Puerto Natales or via the website.

High season is from November to March and low season is April to October. Prices for the trip include full board (vegetarian meals can be requested). Per-person fares, which vary according to the view and whether it is a private or shared bathroom (ranging from the upper-deck AAA room with an en suite bathroom to the least-attractive C class, where only every four berths have windows though some share levels with the higher classes), are as listed in the table (prices converted at time of publication; exchange rates may vary).

Cars are CH$280,000 extra. Bicycles and motorcycles can also be carried along for an additional cost. Travelers prone to seasickness should consider taking medication prior to the 12-hour crossing of Golfo de Penas, which is

NAVIMAG COSTS & SEASONS

Fares below represent Puerto Montt–Puerto Natales. In the opposite direction, fares are slightly less in high season. Discounts of 10% and 15% are available for those with student ID or ISIC, respectively.

CLASS	AAA (CH$)	AA (CH$)	A (CH$)	C (CH$)
Nov-Mar				
Single	1,244,435	1,194,053	1,058,021	–
Double	627,775	604,584	554,201	–
Triple	–	440,842	377,865	–
Quad	–	347,635	297,253	211,604
Apr-Oct				
Single	821,226	735,777	604,584	–
Double	438,323	387,941	317,406	–
Triple	–	277,100	231,757	–
Quad	–	219,161	201,528	151,145

exposed to rolling Pacific swells – particularly in winter. The southern route includes passage by the glacier Pio XI, the largest in South America (it's as big as Santiago), though there are more beautiful and photogenic glaciers along the route.

Naveira Austral sails the *Dom Baldo* Fridays and Sundays to Chaitén. The trip takes eight hours and usually runs overnight and is less than comfortable. Service is scaled back in the winter and is limited in the low season. Prices are CH$16,000 per seat, from CH$29,000 for a berth and CH$88,000 for vehicles.

Cruceros Skorpios (☑275-646; www.skor pios.cl; Av Angelmó 1660) is a legitimate cruise and calls itself 'semi-elegant.' Its most popular trip sails the *Skorpios II* to Laguna San Rafael with departures on Saturdays from Puerto Montt from September to the end of April. The six-day round-trip cruise stops at its exclusive hot-springs resort, Quitralco, and at towns in the Chiloé archipelago. Double occupancy rates, which include abundant buffets, open bar and hotel-class rooms, range from CH$969,000 to CH$1,275,000 in high season.

Auto-passenger ferries from Pargua, 62km southwest of Puerto Montt, go to Chacao (30 minutes), on the northern tip of Chiloé, every 30 minutes or so. Fares are CH$600 for passengers (included in bus fares to Chiloé) or CH$10,000 per car, no matter how many passengers.

❶ Getting Around

ETM (☑256-253; www.busesetm.cl) shuttles go to **Aeropuerto El Tepual** (☑252-019), 16km west of town, from the bus terminal (CH$1900). Catch the bus 1½ hours before your flight's departure. It also offers door-to-door service from the airport (CH$5000). Taxis between the airport and downtown cost CH$10,000.

Car-rental agencies **Europcar** (☑286-277; Antonia Varas 162) and **Antillanca** (☑431-111; www.rent.cl; Av Diego Portales 514) can help get the permission certificate (CH$60,000 plus taxes) to take rental vehicles into Argentina with two days' notice.

Chiloé

Best Places to Eat

» Hostal Omera Comedor
(p299)

» Parador Darwin (p302)

» El Chejo (p292)

» Retro's Pub (p289)

» Mar y Canela (p299)

Best Places to Sleep

» EcoLodge Chepu
Adventures (p292)

» La Refugia (p300)

» Palafito 1326 (p297)

» Parador Darwin (p302)

» Hotel Parque Quilquico
(p300)

Why Go?

When the early-morning fog shrouds misty-eyed and misunderstood Chiloé, it's immediately apparent something different this way comes. Isla Grande de Chiloé is the continent's second-largest island and is home to a fiercely independent, seafaring people who developed culturally and historically in defiance of Santiago.

On the surface you will see changes in architecture and cuisine: *tejuelas,* the famous Chilote wood shingles; *palafitos* (houses mounted on stilts along the water's edge); more than 150 iconic wooden churches (14 of which are Unesco World Heritage sites); and the renowned meat, potato and seafood stew, *curanto.* A closer look reveals a rich spiritual culture that is based on a distinctive mythology of witchcraft, ghost ships and forest gnomes.

All of the above is weaved among landscapes that are windswept and lush, with undulating hills, wild and remote national parks, and dense forests, giving Chiloé a distinct flavor unique in South America.

When to Go
Ancud

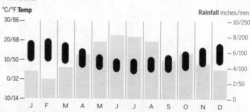

Feb The clearest skies of the year in Chiloé, but you'll still need a poncho.

Sep–Mar Magellanic and Humboldt penguins breed in Monumento Natural Islotes de Puñihuil.

Dec–May Best time of year to catch endangered blue whales off Chiloé's northwest coast.

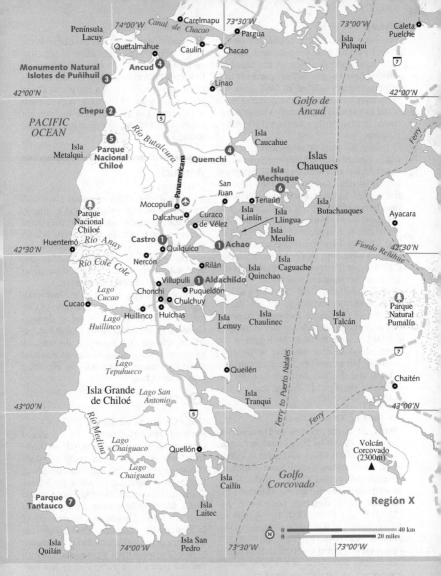

Chiloé Highlights

1 Genuflect in awe upon seeing the interiors of Chiloé's Unesco-listed wooden churches in **Achao** (p295), **Castro** (p297) and **Aldachildo** (p287)

2 Wake up with the sun on a kayak at dawn on a river trip in misty **Chepu** (p291)

3 Spy Magellanic and Humboldt penguins or blue whales at the wild and rugged **Monumento Natural Islotes de Puñihuil** (p291)

4 Tear into a bowl of *curanto* (meat, potato and seafood stew), Chiloé's most traditional dish, in local restaurants such as Kuranton in **Ancud** (p289) and El Chejo in **Quemchi** (p292)

5 Hike along the raging and wild west coast in **Parque Nacional Chiloé** (p301)

6 Wander the picturesque roads of **Isla Mechuque** (p292), an idyllic microcosm of Chiloé on a mini-island

7 Lose yourself on a hut-to-hut trek through **Parque Tantauco** (p303)

History

The islands were first populated by the Chono people, who were pushed towards the Archipelago de Aisén as the Mapuche invaded from the north. The Spaniards took full possession of Chiloé in 1567, some five years after a smallpox epidemic killed much of the indigenous population. A measles epidemic in 1580 further weakened the native influence.

During the wars of independence, Chiloé was a Spanish stronghold; the Spanish resisted criollo attacks in 1820 and 1824 from heavily fortified Ancud, until their final defeat in 1826. In 1843 the schooner *Ancud* left the shores of Chiloé full of islanders, who stuck out four months of sailing to lay Chilean claim to Magallanes at Fuerte Bulnes. The later wool and ranching booms in Magallanes were built on the backs of migrant Chilote labor. Their cultural influence is still felt in the far southern regions.

Chiloé itself stayed off the radar until the 1850s when its proximity to the new Puerto Montt gave the islands increasing commercial importance. It took another century to establish a road running the length of the main island. Fishing was and is the main industry, but is now heavily dominated by salmon and shellfish farming. Tourism has increased significantly during the last two decades.

ⓘ Getting There & Away

Nearly all traffic reaches and leaves Isla Grande de Chiloé by ferry between Pargua, on the mainland 62km southwest of Puerto Montt, and Chacao, a small town of little interest at the northeast corner of the island. Bus fares to/from the mainland include the half-hour ferry crossing; pedestrians pay CH$600, cars CH$10,000. For details on ferries from Quellón to Chaitén, see p304. For bus details from Puerto Montt, see p281. Regularly scheduled flights from Santiago to Aerodrómo Mocopulli near Castro should have begun by the time you read this.

WET WEATHER

When it is not misting or raining in Chiloé, it tends to be sprinkling or drizzling. During the rainiest months (April to August), tourism grinds to a halt. Many agencies, lodgings and churches are closed. Plan accordingly.

ⓘ Getting Around

The easiest way to get around Chiloé is the bus. Buses connect every major destination on the main island with some frequency and link up with ferries to smaller islands. It is also easy to explore with a car, which allows you to visit some of the more remote parts of this land. You can rent a car in Ancud or Castro, or bring one over from the mainland on the ferry.

Ancud

☑ 065 / POP 49,551

Ancud was once a rather wealthy place with gracious buildings, palafitos and a railway line. But the earthquake of 1960 decimated the town and now the sprawling city is built primarily of boxy concrete structures and is not particularly attractive, save the spectacular waterfront, which glistens throughout the better part of each summer day.

Ancud's coup is in its natural surroundings, and for those who want a taste of Chiloé but don't have time to dig as deep as Castro, its spectacular nearby coastline, excellent seafood, cozy hostels and proximity to Monumento Natural Islotes de Puñihuil make it an easy-to-digest base for exploring over a day or two.

⊙ Sights

TOP CHOICE Centro de Visitantes
Inmaculada Concepción   MUSEUM
(Errázuriz 227; www.iglesiasdechiloe.cl; ☺9:30am-7pm) Don't even think about visiting Chiloé's Unesco churches without first stopping in at this excellent museum housed in the former Convento Inmaculada Concepción de Ancud (1875). It's home to wooden scale models of each of Chiloé's Unseco and Patrimonio de la Humanidad churches, which show the workings of the intricate interior woodwork of each. The room itself is gorgeous, too, with rescued pieces from various churches now housed here as museum centerpieces while colorful stained glass contrasts brightly with the wooden interior of the original convent. You'll also find an interesting museum shop, artisan shop and cafe. No English signage or information is available yet.

Museo Regional Aurelio Bórquez
Canobra   MUSEUM
(Museo Chilote; Libertad 370; www.museoancud.cl; adult/child CH$600/300; ☺10am-7:30pm Jan-Feb, 10am-5:30pm Tue-Fri, 10am-2pm Sat & Sun

CHILOÉ'S TOP CHURCHES

Chiloé boasts more than 150 gorgeous wooden *iglesias* (churches) and *capillas* (chapels), one of the region's main attractions; 14 are Unesco World Heritage sites (and two more Patrimonio de la Humanidad). They are almost all built in a similar fashion with a single tower in the front, slanted side roofs, arched entrances and attractive wooden shingles. Some boast amazing exteriors, some gorgeous surroundings, but the truly triumphant moment comes when you step inside – the interiors are completely unorthodox if your comparison is European or North American cathedrals.

For tours to some of the island's less accessible churches, contact Chiloétnico in Castro (p297). The five best:

Achao The oldest of Chiloé's churches (1740)

Castro Neo-Gothic style with interior built entirely of native wood

Tenaún For its dramatic blue-starred exterior

Colo Notable entrance door between two arches

Aldachildo Dramatic interiors with original star-painted ceiling

Other churches of note include Caguach, Chelín, Chonchi, Dalcahue, Detif, Ichuac, Nercón, Quehui, Quetalco, Quinchao, San Juan, Rilán and Villipulli.

Mar-Dec) The excellent Museo Regional Aurelio Bórquez Canobra, casually referred to as Museo Chilote, looks more like a fortress than a museum. It has fantastic displays tracking the history of the island; a full-sized replica of the *Ancud,* which sailed the treacherous fjords of the Strait of Magellan to claim Chile's southernmost territories; and a massive blue whale skeleton.

FREE **Fuerte San Antonio** FORTRESS
(cnr Lord Cochrane & Baquedano; ☺8:30am-9pm Mon-Fri, 9am-8pm Sat & Sun) During the wars of independence, Fuerte San Antonio was Spain's last Chilean outpost. At the northwest corner of town, late-colonial cannon emplacements look down on the harbor from the early-19th-century remains of the fortress. There's not much left but a well-preserved wall, but the views and historical significance are impressive. There's a somewhat secluded beach, Playa Gruesa, behind the north wall.

☞ Tours

Many folks around town run minibus tours to see the penguins at Monumento Natural Islotes de Puñihuil for around CH$13,000.

 Austral Adventures GUIDED TOUR/OUTDOORS
(☎625-977; www.austral-adventures.com; Av Costanera 904) This is the go-to agency for English-speaking tours from Ancud, including extended nature-centric jaunts to see

the penguins and whales, kayaking on the bay and birdwatching – always with a fierce eco-slant. American owner Britt Lewis is impossibly nice and knowledgeable – if you've come to Chiloé for nature, this should be your first stop.

La Red de Agroturismo HOMESTAYS
(www.viajesrurales.cl) Chiloé's agrotourism association organizes excursions to farming and fishing communities, as well as private homes that offer meals and lodging in several small towns that aren't on most maps. Arrangements must be made through the individual family homes. Pick up a catalog at Sernatur (p290).

🛏 Sleeping

The Tower GUESTHOUSE $$
(☎625-977; www.austral-adventures.com; Playa Lechagua; r CH$35,000, cabaña CH$50,000; [P]☺) It's an unconventional choice, but for those with extra pesos and a penchant for solitude, and given the city's lack of a decent midrange or top-end choice, this is Ancud's best bet. Your hosts are Britt from Austral Adventures and his wife, Sandra – a gourmet Peruvian chef – who have built just three lodgings on their property on an isolated beach 6km south of Ancud. The namesake tower offers two stylish apartments with kitchenettes, but sea views are obstructed. The real coup is the new huge beachfront *cabaña* (cabin), where it's just you and the dolphins in the bay. This remote and rustic

Ancud

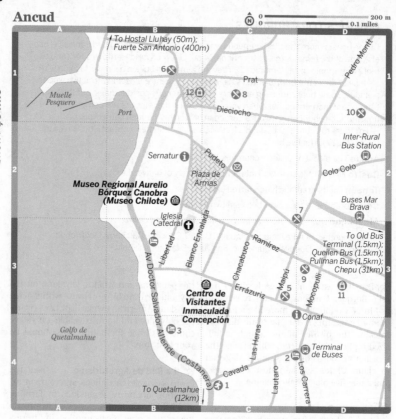

getaway with style and food to boot is only for certain souls. You know who you are.

Hostal Mundo Nuevo
HOSTEL **$**

(☎628-383; www.newworld.cl; Costanera 748; dm CH$11,000, s/d CH$29,000/39,000, s/d without bathroom CH$21,000/29,000; P☀@☎) This Swiss-owned hostel is just a quick walk down the hill and around the corner from the Cruz del Sur bus station and boasts postcard-perfect sunset views over the Bay of Ancud from a big, comfortable bench on its naturally lit front porch. Vistas from the rooms aren't elusive, either: the 12 privates and the six-bed dorm all frame the sea with stupendous results. New feather pillows and duvets insure a good night's rest and decent breakfasts, including homemade multigrain bread, beckon you from bed every morning.

13 Lunas Hostel
HOSTEL **$**

(☎622-106; www.13lunas.cl; Los Carrera 855; dm from CH$8500, s/d CH$15,000/25,000, r with-

out bathroom per person CH$11,000; P☀@☎) Brand new at the time of writing, this helpful hostel can't be missed, situated directly across from the Cruz del Sur bus terminal: its bright-green-and-yellow motif screams artsy Chiloé. Owner Claudio is young, enthusiastic and speaks English. The lovely hostel oozes coziness with bright hardwoods, beacons of natural light, hotel-level bathrooms and a wonderful terrace with views. There's even a late-night drinking den and BBQ. Avoid the less-atmospheric basement rooms if possible.

Hostal Lluhay
GUESTHOUSE **$**

(☎622-656; www.hostal-lluhay.cl; Lord Cochrane 458; r per person CH$12,000; P@☎) Lluhay wins over visitors with its very welcoming owners. Don't be surprised if they start feeding you delicious homemade *küchen* (sweet, German-style cakes), pouring you cocktails by the fireplace or knocking out a few bars

Ancud

on the piano. Bike and kayak rental is now available.

Camping Arena Gruesa CAMPGROUND $
(⏹623-428; www.arenagruesa.cl; Av Costanera Norte 290; campsites per person CH$4500, s/d CH$18,500/29,000; P@☎) Located atop a bluff on the north side of town, city campsites don't get much better views than this. The area is semigrassy and decently maintained with electricity, hot water and tiny *refugios* (rustic shelters) for rainy nights. It's also a minute's walk to the beach. It would be odd to stay here otherwise, but decent rooms do all offer sea views.

Hotel Galeón Azul HOTEL $$
(⏹622-567; www.hotelgaleonazul.cl; Libertad 751; s/d CH$39,800/48,800; P⊖@☎) This yellow beacon of a hotel with its blue trimmings is a relic, but its bright, sky-lit hallway and abundant windows take advantage of the natural light and expansive views over the harbor.

✖ Eating & Drinking

Tucked away next to the Mercado Municipal is the Mercado Gastronómico, a series of downhome market stalls doing *cazuela* (meat and vegetable stew), *chupe* (fish casserole) and set lunch menus for around CH$1500 to CH$2000.

Kuranton CHILEAN, SEAFOOD $
(Prat 94; curanto CH$6000; ⊙lunch & dinner) This institution has an extensive menu of excellent seafood, despite the dumbing down of things with scooped mashed, but it's really all about the *curanto* (see the boxed text, p290), Chiloé's gastronomic bombshell. This hearty stew of mussels, clams, chicken, pork and three types of potatoes is a meal fit for hibernation. Don't miss it.

Retro's Pub BURGERS, MEXICAN $
(Ramírez 317; mains CH$3000-7500; ⊙lunch & dinner Mon-Sat; ☎) Dressed up in new digs inside a cozy home, the best bar in Ancud now spreads itself among several rooms – you can *almost* hear the fireplace cracklin' above the classic rock. The menu is chockfull of Tex-Mex, as well as killer burgers the size of Kansas (fork required) on sourdough-reminiscent buns, stone-cooked pizza, sandwiches, pasta and the like – everything made from scratch, everything a great homesickness remedy. The one major downside is that smoking is allowed throughout, making it *really* retro.

El Embrujo de Chiloé CAFE $
(Maipú 650; sandwiches CH$1200-1900; ⊙lunch & dinner; ☎) This cozy, all-wood cafe is always packed with discerning locals, sipping decent cappuccinos or catching a quick sandwich on the cheap. There's a playful witchcraft undercurrent and it feels more *Chilote* than Botica.

La Botica de Café CAFE $
(Pudeto 277; desserts CH$800-2100; ⊙breakfast, lunch & dinner) A modern coffeehouse serving up the most elusive thing in Ancud: real gourmet espresso (hell, there's even *ristretto!*) and a ridiculously tempting selection of international desserts.

Unimarc SUPERMARKET
(Prat 364) This is the best market for people who are self-catering.

☆ Entertainment

Altrapasueños LIVE MUSIC
(Ramírez 469; ⊙closed Sun) This intimate music venue – the hardwoods make it cozy, the size makes it even more snug – hosts live bands most nights of the week, theater on occasion and at the very least a piano man otherwise. It's two blocks east of Mocopulli.

CURANTO: CHILOÉ'S CULINARY COUP

No words can quite prepare you for the first moment a piping hot bowl of *curanto* lands on the table in front of you, but 'What did I get myself into?' comes in mind. Rest assured, however, your slack-jaw will come in handy when it's time to shove all that food in. Chiloé's most traditional dish is of unknown origins, but historically its preparation harkens back to the earth ovens of Polynesian culinary ancestry. Traditionally *curanto* was made by heating up stones in a hole in the ground and waiting until they crackle, then directly piling on shellfish, pork and chicken, followed by nalca (a rhubarb-like plant) or pangue (a native plant of Chile) leaves and damp cloths before the whole shebang was covered in dirt and grass and left to simmer for nearly two hours. They still prepare it this traditional way, called *curanto al hoyo*, in a few places around the island, including **Restaurant Quetalmahue** (www.restaurantquetalmahueeng.es.tl; curanto CH$7000; ⊙lunch & dinner) in Quetalmahue, a small fishing village 12km from Ancud. If you can't make it there (*curanto* ready from 2pm to 4pm; a taxi runs a negotiable CH$10,000 to CH$15,000 round-trip from Ancud with waiting), the next best thing – minus the pit and dirt – is Kuranton (p289) in Ancud and El Chejo (p292) in Quemchi.

🛍 Shopping

Kelgwo CLOTHING
(www.kelwgo.cl; Ramírez 359; ⊙closed Sun) This boutique does naturally dyed, high-quality woven coats, dresses, scarfs, shawls and tops that put a gorgeous modern take on Chiloé's age-old weaving traditions.

Mercado Municipal MARKET
(cnr Dieciocho & Libertad) Has an abundance of craft markets.

ℹ Information

Banco de Chile (Libertad 621) ATM.
BancoEstado (Ramirez 229) ATM.
Conaf (🗷627-520; Errázuriz 317; ⊙9am-12:15pm & 2:15-5:30pm Mon & Wed, 9am-12:15pm & 2:15-4:30pm Fri) National park info.
Hospital de Ancud (Almirante Latorre 301; ⊙24hr) Located at the corner of Pedro Montt.
Post office (cnr Pudeto & Blanco Encalada; ⊙9am-6pm Mon-Fri, to 12:30pm Sat)
Sernatur (🗷622-665; Libertad 665; ⊙8:30am-7pm Mon-Fri, 9:30am-7pm Sat & Sun) On the Plaza de Armas, this is the only formal national tourist office on the island. It has very helpful staff, brochures, town maps and lists of accommodations.

ℹ Getting There & Away

Ancud has three bus terminals. **Cruz del Sur** (🗷622-265; www.busescruzdelsur.cl) owns and operates the main **Terminal de Buses** (cnr Los Carreras & Cavada), which offers the most departures to Chiloé's more southerly towns, with departures about every hour, and to cities on the Panamericana to the north (including three daily departures to Santiago). It's a five-minute walk from the waterfront and downtown. A taxi to/from the terminal to Av Costanera in downtown costs CH$1500. **Queilen Bus** (🗷621-140) operates out of the old bus terminal at Anibal Pinto 1700, 1.5km from the center.

Cruz del Sur buses go to Punta Arenas every Monday, Tuesday and Saturday at 8:30am in high season, with variable possibilities other times of year. Queilen Bus heads out Monday, Wednesday and Friday at 7:45am year-round. However, travelers going to most southerly regions beyond Chiloé and to Bariloche, Argentina, will do better to take buses from Puerto Montt.

Sample fares and times are as follows (prices can fluctuate with the quality of the bus/ classes):

DESTINATION	COST (CH$)	DURATION (HR)
Castro	2000	1½
Concepción	18,500-25,000	12
Dalcahue	1500	1½
Osorno	5500	4
Puerto Montt	4000	2
Puerto Varas	4300	2½
Punta Arenas	40,000-45,000	32
Quellón	4000	4
Santiago	26,000-37,000	17
Temuco	9500	8
Valdivia	7500	6

Chiloé's more rural destinations to the east, as well as afternoon buses to Chepu, the gateway to the northern end of Parque Nacional Chiloé, are serviced by buses that leave from the small inter-rural bus station on Colo Colo above the Bigger supermarket. The schedule is supposed to be posted near the bathroom (if not, ask at the administration office); simply buy tickets on the bus. **Buses Mar Brava** (☑622-312), departing from the 300 block of Aníbal Pinto, heads to rural destinations to the northwest, including Monumento Natural Islotes de Puñihuil at 6:45am.

Monumento Natural Islotes de Puñihuil

Three islands off the coast of Puñihuil, on the Pacific Ocean, are breeding grounds for Magellanic and the near-extinct Humboldt penguins, and a haven for blue whales. The entire area is now protected as a natural monument and a no-fishing zone has been instituted in the area (a huge step for environmental protection). The best time of year to go for the penguins is when they are breeding, from September to March (you might otherwise be out of luck). Several travel agencies in Ancud organize excursions to the site, or you can grab a Mar Brava bus from central Ancud on your own (except Sunday). No matter how you arrive, your transportation will drive right out onto a magnificent rugged beach. **Ecoturismo Puñihuil** (☑09-8317-4302; adult/child CH$6000/3000) runs 20 trips per day with four local fishing boats between 10:30am and 5:45pm to take tourists out for a closer (but quick) look at the penguins. All-weather gear is provided. Boats can fill up in high season – it's best to book ahead at Austral Adventures in Ancud (p287).

If the rickety rural buses leave too early for you (6:45am), and you're more than one person, an economizing option is **Taxi Tour** (☑09-9643-5201). Owner Luis Cárdenas is bang on time and will take up to four people out to the penguins and back for CH$20,000, not including the boat and tour. Always check ahead with a travel agency or two to make sure that the penguins are actually in the region.

After years of caution and research, **Ecomarine Puñihuil** (☑09-8174-7592; www.ecomarinepinihuil.cl; per person CH$95,000) is finally authorized to operate whale-watching tours in this area, where at least 140 blue whales have been tagged and tracked just a few miles off this coast. At the time of writing, the trip was wildly expensive, and only eight people per day could go, departing at 7am and returning at 11:30am (only one boat makes the trip so far). Prices should come down a bit as boats and competition are added. The best time of year is December to May and tours are weather dependent – it's good to give yourself a few windows of opportunity to go in case of cancellations. Austral Adventures also handles bookings in Ancud.

If you want to make a night of it, **Pinguinland Cabañas** (☑099-019-4273; www.casapunihuil.com; cabins for 4/6 people CH$49,000/65,000; P) offers fantastic cabins with large kitchens, good towels – even bathtubs! – all on top of a bluff with spectacular views of the islet. If you have binoculars or a telescope, you can observe the penguins and, if you're lucky, see whales with your naked eye from here as well.

The road to Puñihuil is being paved, so managing all of this with a sustainable slant is the area's most pressing challenge.

LOCO

Loco, a regional mollusk similar to abalone, is popular at the restaurants at Pingüinera Puñihuil – as well as throughout southern Chile – but it's best avoided as it's fished relentlessly and irresponsibly in most areas in blatant disregard for local fishing restrictions. In some Mapuche strongholds, such as the Osorno coast (p257), *loco* fishing is allowed as a local means of subsistance and is a more ethical choice in those areas, though you will still encounter illegal harvesters in your travels.

Chepu

Previously difficult to access and lacking infrastructure, Chepu, the northern sector of Parque Nacional Chiloé (p301), 38km southwest from Ancud, remains Chiloé's sanctuary of pristine beauty. Arriving here gives you a sense of discovery. You'll find stunning coastline, gorgeous rivers and 128 species of birds, totally untapped by mass tourism thus far, but changing sooner rather than later. In a breathtaking spot overlooking the confluence of three rivers and 140 sq km of sunken forest (a surreal phenomena created by the 1960 quake, which sunk the ground some 2m, allowing salt water to enter the area and kill the trees), you'll find **EcoLodge Chepu Adventures** (☑099-379-2481; www.chepu.cl; campsites for 2 CH$8000, dm per person CH$5000, cabañas CH$30,000; ℗@⊙). Infrared solar showers and wind-generated electricity power this spectacular, nearly self-sufficient eco-campground constructed from wood-alternative recycled fiber. Consummate hosts Fernando and Amory offer mystical self-guided kayak trips at dawn on the Río Puntra (CH$18,000), kayaks for rent during the day (per hour CH$4000) and three, carbon-neutral silent electric Kayachts for birdwatching – they also know their way around the kitchen and barbeque. For noncampers, there are also two Argentine-style *dormis* (mini sleeping rooms) and four upscale *cabañas*.

A step down in wow is **Los Senderos de Chepu** (☑099-260-2423; www.actiweb.es/senderoschepu; full board per person CH$15,000; ℗), with sea views in the distance and family-run hospitality; and **Hospedaje Perez-Diaz** (☑099-8523-6960; www.agroturismochepu.cl; full board with/without bathroom CH$18,000/14,000; ℗), part of the Agroturismo Network, and a Chepu veteran with fine artisanal cheeses made on premises.

Although the most untouched northern sector of Parque Nacional Chiloé is near here, there is no reasonable trail maintenance. You can access the park's borders by a 30-minute boat ride from Chepu and a five-hour coastal hike, but it stops short of the park. There's a small *refugio* for camping at the end of the trail, but getting keys from Conaf is difficult. From there, in theory, you can hike another three hours to Río Pescado, but you'll need a machete and it's really not worth it.

Buses Yañez has two buses on Monday, Wednesday and Friday from Ancud to Chepu. The 6:30am bus picks up folks at the Petrobras gas station on the corner of Prat and Goycolea (it drives by slowly, flag it down!), while the second, at 4pm, leaves from the inter-rural bus station. Buses return to Ancud at 7:45am and 5:45pm (CH$1500, one hour).

Bring supplies – Chepu is rural!

Quemchi

☑065 / POP 9102

On a clear summer day, the snowcapped mountains of southern Chile loom in the distance over misty Quemchi, topping off an already impressive view from the sea wall of this sleepy little town. Quemchi's waterfront is an ideal place to lose yourself for a day, strolling along the bay and passing the hours in one of Chiloé's best restaurants – El Chejo. It has the highest change in tides (7m) on the island, which makes for a surreal scene of beached fishing boats while the water's out.

Rural buses make the trip to Ancud (CH$1500) and Castro (CH$3000, 1½ hours to either destination) every 20 to 45 minutes throughout the day, less on Sunday. Check at the library and adjacent supermarket for schedules.

🍴 Sleeping & Eating

Hospedaje Costanera   GUESTHOUSE $
(☑691-230; Diego Bahamonde 141; per person with/without bathroom CH$10,000/7500, cabañas from CH$20,000; ℗⊙) It isn't the only game in town, but it boasts the best sea views (though some are obstructed by electrical wires) and prime location 50m from El Chejo. Ask for one of the front rooms to get a glimpse, but avoid No 3 as there is no room for luggage! The owner can be a bit gruff, but he's harmless.

TOP CHOICE El Chejo   CHILEAN $
(Diego Bahamonde 251; mains CH$3000-5000; ⊙lunch & dinner) A family-run treasure. El Chejo is no gourmet restaurant, it offers honest food prepared with love by a family that fawns over its patrons. There's no menu – you get what's good that day. That could mean starting with the excellent *empanada de centolla* (a fried pastry filled with king crab) followed by a choice of several locally caught fish, all washed down with a sampling of Chilote fruit liqueurs (try the *murtado,* a medicinal berry). Some of the intimacy has been lost due to expansion, and some personality moved to Chacao with the daughter, Jessica, but service is still brimming with Chilote personality. *Curanto al hoyo* (*curanto* prepared in the traditional way in an earth oven) is served every Sunday (CH$5000).

Isla Mechuque

☑065 / POP 500

The further you venture into Chiloé's smaller islands, the more it feels as if you've traveled back in time. Isla Mechuque is only 45 minutes by boat from Tenaún, but feels like it's caught in a bygone era. A part of the

WORTH A TRIP

TENAÚN & SAN JUAN

Tiny **Tenaún** is rural – 37km northeast along a gravel road from Dalcahue (p293) – but there are two very compelling reasons to visit. The magnificent **Iglesia de Nuestra Señora del Patrocinio** (1837), for which the town is named (Tenaún means 'three mounts'), is one of Chiloé's Unesco gems, meticulously restored down to the last shingle over the last two years. Its three magnificent blue towers, in stark contrast to almost any other church you will ever see, appear to be reflecting the cerulean blue sea that sits right across the street on orders from God himself. Its distinctive stars and trimmings add to the surreal architecture.

Hospedaje Mirella Montaña (☑09-9647-6750; mirellamontana@gmail.com; r with/without bathroom CH$12,000/10,000), located next to the church and part of the Agroturismo Network, makes it worth staying in Tenaún. The indomitable Mirella is an exceptional cook and is serious about making sure her guests enjoy the multicourse meals she prepares (CH$5000). She does *curanto al hoyo* or whatever fresh catch her son, Javier, grabs that day. Try to call ahead. On a clear day, you can see Volcán Corcovado across the Gulf of Ancud from her front porch.

Expresos Tenaún (☑09-9500-3305) runs four buses between Castro and Tenaún Monday to Saturday (CH$1500, 1½ hours), and two on Sunday, stopping in Dalcahue along the way. The schedule is posted on the window of Minimercado Ita on the main road through town.

About 3km before Tenaún coming from Dalcahue is the turn off for San Juan, a tiny village even more off the grid. After 6km, the road plunges into a serene bay surrounded by picturesque pastoral countryside, leading to **Iglesia de San Juan Bautista** (1887), another Unesco wooden house of worship sitting in the tiny grassed village square. **Hospedaje Elizabeth** (☑09-8866-6570; hospedaje.elizabeth-sanjuan@hotmail.com; r without bathroom CH$5000) is dead simple and cramped but offers both sea and church views. Hospedaje Kontiki rents kayaks.

Three buses a day (except Sunday) connect San Juan with Dalcahue and Castro (CH$1500).

Islas Chauques – considered Chiloé's most beautiful island chain – Mechuque is small but stunning. There are two museums, *tejuela* homes, a splendid viewpoint, a picturesque bridge, famous *curanto al hoyo* and *palafitos* – it's like a mini Chiloé offering all of the larger archipelago's attractions condensed down into an area that makes for an easy and memorable day trip.

If you want to spend the night, the new **Hospedaje Maria Humilde** (☑099-612-6233; r per person without bathroom CH$15,000) is a perfectly reasonable option.

The *Ultima Esperanza* II leaves for Isla Mechuque from Dalcahue's fishing dock Tuesday, Thursday and Friday at 1pm (CH$3500), with returns available Monday, Wednesday and Thursday departing Mechuque at 7:30am. Other departures may be available the rest of the week except Sunday, but a tour with Turismo Pehuén (p297) in Castro is the easiest way to explore Mechuque.

Dalcahue

☑065 / POP 8000

In Huilliche, Dalcahue means 'Dalca's Place' and is named after the boats (*dalcas*), constructed by Chiloé's first inhabitants. It's a feisty town facing the inner sea of the island and is known as the departure dock for Isla Quinchao, one of archipelagic Chile's more accessible and interesting islands.

⊙ Sights

Nuestra Señora de Los Dolores
CHURCH

Founded in 1849, this church is another one of the island's 14 Unesco World Heritage sites (take special note of the painting behind the entrance door; the juxtaposition of Jesus with Chiloé's mythological characters was used as Jesuit propaganda to convert the indigenous inhabitants).

MYTHOLOGICAL CREATURES OF CHILOÉ

For centuries Chiloé's distinctive mythology swirled through the foggy towns, blew from one island to the next and gave form to the culture of the Chilote people. Outside the commercial centers, these traditional beliefs are very much alive today. The beliefs, syncretic with the island's Catholicism, weave a story of the creation of the island, tales of destruction on the stormy seas and warnings about straying from the 'clean' way of life.

» **Brujos** (broo-hos) The center of Chiloé's mythology, brujos are warlocks with black-magic powers, bent on corrupting and harming normal Chilote folks. They are based in a secret location (most likely a cave) near Quicavi.

» **Cai-Cai Vilú** (kai-kai-vee-loo) The Serpent God of the Water who waged a battle against Ten-Ten Vilú (Serpent God of the Earth) for supremacy over the domain. Cai-Cai Vilú eventually lost but was successful in covering enough territory with water that Chiloé stayed separated from the mainland.

» **El Caleuche** (el-ka-le-oo-che) A glowing pirate ship piloted by singing, dancing brujos. Their melodious songs draw commercial vessels into El Caleuche's trap. It is capable of sailing into the wind and navigating under the water's surface.

» **Fiura** (fee-oo-ra) A short, forest-dwelling hag with a ravenous sexual appetite and breath that causes sciatica in humans and is enough to kill smaller animals.

» **Invunche** (een-voon-che) The grotesque guardian of the cave of the brujos. Invunche was born human, but the brujos disfigured him as he grew: turning his head 180 degrees, attaching one leg to his spine and sewing one of his arms under his skin. He eats human flesh and cat's milk, and is extremely dangerous.

» **Pincoya** (peen-koi-a) A naked woman of legendary beauty who personifies the fertility of the coasts of Chiloé and its richness of marine life. On the rocky shores she dances to her husband's music. The way that she faces determines the abundance of the sea harvest.

» **Ten-Ten Vilú** (ten-ten-vee-loo) Serpent God of the Earth (see Cai-Cai Vilú).

» **Trauco** (trow-ko) A repugnant, yet powerful, gnome who can kill with a look and fell trees with his stone hatchet. He is irresistible to young virgins, giving them impure erotic dreams and sometimes even a 'mysterious' child out of wedlock.

» **Viuda** (vee-oo-da) Meaning 'the widow,' Viuda is a tall, shadowy woman dressed in black with milk-white bare feet. She appears in solitary places and seduces lonely men. The next day she abandons them where she pleases.

» **La Voladora** (la-vo-la-do-ra) A witch messenger, who vomits out her intestines at night so that she is light enough to fly and deliver messages for the brujos. By the next morning, she swallows her intestines and reassumes human female form.

Crafts Fair MARKET
(9:30am-8pm Sun Jan-Feb, 10am-5:30pm Sun Mar-Dec) You'll find the island's most authentic arts and crafts here, dominated by sweaters, socks, and hats woven from oveja (wool) and dyed with natural pigments made from roots, leaves and iron-rich mud. All the surrounding islands participate.

Sleeping & Eating

Onde Nacho GUESTHOUSE $
(641-201; www.ondenachoturismo.blogspot.com; Freire 490; s/d/t CH$12,000/22,000/25,000, s without bathroom CH$9000; P*@?) A comfortable midrange pension (guesthouse) in a well-appointed home with a three-story, cabaña-like second house for lodgers. The homeowners are quite friendly people, it's a five-minute walk to the church and crafts fair, and beers are CH$800.

Hotel La Isla HOTEL $$
(641-241; Elías Navarro 420; s/d CH$25,410/31,460/41,140; P*@?) The best hotel in town is located inside a cute red-and-blue trimmed cabinlike building a few minutes' walk from the church. The bright rooms are spacious and offer soft beds and showers that are big enough for two people – a miracle in Chiloé.

TOP CHOICE Dalca
CHILEAN $

(mains CH$2300-8900; ☺lunch & dinner Mon-Sat, lunch Sun) Just when you thought you were sick of shellfish, the *caldillo de mariscos* (shellfish stew, CH$2300) at this highly regarded seafood restaurant, above the fishing dock, shows up and restores your faith.

La Cocinera Dalcalhue
CHILEAN $

(mains CH$2000-6000; ☺8am-9pm) Tucked behind the crafts market, this is the place to go for a true taste of local color. It's a collection of eight kitchenette stalls run by grandmotherly types dishing up *curanto*, pounding out *milcao* (potato bread) and dosing out Chilota sweets. Plop yourself down at the counter – locals prefer Doña Lula (No 8) and Delicias Celestiales (No 6) – but go with whatever looks best.

ℹ Information

There is a **tourism office** located on Oscar Freire across from O'Higgins.

ℹ Getting There & Away

There is no bus terminal in Dalcahue. Buses Dalcahue runs buses to Castro (CH$700, 30 minutes) and Mocopulli (CH$500), for airport access, every 15 minutes from a stop on Freire in front of Supermercado Otimarc between Henriquez and Eugenin. You can also catch buses at various points up and down the main street of Freire. **Cruz del Sur** (☎641-050; San Martín 102; ☺8:30am-1pm & 2:30-7pm) has two buses per day to Ancud (CH$1500) and Puerto Montt (CH$5000) leaving at 9:10am and 3:15pm; there's an extra 7pm departure on Sunday. Buses depart from the office on San Martín right next to the church. There are also three buses per day to Tenaún (Expresos Tenaún, CH$1500). Catch them along the main street.

Ferries for Isla Quinchao leave continuously between 6am and 1am. Pedestrians go free, but try and time it so you cross with an Achao-bound bus as you'll need to be on it once you get to the other side. Cars cost CH$3000 (round-trip). Boats also leave here for Isla Mechuque several days per week (see p292).

Isla Quinchao

☎065 / POP 9203

The elongated island of Quinchao, easily accessed via a short ferry crossing from Dalcahue, is a hilly patchwork of pasturelands punctuated by small villages. A good road runs the length of the island and carries you through the island's most popular destinations, Curaco de Vélez and Achao. On a clear day, you have spectacular views to Chiloé to the west and the snowcapped mountains of Northern Patagonia to the southeast.

CURACO DE VÉLEZ

An unexpected treasure lies in wait in the form of lovely Curaco de Vélez, the first town you come to along the main road from the ferry dock on Isla Quinchao. A superbly tranquil town, it's well worth spending an afternoon strolling the streets here, taking in the fascinating two- and three-story ornately shingled wooden homes and eight traditional water mills for which the town is known. On the town square, there's also an interesting church as well as the **Museo Curaco de Vélez** (Calle 21 s/n; ☺9am-12:30pm & 1:30-6pm; admission free), a well-done, less-is-more take on local culture and antiques. And don't miss the underground crypt of War of the Pacific hero Galvarino Riveros Cárdenas – he's buried right in the square!

In the summer, there is a modest crafts fair and **Rincón Gastronomíco** (☺9am-7pm) in a grassy area with picnic benches and sea views next to the plaza. There's *milcao*, cheese empanadas and *chochoca* made here in the traditional way: Chilote potatoes and flour wrapped thin around a long *luma* wood pole and cooked over an open fire for 40 minutes, then stuffed with pork cooked in its own fat (CH$800). Otherwise, head straight for **Ostras Los Troncos** (☺lunch & dinner), an open-air restaurant across the street from the beach. You'll find wooden trunk tables and chairs packed in like sardines with patrons slurping down buckets of fresh oysters (CH$500 each) awash in lemon and salt, chased with *cerveza* (beer). From the main square, follow Calle Francisco Bohle down and to the right.

The buses that run frequently between Achao and Dalcahue stop in Curaco.

ACHAO

When the early-morning fog rolls into the village of Achao, 22km southeast of Dalcahue, it can be an eerie sight, leaving no doubt you are in a remote Chilote seaside town. Though it lacks some of the indisputable charm and stillness of Curaco, Achao, too, is a worthwhile stop for its landmark church and outstanding architecture – not to mention stupendous views across to mainland Chile on a clear day. People from nearby islands come to Achao to sell their wares and produce, creating quite a buzz of activity along its small jetty and adjacent Feria Artisanal.

◉ Sights

Iglesia Santa María de Loreto CHURCH

Achao's 18th-century Jesuit church, Iglesia Santa María de Loreto, on the south side of the Plaza de Armas, is Chiloé's oldest (1740) and also a Unesco World Heritage site. Crowned by a 25m tower, it has alerce shingles and is held together by wooden pegs rather than nails. The church has been slowly restored, with new wood juxtaposing the old, but its restoration has remained faithful to the original design. Its hours are erratic – knock on the door and see if anyone around.

Museo de Achao MUSEUM

(cnr Delicias & Amunátegui; admission CH$300; ⊙10am-1pm & 2-6:30pm Dec-Feb) Museo de Achao highlights aspects of the Chono people of Achao and other indigenous groups in Chiloé. Wood products, weavings, stones and plants used for tinting materials are all elegantly presented with informative material (in Spanish).

Grupo Artesanal Llingua MARKET

(cnr Serrano & Ricardo Jara) The Grupo Artesanal Llingua, artisans from the nearby Isla Llingua, have a well-stocked market of their crafts including woven coffee cups, handbags and breadbaskets. It's only open on days when the ferry comes over from Isla Llingua on Monday, Wednesday and Friday.

⚎ Festivals & Events

Encuentro Folklórico de las Islas del Archipiélago MUSIC

Held in the first week of February, this festival attracts musical groups from throughout the archipelago.

⊨ Sleeping & Eating

In the busy summer season everything can get booked up and most places close down during the winter.

Hospedaje Sol y Lluvias GUESTHOUSE $

(⌸661-383; hospedaje.solylluvias1@gmail.com; Ricardo Jara 9; s without bathroom CH$10,000, r CH$24,000; P☕☎@) The top choice in town sits in a wonderful rust-orange house on the corner of Ricardo Jara and Serrano. It offers all the makings of a well-run home, right down to the substantial breakfasts.

Hostal Plaza GUESTHOUSE $

(⌸661-283; Amunátegui 20; s/d CH$8000/15,000, without bathroom CH$7000/12,000) A super-friendly family home that is right on the plaza above the post office. It's kind of like staying at grandma's house.

Mar y Velas CHILEAN, SEAFOOD $

(Serrano 2; mains CH$3900-7800; ⊙lunch & dinner) Overlooking the bustling jetty (and usually a thick blanket of intimidating fog) is this recommended seafood restaurant with an extensive menu and flirtatious servers. Try the house-style fish smothered in cheese, sausage and mussels. La Nave next door is also good.

ℹ Getting There & Away

The **bus terminal** (cnr Miraflores & Zañartu) is a block south of the church. Buses run daily to Dalcahue (CH$1200) and Castro (CH$1600) every 15 to 30 minutes. Queilen Bus also goes to Puerto Montt (CH$6000) Monday to Saturday at 7am and 1pm Sunday.

Castro

⌇065 / POP 34,537

Using some poetic license here, if there is one place to call Chiloé cosmopolitan, it's Castro, where all the idiosyncrasies and attractions of Chiloé are nicely packaged in the Big City. At times loud and boisterous like some working class towns in Mexico, the capital of the archipelago somehow retains its local Chilote character side by side with a dash of modern development (a new megamall raised all sorts of eyebrows) and comfortable tourism infrastructure. Just 85km south of Ancud, it is located in the dead center of the island, making it the main transportation hub and a perfect base for exploring attractions further afield, and sits on a bluff above its sheltered estuary lined with distinctive *palafito* houses.

The earthquake in 1960 destroyed the port, the railway, the town hall as well as some *palafitos*, but Castro rebounded and turned itself into an easily digestible destination that's easily navigable on foot. Perhaps the greatest single attraction is simply walking down the streets and around the central plaza, soaking up all of Castro's curious energy.

◉ Sights

Castro is the best place to see the *palafitos*. From the street, they resemble any other house in town, but the backsides jut over the water and, at high tide, serve as piers with boats tethered to the stilts. This truly singular architecture, now protected as a national historic monument, can be seen along six areas in town. The postcard view from land is the Puente Gamboa Mirador just west of centro.

TOP CHOICE Iglesia San Francisco de Castro   CHURCH

(San Martín) Italian Eduardo Provasoli chose a marriage of neo-Gothic and classical architecture in his design for the elaborate Iglesia San Francisco, finished in 1912 to replace an earlier church that burned down (which had replaced an even earlier church that had burned down). One of Chiloé's Unesco gems, the church once assaulted the vision with its exterior paint job – salmon with violet trim – but it's in bad need of a touch up these days, colored a more faded marigold with unripe eggplant trim. Inside, the varnished-wood interior is stunning. It is best to visit on a sunny day – if you are lucky enough – as the interior is more charming illuminated by the rows of stained-glass windows.

FREE Museo Regional de Castro   MUSEUM

(Esmeralda 255; ⊙9:30am-5pm Mon-Fri, 9:30am-6:30pm Sat, 10:30am-1pm Sun Jan-Feb, 9:30am-1pm & 3-6:30pm Mon-Fri, 9:30am-1pm Sun Mar-Dec) This museum, half a block from Plaza de Armas, houses a well-organized collection of Huilliche relics, musical instruments, traditional farm implements and Chilota wooden boat models, and exhibits on the evolution of Chiloé's towns. Its black-and-white photographs of the 1960 earthquake help you to understand the impact of the tragic event.

FREE MAM Chiloé   MUSEUM

(Museo de Arte Moderno de Chiloé; www.mam chiloe.cl; Parque Municipal; ⊙10am-6pm Jan-Feb, 11am-2pm Nov-Dec & Mar) Castro's spacious Museum of Modern Art features innovative works by contemporary Chilean artists, many of them Chilotes. It's a fair hike from town, but worth it if you're an art buff.

Tours

TOP CHOICE Chiloétnico   CULTURAL, ADVENTURE TOURS

(☑099-135-3448; www.chiloetnico.cl; Ernesto Riquelme 1228) This highly recommended tri-lingual (fluent English and German) agency is doing the right things in the right places.

Juan Pablo runs great mountain-biking and hiking trips to Parque Nacional Chiloé, Parque Tantauco and nearby islands; cultural trips out to some of Chiloé's more obscure Unesco churches on the less-trampled secondary islands where tourism is still a novelty; and rents camping gear and bikes. It is also the official office of Parque Tantauco in Castro.

Turismo Pehuén   WILDLIFE, GUIDED TOURS

(☑635-254; www.turismopehuen.cl; Latorre 238) Turismo Pehuén is a highly regarded agency that organizes multiday tours to nearby islands such as Mechuque and Parque Nacional Chiloé (both from CH$50,000); and is the official office for Naveira Austral in Castro.

✯✯ Festivals & Events

Festival Costumbrista   CULTURAL

Castro celebrates Festival Costumbrista in mid-February. It is a weeklong party with folk music and dance, as well as traditional foods.

🛏 Sleeping

Castro is well set up for budget and mid-range travelers, with a variety of affordable choices, mostly along San Martín and O'Higgins, their immediate side streets, and the eastern end of Sotomayor, which turns into the wide concrete staircase called Barros Arana with a high concentration of *hospedajes* (budget accommodations).

TOP CHOICE Palafito 1326   BOUTIQUE HOTEL $$

(☑530-053; www.palafito1326.cl; Ernesto Riquelme 1326; s/d from CH$41,000/47,500; P🐕@🛜) Castro's first truly great option, following a Chilote design aesthetic carved entirely from tepú and cypress woods, this *palofito* design hotel has 12 smallish rooms with high-style touches like wool throws from Dalcahue. The fjord-view rooms make you feel like you're sleeping over wetlands, with gaggles of birds and grassy junquillo plants appearing when the tide rolls out. A planned cafe on the extensive top-floor outdoor terrace should be a destination in itself.

Palafito Hostel   HOSTEL $$

(☑531-008; www.palafitohostel.com; Ernesto Riquelme 1210; dm CH$13,000, s/d from CH$21,000/32,000; @🛜) This upmarket hostel sitting on Palafitos Gamboa with spiritual views over the Fiordo de Castro revolutionized the entire neighborhood when it opened in 2008 and was the catalyst for

Castro

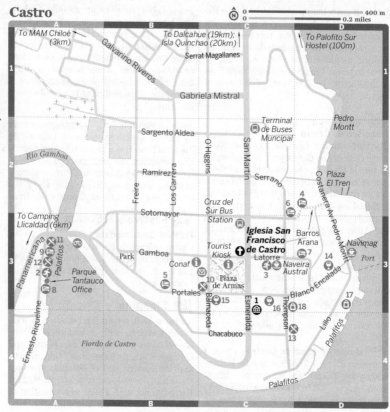

To MAM Chiloé (3km)
To Dalcahue (19km); Isla Quinchao (20km)
To Palofito Sur Hostel (100m)
Galvarino Riveros
Serrat Magallanes
Gabriela Mistral
Pedro Montt
Sargento Aldea
Terminal de Buses Muncipal
Río Gamboa
Ramírerza
O'Higgins
San Martín
Serrano
Plaza El Tren
Costanera Av Pedro Montt
To Camping Llicaldad (6km)
Freire
Los Carrera
Sotomayor
Cruz del Sur Bus Station
Iglesia San Francisco de Castro
Barros Arana
Navimag
Port
Panamericana
Palafitos
Park
Gamboa
Tourist Kiosk
Latorre
Naveira Austral
Parque Tantauco Office
Conaf
Plaza de Armas
Ernesto Riquelme
Portales
Balmaceda
Esmeralda
Thompson
Blanco Encalada
Lillo
Palafitos
Chacabuco
Fiordo de Castro
Palafitos

turning Riquelme into Castro's coolest street. You pay more for a dorm here, but the quality outweighs the difference, with great breakfasts, dreamy views and a cabin-cool feel throughout.

Palafito Sur Hostel
HOSTEL $

(536-472; www.palafitosur.com; dm CH$12,000, r CH$25,000; P@) This design-forward hostel steeped in the architectural details of an original *palafito* home among Castro's northern *palofitos* is a short walk along the *costanera* (lakeshore road) from the port. If they manage to cultivate the vibe, it is Castro's best shot at a traditional hostel. Restored with 120-year-old rescued alerce shingles and utilizing a funky color scheme from Castro's fisherman's association, it sits over the water and offers two- and four-bed dorms and a couple of overpriced private rooms. At high tide, you can take its kayaks right from the terrace.

Hostal Cordillera
GUESTHOUSE $

(532-247; www.hostalcordillera.cl; cnr Serrano & Sotomayor; r per person without bathroom CH$8000, d CH$22,000; P@) The firecracker owner, who musters a bit of English when pressed, smothers you with motherly love at this traveler's hub. You'll get some sea views, large bathrooms, comfy beds and cable TV. Some travelers have complained it's chilly in winter, but central heating is on its way. There's a pleasant little deck out back where you can take in the water views over a few drinks.

Hospedaje Mirador
GUESTHOUSE $

(633-795; www.hostalelmiradorcastro.cl, in Spanish; Barros Arana 127; r per person with/without bathroom CH$26,000/CH$10,000; P@) One of the better Barros Arana choices, Mirador has some seaside views, fantastic bathrooms (by Chiloé standards), hearty breakfasts, a welcoming atmosphere and off-site parking.

Castro

Hostal Central   GUESTHOUSE $

(📞637-026; www.hostalcentraldecastro.com; Los Carrera 316; r per person with/without bathroom CH$15,000 /CH$10,000; P😊@📶) Single travelers could do no better than scoring a bright 3rd-floor room here, but otherwise, what was once one of the nicest of the traditional budget options in town has fallen a bit from grace.

Camping Llicaldad   CAMPING $

(📞635-080; Panamericana Ruta 5 Km6; campsites CH$15,000) The best campground in relation to distance from the city. Sites here have beautiful views overlooking the Fiordo de Castro.

✕ Eating

[TOP CHOICE] **Hostal Omera Comedor**   CHILEAN $

(www.hostalomera.tk; Latorre 120; menu CH$2000; 🕐lunch & dinner Mon-Sat; 📶) You can't eat this well in this cool kind of atmosphere for this price anywhere. How it can be done without bleeding money is an extraordinary question, but this art-fueled lunch hot spot offers three exceptional home-cooked choices per day, including an appetizer, juice and organic fig or barley coffee, for a shocking CH$2000. The entirety of Castro – all races, religions, creeds and classes – converge amid tagged walls and seriously good food. The secret is out.

Mar y Canela   CHILEAN $

(Ernesto Riquelme 1212; www.marycanela.cl; mains CH$3600-8900; 🕐lunch & dinner; 📶) Bless this artsy *palafito* cafe's heart – it is trying hard, sometimes too hard (pesto-tongue or melted goat sandwiches?); and service can be spotty and aloof (maybe it's the Facebooking in the open kitchen?), but for Chiloé, it has raised the bar on creative cuisine. You'll find such unheard-of delicacies as hazelnut-crusted brie and quinoa burgers as well as a small selection of fresh seafood preparations, sandwiches and burgers sized for three, and an intimate atmosphere that punches above Castro's weight class.

Sacho   CHILEAN, SEAFOOD $$

(Thompson 213; mains CH$2500-8500; 🕐lunch & dinner Mon-Sat, lunch Sun) If you lived in Castro and your parents came for a visit, you'd probably take them to this longstanding seafood staple with views, one of Chiloé's best. The atmosphere is semirefined (whimsical tablecloths, linen napkins) and the specialty is *pulmay,* a *curanto*-like shellfish dish featuring clams and mussels, but with a little less meat and potatoes.

Café del Puente   CAFE, BREAKFAST $

(Ruquelme 1180b; mains CH$1200-4200; 🕐breakfast, lunch & dinner; 📶) Breakfast addicts rejoice! This atmospheric baby-blue cafe-teahouse over the water on revitalized Riquelme street does everything you're missing: eggs, bacon, French toast, muesli, whole wheat bread... and does it well.

Brújula del Cuerpo   DINER $

(O'Higgins 308; mains CH$1310-5990; 🕐breakfast, lunch & dinner; 📶) A godsend for those tired of seafood, this Chilota-style diner does pizza, fajitas, American-style breakfast and other *comida rapida* (fast food).

🍷 Drinking

Patrimonial   BAR

(Balmaceda 291; cocktails CH$2000-4000) This intimate spot is the bohemian bar of choice,

PENINSULA DE RILÁN

Previously untapped by tourism, this 100-sq-km peninsula separated from Castro by the Dalcahue Channel is suddenly a hotbed of discerning luxury getaways with attention to design. The stunning **Hotel Parque Quilquico** (☑065-971-000; www.hotelparque quilquico.cl; s/d CH$134,000/190,000, 2-bedroom palafitos CH$380,000; Ⓟ☺@☏☂), opened in 2011, is one of Chiloé's most eye-catching structures. Local architect Eduardo Roja rescued loads of cypress wood and *tejuela* shingles from old Chilote homes to form the circular hotel, designed to take in the views from all angles. If you can't sleep here, come for a meal – the chef comes from Años Luz in Castro, formally the best restaurant in Chiloé before it was swallowed up by big-business drug stores and laundromats.

Nearby, newer and even more remote is **La Refugia** (☑065-772 080; www.refugia.cl; Bahía Pullao, San José; full board s/d US$742/1060; Ⓟ☺@☏), modeled after Chile's successful Explora franchise (in fact, the head guide was poached from there), and a dramatic upscale shelter on the edge of Chiloé's most important wetlands. The building, a striking, environmentally unobtrusive marriage of native woods (certified alerce wood, the sacred wood of the Mapuche; *Ulmo*, Chilean honey wood; and *mamilo*) with unfinished concrete, frames the stunning countryside with 3m-high windows throughout the rooms and common area. A long hallway that seemingly narrows to a trapezoidal window – an architectural illusion only adding to this building's wonder, leads to the 12 rooms. Rates include meals, drinks and all excursions, which include trekking, horseback riding, sailing and kayaking, with an eye and ear for tapping into some of Chiloé's less famous attributes.

warmed by a wood-burning stove and home to just a few tables. It's on the 2nd floor overlooking the plaza and is a good spot to try Chiloé's own craftbrew, Vertus (porter and golden ale) or excellent make-your-own *micheladas* (Mexican beer cocktails).

Kaweshkar Lounge   LOUNGE
(www.kaweshkarlounge.cl; Blanco Encalada 31; cocktails CH$2000-5000) The retro, haphazard design of this diver bar recalls Berlin or New York's East Village. The cocktails are well mixed, but when we came through, its chalkboard read, 'We're not in Lonely Planet but we are great!', despite the fact it has been listed in the guide since 2009.

Ristretto Café   CAFE, BAR $
(Blanco 264; snacks CH$400-1000; ☺closed Sun; ☏) It's a shame the best cafe in Chiloé allows smoking, but in the land of Nescafé, you just have to suck it up. There is an extensive coffee, tea and tapas menu and over 50 international beers that insure it turns into a bar by night.

🛍 Shopping

Feria Artesanal   MARKET
Castro's waterfront Feria Artesanal is by far the island's biggest, but be wary here – much of the merchandise is secretly imported from China, India, Peru and Ecuador. You'll find venders hawking a fine selection of

woolen ponchos and sweaters, caps, gloves, basketry and liquors.

Origenes   HANDICRAFTS
(Thompson 295) This shop stocks beautiful, high-quality ceramics and handicrafts.

Origin Sur   CLOTHING
(Ernesto Riquelme 1212) Located inside the Mar y Canela restaurant, Origin Sur offers beautifully made woolens.

❶ Information

ATMs can be found at the numerous banks on or around the Plaza de Armas.

Conaf (☑547-706; Gamboa 424; ☺8:45am-1pm & 2-5:45pm Mon-Fri) The official Chilean parks department has a limited amount of information in Spanish on Parque Nacional Chiloé.

Hospital de Castro (www.hospitalcastro.gov. cl; Freire 852)

Parque Tantauco office (☑099-135-3448; Ernesto Riquelme 1228) The park is represented in Castro by Chiloétnico.

Police (☑765-366; Portales 457)

Post office (O'Higgins 388; ☺9am-1:30pm & 3-6pm Mon-Fri, 10am-12:30pm Sat) On the west side of Plaza de Armas.

Tourist kiosk (☑547-706; Plaza de Armas) A large kiosk stocking some helpful brochures and maps.

❶ Getting There & Around

Air

Castro's brand new Aeródromo Mocopulli, located 20km north of town, should have opened by the time you read this and will finally connect Chiloé with the rest of the country via commercial flights. Both **Lan** (☑632-866; O'Higgins 412) and **Sky** (☑534-643; Blanco 388) were planning daily flights from Santiago at the time of writing.

Bus

Centrally located Castro is the major hub for bus traffic on Chiloé. There are two main bus terminals. The rural station, **Terminal de Buses Municipal** (San Martín), has the most services to smaller destinations around the island and some long-distance services. Buses to Mocopulli (CH$500), Dalcahue (CH$700), Chonchi (CH$700), Isla Quinchao (CH$1400 to CH$1600) and Tenaún (CH$1500) all leave from here as well as Quemchi. **Queilen Bus** (☑632-173; www.queilenbus.cl) and an office representing Cruz del Sur, Transchiloé, Turibús and others also operates out of here to most destinations of importance, including Punta Arenas and Bariloche. **Buses Ojeda** (☑573-488) and **Union Express** (☑096-668-3531) offer the most departures from here for Cucao and Parque Nacional Chiloé on the west coast, 17 times per day between them (CH$1500). Sit on the right side for most outstanding views of Lago Cucao.

The second terminal, the main depot of **Cruz del Sur** (☑635-152; www.pullmansur.cl; San Martín 486), also houses Transchiloé and Turibús, and focuses on transportation to the main Chilote cities, Quellón and Ancud, and long-distance services.

Sample fares and times are as follows (prices may fluctuate with the quality of the bus/classes):

DESTINATION	COST (CH$)	DURATION (HR)
Ancud	2000	1½
Concepción	27,000	14
Puerto Montt	5500	4
Quellón	2000	½
Quemchi	1300	1½
Santiago	27,000-38,000	16
Temuco	10,500	10
Valdivia	8500	7½
Punta Arenas	45,000	36

Boat

Navimag Cruceros (☑532-434; www.navimagcruceros.cl; Terminal Portuario de Castro, Av Pedro Montt s/n) sails the cruiseship *Mare Australis* to Laguna San Rafael from Castro several times a month from October to March. High-season (January and February) round-trip prices from Castro range from CH$1,662,605 for an AAA single in high season to CH$1,360,313 for B berth.

Summer ferries to/from Chaitén are operated by **Naviera Austral** (☑635-254; www.navieraustral.cl; Latorre 238), which departs Saturday at midnight in January and February. Fares range from CH$16,000 (seat) to CH$25,700 (berth with window). Vehicles cost CH$82,000.

Parque Nacional Chiloé

Running back from the pounding Pacific coastline, and over extensive stands of native evergreen forest, the 430-sq-km **Parque Nacional Chiloé** (adult/child CH$1500/free) is located only 30km west of Chonchi and 54km west of Castro. The park teems with Chilote wildlife, ranging from 110 different types of bird, to foxes and the reclusive pudú (the world's smallest deer), which inhabits the shadowy forests of the contorted tepú tree. Within the park and situated along the eastern perimeter are a number of Huilliche indigenous communities, some of which are involved with the management of campsites within the park.

The park comprises three sections. The northern sector is called **Chepu** (p291) and includes Isla Metalqui (and its sea-lion colony) and is not truly accessible without a machete and a pioneering spirit. In addition, Metalqui is highly restricted because of ecological concerns and can only be visited with special arrangements from the parks service. The middle sector, **Abtao**, is restricted by Conaf and accessible only by an 18km hike from the Pichihué property. The more accessible southern sector, **Chanquín**, contains the majority of the eight official hikes in the park, ranging from quick jaunts to 25km slogs.

Visitors are at the mercy of Pacific storms, so expect lots of rain. The mean annual rainfall at Cucao is 2200mm, and anyone planning more than an hour-long walk should have water-resistant footwear, woolen socks and a decent rain jacket. Insect repellent is not a bad idea, either. There is a **Conaf visitor center** (☉9am-7:30pm Jan-Feb, to 6pm Mar-Dec) 1km past the bridge from Cucao. The center covers flora and fauna extensively and it also houses a small museum.

Cucao is your last chance to pick up supplies, although you will find better prices and wider selections in Chonchi or Castro.

◉ Sights & Activities

The raw beauty of this national park is best appreciated on foot, and there are several hikes that can easily hold your attention for a day or two. The **Sendero Interpretivo El Tepual**, a short 1km nature trail built with tree trunks, branches and short footbridges, loops through dense, gloomy forest. The **Sendero Dunas de Cucao** starts from the visitor center and heads 2km through a remnant of coastal forest to a series of dunes behind a long, white sandy beach.

Day hikers can follow the coast north on a 3km trail to **Lago Huelde** or a shorter 1.5km trek to **Playa Cucao**, a roaring Pacific beach. The most popular route is the **Sendero Chanquín-Cole Cole**, a 25km hike (about five hours one way) located along the coast, past Lago Huelde to Río Cole Cole. Lots of people set out to make this hike and back in one day, but nobody usually makes it further than the indigenous settlement at Huentemó, where there are basic camping facilities as well as a *refugio* for CH$4000 per person (equipped with a kitchen) and a local *hospedaje*. The hike extends another 8km north to **Río Anay**, passing through a stand of arrayán to arrive at another rustic *refugio* in reasonable shape. Keep in mind, you take the gravel highway about 6km past the visitors center before it dead ends on the beach (near the end of this highway, you'll find your last chance for food: El Arco de Noé Café).

Several of the camping sites within the park have been shut down, but you are allowed to camp anywhere you want. In Cole Cole, camping is CH$1000 per person and there's also a basic *refugio* with a kitchen and bathroom for CH$2000 per person.

⌂ Sleeping & Eating

Most accommodations and restaurants are in Sector Chanquín, just past the bridge from Cucao.

⎡TOP⎤
⎣CHOICE⎦ Parador Darwin   GUESTHOUSE $
(☑099-799-9923; Sector Chanquín; s/d CH$20,000 /25,000; ⊗closed Apr-Oct; ▣⊜@⧉) Full of character and charm, this colorful German-owned wooden house surrounded by massive nalca plants is a fantastic midrange choice. But even if you don't give a toss

about the park, come for the restaurant (mains CH$5500 to CH$7000), the best option within miles and miles. It immediately captivates with the sights (fresh loaves of bread everywhere) and smells of something delicious. It features *nueva Chilota* cuisine, which includes a hot smoked salmon you won't soon forget, Hungarian goulash, great pizzas, and chocolate-and-seaweed-flavored German *küchen*. The almost frozen, shot-sized pisco sours are lethally good.

Palafito Cucao Hostel   HOTEL
(☑971-164; www.hostelpalafitosur.cl; Sector Chanquín; s/d CH$36,000/45,000; ⊗closed Apr-Oct; ▣⊜@⧉) This sister hotel of Palafito 1326 and Palafito Hostel in Castro opened in late 2011, bringing along with it a sense of comfort previously unseen in Cucao. It's a beautiful hotel on the Lago Cucao, with stylish rooms, a cozy common area and kitchen, and a lovely wraparound terrace. But whereas in Castro, it's a welcomed change of pace, here it feels a tad too much like forced trendiness.

El Fógon de Cucao   LODGE $$
(☑099-946-5685; Sector Chanquín; campsites per person CH$4000, s/d without bathroom from CH$10,000/20,000; ▣) Another good choice with a variety of rooms on offer. The *hospedaje* is an upscale rustic gem and the campsites sit on the shore of Lago Cucao. The restaurant (open for lunch and dinner; meals CH$6000) across the street does a set fish menu over lake views. It can also arrange excursions on horseback to Lago Huelde (CH$20,000, two hours) or a full day to Río Cole Cole (CH$45,000), and kayaks on Lago Cucao (CH$2500 per hour).

Camping del Parque   CAMPGROUND $
(☑971-027; www.parquechiloe.cl; campsites per person CH$4000, cabins up to 6 people CH$48,000) This Conaf-maintained camping and cabin complex lies about 200m beyond the visitors center and into the park. The sites have privacy, running water, firewood, hot showers and toilets. The cabins are spacious and fully equipped. There is a small cafe (open for breakfast, lunch and dinner, closed in June) on the site that handles reception.

Hospedaje El Paraíso   GUESTHOUSE $
(☑099-296-5465; Laura Vera, Cucao; campsites per person CH$3000, r without bathroom CH$9000; ▣⊜) This is the basic budget option in Cucao, well run by a doting woman,

inside a faded pink house a few hundred meters before the bridge. It offers a fantastic river view.

Hospedaje Chucao GUESTHOUSE $
(☎099-787-7319; Huentemó; r per person without bathroom CH$6000) Simple *hospedaje* for crashing at Huentemó.

Las Terrazes de Cucao CHILEAN $
(Sector Chanquín; mains CH$400-1300; ⊗breakfast, lunch & dinner) A good choice for basic local fare done cheaply across from park entrance. Breakfast here is a must if you are hitting the park for a full day, but it wasn't opening until 9am when we came through.

❶ Getting There & Away

Cucao is 54km from Castro and 34km west of Chonchi via a bumpy gravel road, passable in all but the most inclement weather. There is regular bus transportation between Castro and Cucao. Schedules vary, but there are usually numerous buses daily (CH$1500); see p301 for details of the bus companies.

Quellón

While the southern terminus for one of the world's great highways (the Panamericana Hwy, also known as Hwy 5) and a salmon epicenter, Quellón is for the most part an unsophisticated town, one you're likely only to see coming or going from the ferry to Chaitén.

If you come in on the ferry and have had enough traveling for a day, there are some excellent eats, but an increase in street crime due to the salmon fallout (see the boxed text, p275), and a generally insipid shadiness about the place, makes Quellón a get in, get out town.

Don't wander west of the Naveira Austral office on the *costanera* or around the bus station, especially at night.

🛏 Sleeping

Hotel El Chico Leo HOTEL $$
(☎681-567; ligorina@hotmail.com; Costanera Pedro Montt 325; r per person without bathroom CH$8000, d CH$22,000; ☏⊜@☎) Known for its clean, bright rooms, attentive staff and quality beds, El Chico Leo is a cramped but comfortable choice, though the low-ceilinged bathrooms pose a serious challenge for taller travelers. The justifiably popular restaurant (mains CH$2600 to CH$6500) is known for its seafood, especially the ginormous *curantos*.

Hotel Playa HOTEL $
(☎681-278; Costanera Pedro Montt 427; r per person without bathroom CH$6000, with breakfast CH$7500; ☏☎) The logical budget choice right across the street from the ferry dock to Chaitén. The simple rooms here are actually more spacious than nearly all of the pricier options.

🍴 Eating

On and around the main drag of Ladrilleros, you'll find options. Try Isla Sandwich at Ladrilleros 190 for excellent gourmet sandwiches and El Madero at Freire 430 for innovative contemporary fare.

Taberna Nos SPANISH $
(O'Higgins 150; tapas CH$1500-3000; ⊗dinner-late Mon-Sat) If you spend one night in Quellón, it should be at this local secret run by a Spanish

---

WORTH A TRIP

THE PRESIDENT'S PARK

Among the world's 25 biodiversity hot spots, **Parque Tantauco** (☎065-680-066; www.parquetantauco.cl; Av La Paz 68, Quellón) – created and owned by Chilean business magnate and president, Sebastián Piñera, and run by his foundation (Fundación Cultura y Sociedad) – is a private nature reserve encompassing 1180 sq km west of Quellón, Chiloe. The park is home to native otters, Darwin foxes and pudús (small deer, indigenous to Chile), as well as both the world's largest mammal (blue whales) and its smallest marsupial (*monito del monte* or 'little mountain monkey'), and is a very worthwhile off-the-beaten-track find for hiking, camping and watching wildlife. You won't even find it on most maps, so spending time here usually means you are isolated with nature, sharing air with way more Valdivian temperate rainforest than the North Face set.

Tantauco is the only place outside of Torres del Paine that you traverse a park by hut-to-hut hiking over a multiday trek. For more information, check out the park website or stop in Chiloétnico's offices in Castro (p297) or the park's office in Quellón.

music aficionado. Inside a residential black house, there are excellent tapas and drinks in a bar that's way too cool for its address.

❶ Getting There & Away

Buses to Castro (CH$1200, two hours) are frequent with Cruz del Sur and Transchiloé, which leave from the **bus terminal** (cnr Pedro Aguirre Cerda & Miramar). The last bus leaves for Castro at 7:30pm. There are also services to Puerto Montt (CH$6200) and Temuco (CH$11,000).

Naviera Austral (☑682-506; www.navier austral.cl; Pedro Montt 457) sails the *Don Baldo* to Chaitén on Thursday at midnight throughout the year. Passengers cost CH$16,000 (seat) to CH$25,700 (berth with window) and vehicles CH$82,000. It also sails to Puerto Chacabuco on Monday at 6pm throughout the year. Prices are considerably higher (CH$38,450 for a chair, CH$45,000 for a berth with a window and CH$137,920 for a vehicle). The trip takes 24 hours.

Northern Patagonia

Includes »

Best Places to Eat

» Mamma Gaucha (p323)

» Cocinerías Costumbristas (p313)

» Martín Pescador (p315)

» Carnes Queulat (p324)

» Mi Casita de Té (p318)

Best Places to Stay

» Lodge at Valle Chacabuco (p333)

» Un Destino No Turistico (p331)

» Fundo Los Leones (318)

» Terra Luna (p331)

» Alto Melimoyu B&B (p317)

Why Go?

For a century, Northern Patagonia has been the most rugged and remote part of continental Chile, the place where scant pioneers quietly set forth a Wild West existence. While life here may be tough for its residents, it doesn't lack for scenery. Exuberant rainforest, scrubby steppe and unclimbed peaks crowd the horizon, but the essence of this place is water, from the clear cascading rivers to the turquoise lakes, massive glaciers and labyrinthine fjords. Southbound visitors often bypass Northern Patagonia on a sprint to Torres del Paine, but its backcountry treasures are pay dirt to the adventurous traveler. With the construction of dams and high-tension towers imminent, many feel that the time to see this virgin region is now.

With a few ferry interruptions, the gravel Carretera Austral rumbles from Puerto Montt to Villa O'Higgins, some 1200km south. This chapter runs north to south, from Hornopirén to Villa O'Higgins.

When to Go
Coyhaique

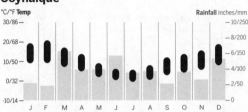

Nov–Mar Warmest months with best bus connections on the Carretera Austral.	**Feb** Festival Costumbrista celebrates pioneer culture with parties in most small towns.	**Jul–Aug** Blue-sky days around Coyhaique, with nearby skiing and snowshoeing.

Northern Patagonia Highlights

1 Explore the misty fjords and trek the temperate rainforests of **Parque Pumalín** (p310)

2 Pedal or drive past farms, rushing rivers and hanging glaciers while tracing the length of the mythic **Carretera Austral** (p309)

3 Giddy-up into **pioneer Patagonia** (p316) on remote Andean trails

4 Face a whirl of white water, rafting the world-class rapids of **Río Futaleufú** (p314)

5 Lose track of time dallying in cool **Caleta Tortel** (p335), a seaside village set on boardwalks

6 Scout for cave paintings and spy on flamingos in the little-known **Reserva Nacional Jeinemeni** (p330)

7 Get up close and personal with **Glaciar San Rafael** (p326) by joining a tour from nearby Puerto Río Tranquilo

46°S

47°S

48°S

RP 18

RN 40

RN 26

Río Mayo

RP 55

RN 26

Paso Alto Coyhaique

Villa Mañihuales

Reserva Nacional Coyhaique

Dos Lagunas

Paso Huemules (502m)

El Portezuelo

Villa Cerro Castillo

Balmaceda Cerro Castillo (2700m)

RP 43

ARGENTINA

Perito Moreno

Cueva de las Manos

Reserva Nacional Río Simpson

Puerto Aisén

COYHAIQUE

Puerto Chacabuco

Fiordo Aisén

Volcán Hudson (2600m)

Reserva Nacional Cerro Castillo

Puerto Ingeniero Ibáñez

Lago Buenos Aires

Los Antiguos

Chile Chico

Mallín Grande

Puerto Murta

Puerto Río Tranquilo

Lago General Carrera

Reserva Nacional Jeinemeni **6**

Archipiélago de los Chonos

Bahía Exploradores

Monte San Valentín (4058m)

Estuario San Francisco

7

Cruce El Maitén

Puerto Bertrand

Valle Chacabuco (Parque Nacional Patagonia)

Puerto Guadal

Paso Roballos (647m)

RP 39

Cordillera de los Andes

Península de Taitao

Campo de Hielo

Laguna San Rafael

Parque Nacional Laguna San Rafael

Campo de Hielo Norte **7**

Glaciar San Rafael

Cochrane

Reserva Nacional Tamango

Lago Cochrane

RP 37

72°W

Lago Strobel

Bajo Caracoles

Santa Cruz

RP 12

70°W

100 km
60 miles

N

Península Tres Montes

Golfo de Penas

Caleta Tortel **5**

El Vagabundo

Puerto Yungay

Región XI

Villa O'Higgins

Campo de Hielo Sur

Lago O'Higgins

Candelario Mansilla

Parque Nacional Bernardo O'Higgins

Reserva Nacional Katalalixar

Ferry to Puerto Natales

74°W

76°W

History

Long isolated and still remote, Northern Patagonia is the youngest area of the Chilean nation and the last to integrate. Chile only started promoting colonization in the early 20th century and many of the towns are barely 50 years old.

For thousands of years, the Chonos and Alacalufes people inhabited the intricate canals and islands, while Tehuelches lived on the mainland steppes. Aisén's rugged geography deterred European settlement, though fortune seekers believed the legendary 'City of the Caesars' to be here. Many expeditions (including one which brought Charles Darwin here) visited the area in the late 18th and early 19th centuries, some in search of a protected passage to the Atlantic Ocean.

In the early 1900s the government granted nearly 10,000 sq km in and around Coyhaique to the Valparaíso-based Sociedad Industrial Aisén as a long-term lease for exploitation of livestock and lumber. The company dominated the regional economy, and colonists trickled into the region to claim remote lands for farming. Encouraged by a Chilean law that rewarded clearance with land titles, the Sociedad and colonists burned nearly 30,000 sq km of forest and destroyed much of Aisén's native southern beech in a series of fires that raged for nearly a decade in the 1940s.

The region is sparsely populated, most notably south of Coyhaique, an area that was devastated by the 1991 eruption of Volcán Hudson. As with Volcán Chaitén's 2008 eruptions, it dumped tons of ash over thousands of square kilometers in both Chile and Argentina, ruining cropland and killing livestock by burying pasture grasses.

Salmon farming is a major industry and Patagonia's cold waters provide optimal farming conditions. The industry continues its exponential growth, creeping south since the practice has contaminated some Lakes District waters past sustainability, with waste from farms causing serious ecological disruption. The lobby for salmon farming is still quite strong and effective, given that there are few other jobs in the region.

A number of controversial hydroelectric projects (see p332) and other industrial plans define the continual push and pull between development and conservation in this region.

National Parks, Reserves & Private Parks

From Valdivia rainforest to glaciers, Northern Patagonia offers diverse parks and few crowds. For verdant green, don't miss Parque Pumalín (p310) or Parque Nacional Queulat (p320), with its signature hanging glacier. A number of reserves around Coyhaique provide adventure near city comforts. For multiday treks, Reserva Nacional Cerro Castillo (p327) offers extensive trails with majestic views. Don't miss the future Parque Nacional Patagonia (p332), a newly inaugurated private park near Cochrane best for wildlife-watching. Only accessed by cruises or boats, Parque Nacional San Rafael (p326) features the magnificent glaciers of Campo de Hielo Norte.

❶ Getting There & Around

The Carretera Austral and its offshoots are remote and mostly unpaved. Most travelers start with a ferry from Puerto Montt or Chiloé to Chaitén or Puerto Chacabuco; fly to Chaitén or Coyhaique; or go overland via Argentina, accessing the region through Futaleufú. In order to drive the length of the Carretera Austral, there are several mandatory ferry crossings. Some bus routes only have services a few days per week, with fewer in low season. In high season, long-distance buses often fill up early in their route and refuse standing passengers. Hitchhiking, not recommended by Lonely Planet, is possible along the Carretera Austral, but difficult for groups or travelers with a lot of luggage.

Hornopirén

📞 065 / POP 2500

Few take advantage of the lush surroundings of this salmon-farming and transport hub. If the ferry is full, you may spend more time here than originally planned. The Ruta Bi-Modal ferry links the roadless northern section of Parque Pumalín to Caleta Gonzalo, where the road continues south.

A **tourist kiosk** (oficinadeturismohualaihue@gmail.com; ⏰9am-7pm Dec-Feb), Conaf office and supermarket are at the main plaza.

🛏 Sleeping

Campgrounds flank the road to Parque Nacional Hornopirén, including a large site at the Hornopirén bridge.

Hotel Hornopirén　　　　　　　HOTEL **$**

(📞217-256; Carrera Pinto 388; r per person CH$12,000; @🛜) With well-worn Patagonian character, water views and the assuring presence of Señora Ollie.

Cabañas Lahuan   CABINS $$
(☑217-239; www.turismolahuan.com; Calle Cahuelmo 40; 5-/8-person cabins CH$60,000/80,000; 🛜) Lovely two-story cabins with wood stoves, grills and big picture windows facing the harbor. There are kayaks for guest use and the owners take groups to the lovely and remote Termas Porcelanas, a 1½-hour boat trip (CH$55,000 per person).

❶ Getting There & Away

Kemelbus (☑253-530; www.kemelbus.cl) has buses daily to and from Puerto Montt (CH$4000, four hours). The bus ticket includes the fee for the ferry across the narrow Estuario de Reloncaví. Passengers can also continue on to Parque Pumalín or Chaitén (CH$14,000, nine

ROAD TRIP!

Ranking among the world's ultimate road trips, the **Carretera Austral** runs 1240 mostly unpaved kilometers alongside ancient forests, glaciers, pioneer farmsteads, turquoise rivers and the crashing Pacific. Completed in 1996, it cost an initial investment of US$300 million, took more than 20 years to build and cost 11 workers their lives. Pinochet's quest to cut a road through Aisén was not based on common sense or a pragmatic plan, it arguably had more to do with the symbolism of a highway that tied together the disparate regions of the country.

Highway may be a glorified name for it – part of the adventure is simply navigating sections of gargantuan ruts and potholes. Yet travelers are drawn here in part because the route is not lined with Subway, Shell stations and Starbucks. Don't skimp on planning and a good dose of prudence.

To the north of the Carretera Austral, ferry service is inadequate for the amount of traffic and only runs regularly during summer – so don't even bother outside summer. The harsh climate can make maintenance a nightmare, with rock slides common and landslides closing sections of the road for days. In the south, the road sits barely 1m above the flood-prone Río Baker, the mightiest of any Chilean river.

While the majority of the traffic is long-distance commercial trucks that rumble up and down the highway, an increasing number of SUVs and pick-ups ply the roads carrying determined anglers, outdoor adventurers and old-fashioned road-trippers. Many courageous cyclists and motorcyclists brave the highway during summer too.

Lastly, isolation makes this region expensive. Be prepared for costs 20% above the rest of Chile. In preparation, we suggest you should:

» Get your vehicle checked out prior to departure.

» When possible, reserve ferry crossings in advance.

» Organize your cash (there are few ATMs, and BancoEstado takes only MasterCard).

» Drive during the day, as curves are not marked with reflectors.

» Carry extra food, water and even gas, as a breakdown or empty tank can leave you marooned. Top off your tank whenever you see a gas station as it may be a long, long time before you find another one.

» Always carry a *neumático* (spare tire) and make sure the vehicle has *una gata* (a car jack).

» Take your time and enjoy the scenery – high-speed turns on loose gravel roads are a recipe for disaster. In most areas, 50km per hour is considered reasonable.

» Stop if someone looks like they might need help.

» Give trucks a wide berth and don't tail anyone too closely as much of the road is made of gravel – broken windshields on the Carretera Austral are as common as parking tickets in Manhattan.

If planning to cross into Argentina, start your trip with all papers in order, permission to take a rental vehicle out of the country and the required insurance. Extra fuel, meat, produce and dairy products can't cross borders. All of the larger towns listed in this chapter have some sort of gas station.

hours), via the Ruta Bi-Modal; bus tickets include ferry costs.

Less than one hour south of Puerto Montt, **Naviera Paredes** (☑ in Puerto Montt 065-276-490; www.navieraparedes.cl; bicycle/car CH$2600/9500; ☺ 7am-8pm) ferry makes the 30-minute crossing from Caleta La Arena to Puelche. Ferries leave every half-hour in high season, with extended hours in summer.

Between Hornopirén and Parque Pumalín, **Naviera Austral** (☑ in Puerto Montt 065-270-430; www.navieraustral.cl; Angelmó 2187, Puerto Montt; per passenger/car CH$5000/30,000) travels the Ruta Bi-Modal, a new system which coordinates two ferry crossings with a short 15km land stretch between them; passengers pay only once. In total, the trip between Hornopirén and Caleta Gonzalo lasts five hours. From the first week of January to the end of February there are two trips daily at 9:30am and 2pm. Summer is busy, so reserve one week ahead by arranging a direct deposit to the Naviera Austral bank account, with passengers' passport information and the license plate. Public buses also do the route.

Parque Nacional Hornopirén

The obscure **Parque Nacional Hornopirén** (admission free) protects a lush wilderness of alpine terrain. Trails to and in the park are marked but at times hard to follow. Still, it offers great scenery and backcountry escapes, though there's no public transportation to it. If planning on making an overnight hike, check in with Conaf before departing town.

About 6km south of Hornopirén, the road forks. The right fork eventually leads to the end of the road at Pichanco. Continue walking another 8km from here along a faintly marked trail to the park's entrance. Three kilometers on, **Lago General Pinto Concha** has a pristine beach where wild camping is possible.

Parque Pumalín

☑ 065

Verdant and pristine, this 2889-sq-km park encompasses vast extensions of temperate rainforest, clear rivers, seascapes and farmland. A remarkable forest-conservation effort, stretching from near Hornopirén to south of Chaitén, Parque Pumalín attracts international visitors in great numbers. Owned by American Doug Tompkins (p334),

it is Chile's largest private park and one of the largest private parks in the world. Agricultural use goes on alongside forest preservation in an innovative park model that perpetuates bee keeping, organic farming and animal husbandry alongside ecotourism. For Chile it's a model park, with well-maintained roads and trails, extensive infrastructure and minimal impact.

The 2008 eruption of Volcán Chaitén (p313) in the park and the ensuing cleanup kept the park closed for several years. It reopened in 2011. While ash is noticeably present (especially on dry, windy days) in parts, the park has managed to recover its excellent infrastructure.

Since the ferry usually requires advance reservations, many people access the park from Chaitén in the south. Caleta Gonzalo, the ferry landing, features cabins and a cafe. A new visitor center is being implemented in the current *guardaparques* (ranger) station 20km south of Chaiten. Fires are prohibited in the park.

🏃 Activities

Check with an information center before finalising your hiking plans as conditions are changeable.

Sendero Cascadas (a three-hour round-trip) is an undulating climb through dense forest that ends at a large waterfall. The river crossing about an hour into the hike can be dangerous at high water.

About 12km south of Caleta Gonzalo, the marked route to **Laguna Tronador** is not so much a trail as it is, often literally, a staircase. Beginning as a boardwalk, it crosses a rushing stream on a *pasarela* (hanging bridge) before ascending a series of wooden stepladders where the soil is too steep and friable for anything else. After about an hour's climb, at the saddle, there's a *mirador* (lookout platform) with fine views of Volcán Michinmahuida above the forest to the south. The trail then drops toward the lake, where there's a two-site campground with sturdy picnic tables (one set on a deck) and a latrine.

One kilometer further south, only a few minutes off the highway to Chaitén, **Sendero los Alerces** crosses the river to a substantial grove of alerce trees, where interpretive signs along the way explain the importance of conserving these ancients. At **Cascadas Escondidas**, 14km south of Caleta Gonzalo,

ALERCE

Waterproof and nearly indestructible, the valuable alerce shingle once served as currency for the German colonists in the south. Known as lahuan in Mapuche, *Fitzroya cupressoides* ranks among the oldest and largest tree species in the world, with specimens reaching almost 4000 years old. This 40m to 60m jolly evergreen giant plays a key role in temperate rainforests, though its prime value as a hardwood (and surefire shelter in a rainy climate) means it was logged to near-extinction. It is no longer legal to harvest live trees, but you can see alerce shingles on Chilote houses and the real deal deep in the Lakes District and Northern Patagonian forests.

a one-hour trail leads from the campground to a series of waterfalls.

Currently the most popular route heads to the **Volcán Chaitén Crater**. Given the volcano's activity in recent history, it's very important to check with rangers before heading out, and preferably go with a guide. The trail is 800m with a 250m change in altitude, a pyroclastic, Mt St Helen's-style trail through forest that burned through heat, not fire. It's near Puente Los Gigos.

At **Michinmahuida**, 33km south of Caleta Gonzalo, a 12km trail leads to the base of the volcano.

In the park's newest sector some 20km south of Chaitén, a flat, open 10km trek to **Ventisquero Amarillo** starts at the Ventisquero campground toward the base of the Michinmahuida Glacier; cross the river at its widest point, closer to the campground.

☞ Tours

Currently the only way to access some of the isolated northern reaches of the park is by boat. A few operators organize boating and kayaking trips through the fjords and to otherwise inaccessible hot springs. In Chaitén, Chaitur (p313) has information on local guides who take hiking groups to the volcano.

Austral Adventures   BOATING
(📞065-625-977; www.austral-adventures.com; Av Costanera 904, Ancud, Chiloé) All-inclusive trips on the *Cahuella*, a 15m Chilote-style wood-

en motor cruiser, sailing around Chiloé's islands and through Pumalín's fjords. Four-day trips from CH$483,000 per person.

Al Sur Expeditions   BOATING
(📞065-232-300; www.alsurexpeditions.com) Specializes in sea-kayaking and provides boat transportation to the remote Cahuelmo Hot Springs.

Yak Expeditions   KAYAKING
(www.yakexpediciones.cl) Kayaking tours.

🛏 Sleeping & Eating

Information centers and the park website have details on all of the campgrounds, some of which are at trailheads.

NORTH PARQUE PUMALÍN (BOAT ACCESS ONLY)

Camping Cahuelmo   CAMPGROUND $
(📞250-079; North Pumalín; campsites per person CH$1500) Cahuelmo has hot springs (CH$3500) and six good tent spaces at the southeast corner of the Cahuelmo Fjord, accessed by boat via Hornopirén or Leptepu. Advance reservations are required.

PENÍNSULA HUEQUI-AYCARA

Avellano Lodge   LODGE $$
(📞576-433, 099-641-4613; www.elavellanolodge.com; Ayacara; per person full board CH$35,000; @🛜) Just outside of the park on the peninsula, this gorgeous hardwood lodge offers an unbeatable combination of access to the park, service and comfort. Hiking, fly-fishing and sea-kayaking tours with all-inclusive packages, including transfer from Puerto Montt, are available.

SOUTH PARQUE PUMALÍN

The following camping options are listed from the north to the south in the south section of Parque Pumalín.

Visitors can eat at Cafe Caleta Gonzalo or possibly arrange *asados* (barbecues) in advance (through reservation) with spit-roasted lamb and fresh farm veggies; for a group of seven it's CH$10,000 per person.

Camping Río Gonzalo   CAMPGROUND $
(Caleta Gonzalo; campsites with fire pit CH$5000) On the shores of Reñihué Fjord, this walk-in campground has a shelter for cooking, and bathrooms with cold showers.

Caleta Gonzalo Cabañas   CABINS $$
(reservas@parquepumalin.cl; s/d/t/q incl breakfast CH$50,000/75,000/95,000/115,000) Cozy cabins

(without kitchen facilities) that overlook the fjord, with cool loft beds for kids.

Café Caleta Gonzalo
CAFE $$$

(lunch CH$12,500; ⊙breakfast, lunch & dinner) The park's only restaurant is this attractive cafe with a huge fireplace. Fresh bread, local honey and organic vegetables put it a notch above average. Homemade oatmeal cookies, honey or picnic boxes are available to go.

Camping Tronador
CAMPGROUND $

(campsites free) Free campsites at the basin of the stunning amphitheater lake on Tronador trail, 1½ hours from the trailhead.

Fundo del Río Cabañas
CABINS $$$

(reservas@parquepumalin.cl; s/d/t/q incl breakfast CH$50,000/75,000/95,000/115,000) Tucked into farmland, these ultraprivate cabins with kitchen facilities have sea or valley views and firewood included.

Cascadas Escondidas
CAMPGROUND $

(covered campsites CH$5000) Features platform sites with roof at the trailhead to Cascadas Escondidas.

Lago Negro
CAMPGROUND $

(campsites per person CH$1500, covered campsites CH$5000) Large camping area close to the lake.

Lago Punta
CAMPGROUND $

(campsites per person CH$1500, covered campsites CH$5000) Room for numerous tents near the lake.

Lago Blanco
CAMPGROUND $

(covered campsites CH$5000) Twenty kilometers south of Caleta Gonzalo and 36km north of Chaitén, Lago Blanco has a few covered sites and great views of the lake. Make sure you hike the short distance to the *mirador* for a better view. There is excellent fishing in the lake, but you'll need to get a permit from a ranger station.

Camping El Volcán
CAMPGROUND $

(campsites per person CH$1500, covered campsites CH$5000) At the southern end of the park before Chaitén, 2.5km before the southern-entrance ranger station, this big camping zone has car camping and information.

Sector Amarillo
CAMPGROUND $

(campsites per person CH$1500) This newest sector south of Chaitén occupies former farmland beyond the Termas El Amarillo, with great views and flat, open sites in three separate areas. It is a couple of days' hiking from other areas or accessible by car.

❶ Information

Two **Centros de Visitantes** (www.pumalinpark.org; Caleta Gonzalo & El Amarillo; ⊙9am-7pm Mon-Sat, 10am-4pm Sun) have park brochures, photographs and environmental information as well as regional artisan goods for sale. For more information before arriving, contact the Pumalín office in **Puerto Varas** (☑065-250-079; Klenner 299; ⊙9am-5pm Mon-Fri) or the **USA** (☑415-229-9339; Bldg 1062, Fort Cronkhite, Sausalito, CA 94965). The website has updated information.

In the El Amarillo sector, **Puma Verde** (Carretera Austral s/n; showers CH$500; ⊙9am-8:30pm Mon-Sat, 10am-8pm Sun) is a park-run general store and gas station – the last one before La Junta. Sells an excellent selection of regional artisan products and reasonably priced provisions, including eggs and produce.

❶ Getting There & Away

The **Naviera Austral** (☑065-270-431) ferries sail daily from Caleta Gonzalo to Hornopirén (five to six hours) at 1:15pm and 5:15pm daily in high season. Bus-boat combos from Puerto Montt can drop visitors in the park on the way to Chaitén. For full details on these options see p333.

Chaitén

☑065 / POP 4000

When an unknown volcano decided to wake up on May 2, 2008, this quiet village underwent a total siege. Residents were able to evacuate, but suffered years of uncertainty as the government formed a response. The initial decision was to rebuild the town 10km north, in the coastal enclave of Santa Bárbara. Yet, as Mother Nature calmed down, plans seem to have shifted. While sections of Chaitén remain lost, much of it is rebuilding. In the meanwhile, there are few lodgings and restaurants, but provisions, gas and camping are easy to find.

Chaitén is the major transport hub for the northern Carretera Austral. Flights and ferries from Puerto Montt and Chiloé arrive here, and it's the starting point for many bus routes south. It's also the main access point for Parque Pumalín.

If you arrive by ferry, the port is a 10-minute walk northwest of town. Chaitén is 56km south of Caleta Gonzalo and 45km northwest of Puerto Cárdenas.

VOLCÁN CHAITÉN WAKES UP

No one even considered it a volcano, but that changed quickly. On May 2, 2008, Volcán Chaitén, 10km northeast of its namesake town, began a month-long eruption with a 20km-high column of ash. During the first week, successive explosions emitted more than a cubic kilometer of rhyolitic ash. The rampage caused flooding and severe damage to homes, roads and bridges, decimated thousands of livestock and spewed ash as far as Buenos Aires. Chaitén's 4000 inhabitants were evacuated. The government sanctioned relocating the town slightly northwest to the village of Santa Barbara (Nuevo Chaitén), but recent improvements in the old town infrastructure has locals returning to recover their homes in Chaitén.

Located in Parque Pumalín, the volcano is easily viewed from sections of the main park road. It's also possible to view forests on the volcano's northeastern flank calcified by pyroclastic flows. The crater has yawned open to 3km in diameter, hosting within it a new complex of quickly formed rhyolitic domes. It's possible to hike to the crater with a local guide though great care should be taken.

The park reopened in 2011, thanks to park rangers who have worked tirelessly in its recovery. At present, Volcán Chaitén remains on yellow alert while under constant monitoring by Sernageomin, the government agency of geology and mining.

◉ Sights & Activities

Termas El Amarillo   HOT SPRINGS
(admission CH$3700) One large cement soaking pool and two smaller, hotter tubs overlook Río Michinmahuida. Day-trippers and families may create daytime congestion, but peace reigns when the gate closes at 9pm and campers (campsites CH$5400) can savor a starlight soak. It's 25km southeast of Chaitén, on a spur north off the Carretera Austral.

Lago Yelcho   FISHING
A brilliant blue under glacial peaks, and fed by the raging Río Futaleufú, the 110-sq-km Lago Yelcho is adored by anglers. The small port of Puerto Cárdenas (62km south of Chaitén) has modest lodging choices, all summer-only, and lodges that provide fishing boats and guides.

Ventisquero Yelcho   HIKING
A 2½-hour hike to a large hanging glacier. Camping is possible near the parking lot, where there is also a *quincho* (barbecue hut) and bathrooms. There are glacier views throughout the hike along the riverbanks. If short on time, hike one hour in for good views. It's 15km south of Puerto Cárdenas. Puente Ventisquero (Glacier Bridge) is the starting point.

☞ Tours

Chaitur   TOUR
(☎097-468-5608; www.chaitur.com; O'Higgins 67) The best source of information in town,

English-speaking Nicholas at Chaitur dispatches most of the buses and arranges trips with bilingual guides to Pumalín, the Yelcho glacier, Termas El Amarillo and beaches with sea-lion colonies. He also runs informative guided hikes to the Chaitén volcano crater with interesting scientific information. Chaitur also rents bikes (CH$3000 for two hours).

🛏 Sleeping & Eating

Hospedaje Don Carlos   GUESTHOUSE $
(☎731-287; doncarlos.palena@gmail.com; Almirante Riveros 53; s/d CH$15,000/25,000, without bathroom CH$10,000/20,000; [P][☎]) Clean, with firm beds, buffed furniture and kitsch details like dolls and plastic fruit. Reserve ahead as it fills fast.

Cielo Mar Camping   CAMPING $
(☎097-468-5608; www.chaitur.com; O'Higgins & Corcovado; campsites per person CH$2500; [☎]) Backyard campsites and hot-water showers, right in the center of town.

TOP CHOICE Cocinerías Costumbristas   SEAFOOD $
(Portales 258; meals CH$4500; ☺breakfast, lunch & dinner) Apron-clad señoras in tiny kitchens serve up piping-hot seafood empanadas, fish platters and fresh *paila marina* (shellfish soup). Come early because it fills up fast with locals.

ℹ Information

BancoEstado (cnr Libertad & O'Higgins) Has an ATM and poor exchange rates on cash.

Hospital de Chaitén (✆731-244; Av Ignacio Carrera Pinto; ⏱24hr) Emergency is open 24 hours.

Tourist kiosk (cnr Costanera & O'Higgins; ⏱9am-9pm Jan-Feb) Has leaflets and a list of accommodations.

❶ Getting There & Away

Air

A provisional airstrip operates on the road from Pumalín to Chaitén (orange cones hold automobile traffic at landing times!). Both **Aerocord** (✆in Puerto Montt 065-262-300; www.aerocord.cl; Costanera s/n) and **Pewen** (✆in Puerto Montt 065-224-000; www.pewenchile.com) fly to Aerodromo La Paloma in Puerto Montt (one-way CH$42,000, 45 minutes). Both fly daily except Sundays, usually at 11am.

Boat

Ferry schedules change, so confirm them before making plans.

The **Naviera Austral** (✆07-976-0342; www.navieraustral.cl; Corcovado 266) auto-passenger ferry sails to Puerto Montt (passenger seat/bunk/car CH$16,000/31,200/88,000, 12 hours) three times a week. In summer, a ferry goes to Quellón (CH$16,000/25,700/82,000, six hours), Chiloé, two times a week. For details on the ferries (with bus combinations) to Hornopirén and Puerto Montt, see p333.

Bus

Transportation for the Carretera Austral change frequently. Unless otherwise indicated, departures are from the main **Chaitur Bus Terminal** (✆097-468-5608; www.chaitur.com; O'Higgins 67). Buses Terra Austral goes to La Junta Friday through Monday at 1pm; from here there are daily early-morning connections to Coyhaique.

All Coyhaique-bound buses stop in Puyuhuapi and other towns on the way. Buses Becker goes to Coyhaique on Wednesdays at 10am. It also goes to Villa Santa Lucía on Sunday at 8:30am (with onward connections to Coyhaique).

Buses Cardenas goes to Futaleufú daily at noon except Thursdays. **Buses Palena** goes to Palena every day except Thursday, leaving the center between 11am and 1pm (depending on flight arrivals).

DESTINATION	COST (CH$)	DURATION (HR)
Coyhaique	CH$24,000	9-10
Futaleufú	CH$8000	3½
La Junta	CH$8500	4
Palena	CH$8500	4
Puyuhuapi	CH$12,000	5
Villa Santa Lucía	CH$4000	2

Futaleufú

✆065 / POP 1800

The Futaleufú's wild, frosty-mint waters have made this modest mountain town famous. Not just a mecca for kayaking and rafting, it also boasts fly-fishing, hiking and horseback riding. Improved roads and growing numbers of package-tour visitors mean it isn't off the map anymore. Just note the ratio of Teva sandals to woolen mantas; that said, it's still a fun place to be.

The town of Futaleufú, a small 20-block grid of pastel-painted houses 155km southeast of Chaitén, is mainly a service center to the Argentine border, only 8km away, and a bedroom community for boaters. Many visitors hop the border to the nearby Argentine towns of Trevelín and Esquel, and to Argentina's Parque Nacional Los Alerces.

🏃 Activities

The Futa or Fu, as it's known, is a technical, demanding river, with some sections only appropriate for experienced rafters. Depending on the outfitter you choose and the services included, rafting the Futaleufú starts at CH$50,000 per person for a half-day section known as Bridge to Bridge with Class IV and IV-plus rapids. A full-day trip for experienced rafters only goes from Bridge to Macul, adding two Class V rapids, starting at CH$75,000.

Ideal for families, rafting trips on the Class III Río Espolón cost about CH$15,000 for the five-hour trip. Novice kayakers can try this river or head to Lago Espolón for a float trip.

Bio Bio Expeditions   RAFTING
(✆800-246-7238; www.bbxrafting.com; Río Azul sector) A pioneer in the region, this ecologically minded group offers river descents, horseback treks and more. It is well established but may take walk-ins.

Expediciones Chile   RAFTING
(✆721-386; www.exchile.com; Mistral 296) A secure rafting operator with loads of experience. Specializes in week-long packages but offers kayaking instruction, canyoning, mountain biking and horseback riding as well.

H2O Patagonia   RAFTING
(✆in USA 888-426-7238; www.h2opatagonia.com) A US-based adventure company that can coordinate your entire trip, including luxurious accommodations on its ranch.

Patagonia Elements   RAFTING
(☑097-499-0296; www.patagoniaelements.com; Cerda 549) With competent Chilean guides, this outfit also offers kayak classes, fly-fishing and horseback riding.

🛏 Sleeping

TOP CHOICE **Las Natalias**   HOSTEL $
(☑096-493-7761; hostallasnatalias.cl; dm/d without bathroom CH$9000/25,000, f CH$30,000; @) Newish and fully decked out, this sprawling home has bunkrooms with plenty of shared bathrooms. There is also a large communal area as well as great mountain views. Breakfast isn't included but there's an ample and well-supplied kitchen. Nate, the friendly American who is at the helm, can help connect travelers with local guides and routes. It's a 10-minute walk from the center. Follow Cerda and the signs for the northeast sector out of town; it's on the right after the hill climb.

Martín Pescador B&B   B&B $
(☑721-279; Balmaceda 603; s/d CH$10,000/20,000, 6-person cabin CH$45,000; 🛜) Behind the restaurant, this cozy home with adobe-style walls and attractive furnishings is a steal. The two-bedroom cabins with narrow staircases are rustic and stylish, with kitchenettes. Mitch, the owner, also works as a freelance outdoor guide.

Adolfo's B&B   GUESTHOUSE $
(☑721-256; O'Higgins 302; d CH$20,000, per person without bathroom CH$8000, 6-person cabin CH$45,000; @🛜) The best bargain digs in town are in this warm wood-finish home of a local school teacher. It's sometimes unattended for stretches of time. Breakfast may include eggs, homemade bread and coffee cake.

Hotel El Barranco   LODGE $$$
(☑721-314; www.elbarrancochile.cl; O'Higgins 172; s/d CH$85,000/100,000; @🛜🏊) At this elegant lodge situated out on the edge of the town grid, rooms are snug with carved woodwork, colonial accents and big beds. There is also a swimming pool, a sauna, a gym and free bikes. The owner Juan Pablo provides great information on outdoor options.

Posada Ely   GUESTHOUSE $$
(☑721-205; posada.ely.futaleufu@gmail.com; Balmaceda 409; s/d CH$15,000/30,000; P🛜) These well-kept rooms sit under the sure guardian-ship of Betty, a dyed-in-the-wool local who makes a mean rosehip jam, served with a breakfast of fresh bread, eggs, juice, tea and more. Cable TV is available.

Hostería Río Grande   HOTEL $$
(☑721-320; O'Higgins 397; s/d/t CH$35,000/55,000/65,000; P🛜) This comfortable shingled lodge caters to sporty gringos who, between raft trips, can pump iron in the attached weight room. Expect bright, carpeted rooms with portable heaters and low-slung beds in deep frames. It also features a small pub with a grassy terrace.

Patago   CABINS $
(☑09-958-9565; gregorioaraya@hotmail.com; Lago Lonconao; r per person CH$10,000, 4-person cabin CH$60,000) A chill spot to crash, this rustic home and adjacent cabin sit on the shores of Lago Lonconao. Gregorio, the warm host, also cooks breakfast (CH$3000) and lunch with an emphasis on vegetarian options.

Cara del Indio   CAMPGROUND $
(☑02-196-4239; www.caradelindio.cl; campsites/refugios per person CH$3000, cabins from CH$25,000) With a spectacular riverfront setting, this adventure base camp is 15km from Puerto Ramiréz and 35km from the Carretera Austral. Run by Luis Toro and his family, the camp boasts 10km of riverfront. Primative *refugios* (rustic shelters) offer some minimal shelter. Sites have access to hot showers, an outdoor kitchen and a wood-burning sauna. Guests can purchase homemade bread, cheese and beer onsite. December and March, on either end of the two-month summer rush, are more peaceful times to be here.

Camping Puerto Espolón   CAMPGROUND $
(☑099-447-7448; www.aldeapuertoespolon.blogspot.com; campsites per person CH$4000, 2-person domes CH$12,000; ⊙Jan & Feb) A gorgeous setting on a sandy riverbank flanked by mountains, just before the entrance to town. Guests get use of an outdoor kitchen and hot showers. There's also the option of geodesic domes (which hold up to eight people) and teepees – bring your own sleeping bag, in both cases.

🍴 Eating

Since most supplies have to be trucked in from afar, fresh vegetables can be in short supply.

DON'T MISS

PIONEER PATAGONIA

When winds roar sidelong and rains persist, take refuge by the woodstove, drink a round of *maté* (tea) and *echar la talla* (pass the time) with the locals. Rural Patagonia offers a rare and privileged glimpse of a fading way of life. To jump-start their slack rural economy, government and nonprofit initiatives have created local guide and homestay associations.

These family enterprises range from comfortable roadside *hospedajes* (budget accommodations) and farm stays to wild country multiday treks and horseback-riding trips through wonderland terrain. Prices are reasonable – starting from CH$10,000 per day for lodging and CH$15,000 per day for guide services – although extras include horses, and only Spanish is spoken.

Travelers can link with rural home stays and guide services through **Casa del Turismo Rural** (www.casaturismorural.cl) in Coyhaique (see p321) or the **Municipalidad de Cochamó** (www.cochamo.cl) in Río Puelo (see p273). Some of the best opportunities are around Cerro Castillo, La Junta, Palena and Llanada Grande (in Sur Chico). It's best to book a week or more in advance, as intermediaries have to make radio contact with the most remote hosts. That's right – no phones, no electricity, no worries.

Another good resource, **Discover Patagonia Circuit** (www.undiscoveredpatagonia.com) is an innovative government-funded project that plans to offer travelers 40 original DIY circuits in rural Patagonia, from Chile's Valle Chacabuco south to El Chaltén, Argentina.

TOP CHOICE **Martín Pescador** FINE DINING **$$**
(☑721-279; Balmaceda 603; mains CH$7500-10,000; ☺dinner; ☎) This circular dining room brims with ambience, from the paintings by local artists to the worn wood beams, log fire and sofas. Regional delicacies like chicken with morel mushrooms, salmon carpaccio or baked crab dishes make it ideal for a special dinner. Extended hours have made it a popular spot for a drink or two.

SurAndes CAFE **$**
(☑721-405; www.surandeschile.cl; Cerda 308; mains CH$4000; ☺breakfast, lunch & dinner; ☎) Real coffee and fresh juices perk up tired travelers who bask in this lovely atmospheric cafe serving fresh omelettes, custom burgers and veggie plates. There is also a cabin and an attractive five-person apartment (CH$15,000 per person) for rent upstairs.

El Encuentro CHILEAN **$$**
(☑721-247; O'Higgins 653; meals CH$7000) Don't think about the plastic-covered lace tablecloths, these are decent home-style meals featuring meat from regional ranches, salmon and chicken in cream sauce.

ⓘ Information

BancoEstado (cnr O'Higgins & Manuel Rodríguez) Bring all the money you'll need; this the only choice for changing money. ATM takes only MasterCard.

Post office (Manuel Rodríguez)

Tourist office (O'Higgins 536; ☺9am-9pm) Helpful, with information on cabins, activities and descriptions of local treks.

ⓘ Getting There & Away

Buses Becker (☑721-360; www.busesbecker.com; cnr Balmaceda & Pratt; ☺9am-1pm & 3-7pm) goes to Villa Santa Lucía (CH$6000, two hours), where you can transfer south to Coyhaique. It also goes once weekly to La Junta (CH$12,000), Puyuhuapi (CH$13,500) and Coyhaique (CH$24,000, nine to 10 hours). Buses Cardenas goes to Chaitén (CH$8000, 3½ hours) daily except Thursdays. **TransAustral** (☑721-360; cnr Balmaceda & Pratt) goes at 8am on Wednesday and Sunday to Puerto Montt (CH$25,000, 12 hours via Argentina). The same office also sells air tickets from Chaiten to Puerto Montt, worth buying in advance.

The **Futaleufú border post** (☺8am-8pm) is far quicker and more efficient than the crossing at Palena, opposite the Argentine border town of Carrenleufú.

There's no gas station in Futaleufú. The grocery store on Sargento Aldea sells fuel by the jug; it's cheaper in Argentina, if you make it.

Palena

A quiet mountain town on its namesake turquoise river, Palena's draw is exploring its verdant valleys on foot or horseback, where you'll find remnants of pioneer lifestyle and real hospitality. The Rodeo de Palena, held on the last weekend in January, and week-long Semana Palena in late February feature cowboy festivities and live music.

On the plaza, the **tourism office** (☑065-741-221; www.palenaonline.cl; Piloto Pardo s/n; ⊙9am-8pm Mon-Sat, to 6pm Sun) arranges horse packing, rafting and fishing trips with local guides. Allow some lead time before your trip, since some rural outfitters must be reached by radio. It can also connect adventurers to the Casanova family farm Rincón de la Nieve in Valle Azul, accessed via hiking or horseback riding. Chill there or continue on a truly incredible five-day round-trip ride to remote Lago Palena (see boxed text, p316); arrange in advance.

Adventuras Cordilleranas (☑065-741-367; deisy_504@hotmail.com; El Malito bridge; s incl breakfast CH$10,000) is run by a friendly family who also offer kayaking on Río Palena. Contact in advance. If arriving from the west, have the bus drop you off 22km before Palena.

Buses Palena (☑065-741-319; Plaza de Armas) goes to Chaitén (CH$5000, four hours) at 6am on Wednesdays and Thursdays.

La Junta

☑067

With the slow feel of a Rocky Mountain backwater, La Junta is a former *estancia* (grazing ranch) that formed a crossroads for ranchers headed to market. Midway between Chaitén and Coyhaique, this dusty town is also an important transfer point for north–south connections, with better lodging options than nearby Puyuhuapi. Unmistakable with its centerpiece monument to Pinochet, it now serves as a major fuel and rest stop for travelers, replete with old-fashioned hardware stores and a rocky butte bookending town.

Visitors can take float trips on Río Palena, go fly-fishing or hike in area reserves. Brown, rainbow and Chinook trout abound at Reserva Nacional Lago Rosselot and Lago Verde. Private hot springs **Termas del Sauce** (☑098-737-5645; Camino a Raul Marin Balmaceda Km17; per person CH$5000) offers pleasant but rustic pools and camping on a brook 17km out of town toward Raúl Marín Balmaceda.

At the end of January, the **Fiesta del los Rios** celebrates the two rivers that converge here, with free floating trips, barbecues and folk performances. There is no bus terminal here; ask locals the schedules and catch a bus passing by.

🛏 Sleeping & Eating

TOP CHOICE **Alto Melimoyu B&B**   B&B $$
(☑314-320; www.altomelimoyu.cl; Carretera Austral 375; s/d CH$36,000/51,000, without bathroom CH$28,000/41,000; ☏) New on the block, this gorgeous B&B combines great design with warm attention. Perhaps the only detraction is its location on the dusty main road – though it's set back enough to almost forget it's there. Guests cozy up by the fire on the wide-wale corduroy couch and enjoy big breakfasts around communal tables hand-made by locals. There's also a wooden hot tub rented by the hour. Run by a young, active couple, with bikes and kayaks for rent and connections to local tours.

Espacio y Tiempo   LODGE $$$
(☑314-141; espacioytiempo.cl; Carretera Austral s/n; s/d/tr CH$53,000/76,000/99,000; ☏) This well-heeled and comfortable lodge relaxes visiting anglers and travelers with classical music, sprawling green gardens and a well-stocked bar. Rooms are recently remodeled, with muted tones and top-quality mattresses. Further perks include private porches and an abundant buffet breakfast with real coffee. The on-site restaurant is popular with locals, specialties include local elk, but there are also enticingly big bowls of salad. The hosts happily arrange local excursions or you can just visit the llamas out back.

Hostería Mirador del Río   FARMSTAY $
(☑314-141, 098-159-2869; www.miradordelrio.cl; Camino a Raul Marin Balmaceda Km6; r per person incl breakfast CH$12,000) For a welcome retreat from the dusty Carretera Austral, get outside of town to this charming farmhouse. The family is lovely and breakfast satisfies with homemade jam and bread hot out of the woodstove. Guests can also do *catanoa* (double canoe) trips (two passengers CH$28.000) down the mellow Río Palena.

Terrazas de Palena   B&B $$
(☑099-415-4274; www.terrazasdelpalena.cl; Carretera Austral s/n; d/q apt CH$40,000/50,000, 2-/5-person cabin CH$50,000/70,000; @) With sweeping views, these cubist cabins and apartments with woodstove provide a nice, tranquil spot to regroup. There's also a restaurant in the works, excursions and airport transfers. Located 2km north of La Junta.

WORTH A TRIP

EXPLORE THE LOST COAST

The long-isolated coastal village of **Raul Marín Balmaceda** finally has road access and it's well worth the detour. At the mouth of the Río Palena, a new watershed preserve, it's teeming with wildlife, such as otters, sea lions and austral dolphins. For the best marine life, paddle out in a kayak or take a boat tour. The village has wide sandy streets and grassy paths to a lovely beach. A wonderful ecotourism option, **Fundo Los Leones** (📞096-597-3986, 097-898-2956; www.fundolosleones.cl; s/d cabin CH$68,000/90,000; 🐾) provides the ultimate retreat in tiny shingled cabins on the Pitipalena Fjord. It also offers meals with organic ingredients from the farm and excursions by kayak and boat. In the village, **Los Lirios** (📞096-242-0180; violaloslirios@gmail.com; r per person with/without bathroom CH$12,000/10,000) offers a comfortable homestay.

From La Junta, buses depart on Monday, Wednesday and Friday at 8:30am. You can also make the two-hour drive on a decent gravel road. There's an obligatory ferry crossing (free): day trippers note that it's only open until 7pm.

Pension Hospedaje Tía Lety   GUESTHOUSE **$**
(📞098-763-5191; Varas 596; r per person incl breakfast CH$10,000) A friendly family setting, with bulky beds in well-kept rooms. Breakfast is filling.

TOP CHOICE **Mi Casita de Té**   CHILEAN **$**
(cnr Varas & Lynch; mains CH$5000; ⊙breakfast, lunch & dinner) At this bustling family restaurant, Eliana and her daughters cook and serve abundant, fresh meals and even espresso. In summer there are lovely salads with organic lettuce. Any time, the beef *cazuela* (stew), with corn cobs, fresh peas and cilantro, is deeply satisfying Chilean comfort food.

❶ Information

Conaf (📞314-128; cnr Patricio Lynch & Manuel Montt) Has details on nearby parks and reserves.

Tourist kiosk (cnr Portales & 1era de Noviembre; ⊙9am-9pm Mon-Fri, 10:30am-7:30pm Sat & Sun) On the plaza, with information on buses, lodgings and activities.

Yagan Expeditions (📞314-386; yagan.expeditions@gmail.com; cnr Lynch & Portales) Small tour operator providing horseback riding, trekking and hot-springs trips, as well as kayaking on Lago Rosselot.

Puyuhuapi

📞067

Tucked into the Jurassic scenery of overgrown ferns and nalca plants, this quaint seaside village is the gateway to Parque Nacional Queulat and Termas de Puyuhuapi, a prestigious hot-springs resort. In 1935 four

German immigrants settled here, inspired by explorer Hans Steffen's adventures. The town sits at the northern end of the Seno Ventisquero, a scenic fjord that's part of the larger Canal Puyuhuapi.

The agricultural colony grew with Chilote textile workers whose skills fed the success of the 1947 German **Fábrica de Alfombras** (www.puyuhuapi.com; Calle Aysén s/n) which sells its high-end handmade carpets online.

There's free wi-fi on the plaza.

◉ Sights

Termas del Ventisquero   HOT SPRINGS
(📞067-325-228; admission CH$14,000; ⊙9am-11pm Dec-Feb & some winter weekends) If you don't have the time or resources to boat out to the other hot springs, this is an excellent alternative. Located roadside on the Carretera Austral, 6km south of Puyuhuapi, this new miniresort has one big pool and three small pools facing the sound, surrounded by umbrellas and lounge chairs. The water is 36°C to 40°C and there are adequate changing rooms with showers and lockers. Food is not allowed but you can grab a bite at the restaurant, which also serves English teas, espresso and pisco sours.

🛏 Sleeping & Eating

Day visitors to the hot springs often lodge in town, but reserve ahead in summer.

TOP CHOICE **Casa Ludwig**   B&B **$$**
(📞325-220; www.casaludwig.cl; Otto Uebel s/n; s CH$16,000-35,000, d CH$24,000-42,000, tr CH$48,000) A historic landmark, this classic home is elegant and snug, with roaring fires in the sprawling living room and big

breakfasts at the communal table. Room prices can vary according to room size, with deep discounts in low season. Browse a big book of activities on offer, or ask the helpful English- and German-speaking owners for information.

Cabañas Aonikenk CABINS $
(☑325-208; aonikenkpuyuhuapi.cl; Hamburgo 16; s/d CH$18,000/24,000, 2-5-person cabins CH$40,000-60,000; 🐕) Hosted by the amicable Veronica, these new all-wood cabins have paraffin stoves, snug white bedding and small balconies. The more economical double is usually reserved. The cafe offers whole-wheat sandwiches, cakes and salads; its lounge space is a nice refuge on a rainy day. Laundry service and bike rentals are also offered.

Hospedaje Ventisquero GUESTHOUSE $
(☑325-130; O'Higgins s/n; r per person CH$6000; @) This rambling white house lets out affordable but bleak rooms without breakfast, luring guests with 15 minutes of free internet.

Camping La Sirena CAMPGROUND $
(☑325-100; Costanera 148; campsites per person CH$2500) Sites are cramped but there are tent shelters, bathrooms and hot showers. Enter via the road passing the playground to the water.

El Muelle SEAFOOD $$
(Otto Ubel s/n; mains CH$5000-8000; ⊙lunch & dinner) If the *merluza* (hake) on your plate were any fresher, it would still be in the fjord. Despite slow service, it's worth hunkering down to a big seafood meal served with mashed potatoes or crisp fries. The shingled house surrounded by overgrown flowerbeds sits in front of the police station.

ℹ Information

Tourist office (Otto Uebel s/n; www.cuenca delpalena-queulat.cl; ⊙noon-2pm & 3-9pm Mon-Sat) Located in front of the park, with comprehensive information on lodgings, hot springs and restaurants. Ask here for a map to the town walking circuit.
Chucao Expeditions (☑098-258-5799, 097-766-1524; chucaoexpeditions@gmail.com; Otto Uebel 36) Offers excursions in kayak and on bicycles, as well as boat trips.

ℹ Getting There & Away

Buses that run between Coyhaique and Chaitén will drop passengers in Puyuhuapi. Buy your re-turn ticket as far ahead as possible, as demand exceeds availability in summer. Buses stop at restaurant **El Muelle** (Otto Ubel s/n; ticket sales 10am-4pm & 7-8pm Mon-Sat, 11am-1pm Sun), where tickets are also sold during limited hours.
Buses Becker (☑232-167, 098-465-2959) goes to Chaitén on Tuesdays at 8am and Futaleufu on Saturdays at 8am; both buses pass through La Junta. **Terra Austral** (☑098-769-9024) leaves at 6am daily for Coyhaique.

DESTINATION	COST (CH$)	DURATION (HR)
Chaitén	CH$12,000	5
Coyhaique	CH$8000	4-5
Futaleufú	CH$12,000	6
La Junta	CH$4000	1

Termas De Puyuhuapi

Chile's leading hot-springs resort, the luxurious **Termas de Puyuhuapi Hotel & Spa** (☑067-325-103/117; 3-night package d CH$700,000) sits in a lush forest on the western shore of the Seno Ventisquero. The only access is by boat. Buildings combine the rustic look of Chilote *palafitos* (houses on stilts) with Bavarian influences, but interiors of standard rooms could be updated. Packages may include boating trips to Glaciar and Laguna San Rafael. Currently package vacationers make up most of the clientele. Independent travelers may have a hard time booking a one-night reservation in the February high season.

Three outdoor baths, including a fern-shaded hot-mud lagoon, sit right by the water, allowing visitors to soak and steam away then jump into the cool sound. The indoor spa is more elaborate but less ambient. Families frequent its cold-water pools, Jacuzzis and one large pool with different jets.

Day use is based on availability, so call the day before. Day trippers pay for boat transfer (adult/child CH$5000/2500) plus use of the outdoor pools (adult/child CH$22,000 /10,000). Spa treatments and massages cost extra. Food is served at the hotel restaurant and a cheaper cafe.

Termas de Puyuhuapi is accessed via boat from the Bahía Dorita mainland dock, 13km south of Puerto Puyuhuapi. Launches leave between 10am and 6pm. Contact **Patagonia Connection** (☑in Santiago 02-225-6489; www.patagonia-connection.com) for information.

Parque Nacional Queulat

The 1540-sq-km **Parque Nacional Queulat** (admission CH$4000) is a wild realm of rivers winding through forests thick with ferns and southern beech. When the sun is out it's simply stunning, with steep-sided fjords flanked by creeping glaciers and 2000m volcanic peaks. The park straddles the Carretera Austral for 70km, midway between Chaitén and Coyhaique.

Created in 1983, the park is extremely popular but its far-flung location keeps it within reach of the select few willing to venture this far. Visitors are also challenged by the almost constant rain (up to 4000mm per year) and impenetrable foliage. Despite its impressive size, hiking trails are few. Conaf has struggled to maintain trailhead signs, most of which are either hidden by the aggressive growth or missing.

The **Centro de Información Ambiental** (☉9am-6pm), 22km south of Puerto Puyuhuapi and 2.5km from the road, at the parking lot for the Ventisquero Colgante, is the main center to the park and where admission fees are collected. It has well-organized, informative displays of plants and glacial activity, and rangers can help with hiking plans.

Activities

Near the information center, there's a quick walk to a lookout of the **Ventisquero Colgante**, the park's most popular attraction. You can also take the bridge across Río Ventisquero and follow a 3.2km trail along the crest of a moraine for great views of the glacier and the crash of ice onto the rocks below. At **Laguna de Los Tempanos**, boat cruises (per person CH$3500, summer only) take you from the boat launch across the lake to view the glacier.

North of the southern entrance, at Km170, a damp trail climbs the valley of the **Río de las Cascadas** through a dense forest of delicate ferns, copihue vines, tree-size fuchsias, podocarpus and lenga. The heavy rainfall never directly hits the ground but seems to percolate through the multistoried canopy. After about half an hour, the trail emerges at an impressive granite bowl, where half a dozen waterfalls drop from hanging glaciers.

Twenty kilometers south of the information center, **Sendero Padre García** is a 100m staircase that drops to an overlook of an impressive waterfall and its transparent pool. Stop on the small shoulder on the left. Padre García was a Jesuit priest who trekked through Queulat in search of the mythical Ciudad de Los Césares. Continuing on, the road zigzags treacherously up the Portezuelo de Queulat between Km175 and Km178, with outstanding views of the Queulat Valley.

Top-notch **fishing** can be found at the larger streams, such as the Río Cisnes, and the glacial fingers of Lago Rosselot, Lago Verde and Lago Risopatrón.

Sleeping

Camping Ventisquero   CAMPGROUND $
(campsites CH$6000) Near the Ventisquero Colgante, this has 10 attractive, private sites with covered barbecues and picnic tables. Firewood is available. Beware: the bathrooms have glacial showers and the sites themselves are a bit rocky for pitching multiple tents.

Camping Angostura   CAMPGROUND $
(Lago Risopatrón; campsites CH$5000) Located in a sopping rainforest, 15km north of Puerto Puyuhuapi, but the facilities are good (cold showers only).

ℹ Getting There & Away

Buses connecting Chaitén and Coyhaique will drop passengers at Puyuhuapi or other points along the western boundary of the park. See p314 for details. Make seat reservations on the next bus you plan to take, and be prepared to wait.

Around Parque Nacional Queulat

After Parque Nacional Queulat, the road splits at the turn-off for Puerto Cisnes. From here to Coyhaique it's all paved. **Villa Amengual** is a pioneer village with a Chilote-style shingled chapel, basic family-run lodgings and basic services. It's at the foot of 2760m Cerro Alto Nevado.

Another 55km south, **Villa Mañihuales** was founded in 1962. It has a couple of *hospedajes* (budget accommodations), including **Residencial Mañihuales** (☎067-431-403; E Ibar 280; r per person CH$10,000), and some simple cafes.

A further 13km south, the Carretera Austral splits. The highway southwest to Puerto Aisén and Puerto Chacabuco is also paved. Access to Coyhaique takes an incredibly

ISLA MAGDALENA

An island sanctuary with hot springs and trails, **Parque Nacional Isla Magdalena** makes an engaging trip for adventurers but there is little infrastructure from Conaf and travel options are expensive. Ask around locally to organize a trip. Travelers can approach other visitors to split boat costs, which run around CH$100,000 for groups of 10. Information on the area can be found at **La Municipalidad de Cisnes** (www.cisnes.org). Acces is via Puerto Cisnes, an industrial salmon-farming area 35km west of the Carretera Austral linked by a paved road. Buses from La Junta (CH$5000, three hours) arrive here daily.

scenic route crossing the Andes through primary forest thick with ferns and lianas.

Coyhaique

📞 067 / POP 44,900

The cow town that kept growing, Coyhaique is the regional hub of rural Aisén, urbane enough to house the latest techie trends, mall fashions and discos. All this is plopped in the middle of an undulating range, with rocky humpback peaks and snowy ranges in the backdrop. For the visitor, it's the launch pad for far-flung adventures, be it fly-fishing, trekking the ice cap or rambling the Carretera Austral to its end at Villa O'Higgins. For those fresh from the rainforest wilderness of northern Aisén, it can be a jarring relapse into the world of semi trucks and subdivisions.

Industry is braced to pounce here, with a number of regional hydroelectric projects in the works and a recently defeated aluminum plant. Rural workers come to join the timber or salmon industries and add to the growing urban mass.

At the confluence of the Río Simpson and Río Coyhaique, the sprawling city center has its plaza at the heart of a pentagonal plan.

◉ Sights & Activities

Mirador Río Simpson　　LOOKOUT
Prime river vistas can be gained here, reached by walking west on JM Carrera.

Lago Elizalde　　LAKE
One of many serene mountain lakes surrounding Coyhaique and great for trout fishing, kayaking or simply time at the beach. It's just 33km from Coyhaique. Buses depart from the bus terminal.

Museo Regional de la Patagonia　　MUSEUM
(📞213-175; cnr Baquedano & Eusebio Lillo) Catalogues pioneer artifacts and Jesuit regalia. It also houses a fine collection of labeled photographs on regional history, including the construction of the Carretera Austral. Currently closed for renovation.

Reserva Nacional Coyhaique　　HIKING
(admission CH$2000) These hiking trails are only 5km from town. Take Baquedano north across the bridge and go right at the gravel road; from the entrance it's 3km to Laguna Verde.

Centro de Ski El Fraile　　SNOW SPORTS
(📞231-690; ☉Jun-Sep) A T-bar and pommel lift access 800m of vertical terrain at this small resort 29km south of Coyhaique. Experts can hike past the lifts to some bowls with heavy, wet snow and lovely tree-skiing. Rental equipment is available.

☞ Tours

Casa del Turismo Rural　　ECOTOUR
(📞524-929; www.casaturismorural.cl; Plaza de Armas) Networks visitors to rural homestays (around CH$10,000 to CH$15,000 per person nightly) and reasonably priced local guide services for a grass-roots approach to trekking, fishing and horseback riding. It can also hook up travelers with glacier trips and visits to the Capilla de Marmol near Lago General Carrera.

GeoSur Expediciones-Patagonia Learning Adventures　　ADVENTURE TOUR
(📞099-264-8671; www.patagonialearning.com; Símon Bolívar 521) Bilingual adventure specialists combine opportunities for learning about the local culture and landscapes of the region with trekking, kayaking, fly-fishing or simply a day in the country at its adventure center. Located 57km south of Coyhaique, the GeoSur Mountain Lodge sits perched above Lago Monreal and Lago Paloma, making a great alternative start to the multiday Cerro Castillo trek.

Coyhaique

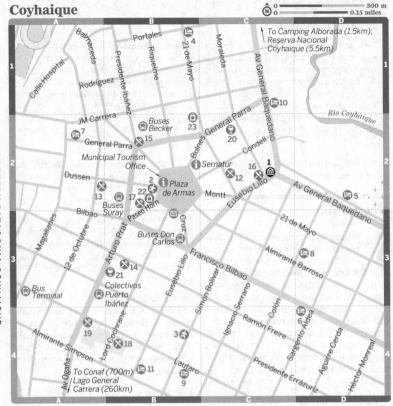

Coyhaique

🛏 Sleeping

TOP CHOICE Patagonia Hostel
HOSTEL $

(📞096-240-6974; www.patagonia-hostel.com; Lautaro 667; dm/d CH$10,000/30,000; @🛜) A welcoming German-run hostel. The rooms are stylish and minimal, but splurge with 2m-long beds and huge pillows. Tea is always available and breakfast includes fruit, cheese, salami and jam. Check out its tour services, which include nearby mountain treks.

TOP CHOICE Hotel El Bagual
BOUTIQUE HOTEL $$$

(📞244-995; www.hotelbagual.cl; General Parra 551; s/d/t CH$55,000/75,000/95,000; @🛜) This lovely oversized house on a quiet street end is the perfect splurge. Think welcoming but subdued, with tasteful, muted colors and modern art. Soft sofas with sheepskin throws invite you to linger around the living room's huge stone fireplace. Rooms are ample and there's a bar and restaurant on-site.

Albergue Las Salamandras
HOSTEL $

(📞211-865; www.salamandras.cl; Teniente Vidal Km1.5; s/d CH$20,000/28,000, dm/s/d without bathroom CH$8500/16,000/20,000, 2-6 person cabins CH$20,000-60,000, campsite per person CH$6000; @🛜) On a wooded bank, this rustic guesthouse offers ample common spaces, two kitchens, and dorm beds weighted in blankets. It can also fire up the wooden hot tub for CH$25,000 extra (group rate). You can also book off-the-beaten-track adventures here. It's 2km south of town; check the website for good directions.

Hostal Español
INN $$

(📞242-580; www.hostalcoyhaique.cl; Sargento Aldea 343; s/d CH$30,000/42,000; 🅿@) Tasteful and modern, this ample wooden house has 10 rooms with fresh quilted bedding, claret carpets and a personal touch. Service is great and there's a comfortable living room to put your feet up by the crackling fire. A frigobar, central heating and wi-fi are other perks.

Kooch Hostel
HOSTEL $

(📞527-186; www.koochhostel.com; Camino Piedra del Indio Km2; dm/s/d CH$10,000/15,000/24,000; @) There are just a few rooms in this big, cozy home with a communal kitchen and patio. Guests choose from twin beds or a four-person dorm; all feature down duvets and bright colors. It's 200m from the turnoff to Piedra del Indio, 10 blocks from the plaza.

El Reloj
INN $$$

(📞231-108; www.elrelojhotel.cl; Baquedano 828; s/d CH$49,000/68,500; @🛜) Comfortably upscale, this lovely lodging is actually a renovated warehouse. Old rustic remnants blend with a smart, clean design. Think cypress walls, colonial furniture and a cozy stone fireplace. Rooms are quiet, with those upstairs boasting better light and views. Use cash to avoid the room tax, technically not necessary for foreigners.

Raices B&B
B&B $$$

(📞210-490, 099-619-5672; www.raicesbedandbreakfast.com; Baquedano 444; s/d CH$45,000/60,000; 🅿🛜) Hosted by the energetic Cecilia, this central lodging has a tasteful, minimalist ethos. Comfortable beds with plush linens are set in large rooms accented by raw wood and rustic fireplaces (lit at your request). In spite of its location on a busy street, many windows look out on verdant greenery.

Doña Herminia
GUESTHOUSE $

(📞231-579; 21 de Mayo 60; r per person without bathroom CH$8000) Surrounded by thick hedges, this ship-shape home gleams from Doña Herminia's mother-hen attention. Guests dig its little extras like reading lamps and big fresh towels.

La Estancia Cabañas
CABINS $$

(📞250-193; cabanasla@hotmail.com; Colón 166; s/d/tr cabins CH$30,000/40,000/50,000; 🛜) These rustic, well-spaced cabins fill a quiet orchard of apple trees. Two-story cabins have tiled floors, wood stoves and kitchenettes. It's a great deal for small groups.

Residencial Mónica
GUESTHOUSE $

(📞234-302; Eusebio Lillo 664; r per person with/without bathroom CH$10,000/8000) Warm and well-attended, this rambling, prim '60s-style home is always full, in the low season it receives a lot of traveling workers.

Camping Alborada
CAMPGROUND $

(📞238-868; campsites per person CH$3000) Besides camping options at nearby Reserva Nacional Coyhaique, this place, only 1km from the city, has exceptionally clean and sheltered sites (with roofs), lots of bathrooms and individual sinks, hot showers, fire pits and electricity.

🍴 Eating

TOP CHOICE Mamma Gaucha
PIZZERIA $$

(📞210-721; Paseo Horn 47; mains CH$4500-8000; ⏲breakfast, lunch & dinner, closed Sun) Fusing

Patagon lore with a sophisticated palette and reasonable prices, Mamma Gaucha could please the fussiest road warrior. Cane ceilings, whitewashed barn-board walls and cartoon menus create a down-home setting. Start with a fresh-mint lemonade, organic wine or a pint of La Tropera, locally brewed upstairs. The mainstay are clay-oven pizzas, but the homemade pastas and salad bowls that are filled with local produce are just as worthy.

Carnes Queulat PARRILLA $$
(☑250-507; www.carnesqueulat.cl; Ramón Freire 327; mains CH$4000-7000; ⊙lunch & dinner, closed Sun) Tucked away down a gravel alleyway, this friendly plain-Jane place happens to serve the best steaks in the region. *Carne a las brasas* – meat attentively grilled over wood fire – is the worthy house specialty, best matched with some piping-hot homemade empanadas and the secret-recipe pisco sour.

El Reloj Restaurant GOURMET $$
(☑231-108; www.elrelojhotel.cl; Baquedano 828; mains CH$9000) Part of an elegant, intimate hotel, this small restaurant offers a finer touch with sumptuous meals made with regional products, such as crab and Austral hake. Check out the wine selection and homemade desserts. If the weather's good, reserve a table in the apple grove.

Café Confluencia CAFE $$
(☑245-080; 25 de Mayo 548; mains CH$4000-7000; ⊙breakfast, lunch & dinner) A chic eatery serving lovely oversized salads, healthy mains and the occasional stir-fry or taco. Mint pisco sours are the standout drinks to order but tea and fresh juices are good daytime fixes.

La Ovejita CAFE $
(cnr Lillo & Moraleda; sandwiches CH$3000; ⊙breakfast, lunch & dinner; ☎) With an inviting dessert case and seafoam-colored walls, this is an ideal nook to settle down with a pot of Dilmah tea and some goodies. Chocolate is made on-site or you can try a raspberry mousse that's lighter than air. Sandwiches like almond chicken or cured ham with chive cream cheese cure you of the same-old, same-old.

Casino de Bomberos CHILEAN $
(General Parra 365; fixed-price lunch CH$4000; ⊙lunch) Call it a cultural experience, this classic but windowless eatery gets packed with locals downing seafood plates or steak and eggs. The one thing it's short of is fresh air, with empanadas and French fries sizzling up the griddle.

Café Holzer CAFE, DESSERTS $
(Dussen s/n; cakes CH$2000; ⊙breakfast & lunch; ☎) According to locals, the best place to go for sweets is this tiny cafe that has a grassy patio. Sumptuous cakes and tarts are flown in from a reputable Santiago bakery. Real coffee is served and you can also sample a gourd of *maté* to see what all the buzz is about.

The two large supermarkets that are situated side by side on Lautaro are ideal for self-caterers.

🍷 Drinking & Entertainment

Coyhaique has a surprisingly active nightlife in the summer months.

Pub Alkimia PUB, CLUB
(Arturo Prat s/n) Behind the plush black curtains there's a club scene trussed up for a younger crowd and well-heeled 30-somethings alike, with upstairs-downstairs lounges.

Piel Roja PUB
(☑237-832; Moraleda 495; ⊙6pm-5am) Rumbling with late-night life, this bar swarms with local youths and the occasional adventure guide. The circular bar downstairs is the best place for wallflowers to hide; upstairs becomes a romping dance floor in the wee hours.

Café Confluencia CAFE
(☑245-080; 25 de Mayo 548) Two-for-one drink specials and live music on the weekends featuring a range of rock and roll bands and Latin acts turn this cool cafe into a crowded nightspot.

🛍 Shopping

Several crafts outlets sell woolens, leather goods and wood carvings. The **Feria Artesanal** (Plaza de Armas) and **Kaienk** (21 de Mayo 383C; www.telaresdelapatagonia.cl), with exquisite hand-woven shawls and scarves, are worth a look.

ℹ Information

Along Condell, between the plaza and Av Baquedano, are a number of banks with ATMs. Get cash here; it is one of the few stops on the Carretera Austral with Visa ATM access.

Cabot (☎230-101; General Para 177) A general service travel agency.

Conaf (☎212-125/225; Av Ogana 1060; ☺9am-8pm Mon-Sat, 10am-6pm Sun) Provides information on area parks and reserves.

Hospital Regional (☎219-100; Ibar 68; ☺24hr) Emergency is open 24 hours.

Municipal Tourism Office (☑Plaza de Armas) Helpful with excursion and accommodations information.

Police (☎215-105; Baquedano 534)

Post office (Lord Cochrane 202) Near Plaza de Armas.

Sernatur (☎240-290; www.chiletravel/en .html; Bulnes 35; ☺8:30am-9pm Mon-Fri, 10am-6pm Sat & Sun summer) This office provides lists of activity, lodging and transportation options and costs. Regional information is also available.

Turismo Prado (☎231-271; 21 de Mayo 417; ☺9am-6pm) Changes currency.

ⓘ Getting There & Away

Air
Lan (☎231-188; General Parra 402) has several daily flights (most leaving in the morning) to Puerto Montt (CH$96,500) and Santiago (CH$203,000) from the Balmaceda airport; note that rates can be deeply discounted if purchased in-country.

Sky Airline (☎240-827; www.skyairline.cl; Arturo Prat 203) flights from Santiago stop at Balmaceda airport on the way to Punta Arenas.

Transporte Aéreo Don Carlos (☎231-981; Cruz 63) flies small craft to Villa O'Higgins (CH$36,000) on Monday and Thursday. Charter flights are available to Parque Nacional Laguna San Rafael, Chile Chico, Caleta Tortel and Cochrane.

Boat
Ferries and cruises to Puerto Montt, Chiloé and Parque Nacional Laguna San Rafael leave from Puerto Chacabuco, one hour west of Coyhaique by bus, but the closest regional offices are in Coyhaique.

For cruises to Parque Nacional Laguna San Rafael, see p326.

Travelers to Chile Chico can purchase ferry tickets in town at **Naviera Sotramin** (☎237-958; Cerda 647; passenger/automobile CH$1960/17,500), the ferry of which crosses Lago General Carrera between Puerto Ingeniero Ibáñez and Chile Chico almost daily, saving drivers a lot of time on bad roads. If you're driving, make reservations a week out in summer.

Bus
Buses operate from the **bus terminal** (☎258-203; cnr Lautaro & Magallanes) and separate offices. Schedules change continuously; check with **Sernatur** (☎233-949; Bulnes 35) for the latest information. Busing in and out of Coyhaique is just about as confusing as getting around the plaza. Companies and departures vary on demand, and unless noted leave from the terminal.

Companies serving destinations north:

Bus Transaustral (☎232-067; bus terminal) Has services to Osorno and south to Comodoro Rivadavia, Argentina, for connections to Punta Arenas.

Buses Becker (☎232-167; www.busesbecker. com; General Parra 335) Pullman run services twice weekly to Puyuhuapi, La Junta, Villa Santa Lucía and Chaitén. To Futaleufú on Saturdays.

Transportes Terra Austral (☎254-355) Puyuhuapi and La Junta.

Buses Suray (☎238-387; Arturo Prat 265; CH$1000) Have hourly services to Puerto Chacabuco.

Queilen Bus (☎240-760; www.queilenbus. cl; bus terminal) Puerto Montt and Chiloé via Argentina.

Companies serving destinations south:

Acuario 13/Buses Sao Paulo (☎255-726) Cochrane.

Buses Don Carlos (☎231-986/1; Cruz 63) Villa Cerro Castillo, Puerto Río Tranquilo, Puerto Bertrand and Cochrane.

Colectivos Puerto Ibáñez (cnr Arturo Prat & Errázuríz) Door-to-door shuttle to Puerto Ingeniero Ibáñez (CH$4000, 1½ hours).

DESTINATION	COST (CH$)	DURATION (HR)
Chaitén	24,000	9-11
Chile Chico	4000	3½ with ferry
Cochrane	13,000	7-10
Futaleufú	20,000	8-9
La Junta	10,000	5-6
Puerto Montt	30,000	23
Puyuhuapi	8000	6

ⓘ Getting Around

To/From the Airport
Door-to-door shuttle service (CH$4000) to Balmaceda airport, 50km southeast of town, leaves two hours before flight departure. Take any airport transfer, or call **Transfer Velasquez** (☎250-413) for pick-up service.

Car & Bicycle
Car rental is expensive and availability limited in summer. However, it's a popular option since

public transportation is infrequent, sometimes inconvenient and focused on major destinations. Shop around for the best price and, if possible, reserve ahead. Try **Traeger** (☑231-648; Baquedano 457), with its own repair shop and tow service, **Automundo AVR** (☑231-621; fax 231-794; Francisco Bilbao 510) or **Los Andes Patagónicos** (☑232-920; Horn 48). The **Automóvil Club de Chile** (☑231-847; JM Carrera 333) is exceptionally friendly and helpful; staff meet clients at the airport and pick up the cars there as well.

Figon (☑234-616; Almirante Simpson 888) rents and repairs bicycles.

Reserva Nacional Coyhaique

Draped in lenga, ñire and coigue, the 21.5-sq-km **Reserva Nacional Coyhaique** (admission CH$2000) has small lakes and the 1361m Cerro Cinchao. The park is 5km from Coyhaique (about 1½ hours), a good day hike, offering excellent views of the town and Cerro Macay's enormous basalt columns in the distance. Take Baquedano north, across the bridge, then go right at the gravel road, a steep climb best accessed by 4WD. Condor Explorer (p321) runs hiking and winter ski trips in the park.

From the park entrance, it's 2.5km to the **Casa Bruja** sector, with five campsites (CH$3500 per site) with fire pits, hot water, showers and bathrooms. You can also hike 4km through coigue and lenga forests to Laguna Verde, where there are picnic sites and camping with basic facilities. Hiking trails also lead to Laguna Los Sapos and Laguna Venus.

Reserva Nacional Río Simpson

Rocky elephant buttes flank the lazy curves of Río Simpson in a broad valley 37km west of Coyhaique. Straddling the highway to Puerto Chacabuco, the 410-sq-km Reserva Nacional Río Simpson is an easily accessed scenic area that is popular with anglers and summer soakers. Conaf's **Centro de Visitantes** (☉10am-4pm Mon-Sat, 11am-2pm Sun), on the Coyhaique–Puerto Aisén road, has a small natural-history museum and botanical garden. A short walk leads to **Cascada de la Virgen**, a shimmering waterfall on the north side of the highway.

Five kilometers east of the Centro de Visitantes, **Camping San Sebastián** (campsites per group CH$7000) has sheltered sites and hot showers. Near the confluence of the Río Simpson and Río Correntoso, 24km west of Coyhaique, **Camping Río Correntoso** (☑067-232-005; campsites per group CH$7000) has 50 spacious riverside sites in a bucolic setting. The showers are rustic, but hot.

To get there, take any of the frequent buses between Coyhaique and Puerto Aisén; for details, see p325.

Monumento Natural Dos Lagunas

On the road to Paso Alto Coyhaique on the Argentine border, this 181-hectare **wetland reserve** (admission CH$1000) hosts diverse birdlife, including black neck swans, coots and grebes; the area is an ecological transition zone from southern beech forest to semiarid steppe. Orchids abound. A short hiking trail goes to Laguna El Toro while a longer loop flanks the northern edge of Laguna Escondida. Near the reserve's entrance Conaf maintains a self-guided nature trail (1km) and a picnic area. While the park lacks regular public transportation, Coyhaique's branch of Conaf may be able to offer suggestions for getting there.

Parque Nacional Laguna San Rafael

Awesome and remote, this **national park** (admission free) brings visitors face to face with the San Valentín glacier in Chile's northern ice field. The glacier dates back 30,000 years. Established in 1959, the 12,000-sq-km Unesco Biosphere Reserve is the region's most impressive and popular attraction. Scientific interest centers on the extreme fluctuation in water level of the glacier-fed lagoon. The park encompasses peaty wetlands, pristine temperate rainforest of southern beech and epiphytes, and 4058m Monte San Valentín, the southern Andes' highest peak.

Until recently, getting here was expensive and time consuming. Most visitors arrived by sea, shifting to smaller craft and rubber rafts to approach the glacier's 60m face. Unfortunately, this approach permits only a few hours at the glacier without exploring the surrounding trails.

Valle Exploradores, a new gravel road from Puerto Río Tranquilo to La Teresa, at Km 75, dramatically improves park access. Now it's possible to take day trips from Río Tranquilo: outfitters provide a necessary boat crossing to continue on from where the road ends. Staying overnight is worth it to hear the sighs, splintering and booms of calving ice.

There is camping near the Conaf office by the airstrip, with five rustic campsites with water and bathrooms. Fires are not allowed and no food is available at the park.

☞ Tours

The following ships sail from Puerto Chacabuco and Puerto Montt. Check websites for departures and student/senior discounts.

Emtrex   GLACIER TOUR
(☑098-259-4017; www.exploradores-sanrafael.cl; per person daytrip/overnight CH$130,000/200,000) Run by a knowledgeable adventure-travel group, these excursions provide access to the glacier in an open Zodiac boat (passengers are provided with flotation suits). Overnights are spent in a well-heeled base camp in the park. Day trips start at Km75 on the Valle Exploradores road. Longer excursions feature hiking.

Destinos Patagonia   GLACIER TOUR
(☑099-158-6044; www.destinospatagonia.cl; per person 2-day package CH$200,000) The tour picks up participants at Km75 on the Valle Exploradores road (overland transfers from Puerto Río Tranquilo extra). It visits the San Rafael Glacier in a covered boat, overnight is spent at a comfortable refuge.

Cruceros Skorpios   CRUISE
(☑in Santiago 02-477-1900; www.skorpios.cl; 6-day, 5-night cruise for 2 from CH$2,100,000) The luxuriant *Skorpios II* sails from Puerto Montt, spending all of the third day at the glacier. A highlight is the stop at Quitralco, Skorpios' private hot-springs resort. On return it visits the island of Chiloé.

Navimag   CRUISE
(☑067-233-306; www.navimagcruceros.cl; Paseo Horn 47-D, Coyhaique; 5-day, 4-night cruise for 2 from CH$1,350,000) *Mare Australis* sails from Puerto Chacabuco to Chiloé and the Laguna San Rafael in five days and four nights. Passengers may choose to finish the trip in Castro, Chiloé.

Catamaranes del Sur   CRUISE
(☑in Santiago 02-231-1902; www.catamaranes delsur.cl; JM Carrera 50, Puerto Chacabuco; 3-day, 2-night package for 2 from CH$1,080,000) Runs a 12-hour day trip from Puerto Chacabuco on the *Catamaran Chaitén* and the smaller *Iceberg Expedition*. Daytime travel ensures great views of the fjords, but with less time at the glacier face. Includes airport transfer and lodging at the exclusive but nondescript Loberías del Sur and visits to its private park Aikén.

Reserva Nacional Cerro Castillo

Cerro Castillo's basalt spires are the crowning centerpiece of **Reserva Nacional Cerro Castillo** (admission CH$1000), a sprawling 1800-sq-km mountain reserve of southern beech forest, 75km south of Coyhaique. The park boasts fine fishing and hiking, along with little foot traffic. Its namesake, the 2700m triple-tier Cerro Castillo, is flanked by three major glaciers on its southern slopes. Hikers can complete a segment of Sendero de Chile with the 16km trail to Campamento Neozelandés. Another recommended four-day trek (described in Lonely Planet's *Trekking in the Patagonian Andes*) leaves from Km75, at the north end of the reserve, and goes to Villa Cerro Castillo at the south end via a high route passing glaciers, rivers and lakes.

Conaf operates a sheltered **campground** (tent CH$3500) at Laguna Chaguay, 67km south of Coyhaique. It has bathrooms and hot showers. Backcountry camping is also possible. Before going into the backcountry, check in with the ranger to avoid seasonal hazards.

Upon request, public buses will stop to leave passengers at the ranger station and campground.

Villa Cerro Castillo

Under the sparkly five-carat face of Cerro Castillo, pioneer town Villa Cerro Castillo has a congenial dusty-heeled feel. It's a good base to explore the reserve and a short distance from the Carretera Austral, 10km west of the Puerto Ingeniero Ibáñez junction. The town's **Festival Costumbrista**, usually held in February, offers an authentic take on Patagonian rodeo and draws artists and artisans from all over Chile and Argentina.

The **tourist office** (Los Antiguos 208; ☺10am-8pm Jan-Feb) is helpful with information.

The clean and comfortable **Cabañas Don Niba** (☎099-474-0408; Los Pioneros 872; d CH$25,000, s/d without bathroom CH$9000/18,000) family lodging dishes out whopping breakfasts and the company of Don Niba, guide, storyteller and grandson of pioneers. He also offers horseback riding, *asados* and hikes. **Camping Refugio Donde Jorge** (☎097-898-8550; cumbresyglaciares@yahoo.es) sits at the start of the multiday Cerro Castillo hike; for hike indications, check out Lonely Planet's *Trekking in the Patagonian Andes.* Guide service **Los Baqueanos** (☎097-562-2911; baqueanosdelapatagonia.cl) leads good horseback treks and practices *domo racional*, a gentle taming method.

For satisfying road food, **La Querencia** (O'Higgins 460; set menu CH$5000; ☺breakfast, lunch & dinner) delivers. If you're too late for the set lunch, Señora Maria will fix you an enormous sandwich.

Buses Don Carlos shuttles daily to and from Coyhaique and twice weekly to Puerto Río Tranquilo (for details, see p325).

Puerto Ingeniero Ibáñez

☎067 / POP 3000

On the north shore of Lago General Carrera, sleepy Puerto Ingeniero Ibáñez serves as a transit station for ferry goers, although many new sport-climbing routes mean it will probably become a hot stop for climbers. Clobbered in Volcán Hudson's 1991 eruption, it has since recovered.

Ferries to Chile Chico, on the lake's south shore, leave from here. If local handicrafts interest you, ask around for pottery artist Señora Marta Aguila or weaver and herbal-remedy specialist Señora Juana Vega. It's that informal. Locals can also point you to cave paintings or the Río Ibáñez falls, 8km away.

Around 1.5km before town, **La Casona** (☎099-294-3413; senderospatagonia@gmail.com; r per person CH$10,000) offers friendly farmhouse lodgings, ideal for cyclists or hikers. Camping may also be available. Campers will find friendly faces at countryside **Maitenal Camping** (☎098-389-2832, 098-532-7680; Camino a Levican Km12; campsites per person CH$2000), with good installations, including showers and artisan beer. Host Lillian is a certified guide and her German husband Gerald maintains the climbs at El Maitenal.

For road transportation from Coyhaique to Puerto Ingeniero Ibáñez, see p325 Ferry schedules seem to change from year to year and season to season. For Chile Chico, the **Naviera Sotramin** (☎099-757-0116; General Carrera 202; passenger/automobile CH$1960/17,500) ferry crosses Lago General Carrera to Chile Chico almost daily; arrive 30 minutes predeparture.

Chile Chico

☎067 / POP 4000

Bordering Argentina, this pint-sized orchard town occupies the windy southern shore of Lago General Carrera. A sunny microclimate makes it a pleasant oasis on the steppe. It is linked to Chile by ferry or a roller-coaster road dotted with gold and silver mines. Locals traditionally earned their living from raising livestock and farming but have turned to mining in numbers. Rumor has it that wi-fi is soon coming to town.

Hikers shouldn't miss the Reserva Nacional Jeinemeni, 60km away, with solitary treks in an arid wonderland of flamingo-filled turquoise mountain lagoons. Travelers tend to zip through town, but there are worthwhile side trips and connections to Los Antiguos and Ruta 40 leading to southern Argentine Patagonia.

Traveling the abrupt curves of Paso Las Llaves, west from Chile Chico to the junction with the Carretera Austral, is one of the region's highlights. Scary and stunning, it hits blind corners and steep inclines on loose gravel high above the lake with no guardrails. If driving, proceed very slowly; in some places the roadway is barely wide enough for a single vehicle.

⊙ Sights & Activities

Casa de la Cultura   MUSEUM
(☎411-355; cnr O'Higgins & Lautaro; admission free) Chile Chico's museum and cultural center, Casa de la Cultura, features a ground-floor collection of works by regional artists and a 2nd-floor assemblage of local artifacts, including minerals and fossils. Outside is the restored *El Andes,* which was built in Glasgow, Scotland, to navigate the Thames, but was brought here to carry passengers and freight around the lake.

Expeditions Patagonia   ADVENTURE TOURS
(☎098-464-1067; www.expeditionspatagonia.com; O'Higgins 333, Galeria Municipal; ☺9am-1pm & 2:30-8pm) Run by Ferdinando Georgia, a

reputable guide and graduate of Escuela de Guias (a rigorous training program in Coyhaique), this outfitter does trekking in Jeinimeni, multiday trips and mountaineering expeditions.

🛏 Sleeping & Eating

Hostería de la Patagonia   FARMSTAY $
(☎411-337; hosteriadelapatagonia.cl; Camino Internacional s/n; campsites per person CH$4000, s/d/tr CH$18,000/32,000/36,000, without bathroom CH$10,000/20,000/30,000) Descendants of Belgian colonists run this sweet farmhouse with gardens and horses. Rooms are light-filled and tidy, some with private bathrooms. Meals cost CH$8000 extra. Look for the yellow roof, leaving town on the way toward Argentina.

La Posada del Río   HOTEL $$
(☎099-647-0968, 099-452-0759; www.chile-chico.cl; Camino Internacional Km5; d/t CH$42,000/48,000) On the open steppe with sweeping views, this new hotel has bright rooms replete with wooden accents. Breakfasts come complete with orange juice, *medialunas* (croissants) and jam. The hotel also owns a 32-passenger boat which provides an alternate mode of travel to Puerto Ibañez (50 minutes, CH$10,000) with almost daily trips in high season.

Hospedaje No Me Olvides   FARMSTAY $
(Sector Chacras; campsites CH$4000, s without bathroom CH$10,000) Rooms are snuggly and ample at this country farmhouse, 200m from town. Attention is quite friendly and guests can use the kitchen. Campers bed down in the orchard. Currently there's no working phone; for directions see the tourism office.

Kon Aiken   GUESTHOUSE $
(☎411-598; Pedro Burgos 6; campsites per person CH$3000, r per person CH$8000, 7-person cabin from CH$35,000) With a family atmosphere, this handy lodging offers good rates. The range of services sometimes give it a busy atmosphere. The kind owners sell firewood, share the bounty of local produce and organize the occasional *asado* or salmon bake. A row of poplars block the winds for campers.

Hospedaje Brisas del Lago   GUESTHOUSE $
(☎411-204; Manuel Rodríguez 443; d CH$22,500, s/d without bathroom CH$10,500/15,000) There are a number of good-sized rooms, both clean and comfortable, but service lacks spark.

Café Elizabeth y Loly   CAFE $
(☎411-451; Pedro González 25; mains CH$2500-5000; ☺lunch & dinner) Considering this is Chile Chico, this quirky stop is a cafe-culture hot spot, serving strong coffee and authentic baklava, opposite the plaza.

ℹ Information

BancoEstado (González 112; ☺9am-2pm Mon-Fri) Changes US cash only and has reasonable rates, but collects a commission on all traveler's checks. The ATM takes only MasterCard.

Conaf (☎411-325; Blest Gana 121; ☺10am-6pm Mon-Fri, 11am-4pm Sat) For information on Reserva Nacional Jeinemeni.

Oficina de Información Turística (☎411-338; www.chilechico.cl; cnr O'Higgins & Blest Ghana; ☺9am-9pm Mon-Fri, 10am-9pm Sat & Sun) Excellent area information.

Post office (Manuel Rodríguez 121)

ℹ Getting There & Away

Drivers should fill up with gas here at the Copec station.

Boat

An almost-daily ferry run by **Naviera Sotramin** (☎237-958; Muelle Chile Chico; passenger/automobile CH$1960/17,500) crosses Lago General Carrera to Puerto Ingeniero Ibáñez, a big shortcut to Coyhaique. If driving, make reservations a week out in summer. Arrive 30 minutes before departure time.

Bus

A number of shuttle buses cross the border to Los Antiguos, Argentina (CH$3000, 20 minutes), just 9km east. Shuttles, which coordinate with buses that run directly to El Chaltén, leave from O'Higgins 420.

From Los Antiguos, travelers can make connections in Argentina to Perito Moreno, Comodoro Rivadavia, El Chaltén and southern Argentine Patagonia.

A bus terminal is under construction. Currently, bus routes are run by private individuals subject to apply for the government concession, thus providers and schedules can vary from year to year.

To Puerto Guadal (CH$6000, three hours), **Seguel** (☎067-431-224, 245-237; O'Higgins 394) goes from Monday and Thursday at 4pm. Going north to Puerto Río Tranquilo (CH$10,000, five hours), **Patricio Aravena** (☎097-750-2351) has pick-up service, leaving on Tuesday and Friday at 10am. South to Cochrane (CH$13,000, five hours), **Alfonso Haeger** (☎097-962-8325) travels Wednesdays and Saturday at 1pm.

Buses Acuña (☑251-579; Rodríguez 143) and **Buses Ali** (☑219-009) to Coyhaique (CH$4000, 3½ hours) make a ferry-bus combination; reserve ahead. You will first take the Naviera Sotramin Ferry to Puerto Ibáñez.

Reserva Nacional Jeinemeni

Turquoise lakes and the rusted hues of the steppe mark the rarely visited **Reserva Nacional Jeinemeni** (admission CH$2000), 52km southwest of Chile Chico. Its unusual wonders range from cave paintings to foxes and flamingos. In the transition zone to the Patagonian steppe, it covers 1610 sq km. Through-hikers can link to Valle Chacabuco via a two-day mountain traverse on **Sendero La Leona**; for information contact Estancia Valle Chacabuco (p332).

Three private **camping areas** (per site CH$5000) are on the banks of the startlingly blue Lago Jeinemeni, about 400m from the Conaf office. **Sendero Lago Verde** takes visitors on a three-hour, 10km-round-trip hike to a gemstone lake. The road into the park is passable only by 4WD vehicles because Río Jeinemeni cuts across the road, causing flooding conditions mid-afternoon. Day-trippers should leave early enough to cross on the way back before 4pm.

En route to the reserve, about 25km south of Chile Chico, an access road leads to **Cueva de las Manos**, Tehuelche cave paintings. Reaching the cave requires a steep uphill climb (unmarked) and is best done with a guide.

Puerto Río Tranquilo

☑067

A village of shingled houses on the windy western shores of Lago General Carrera, Puerto Río Tranquilo is a humble pit stop. For many travelers, it's just a fuel stop, but growing outdoor opportunities are starting to put it on the map. It's the closest access point to Capilla de Marmol's cool marble caves. More recently it's become the launch point for more budget-minded tours to the stunning Glaciar San Rafael.

◉ Sights & Activities

Capilla de Mármol   LANDMARK
(Marble Chapel) Well worth the detour, these sculpted geological formations are accessible by boat on Lago General Carrera.

Trips (from CH$30,000 for five passengers) only go out in calm boating conditions.

Valle Exploradores   DRIVING TOUR
This newly constructed east–west road heads toward Laguna San Rafael, but stops short at a water crossing. Gorgeous but rough, it is still a worthy driving- or biking-tour detour, crowded with glaciers and overgrown nalca plants. Keep an eye out for the overlook to Glaciar Exploradores at Km52. Day trippers to Glaciar San Rafael meet their outfitters at the end of the road.

🛏 Sleeping

TOP CHOICE **El Puesto**   INN $$
(☑satellite 02-196-4555; www.elpuesto.cl; Pedro Lagos 258; s/d CH$47,000/58,000; 🛜) Guests are pampered in this modern wood home, with woolen slippers, hand-woven throws and rockers. There's even a swing set for kids. English-speaking owners Francisco and Tamara run a reputable professional guide service offering ice trekking on Glacier Exploradores and other services. Meals are available with reservations; they also offer massage and rent local cabins.

Residencial Darka   GUESTHOUSE $
(☑419-500; Arrayanes 330; r per person CH$10,000) Family-run, with clean rooms. The pastels and lace provide a good dose of kitsch.

Camping Pudu   CAMPGROUND $
(☑211-085, 098-920-5085; campingpudu@gmail.com; campsites per person CH$4000; ☺Dec-Mar) Beach camping with hot showers and laundry service, 1km south of Puerto Río Tranquilo. Guided fishing and hikes are also available.

ℹ Information

Tourism kiosk (Av Costanera s/n; ☺9am-9pm, Tue-Sun Dec-Mar) Has information about lodging and tours to the Capilla de Mármol.
Casa del Turista (☑096-677-9321; cnr Av Costanera & Pedro Lagos; ☺9am-noon & 4-9pm) Organizes adventure tours and boat trips to Glacier San Rafael.

ℹ Getting There & Away

Regular buses between Coyhaique (CH$8000) and Cochrane (CH$8000) will drop off and pick up passengers here. Coyhaique-bound buses usually pass at around 10am. Those heading further south pass between 1pm and 2pm.
To Chile Chico (CH$8000), the bus passes at around 5pm.

Cruce el Maitén

Cruce el Maitén is little more than a fork in the road where an eastern route branches alongside Lago General Carrera to Chile Chico. **Pasarela Sur Lodge** (☎067-411-425; www.pasarelasurlodge.cl; Km265; cabin per person CH$30,000) has cabins with a hot tub, a public restaurant (meals CH$13,000) and a motorboat ready at the dock for fishing (CH$30,000 per hour with guide). Lakeside **Hacienda Tres Lagos** (☎067-411-323; www.haciendatreslagos.com; Km274; d suite/bungalow CH$178,000/134,000; @☎) offers elegant accommodations, excursions and copious amenities that aim to please all, namely an art gallery, zip line, sauna, Jacuzzi, cafe and game room.

Puerto Guadal

Windy but damn postcard beautiful, Puerto Guadal is located at the southwest end of Lago General Carrera on the road to Chile Chico, 13km east of the Carretera Austral. The village appears to be at siesta at all hours, but cool accommodations, nearby fossil hikes and glaciers can keep a visitor very entertained.

Adventure outfitter **Kalen** (☎067-431-289, 098-811-2535; Los Alerces 557; ⊙9am-9pm) is run by reputable guide Pascual Diaz. He offers horseback riding, glacier trips with hiking (CH$48,000 per person) and hikes to a beautiful fossil bed (CH$20,000 per person plus guide fees). Try to make contact in advance, as the office may be closed for outings.

With rave reviews, ecocamp and hostel **Un Destino No Turistico** (☎098-756-7545; www.destino-noturistico.com; Camino Laguna La Manga Km1; campsites per person CH$4500, dm/d CH$9000/22,000) provides a lovely countryside getaway. Owners Rocio and Manuel are active educators, teaching off-grid living and sharing their useful innovations. The hostel is impeccable, with comfortable beds, each with its own reading lamp, in addition to solar showers and composting toilets. It's situated 1.5km from town, but all downhill when you leave. Cars should park outside the entrance gate.

Lakeside adventure lodge **Terra Luna** (☎067-431-263; www.terra-luna.cl; campsites per person CH$5000, 2-person huts CH$30,000, d/tr/q CH$80,000/90,000/110,000; ☎▥) presents the option of perfect repose or an adrenaline

rush. Lodgings vary from smart apartments to freestanding cabins, with the tempting extra of a lakefront wood-fired hot tub. The restaurant serves a set menu of chef-prepared meals nightly. Adorable budget-oriented huts with kitchen and camp sites suit budget travelers, though spots are few. With sprawling grounds, there is also a play area, guest kayaks and zip lines in the works. Run by Azimut, a French-owned guide service, there are frequent excursions like glacier visits and hikes by jet boat, canyoning and overnighting on the Campo de Hielo Norte. It's 1.5km from Puerto Guadal toward Chile Chico.

Buses leave from **ECA** (☎067-431-224; Las Magnolias 306), heading north to Coyhaique (CH$11,000) Wednesdays and Sundays at around 8am. Bus services that are southbound pass the crossroads just outside of town, to Cochrane (CH$5000) starting at around 2pm.

Seguel (☎067-431-214, Los Notros 560) servicesd travel to Chile Chico (CH$7000, three hours) on Mondays and Thursdays at about 7am. Check locally for other combinations of bus servcies.

Puerto Bertrand

☎067 / POP 1500

On the bank of the ultramarine blue Lago Bertrand below the snow-covered San Valentín and Campo de Hielo Norte, Puerto Bertrand is a show of contrasts. Weathered shingle homes overgrown with rose blossoms and high-end fishing lodges share the space of this humble, dusty stop. Bertrand occupies the southeast shore of the lake, situated 11km south of Cruce el Maitén. It is also the base for mountaineering expeditions to the northern ice field and rafting trips on Río Baker, Chile's most voluminous river.

🏃 Activities

Patagonia Adventure
Expeditions   HORSEBACK RIDING

(☎411-330; www.adventurepatagonia.com) Pioneers of the fantastic Aysén Glacier trail, who takes guests horseback trekking through glacially carved valleys and old lenga forests, forging streams, climbing to Ventisquero Soler, ice climbing and meeting up with gauchos for an *asado*. These lauded trips with bilingual guides focus on 'cultural geography.' It also offers floating on the Río

PATAGONIA'S RIVER DEBATE

Patagonia boasts one of the world's great water reserves, with deep glacial lakes, two of the planet's largest non-polar ice fields and powerful, pristine rivers rushing from the Andes to the Pacific. It's a dream if you're a salmon, a nature lover or kayaker. Or a hydroelectric company.

In May, 2011, a Chilean government commission approved a US$7billion dollar plan to build five dams on what's considered two of the world's wildest rivers – the Aisen region's Baker and Pascua rivers. The dams would provide energy to a country whose growth and industry is clamoring for it. They would also usher in the industrialization of one of the most pristine parts of the planet. Behind the dams is HydroAysén, a Chile-based conglomerate comprised of Spanish-Italian multinational Endesa and the Chilean company Colbún.

Pending approval is the most controversial aspect of the project – building the world's longest transmission lines. Thousands of high-voltage towers would run 2415km to bring power to Santiago and mining operations in the north that consume half of Chile's energy. The towers would require a clear-cut equivalent to the distance from Maine to Florida and change the iconic landscape. In the town of La Junta, resistance to the towers has been so fierce that planners are considering detouring their path to avoid a conflict. In other affected towns, resistance is said to be subsiding with HydroAysén's promises to offer $350million in regional infrastructure, jobs and scholarships.

Chile's peculiar water laws are behind the commercial rush. After the Pinochet regime privatized the national energy company Endesa, it was sold to foreign investors. According to the report *Conflicts Over Water in Chile* (edited by Sara Larrain and Colombina Scaeffer of the Chilean nongovernment organization, Chile Sustenable), 80% of Chile's non-consumptive water rights are foreign-owned.

Energy is a hot topic in Chile, where natural resources are few. Still, the decision of the government commission proved unpopular with the public – a protest march in Santiago attracted an unanticipated 30,000 citizens. If transmission lines are approved, the decade-long construction will begin as early as 2014. Already, the looming possibility has many travelers rushing to see Patagonia in its still-pristine state.

Baker. For more information, check out its Facebook page.

Baker Patagonia Aventura   RAFTING
(www.bakerpatagonia.com; half-day trips CH$30,000) Leads five-day and one day (class III) raft trips on the Río Baker. Currently there's no phone but the office faces Lago Bertrand.

🛏 Sleeping & Eating

Hostería Puerto Bertrand   GUESTHOUSE $
(☑099-219-1532; Costanera s/n; r per person without bathroom CH$10,000) Above the general store, this rickety wood home has a cozy atmosphere with soft armchairs and lace-covered tables. Shop around for a room with ventilation.

Patagonia Green Baker   CABINS $$
(☑in Santiago 02-196-0409; www.greenlodge baker.com; d CH$45,000; 2-/3-/4-person cabins CH$55,000/70,000/75,000) These two-story cabins are a pleasant enough stop. Riverside,

the complex features a hot tub, restaurant and activities like kayaking and horseback riding. Cabins have direct TV and phones. It's located 3km south of Puerto Bertrand.

La Casa del Río Konaiken   CAFE $
(☑098-402-3197; www.konaiken.blog.com; snacks CH$2500, ☑) A great pit stop, with espresso, wholegrain pies and homemade jams. The three rustic three-person cabins (CH$45,000) on the forested shores of Río Baker, 6km south of Puerto Bertrand, are a coveted treat. Dinner for guests includes wine and the option of vegetarian fare. The owner is also a local conservation advocate.

Valle Chacabuco (Parque Nacional Patagonia)

Eighteen kilometers north of Cochrane, this reformed *estancia* is home to flamingo, guanaco, huemul (endangered Andean deer), puma, viscacha and fox. Conservacion Patagonica, the NGO behind the Patagonia

National Park project, began this initiative in 2004. Now dubbed as the Serengeti of the Southern Cone, the 690-sq-km Valle Chacabuco features Patagonian steppe, forests, mountains, lakes and lagoons. The park stretches from the Río Baker to the Argentine border. In a private vehicle, it's possible to cross here at Paso Roballos.

It's still a national park in the making. Combining this valley with Reserva Nacional Jeinimeni to the north and Reserva Nacional Tamango to the south will eventually result in a 2400-sq-km park worthy of one day rivaling Torres del Paine.

Major rehabilitation, with the help of many volunteers, has reinstated the valley as an important wildlife corridor. Already foxes and herds of guanaco are easily spotted. Studies underway in the park look at grasslands ecology and track huemul (endangered deer) populations. Currently the park's roaming population of around 1500 huemul makes up 10% of the entire worldwide population.

The park plans to add many more trails and campgrounds. While infrastructure and services are still under construction, visitors can hike existing trails, drive through and take in the beauty or help restore it by taking part in an extensive volunteer program.

☆ Activities

Lagunas Altas Trail   HIKING
This 26km trail ascends from the Westwind Camping site (close to park headquarters) toward a southern ridge and heads east across open terrain and around small gemstone lakes before winding down toward the administration buildings, with spectacular views of the Chacabuco Valley, San Lorenzo, the northern Patagonian ice field and the Jeinimeni Mountains. Bring plenty of water.

Aviles Valley Trail   HIKING
Starting at the Stone House Camping site, about 25km up valley from the main park headquarters, the Aviles Valley trail connects the Chacabuco Valley with Jeinimeni National Reserve and the town of Chile Chico to the north. Take a day hike up this valley, or plan for a three- to four-day (about 45km) backpack to Lago Jeinimeni.

Valley Drive   WILDLIFE WATCHING
The 72km drive from the Río Baker to the Argentine border climbs through steppe, with flamingos in lagoons and foxes crossing the road. Drive slowly and pull out only where there's room.

🛏 Sleeping & Eating

Visitors can also lodge in nearby Cochrane. A flagship restaurant, the first large stone building at the entrance of the park administration area, should be open for lunch and dinner by the time you read this. In addition to a set menu, it will serve sandwiches and tea. A greenhouse on-site supplies most of the fresh produce.

The Lodge at Valle
Chacabuco   BOUTIQUE HOTEL $$$
(reservas@vallechacabuco.cl; suggested donation per person US$250; ☉mid-Oct–April) Classic and refined, this beautiful stone lodge was modeled on English architecture in southern Argentina. Patterned tiles, handsome wood and large photographic nature prints foster a warm ambience. There are just six guest rooms, mostly doubles with some bunks for families. The lodge will initially open on a donations-only payment system, advance reservations required.

Westwind Camping   CAMPGROUND $
(campsites free) In the valley, this large, grassy campground features eight covered cook shelters and a bathhouse with hot showers. Sites are first-come, first-served. It's 4km from the administrative area.

Stone House Camping   CAMPGROUND $
(campsites free) Part way up the valley drive, it's about 25km from the administrative area. The bathrooms are housed in a historic stone outpost left over from the park's days as a sheep *estancia*.

❶ Information

Visitors can go to **Park Headquarters** (☑065-970-833; www.conservacionpatagonica.org; park entry free) for trail maps and information. The **official blog** (www.conservacionpatagonica.org/blog) offers more information about the project and the region. A natural-history center is in the works.

❶ Getting There & Away

The entrance to the park is 18km north of Cochrane. Look for the sign for Entrada Baker. Buses between Cochrane and Coyhaique can drop passengers at the entrance, but the administrative area is 11km further east on the main road to Paso Roballos.

THE TOMPKINS LEGACY

Ecobarons – the wealthy philanthropists recycling their greenbacks into green causes – have stamped an indelible presence into Southern Cone conservation and none more so than US entrepreneurs Douglas and Kris Tompkins. With holdings in Chile and Argentina, the couple has conserved over two million acres of land, which is more than any individual in history. While this power couple started in the trenches of retail (she as CEO of Patagonia, he as founder of Northface and Esprit), they have turned their industry toward rewilding key ecosystems.

It started in 1991 with Parque Pumalín, a Rhode Island–sized conservation project cobbled together from small Patagonian farms abutting ancient forest. In 2004, Kris Tompkins became a player, purchasing a run-down *estancia* (grazing ranch) near Cochrane through nonprofit Conservación Patagonica. At the time, intensive sheep ranching had resulted in the widespread desertification of the ranch, which had long since ceased profitability. Major rehabilitation has helped reinstate the land as an important wildlife corridor between two other parks. Known as Valle Chacabuco (Parque Nacional Patagonia), the 690-sq-km park features Patagonian steppe, forests, mountains, lakes and lagoons. Re-creating a home on the range was never so hard won. To restore grasslands, invasive plant species that proliferated with livestock were ripped out by hand. Over 644km of fencing was removed so native guanaco and huemul could return – and they did.

Doug Tompkins has also donated two smaller national parks, Corcovado and Tic Toc, to the state, but remains steadfast in his protection of Pumalín (where the couple has a home). Donated to Fundación Pumalín in 2005, it will eventually become a national park.

The couple has inspired copycat contributions, like former Chilean presidential candidate Sebastian Piñera's Parque Tantauco in Chiloé. The Tompkins' sweeping land purchases initially stirred up suspicion and regional resentment in Chile. Yet as time goes by, much of the initial criticism has died down and many Chileans have found the parks to be a worthwhile contribution to their nation.

Cochrane

📞067 / POP 3000

An old ranching outpost, Cochrane is the southern hub of the Carretera Austral. The new bustling of industry comes in anticipation of major proposals for nearby hydroelectric dams. Neighbors are divided over progress that might mean a mini-economic boom but would double the population with itinerant workers and definitively change the landscape.

Visitors should take advantage of activities a spring step away, which include fishing on Lago Cochrane, horseback treks and hiking. Cochrane has the last gas station and is the best place for information along this lonely stretch of road.

🛏 Sleeping & Eating

Residencial Cero a Cero　　GUESTHOUSE $
(📞522-158; Lago Brown 464; s/d CH$15,000/22,000, r per person without bathroom CH$9000) A log home that has ample space, Cero a Cero is a comfortable option with good beds, plenty of windows and a warm, cozy interior.

Latitude 47　　GUESTHOUSE $
(📞098-829-0956; Lago Brown 564; s/d CH$20,000/30,000, r per person without bathroom CH$10,000) With warm hospitality, this big white house has a selection of narrow upstairs rooms with single beds. The recently constructed rooms with bathroom, in an independent area, are worthy upgrades.

Cabañas Sol y Luna　　CABINS $$
(📞098-157-9602, 096-571-0763; xmardonestorres@hotmail.com; 4-person cabins CH$45,000; @) Nice, new and well equipped, these cabins help you achieve a needed rest. There's also a sauna and hot tubs.

Restaurant Ada's　　CHILEAN $
(📞098-399-5889; Teniente Merino 374; mains CH$4500; ◷lunch & dinner) Serving crisp whole fish or tender beef, bottles of wine, salads and potatoes, these big meals add up to a good deal. Service is attentive too.

Café Tamango
CAFE $

(Esmeralda 464; sandwiches CH$4000; ⊘9am-8pm Mon-Sat; ☑) Everything looks good in this cafe, from the homemade candies and ice cream to sandwiches and couscous. It's set back from the road with outdoor seating.

❶ Information

BancoEstado (Esmeralda 460) ATM accepts MasterCard only.

Conaf (☑522-164; Río Nef 417; ⊘10am-6pm Mon-Sat)

Hospital (☑522-131; O'Higgins 755; ⊘24hr) Emergency is open 24 hours.

Post office (Esmeralda 199; ⊘9am-3pm Mon-Fri, 11am-2pm Sat)

Tourist kiosk (☑522-326; turismo@cochrane patagonia.cl; Plaza de Armas; ⊘9am-1pm & 2-9pm Jan & Feb) With the latest bus schedules, fishing guides and taxi information.

❶ Getting There & Away

Buses go daily to Coyhaique, usually at 8am. Companies include **Buses Don Carlos** (☑522-150; Prat 334), **Buses Acuario 13** (☑522-143; Río Baker 349), **Sao Paulo** (☑522-143; Río Baker 349) and **Aguilas Patagonicas** (☑211-288, 522-020; Dr Steffen & Las Golondrinas).

To get to Caleta Tortel, take Buses Acuario 13, which departs at 9:30am on Monday, Wednesday and Sunday.

For Villa O'Higgins, **Buses Aldea** (☑522-143; Río Baker 349) departs at 8am on Thursday and Sunday.

Chile Chico is served by **Transportes Egger** (☑522-448, 522-020; Las Golondrinas 399) twice weekly, with stops in Puerto Bertrand and Puerto Guadal.

DESTINATION	COST (CH$)	DURATION (HR)
Caleta Tortel	CH$6000	3
Chile Chico	CH$13,000	5
Coyhaique	CH$13,000	7-10
Villa O'Higgins	CH$22,000	6

Reserva Nacional Tamango

Boasting Chile's largest population of endangered huemul deer, **Reserva Nacional Tamango** (admission CH$3000; camping per site CH$5000) protects a 70-sq-km transition zone to the Patagonian steppe. Huemul are notoriously shy, but chances of sighting one are better here than anywhere. At the entrance, trails (1.5km to 7km in length) lead to Laguna Elefantina, Laguna Tamanguito and 1722m Cerro Tamango. The reserve is located 6km northeast of Cochrane; there is no public transportation to the entrance. At the corner of Colonia and San Valentín, hikers can take Pasaje No 1 north and then east to access trails to the entrance. Cochrane's Conaf office may have trail maps available.

Caleta Tortel

☑067 / POP 550

A network of creaky boardwalks tracing the milky waters of the glacier-fed sound, Caleta Tortel feels fabled. There are no roads. Dedicated as a national monument, this fishing village cobbled around a steep escarpment is certainly unique. Seated between two ice fields at the mouth of Río Baker, it was first home to canoe-traveling Alacalufes (Qawashqar); colonists didn't arrive until 1955. Still isolated but more outwardly social than other Patagonians, locals live off tourism and cypress-wood extraction. Dependence on a small turbine means that the town has water and electricity shortages in big droughts. Use water sparingly.

The road stops at the edge of town, near the El Rincon sector. Boardwalks and staircases lead to the center and past, to the sector of Playa Ancha, a wide beach. Water taxis help people get around town, but it's best to take minimal luggage and keep in mind the numerous staircases.

◉ Sights & Activities

Imposing glaciers like Glacier Montt (Campo de Hielo Sur) and Glacier Steffens (Campo de Hielo Norte) can only be reached by boat. Motorized boat trips for eight to 10 people cost between CH$250,000 and CH$320,000. Some excursions include hiking or horseback riding. Rates are divided by the number of passengers and departures are dependent on weather.

Paz Austral
GLACIER TOUR

(☑satellite phone 02-196-0270/1; www.entrehielos tortel.cl) Trips to Glacier Steffens and Reserva Katalalixar (on demand) and the mouth of the Río Baker and Isla Los Muertos (daily).

Destinos Patagonia
GLACIER TOUR

(☑099-158-6044; www.destinospatagonia.cl; per person 2-day package CH$200,000) Boat *Qawasqar* visits both glaciers as well as Isla los Muertos.

Junquillo HIKING

Above the Rincon sector of Tortel, this three-hour round-trip offer views of the Baker estuary and canals.

🛏 Sleeping & Eating

TOP CHOICE Entre Hielos B&B $$$

(🖊satellite phone 02-196-0270/1; www.entrehielos tortel.cl; s/d CH$55,000/70,000; 🛜) A lovely cypress home located at the top of a steep staircase, this wonderful lodging boasts both modern style and family warmth. Breakfast includes real coffee and homemade jams. Chef-prepared meals may include local beef or salmon from the Río Baker and there's a great selection of wines. It also runs boat tours.

Brisas del Sur GUESTHOUSE $$

(🖊231-815; Playa Ancha sector; d CH$35,000, r per person without bathroom CH$12,000; 🛜) Señora Valería puts guests at ease in snug rooms with lovely beach views and smells of good cooking wafting up the stairs. Contact this guesthouse through the tourism kiosk.

Residencial Estilo GUESTHOUSE $$

(🖊local line 143; d CH$30,000, r per person without bathroom CH$12,000) Javier Pinella's well-kept wooden house has newish doubles in wood finish.

Playa Ancha Camping CAMPGROUND $

(Playa Ancha; campsites free) Camping is free but primitive with a stunning river-mouth setting; campers can use shower facilities (CH$1500) across the boardwalk at Brisas del Sur.

Sabores Locales CHILEAN $$

(mains CH$6000-10,000; ⊙1pm-1am;🖊) Maritza cooks up a storm of tasty soups, smoked salmon and ceviche dishes in this cute cafe with vegetarian options.

ℹ Information

Telefónica (🖊234-815; ⊙10am-1pm & 3-8pm Mon-Sat) The town's public phone.
Tourism kiosk (🖊231-815; www.munici palidaddetortel.cl; ⊙9am-10pm) Helpful with some English-speaking staff. At the entry to the village, where buses stop.

ℹ Getting There & Away

All buses depart from a stop next to the tourism kiosk in the upper entrance to the village since there is no motorized access to town. To Cochrane (CH$6000, three hours), Buses Aldea departs five days per week at 3pm. To Coyhaique (CH$22,000, 11 hours), Aguilas Patagonicas leaves Thursday and Sunday at 8am.

El Mosco goes to Villa O'Higgins (CH$15,000, four hours) at 4:30pm on Sundays. Robinson Crusoe makes the same trip on Tuesday and Thursday at 4pm.

Charging per trip, not per person, boat taxis leave from the Rincon sector for the center (CH$3000), Playa Ancha (CH$5000) and Isla de los Muertos (CH$35,000); they also do tours of the bay (CH$6000 to CH$20,000).

South to Villa O'Higgins

Wild stretches of rushing rivers and virgin forest flank the curvy road south of El Vagabundo and the access road to Caleta Tortel. Here the Carretera Austral demands constant attention with sectors of washboard road and potential slides. It's best to travel in a high-clearance vehicle.

At **Puerto Yungay**, a government ferry hauls passengers and four cars to the east end of Fiordo Mitchell at Río Bravo, usually three or four times a day at 10am, noon and 6pm (free, one hour) in summer. Space is limited, so if you are driving arrive early and expect to wait, passing the time with a scrumptious empanada from the kiosk. After the ferry crossing, another 100km of rugged road leads to the north end of a narrow arm of Lago O'Higgins (known as Lago San Martín on the Argentine side).

Villa O'Higgins

🖊067 / POP 500

The last stop on the Carretera Austral, this mythic village is alluring in its isolation. First settled by the English (1914–16), the outpost attracted a few Chileans but the road didn't arrive until 1999. The spectacular surroundings can be explored on horseback or foot, and there's world-class fishing. A growing number of trekkers and cyclists are crossing over from El Chaltén, Argentina. Plans to create road access to Argentina via Entrada Mayer (slated for 2013) and add a strip of road between Candelaria Mansilla and Lago del Desierto (which would still require ferry use) will greatly facilitate travel to and from Argentina.

Almost no one uses addresses but locals are happy to point you in the right direction. There's no ATM here so bring the cash you will need.

Tours

Villa O'Higgins

Expediciones   ADVENTURE TOUR
(☑431-821/2; www.villaohiggins.com) Guided horseback riding or trekking trips are available with advance booking through Hans Silva's full-service company, which also rents bikes.

Robinson Crusoe   GLACIER TOUR
(☑431-821/2; www.villaohiggins.com; Carretera Austral s/n; glacier tour CH$80,000; ⊙9am-1pm & 3-7pm Mon-Sat) Departing from Puerto Bahamondez, catamaran *La Quetru* tours to Glaciar O'Higgins, an impressive glacier on the Campo Hielo Sur, with drop-offs at Candelario Mansilla (CH$65,000) for those hiking to Argentina. Available November through March.

🛏 Sleeping & Eating

El Mosco   HOSTEL $
`TOP CHOICE`
(☑431-819; patagoniaelmosco.com; Carretera Austral Km1240; campsites per person CH$5000; d/tr CH$40,000/50,000, dm CH$11,000, s/d without bathroom CH$18,000/28,000, 5-person cabins CH$50,000) Friendly and full-service, this buzzing outpost hosts loads of cyclists, trekkers and even the odd conventional traveler. It's all about the service, and owner Jorge and his busy staff nail it, with good tips for going on outings and a collection of area topographical maps. Worthwhile extras include a private wooden hot tub and a Finnish sauna.

Ecocamp Tsonek   CAMPGROUND $
(☑097-892-9695; www.tsonek.cl; Carretera Austral s/n; campsites per person CH$3000; 🛜) A conservation project in a beautiful beech forest with tent platforms, composting toilets, hot showers and a covered kitchen. It's the dream project of El Pajarero, a talented birdwatching guide who also guides excursions and float trips.

Robinson Crusoe   BOUTIQUE HOTEL $$$
(☑in Santiago 02-334-1503/4; www.robinsoncrusoe.com; Carretera Austral Km1240; d CH$100,000; 🛜) Alone in the upscale niche, this modern prefab construction is made warm with colorful Andean throws and comfortable sofas with yarn cushions. While the hotel overshoots the value of a comfy king-sized bed, it does offer nice amenities like varied buffet breakfasts and two wooden-tub Jacuzzis. Most guests come with an all-inclusive package that includes activities with bilingual guides.

ARGENTINA VIA THE BACK DOOR

Gonzo travelers can skirt the southern ice field to get from Villa O'Higgins to Argentina's Parque Nacional Los Glaciares and El Chaltén (p374). The one- to three-day trip can be completed between November and March. Bring all of your provisions, plus your passport and rain gear. Travel delays are always possible so be prepared. The trip goes as follows:

» Take the 8am bus from Villa O'Higgins to Puerto Bahamondez (CH$2000).

» Take the Hielo Sur catamaran *La Quetru* (CH$65,000, four hours) from Villa O'Higgins to Candelario Mansilla on the south edge of Lago O'Higgins. It goes one to three times a week, most often on Saturdays with some Monday or Wednesday departures. Candelario Mansilla has basic lodging, guided treks and pack-horse rental. Pass through Chilean customs and immigration here.

» Trek or ride to Laguna Redonda (two hours). Camping is not allowed.

» Trek or ride to Laguna Larga (1½ hours). Camping is not allowed.

» Trek or ride to the north shore of Lago del Desierto (1½ hours). Camping is allowed. Pass through Argentine customs and immigration here.

» Take the ferry from the north to the south shores of Lago del Desierto (AR$130, 2¼ hours). Another option is to hike the coast (15km, five hours). Camping is allowed. Check current ferry schedules with Argentine customs.

» Grab the shuttle bus to El Chaltén, 37km away (AR$130, one hour).

For more information, consult **Robinson Crusoe** (☑067-431-821/2; www.villaohiggins.com) in O'Higgins or **Rancho Grande Hostel** (☑54-2962-493-092; www.ranchogrande hostel.com; San Martín 724, El Chaltén) on the Argentine side.

NORTHERN PATAGONIA VILLA O'HIGGINS

Hospedaje Rural   GUESTHOUSE **$**

(☎431-805; r per person without bathroom CH$6000, campsites per person CH$2000) If you're reaching for the final, final frontier, check out this lodging in the southernmost sector of Candelario Mansilla, reached by ferry (p337). Dinner (CH$5000) and breakfast (CH$3000) are extra. Host Don Ricardo can help you explore area trails to glaciers, lakes and rivers.

Hospedaje Patagonia   GUESTHOUSE **$**

(☎431-818; Río Pascua & Lago Christie; d without bathroom CH$10,000) A selection of simple, clean doubles in a rambling house. Meal or tea service may be possible.

Entre Patagones   CHILEAN **$$**

(☎431-810; Av Carretera Austral s/n; set menu CH$8000) This faux-rustic log restaurant and bar serves up tasty and abundant meals of salmon and salad or barbecue specialties. Call ahead to ensure service, it's at the entrance to town. It also rents attractive cabins.

El Campanario   CHILEAN **$**

(Lago O'Higgins 72; set menu CH$3500) Good-value home-cooked meals, though you may have to wait a while.

ℹ Information

Information kiosk (Plaza Cívica; ☉8:30am-1pm & 2:30-7pm Nov-March) May have trekking maps. Located on the plaza where there's also free (but weak) wi-fi.

ℹ Getting There & Away

Transporte Aéreo Don Carlos (in Coyhaique ☎231-981; www.doncarlos.cl) flies from Coyhaique (CH$36,000, 1½ hours) on Monday and Thursday.

For some reason, a bus terminal is under construction. Until then, buses can be caught on the Carretera Austral. Bus Aldea goes to Cochrane (CH$12,000, six hours) on Friday and Monday at 8am. For Caleta Tortel (CH$15,000, four hours), El Mosco travels at 10:30am on Sunday and Robinson Crusoe travels at 8am on Tuesday and Thursday. There are low-season frequency changes.

For information on connecting to Argentina by catamaran, see p337.

Southern Patagonia

Best Places to Eat

» Afrigonia (p356)

» La Marmita (p347)

» Remezón (p347)

» La Tablita (p371)

» La Mesita Grande (p356)

Best Places to Stay

» Ilaia Hotel (p345)

» The Singular Hotel (p353)

» Hotel IF Patagonia (p353)

» Tierra Patagonia (p366)

» Refugio Grey (p365)

Why Go?

Pounding westerlies, barren seascapes and the ragged spires of Torres del Paine – this is the distilled essence of Patagonia. The provinces of Magallanes and Última Esperanza boast a frontier appeal perhaps only matched by the deep Amazon and remote Alaska. Long before humans arrived on the continent, glaciers chiseled and carved these fine landscapes. Now it's a place for travelers to hatch their greatest adventures, whether hiking through rugged landscapes, seeing penguins by the thousands or horseback riding across the steppe.

Parque Nacional Torres del Paine is the region's star attraction. Among the finest parks on the continent, it attracts hundreds of thousands of visitors every year, even some towing wheeled luggage (though we don't recommend it). Throughout the region, it's easy and worthwhile to travel between Argentina and Chile. Included in this chapter are the highlights of Argentine Patagonia.

When to Go
Punta Arenas

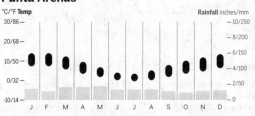

| **Dec–Feb** Warmest months, ideal for *estancia* (grazing ranch) visits and backpacking. | **Mid-Oct–early Mar** Coastal fauna, including penguins and marine birds, abounds. | **Mar–Apr** Blasting summer winds start to die down and brilliant fall colors come in. |

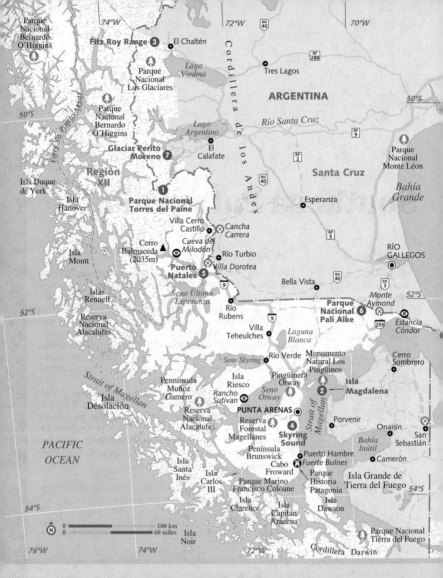

Southern Patagonia Highlights

1 Discover the remote backside of **Parque Nacional Torres del Paine** (p359)

2 Join the march of the penguins on **Isla Magdalena** (p349)

3 Hike the under the toothy **Fitz Roy Range** (p374) near El Chaltén, Argentina's trekking capital

4 Ride the range and trade fireside yarns at a working *estancia* (grazing ranch) at **Skyring Sound** (p350)

5 Enjoy a local microbrew, massage and lovely meals in **Puerto Natales** (p352) after time in Torres del Paine

6 Explore the gnarled volcanic steppe of the little-known **Parque Nacional Pali Aike** (p351)

7 Ice-trek the cool blue contours of 15-story **Glaciar Perito Moreno** (p373) in Argentina

History

Caves in Última Esperanza show that humans, known as the Aonikenk people, have inhabited the region since 10,000 BC. In 1520 Ferdinand Magellan was the first European to visit the region. Development was spurred by the California gold rush, which brought trade via the ships sailing between Europe, California and Australia.

In the late 19th century, *estancias* (grazing ranches) formed, creating a regional wool boom that had massive, reverberating effects for both Chilean and Argentine Patagonia. Great wealth for a few came at the cost of native populations, who were all but wiped out by disease and warfare. With the opening of the Panama Canal in 1914, traffic reduced around Cabo de Hornos and the area's international importance diminished.

Today fisheries, silviculture, small oil reserves and methanol production, in addition to a fast-growing tourism industry, keep the region relatively prosperous.

National Parks & Reserves

Some of the continent's most renowned parks are in this part of Patagonia. Most don't miss an opportunity to see Parque Nacional Torres del Paine (p359). Visits are often combined with a jaunt to Argentina for Parque Nacional Los Glaciares, accessible via El Chaltén (p374) for trekking or El Calafate (p372) to see the Perito Moreno glacier. The more remote Parque Nacional Bernardo O'Higgins (p359) has boat access from Torres del Paine. Near the border is the desolate and utterly distinct Parque Nacional Pali Aike (p351).

ℹ Getting There & Around

The easiest way to get to Southern Patagonia is to fly from Santiago or Puerto Montt to Punta Arenas. There are many flights daily and less-frequent flights from a few other major Chilean cities. Other transportation options include the Navimag ferry from Puerto Montt to Puerto Natales (see p280), or a long bus trip from Puerto Montt that goes to Argentina and then back over to Punta Arenas.

Unlike most of Patagonia, the roads around Punta Arenas are paved and smooth. Buses to major destinations are frequent but should be booked ahead in summer. Travelers must fly or take a ferry to get to Porvenir or Puerto Williams, but be aware that schedules change frequently.

Crossing into Argentina

Transportation between Argentina and Chile is frequent and easy, with crossing the border a normal daily occurrence for locals, on par with a trip to the bank. This chapter includes the most-visited Argentine spots for Chilean travelers. The Chilean entry fee (US$140 for residents of the US and Canada, US$95 for Australian residents) does not have to be paid again upon re-entry as it is valid for the life of the passport. There is no Argentine consulate between Puerto Montt and Punta Arenas, so if you need a visa before you reach either of these towns, get one at the Argentine consulate in Santiago.

Do not cross the border where there are no officials to stamp you through or you will risk expulsion. The most-used border crossings are at Cancha Carrera, between Torres del Paine and El Calafate, and Monte Aymond, between Punta Arenas and Río Gallegos.

Frequent buses link Puerto Natales with the Argentine towns El Calafate and El Chaltén, and Punta Arenas with Ushuaia. If you travel from Ushuaia to Chile's Isla Navarino by boat, make sure to visit customs at the airport.

For expanded coverage of the Argentine destinations, see Lonely Planet's *Argentina*.

MAGALLANES

Hard to believe, but this rugged, weather-battered land has actually been inhabited for hundreds, if not thousands, of years. While modern inhabitants have little in common with the natives who once paddled the channels in canoes and hunted guanacos, they still remain cut off from the rest of the continent by formidable mountains and chilly waters. A supreme sense of isolation (and hospitality) is what attracts most visitors to Magallanes. The only way to get here from the rest of Chile is by air or sea, or by road through Argentine Patagonia.

While the capital, Punta Arenas, offers all of the conveniences of a major Chilean city, its surroundings are raw and desolate. Here visitors will find the end-of-the-world pioneer feeling to be recent and real.

Magallanes' modern economy depends on commerce, petroleum development and fisheries. Prosperity means it has some of the highest levels of employment and school attendance, and some of the best-quality housing and public services in Chile.

Punta Arenas

☑061 / POP 130.136

A sprawling metropolis on the edge of the Strait of Magellan, Punta Arenas defies easy definition. It's a strange combination of the ruddy and the grand, witnessed in the elaborate wool-boom mansions and port renovations contrasted with windblown streams of litter and urban sprawl. Set at the bottom of the Americas, it is downright stingy with good weather – the sun shines through sidelong rain.

Magellanic hospitality still pervades local culture, undeterred (or perhaps nurtured by) nature's inhospitality. The city is remarkably relaxed and friendly. Recent prosperity, fed by a petrochemical industry boom and growing population, has sanded down the city's former roughneck reputation. It would be nice if it were all about restoration but duty-free shopping and mega-malls on the city outskirts are the order of the future.

Easy connections to Tierra del Fuego, Torres del Paine and Argentina, and good travelers' services make Punta Arenas a convenient base for traveling. A growing volume of cruise-ship passengers and trekkers has effectively replaced yesteryear's explorers, sealers and sailors.

History

Little more than 150 years old, Punta Arenas was originally a military garrison and penal settlement conveniently situated for ships headed to California during the gold rush in later years. Compared to the initial Chilean settlement at Fuerte Bulnes, 60km south, the town had a better, more protected harbor, and superior access to wood and water. English maritime charts dubbed the site Sandy Point, and thus it became known as its Spanish equivalent.

In its early years Punta Arenas lived off natural resources, including sealskins, guanaco hides and feathers, as well as mineral products (including coal and gold), guano, timber and firewood. The economy didn't take off until the last quarter of the 19th century, after the territorial governor authorized the purchase of 300 purebred sheep from the Falkland Islands. This successful experiment encouraged others to invest in

Punta Arenas

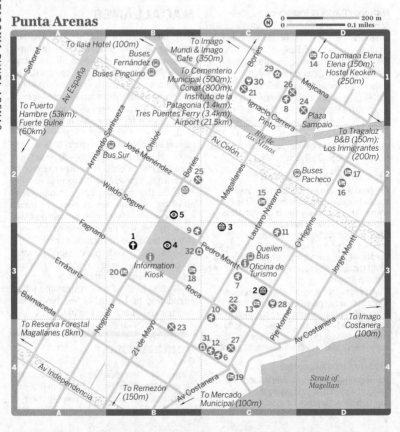

sheep, and by the turn of the century nearly two million animals grazed the territory.

The area's commercial and pastoral empires were built on the backs of international immigrant labor, including English, Irish, Scots, Croats, French, Germans, Spaniards, Italians and others. Many locals trace their family origins to these diverse settlers. Today evidence of this mass migration can be seen in the street names throughout town and on headstones in the cemetery. Church services are still held in English, while the many mansions created by the wealthy are now hotels, banks and museums.

◉ Sights & Activities

Plaza Muñoz Gamero, also known as the Plaza de Armas, is the center of town. Street names change on either side of the plaza, but street addresses fronting the plaza bear the name Muñoz Gamero. Most landmarks and accommodations are within a few blocks of here. Both Av España and Av Bulnes are main thoroughfares to the north of the city (the latter accesses the large duty-free shopping area known as the Zona Franca).

Plaza Muñoz Gamero   PLAZA
A central plaza of magnificent conifers surrounded by opulent mansions. Facing the plaza's north side, the Casa Braun-Menéndez (Sara Braun Mansion) houses the **Club de la Unión** (☎241-489; admission CH$1000; ☺10:30am-1pm & 5-8:30pm Tue-Fri, 10:30am-1pm & 8-10pm Sat, 11am-2pm Sun). The nearby **monument** commemorating the 400th anniversary of Magellan's voyage was donated by wool baron José Menéndez in 1920. Just east is the former **Sociedad Menéndez Behety**, which houses Turismo Comapa. The **cathedral** sits west.

Museo Regional Braun-Menéndez   MUSEUM
(☎244-216; Magallanes 949; admission CH$1500, Sun free; ☺10:30am-5pm Mon-Sat, 10:30am-2pm Sun summer, to 2pm daily winter) This opulent mansion testifies to the wealth and power of pioneer sheep farmers in the late 19th century. The well-maintained interior houses a regional historical museum (ask for booklets in English) and original exquisite French-nouveau family furnishings, from intricate wooden inlaid floors to Chinese vases.

In former servants' quarters, a downstairs cafe is perfect for a pisco sour while soaking up the grandeur.

Cementerio Municipal   CEMETERY
(main entrance at Av Bulnes 949; ☺7:30am-8pm) Among South America's most fascinating cemeteries, Cementerio Municipal contains

SOUTHERN PATAGONIA PUNTA ARENAS

a mix of humble immigrant graves and extravagant tombs under topiary cypresses. In death as in life, the first families of Punta Arenas flaunted their wealth – wool baron José Menéndez's extravagant tomb is, according to Bruce Chatwin, a scale replica of Rome's Vittorio Emanuele monument. But the headstones also tell the stories of Anglo, German, Scandinavian and Yugoslav immigrants. There is also a monument dedicated to the Selk'nam (Onas) and a map posted inside the main entrance gate.

It's an easy 15-minute stroll northeast of the plaza, or catch any taxi *colectivo* (shared taxi with specific route) in front of the Museo Regional Braun-Menéndez on Magallanes.

Museo Naval y Marítimo
MUSEUM
(☏205-479; Pedro Montt 981; adult/child CH$1200/600; ⊙9:30am-12:30pm & 2-5pm Tue-Sat) A naval and maritime museum with historical exhibits which include a fine account of the Chilean mission that rescued Sir Ernest Shackleton's crew from Antarctica. The most imaginative display is a replica ship complete with bridge, maps, charts and radio room.

Museo Regional Salesiano
MUSEUM
(☏221-001; Av Bulnes 336; admission CH$2000; ⊙10am-12:30pm & 3-6pm Tue-Sun) Especially influential in settling the region, the Salesian order collected outstanding ethnographic artifacts, but their museum touts their role as peacemakers between the Yaghan and Ona and settlers.

Instituto de la Patagonia
MUSEUM
Pioneer days are made real again at the Patagonian Institute's **Museo del Recuerdo** (☏207-056; www.umag.cl, in Spanish; Av Bulnes 01890; admission CH$1000; ⊙8:30am-11am & 2:30-6pm Mon-Fri), part of the Universidad de Magallanes. On display are a collection of antique farm and industrial machinery, a typical pioneer house and shearing shed, and a wooden-wheeled shepherds' trailer. The library has historical maps and a series of historical and scientific publications. Any *taxi colectivo* that is heading to the Zona Franca will drop you across the street.

Reserva Forestal Magallanes
HIKING, MOUNTAIN BIKING
(admission free; ⊙daylight hours) Great hiking and mountain biking through dense lenga and coihue, 8km from town.

Tours

Worthwhile day trips include tours to the **Seno Otway pingüinera** (penguin colony; p349), 48km to the north. Tours (from CH$15,000) leave at 4pm daily October through March, weather permitting.

Visits to the town's first settlements at Fuerte Bulnes and Puerto Hambre leave at 10am (admission CH$1000). Both tours can be done in one day; by sharing a rental car and going at opposite times visitors can avoid the strings of tour groups. Most lodgings will help arrange tours – if they don't run their own operation.

Torres del Paine tours are abundant from Punta Arenas, but the distance makes for a very long day; it's best to organize transport from Puerto Natales.

If you have the time, a more atmospheric alternative to Seno Otway is the thriving Magellanic penguin colonies of **Monumento Natural Los Pingüinos** (p349) on Isla Magdalena. Five-hour ferry tours (adult/child CH$25,000/13,000) land for an hour at the island and depart the port on Tuesday, Thursday and Saturday, December through February. Confirm times in advance. Book tickets through **Turismo Comapa** (☏200-200; www.comapa.com; Magallanes 990) and bring a picnic.

Tours also go to destinations such as Parque Nacional Pali Aike.

Frieda Lange & Co
TOUR
(☏613-991; www.friedalange.com; Errázuriz 950; ⊙8am-6pm) Recommended innovative bilingual city tours and trips to Fuerte Bulnes. Also sells a good selection of books on Patagonian history, culture and nature.

Turismo Aonikenk
TOUR
(☏228-332; www.aonikenk.com; Magallanes 619) Recommended English-, German- and French-speaking guides. Offers treks to Cabo Froward (the southernmost point on mainland South America), visits to the king penguin colony in Tierra del Fuego, and cheaper open expeditions geared at experienced participants. Also has information on Estancia Yendegaia.

Inhóspita Patagonia
TOUR
(☏224-510; Lautaro Navarro 1013) Offers trekking trips to Cabo Froward.

Turismo Pali Aike
TOUR
(☏223-301; www.turismopaliaike.com; Lautaro Navarro 1129) Offers standard regional tours.

INDECENT EXPOSURE *Jocelyn Turnbull PhD*

In the mid-1980s British scientists at Halley Station in Antarctica noticed that their ozone-measuring instrument seemed to have gone wrong – ozone levels were vastly lower than had ever been recorded before. Unfortunately, it was not their instrument that had gone wrong, but the ozone itself – ozone levels over Antarctica in springtime were dropping to a fraction of the regular amount.

Soon after, they were able to isolate the culprit: chlorofluorocarbons (CFCs), which are manmade gases used in aerosols, refrigeration, air-conditioning, industrial solvents, asthma inhalers and fire control. Most of the time these gases are innocuous, but in the Antarctic springtime the combination of very cold temperatures and the return of sunshine to the polar region allow the CFCs to rapidly gobble up the stratospheric ozone, resulting in the famed ozone hole. Once the Antarctic temperatures start to warm as spring progresses, the ozone begins to recover, only to be depleted again when the next spring arrives.

Ozone protects the Earth's surface from UV radiation, the stuff that causes sunburn, among other things. Without it, sunburn and skin cancer become very serious concerns. The ozone hole has impacted Southern Patagonia more than any other inhabited area on earth. It is particularly bad during the spring, when the ozone hole is at its worst. Visitors should wear brimmed hats and sunglasses, slather on the sunscreen and be particularly mindful of children.

The adoption and strengthening of the 1987 Montreal Protocol has cut the quantity of CFCs out there and Antarctic ozone levels are beginning to recover, but it's a slow process and it will take another 50 years or so to get back to normal ozone levels.

Turismo Pehoé TOUR
(☎241-373; www.pehoe.com; José Menéndez 918) For standard regional tours.

Turismo Yamana TOUR
(☎221-130; www.yamana.cl; Errázuriz 932) Runs kayaking trips on Magellan Strait.

✦✦ Festivals & Events

Winter Solstice TRADITIONAL
The longest night of the year is celebrated on June 21.

Carnaval de Invierno CULTURAL
(Winter Carnival) This two-day carnival, held in the last week of July, is a big party that kicks off the beginning of the winter season with fireworks, floats and all of the standard carnival fanfare.

🛏 Sleeping

On the cruise-ship circuit, Punta Arenas has a plethora of hotels. Foreigners are not required to pay the additional 18% IVA charge, if paying with US cash, traveler's checks or credit card. Off-season (mid-April to mid-October) prices drop. Rates include breakfast.

TOP CHOICE Ilaia Hotel BOUTIQUE HOTEL $$
(☎723-100; www.ilaia.cl; Ignacio Carrera Pinto 351; d/t CH$60,000/65,000) Playful and modern, this high-concept boutique hotel is run with family warmth. Sly messages are written to be read in mirrors, rooms are simple and chic and an incredible glass lookout room gazes out on the Strait. A yoga studio is in the works; in the meantime, there are various therapies available and healthy breakfasts that include chapati bread, homemade jam, avocados, yogurt and more. But you won't find a TV.

Tragaluz B&B B&B $$
(☎613-938; www.tragaluzpatagonia.com; Mejicana 1194; s/d/t CH$35,000/40,000/48,000, apt CH$50,000; @☎) Homey describes this classic aluminum two-story B&B with mosaic mirrors and warm towel racks. The young American and Chilean hosts Dan and Lorena are superfriendly and knowledgeable about outdoor pursuits. While rooms are standard, the breakfast includes fruit, good coffee and treats like scrambled eggs with veggies or homemade waffles with palm honey. Watch for a greenhouse Jacuzzi in the works.

Hospedaje Magallanes B&B $$
(☎228-616; www.aonikenk.com; Magallanes 570; s/d without bathroom CH$25,000/30,000; ☺@☎) A great, inexpensive option run by a German-Chilean couple who are also Torres del Paine guides with an on-site travel agency. With just a few quiet rooms, there are often

communal dinners or backyard barbecues by the climbing wall. Breakfast includes brown bread and strong coffee.

Hospedaje Independencia GUESTHOUSE $
(227-572; www.chileaustral.com/independencia; Av Independencia 374; campsites/dm CH$2000/5000; @) One of the last diehard backpacker haunts with cheap prices and bonhomie to match. Despite the chaos, rooms are reasonably clean and there are kitchen privileges, camping and bike rentals.

Imago Mundi HOSTEL $
(613-115; www.imagomundipatagonia.cl; Mejicana 252; dm/d CH$10,000/25,000; @) Infused with wanderlust, this rambling house has snug bunks in electric colors and cozy spaces with tables crafted from old doors. Guests should check out the rotating cultural events (like art-house movies and workshops) hosted here.

Hotel Patagonia Pionera INN $$$
(222-045; www.hotelpatagoniapionera.cl; Arauco 786; s/d CH$57,000/68,300; P@令) This immaculate restored brick mansion is an elegant and intimate alternative to the big downtown hotels. Expect crisp white duvets, tangerine accents and hardwood floors. It's in a well-heeled residential neighborhood, only six blocks from the plaza.

Hostal La Estancia GUESTHOUSE $
(249130; www.estancia.cl; O'Higgins 765; d CH$25,000, dm/s/d without bathroom CH$12,000/20,000/30,000; @令) An old downtown house with big rooms, vaulted ceilings and tidy shared bathrooms. Longtime owners Alex and Carmen are eager to help with travel plans. There's a book exchange, kitchen use, a laundry and storage.

Hostal Fitz Roy GUESTHOUSE $
(240-430; www.hostalfitzroy.com; Lautaro Navarro 850; d CH$30,000, dm CH$8000, d without bathroom CH$25,000, 5-person cabin CH$35,000; @) This country house in the city offers rambling, good-value rooms and an inviting, old-fashioned living room to pore over books or sea charts. Rooms have phones and TVs.

Hotel Dreams del Estrecho LUXURY HOTEL $$$
(600-626-0000; www.mundodreams.com/det alle/dreams-punta-arenas; O'Higgins 1235; d/ste CH$97,000/117,000; P@令≋) Parked at the water's edge, this glass oval high-rise brings a little Vegas to the end of the world. It's a glittery atmosphere, with new rooms which

are spacious and luxuriant, but the showstopper is the swimming pool that appears to merge with the ocean. There is also a spa, casino and swank restaurant on site.

Hotel Cabo De Hornos BUSINESS HOTEL $$$
(242-134; www.hoteles-australis.com; Plaza Muñoz Gamero 1025; d CH$109,000; @令) This smart business hotel begins with a cool interior of slate and sharp angles, but rooms are relaxed and bright, with top-notch views. Service is good and the well-heeled bar just beckons you for a nightcap. The on-site restaurant is well regarded too.

Hostal Terrasur INN $$
(243-014; www.hostalterrasur.cl; O'Higgins 723; s/d CH$30,000/40,000; P@令) The slightly upscale Terrasur nurtures a secret-garden atmosphere, from its rooms with flowing curtains and flower patterns to the miniature green courtyard.

El Conventillo HOSTEL $
(242-311; www.hostalelconventillo.com; Pasaje Korner 1034; dm CH$8500; @令) This cool brick hostel in the reviving waterfront district has remodeled carpeted dorms and clean row showers. Bright colors mask the fact that there is little interior light; rooms are windowless. Yogurt and cereal are part of a big breakfast.

Hostel Keoken GUESTHOUSE $
(244-086; www.hostelkeoken.cl, in Spanish; Magallanes 209; s/d CH$17,000/30,000, without bathroom CH$12000/24,000; @) Increasingly popular with backpackers, Hostel Keoken features comfortable beds topped with fluffy white down comforters and homemade pastries for breakfast. The center of town is a few minutes away on foot.

Al Fin del Mundo HOSTEL $
(710-185; www.alfindelmundo.cl; O'Higgins 1026; dm/s/d without bathroom CH$10,000/15,000/20,000; @令) On the 2nd and 3rd floors of a downtown building, these rooms are cheerful but due for updates. All share bathrooms with hot showers, and a large kitchen, as well as a living area with a big TV, pool table and DVD library.

Hotel Plaza HOTEL $$$
(241300; www.hotelplaza.cl; Nogueira 1116; s/d CH$51,000/63,000; @) This converted mansion boasts vaulted ceilings, plaza views and historical photos lining the hall. Inconsistent with such grandeur, the country decor is

unfortunate. But service is genteel and the location unbeatable.

Eating

Local seafood is an exquisite treat: go for *centolla* (king crab) between July and November or *erizos* (sea urchins) between November and July.

La Marmita
TOP CHOICE   CHILEAN $$

(☏222-056; Plaza Sampaio 678; mains CH$6000-10,000; ⊘lunch & dinner Mon-Sat) Recently revamped, this classic bistro enjoys wild popularity for its lovely, casual ambience and tasty fare. Besides fresh salads and hot bread, hearty dishes like casseroles or seafood hearken back to grandma's cooking, Chilean style. There's also a new take-out service.

Remezón
FINE DINING $$$

(☏241-029; www.patagoniasalvaje.cl, in Spanish; 21 de Mayo 1469; mains CH$10,000-15,000; ⊘lunch & dinner) An innovative mainstay with a homey atmosphere. Garlic soup made with fragrant beef broth is a good starter, poured dramatically from a silver tea service. You can share it, too. Innovative game dishes are the house specialty, but the *merluza negra* (black hake) is outstanding – fresh and perfectly prepared, served with *chupe de espinaca* (spinach casserole). Chef Luis also offers group cooking workshops that include a trip to the local market.

Sotito's
SEAFOOD $$$

(☏243-565; O'Higgins 1138; mains CH$5000-15,000; ⊘lunch & dinner) This seafood institution is popular with moneyed locals and cruise-ship travelers in search of a classy king-crab feast. The decor may not be inspiring but the cuisine doesn't disappoint.

Café Almacen Tapiz
CAFE $

(www.cafetapiz.cl; Roca 912; mains CH$5000; ⊘9am-9:30pm; ☏) Cloaked in alerce shingles, this lively cafe makes for an ambient coffee break. In addition to gorgeous layer cakes, there are salads and pita sandwiches with goat cheese, meats or roasted veggies.

Damiana Elena
FINE DINING $$$

(☏222-818; Magallanes 341; mains CH$7000-9000; ⊘dinner Mon-Sat) This elegant restaurant is located in a romantic old house, off the beaten path in a residential neighborhood. The detour is worth it for the warm, sophisticated ambience and first-rate Chilean cuisine: highlights include the salmon ceviche and the grilled tilapia.

Fuente Hamburg
FAST FOOD $

(☏245-375; Errázurriz 856; mains CH$2500-4000; ⊘10:30am-8:30pm Mon-Fri, to 3pm Sat) Shiny barstools flank a massive grill churning out quickie bites. Grab a *churrasco* (thin-sliced beef) topped with tomatoes and green beans, served with fresh mayo on a soft bun.

Los Inmigrantes
CAFE $

(☏222-205; www.inmigrante.cl; Quillota 559; mains CH$5000) In the historic Croatian neighborhood, this cafe serves generous oversized sandwiches of salmon, cured meats or veggies on all kinds of bread, as well as decadent cakes. On display are interesting relics from Dalmatian immigrants.

Lomit's
DINER $

(☏243-399; José Menéndez 722; mains CH$3000; ⊘10am-2:30am) Chile's answer to the sidecar diner is this atmospheric cafe where cooks flip dripping made-to-order burgers at a center-stage griddle. Portions are generous but the service sure dallies.

Mercado Municipal
MARKET $

(21 de Mayo 1465) Fish and vegetable market with cheap 2nd-floor *cocinerías* (eateries).

Secreto de la Patagonia
SELF-CATERING $

(☏245-659; Sarmiento 1029) Locally made artisan chocolates, goat cheese and preserved meats, worthy as gifts or park treats.

Imago Cafe
CAFE $

(Costanera s/n; mains CH$3000; ⊘9am-9pm Mon-Fri, 10am-9pm Sat & Sun) A hip 2nd-story nook overlooking the city, with loose-leaf teas, fair-trade coffee and sandwiches.

Abugosh
SUPERMARKET

(Bories 647) A large, well-stocked supermarket.

Pachamama
SELF-CATERING

(☏226-171; Magallanes 619-A) A natural market with bulk trail-mix munchies and organic products.

Drinking

La Taberna
PUB

(☏241-317; Sara Braun Mansion, Plaza Muñoz Gamero; ⊘7pm-2am, to 3am weekends) This dark and elegant subterranean bar, with polished wood fixtures and cozy nooks reminiscent of an old-fashioned ship, is a classic old-boys' club. The rooms fill with cigar smoke later in the evening, but the opportunity to sip pisco sours in the classy Sara Braun Mansion shouldn't be missed.

Jekus   PUB
(241-851; O'Higgins 1021; 6pm-3am) A restaurant that serves as a popular meeting spot for drinks, with happy hours, karaoke and soccer on the tube.

☆ Entertainment

Kamikaze   CLUB
(248-744; Bories 655; cover incl 1 free drink CH$3000) Tiki torches warm up this most southerly dance club and, if you're lucky, the occasional live rock band.

Cine Estrella   CINEMA
(Mejicana 777) The Estrella shows first-run movies.

🔒 Shopping

The Art Corner   ARTS & CRAFTS
(989045392; Errázuriz 910, 2nd fl) The workshop and store of talented local artist Andrea Araneda. A great place for innovative handmade gifts, with gorgeous woolens, paintings focused on Magellanic themes and crafts.

Zona Franca   MALL
(Zofri; closed Sun) The duty-free zone is a large, polished conglomeration of shops that is worth checking out if you're looking for electronics, outdoor gear, computer accessories or camera equipment. *Colectivos* shuttle back and forth from downtown along Av Bulnes throughout the day.

World's End   BOOKS
(213-117; Plaza Gamero 1011) Stocks maps, photo books, souvenirs and Lonely Planet guides in English and Spanish.

ℹ Information

Travel agencies in the center along Roca and Lautaro Navarro change cash and traveler's checks. All are open weekdays and Saturday, with a few open on Sunday morning. Banks with ATMs dot the city center. Sernatur has a list of recommended doctors.

Conaf (230-681; Bulnes 0309) Has details on the nearby parks.

Hospital Regional (205-000; Angamos 180; 24hr)

Information kiosk (200-610; www.puntaarenas.cl, in Spanish; Plaza Muñoz Gamero; 8am-7pm Mon-Sat, 9am-7pm Sun) South side of the plaza.

Police (241-714; Errázuriz 977)

Post office (Bories 911) Located one block north of Plaza Muñoz Gamero.

Punta Arenas (www.puntaarenas.cl, in Spanish) The municipality's website.

Sernatur (241-330; www.chile.travel/en.html; Lautaro Navarro 999; 8:15am-8pm Mon-Fri Dec-Feb, 8:15am-6pm Mon-Thu, 8:15am-5pm Fri rest of year) With friendly, well-informed, multilingual staff and lists of accommodations and transportation.

ℹ Getting There & Away

The tourist offices distribute a useful brochure which details all forms of transport available.

Air

Punta Arenas' airport (PUQ) is 21km north of town.

LanChile (241-100, 600-526-2000; www.lan.com; Bories 884) flies several times daily to Santiago (CH$229,000) with a stop in Puerto Montt (CH$127,000), and on Saturday to the Falkland Islands (round-trip CH$530,000). A new service goes direct to Ushuaia several times a week in summer. For national flights, book ahead online for the best deals. **Aerolíneas Argentina** (0810-222-86527; www.aerolineas.com.ar) offers flights to various cities in Argentina. **Sky Airline** (710-645; www.skyairline.cl; Roca 935) flies daily between Santiago and Punta Arenas, with a stop either in Puerto Montt or Concepción.

From November to March, **Aerovías DAP** (616-100; www.aeroviasdap.cl; O'Higgins 891) flies to Porvenir (CH$21,000) Monday through Saturday several times daily, and to Puerto Williams (CH$63,000) Monday through Saturday at 10am. Luggage is limited to 10kg per person.

DAP offers Antarctica tours, charter flights over Cabo de Hornos and to other Patagonian destinations, including Ushuaia and Calafate.

DAP also provides shuttle service (CH$2000) to the airport.

Boat

Transbordador Austral Broom (580-089; www.tabsa.cl; Juan Williams 06450) operates three ferries to Tierra del Fuego. The car/passenger ferry *Crux Australis* to/from Porvenir (CH$5500/34,900 per person/vehicle, 2½ to four hours) usually leaves at 9am but has some afternoon departures; check the current online schedule. From Punta Arenas, it's faster to do the Primera Angostura crossing (CH$1600/13,900 per person/vehicle, 20 minutes), northeast of Punta Arenas, which sails every 90 minutes between 8:30am and 11:45pm. Broom sets sail for Isla Navarino's Puerto Williams (reclining seat/

bunk CH$90,000/125,000 including meals, 34 hours) three or four times per month on Wednesday only, returning Saturday.

Cruceros Australis (☑in Santiago 02-442-3110; www.australis.com; ☺Sep-May) runs luxurious four-day and five-day sightseeing cruises to Ushuaia and back (see p392). Turismo Comapa handles local bookings.

Bus

Buses depart from company offices, most within a block or two of Av Colón. Buy tickets several hours (if not days) in advance. The **Central de Pasajeros** (☑245-811; cnr Magallanes & Av Colón) is the closest thing to a central booking office.

Daily destinations and companies include the following:

DESTINATION	COST (CH$)	DURATION (HR)
Puerto Montt	45,000	32
Puerto Natales	4000	3
Río Gallegos	10,000	5-8
Río Grande	20,000	7
Ushuaia	30,000	10

Bus Sur (☑614-221; www.bus-sur.cl; José Menéndez 552) El Calafate, Puerto Natales, Río Gallegos, Ushuaia and Puerto Montt.

Buses Fernández/Buses Pingüino (☑221-429/812; www.busesfernandez.com; Armando Sanhueza 745) Puerto Natales, Torres del Paine and Río Gallegos.

Buses Ghisoni (☑240-646; www.busesbarria.cl; Av España 264) Comfortable buses to Río Gallegos, Río Grande and Ushuaia.

Buses Pacheco (☑242-174; www.busespacheco.com; Av Colón 900) Puerto Natales, Río Gallegos and Ushuaia.

Tecni-Austral (☑222-078; Lautaro Navarro 975) Río Grande.

Turíbus/Cruz del Sur (☑227-970; www.busescruzdelsur.cl, in Spanish; Armando Sanhueza 745) Puerto Montt, Osorno and Chiloé.

Getting Around

To/From the Airport

Buses depart directly from the airport to Puerto Natales. **Transfer Austral** (☑282-854) runs door-to-door shuttle services (CH$3000) to/from town to coincide with flights. Buses Fernández does regular airport transfers (CH$3000).

Bus & Taxi Colectivo

Taxi *colectivos*, with numbered routes, are only slightly more expensive than buses (about CH$800, or a bit more late at night and on Sundays), far more comfortable and much quicker.

Car

Cars are a good option for exploring Torres del Paine, but renting one in Chile to cross the border into Argentina gets expensive due to international insurance requirements. If heading for El Calafate, it is best to rent your vehicle in Argentina. Purchasing a car to explore Patagonia has its drawbacks, as Chilean Patagonia has no through roads that link northern and southern Patagonia, so it is entirely dependent on the roads of Argentina or expensive ferry travel.

Punta Arenas has Chilean Patagonia's most economical rental rates, and locally owned agencies tend to provide better service. Recommended **Adel Rent a Car/Localiza** (☑235-471/2, 09-882-7569; www.adel.cl; Pedro Montt 962) provides attentive service, competitive rates, airport pickup and good travel tips. Other choices include **Budget** (☑225-983; O'Higgins 964), **Hertz** (☑248742; O'Higgins 987) and **Lubag** (☑710-484; Magallanes 970).

DON'T MISS

PENGUIN COLONIES

You don't have to trek to Antarctica for a sizable dose of happy feet. Two substantial Magellanic penguin colonies are easily reached from Punta Arenas. If you have time to make a day of it, we recommend the larger (60,000 breeding pairs) and more interesting **Monumento Natural Los Pingüinos**, accessible only by boat to Isla Magdalena in the Strait of Magellan (p344).

Easier to reach is **Seno Otway** (Otway Sound; www.turisotway.cl; admission CH$5500; ☺8am-6:30pm Oct 15-March), with about 6000 breeding pairs, located around an hour northwest of the city. Tours to Seno Otway usually leave in the afternoon; however, visiting in the morning is best time of the day for photography because the birds are mostly backlit in the afternoon. Arrive via private vehicle or tour. If driving independently, pay attention as you head north on Ruta 9 (RN 9) – it's easy to miss the small sign indicating the turn-off to the penguin colony. It's worth noting that it's in close proximitiy to the airport.

Around Punta Arenas

MONUMENTOS HISTÓRICOS NACIONALES PUERTO HAMBRE & FUERTE BULNES

These two national monuments make up **Parque Historia Patagonia** (☏723-195; www.fuertebulnes.com; Km56 Sur; admission CH$1000; ☺10am-7pm Oct-Mar). Founded in 1584 by Pedro Sarmiento de Gamboa, 'Ciudad del Rey don Felipe' was one of Spain's most inauspicious and short-lived South American outposts. Its inhabitants struggled against the elements and starved to death at what is now known as **Puerto Hambre** (Port Hunger).

In May 1843, Chilean president Manuel Bulnes sent the schooner *Ancud,* manned by Chilotes and captained by John Williams, a former English officer, to Magallanes to occupy this southern area, then only sparsely populated by indigenous peoples. Four months later on September 21, when the *Ancud* arrived at Puerto Hambre, Williams declared the area Chilean territory and began to establish camp on a hilltop, dubbed **Fuerte Bulnes**. The exposed site, lack of potable water, rocky soil and inferior pasture soon made his colony abandon the site and move northward to a more sheltered area, called Sandy Point by the settlers and Lacolet by the Tehuelche.

Trails, a visitors center and lookouts are currently under construction. A paved road (ready in 2013) runs 60km south from Punta Arenas to the restored wooden fort, where a fence of sharpened stakes surrounds the blockhouse, barracks and chapel. There isn't any scheduled public transportation but several tour companies make half-day excursions to Fuerte Bulnes and Puerto Hambre; for details, see p344.

CABO FROWARD

The most southerly point on the continent, Cabo Froward (Cape Froward) is 90km south of Punta Arenas and accessible by a two-day hike along wind-whipped cliffs. At the cape, a 365m hill leads to an enormous cross, originally erected by Señor Fagnano in 1913 but the latest one was erected in 1987 for Pope John Paul II's visit. Camping is possible along the trail; ask about guided hikes at any of the tour companies in Punta Arenas (p344) or Puerto Natales–based Erratic Rock (p352).

Faro San Isidro, about 15km before Cabo Froward, is a lighthouse near the base of Monte Tarn (830m). This rugged area is home to prolific birdlife and some good hiking. It's also a launch point for humpback whale-watching trips to Isla Carlos III in **Parque Marino Francisco Coloane**, Chile's first marine park. Humpbacks and minke whales feed seasonally here between December and May. Package stays are available at **Hostería Faro San Isidro** (☏in Punta Arenas 061-223-725, 099-349-3862; www.hosteriafarosanisidro.cl; 2-day packages per person CH$215,000), including transport from Punta Arenas and activities, such as kayaking and hiking.

RÍO RUBENS

Roughly midway between Villa Tehuelches and Puerto Natales on blustery, paved Ruta 9, Río Rubens is a fine trout-fishing area and, for travelers with their own transport,

---

SKYRING SOUND

Ranch life spills from the pores of **Estancia Río Verde** (☏061-311-131/123; www.estanciarioverde.cl; Ruta Y50 Km97; d incl breakfast CH$80,000), a working sheep ranch and horse-breeding farm on the shores of Skyring Sound, an area with some of the region's best-maintained assemblages of Magellanic architecture. Gracious English-speaking host Josefina keeps a relaxed atmosphere while Sergio runs the ranch hands-on; or maybe it's the other way around. Regardless, a ride around the property affords an interesting close-up of operations. Rodeos are held at the *medialuna* (a traditional half-moon stadium) in summer; there are also sailing, fishing and sightseeing trips on offer. Guests stay in a beautiful restored *casco* (the main house of the *estancia*) with 14 elegant rooms.

The kitchen churns out regional delicacies, including Patagonian lamb, with fresh bread, garden vegetables and plenty of wine. Passers-by can stop for lunch (CH$15,000) and check out the small museum.

You will need a car to make this interesting detour. It's 43km north of Punta Arenas via Route 9; follow gravel road Y50 to Km97.

ENIGMATIC PATAGONIA: CHATWIN'S MASTERPIECE

In 1977 the late English writer Bruce Chatwin penned *In Patagonia,* an indispensable companion for the Patagonian traveler. Three decades after its original publication, the book continues to inspire people to travel to such far-flung places as Ushuaia, Punta Arenas and Puerto Natales.

Chatwin's fascination with Patagonia began in early childhood, when he coveted a scrap of giant sloth skin kept in a 'glass-fronted cabinet' in his grandmother's house in England. The skin, covered in orange hair, had been sent as a gift from his eccentric sea-faring relative Charley Milward, who resided in Punta Arenas. Chatwin was also intrigued by the seemingly out-of-place immigrant communities, such as the Patagonian Welsh, and colorful, free-spirited characters like Robert Leroy Parker and Harry Longabaugh (aka Butch Cassidy and the Sundance Kid). A six-month journey through Patagonia resulted in Chatwin's masterpiece at the age of 37. It recounts his journey and personal encounters while heading south from Buenos Aires to his final destination, Cueva del Milodón – the one-time home of the prehistoric sloth.

While Chatwin mixed fluid storytelling, intriguing regional history, personal portraits and old-fashioned travel memoir, he tossed one last ingredient into the pot: fiction. This was, and continues to be, controversial because there was no acknowledgement that any of the stories were fabricated. *In Patagonia* reads primarily as a nonfiction travel memoir. However, after the publication of the book, a number of Patagonian residents came forward to challenge and contradict events depicted in the book. Many of the conversations and characters that Chatwin reported as true were just figments of his imagination.

Patagonia is a land of mystery and legend: a place that the first European explorers described as being populated by giants. Perhaps the story fits with this fringe of the world that is known as Patagonia; a land with its own pace of time, history and reality.

Chatwin died of AIDS in 1989. He claimed to the end that he was ill due to the bite of a Chinese bat and a tropical fungal infection.

an ideal spot to break the 250km journey from Punta Arenas.

An old-style roadhouse, **Hotel Río Rubens** (☎92547056; www.hotelriorubens.cl, in Spanish; Km183) has a few too many tales told in its worn wooden floors and simple rooms. We like it for the steak sandwiches (CH$5000), served on fresh bread at the buzzing downstairs restaurant.

PARQUE NACIONAL PALI AIKE

Rugged volcanic steppe pocked with craters, caves and twisted formations, Pali Aike means 'devil's country' in Tehuelche. This desolate landscape is a 50-sq-km **park** (admission CH$1000) along the Argentine border. Mineral content made lava rocks red, yellow or green-gray. Fauna includes abundant guanaco, ñandú, gray fox and armadillo. In the 1930s Junius Bird's excavations at 17m-deep **Pali Aike Cave** yielded the first artifacts associated with extinct New World fauna such as the milodón and the native horse *Onohippidium*.

The park has several trails, including a 1.7km path through the rugged lava beds of the **Escorial del Diablo** to the impressive **Crater Morada del Diablo**; wear sturdy shoes or your feet could be shredded. There are hundreds of craters, some four stories high. A 9km trail from Cueva Pali Aike to **Laguna Ana** links a shorter trail to a site on the main road, 5km from the park entrance.

Parque Nacional Pali Aike is 200km northeast of Punta Arenas via Ch (rural road) 9, Ch 255 and a graveled secondary road from Cooperativa Villa O'Higgins, 11km north of Estancia Kimiri Aike. There's also access from the Chilean border post at Monte Aymond. There is no public transport, but Punta Arenas travel agencies (p344) offer full-day tours.

ÚLTIMA ESPERANZA

With a name that translates to Last Hope, the once-remote Última Esperanza fills the imagination with foreboding. Storms wrestle the vast expanse and the landscape falls nothing short of grand; after all, Parque Nacional Torres del Paine and part of the Southern Patagonian Ice Field are in the back yard. Often lumped together with neighboring Magallanes, Última Esperanza is a separate southern province. While it can still be a challenging place to travel in winter, it is no longer so far off the beaten path. In fact, the tourism boom has transformed parts of it from rustic to outright decadent; still, there's something for everyone here.

Puerto Natales

📞 061 / POP 18,000

A formerly modest fishing port on Seno Última Esperanza, Puerto Natales has blossomed into a Gore-Tex mecca. The gateway to Parque Nacional Torres del Paine, this town is reaping the benefits of its business savvy: boutique beers and wine tastings are overtaking tea time, and gear shops have already replaced the yarn sellers. The town now feeds off tourism, and it's an all-you-can-eat feast with unwavering demand. While some sectors cater to international tastes, there's appeal in Natales' corrugated-tin houses strung shoulder to shoulder and cozy granny-style lodgings. Most notably, in spite of a near-constant swarm of summer visitors, the town still maintains the glacial pace of living endemic to Patagonia.

Puerto Natales sits on the shores of Seno Última Esperanza, 250km northwest of Punta Arenas via Ruta 9, and has some striking views out over the mountains. It is the capital of the province of Última Esperanza and the southern terminus of the ferry trip through the Chilean fjords.

◎ Sights & Activities

Museo Histórico MUSEUM
(📞411-263; Manuel Bulnes 285; admission free; ⊗8:30am-12:30pm & 2:30-6pm Tue-Sun) OK for a crash course in local history, the museum is a quick visit. There are natural-history items (mostly stuffed animals), archaeological artifacts, such as stone and whalebone arrowheads and spear points, plus a Yaghan canoe, Tehuelche bolas and historical photographs of Puerto Natales' development.

Eberhard Ranch ESTANCIA
Surrounded by tranquil fjords and looming mountains, the original homestead and *estancia* in the region, this *estancia* is impossibly scenic and gives a taste of the area beyond the outdoor-sports mecca of Puerto Natales. Here you can see *gauchos* (cowboys) at work. It's not a tourist show, but real work, including the slaughter of sheep – so it's not for the faint of heart. To arrange a visit contact Estancia Travel (below).

Mirador Dorotea HIKING
Less than 10km from Natales, this large rocky outcrop just off Ruta 9 provides a good warm-up for the park. A big sign identifies the hike to the lookout at lot 14 just off the road. The hike (two hours round-trip; entrance fee CH$3000) takes you through a lenga forest and up to a splendid view back over Puerto Natales, the glacial valley and the surrounding mountains.

Mandala Andino SPA
(📞414-143; www.mandalapatagonia.com; Eberhard 161; per person per hr CH$10,000; ⊗10am-10pm Oct-Mar) You don't need a gold card to get a little pampering here. This minispa serves hikers fresh off the trail with three large wooden tubs, one in a covered dome, which will warm you to blissfulness. Other therapies include expert deep-tissue or hot-stone massages and quartz singing bowls.

☞ Tours

Antares/Indomita Big Foot ADVENTURE TOUR
(📞414-611; www.antarespatagonia.com; Pedro Montt 161) Guide service specializing in Torres del Paine, Antares can facilitate climbing permits and made-to-order trips. It also has the concession for ice hikes in the park. Indomita Big Foot runs kayak trips in the fjords and park.

Baqueano Zamora HORSEBACK RIDING
(📞613-531; www.baqueanozamora.com, in Spanish; Baquedano 534) Runs horseback-riding trips in Torres del Paine.

Chile Nativo ADVENTURE TOUR
(📞411-835; www.chilenativo.cl; Eberhard 230, 2nd fl) Links visitors with local gauchos, organizes photo safaris and can competently plan your tailor-made dream adventures.

Erratic Rock HIKING
(📞410-355; Baquedano 719) Aims to keep Torres del Paine sustainable with good visitor advice, alternative options, informative talks and gear rentals. Guide service specializes in treks to Cabo Froward, Isla Navarino and lesser-known destinations.

Estancia Travel HORSEBACK RIDING
(📞412-221; www.estanciatravel.com; Bories 13-B, Puerto Bories) Run by a former Chilean equestrian champion, this professional outfit facilitates horseback-riding trips in and out of Torres del Paine.

Fortaleza Expediciones   ADVENTURE TOUR
(☑410-595; www.fortalezapatagonia.cl; Tomás Rogers 235) A knowledgeable outfit that rents camping gear.

Fantastico Sur   PARK TOURS
(☑614-184; www.fantasticosur.com; Esmeralda 661) Runs Refugios Torres, El Chileno, Los Cuernos in Torres del Paine and offers park tours, guiding and trek planning services.

Knudsen Tour   REGIONAL TOURS
(☑414-747; knudsentour@yahoo.com; Blanco Encalada 284) Well regarded, with trips to El Calafate, Torres del Paine and alternative routes along Seno Último Esperanza.

Turismo 21 de Mayo   CRUISES
(☑411-978; www.turismo21demayo.cl, in Spanish; Eberhard 560) Organizes day-trip cruises and treks to the Balmaceda and Serrano glaciers.

Turismo Comapa   FERRY
(☑414-300; www.comapa.com; Bulnes 541; ☉9am-1pm & 3-7pm Mon-Fri, 10am-2pm Sat) Navimag ferry and airline bookings.

Vertice Patagonia   PARK TOURS
(☑412-742; www.verticepatagonia.com; Ladrilleros 209) Runs Refugios Grey, Dickson and Paine Grande in Torres del Paine.

✹ Festivals & Events

Festival de Cine de la Patagonia   FILM FESTIVAL
This week-long festival, held in mid-February, features movies and the Banff Mountain Film Festival, with some features shown in the Cueva del Milodon.

🛏 Sleeping

Options abound, most with breakfast, laundry and lowered rates in the low season. Reserve ahead if arriving on the ferry. Hostels often rent equipment and help arrange park transport.

🍃 Kau   B&B $$
(☑414-611; www.kaulodge.com; Pedro Montt 161; d CH$45,000; 🛜) With a mantra of simplicity, this aesthetic remake of a box hotel is cozy and cool. Thick woolen throws, picnic-table breakfast seating and well-worn, recycled wood lend a kind of blue-jeans intimacy. Rooms boast fjord views, central heating, bulk toiletries and safe boxes. The Coffee Maker espresso bar boasts killer lattes and staff at the agency desk have tons of adventure information on tap.

The Singular Hotel   BOUTIQUE HOTEL $$$
(☑414-040, bookings in Santiago 02-387-1500; www.thesingular.com; Ruta 9, Km 1.5; d incl full board & excursions CH$580,000; P@🛜🏊) A notable newcomer, The Singular reclaims the space of a regional landmark, a former meatpacking and shipping facility on the sound. Vegetarians may not dig the history, but the fine industrial design, heightened with features, such as chairs fashioned from old radiators in the lobby, is mixed with interesting vintage photos and antiques. The snug glass-walled rooms all have water views and the chic bar-restaurant (alongside the museum, open to the public) serves fresh local game. Guests can use the spa with pool and explore the surroundings by bike or kayak. The only downside is that it is too far to browse Natales without making it a trek. It's located in Puerto Bories, 6km from the center.

Hotel IF Patagonia   BOUTIQUE HOTEL $$$
(☑410-312; www.hotelifpatagonia.com; Magallanes 73; d CH$70,000-90,000; P🛜) With brimming hospitality, IF (for Isabel and Fernando) is minimalist and lovely. Its bright, modern interior includes wool throws, down duvets and deck views of the fjord. Rooms can be on the small side. Check out the optional seafood dinners, hauled in with the owners' own fishing boat. Watch for a spa in the works.

Amerindia   B&B $$
(☑411-945; www.hostelamerindia.com; Barros Arana 135; d with/without bathroom CH$40,000/30,000, 6-person apt CH$75,000; ☉closed Jul; @🛜) An earthy retreat with a woodstove, beautiful weavings and raw wood beams. Don't expect a hovering host, the atmosphere is chill. Guests wake up to cake, eggs and oatmeal in a cozy cafe that is open to the public and also sells organic chocolate and teas.

Hotel Indigo   BOUTIQUE HOTEL $$$
(☑413-609; www.indigopatagonia.com; Ladrilleros 105; d/ste CH$130,000/175,000; ☉@🛜) Hikers will head first to Indigo's rooftop Jacuzzis and glass-walled spa, but plush, restful rooms are stocked with apples and tea candles. Materials like eucalyptus, slate and iron overlap the modern with the natural to interesting effect. The star here is the fjord in front of you, which even captures your gaze in the shower.

Puerto Natales

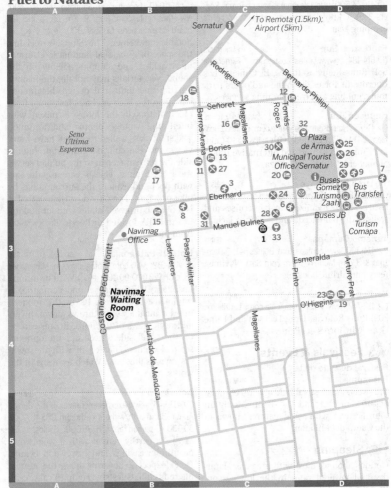

Remota LODGE $$$
(414-040, bookings in Santiago 02-387-1500; www.remota.cl; Ruta 9, Km 1.5; s/d 3 nights incl full board & excursions CH$1,110,000/1,548,000; @ 🛜 🏊) Socialites beware – isolation is the idea here. Unlike most hotels, the exclusive Remota draws your awareness to what's outside: silence broadcasts gusty winds, windows imitate old stock fences and a crooked passageway pays tribute to *estancia* sheep corridors. Though rooms are cozy, you'll probably want to spend all your time at 'the beach' – a glass-walled room with lounge futons that gape at the wild surroundings.

The Singing Lamb HOSTEL $
(410-958; www.thesinginglamb.com; Arauco 779; dm CH$10,000) Sparkling clean and green (with compost, recycling, rainwater collection as well as linen shopping bags), this fresh hostel is run by a motherly Kiwi. The two long dorms feel a little institutional but thoughtful touches, such as central heating, a tasty breakfast (including eggs and homemade wheat toast) and a sunroom compensate. To get here, follow Raimírez one block past Plaza O'Higgins.

and there's a kitchen for cooking and new gear rentals. The dorm rooms are located in an annex across the street.

Temauken Hotel
B&B $$$

(📞411-666; www.temauken.cl; Calle Ovejero 1123; s/d/t/ste CH$55,000/75,000/90,000/110,000; 🛜) A cheerful and elegant choice well away from the center, this new three-story stilted home is plush and modern. Rooms have thick down duvets and woolen throws. The light-filled living room has wicker lounges and panoramic sea views. The restaurant serves gourmet meals.

4Elementos
GUESTHOUSE $$

(📞415-751; www.4elementos.cl, in Spanish; Esmeralda 813; dm CH$10,000, s/d CH$15,000/25,000, s/d without bathroom CH$12,000/20,000) The pioneer of Patagonian recycling, this spare guesthouse has the passionate mission of educating people about proper waste disposal. Its also nothing fancy – except for the Scandinavian breakfast served with careful attention. If you're good, Trauko will get up before dawn to bake you fresh whole-grain bread to take away on your journey. Guide service, park bookings and cool offsite greenhouse tours are available.

Erratic Rock II
B&B $$

(📞414-317; www.erraticrock2.com; Benjamin Zamora 732; d/t CH$35,000/36,000; @🛜) Billed as a 'hostel alternative for couples,' this cozy home offers spacious doubles with throw pillows and tidy bathrooms. Breakfasts in the bright dining room are abundant. It's two blocks east of Plaza O'Higgins.

Yaganhouse
HOSTEL $

(📞414-137; www.yaganhouse.cl; O'Higgins 584; dm/d CH$8,000/18,000; 🛜) Typical of local houses-turned-hostel, with funky additions. Eco-house may be a bit of a stretch, but there are homey shared spaces with colorful throws and rugs, laundry service and equipment rental.

Hostal Dos Lagunas
GUESTHOUSE $

(📞415-733; www.hostaldoslagunas.com; cnr Barros Arana & Bories; dm/d CH$10,000/$25,000) Natales natives Alejandro and Andrea are attentive hosts, spoiling guests with filling breakfasts, steady water pressure and travel tips.

Hostel Natales
HOSTEL $

(📞414-731; www.hostelnatales.cl; Ladrilleros 209; dm/d/tr CH$12,000/24,000/30,000; @) Tranquil

Lili Patagonico's Hostal
HOSTEL $

(📞414-063; www.lilipatagonicos.com; Arturo Prat 479; dm CH$8000, d CH$25,000, d without bathroom CH$18,000; @🛜) A sprawling house with a climbing wall, a variety of dorms and colorful doubles – with brand-new bathrooms and down comforters.

Hostal Nancy
HOSTEL $

(📞410-022; www.natieslodge.cl; Ramírez 543; dm/s/d CH$7000/9000/24,000; @) Nancy is a sweetheart. Rooms in her house are hodge-podge, but also clean and comfortable, with down covers, good mattresses and central heating. Privates have their own bathrooms

Puerto Natales

and toasty, rooms here all have private bathroom. Generic, this spot doesn't have the energy of other hostels, but dorms are good value.

Patagonia Aventura   HOSTEL $
(☑411-028; www.apatagonia.com; Tomás Rogers 179; dm/d CH$8000/20,000; ⊙mid-Sep–mid-May; @) Situated on the plaza, this hostel has ambient dorms with down duvets but bathrooms are in short supply and there is no kitchen access. The attached tour agency also rents bikes.

Casa Cecilia   GUESTHOUSE $$
(☑613-560; www.casaceciliahostal.com; Tomás Rogers 60; d with/without bathroom CH$38,000/25,000; ⊙) Well kept and central, Cecilia is a reliable mainstay with good showers, highly praised service and homemade wheat toast for breakfast. The only drawbacks are a small kitchen and cramped rooms.

Residencial Bernardita   GUESTHOUSE $
(☑411-162; www.residencialbernardita.cl; O'Higgins 765; r per person without bathroom CH$12,000; ☎) Guests highly recommend Bernardita's quiet rooms with central heating and mismatched granny decor. Choose between rooms in the main house or more private

ones in the back annex. There's also kitchen use and breakfast.

✗ Eating

Afrigonia   FUSION $$
(☑412-877; Eberhard 343; mains CH$8000; ⊙lunch & dinner) Outstanding and wholly original – you won't find Afro-Chilean cuisine on any NYC menu. This romantic gem was dreamed up by a hardworking Zambian-Chilean couple. Fragrant rice, fresh ceviche and mint roasted lamb are prepared with succulent precision. Take your time and definitely leave room for the fennel and cardamon bread pudding with rooiboos cream. Next door, a small take-out business of the same name sells wraps and salads, but it lacks the flair of the restaurant.

La Mesita Grande   PIZZERIA $
(Arturo Prat 196; pizzas CH$5500; ⊙lunch & dinner) Happy diners sit at one long, worn table shared by windburned hikers. It's conducive to socializing with seatmates from around the world, between bites of thin-crust pizza and organic salads from a local

greenhouse. There's also local Baguales beer on tap.

Cangrejo Rojo
CAFE $

(☑412-436; Santiago Bueras 782; mains CH$2000-4000; ☺9am-1:30pm & 3-10:30pm, closed Mon) Unfathomably friendly and cheap, this corregated tin cafe serves pies, ice cream, sandwiches and hot claypot dishes like seafood casserole or lamb chops. Service is sweet and personal. To get here, follow Baquedano four blocks south of Plaza O'Higgins to Bueras.

La Casa Magna
CHILEAN $

(☑410-045; Bulnes 370; menu CH$3000; ☺10:30am-midnight) Almost always open, this family-run no-frills eatery offers wonderful home cooking at bargain prices. Hearty stews, with chicken, potatoes and cilantro, satisfy and the service is friendly.

El Living
CAFE $

(www.el-living.com; Arturo Prat 156; mains $5000; ☺11am-11pm Nov-mid April; ☑) Indulge in the London-lounge feel of this chilled-out cafe. There's proper vegetarian fare, stacks of European glossies and a stream of eclectic tunes. In addition to real coffee, tea and fresh juice, organic salads, burritos and soups are served. Wine and local beer are also at the ready. Choose a comfy chair or check out the new garden space.

La Aldea
MEDITERRANEAN $$

(Barros Arana 142; mains CH$7000; ☺8pm-midnight) Chef Pato changes the blackboard offerings daily, but the focus here is fresh and Mediterranean. Think grilled clams, lamb tagine and quinoa dishes. Get here early, there are only eight tables.

Pan Pa Ya
BAKERY $

(☑415-474; Bories 349; ☺9am-8pm) For bread rolls or whole-wheat loaves to take on the trail, check out this bakery with ultrafresh products.

Patagonia Dulce
CAFE $

(☑415-285; www.patagoniadulce.cl, in Spanish; Barros Arana 233; ☺9am-8pm) Coffee and chocolate shop, Patagonia Dulce also serves fresh baked goods, homemade ice creams and velvety hot chocolate.

Asador Patagónico
PARRILLA $$

(☑413-553; Arturo Prat 158; mains CH$8000) If trekking left you with a mastodon appetite, splurge at this upscale Argentine-style grill. Flame-seared lamb, steak and salads, as well as sweetbreads, are served as you wish alongside quality wines.

Drinking

Baguales
BREWERY

(☑411-920; cervezabaguales.cl; Bories 430; ☺7pm-2am daily, weekends only in winter; ☜) Climber friends started this microbrewery as a noble quest for quality suds. They have succeeded. Gringo-style burgers and generous veggie tacos will whet your appetite. Get here early to grab a booth, supplied with its own metered tap and topo map to plan your route.

El Bar de Ruperto
BAR

(☑410863; cnr Bulnes & Magallanes; ☜) A typical bar with foosball, chess and other board games.

Shopping

La Maddera
OUTDOOR GEAR

(☑413-318, 24hr emergency 099-418-4100; Arturo Prat 297; ☺8am-11:30pm; @) You'll find camping gear galore at this friendly shop; also fixes damaged gear and does after-hours business for trekkers with early departures.

Information

Most banks in town are equipped with ATMs. The best bilingual portal for the region is www.torresdelpaine.cl.

Conaf (☑411-438; Baquedano 847) National parks service administrative office.

Gasic (Bulnes 692) Decent rates on cash and traveler's checks.

Hospital (☑411-582; Pinto 537)

Municipal tourist office (☑614-808; Plaza de Armas; ☺8:30am-12:30pm & 2:30-6pm Tue-Sun) In the Museo Histórico, with attentive staff and regionwide lodgings listings.

Post office (Eberhard 429)

Sernatur (☑412-125; www.chile.travel/en.html; Pedro Montt 19 & Plaza de Armas; ☺9am-7pm Mon-Fri, 9:30am-6pm Sat & Sun) There's a second location with the municipal tourist office on the plaza.

Getting There & Away

Air

Puerto Natales' small airport has frequent changes in its services. Currently, only **Sky Airline** (☑toll-free in Chile 600-600-2828; www.skyairline.cl; Bulnes 682) flies to/from Punta Arenas once a week on Saturday (round-trip CH$33,000), with connections to Puerto Montt and Santiago.

Boat

For many travelers, a journey through Chile's spectacular fjords aboard the **Navimag Ferry** (🖉in Santiago 56-02-442-3114; www.navimag. com; Pedro Montt 262, Hotel Costa Australis) becomes a highlight of their trip. This four-day and three-night northbound voyage has become so popular it should be booked well in advance.

You can also try your luck. To confirm when the ferry is due, contact Turismo Comapa (p352) or the Navimag office in Hotel Costa Australis a couple of days before your estimated arrival date. The *Magallanes* transports cars and passengers. It leaves Natales early on Friday and stops in Puerto Edén (or the advancing Glaciar Pía XI on southbound sailings) en route to Puerto Montt. It usually arrives in Natales in the morning of the same day and departs either later that day or on the following day, but schedules vary according to weather conditions and tides. Disembarking passengers must stay on board while cargo is transported; those embarking have to spend the night on board.

High season is November to March, midseason is October and April and low season is May to September. Most folks end up in dorm-style, 22-bed berths, but often wish they had sprung for a private cabin. Fares vary according to view, cabin size and private or shared bathroom, and include all meals (including veggie options if requested while booking, but bring water, snacks and drinks anyway) and interpretive talks. Per-person fares range from CH$200,000 for a bunk berth in low season to CH$945,000 for a triple-A cabin in high season; students and seniors receive a 10% to 15% discount. Check online for current schedules and rates.

Bus

Puerto Natales has no central bus terminal. In high season book at least a day ahead, especially for early-morning departures. Services are greatly reduced in the low season.

A second road has been opened to Torres del Paine and, although gravel, it is much more direct. Several tour operators use it. This alternative entrance goes alongside Lago del Toro to the Administración (park headquarters).

Buses leave for Torres del Paine two to three times daily at around 7am, 8am and 2:30pm. If you are headed to Mountain Lodge Paine Grande in the low season, take the morning bus to meet the catamaran (one way CH$12,000, two hours). Tickets may also be used for transfers within the park, so save your stub. Schedules are in constant flux, so double-check them before heading out.

Companies and destinations include the following:

Bus Sur (🖉614-220; www.bus-sur.cl, in Spanish; Baquedano 668) Punta Arenas, Torres del Paine, Puerto Montt, El Calafate, Río Gallegos and Ushuaia.

Buses Fernández/El Pingüino (🖉411-111; www.busesfernandez.com; cnr Esmeralda & Ramírez) Torres del Paine and Punta Arenas. Also goes direct to Puerto Natales from the airport.

Buses Gomez (🖉415-700; www.busesgomez. com, in Spanish; Arturo Prat 234) Torres del Paine.

Buses JB (🖉410-242; www.busesjb.cl; Arturo Prat 258) Torres del Paine.

Buses Pacheco (🖉414-800; www.busespacheco.com; Ramírez 224) Punta Arenas, Río Grande and Ushuaia.

Buses Transfer (🖉412-616; www.pumatour.cl; Bulnes 518) Torres del Paine, El Calafate and Ushuaia.

Cootra (🖉412-785; Baquedano 244) El Calafate daily at 8:30am.

Turismo Zaahj (🖉412-260/355; www.turismozaahj.co.cl, in Spanish; Arturo Prat 236/270) Torres del Paine and El Calafate.

DESTINATION	COST (CH$)	DURATION (HR)
El Calafate	12,000	5
Punta Arenas	4500	3
Torres del Paine	8000	2
Ushuaia	30,000	13

❶ Getting Around

Many hostels rent bikes. Car rental is expensive and availability is limited; you'll get better rates in Punta Arenas or Argentina. Try **Emsa/Avis** (🖉410-775; Bulnes 632).

Reliable Radio Taxi (🖉412-805; cnr Prat & Bulnes) can even be counted on for after-hours deliveries.

Cueva del Milodón

In the 1890s German pioneer Hermann Eberhard discovered the partial remains of an enormous ground sloth in a cave 25km northwest of Puerto Natales. The slow-moving, herbivorous *milodón,* which stood nearly 4m tall, was supposedly the motivating factor behind Bruce Chatwin's book *In Patagonia* (see the boxed text, p351*).* The 30m-high **Cueva del Milodón** (admission CH$3000) pays homage to its former inhabitant with a life-size plastic replica of the animal. It's not exactly tasteful, but still worth a stop, whether to appreciate the grand setting and ruminate over its wild past or to take an easy walk up to a lookout point. Camping (no fires) and picnicking are possible. In February the cave hosts a cinema festival (see p353).

Torres del Paine buses pass the entrance, which is 8km from the cave proper. There are infrequent tours from Puerto Natales; alternatively, you can hitch or share a *taxi colectivo* (CH$20,000). Outside of high season, bus services are infrequent.

Parque Nacional Bernardo O'Higgins

Virtually inaccessible, O'Higgins remains an elusive cache of glaciers. As it can be entered only by boat, full-day excursions (CH$67,000, with lunch included) to the base of Glaciar Serrano are run by Turismo 21 de Mayo (p352).

You can access Torres del Paine via boat to Glaciar Serrano. Passengers transfer to a Zodiac (a motorized raft) stop for lunch at Estancia Balmaceda and continue up Río Serrano, arriving at the southern border of the park by 5pm. The same tour can be done leaving the park, but may require camping near Río Serrano to catch the Zodiac at 9am. The trip, which includes park entry, costs CH$92,000 with Turismo 21 de Mayo.

Parque Nacional Torres del Paine

Soaring almost vertically more than 2000m above the Patagonian steppe, the granite pillars of Torres del Paine (Towers of Paine) dominate the landscape of what may be South America's finest national park. Before its creation in 1959, the park was part of a large sheep *estancia,* and it's still recovering from nearly a century of overexploitation of its pastures, forests and wildlife.

Most people visit the park for its one greatest hit but, once here, realize that there are other attractions with equal wow power. We're talking about azure lakes, trails that meander through emerald forests, roaring rivers you'll cross on rickety bridges and one big, radiant blue glacier. Variety spans from the vast openness of the steppe to rugged mountain terrain topped by looming peaks.

Part of Unesco's Biosphere Reserve system since 1978, the park is home to flocks of ostrichlike rhea (known locally as the ñandú), Andean condor, flamingo and many

other bird species. Its star success in conservation is undoubtedly the guanaco, which grazes the open steppes where pumas cannot approach undetected. After more than a decade of effective protection from poachers, these large and growing herds don't even flinch when humans or vehicles approach.

When the weather is clear, panoramas are everywhere. However, unpredictable weather systems can sheath the peaks in clouds for hours or days. Some say you get four seasons in a day here, with sudden rainstorms and knock-down gusts part of the hearty initiation. Bring high-quality foul-weather gear, a synthetic sleeping bag and, if you're camping, a good tent. It is always wise to plan a few extra days to make sure that your trip isn't torpedoed by a spot of bad weather.

However, the crowning attraction of this 1810-sq-km park is its highly developed infrastructure, which makes it possible to do the whole 'W' hike (p360) while sleeping in beds, eating hot meals, taking showers and even drinking the random cocktail. It's essential to make reservations ahead of time (for contact details see p364).

If you want to sleep in hotels or *refugios* (rustic shelters), you must make reservations in advance. Plan a minimum of three to seven days to enjoy the hiking and other activities. Guided day trips on minibuses from Puerto Natales are possible, but permit only a glimpse of what the park has to offer.

At the end of 2011, a raging fire burned over 40,000 acres. The fire took weeks to contain, destroyed old forest, killed animals and burned several park structures. An international visitor was charged with accidentally setting the fire while trying to start an illegal campfire. The hiker denied setting the fire but paid a US$10,000 fine and agreed to help with reforestation efforts.

The affected area, mostly between Pehoé and Refugio Grey, is essentially the western leg of the W trek. It is now open for visitation but visitors should should be prepared for a landscape that is charred and ashen. The panoramic views remain, but it may take centuries for the forest to recover.

Be conscientious and tread lightly – you are among hundreds of thousands of yearly guests.

 Activities

Hiking

Torres del Paine's 2800m granite peaks inspire a mass pilgrimage of hikers from

Parque Nacional Torres del Paine

around the world. Most go for the Paine Circuit or the 'W' to soak in these classic panoramas, leaving other incredible routes deserted. The Paine Circuit (the 'W' plus the backside of the peaks) requires seven to nine days, while the 'W' (named for the rough approximation to the letter that it traces out on the map) takes four to five. Add another day or two for transportation connections.

Most trekkers start either route from **Laguna Amarga.** You can also hike from Administración or take the catamaran from Pudeto to Lago Pehoé and start from there; hiking roughly southwest to northeast along the 'W' presents more views of black sedimentary peaks known as Los Cuernos (2200m to 2600m). Trekking alone, especially on the backside of the circuit, is unadvisable. Tour operators in Puerto Natales offer guided treks, which include all meals and accommodations at *refugios* or hotels. Per person rates decrease significantly in groups.

THE 'W'

Most people trek the 'W' from right to left (east to west), starting at Laguna Amarga – accessible by a twice-daily 2½-hour bus ride from Puerto Natales. But hiking west to east – especially between Lago Pehoé and Valle Francés – provides superior views of Los Cuernos. To start the W from the west, catch the catamaran across Lago Pehoé, then head north along Lago Grey or Campamento Italiano, from which point excellent (and pack-free) day hikes are possible. The following segments are some of the W's most memorable.

In 2013–14, Camping Frances will open near the entrance to Valle Frances. Contact Fantastico Sur (p352) for details.

Refugio Las Torres to Mirador Las Torres (Four hours one way) A moderate hike up Río Ascencio to a treeless tarn beneath the eastern face of the Torres del Paine for the closest view of the towers. The last hour is a knee-popping scram-

Parque Nacional Torres del Paine

ble up boulders (covered with knee- and waist-high snow in winter). There are camping and *refugios* at Las Torres and Chileno, with basic camping at Campamento Torres. In summer stay at Campamento Torres and head up at sunrise to beat the crowds.

Refugio Las Torres to Los Cuernos (Seven hours one way) Hikers should keep to the lower trail as many get lost on the upper trail (unmarked on maps). There's camping and a *refugio*. Summer winds can be fierce.

Los Cuernos/Lago Pehoé to Valle Francés (Five hours one way) In clear weather, this hike is the most beautiful stretch between 3050m Cerro Paine Grande to the west and the lower but still spectacular Torres del Paine and Los Cuernos to the east, with glaciers hugging the trail. Camp at Italiano and at Británico, right in the heart of the valley, or at the valley entrance at Campamento Frances, anticipated to open in 2013–14.

Mountain Lodge Paine Grande to Refugio Lago Grey (Four hours one way from Lago Pehoé) A relatively easy trail with a few challenging downhill scampers. The glacier lookout is another half-hour's hike away. It has camping and *refugios* at both ends. This is the primary area which burned in 2011, so expect ash, burned forest and areas in recovery.

Mountain Lodge Paine Grande to Administración (Five hours) Up and around the side of Lago Pehoé, then through

extensive grassland along Río Grey. Not technically part of the 'W,' but after completion of the hike, cut out to the Administración to avoid backtracking to Laguna Amarga. Mountain Lodge Paine Grande can radio in and make sure that you can catch a bus from the Administración back to Puerto Natales. You can also enter the 'W' this way to hike it east to west.

THE PAINE CIRCUIT

For solitude, stellar views and bragging rights over your compadres doing the 'W,' this longer trek is the way to go. This loop takes in the 'W' (described earlier), plus the backside between Refugio Grey and Refugio Las Torres. The landscape is desolate yet beautiful. Paso John Gardner (the most extreme part of the trek) sometimes offers knee-deep mud and snow. There's one basic *refugio* at Los Perros; the other option is rustic camping.

Many hikers start the Paine Circuit by entering the park (by bus) at Laguna Amarga, then hike for a few hours to Refugio and Camping Chileno. From this point, the circuit continues counterclockwise, ending in Valle Frances and Los Cuernos. See the following for more details on hikes within the Paine Circuit.

The Paine Circuit is closed during winter.

Refugio Lago Grey to Campamento Paso (Four hours heading north, two hours going south) Hikers might want to go left to right (west to east), which means ascending the pass rather than slipping downhill.

The 'W'

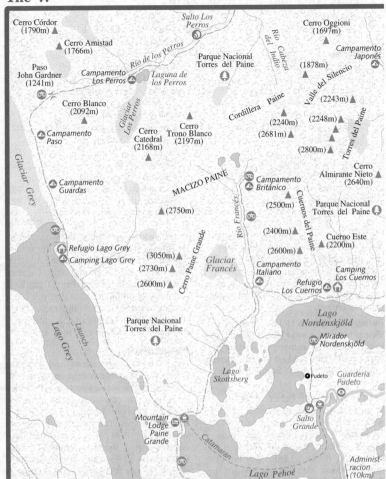

Cerro Córdor (1790m)

Cerro Amistad (1766m)

Salto Los Perros

Cerro Oggioni (1697m)

Campamento Japonés

Río Cabeza del Indio

Paso John Gardner (1241m)

Campamento Los Perros

Río de los Perros

Laguna de los Perros

Parque Nacional Torres del Paine

(1878m)

Valle del Silencio

(2243m)

Cerro Blanco (2092m)

Glaciar Los Perros

Cordillera Paine

(2240m)

(2248m)

Torres del Paine

Campamento Paso

Cerro Catedral (2168m)

Cerro Trono Blanco (2197m)

(2681m)

(2800m)

Cerro Almirante Nieto (2640m)

Campamento Guardas

MACIZO PAINE

Campamento Británico

Parque Nacional Torres del Paine

Glaciar Grey

(2750m)

Río Francés

(2500m)

Cuernos del Paine

Cuerno Este (2200m)

Refugio Lago Grey
Camping Lago Grey

(3050m)

(2730m)

(2600m)

Cerro Paine Grande

(2400m)

(2600m)

Glaciar Francés

Campamento Italiano

Refugio Los Cuernos

Camping Los Cuernos

Launch

Lago Grey

Parque Nacional Torres del Paine

Lago Nordenskjöld

Mirador Nordenskjöld

Lago Skottsberg

Pudeto

Guardería Pudeto

Mountain Lodge Paine Grande

Catamaran

Salto Grande

Administ- racion (10km)

Lago Pehoé

Campamento Paso to Campamento Los Perros (Four hours) This route has plenty of mud and sometimes snow. Don't be confused by what appears to be a campsite right after crossing the pass; keep going until you see a shack.

Campamento Los Perros to Campamento Dickson (Around 4½ hours) A relatively easy but windy stretch.

Campamento Lago Dickson to Campamento Serón (Six hours) As the trail wraps around Lago Paine, winds can get fierce and the trails vague; stay along the trail furthest away from the lake. On the

way, Campamento Coiron has been closed since the 2005 fire.

Campamento Serón to Laguna Amarga (Four to five hours) You can end the trek with a chill-out night and a decent meal at Refugio Las Torres.

OTHER OVERNIGHT HIKES

From Guardería Lago Grey, a four-hour trail follows Río Pingo to Conaf's Camping Zapata, from where hikes (about another 1½ to two hours) continue to a lookout with impressive views of **Glaciar Zapata** and **Lago Pingo**. Many people who have already done

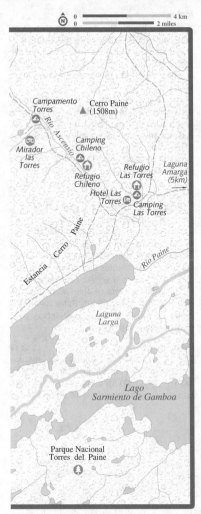

the 'W' hike to Pingo on their second visit to the park (as do a lot of the guides when they aren't working). It is less trafficked and gives a chance to view glaciers.

From Guardería Laguna Amarga a four-hour hike leads to **Laguna Azul**, where camping is possible on the northeastern shore. This area was burnt by the fire in and was closed, so check with Conaf about the state of recuperation before heading out there. After another two-hour hike north the trail reaches **Lago Paine**. Accessibility to meet up with the Paine Circuit trail near the other side of the lake is made impossible by the river.

From the Administración, the three-hour hike to Hostería Pehoé is an easy, mainly flat trail with great views. For more solitude, a four-hour hike branches east after crossing Río Paine, zigzags up the skirt of the Sierra del Toro to access a string of lakes, ending with **Laguna Verde**. There is no camping along this route, but those inclined could splurge for a night at Hostería Mirador del Payne. This is a hike mainly for birdwatching.

DAY HIKES

Walk from Guardería Pudeto, on the main park highway, to **Salto Grande**, a powerful waterfall between Lago Nordenskjöld and Lago Pehoé. Another easy hour's walk leads to **Mirador Nordenskjöld**, an overlook with superb views of the lake and mountains.

For a more challenging day hike, try the four-hour trek leading to **Lago Paine**, the northern shore of which is accessible only from Laguna Azul. The route offers tranquility and gorgeous scenery.

Kayaking

A great way to get up close to glaciers, Indomita Big Foot (p352) leads three-hour tours of the iceberg-strewn Lago Grey from Hotel Grey (CH$45,000) or two-hour tours from the former Refugio Grey (CH$35,000), several times daily in summer. It also offers multiday trips to Río Serrano.

Horseback Riding

The park is certainly a beautiful place to horseback ride. Due to property divisions within the park, horses cannot cross between the western sections (Lagos Grey and Pehoé, Río Serrano) and the eastern part managed by Hostería Las Torres (Refugio Los Cuernos is the approximate cut off). Baqueano Zamora (p352) runs excursions to Lagos Pingo, Paine and Azul, and Laguna Amarga (half-day CH$25,000).

Hotel Las Torres (p366) is part of an *estancia* that comprises the eastern area of the park; it offers full-day horseback-riding trips around Lago Nordenskjöld and beyond.

Ice Trekking

A fun walk through a sculpted landscape of ice, and you don't need experience to go. Antares (p352) is the sole company with a park concession for ice hikes (CH$75,000) on Glacier Grey. Using the Conaf house (former Refugio Grey) as a base, the excursion includes

SOUTHERN PATAGONIA PARQUE NACIONAL TORRES DEL PAINE

a six-hour round-trip hike and three hours on the ice, available from October to May.

Rock Climbing

Rock climbers can contact Puerto Natales outfitters for customized multiday trips. There are not a lot of beginner routes here.

Self-supported climbers must have accident insurance and get permission from the **Dirección de Fronteras y Límites** (Difrol; ☏02-671-4110; www.difrol.cl; Bandera 52, 4th fl, Santiago), which takes about an hour to get if in Santiago and up to 10 days from the Gobernación de Ultima Esperanza in Puerto Natales. Ask for plenty of time for the permission to avoid paying a separate fee each time you enter the park. With these two documents, climbers can obtain a climbing permit at park headquarters.

Avoid delays by arranging the permissions with a climbing outfitter, such as Antares (p352) in Puerto Natales, before arrival in the country.

🛏 Sleeping

Make reservations! Arriving without them, especially in high season, limits you to camping. Travel agencies offer reservations, but it's best to deal directly with the various management companies (see Refugios, p364). Listings feature high-season rates.

Refugios

If you are hiking the 'W' or the Paine Circuit, you will be staying in *refugios* or campsites along the way. It is essential to reserve your spot and specify vegetarian meals in advance. Try to do this as soon as you book your trip.

Refugio rooms have four to eight bunk beds each, kitchen privileges (for lodgers and during specific hours only), hot showers and meals. A bed costs CH$25,000 to CH$35,000, plus sleeping-bag rental and meals (CH$5500 to CH$10,000). Should a *refugio* be overbooked, staff provide all necessary camping equipment. Most *refugios* close by the end of April.

Refugios may require photo ID (ie a passport) upon check-in. Photocopy your tourist card and passport for all lodgings in advance to expedite check-in. Staff can radio ahead to confirm your next reservation. Given the huge volume of trekkers, snags are inevitable, so practice your Zen composure.

These listings match the 'W' hiking description direction (p360). Rates listed are basic – if you want bed linens (versus your own sleeping bag), it's extra.

Refugio Las Torres LODGE $$
(☏in Puerto Natales 061-710-050; www.fantasticosur.com; dm CH$21,500, incl full board CH$44,500; mid-Sep–Apr 30; @) An ample, attractive base camp with solar panels. The 60-bed lodge

TREKKING LIGHTLY

Some 200,000 tourists visit Torres del Paine each year and with the park headlining life adventure lists everywhere, its popularity will only grow. And there is sure to be an impact. Already, in the high season of January and February, trails have traffic jams and campgrounds resemble Woodstock. In that peace-and-love spirit, we've come up with some trip tips:

» Don't drink bottled water, since the bottles become a recycling nightmare (trash is taken out on pack horses, if you can imagine). Instead opt to bring a purifier or use tablets.

» Pack out all garbage, as little scavengers, mainly mice, love to make merry in campgrounds.

» Respect the official camp zones and hike only in designated areas.

» Be extremely mindful of fire from cigarettes, camp stoves, lighters etc. In 2005 and 2011 fires attributed to backpackers destroyed large parts of the park.

» Stay friendly. Park regulars have noted that as traffic increases the community feeling diminishes. But it doesn't have to be that way. So say hi to your fellow hikers and let the fleet-footed ones pass.

Conaf is condisdering organizing groups for postfire reparations. Volunteers also help with trail maintenance, biological studies or an animal census with nonprofit **AMA Torres del Paine** (www.amatorresdelpaine.org).

AVOID THE MULTITUDES

» Most hikers go up to the Torres around 8am and down at 4pm. With full summer light, you can go against traffic by starting a couple of hours earlier or later; inquire about the times of sunset/sunrise at your *refugio* or *guardaparques* (ranger station).

» Hike on less-crowded routes like Glaciar Zapata or the Full Circuit.

» Try joining a multiday trip kayaking Río Serrano or horseback riding; you'll get a completely different perspective and incredible views.

» Hike in the shoulder season, when the weather is still warm enough but the crowds are gone: March is an excellent time in the park; for the hearty, winter can be too.

features a comfortable lounge, restaurant and bar. In high season, an older building nearby is put into use to handle the overflow, at discounted rates.

Refugio Chileno   HUT $$
(☑in Puerto Natales 061-710-050; www.fantastico sur.com; dm CH$19,500, incl full board CH$42,500; ⊙early Oct–mid-Mar) Nearest to the fabled towers, Chileno is one of the smallest *refugios*, with 32 beds and a small provisions kiosk. It's run on wind energy and toilets use composting biofilters.

Refugio Los Cuernos   HUT $$
(☑in Puerto Natales 061-710-050; www.fantastico sur.com; dm CH$19,500, incl full board CH$42,500; ⊙mid-Sep–Apr 30) Filling fast, this mid-W location tends to bottleneck with hikers who are going in either location. But with eight beds per room (stacked high), this small lodge is more than cozy. New separate showers and bathrooms for campers relieve some of the stress and a small water turbine provides much of the power. For a deluxe option, eight two-person cabins with shared bathroom offer privacy, with skylights as well as access to a piping-hot wooden hot tub.

Mountain Lodge Paine Grande   LODGE $$
(☑in Puerto Natales 061-412-742; www.vertice patagonia.cl; dm CH$24,900, incl full board CH$44,500; ⊙year-round; @) Though gangly, this park installation on the 'W' hiking circuit is nicer than most dorms, with sublime Los Cuernos views in all rooms. Its year-round presence is a godsend to cold, wet winter hikers, though meals are not available in winter (May to September). There's on-site camping, a kiosk with basic kitchen provisions and a more deluxe version of camping in domes. The 2nd-floor bar has a

popular happy hour; if you've been hiking for days on end the setting is a bit surreal.

This is the only *refugio* option that can be reached without any hiking (the ferry docks here). Between Lago Grey and Valle Francés, it's a day hike from either and also accessible by ferry across Lago Pehoé.

Refugio Grey   HUT $$
(☑in Puerto Natales 061-412-742; www.verticepat agonia.cl; dm CH$15,000, incl full board CH$35,500; ⊙year-round) Relocated inland from the lake, this deluxe new trekkers' lodge features a decked-out living area with leather sofas and a bar, a restaurant-grade kitchen and snug bunkrooms that house 60, with plenty of room for backpacks. There's also a general store, and covered cooking space for campers. Prices may soon go up to match those of Mountain Lodge Paine Grande. It also runs in winter without meal service (May to September) and has plans to start an extensive recycling program.

Refugio Dickson   HUT $$
(☑in Puerto Natales 061-412-742; www.verticepat agonia.cl; dm CH$15,000, incl full board CH$35,500; ⊙Nov-Mar) One of the oldest refugios and smallest, with 30 beds, in a stunning setting on the Paine Circuit, gazing on Glaciar Dickson.

Camping

The park has both fee camping and free camping. More services can be found at the former. For campground locations, see the Torres del Paine map (p360).

Camping at the *refugios* costs CH$4500 per site. *Refugios* rent equipment – tent (CH$7000 per night), sleeping bag (CH$5000) and mat (CH$1500) – but potential shortages in high season make it prudent to pack your own gear. Small kiosks sell expensive pasta, soup packets and butane gas, and cook shelters (at some campgrounds) prove useful in foul weather. Campgrounds generally operate from mid-October to mid-March, though those on the backside of the Paine Circuit may not open until November due to harsher weather. The decision is made by Conaf.

For bookings, Vertice Patagonia (p352) looks after Camping Grey, Dickson, Perros and Paine Grande. Fantastico Sur (p352) owns camping Las Torres, Chileno and Seron.

Sites on the trekking routes which are administered by Conaf are free but very basic. They do not rent equipment or offer showers. These include: Campamento Británico, Campamento Italiano, Campamento Paso, Campamento Serón, Campamento Torres and Camping Guardas.

Many campers have reported wildlife (in rodent form) lurking around campsites, so don't leave food in packs or in tents – hang it from a tree instead.

Hotels

When choosing lodgings, pay particular attention to location. Lodgings that adjoin the 'W' offer more independence and flexibility for hikers. Most offer multiday packages.

Hotel Lago Grey
HOTEL **$$$**

(⌨712-132; www.lagogrey.cl; booking address Lautaro Navarro 1061, Punta Arenas; d CH$154,000; @) Open year-round, this tasteful hotel has snug white cottages linked by raised boardwalks. The new deluxe rooms are lovely – with lake views and sleek modern style. The cafe (open to the public) overlooks the grandeur. Boat tours visit the glacier, stopping at the Conaf office on the other side of Lago Grey to pick up and drop off passengers.

explora
DESIGN HOTEL **$$$**

(⌨in Santiago 02-206-6060; www.explora.com; d per person 4 nights incl full board & transfers CH$1,390,000; @🟰) Strutting with style, Torres del Paine's most sophisticated (and expensive) digs sit perched above the Salto Chico waterfall at the outlet of Lago Pehoé. Rates include airport transfers, full gourmet meals and a wide variety of excursions led by young, affable, bilingual guides. Views of the entire Paine massif pour forth from every inch of the hotel. But is it worth shelling out? Before you decide, check out the spa with heated lap pool, sauna, massage rooms and open-air Jacuzzi.

Hotel Las Torres
HOTEL **$$$**

(⌨617-450; www.lastorres.com; booking address Magallanes 960, Punta Arenas; d from CH$145,000;

⊘closed Jun) A hospitable and well-run hotel with international standards, spa with Jacuzzi and good guided excursions. Most noteworthy, the hotel donates a portion of fees to nonprofit park-based environmental group AMA. The buffet serves organic vegetables from the greenhouse and organic meat raised on nearby ranches.

Tierra Patagonia
DESIGN HOTEL **$$**

(⌨in Santiago 02-263-0606; www.tierrapatagonia. com; d per person 4 nights incl full board & transfers CH$1,230,000; @🛜🟰) Sculpted into the sprawling steppe, this sleek newcomer is an inviting option. Think luxury lodge, with a lively living and circular bar focused on a grand fire pit and a beautiful oversized artist's rendition of a park map. Large, understated rooms enjoy panoramas of the Paine Massif. Located on Cerro Guido *estancia,* the hotel's ranch-focused activities are a strong asset. All-inclusive rates include airport transfer, daily excursions, and use of spa, meals and drinks. It's on Lago Sarmiento, just outside the national park about 20km from Laguna Amarga.

Hostería Mirador del Payne
INN **$$$**

(⌨226-930; www.miradordelpayne.com; booking address Fagnano 585, Punta Arenas; s/d CH$100,000/122,500) On the Estancia El Lazo in the seldom-seen Laguna Verde sector, this comfortable inn is known for its serenity, proximity to spectacular viewpoints and top-rate service – but not for easy park access. Activities include birdwatching, horseback riding and sport fishing. Call to arrange a ride from the road junction.

Hostería Pehoé
HOTEL **$$$**

(⌨in Santiago 02-296-1238; www.pehoe.cl; d CH$127,095) On the far side of Lago Pehoé, linked to the mainland by a long footbridge, Pehoé enjoys five-star panoramas of Los Cuernos and Paine Grande, but it's a poor-value option with dated rooms reminiscent of a roadside motel. The restaurant and bar are open to the public.

Pueblito Río Serrano
VILLAGE

Heralded as the future of Torres del Paine development, this new 'village' sector sits just outside the park on the new road from Puerto Natales. It occupies a choice spot banked on the s-curves of Río Serrano, with stunning views of the entire Paine massif. It's too bad that there isn't any zoning. Development so far has been fast-paced and rather hodgepodge. It seems rather sad to see a grey fox trotting around a golf course.

Hostería Lago del Toro INN $$$
(☏061-223-351; d/tr incl breakfast CH$85,000/102,500, superior d CH$102,500; @) Sandwiched between two behemoth hotels, this more intimate charmer has fresh carpeted rooms and a warm fire to greet guests. The house, with a corrugated-iron face, resembles an old-fashioned inn, with macramé lace decor and dense wood furniture.

Hotel Cabañas del Paine CABIN $$$
(☏730-177; www.cabanasdelpaine.cl; d CH$142,800) On the banks of the Río Serrano, these cabin-style rooms with great views stand apart as tasteful and well integrated into the landscape.

ℹ Information

Parque Nacional Torres del Paine (www.pntp.cl; admission high/low season CH$15,000/8000) is open year-round, subject to your ability to get there. Transportation connections are less frequent in the low season and winter weather adds additional challenges to hiking. Shoulder seasons of November and March are some of the best times for trekking, with fewer crowds and windy conditions usually abating in March. The website **Torres del Paine** (www.torresdelpaine.com) also has useful information. The main entrance where fees are collected is **Portería Sarmiento** (⊘9am-8pm summer). **Conaf Centro de Visitantes** (⊘9am-8pm summer), located 37km from Portería Sarmiento, has good information on park ecology and trail status. Administración is located also here.

The website **Erratic Rock** (www.erraticrock.com) features a good backpacker equipment list. It also holds an excellent information session every day at 3pm at its Puerto Natales location (p352); go for solid advice on everything from trail conditions to camping.

The best trekking maps, by JLM and Luis Bertea Rojas, are widely available in Puerto Natales. For detailed trekking suggestions and maps, consult Lonely Planet's *Trekking in the Patagonian Andes*.

ℹ Getting There & Away

Parque Nacional Torres del Paine is 112km north of Puerto Natales via a decent road. A newer unpaved road from Puerto Natales to the Administración provides a shorter, more direct southern approach to the park. For details of transportation to the park, see p358.

Argentina is nearby but there is no direct transportation from the park. About 40km south of the main park entrance there is a seasonal border crossing into Argentina called Cancha Carrera at Cerro Castillo. Going to El Calafate from the park on the same day requires joining a tour or careful advance planning, since there is no direct service. Your best bet is to return to Puerto Natales.

ℹ Getting Around

Shuttles (CH$2500) drop off and pick up passengers at Laguna Amarga, at the Hielos Patagónicos catamaran launch at Pudeto and at Administración.

The catamaran leaves Pudeto for Mountain Lodge Paine Grande (one way/round-trip per person CH$12,000/19,000) at 9:30am, noon and 6pm December to mid-March, at noon and 6pm in late March and November, and at noon only in September, October and April. Another launch travels Lago Grey between Hotel Lago Grey and the beach near Refugio Lago Grey (CH$40,000, 1½ to two hours) a couple of times daily; contact the hotel for the current schedule.

ARGENTINE PATAGONIA

Patagonia die-hards won't want to miss the Argentine side, and why not? With easy access to wilderness and a well-developed tourism infrastructure, it combines well with a trip to Chilean Patagonia. In contrast to the Chilean side, here the mountains are surrounded by vast tracts of steppe and plains. Personality-wise it also provides contrast: Argentines are notably more gregarious, a trait that even carries over to competition among tour operators, dining habits and nightlife.

El Calafate

☏02902 / POP 15,000

Named for the berry that, once eaten, guarantees your return to Patagonia, El Calafate hooks you with another irresistible attraction: Glaciar Perito Moreno, 80km away in Parque Nacional Los Glaciares. The glacier is a magnificent must-see but its massive popularity has encouraged tumorous growth and rapid upscaling in the once-quaint Calafate. At the same time, it's a fun place to be, with a range of traveler services. The town's strategic location between El Chaltén and Torres del Paine (Chile) makes it an inevitable stop for those in transit.

The main strip, Av Libertador, is dotted with cutesy knotted-pine constructions of

El Calafate

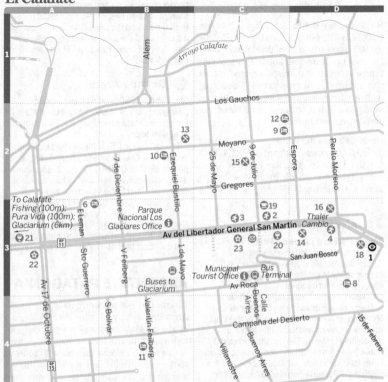

SOUTHERN PATAGONIA EL CALAFATE

souvenir shops, chocolate shops, restaurants and tour offices. Beyond, main-street pretensions melt away quickly; muddy roads lead to ad-hoc developments and open pastures.

January and February are the most popular and costly months to visit, but shoulder-season visits are growing steadily.

◉ Sights & Activities

TOP CHOICE **Glaciarium** MUSEUM
(☑497-912; www.glaciarium.com; adult/child AR$80/55; ☺9am-8pm Sep-May, 11am-8pm Jun-Aug) Unique and exciting, this gorgeous new museum illuminates the world of ice. Displays and bilingual films show how glaciers form, describe continental ice expeditions and discuss climate change. Adults don furry capes for the *bar de hielo* (AR$40 including drink), a blue-lit below-zero ice house serving vodka or fernet and Coke, of course, in glasses made of ice. The gift shop sells handmade and sustainable gifts crafted by Argentine artisans. It also hosts international cinema events. It's 6km from Calafate toward the national park. To get there, take the hourly transfer (round-trip AR$25) from 1ero de Mayo between Av Libertador and Roca.

Centro de Interpretacíon
Historico MUSEUM
(☑497-799; www.museocalafate.com.ar; Av Brown & Bonarelli; admission AR$30; ☺10am-8pm Sep-May, 11am-8pm Jun-Aug) Small but informative, with a skeleton mold of *Austroraptor cabazaii* (found nearby) and Patagonian history displays. The friendly host invites museum-goers for a post-tour *maté* (tea). To get there, walk north on Alem to Av Brown.

Reserva Natural
Laguna Nimez BIRDWATCHING
(binocular rental AR$20; ☺daylight hours) There's prime avian habitat alongside the lakeshore, north of town, with a self-guided trail and

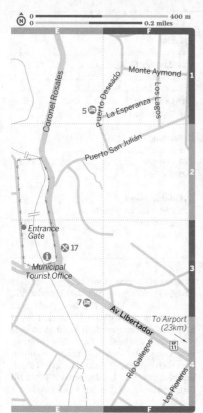

staffed Casa Verde information hut. It's a great place to spot flamingos – but watching birds from El Calafate's shoreline on Lago Argentino can be just as good.

☞ Tours

Some 40 travel agencies arrange excursions to the glacier and other local attractions, including fossil beds and stays at regional *estancias,* where you can hike, ride horses or relax. Tour prices for Glaciar Perito Moreno (around AR$150 per person) don't include the park entrance fee. Ask agents and other travelers about added benefits, such as extra stops, boat trips, binoculars or multilingual guides. For other boat and tour operators based in El Calafate, see p373.

Cal-tur   TOUR
(☑491-368; www.caltur.com.ar; Av Libertador 1080) Specializes in El Chaltén tours and lodging packages.

Chaltén Travel   TOUR
(☑492-212/480; www.chaltentravel.com; Av Libertador 1174) Recommended tours to the glacier, stopping for wildlife viewing (binoculars provided); also specializes in RN 40 trips. Outsources some excursions to **Always Glaciers** (www.alwaysglaciers.com, in Spanish).

Overland Patagonia   TOUR
(☑491-243, 492-243; www.glaciar.com) Operates out of both Hostel del Glaciar Libertador and Hostel del Glaciar Pioneros; organizes the alternative glacier trip (AR$230), which includes hiking and navigating the lake.

Calafate Fishing   FISHING
(☑496-545; www.calafatefishing.com; Av Libertador 1826; ☺10am-7pm Mon-Sat) Offers fun fly-fishing trips to Lago Roca (half-day AR$690) and Lago Strobbel, where you can test rumors that the biggest rainbow trout in the world lives here.

🛏 Sleeping

Rates and availability fluctuate widely by season; high season is January and February, but can extend from early November to April. Most hostels offer pickup from the bus terminal.

TOP CHOICE Lautaro   GUESTHOUSE $
(☑492-698; www.hospedajelautaro.com.ar; Espora 237; dm AR$65, s/d/tr/q AR$180/230/280/340, d without bathroom AR$180; ☺closed Jul; @⑤) Chilled and homey, this refurbished guesthouse reflects the playful efforts of young owners Dario and Belen. It's central, with pretty rooms in a bold palette. Guests can order box lunches made with fresh bread or dine in on home-cooked meals that beat most local restaurants. There are also guest cooking facilities, free coffee, tea and trip planning.

Las Cabañitas   CABINS $
(☑491-118; www.lascabanitascalafate.com; Valentín Feilberg 218; dm AR$80, 2-person cabin AR$250, d without bathroom AR$220; ☺closed Jul; ⑤) A restful spot with snug storybook A-frames with spiral staircases leading to loft beds. The new, energetic owner Gerardo also cooks worthy meals and provides helpful information. Touches include English lavender, a barbecue area and guest cooking facilities.

I Keu Ken Hostel   HOSTEL $$
(☑495-175; www.patagoniaikeuken.com.ar; FM Pontoriero 171; dm AR$80, d/t AR$360/400; @⑤)

El Calafate

Featuring helpful staff, artisan beer and a pet sheep, this quirky hostel has proven popular with travelers. Features include inviting common areas, a deck for lounging and first-rate barbecues (with amnesty for the pet sheep). Its location, near the top of a steep hill, offers views and a workout. Stay tuned - owners are in the process of adding a second location.

Hostal Amancay INN $
(☎491-113; www.hostalamancay.com; Gobernador Gregorio 1457; s/d/tr AR$180/230/290; 🖥) Think small—this tin-front lodging masks a grassy courtyard surrounded by prim motel-style rooms. Owners Cecilia and park guide Marcelo provide warm service and lots of local knowledge. The breakfast room has self-service tea and a treasure trove of books, local guides and maps.

Hotel Posada Los Álamos RESORT $$$
(☎491-144; www.posadalosalamos.com; Moyano 1355; s/d/ste AR$590/620/924; @) A good-value option, Calafate's original resort swims in luxury: plush rooms, overstuffed sofas, spectacular gardens, tennis courts, putting greens and a spa. It's enough to make you almost forget about seeing that glacier.

Hostel de las Manos HOSTEL $
(☎492-996; www.hosteldelasmanos.com.ar; Feruglio 59; dm AR$65, d AR$150; @) Immaculate and personable, this calm hostel alternative is across the footbridge from 9 de Julio.

Hostel del Glaciar Libertador HOSTEL $$
(☎491-792; www.glaciar.com; Av Libertador 587; dm/d AR$76/375; ⊖@) The best deals here are dorm bunks with thick covers. Behind a Victorian facade, modern facilities include a top-floor kitchen, radiant floor heating, new computers and a spacious common area with a plasma TV glued to sports channels. An annex at Los Pioneros 251 is a bit further from the center but similar and even cheaper.

America del Sur HOSTEL $$
(☎493-525; www.americahostel.com.ar; Puerto Deseado 151; dm/d AR$80/420; @) This backpacker favorite boasts a stylish lodge setting with views. It's a social scene that boasts fun times, though lately the service seems a little smug. All-you-can-eat barbecues are put on regularly.

Hotel La Loma INN $$
(☎491-016; www.lalomahotel.com; Av Roca 849; dm/s/d AR$80/390/430; ℙ@⊠) Colonial furnishings and a lovely rock garden enhance this rambling ranch-style retreat with opera on the wi-fi. Dorm rooms are not emphasized. Superior rooms are spacious and bright, antiques fill the creaky hallways and the reception area boasts an open fire and plenty of books. Rates may vary slightly depending on the view.

Eating

For picnic provisions, small shops selling fresh bread, fine cheeses, sweets and wine are found on the side streets perpendicular to Av Libertador. Head to **La Anónima** (cnr Av Libertador & Perito Moreno) for cheap take-out and groceries.

 Pura Vida ARGENTINE **$$**
(493-356; Av Libertador 1876; mains AR$40-70; ☺dinner Thu-Tue; 🖊) Featuring the rare treat of Argentine home cooking, this offbeat, low-lit eatery is a must. Even after years of success, the owners can be found cooking up buttery spiced-chicken pot pies and filling wine glasses. For vegetarians, brown rice and wok veggies or various salads are satisfying, but don't skip the decadent chocolate brownie steeped in warm berry sauce and ice cream for dessert. Reserve ahead.

La Tablita PARILLA **$$**
(491-065; Coronel Rosales 24; mains AR$40-80; ☺lunch Thu-Tue, dinner daily) Steak and spit-roasted lamb are the stars at this satisfying *parrilla* (grill), popular beyond measure for good reason. For average appetites a half-steak will do, rounded out with a good Malbec, fresh salad or garlic fries.

El Cucharón ARGENTINE **$$$**
(495-315; 9 de Julio 145; mains AR$40-84; ☺lunch & dinner) Sophisticated and tucked away, the 'big spoon' is an excellent place to try the regional classic *cazuela de cordero*. The trout with lemon sauce and grilled vegetables is delicious, too.

Viva la Pepa CAFE **$$**
(491-880; Amado 833; mains AR$45; ☺10am-midnight Fri-Wed; 🖊) Decked out in children's drawings, this cheerful café specializes in crepes but also offers great sandwiches with homemade bread (try the chicken with apple and blue cheese), fresh juice and gourds of *mate*. Unfortunately, prices are somewhat inflated.

Casimiro Biguá ARGENTINE **$$$**
(492-590; www.casimirobigua.com; Av Libertador 963; mains AR$48-92; ☺11am-1am) At this chic eatery and *vinoteca* (wine bar) the chef creates wonderful homemade pasta, risotto, lamb stew, and grilled trout and steak. Two new locations have popped up nearby to accommodate the masses: a trattoria and a *parrilla*.

Cambalache CAFE **$**
(492-603; www.cambalacherestobar.com.ar; Moyano 1258; mains AR$35; ☺noon-midnight) A cheerful traveler's hub with inexpensive wine and just average regional dishes like grilled steak and lamb stew.

Drinking

Sholken BREWERY
(Av Libertador 1630; ☺8pm-2am) After a day in the wind and sun, this snug brewpub is a godsend. Beer is brewed onsite and the tiny kitchen churns out heaping trays of meats and cheeses and spicy beef empanadas (mains AR$40). For vegetarians, the endive salad with walnuts, blue cheese and passion-fruit dressing is excellent.

Librobar PUB
(491-464; Av Libertador 1015; ☺10am-3am, closed Tue; 🖊) Situated upstairs in the gnome village, this hip book-bar serves coffee, bottled beers and pricey cocktails. It is a cozy atmosphere to peruse oversized photography books.

el ba'r CAFE
(9 de Julio s/n) This trendy patio cafe is the hot spot for you and your sweater-clad puppy to order espresso, *submarinos* (hot milk with melted chocolate bar), green tea or sandwiches.

Entertainment

La Toldería CLUB
(4914-43; www.facebook.com/LaTolderia; Av Libertador 1177) Small and boisterous, with dancing and live acts.

Don Diego de la Noche LIVE MUSIC
(Av Libertador 1603; ☺to 5am) This perennial favorite serves dinner and features live music like tango, guitar and *folklórico* (Argentine folk music).

Information

Black widow spiders have been spotted in the Laguna Amarga sector. The spiders are hourglass shape and females have a red dot. Avoid encounters by shaking off clothing before putting it on and being careful when handling firewood. If bitten, stay calm but seek medical care immediately.

Withdraw your cash before the weekend rush – it isn't uncommon for ATMs to run out on Sundays. If you are headed to El Chaltén, consider getting extra cash here.

Most agents deal exclusively with nearby excursions and are unhelpful for other areas.

ACA (Automóvil Club Argentino; 491-004; cnr 1 de Mayo & Av Roca) Argentina's auto club; good source for provincial road maps.

Banco Santa Cruz (Av Libertador 1285) Changes traveler's checks and has an ATM.

Hospital Municipal Dr José Formenti (491-001; Av Roca 1487)

Municipal tourist office (491-090/466; www.elcalafate.gov.ar, in Spanish; cnr Rosales & Av Libertador; 8am-8pm) With fairly apathetic service. There's also a kiosk at the bus terminal; both have some English-speaking staff.

Parque Nacional Los Glaciares office (491-005/755; www.parquesnacionales.gov.ar; Av Libertador 1302; 8am-7pm Mon-Fri, 10am-8pm Sat & Sun) Offers brochures and a decent map of Parque Nacional Los Glaciares. It's better to get info here than at the park.

Post office (Av Libertador 1133)

Thaler Cambio (Av Libertador 963; 10am-1pm Mon-Fri, 5:30-7:30pm Sat & Sun) Usurious rates for traveler's checks, but open weekends.

Tiempo Libre (491-207; www.tiempolibreviajes.com.ar; 25 de Mayo 43) Travel agency that books flights.

 Getting There & Away

Air

The modern **Aeropuerto El Calafate** (ECA; 491-220/30) is 23km east of town off RP 11; the departure tax is US$38.

Aerolíneas Argentinas (492-814/16; Av del Libertador 1361) flies every day to Bariloche or Esquel (AR$1414), Ushuaia (AR$692), Trelew (AR$1633), and Aeroparque and Ezeiza in Buenos Aires (AR$1173).

LADE (491-262; bus terminal) flies a few times a week to Río Gallegos (AR$260), Comodoro Rivadavia (AR$408), Ushuaia (AR$641) and Buenos Aires (AR$891).

Lan (495-548; 9 de Julio 57) flies to Ushuaia weekly (round-trip AR$2465).

Bus

El Calafate's hilltop **bus terminal** (Av Roca s/n) is easily reached by a pedestrian staircase from the corner of Av Libertador and 9 de Julio. Book ahead in high season, as outbound seats can be in short supply. Destinations include:

DESTINATION	COST (AR$)	DURATION (HR)
Bariloche	650-700	31
El Chaltén	75	3½
Puerto Natales (Chile)	102	5
Río Gallegos	94-108	4

For Río Gallegos, buses go four times daily, contact **Taqsa** (491-843) or **Sportman** (492-680). Connections to Bariloche and Ushuaia may require leaving in the middle of the night and a change of buses in Río Gallegos.

For El Chaltén, buses leave daily at 8am, 2pm and 6pm. Both **Caltur** (491-368; www.caltur.com.ar; Av Libertador 1080) and **Chaltén Travel** (492-212/480; www.chaltentravel.com; Av Libertador 1174) go to El Chaltén and drive RN 40 to Bariloche (AR$700) in summer.

For Puerto Natales, **Cootra** (491-444) and **Turismo Zahhj** (491-631) depart at 8am and 8:30am daily, crossing the border at Cerro Castillo, where it may be possible to connect to Torres del Paine.

Getting Around

Airport shuttle **Ves Patagonia** (494-355; www.vespatagonia.com) offers door-to-door service (one way/roundtrip AR$33/58).

There are several car-rental agencies at the airport. **Localiza** (491-398; www.localiza.com.ar; Av Libertador 687) and **Servi Car** (492-541; www.servi4x4.com.ar; Av Libertador 695) offer car rentals from convenient downtown offices.

Renting a bike is an excellent way to get a feel for the area and cruise the dirt roads by the lake. Albergue Lago Argentino offers rentals.

Perito Moreno & Parque Nacional Los Glaciares (South)

Among the Earth's most dynamic and accessible ice fields, **Glaciar Perito Moreno** is the stunning centerpiece of the southern sector of **Parque Nacional Los Glaciares** (admission AR$30). The glacier measures 30km long, 5km wide and 60m high, but what makes it exceptional in the world of ice is its constant advance – up to 2m per day, causing building-sized icebergs to calve from its face. In some ways, watching the glacier is a very sedentary park experience but it manages to be nonetheless thrilling.

The glacier formed as a low gap in the Andes and allowed moisture-laden Pacific storms to drop their loads east of the divide, where they accumulated as snow. Over millennia, under tremendous weight, this snow has recrystallized into ice and flowed slowly eastward. The 1600-sq-km trough of Lago Argentino, the country's largest single body of water, is unmistakable evidence that glaciers were once far more extensive than today.

Visiting the Moreno Glacier is no less an auditory than visual experience, as huge icebergs on the glacier's face calve and collapse into the **Canal de los Témpanos** (Iceberg Channel). From a series of catwalks and vantage points on the Península de Magallanes, visitors can see, hear and photograph the glacier safely as these enormous chunks crash into the water. The glacier changes appearance as the day progresses (the sun hits the face of the glacier in the morning).

◉ Sights & Activities

Hielo y Aventura   ICE TREKKING, CRUISE
(✆02902-492-094/205; www.hieloyaventura.com; Av Libertador 935, El Calafate) Runs a cruise, Safari Nautico (AR$70, one hour), and tours to Brazo Rico, Lago Argentino and the south side of Canal de los Témpanos. Catamarans leave hourly between 10:30am and 4:30pm from Puerto Bajo de las Sombras.

To hike on the glacier, try Minitrekking (AR$540, under two hours on ice) or the longer and more demanding Big Ice (AR$770, four hours on ice).

Solo Patagonia S.A.   CRUISE
(✆02902-491-115; www.solopatagonia.com; Av Libertador 867, El Calafate) This cruise outfit offers the All Glacier tour (AR$450) from Punta Bandera, visiting Glaciar Upsala, Glaciar Spegazzini and Glaciar Moreno. If icebergs are cooperating, boats may allow passengers to disembark at Bahía Onelli to walk 500m to iceberg-choked **Lago Onelli**, where the Onelli and Agassiz glaciers merge. Their other all-day tour, Rivers of Ice, takes in glaciers Upsala and Spegazzini (AR$295). Meals are expensive, but you can bring your own picnic.

Cerro Cristal   HIKING
On Lago Roca, a rugged but rewarding 3½-hour hike, with views of Glaciar Moreno and Torres del Paine on clear days. The trail begins at the education camp at La Jerónima, just before the Camping Lago Roca entrance, 55km southwest of El Calafate along RP 15.

Cabalgatas del Glaciar   HORSEBACK RIDING
(✆495-447; www.cabalgatasdelglaciar.com) This outfit offers great day and multiday horseback riding or trekking trips with glacier panoramas to Lago Rocas and Paso Zamora on the Chilean border. These are also available through Cal-tur (p369), located in El Calafate.

🛏 Sleeping & Eating

TOP CHOICE **Camping Lago Roca**   CAMPGROUND $
(✆02902-499-500; www.losglaciares.com/camp inglagoroca; per person AR$44, cabin dm for 2/4 AR$190/290) This full-service campground with restaurant-bar, located a few kilometers past the education camp, makes an excellent adventure base. The clean concrete-walled dorms provide a snug alternative to camping. Hiking trails abound, and the center rents fishing equipment and bikes and coordinates horseback riding at the nearby *estancia*.

Hostería Estancia Helsingfors   ESTANCIA $$$
(✆satellite phone 011-5277-0195; www.helsingfors.com.ar; per person full board AR$1287; ☉Oct-Apr) The location viewing Cerro Fitz Roy from Lago Viedma makes for lots of love-at-first-sight impressions. This former Finnish pioneer ranch is a highly regarded luxury destination, though it cultivates a relaxed, unpretentious ambience. Guests enjoy scenic but demanding mountain treks, rides and visits to Glaciar Viedma. It's on Lago Viedma's southern shore, 170km from El Chaltén and 180km from El Calafate.

Estancia Cristina   ESTANCIA $$$
(✆02902-491-133, in Buenos Aires 011-4803-7352; www.estanciacristina.com; s/d incl full board & activities AR$2553/4220; ☉Oct-Apr) Locals in the know say the most outstanding trekking in the region is right here. Lodging is in bright, modern cabins with expansive views. A visit includes guided activities and boating to Glaciar Upsala. Accessible by boat, it's at Punta Bandera, off the northern arm of Lago Argentino.

Ecocamp Patagonia   CAMPGROUND $$$
(✆011-5199-0401; www.ecocamp-patagonia.com; per person 3-day, 2-night package AR$3904) An all-inclusive nature camp which features hikes and ice trekking on the glacier and overnights in luxury domes with comfortable beds, hot-water showers and all meals (lunch boxes for day trips). Provides transfers.

❶ Getting There & Away

The Moreno Glacier is 80km west of El Calafate via paved RP 11, passing through the breathtaking scenery around Lago Argentino. Bus tours are frequent in summer; or you can simply stroll down Av Libertador. Buses to the glacier leave El Calafate (AR$110 round-trip) in the early morning and afternoon, returning around noon and 7pm.

SOUTHERN PATAGONIA PERITO MORENO & PARQUE NACIONAL LOS GLACIARES (SOUTH)

El Chaltén & Parque Nacional Los Glaciares (North)

☎ 02962 / POP 600

The **Fitz Roy Range**, with its rugged wilderness and shark-tooth summits, is the trekking capital of Argentina. Occupying the northern half of Parque Nacional Los Glaciares, this sector offers numerous well-marked trails with jaw-dropping scenery – that is, when the clouds clear. The town effectively closes down in winter and services are few during the muddy shoulder seasons.

At the entrance to the northern sector, the ragtag village of El Chaltén serves the thousands of visitors who make summer pilgrimages to explore the range. This is a frontier town: it was slapped together in 1985 to beat Chile to the land claim. As Argentina's youngest town, it still has to sort out details like banks (there are no ATMs), roads and zoning but services continue to evolve rapidly.

◉ Sights & Activities

Before heading out, stop by the park ranger office for updated trail conditions. For more information, read Lonely Planet's *Trekking in the Patagonian Andes*.

Laguna Torre   HIKING

If there's little wind and clear skies, make this hike (three hours one way) a priority, since the toothy Cerro Torre is the most difficult local peak to see on normal blustery days. There are two trail options from town. They merge before reaching **Mirador Laguna Torre**, a crest with up-valley views to the extraordinary 3128m rock spire of Cerro Torre, above a sprawling mass of intersecting glaciers.

It's worth pushing on an extra 40 minutes to make camp at **Campamento De Agostini** and further soak in the wonderful setting.

THE ERASURE OF GLACIERS
Carolyn McCarthy with contributions by Ursula Rick

Ribbons of ice, stretched flat in sheets or sculpted by weather and fissured by pressure, glaciers' raw magnificence is boggling to behold. Some of the best places to see, hike or climb these massive conglomerations of ice, snow and rock are here in Patagonia.

During the ice age nearly a third of the planet was under glaciers, now they only cover about 10%. Yet hundreds dot the Patagonian landscape. The most accessible can be found in Argentina's Parque Nacional Los Glaciares (home of the famous Perito Moreno glacier), Chile's Torres del Paine and Bernardo O'Higgins National Parks, along the Beagle Channel and Chile's Patagonian fjords.

Glaciers are much more complex than simple mounds of frozen water. These rivers of ice flow downslope due to gravity, which deforms their layers as they move. Melted ice mixes with rock and soil on the bottom, grinding it into a lubricant that allows the glacier to slide along its bed. Debris from the bed is forced to the side, creating features called moraines. Movement also causes cracks and deformities called crevasses. As snow falls on the accumulation area, it compacts to ice.

When accumulation outpaces melting, the glacier advances; but when there's more melting or evaporation, the glacier recedes. Since 1980, global warming has contributed greatly to widespread glacial retreat. Currently, all the world's small ice caps and glaciers, such as those in Chile and Argentina, contribute about 60% of the sea level rise caused by global ice mass loss.

While the Perito Moreno glacier is advancing, it is an anomaly among the rest of Patagonia's glaciers. Most northern Patagonian glaciers are thinning at a rate of 2m per year; over the past decade some have been retreating hundreds of meters per year. Scientists believe the change is both a product of rising temperatures and a drier climate overall.

Glaciers will play a crucial role in the future of our world. Changes to the atmosphere affect the health of glaciers and changes to glaciers, in turn, affect the health of the atmosphere. The melting of glaciers around the world will affect significant changes to the sea level. Also, as we head into a period of increasing scarcity of potable water, we should remember that 75% of the world's fresh water is contained in glaciers.

Laguna de los Tres   HIKING
One of the most popular destinations, this strenuous hike reaches a high alpine tarn (four hours one way). There are free backcountry campsites at Laguna Capri. The lovely glacial **Laguna de los Tres** sits in close view of 3405m Cerro Fitz Roy.

Loma del Pliegue Tumbado & Laguna Toro   HIKING
A gentle hike heading southwest from the park ranger office, this trail (four to five hours one way) is the only route that allows views of both Cerros Torre and Fitz Roy at once. Prepare for strong winds and carry extra water.

Lago del Desierto & Chile   HIKING
Some 37km north of El Chaltén is Lago del Desierto, near the Chilean border – a nice day-hike for rainy days with no visibility of the Fitz. A 500m trail leads to an overlook with lake and glacier views. A popular way to get to Chile is crossing the border here.

☞ Tours
Most come for the hiking, but don't discount other outdoor opportunities.

Casa de Guias   MOUNTAINEERING
(☎493-118; www.casadeguias.com.ar; Av San Martín 310) Friendly, with AAGM (Argentine Association of Mountain Guides) certified guides who speak English. Offerings include mountain traverses, mountain ascents for the very fit and rock-climbing classes.

El Relincho   HORSEBACK RIDING
(☎493-007, in El Calafate 02902-491961; San Martín 505) Guided tours to the pretty valley of Río de las Vueltas (AR$280, four hours).

Fitzroy Expediciones   MOUNTAINEERING
(☎493-017; www.fitzroyexpediciones.com.ar; Av San Martín 56) Mountaineering- and watersport-oriented, with glacier-trekking excursions and guided kayaking trips on the Río de las Vueltas (half-day) and Río La Leona (two days). Daily trips go to Lago del Desierto for three-hour canoe and kayak excursions.

Patagonia Aventura   MOUNTAINEERING
(☎493-110; www.patagonia-aventura.com.ar, in Spanish; Av San Martín 56) Ice trekking (AR$440) and ice climbing ($550) on Glaciar Viedma.

El Chaltén Mountain Guides   MOUNTAINEERING
(☎493-267; www.ecmg.com.ar; Rio de las Vueltas 218) Licensed guides do ice field traverse and ice-trekking day trips on Glaciar Torre.

Las Lengas   BUS TOUR
(☎493-023; Viedma 95) Minibus service to Lago del Desierto (AR$130), leaving El Chaltén at 8:30am and 3pm daily. All-day trips (AR$150) stay at the lake for six hours. At the south end of the lake, travelers can dine in the inviting restaurant at **Hostería El Pilar** (☎493-002; www.hosteriaelpilar.com.ar).

Patagonia Aventura   BOAT TOUR
(☎493-110; www.patagonia-aventura.com.ar; per person AR$130) Navigates Lago del Desierto. The alternative is a five-hour trek between the south end and the north end of the lake.

🛏 Sleeping
Reservations should be made at least one month in advance for the January-to-February high season, or bring a tent since campgrounds are a sure bet.

TOP CHOICE Nothofagus B&B   B&B $$
(☎493-087; www.nothofagusbb.com.ar; cnr Hensen & Riquelme; s/d/tr AR$280/290/340, s/d/t without bathroom AR$190/200/280; ☺Oct-Apr; ☀☎) Attentive and adorable, this chalet-style inn offers a toasty retreat with hearty breakfast options. Green practices include separating organic waste and replacing towels only when asked. Wooden-beam rooms have carpet and some views, but most have bathrooms shared with one other room.

Camping El Refugio   CAMPGROUND $
(☎493-221; Calle 3 s/n; campsites per person AR$25, dm AR$50) This private campground is attached to a basic hostel with hot showers for campers. Sites are exposed and there is some sparse firewood (fires OK).

El Relincho   CAMPGROUND $
(☎493-007; www.elrelinchopatagonia.com.ar; Av San Martín 505; campsites per person AR$35; vehicles AR$5-10) Another private campground, similarly wind whipped.

Senderos Hostería   B&B $$$
(☎493-336; www.senderoshosteria.com.ar; Perito Moreno s/n; s/d AR$642/752) This contemporary corrugated-tin home offers wonderful amenities for trekkers with a little extra cash to spend on accommodations: a popular on-site wine bar and restaurant, smart rooms with soft white sheets and occasional Fitzroy views.

Anita's House   CABINS $$
(☎493-288; www.anitashouse.com.ar; Av San Martín 249; cabin for 2/3/4 people AR$380/400/450; ☎) A snug spot for groups, couples or

families, smack in the center of town. Kitchens come fully equipped and there's room service and cable TV.

Posada Lunajuim
INN $$$

(☑493-047; www.posadalunajuim.com.ar; Trevisán 45; s/d/tr AR$574/701/838) Combining modern comfort with a touch of the offbeat, this welcoming inn is decorated with monochrome sculptures and textured paintings, and a stone fireplace and library provide a rainy-day escape. Nice touches include DIY box lunches and a big buffet breakfast.

Albergue Patagonia
GUESTHOUSE $

(☑493-019; www.patagoniahostel.com.ar; Av San Martín 493; s/d/tr AR$270/320/360, dm AR$60, d without bathroom AR$190; ⊙Sep-May; ☺) After a recent remodel, this already welcoming wooden farmhouse is gorgeous. Dorms in a separate building are spacious and modern, with good service and a humming atmosphere. It also rents bikes.

Inlandsis
GUESTHOUSE $

(☑493-276; www.inlandsis.com.ar; Lago del Desierto 480; small/large d AR$210/280, cabin for 2/3/4/6 people AR$400/430/460/530; ⊙Oct-Apr) This small, relaxed brick house offers economical rooms with bunk beds (some are airless, check before booking) or larger, pricier doubles with two twin beds or a queen-sized bed. Inlandsis also has bi-level cabins with bathtubs, kitchens and DVD players.

Condor de Los Andes
HOSTEL $

(☑493-101; www.condordelosandes.com; cnr Río de las Vueltas & Halvor Halvorsen; dm/d AR$90/310; ⊙Oct-Apr) This homey hostel has the feel of a ski lodge, with worn bunks, warm rooms and a roaring fire. The guest kitchen is immaculate and there are comfortable lounge spaces.

Rancho Grande Hostel
HOSTEL $

(☑493-092; www.ranchograndehostel.com; Av San Martín 724; dm/d/tr AR$70/270/290; ☺@) Serving as Chaltén's Grand Central Station (Chaltén Travel buses stop here), this bustling backpacker factory has something for everyone, from bus reservations to internet (extra) and cafe service. Clean four-bed rooms are stacked with blankets, and bathrooms sport rows of shower stalls.

✖ Eating & Drinking

Groceries, especially produce, are limited and expensive. Bring what you can from El Calafate.

TOP CHOICE ☆ El Muro
ARGENTINE $$

(☑493-248; Av San Martín 912; mains AR$35-60; ⊙dinner) For exquisite, rib-sticking mountain food (think sweet-and-sour lamb chops or trout with crisp grilled veggies), head to this tiny outpost at the end of the road. Portions are abundant and desserts, such as warm apple pie or bread pudding, should practically be mandatory.

La Cervecería
PUB $

(☑493-109; Av San Martín 320; snacks AR$30; ⊙lunch & dinner till late) That après-hike pint usually evolves into a night out in this humming pub with simpatico staff and a feisty female beer master. Savor a stein of unfiltered blond pilsner or turbid bock with pasta or *locro* (a spicy stew of maize, beans, beef, pork and sausage).

Fuegia Bistro
INTERNATIONAL $$

(☑493-019; Av San Martín 342; mains AR$35-60; ⊙dinner Mon-Sat; ☑) Favored for its warm ambience, this upscale eatery boasts good veggie options and a reasonable wine list. Try the homemade pasta or trout with lemon.

La Lucinda
CAFE $

(☑493-008; Av San Martín 175; sandwiches AR$35; ⊙7am-midnight; ☑) This artsy, cafe is friendly and almost always open. Serves homemade soups and stews, hot sandwiches and a wide selection of coffee, tea and wine.

La Tapera
TAPAS $$

(☑493-195; cnr Antonio Rojo & Riquelme; mains AR$30-70; ⊙lunch & dinner) This ambient eatery specializes in tapas but wintry staples like pumpkin soup and grilled steak are also good options. On cold days, you can sit so close to the open fireplace that you'll have to peel off a layer.

Estepa
PATAGONIAN $$

(☑493-069; cnr Cerro Solo & Av Antonio Rojo; mains AR$35-80; ⊙noon-1am Tue-Sun) Local favorite Estepa cooks up consistent, flavorful dishes like lamb with Calafate sauce, trout ravioli or spinach crepes.

La Chocolatería
CAFE $

(☑493-008; Lago del Desierto 105; snacks AR$15-30) Irresistible, with options ranging from spirit-spiked hot cocoa to wine and fondue.

Patagonicus
PIZZERIA $

(☑493-025; Av MM De Güemes 57; pizza AR$40; ⊙closed Wed & May-Sep) The best pizza in town, with 20 kinds of pie, salads and wine served at sturdy wood tables surrounded by huge picture windows.

Information

Newspapers, cell phones and money exchange have yet to hit El Chaltén, but there's now mercurial satellite internet, a gas station and an ATM. Surf www.elchalten.com for a good overview of the town.

Chaltén Travel (493-092; cnr Av MM De Güemes & Lago del Desierto) Books airline tickets and offers weather-dependent internet service.

Municipal tourist office (493-370; comfomelchalten@yahoo.com.ar; Terminal de Omnibus; ☺8am-8pm) Friendly and extremely helpful, with lodging lists and good information on town and tours. English is spoken.

Park ranger office (493-004/24; ☺9am-8pm) Many daytime buses stop for a short bilingual orientation at this visitor center, just before the bridge over the Río Fitz Roy. Park rangers distribute a map and town directory and do a good job of explaining the park's ecological issues. Climbing documentaries are shown at 3pm daily – great for rainy days.

Puesto Sanitario (493-033; AM De Agostini 70) Provides basic health services.

Viento Oeste (493-200; Av San Martín 898) Sells books, maps and souvenirs and rents a wide range of camping equipment, as do several other sundries shops around town.

Getting There & Away

El Chaltén is 220km from El Calafate via paved roads.

All buses go to the new bus terminal, located near the entrance to town. For El Calafate (AR$75, 3½ hours), **Chaltén Travel** (493-005/92; Av San Martín 635) has daily departures at 7:30am and 6pm in summer. **Cal-tur** (493-079; San Martín 520) and **Taqsa** (493-068; Av Antonio Rojo 88) also make the trip, but neither company will take advance reservations. Service is less frequent in the low season.

Las Lengas (493-023; Antonio de Viedma 95) runs shuttles directly to El Calafate Airport (AR$120) in high season. It also has minivans to Lago Desierto (AR$130), Hostería El Pilar (AR$50) and Río Eléctrico (AR$50).

Hikers can make it to Chile through an overland crossing via Lago del Desierto. The trip takes one to three days, for details, see p337.

Tierra del Fuego

Best Places to Eat

» Kalma Restó (p395)

» Kaupé (p395)

» La Picada de los Veleros (p387)

» María Lola Restó (p395)

» Club Croata (p382)

Best Places to Stay

» Hostería Yendegaia (p382)

» Residencial Pusaki (p386)

» Hotel Lakutaia (p387)

» Lodge Deseado (p384)

» Antarctica Hostel (p394)

Why Go?

At the southern extreme of the Americas, the immense Fuegian wilderness, with its slate-gray seascapes, murky crimson bogs and wind-worn forests, endures as awesome and irritable as in the era of exploration. Shared by Chile and Argentina, this area is also lovely and wild. The remote Chilean side consists of hardscrabble outposts, lonely sheep ranches, and a roadless expanse of woods, lakes of undisturbed trout and nameless mountains.

In contrast, the Argentine side lives abuzz. Antarctica-bound cruisers arriving in Ushuaia find a lively dining scene and dozens of outfitters poised at the ready. Take a dogsled ride, boat the Beagle Channel or carve turns at the world's southernmost resort. When you tire of the hubbub, cross the Beagle Channel to the solitary Isla Navarino.

Uninhabited groups of islands peter out at Cabo de Hornos (Cape Horn). And if Tierra del Fuego is not remote enough, Antarctica remains just a boat ride away.

When to Go
Porvenir

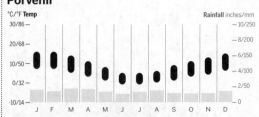

Nov–Mar Warm but windy, best for hiking, penguin-watching and *estancia* (grazing ranch) visits.

Mid-Nov–mid-Apr Fishing season on the Atlantic coast and Chile's remote Lago Blanco.

Jul–Sep Optimal for skiing, snowboarding or dog sledding in Ushuaia.

History

In 1520, when Magellan passed through the strait that now bears his name, neither he nor any other European explorer had any immediate interest in the land and its people. Seeking a passage to the Spice Islands of Asia, early navigators feared and detested the stiff westerlies, hazardous currents and violent seas that impeded their progress. Consequently, the Selk'nam, Haush, Yaghan and Alacalufes people who populated the area faced no immediate competition for their lands and resources.

These groups were hunters and gatherers. The Selk'nam, also known as Ona, and the Haush subsisted primarily on hunting guanaco and dressing in its skins, while the Yaghan and Alacalufes, known as 'Canoe Indians,' lived on fish, shellfish and marine mammals. The Yaghan (also known as the Yamaná) consumed the fungus dubbed Indian bread which feeds off southern beech. Despite inclement weather, they wore little clothing, but constant fires kept them warm. European sailors termed the region 'Land of Fire' for the Yaghan campfires they spotted along the shoreline.

European settlement brought the rapid demise of the indigenous Fuegians. Darwin, visiting the area in 1834, wrote that the difference between the Fuegians and Europeans was greater than that between wild and domestic animals (as a result, he has few fans here). On an earlier voyage, Captain Robert Fitzroy of the *Beagle* had abducted a few Yaghan, whom he returned after several years of missionary education in England.

No European power took any real interest in settling the region until Britain occupied the Falkland Islands (Islas Malvinas) in the 1770s. However, the successor governments of Chile and Argentina felt differently. The Chilean presence on the Strait of Magellan beginning in 1843, along with increasing British evangelism, spurred Argentina to formalize its authority at Ushuaia in 1884. In 1978 Chile and Argentina nearly went to war over claims to three small disputed islands in the Beagle Channel. International border issues in the area were not resolved until 1984 and are still the subject of some discussion.

National Parks, Reserves & Private Parks

Isla Grande is home to Parque Nacional Tierra del Fuego (p398), Argentina's first shoreline national park. Parque Nacional Cabo de Hornos (p388) is usually reached by air tours or cruises. Private parks are developing on the Chilean side, including the remote Estancia Yendegaia (p384), which is difficult to access.

ⓘ Getting There & Away

The most common overland route is the Chilean ferry crossing at Punta Delgada (p348). Roads within Chilean Tierra del Fuego are largely rough and unpaved. Chile is in the process of building a road to the southern end of the island. So far, it links with Lago Fagnano, on the Argentine side, but a 4WD vehicle is required. Those renting a car will need special documents and extra insurance to cross into Argentina; most rental agencies can arrange this paperwork given advance notice.

Visitors can hop on a short flight from Punta Arenas to Porvenir. Most travelers enter the region at Ushuaia (Argentina), a major transportation hub with planes, ferries and buses that access many regional destinations, including Punta Arenas, and Chile's Isla Navarino.

For expanded coverage of the Argentine places mentioned in this guide and for information on destinations further into Argentina, see Lonely Planet's *Argentina*.

ⓘ Getting Around

Half the island is Argentine; have your passport ready for border crossings. Those traveling by bus can make connections through Punta Arenas (p349) or cities in southern Argentina.

CHILEAN TIERRA DEL FUEGO

Foggy, windy and wet, Chile's slice of Tierra del Fuego includes half of the main island of Isla Grande, the far-flung Isla Navarino and a group of smaller islands, many of them uninhabited. Home to only 7000 Chileans, this is the least populated region in Chile. Porvenir is considered the main city, though even that status could be considered an overstatement. These parts can't help but exude a rough and rugged charm and those willing to venture this far can relish its end-of-the-world emptiness. Increasingly, anglers are lured to the little-known inland lakes, and adventurers to the wild backcountry of Estancia Yendegaia. Tourism should ramp up as the road from Estancia Vicuña to Estancia Yendegaia nears completion and a public airport is added.

TIERRA DEL FUEGO

Tierra del Fuego Highlights

1 Trek around the jagged peaks and sculpted landscapes on the five-day circuit of **Dientes de Navarino** (p386)

2 Explore the ancient Fuegian forests of **Parque Nacional Tierra del Fuego** (p398)

3 Splurge on fresh local seafood in one of Argentina's best **restaurants** (p395)

4 Skirt the scenic cliffs of Bahía Inútil while driving the empty back roads around **Porvenir** (p382)

5 Speed through frozen valleys on a **dog-sledding tour** (p390) near Ushuaia

6 Relive grim times in Ushuaia's infamous prison turned museum, **Museo Marítimo & Museo del Presidio** (p390)

7 Ski and snowboard with sublime views at the world's southernmost resort, **Cerro Castor** (p391)

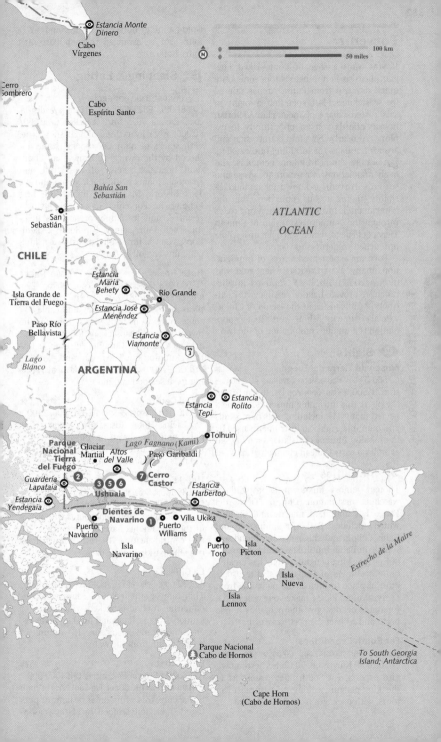

Porvenir

☎061 / POP 5465

If you want a slice of home-baked Fuegian life, this is it. Most visitors come on a quick day trip from Punta Arenas tainted by seasickness. But spending a night in this rusted village of metal-clad Victorian houses affords you an opportunity to explore the nearby bays and countryside and absorb a little of the local life; birdwatchers can admire the nearby king penguins, and lively populations of cormorants, geese and seabirds. Porvenir is known for its inaccessibility (there's no bus route here), but the government is investing in completing roads through the southern extension of Chilean Tierra del Fuego, which will open up a whole untouched wilderness to visitors.

Porvenir experienced waves of immigration, many from Croatia, when gold was discovered in 1879. Sheep *estancias* (grazing ranches) provided more reliable work, attracting Chileans from the island of Chiloé, who also came for fishing work. Today's population is a unique combination of the two.

◉ Sights

Museo de Tierra del Fuego   MUSEUM
(☎580-094/8; Padre Mario Zavattaro 402; admission CH$500; ☺8am-5pm Mon-Thu, to 4pm Fri) On the plaza, this intriguing museum has unexpected materials, including Selk'nam skulls and mummies, musical instruments used by the mission Indians on Isla Dawson and an exhibit on early Chilean cinematography.

🏃 Activities

Though almost unknown as a wildlife-watching destination, Chilean Tierra del Fuego has abundant marine and birdlife, which includes Peale's dolphins around Bahía Chilota and king penguins, found seasonally in Bahía Inútil. The recent discovery of this new king-penguin colony has created quite a stir. As of yet, there's little procedure in place to protect the penguins from overvisitation. Please make your visit with a reputable agency, give the penguins ample berth and respect the nesting season.

Far South Expeditions   BIRDWATCHING
(ecouve@fantasticosur.com; 4-passenger tours CH$60,000) Run by one of Chile's best-known bird experts, Far South offers transport to the king-penguin colony or naturalist-run tours, with packages from Punta Arenas.

Gold-panning, horseback riding and 4WD tours can be arranged through Porvenir's tourist office.

🛏 Sleeping & Eating

TOP CHOICE **Hostería Yendegaia**   B&B $
(☎581-919, 68256521; www.hosteriayendegaia.com; Croacia 702; s/d/tr CH$18,000/30,000/40,000; [P]🛜) Everything a B&B should be, with stacks of naturalist books (some authored by the owner) to browse, an abundant breakfast, views of the strait and spacious rooms with thick down duvets. This historic Magellanic home (the first lodging in Porvenir) has been lovingly restored, and its family of hosts is helpful. Their tour agency, Far South Expeditions, runs naturalist-led trips to see king penguins and other fauna.

Hotel Rosas   GUESTHOUSE $
(☎580-088; hotelrosas@chile.com; Philippi 296; s/d CH$20,000/28,000) Eleven clean and pleasant rooms offer heating and cable TV; some have wonderful views. Alberto, the owner, knows heaps about the region and arranges tours to Circuito del Loro, a historical mining site. The restaurant (*plato del día* CH$4600) gets crowded for meals, serving fresh seafood and more.

Hotel Central   GUESTHOUSE $$
(☎580-077; Philippi 298; s/d CH$15,000/25,000; 🛜) Facing Hotel Rosas, this option brims with matronly charm on the inside. Snug rooms have hardwood floors and good beds. There is a comfortable sitting area as well.

Hotel España   HOTEL $$
(☎580-160; Croacia 698; s/d/t AR$15,000/25,000/36,000; [P]🛜) This ambling hotel has spacious, impeccably kept rooms with views of the bay. Rooms have Berber carpets, TV and central heating. There is a downstairs cafe and parking in the back.

La Chispa   CAFE $
(☎580-054; Señoret 202; plato del día CH$4000) This cafe is situated in a century-old aquamarine firehouse packed with locals for salmon dinners, lamb and mashed potatoes, and other home-cooked fare. It's a couple of blocks uphill from the water.

Club Croata   SEAFOOD $$
(☎580053; Señoret 542; mains CH$4000-8000; ☺11am-4pm & 7-10:30pm Tue-Sun) Traditional to the core, this white-linen restaurant puts together elegant seafood meals at reason-

Porvenir

able prices, in addition to Croat specialties such as pork chops with *chucrut* (sauerkraut). It's all served by bow-tied waiters who take formal to the verge of stuffy. The polished pub stays open until 3am.

ℹ️ Information

Banco de Estado (cnr Philippi & Croacia) Has a 24-hour ATM.

Hospital (☎580-034; Wood, btwn Señoret & Guerrero)

Post office (Philippi 176) Faces the plaza.

Tourist office (☎580-094/8; www.munipor venir.cl; Zavattaro 434; ⊙9am-5pm Mon-Fri, 11am-5pm Sat & Sun) Information is also available at the handicrafts shop on the *costanera* (seaside road) between Philippi and Schythe.

ℹ️ Getting There & Away

Aerovías DAP (☎616-100; www.aerovias dap.cl; O'Higgins 891) Flies to Punta Arenas (CH$21000, 15 minutes) Monday to Saturday from November to March, with fewer flights in the low season. For the airport, 6km north of town, DAP runs a door-to-door shuttle (CH$1800) and taxis charge CH$3500.

Transbordador Austral Broom (☎580-089; www.tabsa.cl) Operates the car/passenger ferry *Crux Australis* to/from Punta Arenas (CH$5500/34,900 per person/vehicle, 2½ to four hours). It leaves at 9am but has some afternoon departures; check the online schedule. The bus to the ferry terminal (CH$500), 5km away, departs from the waterfront kiosk an hour before the ferry's departure.

A good gravel road runs east along Bahía Inútil to the Argentine border at San Sebastián; allow about four hours. From San Sebastián (where

there's gas and a motel), northbound motorists should avoid the heavily traveled and rutted truck route directly north and instead take the route from Onaisín to the petroleum company town of Cerro Sombrero, en route to the crossing of the Strait of Magellan at Punta Delgada–Puerto Espora.

Timaukel

POP 420

Located south of Bahía Inútil (the Useless Bay), the region of Timaukel occupies the southern section of Chilean Tierra del Fuego. It is eagerly trying to reinvent itself as an ecotourism destination – a far rosier option than being logged by US-based Trillium Corporation, which was the plan some years back. Few roads lead into this region, with even less public transportation. On the southern shore of the bay, **Camerón** is a large *estancia* owing its name to a pioneer sheep-farming family from New Zealand. Here, the

FUEGIAN ROAD BUILDING

South of Cameron, access to Chilean Tierra del Fuego once petered out into stark, roadless wilderness and the rugged Cordillera Darwin. But the Ministry of Public Works is working hard to create access to these southern points and develop future tourism destinations. Currently projects are underway to create a link to Ushuaia via Lago Fagnano. In the future the same road will continue to Estancia Yendegaia.

For now there's at least one worthy destination on the road. **Lodge Deseado** (☑91652564; www.lodgedeseado.cl; 2-/3-person cabin CH$135,000/160,000) marks a cozy spot to reel in wild trout, kick back in cool modern cabins and swap stories with the engaging owner Ricardo. It's located on Lago Deseado.

At the time of writing, the road to the western shore of Lago Fagnano was a rough five-hour-plus journey in summer. A 4WD is required for this ultraremote region (also see our tips for Ruta 40). An earlier offshoot connects to the Argentine side via mountain pass Río Bellavista, which is only open from December through March. Check with local police stations (known as *carabineros* in Chile) about the state of roads before heading out.

municipal tourist office may have information on latest developments. To the south, the cherished fly-fishing getaway **Lago Blanco** is accessible only by car, and the only accommodations on offer are the nearby exclusive fishing lodges.

Estancia Yendegaia

Serene glacier-rimmed bays and native Fuegian forest comprise Estancia Yendegaia, a 400-sq-km park. Located in the Cordillera Darwin, it is a strategic conservation link between Argentina's Parque Nacional Tierra del Fuego and Chile's Parque Nacional Alberto de Agostini. A one-time *estancia,* this private park is in the process of removing livestock and rehabilitating trails. Its transformation should be large scale, with an airport in the works and a road soon open to the public. Trails are planned to Glaciar Stoppani and through Valle Lapataia to Paso de Las Lagunas, although the many river crossings make horseback trekking a more viable option. For now only wild camping (without toilets or services) is possible.

Unfortunately, access is difficult and expensive. Visitors should plan to camp and be completely self-supported. There are no provisions available here and there is no onsite phone contact. Transbordadora Austral Broom's ferry between Punta Arenas and Puerto Williams will drop passengers off if given advance notice; for details see p348. From Puerto Williams, the trip takes seven hours. The once-weekly naval boats from

Punta Arenas to Puerto Williams will drop passengers at the southern approach.

The park will soon be donated to Chile and run by Parques Nacionales, but for now, visitor information can be obtained through **Fundación Yendegaia** (☑in Puerto Varas 065-250-079; infoyendegaia@gmail.com).

Isla Navarino

☑061 / POP 2200

For authentic end-of-the-earth ambiance, this remote outpost wins the contest without even campaigning. Isla Navarino is a rugged backpacker's paradise. Located south across the Beagle Channel from Ushuaia, its mostly uninhabited wilderness hosts a rugged terrain of peat bogs, southern beech forest and jagged, toothy spires known as Dientes del Navarino, also a famed trekking route. By a quirk, the island is considered by Santiago to be part of Chilean Antarctica, not Chilean Tierra del Fuego or Magallanes. The naval settlement of Puerto Williams is the only town on the island, the official port of entry for vessels en route to Cabo de Hornos and Antarctica, and home to the last living Yaghan speaker.

A permanent European presence was established on the island by mid-19th-century missionaries who were followed by fortune-seekers during the 1890s gold rush. Current inhabitants include the Chilean navy, municipal employees and octopus and crab fishers. The remaining mixed-race descendants of the Yaghan people live in the small coastal village of Villa Ukika.

PUERTO WILLIAMS
061 / POP 2500

Those stationed here might feel marooned, but for travelers Puerto Williams smarts of great adventure. Not much happens here. In town, action means the wind hurtling debris while oblivious cows graze on the plaza and yards are stacked roof-deep in firewood. With transportation expensive and irregular, Williams feels cut off, but complaints that it's a forgotten burg are far more common from locals than its few tourists, who recognize buried treasure when they see it.

The village centers around a green roundabout and a concrete slab plaza called the Centro Comercial. Walk a few minutes from town and you will be in moss-draped lenga forest, climbing steeply above the tree line. The island's 150km of trails are getting more attention. Plans are in the works to build a *refugio* (rustic shelter). If hiking, take a companion, get directions from locals before heading out and register with the *carabineros* (police), as trail markings may be worn and maps hard to come by.

◉ Sights

Museo Martín Gusinde   MUSEUM
(621-043; cnr Araguay & Gusinde; admission by donation; ⊙9am-1pm & 2:30-7pm Mon-Fri) An attractive museum honoring the German priest and ethnographer who worked among the Yaghans from 1918 to 1923. There is a beautiful authentic bark canoe near the entrance. Focuses on ethnography and natural history.

Parque Etnobotanico Omora   PARK
(www.omora.org) Latin America's southernmost ethnobotanical park has trails with plant names marked in Yaghan, Latin and Spanish. Take the road to the right of the Virgin altar, 4km (an hour's walk) toward Puerto Navarino.

Kipa-Akar   CULTURAL BUILDING
(Villa Ukika) A modest crafts shop that sells Yaghan language books, jewelry and whalebone knives made from found remnants. Ask a villager for help if it's closed.

Yelcho   LANDMARK
Near the entrance to the military quarters is the original bow of the ship that rescued

---

LEAVE IT TO BEAVERS

Forget guns, germs and steel, Canadian beavers have colonized Tierra del Fuego and Isla Navarino using only buck teeth and broad tails.

It all goes back to the 1940s, when Argentina's hapless military government imported 25 pairs of beavers from Canada, hoping they would multiply and, in turn, generate a lucrative fur industry in this largely undeveloped area. Without natural predators, the beavers did multiply, but in turn, felted beaver hats somehow lost their fashion appeal, and the industry collapsed.

Today up to 100,000 beavers inhabit Tierra del Fuego and the surrounding islands, where they are officially considered a plague. Beavers' damaging effects are many. Flooding from beaver dams destroys roads and meadows, ruining infrastructure and creating havoc for livestock. Loggers compete with the rodents for wood, and risk losing their livelihoods. A sole beaver couple has the chewing power to create their own lake, felling hundreds of trees. Beavers also pass giardia into the lakes, which can get into water supplies and work its black magic on human intestines.

After a million-dollar control campaign that offered bounties (US$5 per tail) to trappers with 'humanitarian' traps, the Chilean government is looking into more strategic eradication. In the past the beaver debate has pitted ecologists and loggers against animal-rights activists, and has turned government officials against each other. Somewhere in the middle are tourism companies, who are trying to make beaver-spotting a popular side excursion, but are also worried about devastation to the countryside. On a positive note, since beavers need to live in water, they can only spread so far across the land and they don't reproduce as wildly as rabbits or other rodents.

Busy beavers have already made their way across the Strait of Magellan from where they could spread to the rest of the South American continent. Scientists and forestry officials are in a rush to eradicate populations before they get even further out of hand. Visitors who would like to do their part to eradicate this invader can choose it when they see it on Fuegian menus.

Ernest Shackleton's Antarctic expedition from Elephant Island in 1916.

Activities

TOP CHOICE Dientes de Navarino HIKING

Gaining in popularity, this four- to five-day trekking circuit offers impossibly raw and windswept vistas under Navarino's toothy spires. Beginning at the Virgin altar just outside of town, the five-day, 53.5km trek winds through a spectacular wilderness of exposed rock and secluded lakes. This circuit is normally done in a clockwise direction over a five-day period, but can be extended with numerous possible side trips. Fit hikers can knock out the trek in four days in the (relatively) dry summer months. In some spots, trail markings can be difficult to find: GPS, used in conjunction with marked maps, is a handy navigational tool. Winter hikes are only recommended for the most experienced and prepared trekkers.

For detailed trekking routes, refer to Lonely Planet's *Trekking in the Patagonian Andes*.

Cerro Bandera HIKING

With great views of the Beagle Channel, this four-hour round-trip starts at the Navarino circuit. The trail climbs steeply through lenga to a blustery stone-littered hillside planted with a Chilean flag. Self-supported backpackers can continue on the Dientes circuit.

Lago Windhond HIKING

This remote lake is a lesser-known but worthy alternative to hiking the Dientes circuit, with sheltered hiking through forest and peat bogs. The four-day round-trip is a better bet if there are high winds. For route details, ask at Turismo Shila or go with a guide.

Tours

Fuegia & Co HIKING

(621-251; fuegia@usa.net; Patrullero Ortiz 049) For guided trekking or logistical support, Denis Chevallay offers professional guiding for two people or more (four-day hiking trip per person CH$325,000). He speaks French, German and English and has a wealth of botanical and historical knowledge. Guiding includes porter support and a satellite emergency phone. Day trips to archaeological sites are also available.

Turismo SIM SAILING

(621-150/062; www.simltd.com; Margaño 168) For yacht tours, contact this warm German and Venezuelan couple. Wolf and Jeanette run reputable sailing trips on the Beagle Channel and to Cape Horn. Flying under the Chilean flag, their boats enjoy better access than foreign vessels.

Lancha Patriota BOATING

(621-367; 6-person boat per day US$300) Fishing trips and tailor-made nautical excursions are available through captain Edwin Olivares.

Sleeping

Lodgings often offer meals and can arrange tours of the island or airport transfers.

TOP CHOICE Residencial Pusaki GUESTHOUSE $

(621-118, 098-333-248; pattypusaki@yahoo.es; Piloto Pardo 260; s/d CH$11,500/26,000; @) With legendary warmth, Patty welcomes travelers into this home with comfortable, carpeted rooms, some without bathrooms (with no difference in cost – first come, first served). Mirthful outbreaks and social sprees make it the place to make friends, but it isn't always ideal for getting those 40 winks.

DIENTES PRIMER

While growing in popularity, the Dientes de Navarino hiking circuit requires more navigational skills and backcountry know-how than Torres del Paine. Out here, you're essentially on your own. Before going:

» Consider whether you prefer naturalist guides or local guides and porters.

» When choosing a guide, ask about first-aid certification, language skills and the extent of their experience.

» Remember that planes allow only minimum luggage. You may have to rent gear and buy most of your food on the island. Dry goods are well stocked, but bring energy bars if you need them.

» Make a plan B for bad weather – which might mean a change in destination or extra time.

» Register at the police station (for safety reasons) before starting your trek.

Hotel Lakutaia
HOTEL **$$$**

(📞621-733; www.lakutaia.cl; d CH$65,000) Three kilometers east of town toward the airport, this modern full-service lodge will arrange transportation from Punta Arenas, and can organize day hikes to the Navarino circuit and trips to Cape Horn. The library contains interesting history and nature references. Its only disadvantage is its isolation; you might leave without getting much of a feel for the quirky town. Lunch and dinner are also available.

Refugio El Padrino
HOSTEL **$**

(📞621-136; ceciliamancillao@yahoo.com.ar; Costanera 267; dm CH$10,000; 🖥) Another great choice, backpackers feel right at home at Cecilia's cheery, clean space that's all self-serve (including check-in). It sits right on the channel facing the ferry landing – note that the houses do not go in numerical order.

Hospedaje Paso MaKinley
GUESTHOUSE **$$**

(📞621-124; Piloto Pardo 213; per person CH$15,000; @) Run by the friendly family of an artisan fisherman, this lodging has remodeled rooms in good shape, with cable TV. There's kitchen use and laundry service, but the best feature is fresh fish available for dinners in-house.

Hostal Yagan
GUESTHOUSE **$$**

(📞621-118; hostalyagan@hotmail.com; Piloto Pardo 260; per person CH$15,000; @) An impeccably clean and tidy home run by an ex-navy couple; offers free airport transfers for guests.

🍴 Eating & Drinking

Of the few supermarkets, Simon & Simon is the best, with fresher vegetables, fast food and great pastries.

La Picada del Castor
SANDWICHES **$**

(Plaza de Ancla; mains CH$3500-5000; ⊙10am-10pm, closed Sun) The most likely to be open, serving huge sandwiches and platters of fries at low-lit booths.

La Trattoria de Mateo
ITALIAN **$$**

(Plaza de Ancla; mains CH$4500-7000; ⊙noon-3:30pm & 6-10pm Tue-Sat, 12:30-4pm Sun) An Argentine-run cafe featuring tasty home-made pastas with seafood options as well as pizzas.

La Picada de los Veleros
CHILEAN **$$**

(📞621-118, 098-333-248; Piloto Pardo 260; meals CH$6000-11,000; ⊙sporadic hours) Family-style dinners are served to a menagerie of travelers, visiting workers and whoever makes a

reservation in this home. Patty is a genius when it comes to preparing octopus in garlic and olive oil or *chupe de centolla* (king crab casserole). The jovial environment is best enjoyed if you can speak some Spanish. A bottle of wine is always welcome on the table.

Club de Yates Micalvi
BAR

(beer CH$2500; ⊙open late Sep-May) As watering holes go, this may be like no other. A grounded German cargo boat, the *Micalvi* was declared a regional naval museum in 1976 but found infinitely better use as a floating bar, frequented by navy men and yachties on round-the-world trips.

❶ Information

Near the main roundabout, the Centro Comercial contains the post office, internet access, Aerovías DAP and call centers. ATM, money exchange (US cash only, US$100 minimum) and Visa advances are possible at Banco de Chile.

Sernatur (📞621-011; O'Higgins 165; ⊙8am-1pm & 2-5pm Mon-Fri) Tourist information, including printouts of a hiking map for Dientes de Navarino. It's located in the municipal building.

Turismo Shila (📞097-897-2005; www.turismoshila.cl; cnr O'Higgins & Pratt; ⊙9am-1pm & 4-8pm Mon-Sat) Offers local guides, camping rentals, snowshoes for winter outings and GPS maps. Turismo Shila also sells Fernandez Campbell boat tickets. Located in front of the municipal building.

Turismo SIM (📞621-150; www.simltd.com) Expert sailors with trekking and expedition possibilities south of the 54th parallel, including Cape Horn, the Cordillera Darwin, Isla Navarino, South Georgia Island and the Antarctic Peninsula.

❶ Getting There & Away

Puerto Williams is accessible by plane or boat. Options from Punta Arenas, Chile include:

Aerovías DAP (📞621-051; www.dap.cl; Plaza de Ancla s/n) Flies to Punta Arenas (CH$65,000, 1¼ hours) at 11:30am Monday to Saturday from November to March, with fewer flights in winter. DAP flights to Antarctica may make a brief stopover here.

Transbordador Austral Broom (www.tabsa.cl; Costanera 436) The new ferry *Patagonia* sails from the Tres Puentes sector of Punta Arenas to Puerto Williams three or four times a month on Wednesdays, with departures from Puerto Williams back to Punta Arenas on Saturdays (reclining seat/bunk CH$88,000/105,000 including meals, 38 hours). Travelers rave about the trip: if the weather holds there are good views on deck and the possibility of spotting dolphins or whales.

From Ushuaia, Argentina:

Fernandez Campbell (☐433-232; www.fernan dezcampbell.com; tourist wharf, Ushuaia; one way CH$62,500) Docks directly in Puerto Williams. A comfortable covered boat (with bathroom) goes twice daily in summer with fewer winter departures.

Ushuaia Boating (☐in Argentina 02901-436-193; www.ushuaiaboating.com.ar; one way CH$62,500) Goes daily in Zodiac boats. Tickets include a 40-minute crossing plus an overland transfer from Puerto Navarino. Note: inclement weather often means cancellations.

Cabo de Hornos & Surrounding Islands

If you've made it to Isla Navarino or Ushuaia, you've nearly reached the end of the Americas at Cabo de Hornos (Cape Horn). This small group of uninhabited Chilean islands has long been synonymous with adventure and the romance of the old days of sail (although sailors usually dreaded the rough and brutally cold trip). The cape was 'discovered' in January 1616 by Dutchmen Jakob Le Maire and Willem Schouten aboard the *Unity.* They named the cape for their ship *Hoorn,* which had accidentally burned at Puerto Deseado on the Argentine Patagonian coast. Horn Island, of which the famous cape forms the southernmost headland, is just 8km long. The cape itself rises to 424m, with striking black cliffs on its upper parts. Aerovías DAP has charter flights above Cabo de Hornos that don't land. Potential visitors can also charter a sailboat trip with Turismo SIM (p387).

The South Shetland Islands at the northern end of the Antarctic Peninsula are one of the continent's most visited areas, thanks to the spectacular scenery, abundant wildlife and proximity to Tierra del Fuego, which lies 1000km to the north across the Drake Passage. The largest of the South Shetlands, King George Island, has eight national winter stations crowded onto it. Chile established Presidente Eduardo Frei Montalva station in 1969. Ten years later Chile built Teniente Rodolfo Marsh Martin station less than 1km across the Fildes Peninsula from Frei station. The human population fluctuates between 10 and 20, while the estimated penguin population is around two to three million.

As part of Chile's policy of trying to incorporate its claimed Territorio Chileno Antártico into the rest of the country as much as possible, the government has encouraged families to settle at Frei station, and the first of several children was born there in 1984. Today the station accommodates a population of about 80 summer personnel in sterile, weatherproofed houses.

ⓘ Getting There & Away

All transportation is weather-dependent, although ships are more likely to do the trip in rough conditions than the small airplanes. Plan for the possibility of delays and if you can't wait, don't plan on a refund.

Aerovías DAP (☐061-223-340; www.dap.cl; ◷Nov-April) Flies from Punta Arenas to Frei station on King George Island (a three-hour flight). One- and two-day programs include tours to Villa Las Estrellas, sea-lion and penguin colonies and other investigation stations on the island. Flights to Cabo de Hornos can also be chartered. Check the website for updated departure dates and prices.

Antarctica XXI (☐Punta Arenas 56-61-614-100; www.antarcticaxxi.com; 7 days/6 nights double occupancy per person US$10,800) Runs the only air-cruise combo, flying from Punta Arenas to Chile's Frei station on King George Island, then with a transfer to the 46-passenger ship *Grigoriy Mikheev* for several days of cruising the South Shetlands and peninsula region. There are also shorter and longer programs. It is a member of IAATO, a body that mandates strict guidelines for responsible travel to Antarctica.

ARGENTINE TIERRA DEL FUEGO

In contrast to its Chilean counterpart, this side of the island is bustling, modern and industrial. Argentina's half of the Fuegian pie boasts a paved highway and two major cities with growing economies. That doesn't mean that nature isn't grand here. There are historical *estancias,* excellent Atlantic Coast fly-fishing opportunities, and Antarctic access via Ushuaia. The Cordillera Darwin rises 2500m above Ushuaia, flush with trails and excellent skiing in the winter. Dog sledding and sailing outings offer an alternative to the usual Patagonian fare of trekking and toasting to a hard-day's walk. The island is home to Parque Nacional Tierra del Fuego, Argentina's first shoreline national park.

ANTARCTICA: THE ICE

For many travelers, a journey to Antarctica represents a once-in-a-lifetime adventure. Despite its high price tag, it is much more than just a continent to tick off your list. You will witness both land and ice shelves piled with hundreds of meters of undulating, untouched snow. Glaciers drop from mountainsides and icebergs form sculptures as tall as buildings. The wildlife is thrilling, with thousands of curious penguins and an extraordinary variety of flying birds, seals and whales.

Over 90% of Antarctic-bound boats pass through Ushuaia. In the 2010-to-2011 season, that meant over 36,000 tourists – a stunning contrast to the continent's population of 5000 (summer) or 1200 (winter) scientists and staff. But travel here is not without its costs. On November 23, 2007, the hull of the MV *Explorer* was gashed by ice but evacuated successfully before sinking. The circumstances were highly unusual, although the incident provoked further safety measures.

As long as you've got two or three weeks to spare, hopping on board a cruise ship is not out of the question. Some voyages take in the Falkland Islands and South Georgia (human population of 10 to 20 people, estimated penguin population two to three million); some go just to the Antarctic Peninsula; others focus on retracing historic expeditions. A small but growing handful of visitors reach Antarctica aboard private vessels. All are sailboats (equipped with auxiliary engines).

The season runs from mid-October to mid-March, depending on ice conditions. Most voyages sell out. When shopping around, ask how many days you will actually spend in Antarctica, as crossing the Southern Ocean takes up to two days each way. Also ask how many landings there will be. The smaller the ship, the more landings there are per passenger (always depending on the weather, of course). Tour companies charge anywhere from US$7000 to US$70,000, although some ships allow walk-ons, which can cost as little as US$5000.

Due to Ushuaia's proximity to the Antarctic Peninsula, most cruises depart from here. Last-minute bookings can be made through contacting **Ushuaia Turismo** (☎02901-436-003; www.ushuaiaturismoevt.com.ar; Gobernador Paz 865). Other travel agencies that are offering packages include **Rumbo Sur** (☎02901-422-275; www.rumbosur.com.ar; San Martín 350), **All Patagonia** (☎02901-433-622; www.allpatagonia.com; Juana Fadul 60) and **Canal Fun** (☎02901-437-395; www.canalfun.com; 9 de Julio 118), though there are many more.

Check that your company is a member of **IAATO** (www.iaato.org), which mandates strict guidelines for responsible travel to Antarctica. The following are just a few companies that go.

Adventure Associates (www.adventureassociates.com) Australia's first tour company to Antarctica, with many ships and destinations.

National Geographic Expeditions (www.nationalgeographicexpeditions.com) Highly recommended, with quality naturalists and experts, aboard the 148-passenger *National Geographic Explorer*.

Peregrine Adventures (www.peregrineadventures.com) This outfit offers unique trips that include visiting the Antarctic Circle, with options for kayaking and camping.

Quark Expeditions (www.quarkexpeditions.com) Three kinds of ships, from an icebreaker to a 48-passenger small ship for close-knit groups.

WildWings Travel (www.wildwings.co.uk) UK-based company that focuses on birdwatching and wildlife in Antarctica.

For more information see Lonely Planet's *Antarctica* guidebook. Online, check out www.70south.com for up-to-date information and articles. In Ushuaia consult the very helpful **Oficina Antárctica** (Antarctica tourist office; ☎02901-430015; antartida@tierradelfuego.org.ar) at the pier.

Ushuaia

📞02901 / POP 58,000

Days are long gone since this former missionary outpost and penal colony had to woo or shackle its occupants to stay put. Now a bustling port and adventure hub, Ushuaia draws hundreds of thousands of willing visitors yearly. The city occupies a narrow escarpment between the Beagle Channel and the snowcapped Martial Range. Though remote, it is plugged into modern commerce with a critical mass of shops, cafes and restaurants. While not quite the southernmost city in the world, Ushuaia is the southernmost city of size.

The city caters well to visitors, and its dazzling outdoor options that include hiking, sailing, skiing, dog mushing and kayaking. Also nearby, the spectacular Parque Nacional Tierra del Fuego, with thick stands of native lenga, is a must-see.

Tierra del Fuego's comparatively high wages draw Argentines from all over to resettle here, and some locals lament the loss of small-town culture. Meanwhile, expansion means haphazard development advancing in the few directions the mad geography allows.

◉ Sights

Paralleling the Beagle Channel, Maipú becomes Malvinas Argentinas west of the cemetery, then turns into RN 3, continuing 12km to Parque Nacional Tierra del Fuego. To the east, public access ends at Yaganes, which heads north to meet RN 3 going north toward Lago Fagnano. Most visitor services are on or within a couple blocks of San Martín, a block inland from the waterfront.

Museo Marítimo & Museo del Presidio   MUSEUM

(📞437-481; www.museomaritimo.com; cnr Yaganes & Gobernador Paz; admission AR$70; ◷10am-8pm) Convicts were transferred from Isla de los Estados (Staten Island) to Ushuaia in 1906 to build this national prison, finished in 1920. The spokelike halls of single cells, designed to house 380, actually held up to 800 before closing in 1947. Held here were illustrious author Ricardo Rojas and Russian anarchist Simón Radowitzky. The depiction of penal life here is intriguing, but information is in Spanish.

Another worthwhile exhibit features incredibly detailed scale models of famous ships, spanning 500 years and providing a unique glimpse into the region's history. Remains of the world's narrowest-gauge freight train, which transported prisoners between town and work stations, sit in the courtyard. Guided tours are at 11:30am and 6:30pm.

Museo Yámana   MUSEUM

(📞422-874; Rivadavia 56; admission AR$25; ◷10am-8pm) This small but carefully tended museum has an excellent overview of the Yámana (Yaghan) way of life, including how they survived harsh weather without clothing, why only women knew how to swim and how campfires were kept in moving canoes. Expertly detailed dioramas (in English and Spanish) are based on bays and inlets of the national park; coming here before a park visit offers new bearings.

Museo del Fin del Mundo   MUSEUM

(📞421-863; www.tierradelfuego.org.ar/museo; cnr Maipú & Rivadavia; admission AR$30; ◷9am-8pm) Built in 1903, this former bank has exhibits on Fuegian natural history, birdlife, the life of natives and early penal colonies, and replicas of moderate interest.

Parque Yatana   PARK

(Fundación Cultiva; 📞425-212; cnr Magallanes & 25 de Mayo; admission free; ◷3-6pm Wed-Fri) Part art project, part urban refuge, a city block of lenga forest preserved from encroaching development by one determined family.

The tourist office distributes a free city-tour map with information on the historic houses around town. The 1894 **Legislatura Provincial** (Provincial Legislature; Maipú 465) was the governor's official residence. The century-old **Iglesia de la Merced** (San Martín & Don Bosco) was built with convict labor. **Casa Beban** (cnr Maipú & Plúschow; ◷11am-6pm) was built in 1911 using parts ordered from Sweden, and sometimes hosts local art exhibits.

Activities

Boating can be undertaken year-round. Hiking possibilities should not be limited to Parque Nacional Tierra del Fuego; the entire mountain range behind Ushuaia, with its lakes and rivers, is a hiker's high. However, many trails are poorly marked or not marked at all, and some hikers who have easily scurried uphill have gotten lost trying to find the trail back down. Club Andino Ushuaia (p396) has maps and good information. In an emergency, contact the **Civil Guard** (☎103, 22108).

With the surrounding peaks loaded with powder, winter visitors should jump at the chance to explore the local ski resorts. Accessed from RN 3, resorts offer both downhill and cross-country options. The ski season runs from June to September, with July (winter vacation) the busiest month.

TOP CHOICE / Cerro Castor   SNOW SPORTS
(☎02901-15-605-604/6; www.cerrocastor.com; full-day lift ticket adult/child AR$240/165; ☉mid-Jun–mid-Oct) Fun and incredibly scenic, the largest resort is 26km from Ushuaia, with 15 runs spanning 400 hectares and a number of lodges with cafes and even a hip sushi bar. Rentals are available for skis, boards and cross-country skis. Multiday and shoulder-season tickets are discounted. Clear windbreaks are added to lifts on cold days.

Cerro Martial &
Glaciar Martial   HIKING, SNOW SPORTS
(optional chairlift AR$55; ☉10am-4pm) A hearty all-day hike from the city center leads up to Glaciar Martial, with fantastic panoramas of Ushuaia and the Beagle Channel. The views are more impressive than the actual glacier. Follow San Martín west and keep ascending as it zigzags. When you arrive at the ski run 7km northwest of town, either take the *aerosilla* (chairlift) or walk another two hours to make a full day of it. For the best views, hike an hour above the chairlift terminus. A cozy refuge offers coffee, desserts and beer at the *aerosilla* base. Weather is changeable so take warm, dry clothing and sturdy footwear.

Canopy tours (escuela@tierradelfuego.org.ar; Refugio de Montaña; AR$130; ☉10am-5:15pm Oct-Jun) are run from the base of the *aerosilla* and offer an hour's worth of Tarzan time, zipping through the forest with 11 zip-line cables and two hanging bridges. The highest cable is 8m. It's by reservation only.

Catch a taxi up the hill or jump aboard one of the minivans (AR$35) that leave from the corner of Maipú and Juana Fadul every half-hour from 8:30am to 6:30pm to Cerro Martial.

The winter sports center also rents ski equipment; inquire about snowshoes to take a winter walk.

Beagle Channel   BOATING
Navigating the Beagle Channel's gunmetal-gray waters, with glaciers and rocky isles in the distance, offers a fresh perspective and decent wildlife watching. Operators are found on the tourist wharf on Maipú between Lasserre and Roca. Harbor cruises are usually four-hour morning or afternoon excursions (AR$180 to AR$230) to sea-lion and cormorant colonies. The number of passengers, extent of snacks and hiking options may vary between operators. A highlight is an island stop to hike and look at *conchales,* middens or shell mounds left by the native Yaghan.

Margo Del Sur   SAILING
(☎02901-15-5148-6463; www.magodelsur.com.ar; charter per person per day channel/Antarctica AR$1266/1477) A recommended option for extended sailing trips, captained by Alejandro da Milano, whose lifetime of experience ensures skill and safety at the helm.

Cruceros Australis   CRUISE
(☎in Santiago 02-442-3110; www.australis.com; ☉Sep-May) Luxurious four-day and five-day sightseeing cruises to Punta Arenas and back (starting from US$1498/1894 per person in low/high season), catering mostly to mature travelers. The Saturday departures from Ushuaia include the possibility of disembarking at Cape Horn. Low season is the first and last two months of the season. The cruise visits many otherwise inaccessible glaciers, but time alone and hiking opportunities are limited; the focus is more on nature talks and group excursions. Turismo Comapa (p392) handles local bookings.

Aeroclub Ushuaia   SCENIC FLIGHTS
(☎421-717/892; www.aeroclubushuaia.org.ar; half-hour AR$443) Offers scenic rides over the channel.

Nunatak Adventure   SNOW SPORTS
(☎430-329; www.nunatakadventure.com; RN 3, Km 3018; guided dog sledding AR$140) Snowshoe a beautiful alpine valley or dog-sled with Siberian and Alaskan huskies bumping across Tierra Mayor. For a memorable night, combine either with an evening bonfire (AR$400). It also does guided snowcat rides. See p392 for tours run during summer.

Altos del Valle   SNOW SPORTS
(☎422-234; www.gatocuruchet.com.ar) Gato Curuchet, the first South American in Alaska's Iditarod, teaches dog sledding at this winter resort, also sponsor of popular annual dog-sled races at the end of August, where kids compete too. It also has good cross-country

TIERRA DEL FUEGO USHUAIA

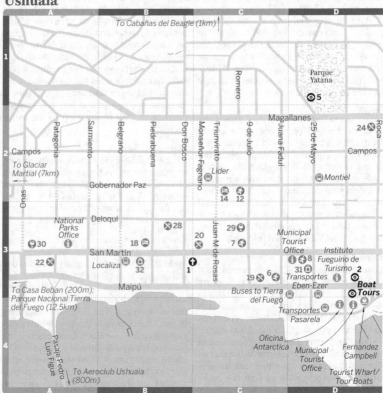

and snowshoeing areas, equipment rentals and full-moon trips. Extreme skiers can check out the snowcat skiing.

Centro de Deportes Invernales
Glaciar Martial   SNOW SPORTS
(☎421-423, 423-340) Located about 7km northwest of town, this family-oriented area has downhill runs well suited for beginners; it also rents equipment.

☞ Tours

Many travel agencies sell tours around the region. You can go horseback riding, hiking, canoeing, visit Lagos Escondido and Fagnano, stay at an *estancia* or spy on birds and beavers.

All Patagonia   GUIDED TOUR
(☎433-622; www.allpatagonia.com; Juana Fadul 60) Amex rep offering more conventional and luxurious trips.

Canal Fun   ADVENTURE TOUR
(☎437-395; www.canalfun.com; 9 de Julio 118) Run by hip young guys, these popular all-day outings include hiking and kayaking in Parque Nacional Tierra del Fuego (AR$425), the famous off-roading adventure around Lago Fagnano (AR$535), and a multisport outing around Estancia Harberton that includes kayaking around Estancia Harberton and a visit to the penguin colony (AR$785).

Compañía de Guías de
Patagonia   WALKING TOUR
(☎437-753; www.companiadeguias.com.ar; San Martín 654) A reputable outfitter organizing excursions in the national park, full-day treks and ice-hiking on Glaciar Vinciguerra (AR$329), and recommended three-day treks to Valle Andorra and Paso la Oveja (AR$2026).

Nunatak Adventure   ADVENTURE TOUR
(☎430-329; www.nunatakadventure.com) Offers competitively priced adventure tours and

TIERRA DEL FUEGO USHUAIA

has its own mountain base. Many travelers have liked the off-roading day trip to Lago Fagnano with canoeing and a full barbecue (AR$460).

**Patagonia Adventure
Explorer**　　　　　　　　　　CRUISE
(☏02901-15-465-842; www.patagoniaadvent.com.
ar; tourist wharf) Comfortable boats with snacks and a short hike on Isla Bridges. For extra adventure, set sail in the 18ft sailboat. Full-day sail trips with wine and gourmet snacks or multiday trips are also available.

Piratour　　　　　　　　　　CRUISE
(☏424-834; www.piratour.com.ar; tourist wharf) Runs 20-person tours that go out to Isla Martillo for trekking around Magellanic and Papúa penguins.

Rumbo Sur　　　　　　　GUIDED TOUR
(☏422-275; www.rumbosur.com.ar; San Martín 350) Ushuaia's longest-running agency special-

izes in more conventional activities, plus a catamaran harbor cruise.

Tango y Che　　　　　　　　CRUISE
(☏02901-15-517967; www.navegandoelbeagle.com; tourist wharf) With two 12-passenger boats, this owner-run tour includes a trek on

Bridges Island and Beagle (what else?) beer on tap served for the cruise back to the harbor – very popular with the hostel crowd.

Tres Marías Excursiones   CRUISE
(☑436-416; www.tresmariasweb.com; tourist wharf) The only outfitter with permission to land on Isla 'H' in the Isla Bridges natural reserve, which has shell mounds and a colony of rock cormorants. Takes only eight passengers.

Tolkar   GUIDED TOUR
(☑431-408/12; www.tolkarturismo.com.ar; Roca 157) Another helpful, popular, all-round agency, affiliated with Tecni-Austral buses.

Turismo Comapa   BOATING
(☑430-727; www.comapa.com; San Martín 245) Confirm Navimag and Cruceros Australis passages here.

Turismo de Campo   GUIDED TOUR
(☑437-351; www.turismodecampo.com, in Spanish; Fuegia Basquet 414) Organizes light trekking, Beagle Channel sailing trips and visits to Estancia Rolito near Río Grande. Also sells a wide variety of nine- to 12-night Antarctica passages.

Ushuaia Turismo   GUIDED TOUR
(☑436-003; www.ushuaiaturismoevt.com.ar; Gobernador Paz 865) Offers last-minute Antarctica cruise bookings.

🛏 Sleeping

Reserve ahead from January to early March. Check when booking for free arrival transfers. Winter rates drop a bit, some places close altogether. Most offer laundry service.

The municipal tourist office (p396) has lists of B&Bs and *cabañas* (cabins), and also posts a list of available lodgings outside after closing time.

Hostels abound, all with kitchens and most with internet access. Rates typically drop 25% in low season (April to October).

Antarctica Hostel   HOSTEL $
(☑435-774; www.antarcticahostel.com; Antártida Argentina 270; dm/d AR$70/125; @🤶) This friendly backpacker hub delivers with a warm atmosphere and helpful staff. It turns out that an open floor plan and beer on tap are conducive to making friends. Guests lounge and play cards in the common room and cook in a cool balcony kitchen. Cement rooms are ample, with radiant floor heating.

Galeazzi-Basily B&B   B&B $$
(☑423-213; www.avesdelsur.com.ar; Valdéz 323; d/t/q cabin AR$390/450/520, s/d without bathroom AR$190/280; @🤶) The best feature of this elegant wooded residence is its warm and hospitable family who will make you feel right at home. Rooms are small but offer a personal touch. Since beds are twin-sized, couples may prefer a modern cabin out back. It's a peaceful spot, and where else can you practice your English, French, Italian and Portuguese?

Cabañas del Beagle   CABIN $$$
(☑432-785; www.cabanasdelbeagle.com; Las Aljabas 375; 2-person cabin AR$1055; 🔄) Couples who are in search of a romantic hideaway delight in these rustic chic cabins that have heated stone floors, crackling fireplaces and full kitchens stocked daily with fresh bread, coffee and other treats. The personable owner, Alejandro, wins high praise for his attentive service. There is a two-night minimum stay. It's located 13 blocks uphill from the center.

Freestyle   HOSTEL $
(☑432-874; www.ushuaiafreestyle.com; Gobernador Paz 866/868; dm with/without bathroom AR$90/80; @🤶) With an MTV vibe you'll either love or not, this tricked-out hostel boasts modern dorms with cozy fleece blankets, a marble-countertop cooking area, and a sprawling living room with pool table, leatherette sofas and panoramic views. Brothers Emilio and Gabriel offer friendly tips and good tour connections.

La Posta   HOSTEL $
(☑444-650; www.laposta-ush.com.ar; Perón Sur 864; dm/d AR$85/135; @🤶) This cozy hostel and guesthouse on the outskirts of town is hugely popular with young travelers thanks to warm service, homey decor and spotless open kitchens. The downside is that the place is far from the town center, but public buses and taxis are plentiful.

Los Cormoranes   HOSTEL $
(☑423-459; www.loscormoranes.com; Kamshen 788; dm/d/tr AR$70/280/330; @🤶) Mellower than the competition, this friendly HI hostel is a 10-minute (uphill) walk north of the center. Good, warm six-bed dorms face outdoor plank hallways – making that midnight bathroom dash bearable. Modern doubles have polished cement floors and bright down duvets – the best is Room 10, with

bay views. The abundant breakfast includes toast, coffee, do-it-yourself eggs and freshly squeezed orange juice.

La Casa de Tere B&B
B&B $$

(☑422-312; www.lacasadetere.com.ar; Rivadavia 620; d AR$337, s/d without bathroom AR$211/253) Tere showers guests with attention, but also gives them the run of the place in this beautiful modern home with great views. Its three tidy rooms fill up fast. Guests can cook, and there's cable TV and a fireplace in the living room. It's a short but steep walk uphill from the center.

Posada Fin del Mundo
B&B $$$

(☑437-345; www.posadafindelmundo.com.ar; cnr Rivadavia & Valdéz; d with/without bathroom AR$527/422) A rambling family home which exudes character, starting with a snug living room with folk art and expansive water views. Eight fresh, tiled rooms tend toward the small side but beds are long. Pricey for its category, at least breakfast is abundant and there's also afternoon tea and cakes. Sometimes booked by entire ski teams in winter.

Cabañas Aldea Nevada
CABIN $$$

(☑422-851; www.aldeanevada.com.ar; Martial 1430; d AR$520; @) You expect the elves to arrive here any minute. This beautiful patch of lenga forest is discreetly dotted with 13 log cabins with outdoor grills and rough-hewn benches contemplatively placed by the ponds. Interiors are rustic but modern, with functional kitchens, wood stoves and hardwood details. There is a two-night minimum stay

Cumbres del Martial
INN $$$

(☑424-779; www.cumbresdelmartial.com.ar; Martial 3560; d/cabin AR$1160/1667; @🛜) This stylish place sits at the base of the Glaciar Martial. Standard rooms have a touch of the English cottage, while the two-story wooden cabins are simply stunners, with stone fireplaces, Jacuzzis and dazzling vaulted windows. Lush robes, optional massages (extra) and your country's newspaper delivered to your mailbox are some of the delicious details.

Yakush
HOSTEL $

(☑435-807; www.hostelyakush.com.ar; Piedrabuena 118; dm AR$85, d with/without bathroom AR$300/240; ⊙mid-Oct–mid-April; 🛜) Exuding warmth and skillfully adorned with whimsical drawings, this colorful hostel is well kept

and exceedingly friendly. Dorms have fresh sheets and good beds, and social spaces include an ample upstairs lounge with futons and slanted ceilings.

🍴 Eating

TOP CHOICE Kalma Resto
FINE DINING $$$

(☑425-786; www.kalmaresto.com.ar; Av Antártida Argentina 57; mains AR$55-105; ⊙8pm-midnight) Creating quite a stir, this tiny chef-owned gem presents Fuegian staples, such as crab and octopus, in a giddy new context. Black sea bass, a rich deep-sea dweller, is combined with a tart tomato sauce for contrast, there are roast lamb stews with earthy pine mushrooms and the summer greens and edible flowers come fresh from the garden. Service is impeccable, with young Chef Jorge making the rounds of the few black-linen tables. For dessert, splurge with a not-too-sweet deconstructed chocolate cake.

Kaupé
INTERNATIONAL $$$

(☑422-704; www.kaupe.com.ar; Roca 470; mains AR$80-120) For an out-of-body seafood experience, head to this candlelit house overlooking the bay. Chef Ernesto Vivian employs the freshest of everything and service is nothing less than impeccable. The new tasting menu (AR$360 with wine and champagne) features two starters, a main dish and dessert, with standouts such as king-crab-and-spinach chowder or black sea bass in blackened butter.

Bodegón Fueguino
PATAGONIAN $$

(☑431-972; www.tierradehumos.com/bodegon; San Martín 859; mains AR$32-82; ⊙Tue-Sun) The spot to sample hearty home-style Patagonian fare or gather for wine and appetizers. This century-old Fueguian home is cozied up with sheepskin-clad benches, cedar barrels and ferns. A *picada* (shared appetizer plate) for two includes eggplant, lamb brochettes, crab and bacon-wrapped plums.

María Lola Restó
ARGENTINE $$

(☑421-185; Deloquí 1048; mains AR$45-70; ⊙noon-midnight Mon-Sat) 'Satisfying' defines the experience at this creative cafe-style restaurant overlooking the channel. Locals pack this silver house for homemade pasta with seafood or strip steak in rich mushroom sauce. Service is good and portions tend toward humongous: desserts can easily be split.

TIERRA DEL FUEGO USHUAIA

Chiko
SEAFOOD **$$**

(☑432-036; Av Antártida Argentina 182; mains AR$38-65; ⊙noon-3pm & 7:30-11:30pm, closed Sun) A boon to seafood lovers. King crab, *paila marina* (shellfish stew) and fish dishes are done up so right that you might not mind the slow service.

Almacen Ramos Generales
CAFE **$**

(☑427-317; www.ramosgeneralesushuaia.com; Maipú 749; mains AR$30-70; ⊙9am-midnight) The real draw of this ambient-rich general store are the croissants and crusty baguettes baked by the French pastry chef. But there's also local beer on tap, a wine list and light, if pricey, fare like sandwiches, soups and quiche.

La Estancia
STEAKHOUSE **$$**

(☑431-241; Godoy & San Martín; mains AR$40-90) For authentic Argentine *asado* (barbecue), it is hard to beat this reliable, well-priced grill. At night it packs in locals and travelers alike, feasting on whole roast lamb, juicy steaks, sizzling ribs and heaping salads.

El Turco
CAFE **$**

(☑424-711; San Martín 1410; mains AR$22-55; ⊙noon-3pm & 8pm-midnight) Nothing fancy, this classic Argentine cafe nonetheless charms with reasonable prices and swift bow-tied waiters game to try out their French on American tourists. Standards include *milanesa* (breaded meat), pizzas, crispy fries and roast chicken.

Lomitos Martinica
FAST FOOD **$**

(San Martín 68; mains AR$22-32; ⊙11:30am-3pm & 8:30pm-midnight) Cheap and cheerful, this greasy spoon with grillside seating serves enormous *milanesa* sandwiches and offers a cheap lunch special.

La Anónima
SUPERMARKET **$**

(cnr Gobernador Paz & Rivadavia) A grocery store with cheap take-out.

Drinking

Geographically competitive drinkers should note that the southernmost bar in the world is not here but on a Ukrainian research station in Antarctica.

Dublin Irish Bar
BAR

(☑430-744; www.dublinushuaia.com; cnr 9 de Julio & Deloquí) Dublin doesn't feel so far away with the lively banter and free-flowing drinks at this dimly lit foreigners' favorite. Look for occasional live music and be sure to try at least one of its three local Beagle beers.

Macario 1910
PUB

(☑422-757; www.macario1910.com; San Martín 1485; sandwiches AR$22; ⊙6pm-late) A welcoming pub with a trans-Atlantic style of polished wood and leather booths. There's tasty locally made Beagle Beer on tap and the above-average pub fare includes fresh tuna sandwiches on homemade bread and plates stacked with shoestring fries made from scratch.

Küar Resto Bar
PUB

(☑437-396; www.kuar.com.ar; Av Perito Moreno 2232; ⊙6pm-late) This chic new log-cabin-style bar welcomes the 'after-ski' crowd for fresh cocktails, local beer and tapas. The interior is stylish but the real highlight, especially at sunset, is the jaw-dropping views over the water. You'll have to catch a cab; Küar is a few kilometers outside of town by the water.

Shopping

Boutique del Libro
BOOKS

(☑432-117, 424-750; 25 de Mayo 62; ⊙10am-9pm) Outstanding selection of Patagonia and Antarctica-themed material, with literature, guidebooks and pictorials (also in English); there's a branch at San Martín 1120.

ⓘ Information

Several banks on Maipú and San Martín have ATMs.

ACA (Automóvil Club Argentino; ☑421-121; cnr Malvinas Argentinas & Onachaga) Argentina's auto club; good source for provincial road maps.

Cambio Thaler (San Martín 209; ⊙10am-1pm & 5-8pm Mon-Sat, 5-8pm Sun) Convenience equals slightly poorer exchange rates.

Club Andino Ushuaia (☑422-335; www. clubandinoushuaia.com.ar, in Spanish; Juana Fadul 50; ⊙9am-1pm & 3-8pm Mon-Fri) Sells maps and bilingual trekking, mountaineering and mountain-biking guidebook. The club occasionally organizes hikes and can recommend guides. Unguided trekkers are strongly encouraged to register here.

Hospital Regional (☑107, 423-200; cnr Fitz Roy & 12 de Octubre)

Immigration office (☑422-334; Beauvoir 1536; ⊙9am-noon Mon-Fri)

Instituto Fueguino de Turismo (Infuetur; ☑421-423; www.tierradelfuego.org.ar; Maipú 505) On the ground floor of Hotel Albatros.

Municipal tourist office (☑432-000, at airport 423-970, outside of Tierra del Fuego 0800-333-1476; www.turismoushuaia.com, in Spanish; San Martín 674) Very helpful, with English- and French-speaking staff, a message board and multilingual brochures, as well as good lodging, activities and transport info. Also at the airport and pier.

National Parks office (Administración de Parques Nacionales; ☑421-315; San Martín 1395; ⊙9am-4pm Mon-Fri)

Post office (cnr San Martín & Godoy)

ⓘ Getting There & Away
Air
Aerolíneas Argentinas (☑421-218; Maipú & 9 de Julio) Jets to Buenos Aires (round-trip AR$2127, 3½ hours) several times daily, sometimes stopping in El Calafate (one-way AR$667, 70 minutes).

LADE (☑421-123; San Martín 542) Flies to Buenos Aires (AR$1091), El Calafate (AR$640), Río Grande (AR$116) and may serve other destinations; prices are one-way.

Lan The best bet for Buenos Aires (round-trip AR$1823). Purchase tickets through local travel agencies.

Boat
A few private yachts charter trips around the channel, to Cape Horn and Antarctica, see p390. These trips must be organized well in advance.

For Puerto Williams, see p387. See Tours (p386) for other maritime transportation.

Bus
Ushuaia has no bus terminal. Book outgoing bus tickets as much in advance as possible; many readers have complained about getting stuck here in high season. Depending on your luck, long waits at border crossings can be expected.

Some destinations served:

DESTINATION	COST (AR$)	DURATION (HR)
Bariloche	774-844	36
Calafate	384	18
Punta Arenas, Chile	130-160	11
Río Gallegos	290-360	12
Río Grande	75-90	4
Tolhuin	50-60	2

Bus Sur (☑430-727; San Martín 245) To Punta Arenas and Puerto Natales, Chile, three times weekly at 5:30am, connecting with Montiel.

Lider (☑436-421; Gobernador Paz 921) Door-to-door minivans to Tolhuin and Río Grande six times daily, with fewer departures on Sunday.

Montiel (☑421-366; Gobernador Paz 605) Door-to-door minivans to Tolhuin and Río Grande with same frequency as Lider.

Taqsa (☑435-453; Godoy 41) Runs to Río Grande at 5am via Tolhuin; to Punta Arenas and Puerto Natales, Chile, three times weekly at 5am; to Río Gallegos, El Calafate and Bariloche daily at 5am.

Tecni-Austral (☑431-408/12; Roca 157) Runs to Río Grande at 5am via Tolhuin; to Punta Arenas three times weekly; to Río Gallegos daily at 5am.

Transportes Pasarela (☑433-712; cnr Maipú & 25 de Mayo) Round-trip shuttles to Lago Esmeralda (AR$40), Lago Escondido (AR$90) and Lago Fagnano (AR$100) depart 10am and return at 2pm and 6:30pm. Pay one way if you want to stay overnight and arrange for pickup.

For transport to Parque Nacional Tierra del Fuego, see p400.

A PIONEER'S GUIDE TO TIERRA DEL FUEGO

It was a childhood too fabulous for fiction. E Lucas Bridges grew up with the Beagle Channel as his backyard, helped his dad rescue shipwrecked sailors and learned survival from the native Yaghan and Selk'nam (Ona) people. His memoir *Uttermost Part of the Earth* fed Bruce Chatwin's boyhood obsession with Patagonia. Now, after decades out of print, this 1947 classic has been rereleased in English.

Bridges' tale starts with his British father establishing an Anglican mission in untamed Ushuaia. *Little House on the Prairie* it wasn't. After the family trades the missionary life for pioneering on an *estancia* (grazing ranch), Bridges' father dies. As a young adult, Bridges tries adventuring with the Selk'nam, which meant surviving on lean guanaco meat, crossing icy rivers and negotiating peace between quarreling factions.

Measles epidemics and sparring with hostile colonists wreaked havoc on Tierra del Fuego's native peoples. By the time the book was first published, their population had nose-dived to less than 150. *Uttermost Part of the Earth* captures the last days of these hardy civilizations and one island's transformation from virgin wilderness to a frontier molded by fortune seekers, missionaries and sheep ranchers.

❶ Getting Around

Taxis to/from the modern airport (USH), 4km southwest of downtown, cost AR$25. Taxis can be chartered for around AR$140 per hour.

There's a local bus service along Maipú.

Rental rates for compact cars, including insurance, start at around AR$464 per day; try **Localiza** (🔲 430-739; Sarmiento 81). Some agencies may not charge for drop-off in other parts of Argentine Tierra del Fuego.

Hourly ski shuttles (round-trip, AR$70) leave from the corner of Juana Fadul and Maipú to resorts along RN 3, from 9am to 2pm daily. Each resort also provides its own transportation from downtown Ushuaia.

Parque Nacional Tierra del Fuego

Banked against the channel, the hush, fragrant southern forests of Tierra del Fuego are a stunning setting to explore. West of Ushuaia by 12km, **Parque Nacional Tierra del Fuego** (via RN 3; admission AR$85), Argentina's first coastal national park, extends 630 sq km from the Beagle Channel in the south to beyond Lago Fagnano (also known as Lago Kami) in the north. However, only a couple of thousand hectares along the southern edge of the park are open to the public, with a miniscule system of short, easy trails that are designed more for day-tripping families than backpacking trekkers. The rest of the park is protected as a *reserva estricta* (strictly off-limits zone). Despite this, a few scenic hikes along the bays and rivers, or through dense native forests of ever-green coihue, canelo and deciduous lenga, are worthwhile. For truly spectacular color, come in the fall when hillsides of ñire burst out in red.

Birdlife is prolific, especially along the coastal zone. Keep an eye out for condors, albatross, cormorants, gulls, terns, oyster-catchers, grebes, kelp geese and the comical, flightless orange-billed steamer ducks. Common invasive species include the European rabbit and the North American beaver, both of which are wreaking ecological havoc in spite of their cuteness. Gray and red foxes, enjoying the abundance of rabbits, may also be seen.

🏃 Activities

Just 3km from the entrance gate, the **Senda Pampa Alta** (5km) heads up a hill with impressive views from the top. A quick 300m

further leads to a *senda* (trail) paralleling the Río Pipo and some waterfalls. A more popular saunter is along the **Senda Costera** (6.5km), accessed from the end of the Bahía Ensenada road. This trail meanders along the bay, once home to Yaghan people. Keep an eye out for shell middens, now covered in grass. The trail ends at the road, which leads 1.2km further to the **Senda Hito XXIV** (5km), a level trail through lenga forest along the northern shore of Lago Roca; this trail terminates at an unimposing Argentine–Chilean border marker. **Senda Cerro Guanaco** (8km) starts at the same trailhead, but climbs up a 970m hill to reach a great viewpoint.

After running 3242km from Buenos Aires, RN 3 takes its southern bow at gorgeous Bahía Lapataia. **Mirador Lapataia** (1km), connecting with **Senda del Turbal** (2km), winds through lenga forest to access this highway terminus. Other walks in this section include the self-guided nature trail **Senda Laguna Negra** (950m), through peat bogs, and the **Senda Castorera** (800m), along which beaver dams, and possibly beavers themselves, can be spotted in the ponds.

🛏 Sleeping

The only fee-based campground and *refugio* is **Lago Roca** (camping per person/dm AR$9/40; ☺year-round), 9km from the park entrance, open except when weather prohibits transport to the park. Both offer hot showers, a good *confitería* (cafe offering light meals) and a tiny (expensive) grocery store. There is plenty of availability for camping at wild sites. Note that water at Lago Roca is not potable; boil it before using.

❶ Getting There & Away

Buses leave from the corner of Maipú and Juana Fadul in Ushuaia every 40 minutes in high season from 9am to 6pm, returning between 8am and 8pm. Depending on your destination, a round-trip fare is around ARS$70, and you need not return the same day. Private tour buses are AR$100 for a round-trip. Taxis shared between groups can be the same price as bus tickets.

The most touristy and, beyond jogging, the slowest way to the park, **El Tren del Fin de Mundo** (🔲02901-431-600; www.trendelfinde mundo.com.ar; adult/child AR$155/50, plus park entrance fee) originally carted prisoners to work camps. It departs (sans convicts) from the Estación del Fin de Mundo, 8km west of Ushuaia (taxis one-way AR$30), three or four times daily

ESTANCIA HARBERTON

Tierra del Fuego's first *estancia* (grazing ranch), **Harberton** (Skype: estanciaharberton. turismo; www.estanciaharberton.com; tour & museum admission adult/child AR$45/free, half-board lodging s/d/t AR$802/1266/1772; ⊙10am-7pm Oct 15–Apr 15) was founded in 1886 by missionary Thomas Bridges and his family. The location earned fame from a stirring memoir written by Bridges' son Lucas, titled *Uttermost Part of the Earth,* about his coming of age among the now-extinct Selk'nam and Yaghan people. Available in English, the book is a good introduction to the history of the region and the ways of native peoples.

In a splendid location, the *estancia* is owned and run by Tomas Bridges' descendants. There's lodging and day visitors can attend guided tours (featuring the island's oldest house and a replica Yaghan dwelling), dine at the restaurant and visit the Reserva Yeca-pasela penguin colony. It's also a popular destination for birdwatchers.

On-site, the impressive **Museo Acatushún** (www.acatushun.com) houses a vast collection of mammal and bird specimens compiled by biologist Natalie Prosser Goodall. Emphasizing the region's marine mammals, the museum has inventoried thousands of mammal and bird specimens; among the rarest specimens is a Hector's beaked whale. Much of this vast collection was found at Bahía San Sebastián, north of Río Grande, where a difference of up to 11km between high and low tide leaves animals stranded. Confirm the museum's opening hours with the *estancia.*

Reserve well in advance as there are no phones at the *estancia*, though Skyping may be possible. With advance permission, free primitive camping is allowed at Río Lasifashaj, Río Varela and Río Cambaceres. Harberton is 85km east of Ushuaia via RN 3 and rough RC-j, a 1½- to two-hour drive one way. In Ushuaia, shuttles leave from the base of 25 de Mayo at Av Maipú at 9am, returning around 3pm. Day-long catamaran tours are organized by local agencies.

in summer and once or twice daily in winter. The one-hour, scenic narrow-gauge train ride comes with historical explanations in English and Spanish. Reserve in January and February, when cruise-ship tours take over. You can take it one way and return via minibus.

Hitchhiking is feasible, but many cars may already be full.

Tolhuin

☎02901 / POP 2000

Named for the Selk'nam word meaning 'like a heart,' Tolhuin is a lake town nestled in the center of Tierra del Fuego, 132km south of Río Grande and 104km northeast of Ushuaia via smooth pavement. This fast-growing frontier town of small plazas and sheltering evergreens fronts the eastern shore of Lago Fagnano, also known as Lago Kami. Most travelers tend to skip right over it, but if you are looking for a unique and tranquil spot, Tolhuin is well worth checking out.

A local highlight – and usually a stop on buses headed towards Ushuaia, **Panadería La Unión** (☎492-202; www.panaderialaunion. com.ar, in Spanish; Jeujepen 450; ☑24hr) serves first-rate pastries and some decent empana-

das. The best spot for basic lodgings and camping is **Camping Hain** (☎15-603-606; Lago Fagnano; campsites per person AR$10, 8-person refugios AR$130), with grassy, sheltered sites, hot-water showers, a huge barbecue pit and *fogon* (sheltered fire pit and kitchen area). Roberto, the conscientious owner, can recommend local excursions and guides.

Río Grande

☎02964 / POP 68,776

The island's petroleum service center has an industrial feel and an addiction to urban sprawl, egged on by its duty-free status. But look further and you will find some of the world's best trout fishing and exclusive lodges that cater to serious anglers. If you didn't come with rod in hand, the longest that you will likely stay in windswept Río Grande is a scant hour to change buses to Ushuaia, 230km southwest.

🛏 Sleeping & Eating

Catering towards suits and anglers, lodging tends to be overpriced, not to mention sparse. High-end places discount 10% for cash.

Posada de los Sauces
HOTEL **$$**

(📞432-895; www.posadadelossauces.com.ar; Elcano 839; s/d/tr AR$350/400/500; @🛜) Catering mostly to high-end anglers, this warm and professional hotel fosters a lodge atmosphere, with fresh scents and woodsy accents. Deluxe rooms have Jacuzzis. The upstairs bar-restaurant, decked out in dark wood and forest green, is just waiting for stogies and tall tales to fill the air.

Hotel Villa
HOTEL **$$**

(📞424-998; hotelvillarg@hotmail.com; San Martín 281; d/tr AR$310/380; 🅿@🛜) Opposite Casino Status, this refurbished place has a popular restaurant, a dozen spacious and stylish rooms outfitted with down duvets, and breakfast with *medialunas* (croissants).

Tante Sara
CAFE **$$**

(Belgrano 402; mains AR$45-88) An upscale chain in Tierra del Fuego, this nonetheless cozy spot hosts both ladies having tea and cake and boys at the varnished bar downing beer and burgers. Salads (like romaine, egg, blue cheese and bacon) are surprisingly good, though service is sluggish.

ℹ️ Getting There & Away

The **airport** (RGA; 📞420-699) is off RN 3, a short taxi ride from town. **Aerolíneas Argentinas** (📞424-467; San Martín 607) flies daily to Buenos Aires (one-way AR$1317). **LADE** (📞422-968; Lasserre 445) flies a couple of times weekly to Río Gallegos (AR$265), El Calafate (AR$457) and Buenos Aires (AR$1091); prices are one-way.

DESTINATION	COST (AR$)	DURATION (HR)
Punta Arenas, Chile	130-160	9
Río Gallegos	265	8
Tolhuin	50-60	2
Ushuaia	75-90	4

Transfer van companies:

Lider (📞420-003, 424-2000; Moreno 635) Best option for Ushuaia and Tolhuin is this door-to-door minivan service, with several daily departures. Call to reserve.

Montiel (📞420-997; www.lidertdf.com.ar 25 de Mayo 712) Ushuaia and Tolhuin.

At **Terminal Fuegina** (Finocchio 1194):

Buses Pacheco (📞421-554) To Punta Arenas three times per week at 10am.

Taqsa (📞434-316) To Ushuaia via Tolhuin.

Tecni-Austral (📞434-316; ticket office Moyano 516) To Ushuaia via Tolhuin three times per week at 8:30am; to Río Gallegos and Punta Arenas three times per week.

Bus Sur (📞420-997; www.bus-sur.cl; ticket office 25 de Mayo 712) To Ushuaia, Punta Arenas and Puerto Natales, Chile, three times weekly at 5:30am, connecting with Montiel.

Easter Island (Rapa Nui)

Best Places to Eat

» Au Bout du Monde (p409)
» Te Moana (p409)
» Kanahau (p409)
» Mikafé (p409)

Best Places to Stay

» Explora en Rapa Nui (p406)
» Te Ora (p406)
» Aloha Nui (p408)
» Cabañas Christophe (p406)
» Cabañas Mana Ora (p407)

Why Go?

Easter Island (Rapa Nui to its native Polynesian inhabitants) is like nowhere else on earth. Historically intriguing, culturally compelling and scenically magical, this tiny speck of land looks like it's fallen off another planet. In this blissfully isolated, unpolished gem it's hard to feel connected even to Chile, over 3700km to the east, let alone the wider world. It's just you, the indigo depths and the strikingly enigmatic *moai* (giant statues) scattered amid an eerie landscape.

When the *moai* have finished working their magic on you, there's a startling variety (for such a small island) of adventure options available. Diving, snorkelling and surfing are fabulous. On land, there's no better ecofriendly way to experience the island's savage beauty than on foot, from a bike saddle or on horseback. But if all you want to do is recharge the batteries, a couple of superb expanses of white sand beckon.

Although Easter Island is world famous and visitors are on the increase, everything remains small and personable – it's all about eco-travel.

When to Go
Hanga Roa

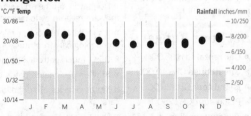

| Jan–Mar Peak season. Highest prices and scarce hotels around February's Tapati Rapa Nui festival. | Jul–Aug Chilly weather, not ideal for beaches but a good time for hiking and horseback riding. | Apr–Jun & Oct–Dec The shoulder season is not a bad time to visit; the climate is fairly temperate. |

AT A GLANCE

Currency Chilean peso (CH$)

Language Spanish, Rapa Nui

Mobile phones Local SIM cards are available and can be used with unlocked GSM phones. Roaming agreements with most operators.

Money A few ATMs

Visas Not required for visitors from most Western countries

Fast Facts

» **Country code** ☎56 32
» **Land area** 117 sq km
» **Main city** Hanga Roa
» **Population** 6700

Exchange Rates

Australia	A$1	CH$505
Canada	C$1	CH$488
Euro	€1	CH$640
Japan	¥100	CH$606
New Zealand	NZ$1	CH$399
UK	UK£1	CH$800
USA	US$1	CH$517

For current exchange rates see www.xe.com.

Set Your Budget

» **Car rental** CH$35,000
» **Guesthouse** CH$40,000
» **Island tour** CH$25,000
» **Pisco sour** CH$2500
» **Two-course dinner** CH$15,000

Connections

Short of sailing your own boat, the only way to and from Easter Island is by air. Flights between Easter Island and Santiago are frequent and last about five hours. There are also less frequent flights to/from Lima (Peru) and to/from Pape'ete (French Polynesia). Public transport is nonexistent on the island. Private minibuses, rental cars and bicycles are the most convenient ways to get around.

ITINERARIES

Four Days

Start the day by visiting the Musée Antropológico Sebastián Englert for some historical background. Next, take a half-day tour to Rano Kau and Orongo ceremonial village and soak up the lofty views. On day two take a full-day tour to marvel at Rano Raraku and Ahu Tongariki. On your return to Hanga Roa head straight to an atmosphere-laden bar on Av Atamu Tekena for the night vibe. Day three is all about Hanga Roa. Hit the *mercado* (market) to put a dent in the wallet and amble down Av Te Pito o Te Henua to enjoy the sunset at Ahu Tahai. Attend a traditional dance show later in the evening. Day four should see you lazing the day away at Anakena beach.

One Week

Follow the four-day agenda then make the most of the island's outdoor adventures. Book a horse-riding excursion along the north coast, spend a day diving off Motu Nui, scramble up and down Maunga Terevaka, and explore Península Poike.

Sustainable Travel

Easter Island is a superb open-air museum, but it's under threat due to the growing number of visitors. A few rules:

» Don't walk on the *ahu* (ceremonial stone platforms), as they are revered by locals as burial sites.

» It's illegal to remove or relocate rocks from any of the archaeological structures.

» Don't touch petroglyphs, as they're very fragile.

» Stay on designated paths to limit erosion.

» Motor vehicles are not allowed on Península Poike or Terevaka.

» Don't pitch your tent in the park.

HANGA ROA

POP 6700

Hanga Roa is the island's sole town. Upbeat it ain't, but with most sights almost on its doorstep and nearly all the island's hotels, restaurants, shops and services lying within its boundaries, it's the obvious place to anchor oneself. It features a picturesque fishing harbor, a couple of modest beaches and surf spots, and a few archaeological sites.

◉ Sights

TOP
CHOICE **Museo Antropológico
Sebastián Englert**   MUSEUM
(☏255-1020; www.museorapanui.cl; Sector Tahai; admission CH$1000; ☺9:30am-5:30pm Tue-Fri, to

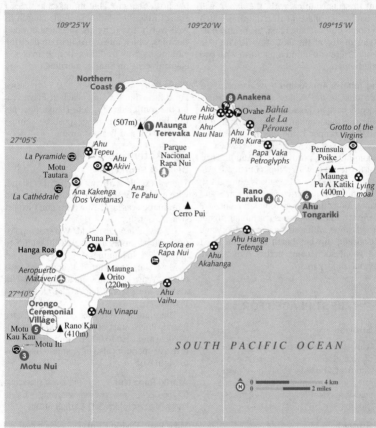

EASTER ISLAND (RAPA NUI) HANGA ROA

Easter Island (Rapa Nui) Highlights

❶ Clip-clop on the flanks of the extinct volcano **Maunga Terevaka** (p411) and feast your eyes on the mesmerising 360-degree views

❷ Hike along the ruggedly beautiful **northern coast** (p405)

❸ Ogle the stunning limpid blue waters of **Motu Nui** on a snorkelling or diving (p404) trip

❹ Take a lesson in archaeology at **Rano Raraku** (p413), the 'nursery' of the *moai*

❺ Ponder over the island's mysterious past at **Orongo ceremonial village** (p411), perched on the edge of Rano Kau

❻ Watch the sun rise at the row of enigmatic statues at **Ahu Tongariki** (p412) while enjoying breakfast

❼ Get hypnotized by the furious and sensual **dance performance** (p410) of a Rapa Nui group

❽ Take a snooze under the swaying palms at **Anakena** (p412)

12.30pm Sat & Sun) This well-organized museum explains the island's history and culture. It displays basalt fishhooks, obsidian spearheads and other weapons, and a *moai* head with reconstructed fragments of its eyes, among others.

Caleta Hanga Roa & Ahu Tautira
ARCHAEOLOGICAL SITE

Your first encounter with the *moai* will probably take place at Ahu Tautira, which overlooks Caleta Hanga Roa, the fishing port in Hanga Roa at the foot of Av Te Pito o Te Henua. Here you'll find a platform with two superb *moai*.

Ahu Tahai & Ahu Akapu
ARCHAEOLOGICAL SITE

Ahu Tahai, in the vicinity of Museo Antropológico Sebastián Englert, is a highly photogenic site that contains three restored *ahu*. Ahu Tahai proper is the *ahu* in the middle, supporting a large, solitary *moai* with no topknot. On the north side of Ahu Tahai is Ahu Ko Te Riku, with a topknotted and eyeballed *moai*. On the other side is Ahu Vai Uri, which supports five *moai* of varying sizes and shapes. Along the hills are foundations of *hare paenga* (traditional houses resembling an upturned canoe, with a single narrow doorway).

Continue further north along the coast and you'll soon come across Ahu Akapu, with its solitary *moai*.

BEST PLACES FOR...

Sunrise

Wake up very early and arrive before dawn at Ahu Tongariki just in time to watch the sun rise behind the superb row of *moai* (giant statues). Afterwards enjoy breakfast near the *ahu* – this is the life!

Sunset

Be sure to come to Ahu Tahai at dusk and watch the big yellow ball sink behind the silhouetted statues – a truly inspiring sight.

Plane-Spotting

Keen plane-spotters should position themselves on the coastal road to Rano Kau, at the western end of the runway, near the landing lights. Find out the exact arrival times of the Santiago–Easter Island plane on the Facebook page of Aeropuerto Mataveri.

Caleta Hanga Piko & Ahu Riata
HARBOR

Easily overlooked by visitors, the little Caleta Hanga Piko is used by local fishers. Come in the early morning, when freshly caught fish are landed and sold on the quay. Facing the *caleta,* the restored Ahu Riata supports a solitary *moai*.

Iglesia Hanga Roa
CHURCH

(Av Tu'u Koihu s/n) The unmissable Iglesia Hanga Roa, the island's Catholic church, is well worth a visit for its spectacular wood carvings, which integrate Christian doctrine with Rapa Nui tradition. It also makes a colorful scene on Sunday morning.

Playa Pea
BEACH

For a little dip, the tiny beach at Playa Pea, on the south side of Caleta Hanga Roa, fits the bill. There's another postage stamp–sized beach near Pea restaurant.

Activities

Diving & Snorkeling

There's excellent diving on Easter Island, with gin-clear visibility in excess of 40m and a dramatic seascape. However, don't expect swarms of fish.

It's diveable year-round. Water temperatures vary from as low as 21°C in winter to almost 27°C in summer.

Most sites are scattered along the west coast. A few favorites include **Motu Nui** and the very scenic La Cathédrale and La Pyramide.

There are three diving centres in Easter Island. Prices start at CH$30,000 for a single dive and CH$40,000 for an introductory dive. All operators also offer snorkeling trips to Motu Nui.

Atariki Rapa Nui
DIVING, SNORKELING

(255-0227; www.atarikirapanui.com; Caleta Hanga Piko s/n; Mon-Sat) A small outfit.

Mike Rapu Diving Center
DIVING, SNORKELING

(255-1055; www.mikerapu.cl; Caleta Hanga Roa s/n; Mon-Sat) A well-established operator.

Orca Diving Center
DIVING, SNORKELING

(255-0877; www.seemorca.cl; Caleta Hanga Roa s/n; Mon-Sat) Has good credentials.

Surfing

Easter Island is hit with powerful swells from all points of the compass throughout the year, offering irresistible lefts and rights – mostly lava-reef breaks, with waves up to 5m. The most popular spots are scattered along the west coast. For beginners, there are a couple of good waves off Caleta Hanga Roa.

A handful of seasonal (usually from December to March) outfits based on the seafront offer surfing courses and also rent surfboards.

Hare Orca   SURFING
(☎255-0877; Caleta Hanga Roa s/n; rental per half day CH$11,000) This shop next to the Orca Diving Center rents bodyboards and surfboards.

Horseback Riding
A network of trails leading to some of the most beautiful sites can be explored on horseback – a typical Rapa Nui experience.

Reliable operators include **Pantu** (☎210-0577; www.pantupikerauri.cl; Sector Tahai s/n) and **Piti Pont** (☎210-0664). Expect to pay about CH$30,000 for a half-day tour and up to CH$70,000 for a full-day tour with a guide.

Hiking
You can take some fantastic trails through the island. A memorable walk is the way marked Ruta Patrimonial, which runs from Museo Antropológico Sebastián Englert up to Orongo ceremonial village (about four hours, 7km). Other recommended walks are the climb to Maunga Terevaka from near Ahu Akivi (about three hours) and the walk around Península Poike (one day). You can also follow the path along the northern coastline from Ahu Tepeu to Anakena beach,. Bring water and food and have a detailed map at hand.

Boat Excursions
Seeing Easter Island from the sea is an exhilarating experience. A couple of operators organize customized tours along the coast. Prices depend on duration and distance. Bookings can be made through your hotel or *residencial* (budget accommodation).

Cycling
Cycling is a superb way of seeing the island at your leisure, provided you're ready to come to grips with the steep and winding roads around the southern parts. An easy loop is from Hanga Roa up to Ahu Tepeu, then east to Ahu Akivi and back to Hanga Roa (about 17km).

Makemake Rentabike   BICYCLE RENTAL
(☎255-2030; Av Atamu Tekena; ◷9am-1pm & 4-8pm) This venture rents mountain bikes in tip-top condition.

WORTH A TRIP

AHU TEPEU TO ANAKENA BEACH
The coastline between Ahu Tepeu and Anakena beach is extremely alluring: vast expanses of chaotic boulders, towering sea cliffs, barren landscapes and sensational ocean views. There are also plenty of archaeological sites dotted along the way as well as caves adorned with impressive petroglyphs. From Ahu Tepeu it takes six to seven hours to reach Anakena beach on foot. Then hitch back or arrange a taxi back to Hanga Roa. It's not marked and the archaeological sites are not signed; you'll definitely need a guide. Contact the tourist office or your lodging to secure one.

☞ Tours
We recommend joining an organized tour since you get the benefit of an English-speaking guide who can explain the cultural significance of the archaeological sites.

Plenty of operators do tours of the sites, typically charging CH$40,000 for a full day and CH$25,000 for a half day. Entrance fees to Parque Nacional Rapa Nui (CH$30,000) aren't included.

Aku Aku Turismo   CULTURAL TOUR
(☎210-0770; www.akuakuturismo.cl; Av Tu'u Koihu s/n) A well-established company that employs competent guides.

Haumaka Tours   CULTURAL TOUR
(☎210-0274; www.haumakatours.com; cnr Avs Atamu Tekena & Hotu Matua) Offers customized tours.

Kava Kava Tours   CULTURAL TOUR
(☎210-0243; www.kavakavatour.cl; Av Tu'u Koihu s/n) A recent company.

Kia Koe Tour   CULTURAL TOUR
(☎210-0852; www.kiakoetour.cl; Av Atamu Tekena s/n) Has good credentials and uses knowledgeable guides

Rapa Nui Travel   CULTURAL TOUR
(☎210-0548; www.rapanuitravel.com; Av Tu'u Koihu) Run by a Rapa Nui–German couple.

🛏 Sleeping
Unless otherwise stated, most places come equipped with private bathroom, and breakfast is included. Air-con is scarce but fans

Hanga Roa

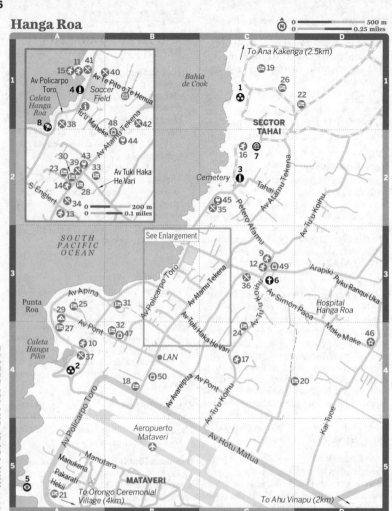

are provided in the hottest months. Airport transfers are included.

Te Ora
CABIN $$

(✆255-1038; www.rapanuiteora.com; Av Apina s/n; r CH$40,000-70,000; 🖥) Although it feels a bit cramped, Te Ora is fine value. All three rooms mix hardwoods and volcanic stones, but the Teora Ora, with great views over the ocean, is a firm favorite. If she's around, the Canadian owner, Sharon, will give you the lowdown on all that's worth seeing on the island – in perfect English, of course. No breakfast is served, but there's a communal kitchen.

Explora en Rapa Nui
LUXURY HOTEL $$$

(✆in Santiago 395-2800; www.explora.com; 3-night all-inclusive packages from s/d US$3360/4770; ✳@🖥🏊) This property blends into a forested patch of volcano-singed countryside. Rooms, all overlooking the Pacific and fiery sunsets, are abundant with indigenous materials. Prices include excursions. One proviso: it feels a bit cut off from the rest of the island (it's about 6km east of Hanga Roa).

Cabañas Christophe
BUNGALOW $$

(✆210-0826; www.cabanaschristophe.com; Av Policarpo Toro s/n; d CH$60,000-70,000; 🖥) This

Hanga Roa

Sights

1 Ahu Akapu C1
2 Ahu Riata A4
3 Ahu Tahai C2
4 Ahu Tautira A1
5 Ana Kai Tangata A5
6 Iglesia Hanga Roa C3
7 Museo Antropológico Sebastián Englert C2
8 Playa Pea A1

Activities, Courses & Tours

9 Aku Aku Turismo C3
10 Atariki Rapa Nui A4
11 Hare Orca A1
Haumaka Tours .... (see 18)
12 Kava Kava Tours C3
13 Kia Koe Tour A2
14 Makemake Rentabike A2
Mike Rapu Dive Center .... (see 15)
15 Orca Diving Center A1
16 Pantu C2
17 Rapa Nui Travel C4

Sleeping

18 Aloha Nui B4
19 Altiplanico C1
20 Atavai–Chez Antoine y Lolita D4
21 Cabañas Christophe A5
22 Cabañas Mana Ora D1
23 Cabañas Nuae Koro A2
24 Gomero C4
25 Hanga Roa Eco Village & Spa A3
26 Hare Swiss C1
27 Hostal Tojika A4
28 Inaki Uhi A2
29 Mihinoa A3
30 Tau Ra'a A2
31 Te Ora B3
32 Teanui B4
33 Vaianny A2

Eating

34 Ariki o Te Pana–Tia Berta A2
35 Au Bout du Monde C2
36 Donde El Gordo C3
37 Haga Piko A4
38 Haka Honu A1
39 Kanahau A2
40 Kuki Varua B1
La Kaleta .... (see 15)
Mahina Nui .... (see 39)
41 Mikafé A1
42 Te Moana B1

Drinking

Haka Honu .... (see 38)
Kanahau .... (see 39)
43 Marau A2
Mikafé .... (see 41)
Te Moana .... (see 42)
44 Topa Tangi Pub B2
45 Vai Te Mihi C2

Entertainment

Ma'ara Nui .... (see 39)
Matato'a .... (see 35)
46 Te Ra'ai D4

Shopping

47 El Baul del To B4
48 Feria Municipal B2
49 Mercado Artesanal C3
50 Mokomae B4

charming venue seduces those seeking character and comfort, with three meticulously maintained rooms that blend hardwoods and volcanic stones. Angle for the upstairs room, which is spacious and inundated with natural light. It's at the start of the Orongo trail, about 1.5km from the centre.

Cabañas Mana Ora BUNGALOW **$$**
(☎210-0769; www.manaora.cl; Sector Tahai; d CH$80,000) This is an adorable nest with two attractively decorated cottages perched on a slope overlooking the ocean. They come equipped with a handy kitchenette and a terrace with sea views. One grumble: bathrooms are miniscule. It's a bit of a schlep from the centre (you'll need a bike).

Hare Swiss BUNGALOW **$$**
(☎255-2221; www.hareswiss.com; Sector Tahai; s/d CH$40,000/60,000; 📶) Just behind the Altiplanico, Hare Swiss is a solid option, with three immaculate bungalows, great sea views and a communal kitchen. If you don't fancy cooking, the driver can drive you to various eateries at dinner.

Hanga Roa Eco Village & Spa LUXURY HOTEL **$$$**
(☎957-0300; www.hotelhangaroa.cl; Av Pont s/n; s/d from CH$145,000/CH$200,000; ❄📶🏊)

TAPATI RAPA NUI

Easter Island's premier festival, the Tapati Rapa Nui, lasts about two weeks in the first half of February and is so impressive that it's almost worth timing your trip around it (contact the tourist office for exact dates). Expect a series of music, dance, cultural and sport contests between two clans that put up two candidates who stand for the title of Queen of the Festival.

After a complete makeover in 2012, this sprawling establishment ranks as one of the best hotels on the island, with an array of creatively designed rooms and suites facing the sea. All units are built of natural materials and their layout is inspired by caves, with curving lines and shapes. They're not just posh and huge, they also blend into the environment. The on-site restaurant serves refined food and the spa is a stunner. It's ecofriendly: there's a water and electricity saving system.

Altiplanico   HOTEL $$$
(255-2190; www.altiplanico.cl; Sector Tahai; s/d US$350/390; @🛜⛲) The best thing about this well-run venture with a boutique feel is its excellent location on a gentle slope in Tahai. Try for bungalows 1, 2, 3, 10, 11 or 17, which have panoramic sea views. The 17 units are all sparkling clean and quirkily decorated, but they're fairly packed together and we found the prices somewhat inflated. The on-site restaurant is elegant but pricey (starters cost US$20). It runs on solar energy.

Aloha Nui   GUESTHOUSE $$
(210-0274; haumakatours@gmail.com; Av Atamu Tekena s/n; s/d CH$35,000/70,000; 🛜) After a complete makeover in 2011, this agreeable place now features six well-equipped rooms and a vast, shared living room. But the real reason you're staying here is to discuss Rapa Nui archaeology in flawless English with Josefina Nahoe Mulloy, who leads reputable tours.

Gomero   HOTEL $$$
(210-0313; www.hotelgomero.com; Av Tu'u Koihu s/n; s/d from CH$60,000/80,000; ❄🛜⛲) This reputable abode has a well-tended little pool nestled in lush gardens, which makes this place a restful spot in summer. Angle for the

superior rooms in the new wing (20 to 23), which are more modern and have air-con, or for the 'standards' (4 to 6, 9 to 11, 16 to 18).

Atavai – Chez Antoine y Lolita   CABIN $$
(210-0145; www.hotel-atavai.com; s/d CH$50,000/65,000; 🛜) This venture offers a soothing collection of white bungalows (nine rooms in total). Quarters are a bit cramped, but otherwise it's serviceable. Evening meals are available on request. The only downside: its location near the airport is not *that* exceptional – you'll need a bike to get to the centre. Look for deals on the website.

Mihinoa   CAMPGROUND $
(255-1593; www.mihinoa.com; Av Pont s/n; campsites per person CH$5000, dm CH$9000, d CH$20,000-25,000; 🛜) Cheap and sometimes cheerful, this backpacker crash pad is a popular spot for budgeteers. You have options here: one of the smallish but well-scrubbed rooms in the two buildings, a six-bed dorm or a campsite on a grassy plot (no shade). The dorm is cramped but serviceable and, joy of joys, has hot showers (mornings and evenings). Perks include tent hire (CH$5500), wi-fi access (CH$5000 for the duration of your stay), a well-equipped communal kitchen and laundry service. And you're just a pebble's throw from the seashore.

Tau Ra'a   HOTEL $$
(210-0463; www.tauraahotel.cl; Av Atamu Tekena s/n; s/d CH$60,000/75,000; 🛜) The 10 rooms are spotless and flooded with natural light, and they come equipped with firm beds and functional bathrooms. Alas, no sea views. The substantial breakfast is a plus. Bill, the Aussie owner, is a treasure trove of local information.

Teanui   CABIN $$
(255-1990; www.teanui.cl; Av Pont s/n; s/d CH$35,000/65,000; 🛜) This well-maintained establishment offers comfortable motel-style rooms as well as two self-contained bungalows in a gardenlike setting.

Inaki Uhi   CABIN $$
(255-1160; www.inakiuhi.com; Av Atamu Tekena s/n; s/d CH$35,000/70,000; 🛜) The 15 boxy rooms here occupy two rows of low-slung buildings facing each other. They feel sterile and the decor is bland but there are four shared kitchens and it's conveniently located on the main drag.

Cabañas Nuae Koro   CABIN $

(☎255-1418; www.nuaekoro.com; off Av Atamu Tekena; s/d CH$20,000/35,000) This budget option doesn't offer much privacy – the wall that separates the two adjoining units is particle board – but it's central and good value.

Hostal Tojika   GUESTHOUSE $

(☎099-358-0810; Av Apina s/n; dm/s/d CH$10,000/20,000/30,000; ☎) Has four rooms, a five-bed dorm and a communal kitchen in a single building overlooking the sea. The rooms lack natural light but the dorm is an excellent bargain.

Vaianny   GUESTHOUSE $

(☎210-0650; www.residencialvaianny.com; Av Tuki Haka He Vari; s/d CH$25,000/35,000; ☎) A good bet for budgeteers, with basic but clean rooms. Mattresses are saggy and bathrooms tiny. It's within hollering distance of some of the town's best bars and restaurants.

Eating

For self-caterers, there are a couple of supermarkets on Av Atamu Tekena.

Mikafé   CAFETERIA, SANDWICHES $

(Caleta Hanga Roa s/n; ice creams CH$1500-2500, sandwiches & cakes CH$2500-4500; ☺9am-8pm) Mmm, try the the *helados artesanales* (homemade ice creams)! Oh, the damn addictive banana cake! Other treats include panini and sandwiches.

Te Moana   CHILEAN $$

(Av Atamu Tekena s/n; mains CH$10,000-17,000; ☺lunch & dinner Mon-Sat) This buzzy restaurant and bar with a cozy interior is renowned for its delectable grilled meat and fish dishes.

Au Bout du Monde   INTERNATIONAL $$$

(Av Policarpo Toro s/n; mains CH$10,000-16,500; ☺lunch & dinner Wed-Mon) In this agreeable venue run by a Rapa Nui–Belgian couple, every visitor ought to try the tuna in vanilla sauce, the homemade tagliatelle or the beef fillet. Leave room for dessert – the Belgian chocolate mousse is divine.

Haga Piko   SEAFOOD $

(Caleta Hanga Piko; mains CH$5500-7700; ☺11am-4pm Mon-Sat) This simple family-run establishment is excellent value. The fish on offer is determined by what's in the nets that day, and the terrace overlooking Caleta Hango Piko is a good place to soak up the atmosphere of the seafront.

Kanahau   SEAFOOD, CHILEAN $$

(Av Atamu Tekena s/n; mains CH$8000-16,000; ☺lunch & dinner) Whether you satisfy yourself with outstanding ceviche or sample the *lomo kanahau* (beef with a homemade sauce), among a variety of hearty dishes, you'll be pleased with the careful preparation and attentive service.

Donde El Gordo   CHILEAN, SANDWICHES $$

(Av Te Pito o Te Henua s/n; mains CH$6000-11,000; ☺lunch Tue-Sun, dinner Tue-Sat) Simple and satisfying are words that come to mind when dining at Donde El Gordo. The menu consists of generous sandwiches, empanadas (from CH$1800), pizzas and copious salads, as well as vitamin-packed fruit juices. A good surprise.

Haka Honu   CHILEAN $$

(Av Policarpo Toro s/n; mains CH$6000-16,000; ☺lunch & dinner Tue-Sun) Fish dishes, steaks, pasta and salads round out the menu at this buzzy eatery. The outside terrace catches every wisp of breeze and is perfect for watching the world surf by.

La Kaleta   SEAFOOD, CHILEAN $$

(Caleta Hanga Roa; mains CH$6500-16,000; ☺lunch & dinner) In a lovely location overlooking the sea, breezy La Kaleta is your spot for salads, pasta, steaks and fish dishes.

Ariki o Te Pana – Tia Berta   CHILEAN $

(Av Atamu Tekena s/n; mains CH$2000-10,000; ☺lunch & dinner Mon-Sat) Surrender to some melt-in-your-mouth empanadas prepared mamma-style in this no-frills den.

Mahina Nui   SEAFOOD, CHILEAN $$

(Av Atamu Tekena s/n; mains CH$6000-16,000; ☺lunch & dinner Mon-Sat) With its flashy facade on the main drag, Mahina Nui is sure to draw your attention. There's a varied menu; the ceviche is recommended.

Kuki Varua   SEAFOOD, CHILEAN $

(Av Te Pito o Te Henua s/n; mains CH$6500-8000; ☺lunch Tue-Sun, dinner Tue-Sat) This place has a wide assortment of set menus. Good sea views from the upstairs terrace.

Drinking

Most restaurants feature a bar section.

Te Moana   BAR

(Av Atamu Tekena s/n; ☺11am-late Mon-Sat) One of Hanga Roa's hottest spots at the time of writing. Come for the good fun, good mix of people and good cocktails.

EASTER ISLAND (RAPA NUI) HANGA ROA

Topa Tangi Pub PUB
(Av Atamu Tekena s/n; ☺6pm-late Wed-Sat) Can get really lively on weekends.

Marau BAR
(Av Atamu Tekena s/n; ☺6:30pm-late) Another hangout of choice, with a loungy feel.

Haka Honu BAR
(Av Policarpo Toro s/n; ☺11am-late Tue-Sun) A cool spot for sunset cocktails.

Kanahau BAR
(Av Atamu Tekena s/n; ☺11am-late) Kick off the night with a strong mojito at this cheerful hangout decked in wood.

Mikafé CAFE
(Caleta Hanga Roa s/n; ☺9am-8pm) In search of a real espresso? Mikafé is your answer.

Vai Te Mihi BAR
(Av Policarpo Toro s/n; ☺6pm-late) Gets lively on Friday and Saturday nights. Also features traditional dance shows.

Explora en Rapa Nui BAR
(☺9am-late) Order a pisco sour and watch the sun set – a magical experience.

🛍 Shopping

Hanga Roa has numerous souvenir shops, mostly on Av Atamu Tekena and on Av Te Pito o Te Henua.

Feria Municipal ARTS & CRAFT
(cnr Avs Atamu Tekena & Tu'u Maheke; ☺Mon-Sat) Good prices.

Mercado Artesanal ARTS & CRAFT
(cnr Avs Tu'u Koihu & Ara Roa Rakei; ☺Mon-Sat) Across from the church. Has a bit of everything.

El Baul del To ARTS & CRAFT
(Av Pont; ☺10am-8:30pm) This 'cultural centre' sells locally made handicrafts and traditional Rapa Nui costumes. Also offers body painting.

Mokomae TATTOO PARLOR
(☎099-292-1591; Av Atamu Tekena s/n; ☺by appointment) For traditionally designed tattoos head to this highly rated tattoo studio. Mokomae also sells woodcarvings.

ℹ Information

BancoEstado (Av Pont s/n; ☺8am-1pm Mon-Fri) Changes US dollars and euros. Charges a CH$1500 commission on traveler's cheques. There's also an ATM but it only accepts MasterCard. Visa holders can get cash advances at the counter during opening hours (bring your passport); the bank charges a CH$2000 fee for the service.

Banco Santander (Av Apina; ☺8am-1pm Mon-Fri) On the waterfront. Currency exchange, and has two ATMs that accept Visa and MasterCard. Also has an ATM at the airport (in the departure area).

Farmacia Cruz Verde (Av Atamu Tekena; ☺9am-7:30pm Mon-Sat) Large and well-stocked pharmacy.

Hospital Hanga Roa (☎210-0215; Av Simon Paoa s/n)

Mana@net (Av Atamu Tekena s/n; per hr CH$1200; ☺9am-10pm) Internet cafe and call centre.

Omotohi Cybercafé (Av Te Pito o Te Henua s/n; per hr CH$1000; ☺9am-10pm) Internet and wi-fi access, and call centre.

Police (☎133)

Post office (Av Te Pito o Te Henua s/n; ☺9am-1pm & 2.30-6pm Mon-Fri, 9am-12:30pm Sat)

Puna Vai (Av Hotu Matua; ☺8:30am-1pm & 3-8pm Mon-Sat, 9am-1pm Sun) This petrol station also doubles as an exchange office. Much more convenient than the bank (no queues, better rates, longer opening hours, no commission on traveler's cheques). There's an ATM inside (MasterCard only).

Sernatur (☎210-0255;www.chile.travel/en.html; Tu'u Maheke s/n; ☺9am-6pm Mon-Fri, 10am-5pm Sat) Has various brochures and maps of the island. Staff speak some English.

DON'T MISS

TRADITIONAL DANCE SHOWS

If there's one thing you absolutely *have* to check out while you're on Easter Island it's a traditional dance show. There are about six groups that usually perform three times a week. Shows cost about CH$10,000. A few favorites:

» **Kari Kari** (☎210-0767; Av Atamu Tekena s/n) Performs at a venue called Ma'ara Nui.

» **Matato'a** (☎255-2060; www.matatoa.com) At the Au Bout du Monde restaurant, upstairs.

» **Te Ra'ai** (☎255-1460; www.teraai.cl) Includes an *umu* (underground oven) feast and cultural demonstrations.

LEARN HOW TO TELL YOUR AHU FROM YOUR MOAI

You don't need a university degree to appreciate the archaeological remains on Easter Island. The following explanations should suffice.

Ahu

Ahu were village burial sites and ceremonial centres and are thought to derive from altars in French Polynesia. Some 350 of these stone platforms are dotted around the coast. *Ahu* are paved on the upper surface with more or less flat stones, and they have a vertical wall on the seaward side and at each end.

Moai

Easter Island's most pervasive image, the enigmatic *moai* are massive carved figures that probably represent clan ancestors. From 2m to 10m tall, these stony-faced statues stood with their backs to the Pacific Ocean. Some *moai* have been completely restored, while others have been reerected but are eroded. Many more lie on the ground, toppled over.

Topknots

Archaeologists believe that the reddish cylindrical *pukao* (topknots) that crown many *moai* reflect a male hairstyle once common on Rapa Nui.

PARQUE NACIONAL RAPA NUI

Since 1935, much of Rapa Nui's land and all of the archaeological sites have been a **national park** (admission non-Chileans CH$30,000) administered by **Conaf** (210-0236; www.conaf.cl), which charges admission at Orongo and Rano Raraku that is valid for the whole park for five days as of the first day of entrance. In theory, you're allowed one visit to Orongo and one visit to Rano Raraku; in practice, most rangers allow repeat visits if you ask nicely.

There are ranger information stations at Orongo, Anakena and Rano Raraku.

Northern Circuit

North of Ahu Tahai, the road is rough but passable if you drive slowly. Your best bet is to explore the area on foot, on horseback or by mountain bike, but there are no signs marking the sites.

Ana Kakenga   CAVE

About 2km north of Tahai is Ana Kakenga, or Dos Ventanas. This site comprises two caves opening onto the ocean (bring a torch).

Ahu Tepeu   ARCHAEOLOGICAL SITE

This large *ahu* has several fallen *moai* and a village site with foundations of *hare paenga* (elliptical houses) and the walls of several round houses.

Ana Te Pahu   CAVE

Off the dirt road to Akivi, Ana Te Pahu is a former cave dwelling with an overgrown garden of sweet potatoes, taro and bananas.

Ahu Akivi   ARCHAEOLOGICAL SITE

Unusual for its inland location, Ahu Akivi, restored in 1960, sports seven restored *moai*. They are the only ones that face towards the sea, but, like all *moai,* they overlook the site of a village, traces of which can still be seen.

TOP CHOICE Maunga Terevaka   MOUNTAIN

Maunga Terevaka is the island's highest point (507m). This barren hill is only accessible on foot or on horseback (see p405).

Puna Pau   ARCHAEOLOGICAL SITE

The volcanic Puna Pau quarry was used to make the reddish, cylindrical *pukao* (topknots) that were placed on many *moai*.

Southwest Circuit

Ana Kai Tangata   CAVE

Past the Hotel Iorana in Hanga Roa, a sign points the way to Ana Kai Tangata, a vast cave carved into black cliffs that sports beautiful rock paintings. However, entrance is forbidden due to falling rocks.

TOP CHOICE Rano Kau   CRATER LAKE

Nearly covered in a bog of floating totora reeds, this crater lake resembles a giant witch's cauldron – awesome! Perched 400m

EASTER ISLAND (RAPA NUI) PARQUE NACIONAL RAPA NUI

LOCAL KNOWLEDGE

SERGIO RAPU, ARCHAEOLOGIST

A former governor of Rapa Nui, Sergio Rapu is one of the island's most respected archaeologists and has conducted numerous experiments and measurements in the field.

What special experience do you recommend? Go to the crater rim at Rano Kau half an hour before sunset and bring a bottle of pisco sour. If you're lucky, you'll see the moon rising.

Most powerful archaeological site on the island? Rano Raraku has special vibes – come here early morning or late afternoon and you could almost feel the presence of spooky beings watching you...

Best time for a visit? February, when the Tapati Rapa Nui festival is held. This truly genuine cultural event is a great chance for foreigners to immerse themselves in local culture. My favorite contest is the Haka Pei: on the flanks of the Cerro Pui, a dozen male contestants run downhill on a makeshift sled at a speed that can reach 70km/h. Just thinking about it makes my spine tingle!

above, on the edge of the crater wall on one side and abutting a vertical drop plunging down to the cobalt-blue ocean on the other side, **Orongo ceremonial village** (admission CH$30,000; ⊙9am-5pm) boasts one of the South Pacific's most dramatic landscapes. It overlooks several small *motu* (offshore islands), including Motu Nui, Motu Iti and Motu Kau Kau. Built into the side of the slope, the houses have walls of horizontally overlapping stone slabs, with an earth-covered arched roof of similar materials, making them appear partly subterranean. Orongo was the focus of an islandwide bird cult linked to the god Makemake in the 18th and 19th centuries. Birdman petroglyphs are visible on a cluster of boulders between the cliff top and the edge of the crater.

Orongo is either a steepish climb or a short scenic drive 4km from the centre of town.

Ahu Vinapu ARCHAEOLOGICAL SITE
Beyond the eastern end of the airport runway, a road heads south past some large oil tanks to this ceremonial platform, with several toppled *moai*.

Northeast Circuit

TOP CHOICE **Anakena** BEACH
Beach bums in search of a place to wallow will make a beeline for this picture-postcard-perfect, white-sand beach. It also forms a perfect backdrop for **Ahu Nau Nau**, which comprises seven *moai*, some with topknots. On a rise south of the beach stands **Ahu Ature Huki** and its lone *moai*.

Ovahe BEACH
This beach offers more seclusion than Anakena for wannabe Robinson Crusoes but is considered dangerous because of falling rocks.

Ahu Te Pito Kura ARCHAEOLOGICAL SITE
Beside Bahía de La Pérouse, a nearly 10m long *moai* lies face down with its neck broken; it's the largest *moai* moved from Rano Raraku and erected on an *ahu*.

Papa Vaka Petroglyphs ARCHAEOLOGICAL SITE
About 100m off the coastal road (look for the sign), you'll find a massive basaltic slab decorated with prolific carvings.

Península Poike PENINSULA
At the eastern end of the island, this high plateau is crowned by the extinct volcano **Maunga Pu A Katiki** (400m) and bound in by steep cliffs. The landscape is stark, with huge fields of grass, free-roaming horses and intimidating cows. The best way to soak up the primordial rawness of Península Poike is to take a two-day horseback excursion from Hanga Roa, or a day hike from the main road. Ask your guide to show you a series of small *moai* that lie face down, hidden amid the grass, as well as the **Grotto of the Virgins** (Ana O Keke), carved into the cliffs.

TOP CHOICE **Ahu Tongariki** ARCHAEOLOGICAL SITE
The monumental Ahu Tongariki has plenty to set your camera's flash popping. With 15 imposing statues, it is the largest *ahu* ever built. The statues gaze over a large, level village site, with ruined remnants scattered about and some petroglyphs nearby.

TOP CHOICE **Rano Raraku**   ARCHAEOLOGICAL SITE

Known as 'the nursery', the volcano of Rano Raraku, about 18km from Hanga Roa, is the quarry for the hard tuff from which the *moai* were cut. You'll feel as though you're stepping back into early Polynesian times, wandering among *moai* in all stages of progress studded on the southern slopes of the volcano. At the top the 360-degree view is truly awesome. Within the crater are a small, glistening lake and about 20 standing *moai*.

UNDERSTAND EASTER ISLAND

Easter Island Today

In 2008 Easter Island was granted a special status. It is now a *territoria especial* (special territory) within Chile, which means greater autonomy for the islanders. But independence is not the order of the day – ongoing economic reliance on mainland Chile renders this option unlikely in the foreseeable future.

The main claim is for the return of native lands, and the new status should help settle these matters in the forthcoming years. Indigenous Rapa Nui control almost no land outside Hanga Roa. A national park (designated in 1935) comprises more than a third of the island, and nearly all the remainder belongs to Chile. Native groups have asked the Chilean government and the UN to return the park to aboriginal hands. In 2010 a land dispute opposed one Rapa Nui clan to the owners of the Hanga Roa hotel. The occupation of the hotel and several administrative buildings by Rapa Nui individuals was followed by violent confrontations between police and demonstrators.

The Rapa Nui are also concerned about the development and control of the tourism industry. Mass tourism it ain't, but the rising number of visitors – approximately 65,000 tourists each year – has an impact on the environment.

The recent influx of mainland Chileans (mostly made up of construction workers) has fostered tensions with some locals, who see mainland Chileans as 'troublemakers'. In August 2009 a group of Rapa Nui people blocked the airport for a few days to protest against what they perceive as 'uncontrolled immigration'.

History

The first islanders arrived either from the Marquesas, the Mangarevas, the Cooks or Pitcairn Island between the 4th and 8th centuries.

The Rapa Nui developed a unique civilisation, characterized by the construction of the ceremonial stone platforms called *ahu* and the famous Easter Island statues called *moai* (see p411). The population probably peaked at around 15,000 in the 17th century. Conflict over land and resources erupted in intertribal warfare by the late 17th century, only shortly before the arrival of Europeans, and the population started to decline. More recent dissension between different clans led to bloody wars and cannibalism, and many *moai* were toppled from their *ahu*. Natural disasters, such as earthquakes and tsunamis, may have also contributed to the destruction. The only *moai* that are left standing today were restored during the last century.

European Arrival

When the Dutch admiral Jacob Roggeveen arrived on Easter Sunday 1722, many of the great *moai* were still standing, but there was no sign of any modern implements, suggesting the islanders did not trade with the outside world.

In 1774 the celebrated English navigator James Cook led the next European expedition to land on Rapa Nui. His account is the first to mention that many *moai* had been damaged, apparently as a result of intertribal wars.

Fourteen years later French explorer La Pérouse found the people prosperous and calm, suggesting a quick recovery.

European Takeover

Contact with outsiders nearly annihilated the Rapa Nui people. A raid by Peruvian blackbirders (slavers) in 1862 took 1000 islanders away to work the guano (manure) deposits of Peru's Chincha islands. After intense pressure from the Catholic Church, some survivors were returned to Easter Island, but disease and hard labor had already killed about 90% of them.

A brief period of French-led missionary activity saw most of the surviving islanders converted to Catholicism in the 1860s. Commercial exploitation of the island began in 1870, when French adventurer Jean-Baptiste Dutroux-Bornier introduced the wool trade to Rapa Nui and sent many islanders to work on plantations in Tahiti. Conflicts arose with the missionaries, who were at the same time deporting islanders to missions on Mangareva (in the Gambier Archipelago). Dutroux-Bornier was assassinated by an islander in 1877.

Annexation by Chile

Chile officially annexed the island in 1888 during a period of expansion that included the acquisition of territory from Peru and Bolivia after the War of the Pacific (1879–84).

By 1897 Rapa Nui had fallen under the control of a single wool company, which became the island's de facto government, continuing the wool trade until the middle of the 20th century.

In 1953 the Chilean government took charge of the island, continuing the imperial rule to which islanders had been subject for nearly a century. With restricted rights, including travel restrictions and ineligibility to vote, the islanders felt they were treated like second-class citizens. In 1967, the establishment of a regular commercial air link between Santiago and Tahiti, with Rapa Nui as a refuelling stop, opened up the island to the world and brought many benefits to Rapa Nui people.

The Culture

Rapa Nui is a fairly conservative society, and family life, marriage and children still play a central role in everyday life, as does religion.

A third of the population is from mainland Chile or Europe. The most striking feature is the intriguing blend of Polynesian and Chilean customs. Although they will never admit it overtly, the people of Rapa Nui have one foot in South America and one foot in Polynesia.

Despite its unique language and history, contemporary Rapa Nui does not appear to be a 'traditional' society – its continuity was shattered by the near extinction of the population in the last century. However, although they have largely adapted to a Westernized lifestyle, Rapa Nui people are fiercely proud of their history and culture, and they strive to keep their traditions alive.

Arts

As in Tahiti, traditional dancing is not a mere tourist attraction but one of the most vibrant forms of expression of traditional Polynesian culture. A couple of talented dance groups perform regularly at various hotels. Tattooing is another aspect of Polynesian culture, and it has enjoyed a revival among the young generation since the late 1980s.

There are also strong carving traditions on Easter Island. Carvings incorporate human, bird, fish and other animal motifs, often in combination.

Environment

Easter Island is roughly triangular in shape, with an extinct volcanic cone in each corner – Maunga (Mt) Terevaka, in the northwest corner, is the highest point at 507m. The island's maximum length is just 24km, and it is only 12km across at its widest point. Much of the interior of Easter Island is grassland, with cultivable soil interspersed with rugged lava fields. Wave erosion has created steep cliffs around much of the coast, and Anakena, on the north shore, is the only broad sandy beach.

Erosion, exacerbated by overgrazing and deforestation, is the island's most serious problem. To counteract the effects of erosion, a small-scale replanting program is under way on Península Poike.

SURVIVAL GUIDE

Directory A–Z

Accommodations

If you come here from mainland Chile, be prepared for a shock. Despite a high number of establishments – about 90 when we visited – accommodations on Easter Island are fairly pricey for what you get. All accommodations options are located in Hanga Roa except the Explora en Rapa Nui. *Residenciales* (homestays) form the bedrock of accommodation on the island but there's a growing number of luxury options. At the other end of the scale, there are also a couple of camping grounds in Hang Roa. Note that wild camping is forbidden in the national park.

These review price ranges refer to a double room with private bathroom and breakfast.

$ less than CH$40,000

$$ CH$40,000–CH$80,000

$$$ more than CH$80,000

Business Hours

The following are normal opening hours for Easter Island. Reviews in this chapter do not list business hours unless they differ from these standards.

Offices 9am to 5pm Monday to Friday

Restaurants 9am to 9pm Monday to Saturday

Food

Restaurant review price indicators are based on the cost of a main course.

$ less than CH$8000

$$ CH$8000–CH$12,000

$$$ more than CH$12,000

Internet Access

You'll find internet cafes in Hanga Roa. Wi-fi is also available at most hotels and guesthouses but connections can be slow at times.

Internet Resources

Easter Island Foundation (www.islandheritage.org)

Easter Island home page (www.netaxs.com/trance/rapanui.html)

Lonely Planet (www.lonelyplanet.com/chile/rapa-nui-easter-island)

Money

The local currency is the Chilean peso (CH$). A number of businesses on Rapa Nui, especially *residenciales,* hotels and rental agencies, accept US cash (and euros, albeit at a pinch). Travellers from Tahiti must bring US cash (or euros) as Tahitian currency is not accepted.

ATMs Easter Island has only five ATMs, two of which accept only MasterCard. Don't rely solely on your credit card and make sure you keep some cash in reserve.

Credit Cards Many *residenciales,* hotels, restaurants and tour agencies accept credit cards but they usually charge an additional 5% to 10% commission.

PRACTICALITIES

» *Mercurio,* the national daily newspaper, can be purchased at various shops in Hanga Roa. Easter Island also has its own newspaper, *El Correo del Moai.*

» Chilean shows of the government-owned Television Nacional (TVN) are beamed to the island via satellite.

» Easter Island uses the NTSC system for videos.

» Electricity is supplied at 240V, 50Hz AC.

» Easter Island follows the metric system.

Moneychangers There are two banks and an exchange office in Hanga Roa. US dollars are the best foreign currency to carry, followed by euros. Note that exchange rates on Easter Island are lower than those offered in mainland Chile.

Taxes All prices given in this chapter are inclusive of tax.

Tipping & Bargaining Tipping and bargaining are not traditionally part of Polynesian culture.

Telephone

Easter Island's international telephone code is the same as Chile's (☏56), and the area code (☏32) covers the whole island. International calls (dial ☏00) start at around US$0.50 per minute. You'll find several private call centres in town. Entel offers GSM cell-phone service, and prepaid SIM cards are available for purchase.

TRANSPORTATION

Getting There & Away

Air

The only airline serving Easter Island is **LAN** (☏210-0920; www.lan.com; Av Atamu Tekena s/n; ⊙9am-4.30pm Mon-Fri, to 12.30pm Sat). It has daily flights to/from Santiago, one weekly flight to/from Pape'ete (Tahiti) and twice weekly flights to/from Lima (Peru). A standard economy round-trip fare from Santiago can range from US$600 to US$900.

EASTER ISLAND (RAPA NUI) TRANSPORTATION

Sea

Few passenger services go to Easter Island. A few yachts stop here, mostly in January, February and March. Anchorages are not well sheltered.

Getting Around

Outside Hanga Roa, nearly the entire east coast road and the road to Anakena are paved. Other roads are not paved but are in decent enough condition.

To/From the Airport

The airport is just on the outskirts of Hanga Roa. Accommodation proprietors wait at the airport and will shuttle you for free to your hotel or *residencial*.

Bicycle

Mountain bikes can be rented in Hanga Roa for about CH$12,000 per day. Ask at your *residencial* or hotel.

Car & Motorcycle

Some hotels and agencies rent 4WDs for CH$25,000 to CH$45,000 per eight-hour day, and CH$35,000 to CH$60,000 for 24 hours depending on the vehicle. A word of warning: insurance is *not* available, so you're not covered should the vehicle get any damage. Don't leave valuables in your car.

Scooters and motorcycles are rented for about CH$20,000 to CH$25,000 a day.

You can contact the following outfits.

Haunani (210-0353; Av Atamu Tekena s/n)

Oceanic Rapa Nui Rent a Car (210-0985; www.rapanuioceanic.com; Av Atamu Tekena s/n)

Rent a Car Insular (210-0480; www.rentainsular.cl; Av Atamu Tekena s/n)

Taxi

Taxis cost a flat CH$1500 for most trips around town. Longer trips around the island can be negotiated.

Understand Chile

population per sq km

CHILE   USA   UK

= 1 person

Chile Today

Too bad there is no award for the most dogged country, because Chile would be a serious candidate. After an 8.8 earthquake hit off the central coast in February 2010, Chile dug in. The earthquake carried the power of 10,000 Hiroshima bombs: with the ensuing tsunami it was responsible for hundreds of deaths and US$30 billion dollars in damage. Yet two months later, students returned to school, and the affected roads, ports and airports were up. In large part the recovery depended on citizens who helped each other with no formal emergency response in place.

Chile is no stranger to natural disaster (it was witness to the 2011 eruptions of Cordon Caulle, which also buried parts of Argentina under ash), but it is a survivor. In recent times, the country has also had to deal with another kind of aftershock – the consequence of prosperity.

Mind the Gap

In 2010 Chile became the first South American country to earn membership in the Organization for Economic Cooperation and Development (OECD). Chile is now ranked as the world's 40th most developed country; healthcare has improved and life expectancy is up.

Yet there is room for improvement. Of all OECD members, Chile has the greatest levels of inequality. The number of millionaires in Chile doubled in the early 2000s, but the number of those living in extreme poverty is over 600,000. Although poverty has declined in the past decade by nearly a third, critics argue that the national poverty line is just too low for an accurate picture.

Behind the problem, many say, is education. There is little assistance for middle- or lower-class children to attend college. Tired of this, students in 2011 took to the streets. When the Piñera government turned a deaf ear, protesters broke out into Michael Jackson's *Thriller* and pa-

» Population: 17 million

» Median age: 32

» Internet users: 7 million

» Adult literacy: 96%

» Unemployment: 6.9%

» Life expectancy: 78.8 years

» Inflation rate: 3.3%

» GDP: $281 billion

Top Films

The Maid (2009) A maid questions her lifelong loyalty
Violeta Went to Heaven (2012) Emotional, unflinching biopic of rebel icon Violeta Parra
Mi Mejor Enemigo (2005) Lost Argentine and Chilean soldiers cobble out a truce

Top Travelogues

Voyage of the Beagle (Charles Darwin) Observes native fauna and volcanoes
Motorcycle Diaries (Che Guevera) The road trip that made a revolutionary
In Patagonia (Bruce Chatwin) Iconic work on Patagonian ethos

Say What?

Chilean Spanish is rife with local lingo. Brush up with:
Chilenismos: A Dictionary and Phrasebook for Chilean Spanish (Daniel Joelson)
How to Survive in the Chilean Jungle (John Brennan & Alvaro Taboada)

belief systems
(% of population)

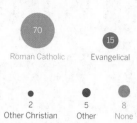

70
Roman Catholic

15
Evangelical

2
Other Christian

5
Other

8
None

if Chile were
100 people

95 would be white or white and Amerindian
4 would be Mapuche
1 would be other Indigenous groups

raded as zombies outside the presidential palace. The Chilean Winter became the largest public protests in decades.

They were led by Camila Vallejo, a 23-year-old University of Chile student activist. First cast as upstarts, the students eventually gained access to La Moneda for negotiations. But the fairy tale stops there. Negotiations have hit a stalemate, though Chilean public opinion has swayed in the students' favor. It doesn't hurt either that *Time, Newsweek* and the *Guardian* have all paid homage to Vallejo, a honor that even billionaire President Sebastian Piñera could not buy.

69 Days Underground
The world was watching on October 13, 2010 when 33 Chilean miners who had been trapped for 69 days in the San José mine were hauled up one by one from 700m down in the earth. They emerged stumbling, blind as moles in the desert glare, into the bosoms of waiting wives and lovers (some even attending the same man). The universe sighed in collective relief.

Their survival was only possible because of a borehole that had penetrated their chamber 17 days into their ordeal. After the hole came a tube and what the Chileans called *palomas* – messenger doves. In these capsules, videos and love letters went up, baked pies and medication went down. It was the line that connected the surface to the depths, life to a world devoid of it, and billions of viewers to 33 anxious souls. Above ground, the line was no longer necessary but had instead become symbolic. Chile, no stranger to struggle, had something else. Solidarity.

While trapped underground, the 33 miners requested wine and cigarettes to help cope with the stress. But their NASA doctor sent nicotine patches instead.

Records
Torre Gran Costanera This 70-story Santiago skyscraper will be the tallest building on the continent
Campos de Hielo Chile boasts over 80% of South America's glaciers

Observatorio Astronómico Andino (OAA) The largest non-professional observatory on the continent, just outside Santiago

New in Santiago
Centro Cultural Gabriela Mistral (www.gam.cl) Urban arts complex
Museo de la Moda (www.museodelamoda.cl) The museum of fashion
Parque Bicentenario Local version of NYC's Central Park

History

With the oldest inhabited site in the Americas, Chile's astounding past is only starting to be unearthed and understood. Though yet to tick off two centuries as a country, Chile has come far from its first days as a backwater of the Spanish empire. Progress has inched forward in imperceptible steps, with major issues that often stalled for decades before resolving. Today's culture still bears the mark of having a small landowning elite, a long industry of mineral exploitation, and politics which both thwarted and strove for reform. Its ultimate resilience has led Chile to become one of the most stable and influential countries of Latin America.

The Chinchorro culture began mummifying their dead some 2000 years before the Egyptians. The oldest known mummy dates from around 5050 BC.

Beginnings

A small child's footprint left in a marshy field rocked the foundations of American archaeology during the 1980s. The 12,500-year-old print proved human habitation in Monte Verde, near Puerto Montt. Other evidence dated back as far as 33,000 years. These highly controversial dates negate the long-accepted Clovis paradigm, which stated that the Americas were populated via the Bering land bridge some 11,500 years ago, after which the Clovis people scattered southwards. New theories suggest multiple entries, different routes, or coastal landings by the first peoples. Following a landmark 1998 convention, the Monte Verde site was acknowledged as the oldest inhabited site in the Americas, although more recent discoveries, notably in New Mexico, date back as far as 40,000 years.

So, you don't say...the ancients did drugs? Ancient Atacameños had a hallucinogenic habit, but all that remains are the accessories: mini spatulas, snuff boards, tubes, little boxes and woolen bags.

Early Cultures

Most pre-Columbian remains have been recovered in the north of Chile, preserved by the extreme desert aridity. The nomadic Chinchorro culture left behind the oldest known intentionally preserved mummies. In north desert canyons, Aymara farmers cultivated maize, grew potatoes and tended llama and alpaca; their descendants still practice similar

TIMELINE

12,500 BC

A child's footprint discovered in Monte Verde outside Puerto Montt – the oldest inhabited site in South America – disproves the supposed human migration from the Bering land bridge.

1520

After his fleet faces mutiny and shipwreck, Ferdinand Magellan is the first European to sight Chilean territory on November 1, 1520 while sailing the strait now named for him.

1535

Conquistador Diego de Almagro marches on Chile with 500 men, 100 African slaves and 10,000 Indian porters. Many freeze to death on Andean passes. Finding no riches, Almagro abandons his claim.

COLD HARD FACTS

Little is known about the Selk'nam (Ona) people who once inhabited Magallanes, but it is well documented that they withstood extreme temperatures wearing little or no clothing. On the **Chilean Cultural Heritage Site** (www.nuestro.cl), anthropologist Francisco Mena recounts, 'An investigator of the 19th century writes that he once met a naked man, and asked him how come he felt no cold. And the Selk'nam answered: My whole body has become face.'

For more interesting historical anecdotes, explore the website, which also has an English version.

agricultural techniques around Parque Nacional Lauca. Also in Chile's northern reaches, the Atacameño culture left remarkably well-preserved remains, from mummies to ornate tablets used in the preparation of hallucinogenic substances. The El Molle and Tiwanaku left enormous geoglyphs, rock etchings and ceramics, still visible in Chile's northern reaches. Meanwhile, Chango fisherfolk occupied northern coastal areas, and Diaguita peoples inhabited the inland river valleys.

The invasive Inka culture enjoyed a brief ascendancy in northern Chile, but its rule barely touched the central valley and the forests of the south, where the sedentary farmers (Picunche) and shifting cultivators (Mapuche) fiercely resisted any incursions. Meanwhile the Cunco fished and farmed on the island of Chiloé and along the shores of the gulfs of Reloncaví and Ancud.

Invasion

In 1495, unbeknownst to indigenous populations, the Americas were earmarked by two superpowers of the day – Spain and Portugal. The papal Treaty of Tordesillas delivered all the territory west of Brazil to Spain. By the mid-16th century, the Spaniards dominated most of the area from Florida and Mexico to central Chile. Though few in number, the conquerors were determined and ruthless, exploiting factionalism among indigenous groups and intimidating native peoples with their horses and firearms. But their greatest ally was infectious disease, to which the natives lacked immunity.

The Spaniards' first ill-fated foray into northern Chile was led over frozen Andean passes in 1535 by Diego de Almagro. Though a failure, it laid the groundwork for Pedro de Valdivia's 1540 expedition. After surviving the parched desert, they reached Chile's fertile Mapocho Valley in 1541. After subduing local indigenous groups, Valdivia founded the city of Santiago on February 12. Six months later the indigenous peoples struck

Isabel Allende's historical novel *Inés of My Soul* is based on facts from the real-life *conquistadora* and former seamstress who fatefully trailed Pedro de Valdivia to the future Chile.

1535–1880	1540	1541	1548
The Arauco War marks the Mapuches' 300-year resistance. Most meet Chile's revolt from the Spanish crown with indifference. The area south of the Río Biobío remains their stronghold.	After crossing the Atacama Desert and facing its blistering extremes, Pedro de Valdiva and a group of 150 Spaniards start a colony on the banks of the Río Mapocho.	Santiago is officially founded on September 11, despite fierce resistance by indigenous Araucanians, numbering around 500,000. The presence of colonists brings disease and death to the indigenous.	Wine comes to Chile via missionaries and conquistadores. Jesuit priests cultivated early vineyards of rustic *pais* grapes; today Chile has more than 70 wineries and international distribution.

back, razing the town and all but wiping out the settlers' supplies. But the Spaniards clung on, and the population burgeoned. By the time of his death in 1553, at the hands of Mapuche forces led by the famous *caciques* (chiefs) Caupolicán and Lautaro, Valdivia had founded numerous settlements and laid the groundwork for a new society.

Colonial Chile

Lust for gold and silver was always high on the Spaniards' agenda, but they soon realized that the true wealth of the New World consisted of the large indigenous populations. The *encomienda* system granted individual Spaniards rights to indigenous labor and tribute. It was easily established in northern Chile (then part of Peru) where the indigenous population were highly organized and even accustomed to similar forms of exploitation.

The Spaniards also established dominance in central Chile, but the semisedentary and nomadic peoples of the south mounted vigorous resistance. Feral horses taken from the Argentine pampas greatly aided the Mapuche, whose new mobility enhanced their ability to strike.

Despite the Crown's distant disapproval, Valdivia began rewarding his followers with enormous land grants. Such *latifundios* (estates) became an enduring feature of Chilean agriculture and society, with many intact as late as the 1960s.

Mestizo children of mixed Spanish and indigenous parentage soon outnumbered indigenous, whose population declined after epidemics, forced-labor abuses and warfare. Chile's neoaristocracy encouraged the landless *mestizo* population to attach themselves as *inquilinos* (tenant farmers) to large rural estates.

Revolution

Independence movements sparked between 1808 and 1810 were born from the emergence of the *criollo* (creole) class – American-born Spaniards pushing for self-government. To facilitate tax collection, Madrid decreed that all Spanish trade pass overland through Panama rather than directly by ship. This cumbersome system hampered commerce and eventually cost Spain its empire.

During colonial times, Chile was judged a subdivision of the Lima-based Viceroyalty of Peru. Called the Audiencia de Chile, it reached from present-day Chañaral south to Puerto Aisén, plus the present-day Argentinean provinces of Mendoza, San Juan and San Luis. Chile developed in near isolation from Peru, creating a wholly distinct identity.

By the 1820s, independence movements were igniting throughout South America. From Venezuela, a *criollo* army under Simón Bolívar fought its way toward Peru. The Argentine liberator José de San Martín

---

Caupolicán led the Mapuches in their first uprising against the Spanish conquistadores. It's believed he became a *toqui* (military leader) by holding a tree trunk for three days and nights and improvising a poetical speech to incite Mapuches to defense.

Chile may seem homogenous but black culture dates back to early Arica where a black mayor was elected in 1620 (the viceroy of Peru later annulled the victory). Today *Foundación Oro Negro* preserves black cultural heritage.

1553

Conquistador Pedro de Valdivia is captured in the Battle of Tucapel, when 6000 Mapuche warriors attack Spanish forts in the south. Valdivia is bound to a tree and beheaded.

1818

With independence movements sweeping the continent, Argentine José de San Martín liberates Santiago. Bernardo O'Higgins, the illegitimate son of an Irishman, becomes 'supreme director' of the Chilean republic.

RICHARD CUMMINS / LONELY PLANET IMAGES ©

1834–35

HMS *Beagle* sails along Chile's coast with Charles Darwin on board; the planned two-year expedition actually lasts five, giving Darwin fodder for his later-developed theory of evolution.

» Bernardo O'Higgins

marched over the Andes into Chile, occupied Santiago and sailed north to Lima.

San Martín appointed Bernardo O'Higgins second-in-command of forces. O'Higgins, the illegitimate son of an Irishman who had served the Spaniards as Viceroy of Peru, became supreme director of the new Chilean republic. San Martín helped drive Spain from Peru, transporting his army in ships either seized from the Spaniards or purchased from Britons or North Americans seeking commercial gain. Thus it was that Scotsman Thomas Cochrane, a colorful former Royal Navy officer, founded and commanded Chile's navy.

The Early Republic

Battered but buoyed by independence, Chile was a fraction of its present size, sharing ambiguous boundaries with Bolivia, Argentina and the hostile Mapuche nation south of the Río Biobío.

Politically stable, Chile rapidly developed agriculture, mining, industry and commerce. O'Higgins dominated politics for five years after formal independence in 1818, but the landowning elite objected to increased taxes, abolition of titles and limitations on inheritance. Forced to resign in 1823, O'Higgins went into exile in Peru.

Diego Portales was interior minister and de facto dictator until his execution following a 1837 uprising. His constitution centralized power in Santiago, limited suffrage to the propertied and established indirect elections for the presidency and senate. It lasted until 1925.

The end of the 19th century was an era of shifting boundaries. Treaties with the Mapuche (1881) brought temperate southern territories under Chilean authority. Chile focused much of its energy on northern expansion and the War of the Pacific. Forced to abandon much of Patagonia to Argentina, Chile sought a broader Pacific presence, and annexed the tiny remote Easter Island (also known as Rapa Nui) in 1888.

Civil War

Mining expansion created a new working class, as well as a class of nouveau rich, both of which challenged the political power of the landowners. The first political figure to tackle the dilemma of Chile's badly distributed wealth was President José Manuel Balmaceda, elected in 1886. Balmaceda's administration undertook major public-works projects, revolutionizing infrastructure and improving hospitals and schools. In 1890, a conservative Congress voted to depose him.

Naval Commander Jorge Montt was elected to head a provisional government. In the ensuing civil war, Montt's navy controlled the ports and eventually defeated the government, despite army support for Balmaceda. Over 10,000 died and Balmaceda shot himself.

If you read Spanish, check out the detailed biographies of early Chilean heroes such as O'Higgins and Cochrane on the Chilean Navy website, www.armada.cl. If not, Wikipedia also does a fine job.

Robert Harvey's extremely readable *Liberators: South America's Struggle for Independence* (2002) tells the epic history of colonial Latin America through larger-than-life heroes and swashbucklers such as O'Higgins, San Martín and Lord Cochrane.

1860	1879–84	1881	1885–1900
French adventurer Orélie-Antoine de Tounens befriends Mapuche leaders and assumes the title King of Araucania and Patagonia. This seemingly protective act ends in his confinement to an insane asylum.	Chile's active development of nitrate deposits in Peruvian and Bolivian territories leads to the War of the Pacific; Chile increases its territory by one-third after defeating both countries.	While focusing on northward expansion, Chile signs a treaty with Argentina conceding all of eastern Patagonia but retaining sovereignty over the Strait of Magellan.	British, North American and German capital turn the Atacama into a bonanza, as nitrates bring some prosperity, create an urban middle class and fund the government.

MINING FOR PROSPERITY

Chile's wealth and prosperity is owed in part to its wrangling of the north in 1879. In the five-year War of the Pacific (1879–84) Chile annexed vast areas of land from Peru and Bolivia. The battles began after Bolivia prohibited a Chilean company from exploiting the nitrate deposits in Atacama, then owned by Bolivia. Chile retaliated by seizing the Bolivian port of Antofagasta and wresting the Tacna and Arica provinces from Peru, thus robbing the Bolivians of all access to the Pacific. This fiercely fought campaign is still celebrated by Chileans with as much gusto as it is bitterly resented by Peruvians and Bolivians. And it's still a prickly thorn in their neighborly relations today.

Santiago's intervention proved a bonanza. The nitrate boom allowed Chile's high society to lavishly prosper. British, North American and German investors supplied most of the capital. Railroads revolutionized infrastructure, and the economy boomed. The addition of ports such as Iquique and Antofagasta only augmented Chile's success.

When the nitrate bubble eventually burst, copper was there to replace it as the force which still propels the Chilean economy.

Twentieth Century

The Chilean economy was hit for its crippling dependence on nitrates, which were being replaced by new petroleum-based fertilizers. The 1914 opening of the Panama Canal made the Cape Horn route, and its many Chilean ports, nearly obsolete.

After periods of poor leadership, several leftist groups briefly imposed a socialist republic and merged to form the Socialist Party. Splits divided the Communist Party, while splinter groups from radical and reformist parties created a bewildering mix of new political organizations. For most of the 1930s and '40s the democratic left dominated Chilean politics.

Meanwhile, the early 20th century saw North American companies gain control of the copper mines, the cornerstone – then and now – of the Chilean economy. WWII augmented the demand for Chilean copper, promoting economic growth even as Chile remained neutral.

Land Reform

In the 1920s, haciendas (large rural landholdings) controlled 80% of the prime agricultural land. *Inquilinos* remained at the mercy of landowners for access to housing, soil and subsistence. Even their votes belonged to landowners. Haciendas had little incentive to modernize, and production stagnated – a situation that changed little until the 1960s.

Reformist sentiment stirred fear in the old order. Conservative and liberal parties decided to join forces. Their candidate, Jorge Alessandri,

1888–1960s	1890–91	1927	1938–46
Chile annexes Easter Island and confines Rapa Nui people to Hanga Roa. The rest of the island becomes a sheep ranch, not reopening to its own citizens until the 1960s.	Tackling unequally distributed wealth and power with reforms, President José Manuel Balmaceda ignites congressional rebellion in 1890; it results in a civil war with 10,000 deaths and Balmaceda's suicide.	General Carlos Ibáñez del Campo establishes a de facto dictatorship, which will prove to be one of the longest lasting of 10 governments in the unstable decade.	Communists, socialists and radicals form the Popular Front coalition, rapidly becoming popular with the unionized working class and playing a leading role in the Chilean labor movement.

son of former president Arturo Alessandri, scraped through the 1958 election with less than 32% of the vote. An opposition Congress forced Alessandri to accept modest land-reform legislation, beginning a decade-long battle with the haciendas.

The 1964 presidential election was a choice between socialist Salvador Allende and Christian Democrat Eduardo Frei Montalva, who drew support from conservative groups. Both parties promised agrarian reform, supported rural unionization and promised an end to the hacienda system. Allende was undermined by leftist factionalism and Frei won comfortably.

Christian Democratic Period

Committed to social transformation, the Christian Democrats attempted to control inflation, balance imports and exports and implement reforms. However, their policies threatened both the traditional elite's privileges and the radical left's working-class support.

The country's economy had declined under Alessandri's presidency, driving the dispossessed to the cities, where squatter settlements, known as *callampas* (mushrooms), sprang up almost overnight. Attacks increased on the export sector, then dominated by US interests. President Frei advocated 'Chileanization' of the copper industry (getting rid of foreign investors), while the Allende camp supported placing the industry under state control.

The Christian Democrats also faced challenges from violent groups such as the Movimiento de Izquierda Revolucionario (MIR; Leftist Revolutionary Movement), which began among upper-middle-class students in Concepción. Urban laborers joined suit, forming the allied Frente de Trabajadores Revolucionarios (Revolutionary Workers Front). Activism also caught on with peasants who longed for land reform. Other leftist groups supported strikes and land seizures by the Mapuche and rural laborers.

Frei's reforms were too slow to appease leftists and too fast for the conservative National Party. Despite better living conditions for many rural workers and gains in education and public health, the country was plagued by inflation, dependence on foreign markets and capital, and inequitable income distribution. The Christian Democrats could not satisfy rising expectations in Chile's increasingly militant and polarized society.

Allende's Rise to Power

In this discomforting political climate, a new leftist coalition coalesced. With Allende at its head, the Unidad Popular (UP) was shaping a radical program that included the nationalization of mines, banks and insurance, plus the expropriation and redistribution of large landholdings. In

Watch the intense movie *Sub Terra* (2003) for a savage indictment of the exploitation that used to go on in Chile's mining industry, often at the hands of gringos.

In 1915, the British Royal Navy took down the German SMS *Dresden* in the harbor of Isla Robinson Crusoe. The infamous war cruiser had successfully slipped detection throughout WWI, only to be discovered because its sailors had joined a soccer match on shore.

1945	1952	1948–58	1960
Poet and foreign consul Gabriela Mistral becomes the first Latin American and fifth woman to win the Nobel Prize (for literature). Her start was as a shy rural schoolmistress.	Ibáñez returns, this time as an elected president promising to sweep out corruption. He revokes the Communist Party ban but sweeps himself out with plans for an auto-coup.	The Communist Party is banned due to the spreading fear that its electoral base is getting too strong amid the growing conservative climate of the Cold War.	The strongest earthquake ever recorded takes place in southern Chile. It flattens coastal towns between Concepción and Chiloé and creates a tsunami that hits Hawaii and Japan.

the 1970 election, Allende squeezed 36% of the vote against the National Party's 35%, becoming the world's first democratically elected Marxist president.

But the country – and even Allende's own coalition – was far from united. The UP consisted of socialist, communist and radical parties conflicted over objectives. Allende faced an opposition Congress, a suspicious US government, and right-wing extremists who even advocated his overthrow by violent means.

Allende's economic program, accomplished by evading rather than confronting Congress, included the state takeover of many private enterprises and massive income redistribution. By increasing government spending, the new president expected to bring the country out of recession. This worked briefly, but apprehensive businesspeople and landowners, worried about expropriation and nationalization, sold off stock, machinery and livestock. Industrial production nose-dived, leading to shortages, hyperinflation and black marketeering.

Peasants, frustrated with an agrarian reform, seized land and agricultural production fell. The government had to use scarce foreign currency to import food. Chilean politics grew increasingly polarized and confrontational, as many of Allende's supporters resented his indirect approach to reform. The MIR intensified its guerrilla activities, and stories circulated in Santiago's factories about new armed communist organizations.

Expropriation of US-controlled copper mines and other enterprises, plus conspicuously friendly relations with Cuba, provoked US hostility. Later, hearings in the US Congress indicated that President Nixon and Secretary of State Kissinger had actively undercut Allende by discouraging credit from international finance organizations and supporting his opponents. Meanwhile, according to the memoirs of a Soviet defector published in 2005, the KGB withdrew support for Allende because of his refusal to use force against his opponents.

Faced with such difficulties, the Chilean government tried to forestall conflict by proposing clearly defined limits on nationalization. Unfortunately, neither extreme leftists, who believed that only force could achieve socialism, nor their rightist counterparts, who believed only force could prevent it, were open to compromise.

Rightist Backlash

In 1972 Chile was paralyzed by a widespread truckers' strike, supported by the Christian Democrats and the National Party. As the government's authority crumbled, a desperate Allende invited constitutionalist army commander General Carlos Prats to occupy the critical post of interior minister, and he included an admiral and an air-force general in his cabinet. Despite the economic crisis, results of the March 1973 congressional

Norwegian Thor Heyerdahl explored Easter Island while crossing the Pacific in the 1950s; it became the centerpiece of his theories about the South American origins of Polynesian civilization. For more details, read *Aku Aku* and *Kon Tiki*.

The strongest earthquake ever recorded, on May 22, 1960, measured between 8.6 and 9.5 on the Richter scale and rattled Chile from Concepción to southern Chiloé. The resulting tsunami wreaked havoc 10,000km away in Hawaii and Japan.

1964
On Easter Island, the Rapa Nui (native islanders) are granted full Chilean citizenship and the right to vote. Three years later commercial flights will open it up to the world.

1970
Salvador Allende becomes the world's first democratically elected Marxist president; radical social reform follows, the state takes control of private enterprises alongside massive income redistribution.

1973
A military coup on September 11, 1973 overthrows the UP government, resulting in Allende's death (an apparent suicide) and the death of thousands of his supporters.

JAN STROMME / LONELY PLANET IMAGES ©

» Rapa Nui men

elections demonstrated that Allende's support had actually increased since 1970 – but the unified opposition nevertheless strengthened its control of Congress, underscoring the polarization of Chilean politics. In June 1973 there was an unsuccessful military coup.

The next month, truckers and other rightists once again went on strike, supported by the entire opposition. Having lost military support, General Prats resigned, to be replaced by the relatively obscure General Augusto Pinochet Ugarte, whom both Prats and Allende thought loyal to constitutional government.

On September 11, 1973 Pinochet unleashed a brutal *golpe de estado* (coup d'état) that overthrew the UP government and resulted in Allende's death (an apparent suicide) and the death of thousands of Allende supporters. Police and the military apprehended thousands of leftists, suspected leftists and sympathizers. Many were herded into Santiago's National Stadium, where they suffered beatings, torture and even execution. Hundreds of thousands went into exile.

The military argued that force was necessary to remove Allende because his government had fomented political and economic chaos and because – so they claimed – he himself was planning to overthrow the constitutional order by force. Certainly, inept policies brought about this 'economic chaos,' but reactionary sectors, encouraged and abetted from abroad, exacerbated scarcities, producing a black market that further undercut order. Allende had demonstrated commitment to democracy, but his inability or unwillingness to control factions to his left terrified the middle class as well as the oligarchy.

Military Dictatorship

Many opposition leaders, some of whom had encouraged the coup, expected a quick return to civilian government, but General Pinochet had other ideas. From 1973 to 1989, he headed a durable junta that dissolved Congress, banned leftist parties and suspended all others, prohibited nearly all political activity and ruled by decree. Assuming the presidency in 1974, Pinochet sought to reorder the country's political and economic culture through repression, torture and murder. The Caravan of Death, a group of military that traveled by helicopter from town to town, mainly in northern Chile, killed many political opponents, several of whom had voluntarily turned themselves in. Detainees came from all sectors of society, from peasants to professors. Around 35,000 were tortured and 3000 were 'disappeared' during the 17-year regime.

The CNI (Centro Nacional de Informaciones or National Information Center) and its predecessor DINA (Directoria de Inteligencia Nacional or National Intelligence Directorate) were the most notorious practitioners of state terrorism. International assassinations were not unusual

HISTORY MILITARY DICTATORSHIP

In Santiago's poor urban neighborhood of La Victoria, the protest murals by the BRP (Brigada Ramona Parra) have appeared since the 1940s, stirring up subversive thought. View them along Avenida 30 de Mayo.

The Pinochet File by Peter Kornbluh (2003) is a surprising and revealing look at US involvement in Chilean politics in the run-up to the military dictatorship of 1973 to 1989.

1973–89	1978	1980	1989
General Augusto Pinochet heads a durable junta that dissolves Congress, bans leftist parties and suspends all others, prohibiting nearly all political activity and ruling by decree.	Chile and Argentina almost go to war over three small islands in the Beagle Channel. The Beagle Conflict is finally settled by papal mediation in 1979.	Pinochet submits a new, customized constitution to the electorate which will ratify his presidency until 1989. It passes though many voters protest by abstaining to vote.	The Concertación para la Democracia (Consensus for Democracy) is formed of 17 parties and its candidate, Christian Democrat Patricio Aylwin, ousts Pinochet in the first free elections since 1970.

SEPTEMBER 11

September 11 is as of much significance to Chileans as North Americans. The date of the 1973 coup, it's commemorated with a major avenue in Santiago.

– a car bomb killed General Prats in Buenos Aires a year after the coup, and Christian Democrat leader Bernardo Leighton barely survived a shooting in Rome in 1975. Perhaps the most notorious case was the 1976 murder of Allende's foreign minister, Orlando Letelier, by a car bomb in Washington, DC.

By 1977 even air-force general Gustavo Leigh, a member of the junta, thought the campaign against 'subversion' so successful that he proposed a return to civilian rule, but Pinochet forced Leigh's resignation, ensuring the army's dominance and perpetuating himself in power. By 1980 Pinochet felt confident enough to submit a new, customized constitution to the electorate and wagered his own political future on it. In a plebiscite with narrow options, about two-thirds of the voters approved the constitution and ratified Pinochet's presidency until 1989, though many voters abstained in protest.

Return to Democracy

The cracks in the regime began to appear around 1983, when leftist groups dared to stage demonstrations and militant opposition groups began to form in the shantytowns. Political parties also started to regroup, although they only began to function openly again in 1987. In late 1988, trying to extend his presidency until 1997, Pinochet held another plebiscite, but this time voters rejected him.

In multiparty elections in 1989, Christian Democrat Patricio Aylwin, compromise candidate of a coalition of opposition parties known as the Concertación para la Democracia (Concertación for short), defeated a conservative economist. Consolidating the rebirth of democracy, Aylwin's term was followed by another Concertación president, Eduardo Frei Ruiz-Tagle.

The Concertación maintained Pinochet's free-market reforms, but Pinochet's military senate appointees could still block other reform. Pinochet assumed a senate seat upon retirement from the army in 1997 – at least in part because it conferred immunity from prosecution in Chile.

This constitutional hangover from the dictatorship was finally swept away in July 2005 when the president was granted the right to fire armed-forces commanders and abolish unelected senators.

The Pinochet Saga

The September 1998 arrest of General Pinochet in London at the request of Spanish judge Báltazar Garzón, who was investigating deaths and disappearances of Spanish citizens in the aftermath of the 1973 coup, caused an international uproar.

Following the arrest, US president Bill Clinton released files showing 30 years of US government covert aid to undermine Allende and

1994	1998	2000	2002
The new president, Christian Democrat Eduardo Frei, ushers in a leftist era but struggles with a limiting constitution in which the military still holds considerable power.	Pinochet is arrested in UK on murder charges relating to his regime. It's one of the first arrests of a dictator based on universal jurisdiction. Seven years of legal battles ensue.	Defeating a former aide to Pinochet, the moderate leftist Ricardo Lagos is elected president, joining a growing breed of left-leaning governments elected across South America.	Chile loosens up – despite bitter cold, over 3000 eager citizens volunteer for artist Spencer Tunick's call for naked bodies for a now infamous outdoor Santiago photo shoot.

DOCUMENTING THE PINOCHET YEARS

» Chilean Director Andrés Wood's hit *Machuca* (2004) depicts the bittersweet coming-of-age of two very different boys during the class-conscious and volatile Santiago of 1973.

» Epic documentary *La Batalla de Chile,* by Patricio Guzman, brilliantly chronicles the year leading up to the military coup of 1973. Filmed partly in secret on stock sent from abroad, the footage had to be smuggled out of Chile.

» March Cooper, Allende's translator, takes an insightful and poignant look at Chile's politics and society from the coup to today's cynical consumer society in *Pinochet and Me: A Chilean Anti-Memoir* (2002).

set the stage for the coup d'état. Pinochet was put under house arrest, and for four years lawyers argued whether or not he was able to stand trial for crimes committed by the Caravan of Death, based on his health and mental condition. Both the Court of Appeals (in 2000) and the Supreme Court (2002) ruled him unfit to stand trial. As a consequence of the court's decision – that he suffered from dementia – Pinochet stepped down from his post as lifetime senator.

It seemed the end of judicial efforts to hold him accountable for human rights abuses. But in 2004 Pinochet gave a TV interview in which he appeared wholly lucid. A string of court decisions subsequently stripped Pinochet of his immunity from prosecution as a former head of state. One of the key human rights charges subsequently brought against him revolved around his alleged role in Operation Condor, a coordinated campaign by several South American regimes in the 1970s and 1980s to eliminate leftist opponents.

Chileans then witnessed a string of yo-yoing court decisions that first stripped his immunity, subsequently reversed the ruling, then again decided that he could stand trial. Revelations made in early 2005 about Pinochet's secret foreign bank accounts – in which he squirreled away more than US$27 million – added to the charges against him and implicated his wife and son. It was also revealed that the judge investigating the former dictator's bank accounts had received death threats.

Despite the intense legal activity, Pinochet never reached trial. He died on December 10, 2006 at the age of 91. In Santiago's Plaza Italia, 6000 demonstrators gathered to celebrate, tossing confetti into the air and drinking champagne, but there were also violent riots. Tens of thousands of Pinochet supporters attended his funeral and honored him as a patriot who gave Chile a strong economic future.

2002	2003	2004	2005
Portraying Chile's disaffected urban youth, the young novelist Alberto Fuget lands the cover of *Newsweek*; he claims the era of Latin American magic realism dead.	With the economy booming, Chile makes a controversial move and becomes the first South American country to sign a free-trade deal with the USA.	In a break with ultraconservative Catholic tradition, Chile establishes the rights of its citizens to divorce; the courts are flooded with cases and proceedings backlog.	The senate approves more than 50 constitutional reforms to fully restore democracy, allowing the president to dismiss nonelected senators (known as 'senators for life') and military commanders.

ECONOMIC CRISIS

The Rise of the Left

The Concertación narrowly scraped through the 2000 elections for its third term in office. Its candidate, the moderate leftist Ricardo Lagos, joined a growing breed of left-leaning governments elected across South America, all seeking to put space between themselves and Washington. Lagos became an important figure in this shift in 2003 when he was one of the most determined members of the UN Security Council to oppose war in Iraq.

In these years, Chile began to shed much of its traditional conservatism. The death penalty was abolished in 2001 and a divorce law was finally passed in 2004 (although the morning-after pill still provokes decisive controversy). The arts and free press began once again flourishing and women's rights were increasingly recognized in law.

The 2006 election of Michelle Bachelet, former minister of defense under Lagos, was a watershed event. Not only because she is a woman, but because as an agnostic, socialist single mother she represented everything that Chile superficially was not. Her father was an air-force general who died under the hands of Pinochet's forces; she was also detained and tortured but released, and lived in exile abroad. Her skill as a consensus builder helped her heal old wounds with the military and the public. For voters, she represented a continuum of the policies of Lagos, moving forward Chile's already strong economy.

Bachelet took the presidency with initially strong approval ratings, but increasing divisions within her coalition (La Concertación Democratica) made reforms difficult. She also was tested by emerging crises with no easy answer. An upgrade of urban buses to Transantiago abruptly consolidated and eliminated routes, leaving many riders stranded on the curb. The student protests of 2006–07 also put the government on the defensive. It took a massive natural disaster for the public to once again rally around Bachelet.

A Seismic Shift

In the early hours of February 27, 2010, one of the largest quakes ever recorded in history hit off the coast of Central Chile. The 8.8 earthquake caused massive destruction, triggering tsunamis on the coast and Archipiélago Juan Fernández and claiming 525 lives. Many homes and highways were destroyed, insurance companies estimated billions of dollars worth of damages.

After some initial looting in affected areas, order returned quickly. Chile's Teletón, a yearly charity fundraising event, raised an unprecedented US$39 million for the cause. Currently, legal suits are pending against several government officials for failing to warn Archipiélago Juan Fern-

> When the world economic crisis hit in 2008, Chile stepped up to the plate and offered loans to the United States, a role reversal which played well for then-president Bachelet.

2006	2006	2007	2009
Michelle Bachelet is elected the first female president of Chile and faces key crises: massive student protests seeking education reform and Santiago's traffic paralysis during transportation reform.	At the age of 91, General Augusto Pinochet dies, having never reached trial. He is denied a state funeral. At his burial, President Bachelet is noticeably absent.	Santiago's youth get radical, from a penchant to protest to the emergence of Pokemones – a short-lived trend of Goth-inspired youth who embrace in public kissing parties.	China displaces the US as the top trading partner of Chile; by the end of 2010 China's investment in Chile reached US$440 million.

ándezof the tsunami. Although there was some debate about whether she should be considered responsible, ex-president Bachelet was ultimately not charged. Overall, the government was praised for its swift action in initial reparations. At the same time, the outpouring of solidarity demonstrated by the Chilean people was a boost to national pride.

Bachelet's tenure was nearly over at the time of the earthquake. After 20 years of rule by the liberal Concertacíon, Chile had elected conservative billionaire businessman Sebastian Piñera from the center-right Alianza por Chile. While Piñera took his oath of office, a 6.9 magnitude aftershock rocked Santiago. Liberal commentators, including novelist Isabel Allende, seized the metaphor, but around the globe observers were curious what the first right-wing government since Pinochet would herald.

Chile rebounded onto the world stage six months later when 33 miners became trapped 700m underground in the Atacama desert. After 17 days they had been feared dead when a borehole broke through their emergency shelter. Miners relayed a scrawled message read live on TV by President Piñera himself: 'We are well in the shelter. The 33.'

Awaiting the rescue, the miners' families and world media held vigil nearby, in the desert 45km north of Copiapó. World attention and an outpouring of public empathy encouraged the government to take over the flailing rescue, with help from NASA and private companies, but complications drew out the drama. On October 13, after enduring 69 days underground, the 33 were finally rescued.

Mining reforms were expected in the aftermath of the incident. Initially President Piñera had promised to adopt the International Labour Organization's (ILO) convention on mining safety, which establishes rights for workers to refuse to work under unsafe conditions. Two years after the incident, the measure had yet to be ratified. While mine inspections have doubled, little else had been done to safeguard one of Chile's biggest industries.

Taking it to the Streets

Starting under the term of Bachelet, Chilean students – nicknamed *pinguinos* (penguins) for their uniforms, began to protest the dismal quality of state schooling en masse. Violence marred some protests yet they eventually succeeded in shaming the government into implementing improvements in primary and secondary education.

Inequity has driven the issue: on a national test, private-school fourth-graders were outperforming their public-school counterparts by 50%. Less than half of Chilean students attend the underfunded public schools, while those who can afford private education gain significant advantages. The Bachelet administration promised reform in the form of

SALTPETER

Naturally occurring nitrate or 'saltpeter' created an early-20th-century boom. Today the Atacama Desert is home to 170 nitrate ghost towns – only one, María Elena, remains open.

2010	2010	2010	2011
On February 27, an 8.8 earthquake and tsunami claims 525 lives and creates massive destruction, with its epicenter 70 miles from the city of Concepción.	Inaugurated just 11 days post earthquake, billionaire businessman Sebastian Piñera becomes the first right-wing president since the Pinochet years. His first task is rebuilding Chile.	The world is captivated by the saga of 33 Chilean miners trapped for 69 days 700m underground near Copiapó – the longest entrapment in history.	In an attempt to solve Chile's greatest unsolved mystery, the remains of ex-president Salvador Allende are exhumed to investigate whether his death had in fact been suicide.

state grants and a new quality agency for monitoring. Yet the issue has persisted into the administration of Sebastian Piñera, this time focused more tightly on the cost of higher education, which remains beyond the means of the poor and much of the middle class.

Mapuche unrest has been another constant. In 2011–12, land disputes with forestry companies resulted in arson fires that killed seven firemen and burned 500 sq km in one week alone. Relations with the state were already poor since police killings of Mapuche youth in 2005 and 2008, which had sparked massive demonstrations and vandalism. Tensions show no sign of abating between the state and the Mapuche indigenous community, who today number around one million.

Brave New World

In spite of domestic woes, in the first decade of the millennium Chile rose as an economic star – boosted by record prices for its key export, copper. When the world economic crisis hit, Chile remained in good standing. Chile was the first South American state to go free trade with the US, though China is now the country's number-one trading partner, boosting the price of copper thanks to its rapid industrialization. As hard as Chile tries to diversify, copper still accounts for a whopping 55% of exports.

After the student protests of the Chilean Winter, President Piñera's approval rating dropped to 26%, the lowest of any postdictatorship administration. Navigating its way through financial highs and domestic snags, Chile may have to reset its north to find its way through mounting social, ecological and economic issues; it's complicated, but par for the course of progress.

2011

A devastating military plane crash off Isla Robinson Crusoe kills 21, including a Chilean TV icon and nonprofit leaders inaugurating the island for tourism post-tsunami.

» Isla Robinson Crusoe

2011

After student protests demanding better education reach a fever pitch, their 23-year-old university-student leader Camila Vallejo dialogues with the government and becomes an international icon.

2012

Progressives anticipate the belated inauguration of the tallest building on the continent, the 70-story Gran Torre Santiago. Delays had plagued the project after the 2008 world financial crisis.

Life in Chile

Isolation may have nurtured Chilenos for decades on this supposed island between the Andes and the sea, but globalization has arrived. Internet, malls and Direct TV have radically recalibrated the tastes and social norms in even the most rural outposts of this once superconservative society. Innovation and creativity keep the culture abuzz, but there's a consumer hangover to deal with. There is still much to be said for the sacred backyard barbecue, and Sundays continue to be reserved for family, all generations included. One thing is for sure: while Chile sits at a cultural crossroads, it leaves the visitor with much to see, enjoy, debate and process.

The National Psyche

Centuries with little outside exposure, accompanied by an especially influential Roman Catholic Church, fostered a high degree of cultural conformity and conservatism in Chile. If anything, this isolation was compounded during the Pinochet years of repression and censorship. Perhaps for this reason outsiders often comment on how Chileans appear more restrained than other Latin American nationalities: they seem a less verbal, more heads-down and hard-working people.

But the national psyche is now at its most fluid, as Chile undergoes radical social change. The Catholic Church's iron grip has loosened. Society is opening up, introducing liberal laws and challenging conservative values. Nowhere is this trend more evident than with the urban youth.

In the past, Chileans were known for compliance and passive political attitudes, but read today's news and unrest simmers. Social change comes at the impetus of Generations Y and Z – the first to grow up without the censorship, curfew or restrictions of the dictatorship. As a result, they are far more questioning and less discouraged by theoretical consequences. Authorities may perceive it as a threat, but Chile's youth has stood up for what's theirs in a way their predecessors would not have. The momentum has also influenced the provinces, namely Magellanes and Aisén, to protest higher costs and general neglect by the central government.

The most lasting impression you'll take away of Chileans is undoubtedly their renowned hospitality, helpfulness, genuine curiosity and heartfelt eagerness to make travelers feel at home.

For an inside scoop on Mapuche culture and issues, check out the four-language Mapuche international site (www.mapuche-nation.org), created with foreign collaboration.

MAPUCHE CULTURE

Lifestyle

Travelers crossing over from Peru or Bolivia may wonder where the stereotypical 'South America' went. Superficially, Chilean lifestyle has many similarities to Europe. Dress is conservative, leaning towards business formal; the exception being teens. And while most Chileans are proud of their traditional heritage, there's a palpable lack of investment in it.

The average Chilean focuses energy on family, home and work. Children are not encouraged to grow up too quickly, and families spend a

LIFE IN CHILE

DOS AND DON'TS

» Keep your behavior circumspect around indigenous peoples, especially in the altiplano and in the Mapuche south.

» Upon greeting and leaving, cheek kisses are exchanged between men and women and between women. Both parties gently touch cheek to cheek and send the kiss to the air. Men exchange handshakes.

» For Chileans, their dictatorship past is old news. Discussions should start with a focus on more contemporary issues.

» Chileans often reserve strong opinions out of politeness. Quickly asserting an opinion is frowned upon.

great deal of time together. Independence isn't nearly as valued as family unity and togetherness. Regardless, single motherhood is not uncommon. Still a very traditional society, it is one of a handful where abortion is still illegal. The legalization of divorce has created a backlog of cases in the courts. While not aggressively antigay, Chile offers little public support for alternate lifestyles.

Generally, the famous Latin American *machismo* (chauvinism) is subtle in Chile and there's a great deal of respect for women. However, this doesn't mean that it's exactly liberal. In Chile, traditional roles still rule.

Chileans have a strong work ethic, and often work six days a week, but are always eager for a good *carrete* (party). Military service is voluntary, though the right to compulsory recruitment is retained. More women are joining the military.

A yawning gulf separates the highest and lowest incomes in Chile, resulting in a dramatic gap of living standards and an exaggerated class consciousness. Lifestyles are lavish for Santiago's *cuicos* (upper-class yuppies), with swish apartment blocks and a couple of maids, while at the other end of the scale people live in precarious homes without running water. That said, poverty has been halved in the last 18 years, while housing and social programs have eased the burden on Chile's poorest.

A lack of ethnic and religious diversity in Chile makes racism less of an issue, although Mapuche still face prejudice and marginalization, and class barriers are as formidable as ever.

Explore everything from tripe stew to tonguetwisters and dirty riddles at www. folklore.cl, a website that aims to rescue Chile's folkloric traditions.

Population

While the vast majority of the population is of Spanish ancestry mixed with indigenous groups, several moderate waves of immigrants have also settled here – particularly British, Irish, French, Italians, Croatians (especially IN Magallanes and Tierra del Fuego) and Palestinians. Germans also began immigrating in 1848 and left their stamp on the Lakes District.

The northern Andes is home to around 69,200 indigenous Aymara and Atacameño peoples. Almost 10 times that amount (around 620,000 people) are Mapuche, mainly from La Araucanía. Their name stems from the words *mapu* (land) and *che* (people). About 3800 Rapa Nui, of Polynesian ancestry, live on Easter Island.

About 75% of Chile's population occupies just 20% of its total area, in the main agricultural region of Middle Chile. This region includes Gran Santiago (the capital and its suburbs), where over a third of the country's estimated 17 million people reside. More than 85% of Chileans live in cities. In Patagonia, the person-per-square-kilometer ratio in Aisén is just 1:1 – in the Región Metropolitana that ratio is closer to 400:1.

Chilean Wine

Grant Phelps
Grant Phelps is the chief winemaker at Viña Casas del Bosque

Many happy factors coincide to make Chile a winemaker's paradise. It happens to be the only country in the world free of the two most destructive grapevine pests – downy mildew and the infamous root louse phylloxera. The climate of Chile also strikes a fine balance that favors winemaking. In all of the major grape-growing regions, rain is virtually unheard of during the entire growing season (from mid-September until mid-May), which has allowed Chilean producers to turn increasingly to organic and biodynamic viticulture. Add to this moderate summer temperatures (due to the cooling influence of the Pacific Ocean and snowcapped Andes), unprecedented amounts of sunshine (more than 250 days per year), an influx of new winemaking technology, and low costs in labor and land, and it is not surprising that Chilean wine has been taking the world by storm.

Although Chile initially made its name internationally with cheap, drinkable reds, it is becoming recognized for superpremium wines increasingly grown on low-yielding hillside vineyards. Travelers will find that Chilean wineries are catching on to the culture of wine touring and there are a variety of wonderful options to explore.

Need a primer on Chilean wine? Start at www.winesofchile.org, a resource for everything from special events and production information to vineyard maps. Wine enthusiasts pour forth on vintages and valley tours at www.chileanwines.survino.com.

A Tale of Boom & Bust

As in many parts of the New World it was Christianity that originally brought the grapevine to Chile. The first-recorded plantings in the country were made in 1548 by the catholic priest Francisco de Carabantes, who brought a selection of vines from Spain. These *pais* grapes, similar to California's mission grapes, were sturdy but lacking finesse, best for table wine.

Quality wine production only began during the last half of the 19th century with the introduction of noble French vines such as Cabernet Sauvignon and Merlot. Technical know-how soon followed with the sudden arrival of French winemakers, desperate for work after phylloxera had left so many of Europe's vineyards decimated.

By 1877 winegrowing had become the most prosperous agricultural activity and Chilean wineries were already exporting to Europe. In the following 20 years production doubled and by 1900 Chile had 400 sq km of vineyards producing some 275 million liters. At this point, Chile's annual wine consumption had reached a historical high of 100L per capita, sending alcoholism spiraling. To combat this, the government introduced an aggressive alcohol tax in 1902, which was followed by a second law in 1938 prohibiting the planting of new vineyards, leading to more than 30 years of stagnation.

In 1974, under Pinochet's free-market reforms, new vineyards were finally permitted. However, this sudden freedom resulted in a planting boom. Overproduction marked the early '80s, causing an eventual collapse of wine prices. By 1986 almost half of the country's vineyards had been

RESOURCES

uprooted and many of the most famous wineries were on the verge of bankruptcy.

Chile's fortunes turned, however, with the arrival of foreign companies such as Miguel Torres of Spain and Baron Rothschild of Bordeaux. These companies brought not only technical expertise but also modern wine-making equipment – notably temperature-controlled stainless-steel tanks and imported oak barrels. The result was a rapid improvement in wine quality. Seeing the potential to exploit new export markets, traditional Chilean producers soon followed suit. By the mid-1990s good fortune was once again smiling on Chile and exports were booming. Between 2000 and 2010 grape plantations increased more than 80%. Chile exports over 70% of its total production in what has become a $1.7 billion industry. Chilean wine is exported to a total of 150 different countries and reaches 1.5 billion consumers each year, making it the world's fifth biggest exporter.

Wine Regions

Wine grapes are grown throughout much of the country from the Elquí Valley to the Bio Bío region in the south, a total distance of about 1200km. The principal wine regions are all located in valleys. Most are named after the main river running through them on its journey from the snowcapped Andes to the Pacific Ocean. From north to south they are: Elqui, Limari, Aconcagua, Casablanca, San Antonio/Leyda, Maipo, Cachapoal, Colchagua, Curicó, Maule and Bio Bío.

Wine enthusiasts will find some of the most important regions in terms of quality are also the most accessible: Maipo Valley (see the boxed text, p82), immediately south of Santiago; Casablanca Valley (see the boxed text, p107), on the main road from Santiago to Valparaiso; and Colchagua Valley (p113), the hub of which is the town of Santa Cruz. A bit further south, the Maule Valley (p118) also has a well-organized wine route.

Chilean Specialties

In spite of recent fascination with lesser-known grape varieties, Chile's number-one red grape continues to be Cabernet Sauvignon. The two best areas for Cab production are undeniably the Maipo and Colchagua Valleys, and most wines under CH$10,000 from these areas will generally

THE BIG SPILL

On February 27, 2010, the wine-growing Maule Region was the epicenter of an 8.8 earthquake that shook Chile's wine industry. At 3:34am, the country awoke to chaos. In three minutes, cracks zippered Hwy 5, houses collapsed and bridges fell. Even though modern constructions in Chile were designed to withstand earthquakes, the more historic winery buildings (primarily constructed of adobe) along with the tanks and stacks of barrels weren't. Walls crumbled, tanks split their seams and tens of thousands of oak casks simultaneously hit the ground. In total, between 125 million and 200 million liters, worth an estimated US$250 million, were lost. Yet, had the quake happened just a few weeks later after harvest, the losses would have been triple that.

Though nature has been the least affected, some wineries lost their entire collections – their whole history, in the quake. The worst damage was concentrated in the Colchagua, Cachapoal and Maipo valleys. Yet, devastation wasn't the end of the story. Winemakers started innovating. Enologists had to get creative, creating new blends and using lesser-known grapes. To meet orders, wineries supplemented stock from other vineyards. With just days remaining until the start of harvest, winemakers and cellar-hands toiled around the clock to patch up tanks. Old rivalries were forgotten as neighbors helped each other make it through harvest in once piece.

Remarkably, the 2010 harvest was received with critical acclaim by the international wine press.

OUR BEST PICKS UNDER CH$5000 (US$10)

Sparkling Viña Mar, Premium Brut

Sauvignon Blanc Ventisquero, Reserva

Chardonnay Caliterra, Reserva

Rosé Miguel Torres, Las Mulas Reserva

Syrah Ramirana, Reserva

Carmenere Ventisquero, Reserva

Cabernet Sauvignon Emiliana, Adobe

Red Blend Estampa, Estate Carmenere/Malbec

CHILEAN WINE

be solid value. However, if you wish to splurge, some standout examples are: Viu Manent, Single Vineyard La Capilla (CH$13,000), Haras de Pirque, Elegance (CH$30,000) and the stunning Los Vascos, Le Dix (CH$50,000).

Chile's darling grape variety is definitely Carmenere. A little-known grape originally from the Bordeaux region of France, Carmenere largely disappeared in the 19th century due to its tendency to ripen poorly in Bordeaux's uneven climate. It was widely planted in Chile in the late 18th century where it was for a long time mistaken for Merlot. It was not until 1994 that Carmenere was 'rediscovered' in Chile and since then it has proven itself to be capable of producing some exceptional wines here. Classic examples of this variety to try are: Odjfell, Orzada (CH$10,000), De Martino, Single Vineyard Alto de Piedras (CH$17,000) or Viu Manent, El Incidente (CH$30,000).

While hotter climate styles of Syrah made inroads in world markets for well over a decade, it's the freshness and natural acidity of Syrah's cool-climate exponents that have been grabbing recent headlines. Try Matetic, Cor
alillo (CH$11,000), Emiliana, Signos de Origin (CH$12,000) or Tabali, Payen (CH$35,000) for a good round-up of what is being done in Chile right now with this style.

Chilean Pinot Noir surged in popularity following the 2005 hit indie film *Sideways* and nowhere does it better than the cool-climate regions of Casablanca and San Antonio. Wines to try are the Casas del Bosque, Gran Reserva (CH$10,000), Veramonte, Ritual (CH$15,000) and Matetic, EQ (CH$23,000).

Although Chile is best known for its reds, it also produces some exceptional white wines, especially Sauvignon Blanc and Chardonnay from the cooler coastal valleys of Casablanca and San Antonio along with the Limari region. The following Sauvignons are all top notch: Montes, Limited Selection (CH$6,000), Leyda, Single Vineyard Garuma (CH$7,000) and Casa Marin, Cipreses Vineyard (CH$16,000). For Chardonnay try Tabali, Talinay Camanchaca (CH$12,000), Lapostolle, Cuvée Alexandre (CH$16,000) and De Martino, Single Vineyard Quebrada Seca (CH$17,000).

For the latest on Chile's garage wine movement, check out www.movi.cl, where you'll find podcasts, harvest reports and editorials from independent vintners.

Literature & Cinema

While poetry has long been the golden nugget of this narrow country, Chilean cinema is gaining world recognition. In the last generation, the military dictatorship prompted an artistic exodus and censorship, but modern Chile has rebounded with a fresh and sometimes daring emphasis on the arts.

Literature & Poetry

Twentieth-century Chile has produced many of Latin America's most celebrated writers. The most acclaimed are poets Pablo Neruda (see the boxed text, opposite) and Gabriela Mistral, both Nobel Prize winners.

Mistral (born Lucila Godoy Alcayaga; 1889–1957) was a shy young rural schoolmistress from Elqui Valley who won great acclaim for her compassionate, reflective and mystical poetry. She became South America's first Nobel Prize winner for literature in 1945.

Nicanor Parra (b 1914) drew Nobel Prize attention for his hugely influential and colloquial 'antipoetry.' *De Hojas de Parra* (From the Pages of Parra) and *Poemas y antipoemas* (Poems and Antipoems) are his most well known. Bohemian Jorge Tellier (1935–96) wrote poetry of teenage angst and solitude.

Fragile social facades were explored by José Donoso (1924–96). His celebrated novel *Curfew* offers a portrait of life under the dictatorship through the eyes of a returned exile, while *Coronación* (Coronation), made into a hit film, follows the fall of a dynasty.

Chile's most famous contemporary literary export is Isabel Allende (b 1942), niece of late president Salvador Allende. She wove 'magical realism' into best-selling stories with Chilean historic references, such as *House of the Spirits, Of Love and Shadows, Eva Luna, Daughter of Fortune, Portrait in Sepia* and *Maya's Notebook*. *My Invented Country* (2004) gives insight into perceptions of Chile and Allende herself.

US resident Ariel Dorfman (b 1942) is another huge literary presence, with plays *La Negra Ester* (Black Ester) and *Death and the Maiden,* set after the fall of a South American dictator, also an acclaimed movie.

Novelist Antonio Skármeta (b 1940) became famous for *Ardiente Paciencia* (Burning Patience), inspired by Neruda and adapted into the award-winning film *Il Postino* (The Postman).

Luis Sepúlveda (b 1949) is one of Chile's most prolific writers, with such books as *Nombre de Torero* (The Name of the Bullfighter), a tough noir set in Germany and Chile; and the excellent short-story collection *Patagonia Express*. For a lighter romp through Chile, Roberto Ampuero (b 1953) writes mystery novels, such as *El Alemán de Atacama* (The German of Atacama), whose main character is a Valparaíso-based Cuban detective.

Chile: A Traveler's Literary Companion (2003), edited by Katherine Silver, is an appetite-whetting whiz through Chile's rich literary tradition, with snippets from the work of many top writers, including Neruda, Dorfman, Donoso and Rivera Letelier.

LITERARY COMPANION

The work of Roberto Bolaño (1955–2005) is enjoying a renaissance; the posthumous publication of encyclopedic *2666* (released in waves) seals his cult-hero status, but it's worth checking out other works.

Bestselling author Marcela Serrano (b 1951) tackles women's issues in books such as *Antigua Vida Mia* (My Life Before: A Novel) and others. Homosexuality and other taboo subjects are treated with top-notch shock value by Pedro Lemebel (b 1950), author of novel *Tengo Miedo Torero* (My Tender Matador).

Younger writers rejecting the 'magical realism' of Latin literature include Alberto Fuguet (b 1964), whose *Sobredosis* (Overdose) and *Mala Onda* (Bad Vibes) have earned acclaim and scowls. Among other contemporary talents, look for the erotic narratives of Andrea Maturana, novelist Carlos Franz, Gonzalo Contreras and Claudia Apablaza.

Sex, drugs, and poetry recitation drive *Los Detectives Salvajes* (The Savage Detectives), late literary bad boy Roberto Bolaño's greatest novel. Like him, the main character is a Chilean poet exiled in Mexico and Spain.

Cinema

Before the 1973 coup Chilean cinema was among the most experimental in Latin America and it is now returning to reclaim some status. Alejandro Jodorowsky's kooky *El Topo* (The Mole; 1971) is an underground cult classic mixing genres long before Tarantino.

There was little film production in Chile during the Pinochet years, but exiled directors kept shooting. Miguel Littín's *Alsino y el Condor* (Alsino and the Condor; 1983) was nominated for an Academy Award. Exiled documentary-maker Patricio Guzmán has often made the military dictatorship his subject matter. The prolific Paris-based Raúl Ruiz is another exile. His English-language movies include the psychological thriller *Shattered Image* (1998).

Post-dictatorship, Chile's weakened film industry was understandably preoccupied with its after-effects. Ricardo Larrain's *La Frontera* (The

POET-POLITICIAN PABLO NERUDA

The combative, sentimental, surreal and provocative poetry of Pablo Neruda (1904–73) tells much about the soul of Chile while his own life story has played an intimate part in its history.

Born in a provincial town as Neftalí Ricardo Reyes Basoalto, Neruda devised his famous alias fearing that his blue-collar family would mock his ambition. The leftist poet led a flamboyant life, building gloriously outlandish homes in Santiago, Valparaíso and Isla Negra. HIs most famous house, La Chascona (see p51), was named after his third wife Matilde Urrutia's perpetually tangled shock of hair.

Awarded a diplomatic post after early literary success, he gained international celebrity wearing his political opinions on his sleeve. He helped political refugees flee after the Spanish Civil War and officially joined the Communist Party once back in Chile, where he was elected senator. After helping Gabriel González Videla secure the presidency in 1946, he had to escape over the Andes into exile when the president outlawed the Communist Party.

All the while Neruda wrote poems. A presidential candidate in 1969, he pulled out of the race in support of Salvador Allende. While serving as Allende's ambassador to France, he received a Nobel Prize, becoming only the third Latin American writer to win the award.

Shortly afterward he returned to Chile with failing health. Pressure was mounting on Allende's presidency. Mere days after the 1973 coup, Neruda died of cancer and a broken heart. His will left everything to the Chilean people through a foundation. The Pinochet regime set about sacking and vandalizing his homes. Later his widow lovingly restored them, and they are now open to the public.

Neruda's work includes *Heights of Macchu Picchu, Canto General* and *Passions and Impressions,* available in English translation.

ANDRÉS WOOD

Chile's hottest film-maker may have studied in New York, but his subject matter is purely Chileno, from *Fiebre de Locos* (Loco Fever), the story of a Patagonian fishing village, to the acclaimed *Machuca* and Sundance Jury Prize–winner *Violeta Se Fue a Los Cielos* (Violeta; 2012), about artist-musician Violeta Parra.

You tell stories from a microperspective that also reflects a globalized Chile... Do you think that perspective is missing in Chilean cinema? It's very difficult to generalize...but we are more interested in what foreigners think of us, and gaining approval in their eyes. It's a country with a kind of identity crisis, caused by different factors, but with insecurity in our own thoughts and feelings.

Chilean cinema is having a lot of international success. Is this a good moment? The younger generations are more profoundly connected to the world, making barriers more and more invisible. The problem is that often we find ourselves creating works to explain who we are to the world rather than being mirrors that can allow us to think, argue and self-reflect. This gap needs to close for us to better connect with our audiences.

Are there certain characteristics that define Chilean cinema? We don't have a solid body of work but that's fine by me. Chilean film is pretty heterogeneous in aesthetics and subject matter.

Borderland; 1991) explored internal exile, and Gonzalo Justiniano's *Amnesia* (1994) used the story of a Chilean soldier forced to shoot prisoners to challenge Chileans not to forget past atrocities.

Then the mood lightened somewhat. The most successful Chilean movie to date, Cristian Galaz's *El Chacotero Sentimental* (The Sentimental Teaser; 1999) won 18 national and international awards for the true story of a frank radio host whose listeners reveal their love entanglements. Silvio Caiozzi, among Chile's most respected veteran directors, adapted a José Donoso novel to make *Coronación* (Coronation; 2000), about the fall of a family dynasty. Comedy *Taxi Para Tres* (Taxi for Three; 2001), by Orlando Lubbert, follows bandits in their heisted taxi. Pablo Larraín's *Tony Manero* (2008) sends up a disco-obsessed murderer.

The film industry has worked through Chile's traumatic past in a kind of celluloid therapy, while gaining international success. *Machuca* (2004), directed by Andrés Wood, shows two boys' lives during the coup. *Sub Terra* (2003) dramatizes mining exploitation. *Mi Mejor Enemigo* (My Best Enemy; 2004), a collaboration with Argentina and Spain, is set in Patagonia during the Beagle conflict (a 1978 territorial dispute between Argentina and Chile over three islands in the Beagle channel).

It's not all war, torture and politics though. Leading the new breed of globally influenced teen flicks is *Promedio Rojo* (loosely translated as Flunking Grades; 2005) from director Nicolás López. Director Matías Bize's *La Vida de los Pesces* (The Life of Fish, 2010) and *En La Cama* (In Bed, 2005) both gained attention abroad. Another filmmaker to watch for is Alicia Scherson.

Social class is another emerging theme. Darling of the Sundance Film Festival, *La Nana* (2009) tells the story of a maid whose personal life is too deeply entwined with her charges.

Fabulous scenery makes Chile a dream location for foreign movies too; contemporary films to have been shot here include *The Motorcycle Diaries* (2004) and the Bond movie *Quantam of Solace* (2008).

The Natural World

With even Santiago skyscrapers dwarfed by the high Andean backdrop, nature can't help but prevail in visitors' impressions of Chile. Geography students could cover almost their entire syllabus in this slinky country: some 4300km long and 200km wide, Chile is bookended by the Pacific Ocean and the Andes. Stunning in variety, it features the driest desert in the world, temperate rainforest and an ice-capped south, linked by 50 active volcanoes and woven together by rivers, lakes and farmland. In recent years, mining, salmon farming and hydroelectric proposals have put many parts of this once-pristine environment under imminent threat.

The Land

Chile's rugged spine, the Andes began forming about 60 million years ago. While southern Chile was engulfed by glaciers, northern Chile was submerged below the ocean: hence today the barren north is plastered with pastel salt flats and the south is scored by deep glacially carved lakes, curvaceous moraine hills, and awesome glacial valleys.

Still young in geological terms, the Chilean Andes repeatedly top 6000m and thrust as high as 6893m at Ojos del Salado, the second-highest peak in South America and the world's highest active volcano.

Much like a totem pole, Chile can be split into horizontal chunks. Straddling the Tropic of Capricorn, the Norte Grande (Big North) is dominated by the Atacama Desert, the driest in the world with areas where rainfall has never been recorded. The climate is moderated by the cool Humboldt Current, which parallels the coast. High humidity conjures up a thick blanket of fog known as *camanchaca,* which condenses on coastal ranges. Coastal cities here hoard scant water from river valleys, subterranean sources and distant stream diversions. The canyons of the precordillera (foothills) lead eastwards to the altiplano (high plains) and to high, snowy mountain passes. Further south, Norte Chico (Little North) sees the desert give way to scrub and pockets of forest. Green river valleys that streak from east to west allow for agriculture.

South of the Río Aconcagua begins the fertile heartland of Middle Chile, carpeted with vineyards and agriculture. It is also home to the capital, Santiago (with at least a third of the country's population), vital ports and the bulk of industry.

Descending south another rung, the Lakes District undulates with green pastureland, temperate rainforest and foothill lakes dominated by snowcapped volcanoes. The region is drenched by high rainfall, most of which dumps between May and September, but no month is excluded. The warm but strong easterly winds here are known as *puelches*. Winters feature some snow, making border crossings difficult.

Did you know that Chile contains approximately 10% of all the world's active volcanoes?

VOLCANOES

IN DEFENSE OF THE BIG GUYS

The largest animal in the world came perilously close to extinction just a few decades ago. So it was with great excitement in 2003 that what seems to be a blue whale 'nursery' was discovered in sheltered fjords just southeast of Chiloé in the Golfo de Corcovado. More than 100 whales gathered here to feed, including 11 mothers with their young. Since then, calls for Chile's government to create Area Marina y Costera de Multiples Usos de Chiloé, Guaitecas y Palena, a protected area, have been intensifying. It's hoped that this area could eventually become a world-class ecotourism destination. Moving toward this effort, Chile banned whale hunting off the entire length of its coast in September 2008. For news and detailed conservation information, try **Centro Ballena Azul** (www.ballena zul.org, in Spanish) and the **Whale and Dolphin Conservation Society** (www.wdcs.org).

Whale-watching is increasingly popular in Patagonia. A variety of species can be spotted, including fin, humpback, killer and sperm whales. Current hubs for Patagonian whale-watching trips include Raul Marín Balmaceda, and in Argentina Puerto Madryn.

The country's largest island, Isla Grande de Chiloé, hangs off the continent here, battered by Pacific winds and storms. The smaller islands on its eastern flank make up the archipelago, but there's no escaping the rain: up to 150 days per year.

The Aisén region features fjords, raging rivers, impenetrable forests and high peaks. The Andes here jog west to meet the Pacific and the vast Campo de Hielo Norte (Northern Ice Field), where 19 major glaciers coalesce, nourished by heavy rain and snow. To the east, mountainous rainforest gives way to barren Patagonia steppe. South America's deepest lake, the enormous Lago General Carrera, is shared with Argentina.

The Campo de Hielo Sur (Southern Ice Field) separates the mainland from sprawling Magallanes and Tierra del Fuego. Weather here is exceedingly changeable and winds are brutal. At the foot of the continent, pearly blue glaciers, crinkled fjords, vast ice fields and mountains jumble together before reaching the Magellan Strait and Tierra del Fuego. The barren eastern pampas stretches through northern Tierra del Fuego, abruptly halting by the Cordillera Darwin.

In Inka times there were millions of vicuña that ranged throughout the Andes. Today in Chile, there are only 25,000.

Wildlife

A bonus to Chile's glorious scenery is its fascinating wildlife. Bounded by ocean, desert and mountain, the country is home to a unique environment that developed much on its own, creating a number of endemic species.

Animals

Chile's domestic camelids and their slimmer wild cousins inhabit the northern altiplano (see the boxed text, p443). Equally unusual are creatures such as the ñandú (ostrichlike rhea), found in the northern altiplano and southern steppe, and the plump viscacha (a wild relative of the chinchilla) that hides amid the rocks at high altitude.

Though rarely seen, puma still prowl widely through the Andes. Pudú, rare and diminutive deer, hide out in thick forests throughout the south. Even more rare is the huemul deer, an endangered species endemic to Patagonia.

Chile's long coastline features many marine mammals, including colonies of sea lions and sea otters, as well as fur seals in the south. Playful dolphin pods and whales can be glimpsed, while seafood platters evidence that fish and shellfish are abundant.

Birdwatchers will be well satisfied. The northern altiplano features interesting birdlife from Andean gulls to giant coots. Large nesting colonies of flamingos speckle highland lakes pink, from the far north down to Torres del Paine. The three species here include the rare James variety (*parina chica,* in Spanish). Colonies of endangered Humboldt and Magellanic penguins scattered along Chile's long coastline are another crowd-pleaser seen at Parque Nacional Pingüino de Humboldt, off the northwestern coast of Chiloé and near Punta Arenas. Recently, a colony of king penguins was discovered on Tierra del Fuego.

The legendary Andean condor circles on high mountain updrafts throughout Chile. The ibis, with its loud knocking call, is commonly seen in pastures. The queltehue, with black, white and grey markings, has a loud call used to protect its ground nests – people claim they are better than having a guard dog.

Plants

Chile has a wealth of interesting and unique plant life. While few plants can eke out an existence in its northern desert, those that manage to do so by extraordinary means. More than 20 different types of cacti and succulents survive on moisture absorbed from the ocean fog. One of the most impressive varieties is the endangered candelabra cactus, which reaches heights up to 5m.

The high altiplano is characterized by patchy grassland, spiky scrub stands of queñoa and ground-hugging species like the lime-green llareta, a dense cushiony shrub. The native tamarugo tree once covered large areas of Chile's northern desert; it digs roots down as far as 15m to find water.

The desert's biggest surprise comes in years of sudden rainfall in Norte Chico. Delicate wildflowers break through the barren desert crust in a glorious phenomenon called the *desierto florido,* which showcases rare and endemic species (see the boxed text, p205).

From Norte Chico through most of Middle Chile, the native flora consists mostly of shrubs, the glossy leaves of which conserve water during the long dry season. However, pockets of southern beech (the *Nothofagus* species) cling to the coastal range nourished by the thick ocean fog. Few stands of the grand old endemic Chilean palm exist today, best viewed in Parque Nacional La Campana.

When heading into the wild, grab a great field guide like *Birds of Patagonia, Tierra del Fuego & Antarctic Peninsula* (2003) and *Flora Patagonia* (2008), formerly published by Fantástico Sur.

THE NATURAL WORLD WILDLIFE

ANDEAN CAMELIDS

For millennia, Andean peoples have relied on the New World camels – the wild guanaco and vicuña; the domesticated llama and alpaca – for food and fiber.

The delicate guanaco, a slim creature with stick-thin legs and a long, elegant neck, can be found in the far north and south, at elevations from sea level up to 4000m or more. It is most highly concentrated in the plains of Patagonia, including Parque Nacional Torres del Paine. It is less common and flightier in the north, where you're most likely to get photos of guanaco behinds as they hightail it to a safe distance.

The leggy vicuña is the smallest camelid, with a swan neck and minuscule head. It lives only above 4000m in the puna and altiplano, from south-central Peru to north-western Argentina. Its fine golden wool was once the exclusive property of Inka kings, but after the Spanish invasion it was hunted mercilessly. In Parque Nacional Lauca and surrounds, conservation programs have brought vicuña back from barely a thousand in 1973 to over 25,000 today.

Many highland communities in northern Chile still depend on domestic llamas and alpacas for their livelihood. The taller, rangier and hardier llama is a pack animal whose relatively coarse wool serves for blankets, ropes and other household goods, and its meat makes good *charqui* (jerky). It can survive – even thrive – on poor, dry pastures.

The slightly smaller but far shaggier alpaca is not a pack animal. It requires well-watered grasslands to produce the fine wool sold at markets in the north.

Southern Chile boasts one of the largest temperate rainforests in the world. Its northern reaches are classified as Valdivian rainforest, a maze of evergreens, hugged by vines and its roots lost under impenetrable thickets of bamboolike plants. Further south, the Magellanic rainforest has less diversity but hosts several important species. Equally breathtaking is the araucaria forest, home to the araucaria – a grand old pine that can age up to 1000 years. The English name became 'monkey puzzle,' since its forbidding foliage and jigsawlike bark would surely stump a monkey.

Meanwhile in the southern lakes region, the alerce is one of the longest-living trees in the world, growing for up to 4000 years. You can admire them in Parque Nacional Alerce Andino and Parque Pumalín (p311).

On Chiloé, in the Lakes District and Aisén, the rhubarblike nalca is the world's largest herbaceous plant, with enormous leaves that grow from a single stalk; the juicy stalk of younger plants is edible in November.

The Archipiélago Juan Fernández is a major storehouse of biological diversity: of 140 native plant species found on the islands, 101 are endemic.

Environmental Issues

With so much recent growth in industry, Chile is facing a spate of environmental issues. Along with Mexico City and Sao Paolo, Santiago is one of the Americas' most polluted cities. The smog blanket is at times so severe that people sport surgical face masks, schools suspend sports activities and the elderly are advised to stay indoors. Significant recent efforts to reduce pollution include a major overhaul of the city's bus system and the creation of no-drive days for private cars (see p470), but there is still room for improvement.

Chile's forests continue to lose ground to plantations of fast-growing exotics, such as eucalyptus and Monterey pine. Caught in a tug-of-war between their economic and ecological value, native tree species have also declined precipitously due to logging. The alerce is protected by laws which prohibit its export and the felling of live trees. But loggers and traffickers of the wood continue undaunted, finding ways around the laws or ignoring them.

Canadian beavers, first introduced for their fur, have caused extensive environmental damage across Tierra del Fuego (see the boxed text, p385), and now are heading to the mainland continent. A plague of introduced mink has also forced the government to take action in southern Chile.

Water and air pollution caused by the mining industry is a longtime concern. Some mining towns have suffered such severe contamination that they have been relocated. Part of the problem is that the industry also demands huge energy and water supplies, and mining locations can interfere with water basins. In 2006, the Chilean government approved a proposal by Canadian mining company Barrick Gold, which furthered a mining agreement between Chile and Argentina called the Pascua Lama treaty. Farmers and environmental groups are opposed to the operation, which has contaminated the Río Alto del Carmen. At the time of writing, extraction still continues.

The south of Chile, with its many rivers and heavy rains, is considered ideal for dams. However, these projects also have major social and environmental drawbacks. In 2011, the government approved a series of controversial dams on Río Baker and Río Pascua, among other Patagonian rivers (see the boxed text, p332). Concerns have also been raised over building large dams in earthquake-prone areas. Approval is still pending for the transmission lines, which would be the longest in the world.

Ancient Forest International's *Chile's Native Forests: A Conservation Legacy,* by Ken Wilcox, provides an accessible overview of the history and description of Chile's forests and the environmental issues affecting them.

Another issue is the intensive use of agricultural chemicals and pesticides to promote Chile's flourishing fruit exports, which during the southern summer furnish the northern hemisphere with fresh produce. In 2011, the Chilean government approved the registration of genetically modified seeds, opening the door for the controversial multinational Monsanto to shape the future of Chilean agriculture. Likewise industrial waste is a huge problem. A Celco paper-pulping plant near Valdivia is a much-publicized example; its emissions killed thousands of swans in a nearby nature sanctuary. After being temporarily shut, the plant reopened with plans to direct its arsenic-heavy waste out to sea.

The continued expansion of southern Chile's salmon farms is polluting water, devastating underwater ecology and depleting other fish stocks (see the boxed text, p275). Some Lakes District areas have become too polluted for sustainable production; in response, farming operations are moving further south to Aisén. A 2007 *New York Times* report revealing widespread virus outbreaks in Chilean salmon and questioning aquaculture practices rocked the industry and inspired tighter government controls and monitoring. Yet production grew 60% in Chile, spiking global farmed salmon production in 2012.

Forest fires continue to threaten many of Chile's wild areas and parks. The 2011 Torres del Paine blaze (allegedly ignited accidentally by an illegal camper; see p359) brought to public attention the lack of funding for professional firefighting, though high winds also contributed to a drawn-out battle with the fire. Though some of the trails were scorched and much of the forest will take centuries to regenerate, the park remains operative.

Easter Island (Rapa Nui) is under mounting pressure from increasing numbers of visitors. Limited natural resources mean that the island must depend on the distant mainland for all supplies and fuel.

The growing hole in the ozone layer over Antarctica has become such an issue that medical authorities recommend wearing protective clothing and heavy sunblock to avoid cancer-causing ultraviolet radiation, especially in Patagonia (see the boxed text, p345).

Global warming is also having a significant impact on Chile. Nowhere is it more apparent than with the melting of glaciers. Scientists have documented many glaciers doubling their thinning rates in recent years while the northern and southern ice fields continue to retreat. In particular, the Northern Patagonian Ice Field is contributing to rising ocean levels at a rate one-quarter higher than formerly believed. In fact, reports say that glaciers are thinning more rapidly than can be explained by warmer air temperatures and decreased precipitation. The change also stands to impact plant and animal life, water levels in lakes and rivers, and overall sustainability.

You can catch up with the latest conservation headlines through English-language news portal the *Santiago Times*, www.santiagotimes.cl, by selecting its Environment header.

THE NATURAL WORLD ENVIRONMENTAL ISSUES

THE DISAPPEARING LAKE

In April 2008, Lago Cachet 2 drained its 200 million cu meter of water in just a matter of hours, releasing big water downstream to the Baker, Chile's highest volume river and generating a downstream wave that rolled on out to the Pacific. In nature, strange things happen. But following this mysterious one, the event repeated a total of seven times in two years.

According to *Nature* magazine, the cause is climate change. Called a glacial-lake outburst flood (GLOF), it results from the thinning and receding of nearby Patagonian glaciers, weakening the natural dam made by the glaciers. After the lake drains, it fills again with glacial melt. It's a constant threat to those who live on the banks of the Río Colonia, though with assistance from NASA and a German university, monitoring systems are now in place.

Environmental Organizations

Ancient Forest International (AFI; ☎707-923-4475; www.ancientforests.org) US-based organization with close links to Chilean forest-conservation groups.

Codeff (Comité Pro Defensa de la Fauna y Flora; ☎02-777-2534; www.codeff.cl, in Spanish; Ernesto Reyes 035, Providencia, Santiago) Campaigns to protect the country's flora and fauna, especially endangered species. Trips, seminars and work projects are organized for volunteers.

Defensores del Bosque Chileno (☎02-204-1914; www.elbosquechileno.cl, in Spanish; Diagonal Oriente 1413, Ñuñoa) Defending the native forests through education, lobbying, promoting the planting of native species over exotics, and taking legal action against logging interests.

Greenpeace Chile (☎02-634-2120; www.greenpeace.cl, in Spanish; Agromedo 50, Centro, Santiago) Focuses on forest conservation, ocean ecology and dealing with toxic waste.

Patagonia Sin Represas (Patagonia Without Dams; www.patagoniasinrepresas.cl) A coalition of Chilean environmental groups supporting the anti-dam movement in Patagonia.

Terram (☎02-269-4499; www.terram.cl; Bustamente 24, Providencia, Santiago) One of the biggest-hitting pressure groups at the moment.

WWF (☎063-244-590; www.wwf.cl; Carlos Andtwander 624, Casa 4, Valdivia) Involved with the preservation of the temperate rainforests around Valdivia, conservation in southern Patagonia and protection of the native wildlife.

Spanish-language picture book *Patagonia Chile ¡Sin Represas!*, edited by Chilean environmentalist Juan Pablo Orrego, uses before and after images to illustrate the impact of proposed hydro-electric projects in Patagonia.

National Parks

Twenty percent of Chile is preserved in 100 national parks, national monuments and nature reserves. Among Chile's top international attractions, the parks receive around two million visitors yearly, almost doubling visitation in the last decade. But while scene-stealing parks such as Torres del Paine are annually inundated, the majority of Chile's protected areas remain underutilized, wild and begging to be explored. Hikers have their pick of trails, and solitude is easily found, especially if you avoid the summer high season of January and February.

Chile's 95 protected areas are divided into three different categories: *parques nacionales* (national parks); *reservas nacionales* (national reserves), which are open to limited economic exploitation; and *monumentos naturales* (natural monuments), which are smaller but strictly protected areas or features.

National parks and reserves are administered by **Conaf** (Corporacíon Nacional Forestal; www.conaf.cl), the National Forestry Corporation. Different from a National Parks Service, the main focus of Conaf is managing Chile's forests and their development. Because of this distinction, tourism is not often a primary concern of the organization. Advocates are lobbying for a National Parks Service to be created but for the time being, the status quo remains.

In Santiago, visit Conaf's central **information office** (☎02-390-0282; Av Bulnes 285, Centro; ☉9:30am-5:30pm Mon-Fri) for basic maps and brochures. Increasingly, in-park amenities like *refugios* (rustic shelters), campgrounds and restaurants are being run by private concessionaires. Conaf is chronically underfunded and many parks are inadequately protected, which makes issues like forest fires a particularly serious concern. However, other government-financed projects are showing a commitment to ecotourism, including the mega-long **Sendero de Chile** (www.senderodechile.cl, in Spanish), which links 8000km of trails from Chile's top to bottom.

Available from Conaf, a new Parks Pass covers all national parks with the exception of Torres del Paine and Parque Nacional Rapa Nui. One year is CH$10,000 per individual and CH$30,000 per family.

Private Protected Areas

Chilean law permits private nature reserves: *áreas de protección turística* (tourist protection areas) and *santuarios de la naturaleza* (nature sanctuaries). But private parks started making Chilean headlines when

TORRES IN FLAMES

On December 27, 2011, a forest fire in Torres del Paine consumed 42,000 acres. A camper was charged with the fire. Under Chile's current forest laws, tourists can only be charged US$300 for an accidental fire in national parks. In this case, while he maintained his innocence, the hiker agreed to pay US$10,000 and plant 50,000 trees. Still, park advocates are clamoring to update the laws to more appropriate fines and better fund emergency responses.

CHILE'S NATIONAL PARKS

PROTECTED AREA	FEATURES
Parque Nacional Alerce Andino	mountainous alerce forest; pumas, pudú, condors, kingfishers, waterfowl
Parque Nacional Archipiélago Juan Fernández (p140)	remote archipelago, ecological treasure trove of endemic plants
Parque Nacional Bernardo O'Higgins (p359)	remote ice fields, glaciers, waterfalls; cormorants, condors
Parque Nacional Bosques de Fray Jorge (p222)	cloud forest in dry desert, coastline
Parque Nacional Chiloé (p301)	coastal dunes, lagoons and folklore-rich forest; rich birdlife, pudú, sea lions
Parque Nacional Conguillío (p231)	mountainous araucaria forests, lakes, canyons, active volcano
Parque Nacional Huerquehue (p247)	forest, lakes, waterfalls and outstanding views
Parque Nacional La Campana (p108)	coastal cordillera: oak forests and Chilean palms
Parque Nacional Laguna del Laja (p132)	Andean foothills, waterfalls, lakes, rare trees; condors
Parque Nacional Laguna San Rafael (p326)	glaciers reach the sea at this stunning ice field
Parque Nacional Lauca (p159)	altiplano volcanoes, lakes, steppe; abundant birdlife and vicuñas
Parque Nacional Llanos de Challe (p205)	coastal plains; 'flowering desert' occurs after heavy rains; guanaco
Parque Nacional Nahuelbuta (p135)	high coastal range of araucaria forests, wildflowers; pumas, pudú, rare woodpeckers
Parque Nacional Nevado Tres Cruces (p202)	volcano Ojos del Salado; flamingos, vicuñas, guanacos
Parque Nacional Pan de Azúcar (p195)	coastal desert; penguins, otters, sea lions, guanacos and cacti
Parque Nacional Puyehue (p259)	volcanic dunes, lava rivers, forest
Parque Nacional Rapa Nui (p411)	isolated Polynesian island with enigmatic archaeological treasures
Parque Nacional Torres del Paine (p359)	Chile's showpiece park of spectacular peaks, forest, glaciers; guanacos, condors, ñandú, flamingos
Parque Nacional Vicente Pérez Rosales (p270)	Chile's oldest national park, crowded with lakes and volcanoes
Parque Nacional Villarrica (p244)	smoking volcanic cone overlooking lakes and resorts
Parque Nacional Volcán Isluga (p171)	remote altiplano, volcanoes, geysers, unique pastoral culture; rich birdlife

HIGHLIGHTS	BEST TIME TO VISIT
hiking	Dec-Mar
hiking, boat trips, diving, flora	Dec-Mar
boat trips	Dec-Mar
hiking, flora	year-round
hiking, wildlife watching, kayaking, horse-trekking	Dec-Mar
hiking, climbing, skiing, boating, skiing	Jun-Oct
hiking	Dec-Mar
hiking, flora	Nov-Feb
hiking	Dec-Mar
boat trips, flights, hiking, climbing	Sep-Mar
hiking, wildlife watching, traditional villages, hot springs	year-round
flora and fauna	Jul-Sep in rainy years
hiking	Nov-Apr
climbing, hiking, wildlife	Dec-Feb
boat trips, wildlife, swimming, hiking	year-round
hiking, skiing, hot springs, biking, lake canoeing	hiking Dec-Mar, skiing Jun-Oct
archaeology, diving, hiking, horseback riding	year-round
trekking, wildlife watching, climbing, glacier trekking, kayaking, horseback riding	Dec-Mar
hiking, climbing, skiing, boat trips, rafting, kayaking, canyoning, skiing	Jun-Oct
trekking, climbing, skiing	hiking Dec-Mar, skiing Jun-Oct
villages, hiking, birdwatching, hot springs	year-round

American businessman Douglas Tompkins (see the boxed text, p334) purchased an area the size of Rhode Island to create Parque Pumalín. In 2005 Pumalín was donated to a Chilean foundation (Fundación Pumalín) and became a bona fide nature reserve. Tompkins may have ignited a great debate about land ownership and use, but he has also inspired others, including Kris Tompkins, his wife, to preserve Patagonia's Valle chacabuco (Parque Nacional Patagonia; p332), and President Sebastián Piñera to create Chiloé's Parque Tantauco (see p303).

Chile has around 133 private parks, totalling almost 4000 sq km. **Codeff** (www.codeff.cl, in Spanish) maintains a database of properties which have joined together to create Red de Areas Protegidas Privadas (RAPP; Network of Private Protected Areas).

Survival Guide

>

Directory A–Z

Accommodations

Chile has accommodations to suit every budget. Listings are organized in order of our preference considering value for cost. All prices listed are high-season rates for rooms that include breakfast and a private bathroom, unless otherwise specified.

In tourist destinations, prices may double during the height of high season (late December to mid-March), and extrahigh rates are charged at Christmas, New Year and Easter week. If you want to ask about discounts or cheaper rooms, do so at the reservation phase. Bargaining for better accommodation rates once you have arrived is not common and frowned upon.

At many midrange and top-end hotels, payment in US dollars (either cash or credit) legally sidesteps the crippling 19% IVA (*impuesto de valor agregado*, value-added tax). If there is any question as to whether IVA is included in the rates, clarify before paying. A hotel may not offer it without your prodding. In theory, the discount is strictly for those paying in dollars or with a credit card.

If trying to reserve a room, note that hotels in Chile may be less responsive to emails than in other areas. If you want it done, it's best to call.

Cabins

Excellent value for small groups or families, Chile's *cabañas* are common in resort towns and national park areas, and integrated into some campgrounds. Most come with a private bathroom and fully equipped kitchen. Resort areas cram *cabañas* into urban properties, so if you're looking for

privacy, check on the details when booking.

Camping

Chile has a developed camping culture, though it's more of a sleepless, boozy sing-along atmosphere than a back-to-nature escape. Most organized campgrounds are family-oriented with large sites, full bathrooms and laundry, fire pits, a restaurant or snack bar and grill for the essential *asado* (barbecue). Many are costly because they charge a five-person minimum. Try asking for per person rates. Remote areas have free camping, often without potable water or sanitary facilities.

Camping equipment is widely available in Chile but international brands have a significant markup. In rainy regions like Patagonia, a synthetic sleeping bag is preferable over down since it will dry much more quickly. White gas (*bencina blanca*) for camp stoves can be hard to find but butane cartridges are common in the outdoors section of big department stores or small hardware stores (*ferreterías*).

Wild camping may be possible. In rural areas, ask landowners if you can stay. In the north, police are cracking down on guerilla camping. Never light a fire without permission to have one and use an established fire ring.

Santiago's **Sernatur** (www.chile.travel/en.html) has a free pamphlet listing camp-sites throughout Chile.

Guesthouses & Rural Homestays

For more local culture, stay at a *casa de familia* (guesthouse). Particularly in the south, where tourism is less formal, it's common for families and rural farms to open up their homes. Guests do not always have kitchen privileges but usually can pay fair prices for abundant meals or laundry service. Tourist offices maintain lists of such accommodations.

BOOK YOUR STAY ONLINE

For more accommodations reviews by Lonely Planet authors, check out http://hotels.lonelyplanet.com. You'll find independent reviews, as well as recommendations on the best places to stay. Best of all, you can book online.

There are many organized networks in the south, most notably in Chiloé, Lago Ranco, around Pucón and Patagonia. For Patagonia, check out Coyhaique's **Casa de Turismo Rural** (www.casaturismorural.cl). For countrywide options, visit **Viajes Rurales** (www.viajesrurales.cl) or inquire at tourist offices.

Hospedajes

Both *hospedajes* and *residenciales* (budget accommodation options) offer homey, simple accommodations, usually with foam-mattress beds, hard pillows, clean sheets and blankets. Never hesitate to ask to see a room before making a decision.

Room rates may be the same for single or double occupancy. There is sometimes a price difference between a double with two beds and one *matrimonial* bed (often with the *matrimonial* bed being more expensive). Bathrooms and shower facilities are usually shared, but a few will have rooms with a private bathroom, usually with a *matrimonial* double bed for couples. Mostly in the north, but not exclusively, you may have to ask staff to turn on the *calefón* (hot-water heater) before taking a shower.

Breakfast is usually coffee and rolls. Sernatur and most tourist offices have lists of licensed budget lodgings.

Hostels

Stylish and savvy hostels have dramatically improved budget options in Chile, particularly in urban or touristy areas. These dorm-style lodgings usually set aside a few more expensive doubles for couples who want a social atmosphere but greater creature comforts.

Independent backpackers hostels are increasingly joining forces to advertise their existence. Look for pamphlets for **Backpackers Chile** (www.backpackerschile.com), which has many European-run listings and a good standard of quality.

Most places don't insist on a Hostelling International (HI) card, but charge a bit more for nonmembers. The local affiliate of HI is **Asociación Chilena de Albergues Turísticos Juveniles** (☎02-411-2050; www.hostelling.cl; Hernando de Aguirre 201, Oficina 602, Providencia, Santiago). One-year membership cards are available at the head office for CH$12,000.

Hotels

From one-star austerity to five-star luxury, Chile has a wide range of hotels. However, correlation between these categories and their standards is less than perfect; many midrange options seem to be better value than their high-end brethren. Most hotels provide a room with private bathroom, a telephone, wi-fi or computer access and cable or satellite TV. Breakfast is always served, even if basic, and often included.

Reservations are usually necessary if you'll be arriving at an awkward hour, during the summer high season or over a holiday weekend.

In South America the term 'motel' can also be a euphemism for a 'love hotel,' catering to couples with no other alternative for privacy. Surrounding privacy walls usually give the game away.

Refugios

Within some national parks, **Conaf** (Corporación Nacional Forestal; ☎02-663-0000; www.conaf.cl, in Spanish; Av Bulnes 285, Centro; ☺9:30am-5:30pm Mon-Thu, to 4:30pm Fri) maintains *refugios* (rustic shelters) for hikers and trekkers. Many lack upkeep due to Conaf's limited budget. There is a growing trend, already in place in Torres del Paine, for private concessions to manage *refugios* and park restaurants. Private reserves sometimes have *refugios* for hut-to-hut trekking.

Rental Accommodations

For long-term rentals in Santiago, check listings in Sunday's **El Mercurio** (www.elmercurio.cl, in Spanish), **Santiago Craigslist** (http://santiago.en.craigslist.org) or the weekly classified listing **El Rastro** (www.elrastro.cl, in Spanish). In vacation areas such as Viña del Mar, La Serena, Villarrica or Puerto Varas, people line the highway approaches in summer to offer housing. You can also check tourist offices, bulletin boards outside grocery stores or local papers.

Addresses

Names of streets, plazas and other features are often unwieldy, and usually appear abbreviated on maps. So Avenida Libertador General Bernardo O'Higgins might appear on a map as Avenida B O'Higgins, just O'Higgins or even by a colloquial alternative (Alameda). The common address *costanera* denotes a coastal road.

Some addresses include the expression *local* (locale) followed by a number. *Local* means it's one of several offices at the same street address. Street numbers may begin with a zero, eg Bosque Norte 084. This confusing practice usually happens when an older street is extended in the opposite direction, beyond the original number 1.

The abbreviation 's/n' following a street address stands for *sin número* (without number) and indicates that the address has no specific street number.

Business Hours

Tourist offices stay open long hours daily in summer, but have abbreviated hours in the low season. In many provincial cities and towns, restaurants and services are closed on Sunday. Reviews won't list business hours unless they differ from these standards:

banks	9am-2pm weekdays, sometimes 10am-1pm Sat
government offices & businesses	9am-6pm on weekdays
museums	often close on Mon
restaurants	noon to 11pm, many close 4-7pm
shops	10am-8pm, some close 1-3pm

Customs Regulations

Check **Chilean customs** (www.aduana.cl/prontus_aduana_eng/site/edic/base/port/foreign_travelers.html, in English) for what and how much you can take in and out of the country.

There are no restrictions on import and export of local and foreign currency. Duty-free allowances include purchases of up to US$500.

Inspections are usually routine, although some travelers have had more thorough examinations. Travelers leaving the duty-free Regións I and XII are subject to internal customs inspections.

When entering the country, check your bags for food. There are heavy fines for fruit, dairy, spices, nuts, meat and organic products. SAG (Servicio Agrícola-Ganadero; Agriculture and Livestock Service) checks bags and levies fines to prevent the spread of diseases and pests that might threaten Chile's fruit exports.

X-ray machines are used at major international border crossings, such as Los Libertadores (the crossing from Mendoza, Argentina) and Pajaritos (the crossing from Bariloche, Argentina).

Discount Cards

An ISIC international student card or youth card will grant you varying discounts at some museums and tourist sites, though most national parks do not offer reductions. Some bus companies offer 25% discounts to students. Senior discount cards are not generally used.

Electricity

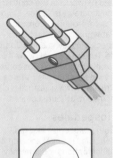

220V/50Hz

220V/50Hz

Embassies & Consulates

Argentina Antofagasta (✆055-220-440; Blanco Encalada 1933); Puerto Montt (✆065-253-996; Pedro Montt N 160, Piso 6, Oficina 50B); Punta Arenas (✆061-261-912; 21 de Mayo 1878); Santiago (✆02-582-2606; www.embargentina.cl; Vicuña Mackenna 41, Centro)

Australia (✆02-500-3500; consular.santiago@dfat.gov.au; Isidora Goyenechea 3621, 12th fl, Las Condes)

Bolivia Antofagasta (✆055-259-008; Jorge Washington 2675); Arica (✆058-231-030; www.rree.gov.bo; Patricio Lynch 298); Calama (✆055-341-976; Latorre 1395); Iquique (✆057-421-777; Gorostiaga 215, Dept E, Iquique); Santiago (✆02-232-8180; cgbolivia@manquehue.net; Av Santa María 2796, Las Condes)

Brazil (✆02-698-2486; www.embajadadebrasil.cl; Alonso Ovalle 1665, Centro, Santiago)

Canada (✆02-362-9660; enqserv@dfait-maeci.gc.ca; Tajamar 481, 12th fl, Las Condes)

France (✆02-470-8000; www.france.cl; Av Condell 65, Providencia)

Germany Arica (✆058-231-657; Arturo Prat 391, 10th fl, Oficina 101); Santiago (✆02-463-2500; www.embajada dealemania.cl; Las Hualtatas 5677, Vitacura)

Peru Arica (✆058-231-020; 18 de Septiembre 1554); Iquique (✆057-411-466; Zegers 570, 2nd fl, Iquique); Santiago (✆02-235-4600; conpersantiago@adsl.tie.cl; Padre Mariano 10, Oficina 309, Providencia)

Spain (✆061-243-566; Jose Menéndez 910, Punta Arenas)

UK Punta Arenas (✆061-244-727; Cataratas del Niagara 01325); Santiago (✆02-370-4100; consular.santiago@fco.gov.uk; Av El Bosque Norte 0125, 3rd fl, Las Condes)

USA (✆02-232-2600; http://santiago.usembassy.gov; Av Andrés Bello 2800, Las Condes)

Food

Restaurant listings are organized according to author preference, considering value for cost.

Travelers should note that current nonsmoking laws allow restaurants and bars to choose to be nonsmoking (with or without a dedicated, separate smoking area) or smoking-only. Smoking-only establishments may refuse entry to children.

Those interested in food tours and a comprehensive Chilean food blog in English should check out **Foody Chile** (www.foodychile.com).

Meals

In general, Chilean food is hearty and traditional. Soups, meat and potatoes, and wonderful casseroles, such as *pastel de choclo* (maize casserole) and *chupe de jaiva* (crab casserole), are staples. Most coastal towns have a *mercado de mariscos* (seafood market) where you can buy fresh fish or eat at small kitchens. If you like spice, seek out the Mapuche *merkén* (spice-smoked chili powder) or *ají Chileno*, a just-passable hot sauce sometimes found in restaurants.

Breakfast usually consists of white rolls with butter and jam, tea and instant coffee. Whole bean coffee is referred to as *café en grano*, available at some cafes and lodgings.

Lunch usually comes in supersized portions. Set meals, known as *menú del dia*, are a good deal. They include a starter or dessert and main dish.

At home, people often eat light in the evening, with a sort of tea time that may include bread, tea, cheese and ham. Known as *onces* (elevenses) tea time is also popular in the south, where German influence adds *küchen* (sweet, German-style cakes) to the mix.

PRICE RANGES

The following price ranges refer to a standard main course.
$ less than CH$6000
$$ CH$6000–CH$12,000
$$$ more than CH$12,000

Drinks

Wine may have center stage (see p435), but there is plenty more to try. Pisco, a grape brandy, is Chile's national alcohol, grown in the dry soil of the north. Pisco sours are a popular start to cocktail hours, and consist of pisco, sugar and fresh *limon de pica*. Students prefer pisco-las, mixing the alcohol with Coke or other soft drinks.

Draft beer is known as *schop*. Microbrews have become popular, particularly in the south where German influence remains. Try brews made by Szot, Kross and Kuntsmann.

Gay & Lesbian Travelers

Chile is still a very conservative, Catholic-minded country yet recent strides in tolerance have been made, particularly in urban areas. Santiago has an active gay scene, with most gay bars and nightclubs found in Barrio Bellavista. For more information see p62. Chilean males are often more physically demonstrative than their counterparts in Europe or North America, so behaviors like a vigorous embrace will seem innocuous.

Gay Chile (www.gaychile.com) has the lowdown on all things gay, including current events, Santiago nightlife, lodging recommendations, legal and medical advice and personals. While in Santiago, keep an eye out for Chile's first magazine oriented toward gays and other socially disenfranchised groups, **Opus Gay** (www.opusgay.cl, in Spanish), teasingly named after the conservative Catholic Opus Dei group.

Chile's main gay-rights organization is **Movimiento Unificado de Minorías Sexuales** (MUMS; www.orgul logay.cl, in Spanish).

Health

Travelers who follow basic, common-sense precautions should have few problems traveling in Chile. Chile requires no special vaccines but travelers should be up to date with routine shots. In temperate South America, mosquito-borne illnesses are generally not a problem, while most infections are related to the consumption of contaminated food and beverages.

Availability & Cost of Health Care

There are two modern facilities in Santiago that offer 24-hour walk-in service for urgent problems, as well as specialty care (by appointment) and inpatient services: **Clínica Las Condes** (210-4000; Lo Fontecilla 441, Las Condes) and **Clínica Alemana** (212-9700; Av Vitacura 5951, Vitacura). For a list of additional physicians, dentists and laboratories in Santiago, go to the website of the **US Embassy** (http://santiago.usembassy.gov).

Medical care in Santiago and other cities is generally good, but it may be difficult to find assistance in remote areas. Most doctors and hospitals expect payment in cash, regardless of whether you have travel health insurance.

If you develop a life-threatening medical problem, you'll probably want to be evacuated to a country with state-of-the-art medical care. Since this may cost tens of thousands of dollars, be sure you have insurance to cover this before you depart. You can find a list of medical evacuation and travel insurance companies on the website of the **US State Department** (http://travel.state.gov).

Most pharmacies are well stocked and have trained pharmacists. Medication quality is generally comparable to other industrialized countries. Drugs that require a prescription elsewhere may be available over the counter in Chile. If you're taking medication on a regular basis, have its generic (scientific) name handy for refills.

Medical care on Easter Island is extremely limited. There is a hospital but the quality of care is unreliable and supplies are often inadequate. Serious medical problems require evacuation to the mainland.

Infectious Diseases & Environmental Hazards

BARTONELLOSIS (OROYA FEVER)

This is carried by sand flies in the arid river valleys on the western slopes of the Andes, between altitudes of 800m and 3000m. (Curiously, it's not found anywhere else in the world.) The chief symptoms are fever and severe body pains. Complications may include marked anemia, enlargement of the liver and spleen, and sometimes death. The drug of choice is chloramphenicol, though doxycycline is also effective.

HANTA VIRUS

A rapidly progressive, life-threatening infection acquired through exposure to the excretion of wild rodents. An outbreak was reported from rural areas in the southern and central parts of Chile in late 2010. Sporadic cases have been reported since that time. The disease occurs in those who live in close association with rodents.

It is unlikely to affect most travelers, though those staying in forest areas may be at risk. Backpackers should never camp in an abandoned *refugio* (rustic shelter), where there may be a risk of exposure to infected excretion. Pitching a tent is the safer option. If backpacking in an area with hanta virus, campers can get more information from ranger stations.

ALTITUDE SICKNESS

Altitude sickness may develop in those who ascend rapidly to altitudes greater than 2500m. Symptoms may include headaches, nausea, vomiting, dizziness, malaise, insomnia and loss of appetite. Severe cases may be complicated by fluid in the lungs (high-altitude pulmonary edema) or swelling of the brain (high-altitude cerebral edema).

The best treatment for altitude sickness is descent. If you are exhibiting symptoms, do not ascend. If symptoms are severe or persistent, descend immediately.

When traveling to high altitudes, it's also important to avoid overexertion, eat light meals and abstain from alcohol. Some high-altitude areas have a clinic where oxygen is available.

CHILEAN RECLUSE SPIDER

Found throughout the country, the Chilean recluse spider is not aggressive. Its venom is very dangerous; reactions can include lesions, renal failure and even death. Chilean recluse spiders are 8mm to 30mm long (including legs) and are identified by their brown color, violin-like markings and unusual six eyes (most spiders have eight). If bitten, put ice on the bite and get immediate medical attention.

WATER

The tap water in Chile's cities is generally safe but has a high mineral content that can cause stomach upsets; bottled water is a good idea for delicate stomachs and in rural areas.

Vigorous boiling for one minute is the most effective

means of water purification. At altitudes greater than 2000m, boil for three minutes. You can also disinfect water with iodine pills, a water filter or Steripen.

Insurance

In general, signing up for a travel-insurance policy is a good idea. For Chile, a basic theft/loss and medical policy is recommended. Read the fine print carefully because some companies exclude dangerous activities from coverage, which can include scuba diving, motorcycling, and even trekking. You may prefer a policy that pays doctors or hospitals directly rather than you having to pay on the spot and make a claim later.

Make copies of all insurance information in the event that the original is lost. For information on health insurance, see opposite and for car insurance, see p470.

Internet Access

Most regions have excellent internet connections and reasonable prices; it is typical for hotels and hostels to have wi-fi or computer terminals. Family guesthouses, particularly outside urban areas, lag behind in this area, though free public wi-fi is available in some communities. Internet cafes can be found pretty well everywhere, even in villages where they provide the only Friday-night entertain-

ment for youth. Rates range from CH$500 to CH$1200 per hour, with very high rates only in remote areas.

In this book, the symbol @ indicates the presence of computer terminals and ⊚ indicates wi-fi access.

Language Courses

Spanish-language courses can be found in major cities and resort areas. For details of schools and programs, see the listings in Santiago (p58), Arica (p147), Iquique (p166), La Serena (p208), Valparaíso (p96) and Puerto Varas (p266). Lonely Planet's *Latin American Spanish Phrasebook* is helpful for beginners.

Legal Matters

Chile's *carabineros* (police) have a reputation for being professional and polite; they cherish the slogan *'siempre un amigo'* (always a friend), although this usually brings a wry smile to the face of motorists. Penalties for common offences are similar to those given in much of Europe and North America. However, the possession, use or trafficking of drugs – including soft drugs such as cannabis – is treated very seriously and results in severe fines and imprisonment.

Police can demand identification at any time, so carry your passport. Throughout the country, the toll-free emergency telephone number for the police is ☏133.

Chileans often refer to police as *pacos*, a disrespectful (though not obscene) term that should *never* be used to a police officer's face.

Members of the military take themselves seriously, so avoid photographing military installations.

If you are involved in any automobile accident, your license (usually your international permit) will be confiscated until the case is

resolved, although local officials will usually issue a temporary driving permit within a few days. A blood-alcohol test is obligatory; purchase a sterile syringe at the hospital or clinic pharmacy when the police take you there. After this, you will be taken to the station to make a statement and then, under most circumstances, released. Ordinarily you cannot leave Chile until the matter is resolved; consult your consulate, insurance carrier and a lawyer at home.

Police do not harass drivers for minor equipment violations but they can be uptight about parking violations. Don't *ever* make the error of attempting to bribe the police, whose reputation for institutional integrity is high.

Maps

In Santiago, the **Instituto Geográfico Militar** (IGM; ☏02-460-6800; www.igm.cl, in Spanish; Dieciocho 369, Centro; ⊙9am-5:30pm Mon-Fri), just south of the Alameda, produces excellent maps, which can be ordered through the website or bought directly. Its *Guía Caminera* is a good highway map, with scales ranging from 1:500,000 to 1:1,500,000. It also produces an easy-to-navigate city street-finder of Santiago, *Guia de Calles de Santiago*, and a map that charts the entire length of the Carretera Austral at a scale of 1:1,000,000. The IGM's 1:50,000 topographic series is valuable for trekkers, although the maps are out of date and those of sensitive border areas (where most national parks are) may not be available.

JLM Mapas publishes good maps for all of the major regions and trekking areas at scales ranging from 1:50,000 to 1:500,000. The maps are widely distributed, easy to use and provide decent information, but they don't claim to be perfectly accurate.

Copec driving guides contain detailed highway maps and excellent plans of Chilean cities, towns and even many villages, though many maps lack scales. The guides are annually updated but published in Spanish only, with separate regional volumes. They are available in Copec gas stations.

In most major Chilean cities the Automóvil Club de Chile (Acchi) has an office that sells highway maps, although not all of them are equally well stocked.

Online maps vary in quality: **Plano Digital de Publiguías** (www.planos.cl, in Spanish) has online city maps but it is a frustrating website to navigate. Santiago maps are available on **Map City** (www.mapcity.cl, in Spanish). Drivers might find maps by **Compass** (www.mapascompass.cl) useful. Some local government websites have interactive maps that allow you to search for a street address in major cities.

Money

The Chilean unit of currency is the peso (CH$). Bank notes come in denominations of 500, 1000, 2000, 5000, 10,000 and 20,000 pesos. Coin values are one, five, 10, 50, 100 and 500 pesos, although one-peso coins are fast disappearing, and even fives and tens are uncommon. Carry small bills with you; it can be difficult to change large bills in rural areas. Gas stations and liquor stores are usually able to, just make an apologetic face and ask, '¿Tiene suelto?'.

Exchange rates are usually best in Santiago, where there is also a ready market for European currencies. Chile's currency has been pretty stable in recent years. The value of the dollar seems to decline during peak tourist season and shoot back up

again come March. Paying a bill with US cash is sometimes acceptable, especially at tour agencies (check their exchange rate carefully). Many top-end hotels publish rates in US dollars with a lower exchange rate than the daily one. It's best to pay all transactions in pesos.

Money transferred by cable should arrive in a few days; Chilean banks can give you money in US dollars on request. Western Union offices can be found throughout Chile, usually adjacent to the post office.

ATMs

Chile's many ATM machines, known as redbanc, are the easiest and most convenient way to access funds. Your bank will likely charge a small fee for each transaction. Most ATMs have instructions in Spanish and English. Choose the option tarjeta extranjera (foreign card) before starting the transaction. You cannot rely on ATMs in San Pedro de Atacama (the one ATM breaks down), Pisco Elqui, Bahía Inglesa or in small Patagonian towns. Throughout Patagonia, many small villages only have one bank, the Banco del Estado, which only accepts MasterCard affiliates at ATMs.

Note that ATMs now charge up to CH$3500 per transaction. Some foreign banks have accounts that will reimburse these fees. Also, withdrawals are limited to a sum of CH$200,000.

Cash

A few banks will exchange cash (usually US dollars only); casas de cambio (exchange houses) in Santiago and more tourist-oriented destinations will also exchange. However, they also charge some commission or have less-agreeable rates. More costly purchases, such as tours and hotel bills, can sometimes be paid in US cash.

Credit Cards

If you've got plastic in your pocket (especially Amex, Visa and MasterCard), you'll be welcome in most established businesses; however, it's best not to depend on credit. Many businesses will charge up to 6% extra to cover the charge they have to pay for the transaction. Credit cards can also be useful to show 'sufficient funds' before entering another South American country.

Tipping

It's customary to tip 10% of the bill in restaurants. Taxi drivers do not require tips, although you may round off the fare for convenience.

Post

Correos de Chile (☑800-267-736; www.correos.cl, in Spanish), Chile's national postal service, has reasonably dependable but sometimes slow postal services. Within Chile, it costs around CH$120 to send a letter.

Receiving Mail

You can receive mail via lista de correos (poste restante; equivalent to general delivery) at any Chilean post office. Some consulates will also hold correspondence for their citizens. To collect your mail from a post office or embassy, you need your passport as proof of identity. Instruct correspondents to address letters clearly and to precede your name with either Señora or Señor, as post offices divide lists of correspondence by gender. There is usually a small charge, about CH$200 per item. Mail is held for one month.

Sending Mail

Chilean post offices are generally open 9am to 6pm Monday to Friday and 9am to noon Saturday. Send important overseas mail certificado (registered) to ensure its arrival; this costs around CH$500. Airmail takes around a week to both Europe and the US.

Sending parcels is straightforward, although a customs official may have to inspect your package before a postal clerk will accept it. Vendors in or near the post office will wrap parcels upon request. International courier services are readily available in Santiago, less so outside the capital.

To send packages within Chile, sending via *encomienda* (the bus system) is much more reliable. Simply take the package to a bus company that goes to the destination. Label the package clearly with the destination and the name of the person who will pick it up, on arrival or from the company's office.

Public Holidays

National holidays, when government offices and businesses are closed, are listed below. There is pressure to reduce these or to eliminate so-called sandwich holidays, which many Chileans take between an actual holiday and the weekend, by moving some to the nearest Monday.

Año Nuevo (New Year) January 1

Semana Santa (Easter Week) March or April

Día del Trabajo (Labor Day) May 1

Glorias Navales Commemorating the naval Battle of Iquique; May 21

Corpus Christi May/June; dates vary

Día de San Pedro y San Pablo (St Peter and St Paul's Day) June 29

Asunción de la Virgen (Assumption) August 15

Día de Unidad Nacional (Day of National Unity) First Monday of September

Día de la Independencia Nacional (National Independence Day) September 18

Día del Ejército (Armed Forces Day) September 19

Día de la Raza (Columbus Day) October 12

Todo los Santos (All Saints' Day) November 1

Inmaculada Concepción (Immaculate Conception) December 8

Navidad (Christmas Day) December 25

Safe Travel

Compared with other South American countries, Chile is remarkably safe. Petty thievery is a problem in larger cities, bus terminals and at beach resorts in summertime, so always keep a close eye on all belongings. Photographing military installations is strictly prohibited.

Dogs & Bugs

Chile's stray canines are a growing problem. Scabies can be common in street dogs; don't pet those that have bad skin problems, it's highly contagious. If driving, be prepared for dogs barking and running after the bumper.

Summertime in the south brings about the pesty *tábano*, a large biting horsefly that is more an annoyance than a health risk. Bring along insect repellent and wear light-colored clothing.

Natural Hazards

Earthquakes are a fact of life for most Chileans. Local construction often does not meet seismic safety standards; adobe buildings tend to be especially vulnerable. The unpredictability of quakes means there is little that a traveler can do to prepare.

Active volcanoes are less likely to threaten safety, since they usually give some warning. Nevertheless, the unexpected eruptions of Volcán Chaitén and Volcán Llaima in 2008 have the country monitoring more closely than ever.

Many of Chile's finest beaches have dangerous offshore rip currents, so ask before diving in and make sure someone on shore knows your whereabouts. Many beaches post signs that say *apto para bañar* (swimming OK) and *no apto para bañar* (swimming not OK) or *peligroso* (dangerous).

In the winter, the smog in Santiago can become a health risk. The city declares 'pre-emergency' or 'emergency' states when the level of smog is dangerously high and takes measures to limit emissions. Children, senior citizens and people with respiratory problems should avoid trips to downtown Santiago at these times.

Personal Security & Theft

Crime is more concentrated in the dense urban areas, though picks up in tourist destinations in summer. Those staying in cabins should close and lock windows before heading out, particularly in popular resort towns. At the beach, be alert for pickpockets and avoid leaving valuables around while you go for a swim. Never leave an unattended car unlocked and keep all valuables in the trunk.

Don't fall for distractions, such as a tap on the shoulder,

GOVERNMENT TRAVEL ADVICE

The following government websites offer travel advisories and information on current hot spots.
Australian Government (www.smartraveller.gov.au)
Canadian Government (www.travel.gc.ca)
UK Foreign & Commonwealth Office (www.fco.gov.uk/en/travel-and-living-abroad)
US State Department (www.travel.state.gov)

spitting or getting something spilled on you; these 'accidents' are often part of a team effort to relieve you of some valuables. Be mindful of your belongings and avoid conspicuous displays of expensive jewelry.

Baggage insurance is a good idea. Do not leave valuables such as cash or cameras in your room. Some travelers bring their own lock. Upmarket hotels often have secure strongboxes in each room.

Senior Travelers

Senior travelers should encounter no particular difficulties traveling in Chile, where older citizens typically enjoy a great deal of respect. On crowded buses, for instance, most Chileans will readily offer their seat to an older person.

Folks over 50 may want to check out tour operators that cater to them. Two of the most established are **Elderhostel** (☎800-454-5768; www.elderhostel.org; Boston, MA) and **Eldertreks** (☎800-741-7956; www.eldertreks.com; Ontario).

Shopping

Chile is one of only two countries in the world where the semiprecious stone lapiz lazuli is found. It is a deep navy-blue color and makes sophisticated jewelry that can be bought in most Chilean jewelers and a few *ferias* (artisans' markets). However, this unique stone can empty your wallet in a flash: expect a pair of good-quality earrings to cost around CH$20,000. Check the quality of the setting and silver used – they are often only silver plated and very soft.

Craft markets can be found throughout the country. In the north, artisans put shaggy llama and alpaca wool to good use by making thick jumpers, scarves,

and other garments to take the bite off the frigid highland nights. Many of these goods are similar to those in Bolivia and Peru. You'll also see crafts made with cactus wood, and painstakingly crafted leather goods in Norte Chico.

In Chiloé and Patagonia, hand-knit woolens such as bulky fishermen's sweaters and blankets are reasonably priced and useful in winter. In the Araucanía, look for jewelry based on Mapuche designs, which are unique to Chile. They also produce quality weavings and basketry. In the Lakes District and Patagonia, artisans carve wooden plates and bowls out of the (sustainable) hardwood raulí.

Wine lovers will not want for Chilean wines to choose from: stick to the boutique wineries with wines that you can't find in your own country, or pick up bottles of the powerful grape-brandy pisco, which is difficult to find outside of Chile. Other artisanal edibles include *miel de ulmo*, a very aromatic and tasty honey special to Patagonia, and *mermelada de murtilla*, a jam made of a tart red berry. As long as such goods are still sealed, there shouldn't be a problem getting through international customs.

Many cities have good antiques markets, most notably Santiago's Mercado Franklin and Valparaíso's Plaza O'Higgins. Flea markets are commonly known as *ferias persas* (Persian fairs).

For a preview, check out the website of **Fundación Artesanías de Chile** (Chilean Craft Foundation; www.artesaniasdechile.cl) to see a selection of local *artesanía*.

Bargaining

Buying items in a crafts market is the only acceptable time to bargain. Transport and accommodation rates are generally fixed and prominently displayed. Moreover, Chileans can be

easily offended by aggressive haggling as it isn't part of the culture.

Solo Travelers

Solo travelers will have no trouble avoiding or hooking up with companions as the mood strikes them. Chileans are generally more reserved than other Latin Americans but they are friendly and eager to help if you strike up a conversation. Inexpensive hostels with communal kitchens encourage social exchange, while a large number of language schools, tours and volunteer organizations provide travelers with an opportunity to meet others. However, it isn't recommended to undertake long treks in the wilderness by yourself.

Telephone

Throughout Chile there are call centers with private cabins and reasonable international rates, although these are rapidly being replaced by internet cafes with Skype. Remote tour operators and lodges have satellite phones with a Santiago prefix.

Cell Phones

Cell-phone numbers have eight digits, plus the two-digit prefix ☎09. The prefix must be used when calling from a land line or Skype-type calling service. Throughout this book, cell numbers are listed with their prefix. Drop the ☎09 prefix when calling cell-to-cell. If calling cell-to-landline, add the landline's area code.

Cell phones sell for as little as CH$12,000 and can be charged up by prepaid phone cards. Cell phones have a 'caller-pays' format. Calls between cell and landlines are expensive and quickly eat up prepaid card amounts.

Do your homework if you want to bring your own cell phone: you'll need a SIM-unlocked GSM-compatible phone that operates on a frequency of 850MHz or 1900MHz (commonly used in the US). If you have such a phone you can buy a new SIM card from a Chilean operator such as Entel or Movistar. Then purchase phone credit from the same carrier in kiosks or at supermarket check-outs. Movistar offers unlimited emails for Blackberries, charged at a reasonable monthly rate. Note that if you will spend a lot of time in Patagonia, Entel has much better coverage than other companies.

You'll get reception in most inhabited areas but reception is scarce in the middle of the Atacama Desert and in parts of Patagonia.

Phone Codes

Chile's country code is ⌨56. All telephone numbers in Santiago and the Metropolitan Region have seven digits; all other telephone numbers have six digits except for certain toll-free and emergency numbers. The toll-free number for the police is ⌨133, ambulance is ⌨131. You'll reach directory assistance at ⌨103.

Long-distance calls are based on a carrier system: to place a call, precede the number with the telephone company's code: **Entel** (⌨123), for example. To make a collect call, dial ⌨182 to get an operator.

Time

For most of the year, Chile is four hours behind GMT, but from mid-December to late March, because of daylight-saving time (summer time), the difference is three hours. The exact date of the changeover varies from year to year. Because of Chile's great latitudinal range, the summer sunrise in the desert tropics of Arica, where the durations of day and night are roughly equal throughout the year, occurs after 8am. Easter Island is two hours behind the mainland. Chileans commonly use the 24-hour clock.

Toilets

Pipes and sewer systems in older buildings are quite fragile: used toilet paper should be discarded in wastebaskets. Cheaper accommodations and public toilets rarely provide toilet paper, so carry your own wherever you go. Better restaurants and cafes are good alternatives to public toilets, which are often dirty.

Tourist Information

Every regional capital and some other cities have a local representative of **Sernatur** (⌨02-731-8310; www.chile.travel/en.html), the national tourist service. Offices vary in usefulness – some have astonishingly knowledgeable multilingual staff, but others bury visitors in dusty brochures and leaflets instead of actually answering their questions.

Many municipalities also have their own tourist office, usually on the main plaza or at the bus terminal. In some areas, these offices may be open during the summer only.

Some official international representatives for Chilean

tourism can be found abroad. Consulates in major cities may have a tourist representative, but more accessible and comprehensive information can be found through specialized travel agencies and on the internet.

Chile has a few general travel agencies that work with affiliates around the world. **Chilean Travel Service** (CTS; ⌨02-251-0400; www.ctsturismo.cl; Antonio Bellet 77, Providencia, Santiago) has well-informed multilingual staff and can organize accommodations and tours all over Chile through your local travel agency.

Travelers With Disabilities

Travel within Chile is still a robust challenge for those with disabilities, though patient planning can open a lot of doors. Even top-end hotels and resorts cannot be relied upon to have ramps or rooms adapted for those with impaired mobility; an estimated 10% of hotels in Santiago cater to wheelchairs. Lifts are more common in large hotels and the law now requires new public buildings to provide disabled access.

Santiago's **Metro** (www.metrosantiago.cl, in Spanish) is in the process of making subway lines more accessible. At present, Línea 5 and Línea 4 have been refitted, as well as the extensions of Líneas 2 and 5, the *línea* to Maipú and the extension of Línea 1 to Plaza Los Dominicos. Public bus company **Transantiago** (www.transantiago.cl, in Spanish) has access ramps and spaces for wheelchairs on new buses. Some street lights have noise-indicated crossings for the blind. Those in wheelchairs will find Chile's narrow and poorly maintained sidewalks awkward to negotiate. Crossing streets is also tricky, but most Chilean drivers are remarkably courteous toward pedestrians – especially those with obvious handicaps.

Santiago's **Tixi Service** (☎toll-free 800-372-300, 02-481-3235; www.tixi.cl, in Spanish) has taxi vans which cater to disabled individuals, with hydraulic elevators to accommodate wheelchairs. American organization **Accessible Journeys** (☎in USA 800-846-4537; www.disabilitytravel.com) organizes independent travel to Chile for people with disabilities.

National parks are often discounted and sometimes free for disabled visitors (check ahead with Conaf). Cruises or ferries such as Navimag sometimes offer free upgrades to disabled travelers, and some of the ski resorts near Santiago have outrigger poles for disabled skiers.

Visas

Nationals of the US, Canada, Australia and the EU do not need a visa to visit Chile. Passports are obligatory and are essential for cashing traveler's checks, checking into hotels and other routine activities.

The Chilean government collects a US$140/95/140 'reciprocity' fee from arriving US/Australian/Canadian citizens in response to these governments imposing a similar fee on Chilean citizens applying for visas. The payment applies only to tourists arriving by air in Santiago and is valid for the life of the passport. Payment must be made in cash; exact change necessary.

It is advisable to carry your passport: Chile's police can demand identification at any moment, and many hotels require you to show it upon check-in.

If your passport is lost or stolen, notify the police, ask them for a police statement,

and notify your consulate as soon as possible.

Tourist Cards

On arrival, you'll be handed a 90-day tourist card. Don't lose it! If you do, go to the **Policía Internacional** (☎02-737-1292; Gral Borgoño 1052, Santiago; ⏰8:30am-5pm Mon-Fri) or the nearest police station. You will be asked for it upon leaving the country.

It costs US$100 to renew a tourist card for 90 more days at the **Departamento de Extranjería** (☎02-550-2484; www.extranjeria.gob.cl; Agustinas 1235, 2nd fl, Santiago; ⏰8:30am-2pm Mon-Fri). Take with you photocopies of your passport and tourist card. You can also visit the Departamento de Extranjería in any of Chile's regional capitals. Many visitors prefer a quick dash across the Argentine border and back.

Volunteering

Experienced outdoor guides may be able to exchange labor for accommodations during the busy high season, if you can stick out the entire season. Language schools often place students in volunteer work as well. At Parque Nacional Torres del Paine, volunteers can help with trail maintenance, biological studies or an animal census. Spanish-language skills are always a plus.

AMA Torres del Paine (www.amatorresdelpaine.org) Located in the national park, works with a limited number of volunteers.

Experiment Chile (www.experiment.cl) Organizes 14-week language-learning/volunteer programs.

Global Community Project (www.globalcommunityproject.blogspot.com) USA-based outfit that takes

student-exchange volunteers with advance notice.

Go Voluntouring (www.govoluntouring.com) International organization that consolidates listings from various NGOs, such as Earthwatch, in addition to social and teaching programs.

Renace (Red Nacional de Acción Ecológica; www.renace.cl, in Spanish) Publishes the annual *Directorio de Organizaciones Miembros* which lists environmental organizations.

Un Techo Para Chile (www.untechoparachile.cl, in Spanish) Nonprofit organization that builds homes for low-income families throughout the country.

Work

It's increasingly difficult to obtain residence and work permits for Chile. Consequently, many foreigners do not bother to do so, but the most reputable employers will insist on the proper visa. If you need one, go to the **Departamento de Extranjería** (☎02-550-2484; Agustinas 1235, Santiago; ⏰8:30am-2pm Mon-Fri).

In Santiago, many youth hostels offer work, an offer usually stated on their websites. **Contact Chile** (www.contactchile.cl) lists internship opportunities online, they are mainly in the service sector. It is not unusual for visiting travelers to work as English-language instructors in Santiago. Industries with an international trading focus, such as salmon farming and fishmeal processing, have a growing need for English-language instruction around Puerto Montt. In general, wages aren't very good and full-time employment is hard to come by without a commitment to stay for some time.

Transportation

GETTING THERE & AWAY

Entering the Country

Most short-term travelers touch down in Santiago, while those on a South American odyssey come via bus from Peru, boat or bus from Argentina, or 4WD trip from Bolivia. Entry is generally straightforward as long as your passport is valid for at least six months beyond your arrival date. For general information on visas and tourist tickets, see p462.

Onward Tickets

Chile requires a return or onward ticket for travelers who are arriving, and officials sometimes ask for evidence of an onward ticket. Not having an onward ticket can also pose a problem at the flight counter in your departure country. If the agent is a stickler, they can refuse to board you. The solution is to either purchase a refundable return air ticket or get the cheapest possible onward bus ticket from a bus company that offers online sales and print your receipt.

Air

Chile has direct connections with North America, the UK, Europe, Australia and New Zealand, in addition to its neighboring countries. International flights within South America tend to be fairly expensive unless they are purchased as part of intercontinental travel, but there are bargain round-trip fares between Buenos Aires or Lima and Santiago.

Airports & Airlines

Most long-distance flights to Chile arrive at Santiago, landing at **Aeropuerto Internacional Arturo Merino Benítez** (☎02-690-1752; www.aeropuertosantiago.cl) in the suburb of Pudahuel. There are also flights from neighboring countries to regional airports such as Arica, Iquique, Temuco and Punta Arenas.

Many major national and international airlines have offices or representatives in Santiago.

Aerolíneas Argentinas (www.aerolineas.com.ar)

Air Canada (www.aircanada.com)

Air France (www.airfrance.com)

Alitalia (www.alitalia.com)

American Airlines (www.aa.com)

Avianca (www.avianca.com)

British Airways (www.britishairways.com)

Copa (www.copaair.com)

Delta (www.delta.com)

Gol (www.voegol.com)

Iberia (www.iberia.com)

Lan (www.lan.com) See p467 for addresses.

Lufthansa (www.lufthansa.com)

Taca (www.taca.com)

United Airlines (www.united.com)

CLIMATE CHANGE & TRAVEL

Every form of transport that relies on carbon-based fuel generates CO_2, the main cause of human-induced climate change. Modern travel is dependent on airplanes, which might use less fuel per kilometer per person than most cars but travel much greater distances. The altitude at which aircraft emit gases (including CO_2) and particles also contributes to their climate change impact. Many websites offer 'carbon calculators' that allow people to estimate the carbon emissions generated by their journey and, for those who wish to do so, to offset the impact of the greenhouse gases emitted with contributions to portfolios of climate-friendly initiatives throughout the world. Lonely Planet offsets the carbon footprint of all staff and author travel.

DEPARTURE TAX & ARRIVAL FEES

The Chilean departure tax for international flights of under/over 500km is US$8/26 or its equivalent in local currency.

Note that *arriving* US air passengers pay a one-time fee of US$140, valid for the life of the passport. Chilean authorities imposed this fee after US officials increased a visa application fee for Chilean nationals, and have since applied a similar system to Australians (US$95) and Canadians (US$140). This must be paid in cash and in US dollars or Chilean pesos. Also note that the officials collecting the fee most often won't have change; bring exact cash if possible.

Tickets

To cut ticket costs, take advantage of seasonal discounts and avoid peak times, such as Christmas, New Year or Easter. You will probably find the best deal if you purchase your airline tickets in advance.

INTERCONTINENTAL (RTW) TICKETS

Most intercontinental airlines traveling to Chile also offer round-the-world (RTW) tickets in conjunction with the airlines they have alliances with. Other companies, such as **Airtreks** (☑North America 415-977-7100, toll-free 877-247-8735; www.airtreks.com), offer more flexible, customized RTW tickets that don't tie you into airline affiliates. Similar 'Circle Pacific' fares allow you to take excursions between Australasia and Chile, often with a stop at Easter Island. Check the fine print carefully for any restrictions that may apply. The following websites advertise RTW tickets:

Airfare (www.airfare.com.au)

Ebookers (www.ebookers.com)

Flight Centre (www.flightcentre.com)

STA (www.statravel.com)

Trailfinders (www.trailfinders.co.uk)

Travel Bag (www.travelbag.co.uk)

Australia & New Zealand

Lan and Qantas share a flight from Sydney to Santiago, stopping in Auckland. **Lan** (☑1300-361-400; 64 York St, Sydney) also has an office in Australia.

Canada

Air Canada flies to Santiago from Toronto, or connect via US cities with other airlines.

Continental Europe

There are regular direct flights from Madrid to Santiago with Lan and Iberia, and several airlines have flights from major European cities via Argentina or Brazil, including Lufthansa. **STA Travel** (www.statravel.com) has offices in Austria, Denmark, Finland, Sweden, Switzerland and Germany.

French Polynesia

Lan flies once a week to and from Papeete, Tahiti, stopping in Easter Island.

South America

Many airlines fly daily between Santiago and Buenos Aires, Argentina, for a standard fare of about US$250 round-trip. However, European airlines that pick up and discharge most of their passengers in Buenos Aires sometimes try to fill empty seats by selling cheap round-trips between the Argentine and Chilean capitals.

There are reasonable Lan flights from Santiago to Mendoza (round-trip US$150, twice daily) and to Córdoba (round-trip US$185, twice daily).

Lan and Taca have numerous daily flights from Lima, Peru, to Santiago for about US$450 (round-trip), and many discount fares pop up on this route. From Lima, Lan also goes direct to Easter Island. Lan also flies from Lima to the southern city of Tacna, only 50km from the Chilean border city of Arica, for CH$150,000 one way. Lan flies daily from Santiago to La Paz (round-trip US$300) with a stop in northern Chile.

Taca and Avianca link Santiago with Bogotá, Colombia, daily (round-trip US$600), sometimes with another South American stop. Lan flies to Montevideo, the Uruguayan capital (round-trip US$300). Gol and TAM fly to Brazilian and Paraguayan destinations.

Recommended agencies: **ASATEJ** (☑011-4114-7544; www.asatej.com) In Argentina. **Student Travel Bureau** (☑011-3038-1555; www.stb.com.br) In Brazil.

UK & Ireland

At the time of writing there were no direct flights between London and Santiago. Connections from the UK go through Madrid, Buenos Aires and the US. Prices average between £760 and £900, depending on the time of year. **Journey Latin America** (☑020-8747-3108; www.journeylatinamerica.co.uk) is a reputable agency.

USA

From the USA, the principal gateways to South America are Miami, New York, Los Angeles, Atlanta and Dallas. For those who plan to travel in the Atacama Desert, one time-saving alternative to landing in Santiago is to fly to Lima, Peru, and on to the Peruvian border city of Tacna, or to Arica (in northern Chile). **Exito** (www.exitotravel.com) is recommended for online bookings.

Land

Border Crossings

Chile's northern border touches Peru and Bolivia, while its vast eastern boundary hugs Argentina. Of the numerous border crossings with Argentina, only a few are served by public transportation. Most international buses depart from Terminal de Buses in Santiago.

For more information on visas, see p462

Bus

There are buses to almost every country on the continent, but only masochists are likely to attempt the 4½- to 10-day marathons to destinations like Quito, Ecuador and Caracas, Venezuela. Common destinations are served by the following bus companies, all located in the **Terminal de Buses Santiago** (www.terminaldebuses santiago.cl):

ARGENTINA

Andesmar (☎02-779-6839; www.andesmar.com) Mendoza.

Buses Ahumada (☎02-784-2515) Buenos Aires.

Cata (☎02-779-3660; www.catainternacional.com) Mendoza.

Crucero del Norte (☎02-776-2416; www.crucerodel norte.com.ar) Also goes to Brazil and Paraguay.

El Rápido (☎02-779-0316; www.elrapidoint.com.ar) Also goes to Uruguay.

Via Bariloche (www.viabar iloche.com.ar) Bariloche from Chilean Lakes District.

BRAZIL

Chilebus Internacional (☎02-776-5557)

Pluma (☎02-779-6054; www.pluma.com.br)

PERU

Ormeño (☎02-779-3443) Also goes to Ecuador and Argentina.

Tas-Choapa (☎02-776-7307; www.taschoapa.cl) Lima, also goes to Argentina.

See the table below for sample bus costs and trip times.

From Terminal Santiago, travelers can also ask about less frequent *colectivos* (shared taxis) to Mendoza (CH$15,000) with **Chi-Ar** (☎02-776-0048). Drivers may stop on request for photo opportunities on the spectacular Andean crossing.

Car & Motorcycle

There can be additional charges and confusing paperwork if you're taking a hired car out of Chile; ask the rental agency to talk you through it. See p469 for road rules and further information about fuel and insurance.

From Argentina

Unless you're crossing from Chile's extreme south there's no way to avoid the Andes. Public transportation is offered on only a few of the crossings to Argentina, and many passes close in winter.

NORTHERN ROUTES

Calama to Jujuy and Salta A popular year-round route over the Andes via San Pedro de Atacama, Ruta 27 goes over the Paso de Jama. It has a regular bus service (with advance booking highly advisable). Slightly further south, on Ruta 23, motorists will find the 4079m Paso de Lago Sico a rougher but passable summer alternative. Chilean customs are at San Pedro de Atacama.

Iquique to Oruro A few scattered bus services run along a paved road from Iquique past the Parque Nacional Volcán Isluga to the Paso Colchane; catch a truck or bus on to Oruru from here (on an unpaved road).

Copiapó to Catamarca and La Rioja There is no public transportation over the 4726m Paso de San Francisco; it's a dirt road which requires high clearance, but rewards with spectacular scenery – including the luminous Laguna Verde.

La Serena to San Juan Dynamited by the Argentine military during the Beagle Channel dispute of 1978–79, the 4779m Paso del Agua Negra is a beautiful route, but the road is unpaved beyond Guanta and buses eschew it. It is a good bicycle route and tours run to hot springs that are on the Argentine side.

SAMPLE BUS COSTS & TRIP TIMES

DESTINATION	COST (CH$)	DURATION (HR)
Asunción, Paraguay	$59,000	45
Buenos Aires, Argentina	$60,000	22
Córdoba, Argentina	$32,000	17
Lima, Peru	$80,000	48
Mendoza, Argentina	$27,000	7
Montevideo, Uruguay	$56,000	32
Río de Janeiro, Brazil	$98,000	72
São Paulo, Brazil	$55,000	55

MIDDLE CHILE

Santiago or Valparaíso to Mendoza and Buenos Aires
A dozen or more bus companies service this beautiful and vital lifeline to Argentina, along Ruta 60 through the Los Libertadores tunnel. Winter snow sometimes closes the route, but rarely for long.

Talca to Malargüe and San Rafael
There's no public transportation through Ruta 115 to cross the 2553m Paso Pehuenche, southeast of Talca. Another crossing from Curicó over the 2502m Paso Vergara is being developed but is still hard to access.

SOUTHERN MAINLAND ROUTES
Several scenic crossings squeeze through to Argentina from Temuco south to Puerto Montt, some involving bus-boat shuttles that are popular in summer (book ahead).

Temuco to Zapala and Neuquén
A good road crosses over the 1884m Paso de Pino Hachado, directly east of Temuco along the upper Río Biobío. A secondary unpaved route just south of here is the 1298m Paso de Icalma, with occasional bus traffic in summer.

Temuco to San Martín de los Andes
The most popular route from Temuco passes Lago Villarrica, Pucón and Curarrehue en route to the Paso de Mamuil Malal (known to Argentines as Paso Tromen). On the Argentine side, the road skirts the northern slopes of Volcán Lanín. There is a regular summer bus service, but the pass may close in winter.

Valdivia to San Martín de los Andes
This mix-and-match route starts with a bus from Valdivia to Panguipulli, Choshuenco and Puerto Fuy, followed by a ferry across Lago Pirihueico to the village of Pirihueico. From Pirihueico a local bus goes to Argentine customs at 659m Paso Huahum, where travelers can catch a bus to San Martín.

Osorno to Bariloche via Paso Cardenal Samoré
This crossing, commonly known as Pajaritos, is the quickest land route in the southern Lakes District, passing through Parque Nacional Puyehue on the Chilean side and Parque Nacional Nahuel Huapi on the Argentine side. It has a frequent bus service all year.

Puerto Varas to Bariloche
Very popular in summer but open all year, this bus-ferry combination via Parque Nacional Vicente Pérez Rosales starts in Puerto Varas. A ferry goes from Petrohué, at the western end of Lago Todos Los Santos, to Peulla, and a bus crosses 1022m Paso de Pérez Rosales to Argentine immigration at Puerto Frías. After crossing Lago Frías by launch, there's a short bus hop to Puerto Blest on Lago Nahuel Huapi and another ferry to Puerto Pañuelo (Llao Llao). From Llao Llao there is a frequent bus service to Bariloche.

SOUTHERN PATAGONIAN ROUTES

Puerto Ramírez to Esquel
There are two options here. From Villa Santa Lucía on the Carretera Austral, a good lateral road forks at Puerto Ramírez. The north fork goes to Futaleufú, where a bridge crosses the river to the Argentine side with *colectivos* to Esquel. The south fork goes to Palena and Argentine customs at Carrenleufú, with less-frequent buses to Trevelin and Esquel. The more efficient crossing is Futaleufú.

Coyhaique to Comodoro Rivadavia
There are several buses per week, often heavily booked, from Coyhaique to Comodoro Rivadavia via Río Mayo. For private vehicles, there is an alternative route from Balmaceda to Perito Moreno via the 502m Paso Huemules.

Chile Chico to Los Antiguos
From Puerto Ibáñez take the ferry to Chile Chico on the southern shore of Lago Carrera and a shuttle bus to Los Antiguos, which has connections to Atlantic coastal towns and Ruta 40. There is bus service to Chile Chico from Cruce el Maitén at the southwestern end of Lago General Carrera.

Cochrane to Bajo Caracoles
Linking Valle Chacabuco (Parque Nacional Patagonia), 647m Paso Roballos links Cochrane with a flyspeck outpost in Argentina's Santa Cruz province.

Puerto Natales to Río Turbio and El Calafate
Frequent year-round buses connect Puerto Natales to Río Gallegos and El Calafate via Río Turbio. Buses from Puerto Natales go direct to El Calafate, the gateway to Parque Nacional Los Glaciares, via Paso Río Don Guillermo.

Punta Arenas to Río Gallegos
Many buses travel between Punta Arenas and Río Gallegos. It's a five- to eight-hour trip because of slow customs checks and a rough segment of Argentine Ruta Nacional (RN) 3.

Punta Arenas to Tierra del Fuego
From Punta Arenas a 2½-hour ferry trip or a 10-minute flight takes you to Porvenir, on Chilean Tierra del Fuego, but there are currently no buses which continue to the Argentine side. The best option is direct buses from Punta Arenas to Ushuaia via Primera Angostura, with shorter and more frequent ferry service.

Puerto Williams to Ushuaia
Year-round passenger boat service from Puerto Williams, on Isla Navarino (reached by plane or boat from Punta Arenas), to the Argentine city of Ushuaia is weather dependent.

From Bolivia
Road connections between Bolivia and Chile have im-

proved, with a paved highway running from Arica to La Paz. The route from Iquique to Colchane is also paved – although the road beyond to Oruro is not. There are buses on both routes, but more on the former.

It's possible to travel from Uyuni, Bolivia, to San Pedro de Atacama via the Portezuelo del Cajón on organized jeep trips.

From Peru

Tacna to Arica is the only overland crossing, with a choice of bus, colectivo, taxi or train. For details, see p153.

GETTING AROUND

Traveling from head to tail in Chile is easy, with a constant procession of flights and buses connecting cities up and down the country. What is less convenient is the service widthwise and south of Puerto Montt, where the country turns into a labyrinth of fjords, glaciers and mountains. However, routes are improving.

Air

Time-saving flights have become more affordable in Chile and are sometimes cheaper than a comfortable long-distance bus. Consider flying from Arica to Santiago in a few short hours, compared to a crippling 28 hours on board a bus. Other than slow ferries, flights are often the only way to reach isolated southern regions in a timely manner. Always get quotes for round-trip fares since they're often cheaper.

Airlines in Chile

There are two principal domestic airlines within Chile.

Lan (☑600-526-2000; www. lan.com) Centro (Paseo Huérfanos 926-B); Las Condes (Av El Bosque Norte 0194); Providencia (Providencia 2006) The

dominant carrier of South America, with the most extensive system of connecting cities, including flights to Easter Island.

Sky Airline (☑600-600-2828; www.skyairline.cl; Huerfanos 815) Can be cheaper.

Regional airlines and air taxis connect isolated regions in the south and the Juan Fernández archipelago. See regional chapters for details.

Most Chilean cities are near domestic airports with commercial air service. Santiago's Aeropuerto Internacional Arturo Merino Benítez has a separate domestic terminal; Santiago also has smaller airfields for air-taxi services to the Juan Fernández archipelago.

For domestic flights, tickets include departure tax.

Air Passes

The best rates with Lan are found on its Chilean website, accessed only in-country, where weekly specials give cut-rate deals with as much as 40% off, especially on well-traveled routes such as Puerto Montt to Punta Arenas. Booking ahead and buying round-trips can save some money.

LanPass offers miles on the One World alliance, with partners such as American Airlines, British Airways, Iberia and Qantas.

DESTINATION	COST (ROUND-TRIP, CH$)
Antofagasta	125,000
Arica	168,000
Calama	125,000
Concepción	75,000
Copiapó	70,000
Coyhaique	125,000
Iquique	130,000
La Serena	65,000
Puerto Montt	80,000
Punta Arenas	150,000
Temuco	85,000

Bicycle

To peddle your way through Chile, a todo terreno (mountain bike) or touring bike with beefy tires is essential. The climate can be a real challenge: from Temuco south, you must be prepared for rain and occasional snow; from Santiago north, especially in the vast expanses of the Atacama Desert, water sources are infrequent and towns are separated by long distances. In some areas the wind can slow your progress to a crawl; north to south is generally easier than south to north, but some readers report strong headwinds southbound in summer. Chilean motorists are usually courteous, but on narrow two-lane highways without shoulders, passing cars can be a real hazard.

Car ferries in Patagonia often charge a bicycle fee. Most towns outside the Carretera Austral have bike-repair shops. Buses will usually take bikes though airlines may charge extra; check with your airline for details.

Hire

Most of Chile's more touristy towns rent bikes, although their quality may vary. There are relatively few bike-rental shops, but hospedajes (budget accommodations) and tour agencies often have a few handy. Expect to pay between CH$5000 and CH$10,000 per day. A quality mountain bike with front suspension and decent brakes can cost CH$15,000 per day or more, but you're only likely to find them in outdoor activity destinations such as the Lakes District and San Pedro de Atacama.

It's common to leave some form of deposit or guarantee: an ID will often suffice.

Purchase

Bikes are not especially cheap in Chile. A decent mountain bike with suspension sells for CH$100,000 and up. If you're looking to sell your wheels at the end of your trip, try approaching tour agencies that rent bikes.

Boat

Chile's preposterously long coastline is strung with a necklace of ports and harbors, but opportunities for travelers to get about by boat are concentrated in the south.

Navigating southern Chile's jigsaw-puzzle coast by ferry is about more than just getting from A to B – it's an essential part of the travel experience. From Puerto Montt south, Chilean Patagonia and Tierra del Fuego are accessed by ferries traveling the intricate maze of islands and fjords with spectacular coastal scenery.

Note that the end of the high season also marks limited ferry service.

Navimag's ferry service that runs from Puerto Montt to Puerto Natales (see p280) is one of the continent's great travel experiences. The following information lists only the principal passenger-ferry services. Also on offer are a few exclusive tour operators that run their own cruises; see p471. More details about the routes listed below are given under the respective destination sections.

Naviera Austral (☎065-270-430; www.navieraustral.cl, in Spanish; Angelmó 2187, Puerto Montt)

Naviera Sotramin (☎067-237-958; Cerda 647, Coyhaique)

Navimag (☎02-442-3120; www.navimag.com; Av El Bosque Norte 0440, 11th fl, Las Condes)

Transbordador Austral Broom (☎061-218-100; www.tabsa.cl; Av Bulnes 05075, Punta Arenas)

Transmarchilay (☎065-270-000; www.transmarchilay.cl, in Spanish; Angelmó 2187, Puerto Montt)

Common routes include:

Castro to Laguna San Rafael Navimag cruises *Mare Australis* to the stunning Laguna San Rafael.

Chiloé to Chaitén Transmarchilay, Naviera Austral and Navimag run between Quellón, on Chiloé, and Chaitén in summer. There are also summer services from Castro to Chaitén.

Hornopirén to Caleta Gonzalo In summer, Naviera Austral ferries take the Ruta Bi-Modal, two ferries linked by a short land stretch in the middle, to Parque Pumalín's Caleta Gonzalo, about 60km north of Chaitén.

La Arena to Puelche Ferries shuttle back and forth across the gap, about 45km southeast of Puerto Montt, to connect two northerly segments of the Carretera Austral.

Mainland to Chiloé Regular ferries plug the gap between Pargua and Chacao, at the northern tip of Chiloé.

Puerto Ibáñez to Chile Chico Sotramin operates automobile/passenger ferries across Lago General Carrera, south of Coyhaique. There are shuttles from Chile Chico to the Argentine town of Los Antiguos.

Puerto Montt to Chaitén Naviera Austral runs car-passenger ferries from Puerto Montt to Chaitén.

Puerto Montt to Laguna San Rafael Expensive cruises with Catamaranes del Sur and Cruceros Skorpios go direct to take a twirl about Laguna San Rafael.

Puerto Montt to Puerto Chacabuco Navimag goes from Puerto Montt to Puerto Chacabuco; buses continue on to Coyhaique and Parque Nacional Laguna San Rafael.

Puerto Montt to Puerto Natales Navimag departs Puerto Montt weekly, taking about four days to puddle-jump to Puerto Natales. Erratic Patagonian weather can play havoc with schedules.

Puerto Williams to Ushuaia This most necessary connection still has no regular ferry but does have regular motorboat service.

Punta Arenas to Tierra del Fuego Transbordador Austral Broom runs ferries from Punta Arenas' ferry terminal Tres Puentes to Porvenir; from Punta Delgada, east of Punta Arenas, to Bahía Azul; and from Tres Puentes to Puerto Williams, on Isla Navarino.

Bus

Long-distance buses in Chile have an enviable reputation for punctuality, efficiency and comfort, although prices and classes vary significantly between companies. Most Chilean cities have a central bus terminal but in some the companies have separate offices. The bus stations are well organized with destinations, schedules and fares prominently displayed. Major highways and some others are paved (except for large parts of the Carretera Austral), but many secondary roads are gravel or dirt. Long-distance buses generally have toilet facilities and often serve coffee, tea and even meals on board; if not, they make regular stops. By European or North American standards, fares are inexpensive. On Chile's back roads transportation is slower and *micros* (buses) are less frequent, older and more basic.

The nerve center of the country, Santiago, has four main bus terminals, from which buses leave to northern, central and southern destinations.

Chile's biggest bus company is **Tur Bus** (☎600-660-6600; www.turbus.cl), with an all-embracing network of services around the country. It is known for being extremely punctual. Discounts are given for tickets purchased online (later retrieve your ticket at the counter).

Its main competitor is **Pullman** (☑600-320-3200; www.pullman.cl), which also has extensive routes throughout the country.

Specifically aimed at backpackers, **Pachamama by Bus** (☑02-688-8018; www.pachamamabybus.com; Agustinas 2113, Barrio Brasil, Santiago) is a hop-on hop-off service with two long routes exploring the north and south respectively. It's not cheap (for example, it costs CH$119,000 for a seven-day pass in the south), but it takes you straight to many out-of-the-way national parks and other attractions not accessible by public transport. It also offers pick-up and drop-off at your chosen hostel, and camping equipment at isolated overnight stops.

Argentina's **Chalten Travel** (www.chaltentravel.com) provides transportation between El Calafate and Torres del Paine and on Argentina's Ruta 40.

Classes

An array of bewildering names denotes the different levels of comfort on long-distance buses. For a classic experience, *clásico* or *pullman* has around 46 ordinary seats that barely recline, two on each side of the aisle. Don't expect great bathrooms. The next step up is *executivo* and then comes *semi-cama,* both usually mean around 38 seats, providing extra leg room and calf rests. *Semi-cama* has plusher seats that recline more fully and buses are sometimes double-decker. The pinnacle of luxury, *salón cama* sleepers seat only 24 passengers, with only three seats per row that almost fully recline. Superexclusive infrequent *premium* services enjoy seats that flatten with fold-down leg rests to resemble a flat bed. Note that movie quality does not improve with comfort level. On overnighters breakfast is usually included but you can save a few bucks by not ordering dinner and bringing a deli picnic. If you have any doubt about the type of service offered, ask for a seating diagram.

Normally departing at night, the *salón cama* and *premium* bus services cost upwards of 50% more than ordinary buses, but you'll be thankful on long-haul trips. Regular buses are also comfortable, especially in comparison to neighboring Peru and Bolivia. Smoking is prohibited on all buses.

Costs

Fares vary dramatically among companies and classes, so shop around. *Ofertas* (promotions) outside the high summer season can reduce normal fares by half and student fares by 25%. For more information, see p76.

Reservations

Except during the holiday season (Christmas, January, February, Easter and mid-September's patriotic holidays) or on Fridays and Sundays, it is rarely necessary to book more than a few hours in advance. On very long trips, like Arica to Santiago, or rural routes with limited services (along the Carretera Austral, for instance), advance booking is a good idea.

Car & Motorcycle

Having your own wheels is often necessary to get to remote national parks and off the beaten track, especially in the Atacama Desert and the Carretera Austral. Security problems are minor, but always lock your vehicle and leave valuables out of sight. Note that, because of smog problems, Santiago and the surrounding region have frequent restrictions (see p470).

The annual Copec guides (p457) are a good source of recent changes, particularly with regard to newly paved roads.

Automobile Associations

The **Automóvil Club de Chile** (Acchi; ☑600-464-4040, 02-431-1000; www.automovilclub.cl; Andres Bello 1863, Santiago) has offices in most major Chilean cities, provides useful information, sells highway maps and rents cars. It also offers member services and grants discounts to members of its foreign counterparts, such as the American Automobile Association (AAA) in the USA or the Automobile Association (AA) in the UK. Membership includes free towing and other roadside services within 25km of an Automóvil Club office.

Bring Your Own Vehicle

It's possible to ship an overseas vehicle to Chile but costs are high. Check your local phone directory under Automobile Transporters. When shipping, do not leave anything of value in the vehicle.

Permits for temporarily imported tourist vehicles may be extended beyond the initial 90-day period, but it can be easier to cross the border into Argentina and return with new paperwork.

For shipping a car from Chile back to your home country, try the consolidator **Ultramar** (☑02-630-1000; www.ultramar.cl).

Driver's License

Bring along an International Driving Permit (IDP) as well as the license from your home country. Some rental-car agencies don't require an IDP. Police at highway checkpoints or on the road are generally firm but courteous and fair. *Never* attempt to bribe them.

Fuel & Spare Parts

The price of *bencina* (gasoline) starts from about

CH$815 per liter, depending on the grade, while *gas-oil* (diesel fuel) costs less.

Even the smallest of hamlets always seem to have at least one competent and resourceful mechanic.

Hire

Major international rental agencies like **Hertz** (☑02-360-8600; www.hertz.cl), **Avis** (☑600-368-2000; www.avis.cl) and **Budget** (☑600-441-0000; www.budget.cl) have offices in Santiago (see p79 for more information), as well as in major cities and tourist areas. The Automóvil Club de Chile also rents cars at some locations. To rent a car you must have a valid international driver's license, be at least 25 years of age (some younger readers have managed to rent cars, however) and have either a major credit card (such as Master-Card or Visa) or a large cash deposit. Travelers from the USA, Canada, Germany and Australia are not required to have an international driver's license to rent a car but, to avoid confusion, it is best to carry one.

Even at smaller agencies, rental charges are high, with the smallest vehicles going for about CH$20,000 per day with 150km to 200km included, or sometimes with unlimited mileage. Adding the cost of any extra insurance, petrol and the crippling 19% IVA (*impuesto de valor agregado*), value-added tax (VAT), it becomes very pricey to operate a rental vehicle. Weekend or weekly rates, with unlimited mileage, are a better bargain.

One-way rentals can be awkward or impossible to arrange. Some companies will arrange such rentals but with a substantial drop-off charge. With smaller local agencies this is next to impossible. Some smaller agencies will, however, usually arrange paperwork for taking cars into Argentina, so long as the car is returned to the original office. There may be a substantial charge for taking a car into Argentina and extra insurance must be acquired.

When traveling in remote areas, where fuel may not be readily available, carry extra fuel. Rental agencies often provide a spare *bidón* (fuel container) for this purpose.

Insurance

All vehicles must carry *seguro obligatorio* (minimum insurance) and additional liability insurance is highly desirable. Car-hire companies offer the necessary insurance. Check if there are any limitations to your policy. Traveling on a dirt road is usually fine (indeed necessary in many parts of the country), but off-roading is strictly off limits. Check before renting to see if your credit card includes some sort of car-rental insurance.

In order to go into Argentina, special insurance is required (try any insurance agency; the cost is about CH$15,000 for seven days).

Parking

Drivers should note that many towns charge for street parking (from CH$200 per hour). Street attendants leave a slip of paper under your windshield wiper with the time of arrival and charge you when you leave. Usually parking is free on the weekends –though attendants may still be there, payment is voluntary.

Purchase

For a trip of several months, purchasing a car merits consideration. Once purchased, you must change the vehicle's title within 30 days or risk a hefty fine; you can do this through any notary by requesting a *compraventa* for about CH$5000. You'll need a RUT (Rol Unico Tributario) tax identification number, available through **Impuestos Internos** (www.sii.cl, in Spanish), the Chilean tax office; issuance takes about 10 days. Chilean cars may not be sold abroad.

Note that, while many inexpensive vehicles are for sale in the duty-free zones of Regiónes I and XII (Tarapacá and Magallanes), only legal permanent residents of those regions may take a vehicle outside of those regions, for a maximum of 90 days per calendar year.

Road Conditions

The Panamericana has quality roads and periodic toll booths *(peajes)*. There are two types: tolls you pay to use a distance of the highway (CH$500 to CH$1800), and the tolls you pay to get off the highway to access a lateral to a town or city (CH$600). Paying the former sometimes voids the need to pay the latter. You'll find a list of tolls (in Spanish) on www.turistel.cl.

Many roads in the south are in the process of being paved. Distance markers are placed every 5km along the Panamericana and the Carretera Austral. Often people give directions using these as landmarks.

Road Hazards

Stray dogs wander around on the roads – even highways – with alarming regularity, and visitors from European and North American countries are frequently disconcerted by how pedestrians use the motorway as a sidewalk.

Road Rules

Chilean drivers are restrained in comparison to the horn-happy racers of many South American countries; they are especially courteous to pedestrians. However, city drivers have a reputation for jumping red lights and failing to signal, so keep your wits about you. Driving after dark is not recommended, especially in rural areas in southern Chile, where pedestrians, domestic animals and wooden carts are difficult to see on or near the highways. If you are involved in an automobile accident, see p457. Speed limits are enforced with CH$35,000 fines; bribing them is not an option.

In Santiago, cars are subject to *restricción vehicular* (vehicular restrictions), according to smog levels. The system works according to the last digits on a vehicle's license plates: the chosen numbers are announced in the news on the day before those vehicles will be subject to restrictions. Violators are subject to fines; for more details and current restrictions, see www.uoct.cl (in Spanish).

Hitchhiking

Thumbing a ride is common practice in Chile, and this is one of the safest countries in Latin America to do it. However, in summer Chilean vehicles are often packed with families on vacation, and a wait for a lift can be long. Some backpackers try to solicit rides at *servicentros* (service centers) on the outskirts of Chilean cities on the Panamericana, where truckers gas up their vehicles. That said, hitchhiking is never entirely safe, and Lonely Planet does not recommend it. People who do choose to risk hitchhiking will be safer if they travel in pairs and let someone know of their plans.

Few drivers stop for groups and even fewer appreciate aggressive tactics. In Patagonia, where distances are great and vehicles few, hitchhikers should expect long waits and carry warm, windproof clothing. In the Atacama you may wait for some time, but almost every ride will be a long one. It's also a good idea to carry some snack food and plenty of water, especially in the desert north.

Local Transportation

Bus

Even small towns usually have a chaotic jumble of bus routes that can be intimidating to the novice rider. Prices

are cheap (around CH$500 for a short trip). *Micros* are clearly numbered and usually carry a placard indicating their final destination. Since many identically numbered buses serve slightly different routes, pay attention to these placards. On boarding, mention your final destination and the driver will tell you the fare and give you a ticket. Do not lose this ticket, which may be checked en route. Buses are often crammed with jostling people, so keep an eye on your pockets and bags.

Santiago's reformed bus system, **Transantiago** (www.transantiagoinforma.cl), has automatic fare machines although passengers complain about waits between buses. You can map your route online. For details see p80.

Colectivo

Nearly all Chilean cities have handy *taxi colectivos*, which resemble normal taxis but run on fixed routes much like buses: you'll see a roof sign or placard in the window indicating the destination. They are fast, comfortable and not a great deal more expensive than buses (usually CH$500 to CH$800 within a city).

Commuter Rail

Both Santiago and Valparaíso have commuter rail networks. Santiago is the modern *metrotren* line running from San Fernando through Rancagua, capital of Región VI, to Estación Central, on the Alameda in Santiago; while Valparaíso runs between Viña del Mar and Valparaíso. For details, see the respective city entries.

Metro

Santiago is blessed with a superefficient subway, the metro. It is clean, cheap and fast expanding. Try to avoid peak hours, which can get very crowded. For details, see p80.

Taxi

Most Chilean cabs are metered, but fares vary. In

Santiago it costs CH$250 to *bajar la bandera* (lower the flag), plus CH$80 per 200m. Each cab carries a placard indicating its authorized fare.

In touristy areas cabs may cost twice as much. In others, meters are less common, so it is wise to agree upon a fare in advance. Taxis may charge more late at night. Tipping is not necessary, but you may tell the driver to keep small change.

Tours

Adventure-tour operators have mushroomed throughout Chile; most have offices in Santiago and seasonal offices in the location of their trips. There are many more listed in regional chapters throughout the book.

Altué Active Travel (☎02-235-1519; www.altue.com) One of Chile's pioneer adventure-tourism agencies; it covers almost any outdoor activity but specialties include sea kayaking and cultural trips in Chiloé.

Austral Adventures (☎065-625-977; www.austral-adventures.com) Specializes in cruises around the Pumalín fjords, fishing, kayaking and customized cultural trips around Chiloé.

Azimut 360 (☎02-235-1519; www.azimut.cl) Offers volcano climbing, mountain biking and sightseeing in the northern altiplano, as well as multiactivity trips in Patagonia.

Cruceros Australis (☎02-442-3110; www.australis.com) Runs large luxury cruises between Punta Arenas and Ushuaia – a trip that lasts five days.

Cruceros Skorpios (☎065-252-996; www.skorpioscruises.com; Av Angelmó 1660, Puerto Montt) Arranges slick luxury cruises from Puerto Montt and Puerto Chacabuco to Laguna San Rafael, stopping in its own private reserve with hot springs. More southerly cruises include Puerto Natales.

Explora (☑02-206-6060; www.explora.com) Exclusive resorts in Parque Nacional Torres del Paine, Easter Island and San Pedro de Atacama, with all-inclusive packages with swish accommodations and excursions.

Geoturismo Patagonia (☑067-233-439; www.geoturismopatagonia.cl) Reputable specialists in the Carretera Austral with good insider knowledge.

Opentravel (☑065-260-524; www.opentravel.cl) Offers excellent trekking trips and horseback-riding adventures to remote areas in Northern Patagonia and across the Andes to Argentina.

Pared Sur (☑02-207-3525; www.paredsur.cl) This is all about mountain biking, with a wide variety of challenges throughout Chile.

Patagonia Connection (☑02-225-6489; www.patagonia-connection.com) Sells luxury spa packages in Northern Patagonia and trips along the Carretera Austral or to Laguna San Rafael via catamaran.

Trails of Chile (☑065-330-737; www.trailsofchile.cl) Specializes in top-shelf, professional tours and adventure travel with excellent service.

Train

Chile's railroads blossomed in the late 19th century courtesy of the country's rich mines. In the early 20th century thousands of hectares of native forest were felled to make way for lines running from Santiago to Puerto Montt. Yet, despite the early investment and sacrifices, Chile's train system went into decline for a century and most tracks now lie neglected or abandoned.

The promised railway renovations south of Santiago haven't made it past Chillán. There is service throughout Middle Chile, however, and a *metrotren* service goes from Santiago as far as San Fernando (see p471).

Train travel has fewer departures and is slower and more expensive than bus travel. See p77 for details and prices or check the website of **Empresa de Ferrocarriles del Estado** (EFE; ☑600-585-5000; www.efe.cl).

There are no long-distance passenger services north of Santiago. It's difficult but not impossible to travel by freight train from Baquedano (on the Panamericana northeast of Antofagasta) to the border town of Socompa, and on to Salta, in Argentina.

Language

Spanish pronunciation is easy, as most sounds have equivalents in English. Read our pronunciation guides as if they were English, and you'll be understood. Note that kh is a throaty sound (like the 'ch' in the Scottish *loch*), v and b are like a soft English 'v' (between a 'v' and a 'b'), and r is strongly rolled. The stressed syllables are indicated with an acute accent in written Spanish (eg *días*) and with italics in our pronunciation guides.

The polite form is used in this chapter; where both polite and informal options are given, they are indicated by the abbreviations 'pol' and 'inf'. Where necessary, both masculine and feminine forms of words are included, separated by a slash and with the masculine form first, eg *perdido/a* (m/f).

BASICS

Hello.	Hola.	o·la
Goodbye.	Adiós.	a·dyos
How are you?	¿Qué tal?	ke tal
Fine, thanks.	Bien, gracias.	byen gra·syas
Excuse me.	Perdón.	per·don
Sorry.	Lo siento.	lo syen·to
Please.	Por favor.	por fa·vor
Thank you.	Gracias.	gra·syas
You're welcome.	De nada.	de na·da
Yes./No.	Sí./ No.	see/ no

I don't understand.
Yo no entiendo.   yo no en·*tyen*·do

My name is ...
Me llamo ...   me *ya*·mo ...

What's your name?
¿Cómo se llama Usted?   ko·mo se ya·ma oo·*ste* (pol)
¿Cómo te llamas?   ko·mo te *ya*·mas (inf)

Do you speak English?
¿Habla inglés?   a·bla een·*gles* (pol)
¿Hablas inglés?   a·blas een·*gles* (inf)

ACCOMMODATIONS

I'd like a single/double room.
Quisiera una   kee·*sye*·ra oo·na
habitación   a·bee·ta·*syon*
individual/doble.   een·dee·vee·*dwal*/do·ble

How much is it per night/person?
¿Cuánto cuesta por   kwan·to kwes·ta por
noche/persona?   no·che/per·so·na

Does it include breakfast?
¿Incluye el   een·*kloo*·ye el
desayuno?   de·sa·*yoo*·no

air-con	aire acondi-cionado	ai·re a·kon·dee·syo·na·do
bathroom	baño	ba·nyo
bed	cama	ka·ma
cabin	cabaña	ka·ba·nya
campsite	terreno de cámping	te·re·no de kam·peeng
guesthouse	pensión/ hospedaje	pen·syon/ os·pe·da·khe
hotel	hotel/hostal	o·tel/os·tal
inn	hostería	os·te·ree·ya
youth hostel	albergue juvenil	al·ber·ge khoo·ve·neel
window	ventana	ven·ta·na

WANT MORE?
For in-depth language information and handy phrases, check out Lonely Planet's *Latin American Spanish Phrasebook*. You'll find it at **shop.lonelyplanet.com**, or you can buy Lonely Planet's iPhone phrasebooks at the Apple App Store.

RAPA NUI LANGUAGE

Although the Rapa Nui of Easter Island speak Spanish, among themselves many of them use the island's indigenous language (also called Rapa Nui). Due to the island's isolation, the Rapa Nui language developed relatively untouched but retains similarities to other Polynesian languages, such as Hawaiian, Tahitian and Maori. These days the language increasingly bears the influence of English and Spanish. The hieroglyph-like Rongorongo script, developed by the Islanders after the Spanish first arrived in 1770 and in use until the 1860s, is believed to have been the earliest written form of Rapa Nui. The written Rapa Nui used today was developed in the 19th century by missionaries, who transliterated the sounds of the language into the Roman alphabet. Sadly, while most understand Rapa Nui, few of the younger Islanders speak it fluently, though work is being done to keep this endangered language, and the culture it carries, alive.

Rapa Nui pronunciation is fairly straightforward, with short and long vowels pronounced as they would be in Spanish or Italian. There are only ten consonants, plus a glottal stop ('), which is pronounced like the pause in the word 'uh-oh.' Any attempt at a few basic Rapa Nui greetings and phrases will be greatly appreciated by the locals, whatever your level of mastery. For more extensive Rapa Nui coverage, pick up a copy of Lonely Planet's South Pacific Phrasebook. To learn more, and to read about efforts to preserve the local culture, check out the Easter Island Foundation website www.islandheritage.org.

Hello.	'Iorana.		My name's ...	To'oku ingoa ko ...
Goodbye.	'Iorana.		What?	Aha?
How are you?	Pehē koe/kōrua? (sg/pl)		Which?	Hē aha?
Fine.	Rivariva.		Who?	Ko āi?
Thank you.	Maururu.		How much is this?	'Ehia moni o te me'e nei?
What's your name?	Ko āi to'ou ingoa?		To your health!	Manuia paka-paka.

DIRECTIONS

Where's ...?
¿Dónde está ...?   don·de es·ta ...

What's the address?
¿Cuál es la dirección?   kwal es la dee·rek·syon

Could you please write it down?
¿Puede escribirlo,   pwe·de es·kree·beer·lo
por favor?   por fa·vor

Can you show me (on the map)?
¿Me lo puede indicar   me lo pwe·de een·dee·kar
(en el mapa)?   (en el ma·pa)

at the corner	en la esquina	en la es·kee·na
at the traffic lights	en el semáforo	en el se·ma·fo·ro
behind ...	detrás de ...	de·tras de ...
far	lejos	le·khos
in front of ...	enfrente de ...	en·fren·te de ...
left	izquierda	ees·kyer·da
near	cerca	ser·ka
next to ...	al lado de ...	al la·do de ...
opposite ...	frente a ...	fren·te a ...
right	derecha	de·re·cha
straight ahead	todo recto	to·do rek·to

EATING & DRINKING

Can I see the menu, please?
¿Puedo ver el menú,   pwe·do ver el me·noo
por favor?   por fa·vor

What would you recommend?
¿Qué recomienda?   ke re·ko·myen·da

Do you have vegetarian food?
¿Tienen comida   tye·nen ko·mee·da
vegetariana?   ve·khe·ta·rya·na

I don't eat (red meat).
No como (carne roja).   no ko·mo (kar·ne ro·kha)

That was delicious!
¡Estaba buenísimo!   es·ta·ba bwe·nee·see·mo

Cheers!
¡Salud!   sa·loo

The bill, please.
La cuenta, por favor.   la kwen·ta por fa·vor

I'd like a table for ...	Quisiera una mesa para ...	kee·sye·ra oo·na me·sa pa·ra ...
(eight) o'clock	las (ocho)	las (o·cho)
(two) people	(dos) personas	(dos) per·so·nas

breakfast	desayuno	de·sa·yoo·no
lunch	comida	ko·mee·da
dinner	cena	se·na
restaurant	restaurante	res·tow·ran·te

EMERGENCIES

Help!	¡Socorro!	so·ko·ro
Go away!	¡Vete!	ve·te

Call ...!	¡Llame a ...!	ya·me a ...
a doctor	un médico	oon me·dee·ko
the police	la policía	la po·lee·see·a

I'm lost.
Estoy perdido/a.   es·toy per·dee·do/a (m/f)

I'm ill.
Estoy enfermo/a.   es·toy en·fer·mo/a (m/f)

It hurts here.
Me duele aquí.   me dwe·le a·kee

I'm allergic to (antibiotics).
Soy alérgico/a a   soy a·ler·khee·ko/a a
(los antibióticos).   (los an·tee·byo·tee·kos) (m/f)

Where are the toilets?
¿Dónde están los   don·de es·tan los
baños?   ba·nyos

SHOPPING & SERVICES

I'd like to buy ...
Quisiera comprar ...   kee·sye·ra kom·prar ...

I'm just looking.
Sólo estoy mirando.   so·lo es·toy mee·ran·do

Can I look at it?
¿Puedo verlo?   pwe·do ver·lo

I don't like it.
No me gusta.   no me goos·ta

How much is it?
¿Cuánto cuesta?   kwan·to kwes·ta

That's too expensive.
Es muy caro.   es mooy ka·ro

Can you lower the price?
¿Podría bajar un   po·dree·a ba·khar oon
poco el precio?   po·ko el pre·syo

There's a mistake in the bill.
Hay un error   ai oon e·ror
en la cuenta.   en la kwen·ta

ATM	cajero automático	ka·khe·ro ow·to·ma·tee·ko
internet cafe	cibercafé	see·ber·ka·fe
market	mercado	mer·ka·do
post office	correos	ko·re·os
tourist office	oficina de turismo	o·fee·see·na de too·rees·mo

TIME & DATES

What time is it?   ¿Qué hora es?   ke o·ra es

It's (10) o'clock.   Son (las diez).   son (las dyes)

It's half past (one).   Es (la una) y media.   es (la oo·na) ee me·dya

morning	mañana	ma·nya·na
afternoon	tarde	tar·de
evening	noche	no·che
yesterday	ayer	a·yer
today	hoy	oy
tomorrow	mañana	ma·nya·na

Monday	lunes	loo·nes
Tuesday	martes	mar·tes
Wednesday	miércoles	myer·ko·les
Thursday	jueves	khwe·ves
Friday	viernes	vyer·nes
Saturday	sábado	sa·ba·do
Sunday	domingo	do·meen·go

TRANSPORTATION

boat	barco	bar·ko
bus	autobús	ow·to·boos
(small) bus	micro	mee·kro
plane	avión	a·vyon
shared taxi	colectivo	ko·lek·tee·vo
train	tren	tren
first	primero	pree·me·ro
last	último	ool·tee·mo
next	próximo	prok·see·mo

A ... ticket, please.   Un billete de ..., por favor.   oon bee·ye·te de ... por fa·vor

1st-class	primera clase	pree·me·ra kla·se
2nd-class	segunda clase	se·goon·da kla·se
one-way	ida	ee·da
return	ida y vuelta	ee·da ee vwel·ta

Signs	
Abierto	Open
Cerrado	Closed
Entrada	Entrance
Hombres/Varones	Men
Mujeres/Damas	Women
Prohibido	Prohibited
Salida	Exit
Servicios/Baños	Toilets

I want to go to ...
Quisiera ir a ... — kee·sye·ra eer a ...

Does it stop at ...?
¿Para en ...? — pa·ra en ...

What stop is this?
¿Cuál es esta parada? — kwal es es·ta pa·ra·da

What time does it arrive/leave?
¿A qué hora llega/sale? — a ke o·ra ye·ga/sa·le

Please tell me when we get to ...
¿Puede avisarme cuando lleguemos a ...? — pwe·de a·vee·sar·me kwan·do ye·ge·mos a ...

I want to get off here.
Quiero bajarme aquí. — kye·ro ba·khar·me a·kee

airport	*aeropuerto*	a·e·ro·pwer·to
aisle seat	*asiento de pasillo*	a·syen·to de pa·see·yo
bus stop	*parada de autobuses*	pa·ra·da de ow·to·boo·ses
cancelled	*cancelado*	kan·se·la·do
delayed	*retrasado*	re·tra·sa·do
platform	*plataforma*	pla·ta·for·ma
ticket office	*taquilla*	ta·kee·ya
timetable	*horario*	o·ra·ryo
train station	*estación de trenes*	es·ta·syon de tre·nes
window seat	*asiento junto a la ventana*	a·syen·to khoon·to a la ven·ta·na

I'd like to hire a ...	*Quisiera alquilar ...*	kee·sye·ra al·kee·lar ...
4WD	*un todo-terreno*	oon to·do·te·re·no
bicycle	*una bicicleta*	oo·na bee·see·kle·ta
car	*un coche*	oon ko·che
motorcycle	*una moto*	oo·na mo·to
child seat	*asiento de seguridad para niños*	a·syen·to de se·goo·ree·da pa·ra nee·nyos

Question Words

How?	*¿Cómo?*	ko·mo
What?	*¿Qué?*	ke
When?	*¿Cuándo?*	kwan·do
Where?	*¿Dónde?*	don·de
Who?	*¿Quién?*	kyen
Why?	*¿Por qué?*	por ke

Numbers

1	*uno*	oo·no
2	*dos*	dos
3	*tres*	tres
4	*cuatro*	kwa·tro
5	*cinco*	seen·ko
6	*seis*	seys
7	*siete*	sye·te
8	*ocho*	o·cho
9	*nueve*	nwe·ve
10	*diez*	dyes
20	*veinte*	veyn·te
30	*treinta*	treyn·ta
40	*cuarenta*	kwa·ren·ta
50	*cincuenta*	seen·kwen·ta
60	*sesenta*	se·sen·ta
70	*setenta*	se·ten·ta
80	*ochenta*	o·chen·ta
90	*noventa*	no·ven·ta
100	*cien*	syen
1000	*mil*	meel

diesel	*petróleo*	pet·ro·le·o
helmet	*casco*	kas·ko
hitchhike	*hacer botella*	a·ser bo·te·ya
mechanic	*mecánico*	me·ka·nee·ko
petrol/gas	*bencina/ gasolina*	ben·see·na ga·so·lee·na
service station	*gasolinera*	ga·so·lee·ne·ra
truck	*camion*	ka·myon

Is this the road to ...?
¿Se va a ... por esta carretera? — se va a ... por es·ta ka·re·te·ra

(How long) Can I park here?
¿(Cuánto tiempo) Puedo aparcar aquí? — (kwan·to tyem·po) pwe·do a·par·kar a·kee

The car has broken down (at ...).
El coche se ha averiado (en ...). — el ko·che se a a·ve·rya·do (en ...)

I had an accident.
He tenido un accidente. — e te·nee·do oon ak·see·den·te

I've run out of petrol.
Me he quedado sin gasolina. — me e ke·da·do seen ga·so·lee·na

I have a flat tyre.
Tengo un pinchazo. — ten·go oon peen·cha·so

GLOSSARY

RN indicates that a term is Rapa Nui (Easter Island) usage.

ahu (RN) – stone platform for *moai* (statues)

alameda – avenue/boulevard lined with trees

albergue juvenil – youth hostel

alpaca – wool-bearing domestic camelid, related to llama

altiplano – high plains of northern Chile, Bolivia, southern Peru and north-western Argentina

anexo – telephone extension

apunamiento – altitude sickness

Araucaníans – groups of indigenous peoples, including Mapuche, Picunche and Pehuenche

arroyo – watercourse

asado – barbecue

ascensor – funicular (cable car)

Ayllu – indigenous community of Norte Grande

Aymara – indigenous inhabi-tants of Andean *altiplano* of Peru, Bolivia and northern Chile

bahía – bay

balneario – bathing resort or beach

barrio – neighborhood

bencina – petrol or gasoline

bencina blanca – white gas for camping stoves

bidón – spare fuel container

bodega – cellar or storage area for wine

bofedal – swampy alluvial pasture in altiplano

cabañas – cabins

cacique – Indian chieftain

calefón – hot-water heater

caleta – small cove

callampas – shantytowns, literally 'mushrooms'

cama – bed; also sleeper-class seat

camanchaca – ocean fog along coastal desert

camarote – sleeper class on ship

carabineros – police

caracoles – winding roads; literally 'snails'

carretera – highway

casa de cambio – money exchange

casa de familia – modest family accommodation

cerro – hill

chachacoma – native Andean plant; said to relieve altitude sickness

Chilote – inhabitant of Chiloé; sometimes connotes 'bumpkin'

ciervo – deer

ciudad – city

cobro revertido – collect (reverse-charge) phone call

cocinerías – greasy-spoon cafes/kitchens

Codelco – Corporación del Cobre, state-owned enterprise overseeing copper mining

colectivo – shared taxi, also called *taxi colectivo*

comparsa – group of musicians or dancers

comuna – local governmental unit

congregación – colonial-era concentration of diverse native populations in a town, see also *reducción*

cordillera – chain of mountains

costanera – coastal road; also along river or lakeshore

criollo – colonial term for American-born Spaniard

desierto florido – rare and ephemeral desert wildflower display in Norte Chico

DINA – National Intelligence Directorate; feared agency created after 1973 coup to oversee police and military intelligence

elaboración artesanal – small-scale production, often by family

empanada – a turnover with a sweet or savory filling

encomienda – colonial labor system in which indigenous communities worked for Spanish *encomenderos*

esquí en marcha – cross-country skiing

estancia – extensive cattle- or sheep-grazing establishment with resident labor force

estero – estuary

feria – artisans' market

Frontera – region of pioneer settlement, between Río Biobío and Río Toltén, dominated by Araucanían indigenous groups until late 19th century

fuerte – fort

fundo – *hacienda;* smaller irrigated unit in central heartland

garúa – coastal desert fog

geoglyph – large pre-Columbian figures or designs on desert hillsides

golfo – gulf

golpe de estado – coup d'état

guanaco – wild camelid related to llama; also police water cannon

hacienda – large rural landholding, with dependent resident labor force

hare paenga (RN) – elliptical (boat-shaped) house

hospedaje – budget accommodations, usually family home with shared bathroom

hostal – hotel, hostel

hostería – inn or guesthouse that serves meals

hotel parejero – short-stay 'love motels' aimed at couples needing privacy

huaso – horseman, a kind of Chilean gaucho or cowboy

IGM – Instituto Geográfico Militar; mapping organization

intendencia – Spanish colonial administrative unit

invierno boliviano – 'Bolivian winter'; summer rainy season in Chilean *altiplano*

isla – island

islote – small island, islet

istmo – isthmus

IVA – *impuesto de valor agregado*, value-added tax (VAT)

küchen – sweet, German-style cakes

lago – lake

laguna – lagoon

latifundio – large landholding, such as *fundo*, *hacienda* or *estancia*

lista de correos – poste restante

llareta – dense shrub in Chilean *altiplano* with deceptive, cushionlike appearance

local – part of address indicating office number where there are several in the same building

lomas – coastal desert hills

maori (RN) – learned men, reportedly able to read Rongo–Rongo tablets

Mapuche – indigenous inhabitants of the area south of Río Biobío

marisquería – seafood restaurant

matrimonial – double bed

matua (RN) – ancestor, father; associated with leader of first Polynesian immigrants

media pensión – half board in hotel

mestizo – person of mixed Indian and Spanish descent

micro – small bus

minga – reciprocal Mapuche Indian labor system

mirador – lookout point

moai (RN) – large anthropomorphic statues

moai kavakava (RN) – carved wooden 'statues of ribs'

motu (RN) – small offshore islet

municipalidad – city hall

museo – museum

ñandú – rhea; large flightless bird similar to ostrich

nevado – snowcapped mountain peak

oferta – promotional fare, often seasonal, for plane or bus travel

oficina – 19th- and early 20th-century nitrate-mining enterprise

onces – 'elevenses'; Chilean afternoon tea

palafitos – rows of houses built on stilts over water in Chiloé

pampa – vast desert expanse

parada – bus stop

parrillada – a mix of grilled meats

peatonal – pedestrian mall

peña folclórica – folk music and cultural club

penquista – inhabitant of Concepción

pensión – family home offering short-term accommodations

pensión completa – full board in hotel

picada – informal family restaurant

pingüinera – penguin colony

playa – beach

Porteño – native or resident of Valparaíso

portezuelo – mountain pass

posta – clinic or first-aid station

precordillera – foothills

propina – tip

puente – bridge

puerto – port

pukao (RN) – topknot on head of a *moai*

pukará – pre-Columbian hilltop fortress

puna – Andean highlands, usually above 3000m

punta – point

quebrada – ravine

quinoa – native Andean grain grown in northern *precordillera*

Rapa Nui – Polynesian name for Easter Island

reducción – colonial-era concentration of indigenous peoples in towns for purposes of political control or religious instruction

refugio – rustic shelter in national park or remote area

residencial – budget accommodations

rhea – flightless bird similar to ostrich; *ñandú* in Spanish

río – river

rodeo – annual cattle roundup on *estancia* or *hacienda*

Rongo–Rongo (RN) – indecipherable script on wooden tablets

ruka – traditional thatched Mapuche house

ruta – route, highway

salar – salt lake, salt marsh or salt pan

salón de cama – bus with reclining seats

salón de té – literally 'teahouse,' but more upscale café

Santiaguino – native or resident of Santiago

seno – sound, fjord

sierra – mountain range

s/n – 'sin número'; street address without number

soroche – altitude sickness

tábano – horsefly

tabla – shared plate of appetizers

tejuelas – shingles, typical of Chiloé architecture

teleférico – gondola cable car

termas – hot springs

todo terreno – mountain bike

toqui – Mapuche chief

torres – towers

totora (RN) – type of reed used for making rafts

Unidad Popular – leftist coalition that supported Salvador Allende in 1970 presidential election

ventisquero – glacier

vicuña – wild relative of llama, found at high altitudes in the north

villa – village, small town

viscacha – wild Andean relative of chinchilla

volcán – volcano

Yaghans – indigenous inhabitants of Tierra del Fuego archipelago

zampoña – panpipe

zona franca – duty-free zone

behind the scenes

SEND US YOUR FEEDBACK

We love to hear from travelers – your comments keep us on our toes and help make our books better. Our well-traveled team reads every word on what you loved or loathed about this book. Although we cannot reply individually to postal submissions, we always guarantee that your feedback goes straight to the appropriate authors, in time for the next edition. Each person who sends us information is thanked in the next edition – the most useful submissions are rewarded with a selection of digital PDF chapters.

Visit **lonelyplanet.com/contact** to submit your updates and suggestions or to ask for help. Our award-winning website also features inspirational travel stories, news and discussions.

Note: We may edit, reproduce and incorporate your comments in Lonely Planet products such as guidebooks, websites and digital products, so let us know if you don't want your comments reproduced or your name acknowledged. For a copy of our privacy policy visit lonelyplanet.com/privacy.

OUR READERS

Many thanks to the travelers who used the last edition and wrote to us with helpful hints, useful advice and interesting anecdotes:

Daniel Alton, Carla Artuso, Timoshenko Aslanides, David Atchason, Roberta Attenhofer, Markus Averes, Carina Baskett, Anna Becke, Frank Beer, Julia Bender, Patty Benjamin, Susannah Bennett, Yvonne Bierings, Ulrik Bjerre Holm, Eric Bodden, Bernd Breugem, David Brewer, Joanna Burton, Anne Callan, Marina Carrascosa, Paula Carvalho, Heino and Tilo Caspelherr, Flavio Chaimowicz, Kenneth Crosby, Rikkert Dahmen, Owen Davies, Chris de Sharks, Sergio de la Barrera, Peter Dobbinga, Su Dore, Alexandru Dumitru, Hilde Dunker, Jennifer Durst, Henk Edelman, Bini Elhanan, Bettina Freie, Susan Fussell, Anna Galluccio, Miguel Garcia-Valenzuela, Roberto Garretón, Filip Geirnaert, Lori Gibson, Tina Goldbach, James Grant-Peterkin, Gemma Grau Colom, Rico Guler, Kathleen Hanley, Amanda Helderman, Kay Henderson, Timo Hettinger, Julie Hilton, Ward Hobert, Luise Hoffmann-Briel, Gerlinde Hruza, John Joosten, Jane Jowitt, Pieter Klootwijk, Mike Knife, Katrina Korfmacher, Andreas La Rosé, Martha Labadie, Cestmir Lang, Lara le Saux, Nando Leerentveld, Laurent Lemasson, Chris Leverington, Dave Liston, Raymond L'Italien, Marion Londres, Julia Lutte, Bruno Maia, Irene Maldonado, Ben Martin, Donna Mccready, Ciaran Mcintyre, Lachlan Mckenzie, Petra Melling, Corina Merboth, Aisha Moinuddin, Eduardo Mondragón Vial, Melanie Morcom, Kathi Morrison, Sebastian Müller, Marja Myllykoski, Seagan Ngai, Bill Nicholson, Michel Niggemann, Sandra Olsson, Kerian Parry, Joshua Paul, Samuel Peak, Ellie Pegler, Matt Pepe, Davide Pianezze, Jason Pietryga, Margaretha Polzin, Ture Rademacher, John L Rector, Ricardo Rodriguez, Vassen Romain, Patrick Roman, David Rousseau, Robert Runyard, Malula Sanchez, Alex Scheelke, Anne-Marie Schweizer, Ricardo Sepulveda, Christian Sigl, Yerka Siglic, Hans Simon, Mike Sinclair, Alfonso Spoliansky, Paul Steele, Nicolas Sternsdorff, Katie Stetson, Silvia Stock, Adam Stoffel, Ben Strom, Trevor Sze, Sergi Teixido Baste, Frauke Thorade, Alvaro Toro, Kariina Tshursin, Tuhiira Tuki, Denise Turcinov, Sarah Turner, Fran Ugalde, Hans van Kleef, Marianne van der Walle, Jefferson Vasconcelos, Carla Veloso, Ivan Verunica, Margaret Vile, Greg Vlacich, Brenda Walker, Frank Weidemann, Marlies Weidenfeller, Nikola Weiss, Shane White, Francesca Whitlock, Mirijam Wiedenmann, Mariëtte Wilmes, Adam Wolf, Jonathan Wright, Julia Yada, Natasha Young, Julie Zack, Andrea Zanghellini, Andrew Zimet, May Zimmerli, Oliver Zoellner, Andrew Zur & Jonathan Zwart

AUTHOR THANKS

Carolyn McCarthy

A trip to Patagonia is a reminder of what's good in the world. Many thanks go to Pancho Vio, Alejandro Gonzalez, Cristian Solis, Trace Gale, Nicolas, LaPenn, Hernan Jofre, Nadine Lehner, Philippe Reuter, Christel, Mery Bravo and Mirella Delgado. Gratitude goes out to Andres on the Zapata tábano expedition. I am also thankful for the great contributions of my co-authors. Every time I go to Patagonia a car breaks. So thank you, Subarito, for not failing me on the Carretera Austral.

Jean-Bernard Carillet

Heaps of thanks to the team at Lonely Planet, especially Maryanne and Errol, for their trust and to the editorial and cartography teams. Coordinating author Carolyn deserves a *grand merci* for her support. In Easter Island, special thanks to Antoine, Ema, Sergio Rapu, Tita, Lionel and the people at Sernatur. On the home-front, well-deserved *bisous* to my daughter Eva and Christine, who are always supportive.

Bridget Gleeson

Thank you to my Chilean brother-in-law, Germán Parra, for introducing me to his culture, and to his family, especially Emelina Nanjari, for welcoming me into her home, improving my Spanish, and teaching me what the perfect *paila marina* should taste like.

Anja Mutić

Obrigada, Hoji for joining this adventure and being by my side through the ups and downs; you make the journey infinitely more fun. *Hvala mama*, for always being in the background as my biggest cheerleader. Thanks to all the great Lonely Planet people, especially my commissioning editor Kathleen and co-author Carolyn. And to all the kindred spirits I met on the road, most notably Eileen Smith in Santiago, who gave me endless insider tips, Ercio in Copiapo and Marcelo in Elqui Valley.

Kevin Raub

Special thanks to my wife, Adriana Schmidt Raub, who I might try and convince to move to Chile. On the road, Carolyn McCarthy, Tracy Katelman, Megan Vibet, Margarita Gross, Britt Lewis, Juan Pablo Mansilla, Karin Terrsy, Alfonso Spoliansky, Amory Uslar, Fernando Claude, Rodrigo Venturelli, Ernesto Palm de Curto, Catherine Bérard and all at Secret Patagonia, Kurt Shillinger, Tracy Katelman, Macarena Bruce, Diego Meier, Renato Arancibia, Diego Meier, Mark McMonigal and Sirce Santibeñez.

ACKNOWLEDGMENTS

Climate map data adapted from Peel MC, Finlayson BL & McMahon TA (2007) 'Updated World Map of the Köppen-Geiger Climate Classification', *Hydrology and Earth System Sciences*, 11, 163344.

Cover photograph: Lago Pehoé and Los Cuernos in Parque Nacional Torres del Paine, Chilean Patagonia, Dede Vargas/Getty Images. Many of the images in this guide are available for licensing from Lonely Planet Images: www.lonelyplanetimages.com.

BEHIND THE SCENES

This Book

This 9th edition of Lonely Planet's *Chile & Easter Island* guidebook was researched and written by Carolyn McCarthy, Jean-Bernard Carillet, Bridget Gleeson, Anja Mutić and Kevin Raub. The previous two editions were also written by Carolyn McCarthy, Jean-Bernard Carillet and Kevin Raub along with Greg Benchwick and Victoria Patience. This guidebook was commissioned in Lonely Planet's Oakland office, and produced by the following:

Commissioning Editor Kathleen Munnelly

Coordinating Editors Alison Ridgway, Sophie Splatt

Coordinating Cartographer Andrew Smith

Coordinating Layout Designer Carlos Solarte

Managing Editors Barbara Delissen, Bruce Evans

Managing Cartographer Alison Lyall

Managing Layout Designer Chris Girdler

Assisting Editors Carly Hall, Anne Mulvaney, Charlotte Orr

Assisting Cartographers Joelene Kowalski

Assisting Layout Designer Wendy Wright

Cover Research Naomi Parker

Internal Image Research Frank Deim, Claire Gibson

Language Content Branislava Vladisavljevic

Thanks to Ryan Evans, Larissa Frost, Gerard Walker

NOTES

NOTES

486

NOTES

index

how to use this book

These symbols will help you find the listings you want:

- ◉ Sights
- 🏊 Beaches
- 🏃 Activities
- 🥊 Courses
- 👉 Tours
- 🎊 Festivals & Events
- 🛏 Sleeping
- ✗ Eating
- 🍺 Drinking
- ☆ Entertainment
- 🔒 Shopping
- ℹ Information/Transport

These symbols give you the vital information for each listing:

- ♪ Telephone Numbers
- ☉ Opening Hours
- P Parking
- ⊖ Nonsmoking
- ❄ Air-Conditioning
- @ Internet Access
- 📶 Wi-Fi Access
- ≋ Swimming Pool
- 🥗 Vegetarian Selection
- 📖 English-Language Menu
- 👪 Family-Friendly
- 🐾 Pet-Friendly
- 🚌 Bus
- ⛴ Ferry
- Ⓜ Metro
- Ⓢ Subway
- ⊖ London Tube
- 🚊 Tram
- 🚆 Train

Reviews are organised by author preference.

Map Legend

Sights
- 🏖 Beach
- 🛕 Buddhist
- 🏰 Castle
- ✝ Christian
- ☪ Hindu
- ☪ Islamic
- ✡ Jewish
- ❶ Monument
- 🏛 Museum/Gallery
- 🏚 Ruin
- 🍇 Winery/Vineyard
- 🐾 Zoo
- ◉ Other Sight

Activities, Courses & Tours
- 🤿 Diving/Snorkelling
- 🛶 Canoeing/Kayaking
- ⛷ Skiing
- 🏄 Surfing
- 🏊 Swimming/Pool
- 🚶 Walking
- 🏄 Windsurfing
- ➕ Other Activity/Course/Tour

Sleeping
- 🛏 Sleeping
- ⛺ Camping

Eating
- ✗ Eating

Drinking
- ☕ Drinking
- ☕ Cafe

Entertainment
- 🎭 Entertainment

Shopping
- 🛍 Shopping

Information
- ✉ Post Office
- ℹ Tourist Information

Transport
- ✈ Airport
- ⊗ Border Crossing
- 🚌 Bus
- 🚡 Cable Car/Funicular
- 🚲 Cycling
- ⛴ Ferry
- Ⓜ Metro
- 🚝 Monorail
- P Parking
- Ⓢ S-Bahn
- 🚕 Taxi
- 🚆 Train/Railway
- 🚊 Tram
- ⊖ Tube Station
- Ⓤ U-Bahn
- • Other Transport

Routes
- Tollway
- Freeway
- Primary
- Secondary
- Tertiary
- Lane
- Unsealed Road
- Plaza/Mall
- Steps
- Tunnel
- Pedestrian Overpass
- Walking Tour
- Walking Tour Detour
- Path

Boundaries
- International
- State/Province
- Disputed
- Regional/Suburb
- Marine Park
- Cliff
- Wall

Population
- ⊕ Capital (National)
- ◉ Capital (State/Province)
- ● City/Large Town
- ● Town/Village

Geographic
- 🏠 Hut/Shelter
- 🗼 Lighthouse
- 👁 Lookout
- ▲ Mountain/Volcano
- 🌴 Oasis
- 🌳 Park
-)(Pass
- 🌳 Picnic Area
- 💧 Waterfall

Hydrography
- River/Creek
- Intermittent River
- Swamp/Mangrove
- Reef
- Canal
- Water
- Dry/Salt/Intermittent Lake
- Glacier

Areas
- Beach/Desert
- +++ Cemetery (Christian)
- ××× Cemetery (Other)
- Park/Forest
- Sportsground
- Sight (Building)
- Top Sight (Building)

Kevin Raub

Sur Chico, Chiloé Kevin Raub grew up in Atlanta and started his career as a music journalist in New York, working for *Men's Journal* and *Rolling Stone* magazines. The rock 'n' roll lifestyle took its toll, so he needed an extended vacation and took up travel writing while ditching the States for Brazil. Despite a dog chewing off a corner of his rental car license plate in Chile, he survived unscathed on this, his second time through Sur Chico and Chiloé. This is Kevin's 19th Lonely Planet guide. You can find him at www.kevinraub.net.

Contributing Author

Grant Phelps trained in the art of winemaking in his native New Zealand and embarked on a 10-year career as a 'flying winemaker', working harvests in seven different countries before experiencing a wine-fuelled epiphany in Chile. Now resident in Valparaíso, he has been making wine in Chile for 12 years and is currently chief winemaker for Viña Casas del Bosque, in the Casablanca Valley.

OUR STORY

A beat-up old car, a few dollars in the pocket and a sense of adventure. In 1972 that's all Tony and Maureen Wheeler needed for the trip of a lifetime – across Europe and Asia overland to Australia. It took several months, and at the end – broke but inspired – they sat at their kitchen table writing and stapling together their first travel guide, *Across Asia on the Cheap*. Within a week they'd sold 1500 copies. Lonely Planet was born.

Today, Lonely Planet has offices in Melbourne, London and Oakland, with more than 600 staff and writers. We share Tony's belief that 'a great guidebook should do three things: inform, educate and amuse'.

OUR WRITERS

Carolyn McCarthy

Coordinating Author; Northern Patagonia, Southern Patagonia, Tierra del Fuego
Carolyn has suffered from a severe case of Chilenisis since working as a hiking guide in the Lakes District some years ago. For this trip, she motored the Carretera Austral and hiked in Torres del Paine and Isla Navarino. She has also authored Lonely Planet's *Argentina, Panama, Yellowstone & Grand Teton National Parks, The Travel Book, Best in Travel* and *Trekking in the Patagonian Andes*. Carolyn has contributed to *National Geographic, Outside* and *Lonely Planet Magazine*, among other publications. You can follow her Americas blog at www.carolynswildblueyonder.blogspot.com.

Jean-Bernard Carillet

Easter Island (Rapa Nui) Journalist and photographer Jean-Bernard is a die-hard island lover and diving instructor. He's made many trips to the South Pacific, including four to Easter Island. On this gig, he searched for the most enjoyable hikes, the most stupendous vistas, the best-value accommodations and the most potent pisco sour. His favourite experiences included enjoying a picnic at sunrise at Ahu Tongariki and walking along the rugged north coast. Jean-Bernard has contributed to many Lonely Planet titles and writes for travel and dive magazines.

Bridget Gleeson

Santiago, Middle Chile Based in Buenos Aires, Bridget was just starting out as a travel writer when her sister fell in love with a Chilean. She's been crossing the Andes ever since to visit the Santiago branch of the family, learning how to mix the perfect pisco sour and negotiate the price of fresh *machas* (razor clams) along the way. She writes about Latin American food, wine and travel for Lonely Planet, *Budget Travel, Afar*, Jetsetter and BBC Travel.

Read more about Bridget at:
lonelyplanet.com/members/bridgetgleeson

Anja Mutić

Norte Grande, Norte Chico While growing up in Croatia, New York–based Anja Mutić had a deep fascination with the ancient civilizations of South America. The appeal grew even more when she first visited the continent in 2001. She has since been returning regularly, for work and for play. On the last two-month jaunt around Chile, she was consistently rained out in the Atacama, said to be the driest desert in the world.

OVER MORE
PAGE WRITERS

Published by Lonely Planet Publications Pty Ltd
ABN 36 005 607 983
9th edition – October 2012
ISBN 978 1 74179 583 7
© Lonely Planet 2012   Photographs © as indicated 2012
10 9 8 7 6 5 4 3 2 1
Printed in China